STA ... **S0-AVW-420**
The Ultimate Rock Reference

This book is the only compendium of rock reference which is an encyclopaedic run-down on the current scene. Every record in
    the TOP 50 UK ALBUM CHARTS
    the TOP 200 US ALBUM CHARTS
    the TOP 100 US SINGLES CHARTS
    the TOP 50 UK SINGLES CHARTS
Previous compendiums have always been a year or two out of date. Never before has there been so exhaustive a run-down on artists, writers, producers (now so important to the *sound* of a record), and *most* important, CATALOGUE NUMBERS. Record collectors who have missed a gem or two through the year can, as a result, order their choice quickly and easily from any reputable shop.
From the publishers who gave you the NME BOOK OF ROCK 2, comes a *must* for your personal book collection.

STAR FILE

Compiled by Dafydd Rees

Foreword by Derek Taylor

Introduction by John Tobler

Incorporating the year's record information from
Billboard and Music Week

A STAR BOOK

published by
the Paperback Division of
W. H. ALLEN & Co. Ltd.

A Star Book
Published in 1977
by the Paperback Division of W. H. Allen & Co. Ltd.
A Howard and Wyndham Company
123 King Street, London W6 9JG

Copyright © 1977 by Dafydd Rees

Printed in Great Britain by
Cox & Wyman Ltd.
London, Reading and Fakenham
Photosetting by Templering Ltd., Mitcham, Surrey

ISBN 0 352 39573 7

FOREWORD by Derek Taylor

This sort of book improves with keeping. Now that we are all looking back, and even, say, 1973 seems (is?) old hat, reference books, particularly those relating to matters beloved of the young and enthusiastic, become more and more fascinating as the years pass. Was it only three years since Ralph McTell was number one with 'Streets of London'? Or does it seem aeons ago? (To me it seems a lifetime ago.) And was it actually number one? Well, was it? Well no, it wasn't. It was number two, only it did so well for so long, and it was so popular and played so often that it seemed like number one.

Anyway, anyway, the point is that people do like to know these things; they like to know them very much. I do myself. Maybe it isn't really important. Maybe it doesn't 'matter', but if you care, then it does *matter* and it is absolutely crucial that if one is going to get involved with facts, then the facts should be available and *factual* and easily cross-referenced. Bets can be settled, scores evened and bullies, cheats, bullshitters, knowalls and plain liars silenced. Opinions are free but facts and figures are 'sacred'.

In my own curious life (now that I have crossed the line from living in fantasy to reading computer printouts with an astonishing pleasure and joyful ease) I have become ever more fascinated by who did what when and for how long. I am no good at all at assembling and tabulating such things but this is not the point. The point is that I know what I know—which is not nearly enough—(and I guess the same goes for most of you) and it is for young men like Dafydd Rees, *born* with a cross-index-file in their heads, to assemble these things and make life easier for the statistic freaks. I don't know why they want to do it—it seems such a tough way of life, but they do want to do it and I am glad for them.

Record companies (and the one which employs me to whom, daily, I pay obeisance for their catalogue, and the benevolence of their leadership) usually have on their staffs a Dafydd Rees, (men or women with mines of catalogue numbers, seams of hot producers, both sides of the brain transmitting chart placings). But because they are busy living in the right-now, the 'facts freaks' never rely on themselves—they buy books like Mr. Rees' excellent work, just to be sure.

And not only this, for many lay people relate what they were doing (and with or to whom) to a certain song (terribly pissed when 'Instant Karma' stopped in the teens—what was *its* highest placing? Anyone remember?—unbearably in love when Liverpool Express had their first chart success with—what was it? How long was it in the charts and how high did it get and who wrote and, incidentally, produced it?) So for those people this book has merit too. They can chart their own year by the music of the year. It is for idle reading, it is for diligent seekers after truth and as an industry handbook for the year 1976, it is without equal, so far as I can see, which is no further than this typewriter right now.

I am particularly impressed that Mr. Rees has taken pains to *cross-refer* each section of the six he has chosen, to show us what happened in this busy, busy industry in 1976 (a year, which, looking back, appears not to have been, musically, quite as bad as we were led to believe by all those surrogate pop-bibles which weekly tell us where it is or is not at).

Most of us need our compilers of facts to make life easy for us and Mr. Rees does this. Television has (for example *The Money Programme, Weekend World* and so on) for so long made difficult factors so easy to assimilate that the printed word itself must now come alive and this is why Mr. Tobler (yes, John Tobler, archivist in extremis) has written an introductory survey.

5

I am pleased that Mr. Rees cares to place his emphasis on the United States for, much as I love England, and its rolling hills and its *Whistle Test* and *Melody Maker* and honey still for tea in Manchester, it is from America that much of the best music now comes and certainly the volume of business there is staggering, bionic even.

I am not sure why I was asked to write this introduction, there are others better qualified—but as a person whose mind is cramped, sometimes beyond endurance by minutiae, the book grabs me—every page is a treat, a mind boggler, never a bore. What the devil I shall do with the information I shall never know. I don't make bets, I don't want to be right in an argument, but I do like to *know*. Also, it is good having something on the train which is an 'open any page' book there is some fun therein.

My life as a newspaper man was bad for me. It gave me a monkey brain. I read the first paragraph of a story, then the last and I had the drift, then maybe I read the middle. (Who cares, most of it is guesswork.) But not in books like this. No...open at any page and you will learn *precisely* what went on.

It is a reference book but it is more. It is a friend. It could do as well on the table in the dentist's as in the office of whoever is running R.C.A. right now. Without a book like this where else is the man who believes himself to be old (because he is going bald and in pain with a badly-set crown and because he is the same age as the Beatles) going to find the reassuring news that in 1976 the Beatles had six singles in the charts. What were they? What label were they? Read this book and find out.

I hope this becomes an annual event. It deserves to. Soon it will be 1983 and many of the records in this book will be classics, out of stock, deleted, unavailable, whatever. Maybe you will remember the tune, but not the title and you will want to buy it so badly that it hurts. Try going to your local record store and asking for, it, try asking the cheery youth behind the Monday morning counter—hungover and crazed, taking delivery of 500 new Zeppelin, 500 Eagles and 25 of the latest fave rave whose name (such is the magnificently mercurial nature of this music world over which we all swarm) is still thoroughly anonymous and its members probably still in junior school. Try asking if he has got that record by can't remember the name but it was late 1976, Top Ten, some new band from London, you remember, played the pubs and had a great guitar break near the end and a long fade and went something like this. Bom, de boom de boom, sax solo, and you will probably wish you had not bothered to get up and so will your busy dealer.

But go in with your book and ask for (jab your finger) 'this record' and there is every chance that he will order it for you, for there are many good dealers who are themselves record freaks, and there is every chance that the record company will still have it in stock, for there are some good record companies and all of them have at least one or more persons who actually like records. At W.E.A. we *all* like records. (I lie—there are two people who don't).

The man who has written the work, researched it, and was kind enough to ask me to write these few lines obviously cares. So do I. So dig this book, dig the facts and dig the music.

DEREK TAYLOR: 2272986/ZKO648830/LFAE 154-8/04383608/
7-6-32
(Army, National Insurance, Identity Card,
Bank Account and Date of Birth—all
numbers, all minutiae, all ever-so-slightly
inaccurate and all mine.)

INTRODUCTION by John Tobler

1976 was a year when the music papers were falling over themselves to discover a new act with the charisma of the Beatles while record buying members of the public steadfastly ignored almost everyone but the acts which in their eyes were trusted and true.

This led to the fact that the biggest hit makers of the year were the Beatles themselves. Seven singles and five albums were UK hits, plus two singles and six albums in the States. Add to that the fact that Paul McCartney was the most successful songwriter, with thirteen chart entries in that capacity, and you could be forgiven for thinking that we were talking about 1966...

It didn't stop with the Beatles either. John Denver, with his easily assimilable, wide open spaces songs, did not have a hit single in Britain, although five of his albums charted, while in America, his score amounted to six singles and seven albums in the chart. There was definitely a deja vu feeling about the charts, with familiar names from the last decade always in evidence—Chicago, Bob Dylan, Peter Frampton, Wings, Led Zeppelin, Rolling Stones, Fleetwood Mac, Stevie Wonder, Diana Ross, Paul Simon, Steve Miller, the Four Seasons—the list is endless.

The only sign of any sort of new order arriving was in the list of those who on the strength of this year's charts, appear to be on the decline. Slade all but vanished, Sweet were far less successful as a singles act (although they had an album on the chart for 44 weeks), Marc Bolan made the charts, but much lower than in 1975, and Carpenters had a bad year. Interestingly enough, two American acts, on the decline in their own country, greatly improved their status here. The Stylistics had five hit singles and four hit albums in Britain, while only managing two of each in the U.S.A., while the Fatback Band's four British hit singles were four more than they got in their native land.

European music had a bonanza year in Britain, with Abba and Pussycat in the top spot in the chart for 16 weeks between them. Add the one week Demis Roussos held that position, and a third of the year belongs to the continent, while Abba's 'Greatest Hits' LP was top of the album chart for eleven weeks. The Munich sound from Germany also caught on strongly, with both Silver Convention and Donna Summer scoring several hits on both sides of the Atlantic, and other European chart entries by such diverse acts as Can, Kayak, Triumvirat, Nektar and Boney M. However, Abba have so far failed to match in America their incredible success in this country.

Of the 618 U.S. single chart entries, and 397 in the U.K., only 117 were common to both charts, indicating a growing divergence of taste. Nevertheless, several deserving cases who had only previously been successful in one country or the other finally got into both charts, with Cliff Richard making inroads into America, and Boz Scaggs finally making it here. LPs connected with television were huge in Britain, with a vast number of records advertised on the box making it very big, while the 'actors making records' syndrome increased its influence, with the 'Rock Follies' album getting to the top of the charts here, and David Soul of *Starsky and Hutch* having a number one single. In America, the pattern was similar, with Mary Kay Place of the *Mary Hartman* series charting strongly, the *Happy Days* theme doing likewise, and the welcome return of John Sebastian with the appropriately titled 'Welcome Back'.

Those who look destined to be one hit wonders were, as ever, present in force. We may never again see chart records by J. J. Barrie, Ethna Campbell, Simon May, Laurie Lingo and the Dipsticks, Paul Davidson, Harpo, Juggy Jones,

7

Billy Howard and so on, but the same might have been said of Chris Hill last year, and he certainly came back strongly around Christmas.

Britain remains unconvinced about Aerosmith and Kiss, on the evidence of the 1976 charts. Aerosmith had four hit records in each U.S. chart, Kiss five singles and six LPs, but neither group approached that kind of success here, with two brief album entries by Kiss, and absolutely nothing from Aerosmith. However, there was no doubt that the Californian music of Jackson Browne and Linda Ronstadt finally took off here, and the Eagles had their best year yet. However, we still don't see soul music in the same way as the Americans—while the Commodores and Earth, Wind and Fire continue to be big in the States, the British record buyer seems to prefer the Real Thing, Sheer Elegance and the Drifters. America also had a jazz album at the top of its chart, certainly a rare occurrence. The artist involved, George Benson, in fact appeared on three different labels, Warner Bros., CTI and A&M, which may be another kind of record...

Small labels did well in the both British and American singles charts. While the CBS group were dominant in the UK with 43 hits, GTO had eleven, Riva 4 out of 6 releases, and RAK 7. In the US Motown, scored with six consecutive singles by different artists, and RSO had five consecutive singles. The Wombles disappeared in 1976, but Mike Batt scored with several production hits including Steeleye Span and the Kursaal Flyers. Heavy breathing rock was big, represented by Donna Summer, Silver Convention and Andrea True Connection, while citizen's band radio inspired several hits in the U.S. including one we can look forward to for 1977, by Rod Hart, in which a policeman pretends to be a homosexual citizen's band user.

Among those who improved their positions considerably during the year were Gallagher and Lyle, Gladys Knight, Joan Armatrading, the two doctors, Hook and Feelgood, Be-Bop Deluxe, Electric Light Orchestra, and finally Jefferson Starship, achieving their best results for several years. Comedy was as big as usual in the States, with Cheech and Chong, Richard Pryor, Redd Foxx and George Carlin, but Britain only had Mike Harding, and, depending on your viewpoint, Pam Ayres.

As far as producers went, the main men were Freddie Perren (Sylvers and Tavares), Kenny Gamble and Leon Huff with the Philly stable, Tom Dowd, David Rubinson (and Friends Inc.), Jack Douglas, Arif Mardin and George Martin, who with the help of the Beatles achieved 13 hit albums in the U.S.

Finally, the statistics—828 records in the U.S. album charts, 618 in the singles, while the U.K. had 285 albums in the chart, plus 397 singles—or 396, if you count the fact that 'Leader Of The Pack' was a hit on two labels!

All we have to do now is wait to see whether punk rock has taken over the 1977 charts, or whether Pam Ayres and her ilk have beaten them back...

COMPILER'S NOTE

Having decided to embark on this book, it seemed vital to cover ground that previous chart books had not. Obviously aspects of those other books had to be added to, in order to make what would hopefully be the definitive work on this fascinating subject. Those aspects included listing, under different headings —all chart information, titles, artists, composers, producers, catalogue numbers, publishers, musicians and recording dates and locations. The last three ideas were discarded, as songs change publishing hands with such regularity that the information would be out of date by the time you read this. Musician and recording details are inadequate because that sort of information is often undocumented, besides which there are probably many musicians who do not wish anyone to know they played on certain records!

Everything else has been included except a catalogue listing of albums. The idea behind listing records under catalogue numbers is to give some indication of how a particular record company has fared that year. This assessment could not be made of albums, as many of them—especially in the U.S.— stay in the charts for upwards of three or four years. A single's lifespan is, at maximum, six months. A table showing a record's performance throughout its chart history was to be included, but had to be left out owing to lack of space.

The book is divided into two parts. The first part contains the Music Week Top 50 singles and Top 50 albums charts for the U.K., and the second part the Billboard Top 100 singles and Top 200 albums charts for the U.S. Both parts cover the charts from January 3, 1976 to December 25, 1976. So a record that entered the charts in late 1976 and climbed to number one during early 1977 will have its position on December 25, 1976 as its highest chart placing.

Each part of the book is divided into six different sections.

1   TITLE SECTION, which shows the week and position of chart entry, the highest placing and week, duration on chart, title of record, artist and catalogue number of all singles.

2   ARTIST SECTION, lists the same records as above but under artists.

3   LABEL SECTION, does likewise but under alphabetical order of record company.

4   WRITER SECTION, lists the same records under their writers credits.

5   ALBUM SECTION, shows the week and position of chart entry, the highest placing and week, duration on chart, artists, title, catalogue number and producers of all albums.

6   PRODUCER SECTION, includes both singles and albums under producers. Albums are denoted by (LP) after the title.

Part Two of the book covers the same information as Part One but for the U.S. instead. Each section will be preceded by a short introduction by way of explanation. There is also a MISCELLANEOUS SECTION at the end of the book, which includes listings of the Top 50 best selling singles and albums of 1976, Platinum and Gold Disc awards for 1976 and all single and album chart toppers for 1976.

All information has been thoroughly checked on record labels and sleeves. Where this has not been possible, record company label copy and publishers have been consulted, notably with records that have spent a couple of weeks in the lower reaches of the U.S. chart, information has been accepted as being correct if *Billboard, Cashbox* and *Record World* all list the same credits.

Certain licence has been taken on occasion, most notably with producers. It has been immensely difficult to credit them correctly, with such terms as co-producer, associate producer, produced in association with etc., being used. Therefore only those actually credited as Producer are listed, although there are exceptions. Where a production company has been credited, all attempts have been made to find the individuals concerned and list them instead. There are pieces of information which are not the same as on record, e.g. Robert Palmer's 'Man Smart, Woman Smarter' credited to D. Kleiber on the record, but in fact written by Joseph Kuhm.

Apologies to all those who feel they should have been listed in this book but have not been, and congratulations to those who have been when they shouldn't have. As record sleeves rarely agree on how to spell people's names, a general consensus of sleeves has been taken.

Many thanks to all those in the copyright and index departments of the many record and publishing companies who have supplied information, as far afield as America and Japan. Thanks also to the Performing Rights Society and the Mechanical Copyright Protection Society Ltd. in London, and the Broadcast Music Inc. and the American Society of Composers, Authors and Publishers in New York. Additional thanks to Derek Taylor, Cathy McKnight and John Tobler, without whom etc...

DAFYDD REES
January, 1977

Part One

Section 1

UK Title Section

(*Music Week* Top 50 Singles Chart)

This section lists the position and week of entry, highest placing and week, duration on chart, title, artist and catalogue number of all singles that made the *Music Week* Top 50 chart during 1976.

These charts are based on the *Music Week*/British Market Research Bureau figures, (and are also used by the BBC for *Top of the Pops).* The sales are based on the previous week's chart to that printed—i.e. the chart for *Music Week* ending July 17, 1976 will be for the sales of Saturday, July 3 to Friday, July 9. However the chart positions correspond to the *Music Week* publication date, and not to the previous week's sales figure date. (The LP charts differ—see Section 5 for details). *Music Week* is not published during Christmas week therefore an additional week's chart placing is added to all those singles that were on the chart the previous week. Numbers in italics denote 1975 entry. *denotes record still in chart on January 1, 1977.

If you wish to find out the composer or producer of a song check under the title in this section alongside which you will find the artist. Then cross-refer to Section 2 and you will find the title under the artist. In the two columns next to the title you will find the composers and producers. If you wish to know all the other records that an individual might have written or produced, refer to Sections 4 and 6 where the information will be listed under that individual. Cross-referencing of all record labels is included, and the information in that respect can be found in Section 3. The six sections of Part 1 do not cross-refer with those of Part 2.

Position and date of entry	Highest position and date	Wks.	Title	Artist(s)	Cat. No.
47(7/ 8)	18(4/ 9)	10	Afternoon Delight	Starland Vocal Band	RCA 2716
42(15/11)	5(6/12)	9	All Around My Hat	Steeleye Span	Chrysalis CHS 2078
46(10/ 4)	12(8/ 5)	7	All By Myself	Eric Carmen	Arista 42
45(29/11)	37(6/12)	3	Alright Baby	Stevenson's Rocket	Magnet MAG 47
43(11/12)	38(18/12)	3	*Anarchy In The U.K.	Sex Pistols	EMI 2566
41(17/ 1)	9(14/ 2)	7	Answer Me (Are You Ready) Do The Bus Stop *see under* Do	Barbara Dickson	RSO 2090 174
44(21/ 8)	5(18/ 9)	11	Aria	Acker Bilk, His Clarinet & Strings	Pye 7N 45607
50(3/ 4)	5(22/ 5)	12	Arms Of Mary	Sutherland Brothers & Quiver	CBS 4001
49(29/11)	5(17/ 1)	10	Art For Art's Sake	10cc	Mercury 6008 017
45(10/ 7)	39(24/ 7)	5	At The Hop	Danny & The Juniors	ABC 4123
30(24/ 1)	12(14/ 2)	7	Baby Face	Wing & A Prayer Fife & Drum Corps	Atlantic K10705
48(11/ 9)	43(2/10)	5	Baby I Love Your Way	Peter Frampton	A&M AMS 7246
49(17/ 4)	33(1/ 5)	6	Baby I'm Yours	Linda Lewis	Arista 43
29(21/ 8)	15(11/ 9)	7	Baby, We Better Try And Get It Together	Barry White	20th Century BTC 2298
35(10/ 7)	19(24/ 7)	6	Back In The U.S.S.R.	Beatles	Parlophone R6016
44(23/10)	13(13/11)	9	Beautiful Noise	Neil Diamond	CBS 4601
49(25/ 9)	37(9/10)	5	Benny And The Jets	Elton John	DJM DJS 10705
37(18/ 9)	10(16/10)	9	Best Disco In Town, The	Ritchie Family	Polydor 2058 777
44(31/ 7)	42(7/ 8)	4	Better Use Your Head	Little Anthony and the Imperials	United Artists UP 36141
43(4/12)	10(25/12)	4	*Bionic Santa	Chris Hill	Philips 6006 551
41(28/ 8)	6(25/ 9)	10	Blinded By The Light	Manfred Mann's Earthband	Bronze BRO 29
49(24/ 4)	41(1/ 5)	5	Blueberry Hill	Fats Domino	United Artists UP 35797
47(8/11)	1(29/11)	17	Bohemian Rhapsody	Queen	EMI 2375
45(19/ 6)	13(24/ 7)	10	Boston Tea Party, The	Sensational Alex Harvey Band	Mountain TOP 12
40(3/ 1)	25(24/ 1)	6	Both Ends Burning	Roxy Music	Island WIP 6262
48(29/ 5)	8(3/ 7)	10	Boys Are Back In Town, The	Thin Lizzy	Vertigo 6059 139
43(11/ 9)	35(25/ 9)	4	Breakaway	Gallagher & Lyle	A&M AMS 7245
48(29/11)	10(10/ 1)	10	Can I Take You Home Little Girl	Drifters	Bell 1462

Position and date of entry	Highest position and date	Wks.	Title	Artist(s)	Cat. No.
37(4/ 9)	2(25/ 9)	10	Can't Get By Without You	Real Thing	Pye 7N 45618
40(24/ 4)	4(22/ 5)	7	Can't Help Falling In Love	Stylistics	Avco 6105 050
49(28/ 2)	35(20/ 3)	5	Can't Say How Much I Love You	Demis Roussos	Philips 6042 114
46(25/12)	46(25/12)	1	*Car Wash	Rose Royce	MCA 267
47(11/12)	47(11/12)	2	Champion, The	Willie Mitchell	London HL-U 10545
47(6/12)	14(3/ 1)	7	Christmas In Dreadland/Come Outside	Judge Dread	Cactus CT 80
37(20/ 3)	24(27/ 3)	4	City Lights	David Essex	CBS 4050
50(14/ 2)	31(28/ 2)	5	Cloud 99	St. Andrew's Chorale	Decca F13617
33(15/ 5)	1(12/ 6)	13	Combine Harvester, The (Brand New Key)	Wurzels	EMI 2450
42(16/10)	24(6/11)	6	Coming Home	David Essex	CBS 4486
40(6/ 3)	11(27/ 3)	7	Concrete and Clay	Randy Edelman	20th Century BTC 2261
45(5/ 6)	16(3/ 7)	8	Continental, The	Maureen McGovern	20th Century BTC 2222
41(14/ 2)	2(20/ 3)	10	Convoy	C.W. McCall	MGM 2006 560
50(17/ 4)	4(8/ 5)	7	Convoy GB	Laurie Lingo & the Dipsticks	State STAT 23
45(29/ 5)	40(19/ 6)	7	Could It Be Magic	Donna Summer	GTO GT 60
47(9/10)	10(20/11)	9	Couldn't Get It Right	Climax Blues Band	BTM SBT 105
49(18/12)	31(25/12)	2	*Daddy Cool	Boney M	Atlantic K10827
43(21/ 8)	6(2/10)	13	Dance Little Lady Dance	Tina Charles	CBS 4480
49(13/12)	37(20/12)	8	Dance Of The Cuckoos	Band of the Black Watch	Spark SRL 1135
49(5/ 6)	31(26/ 6)	6	Dance The Body Music	Osibisa	Bronze BRO 26
23(21/ 8)	1(4/ 9)	15	Dancing Queen	Abba	Epic EPC 4499
49(9/10)	8(6/11)	9	Dancing With The Captain	Paul Nicholas	RSO 2090 206
46(7/ 2)	6(6/ 3)	8	Dat	Pluto Shervington	Opal PAL 5
42(29/ 5)	30(19/ 6)	5	Dawn	Flintlock	Pinnacle P-8419
28(31/ 1)	1(21/ 2)	10	December, 1963 (Oh, What A Night)	Four Seasons	Warner Bros K16688
40(17/ 1)	25(7/ 2)	7	Deep Purple	Donny & Marie Osmond	MGM 2006 561
43(18/ 9)	41(25/ 9)	3	Destiny	Candi Staton	Warner Bros K 16806
41(8/ 5)	9(5/ 6)	8	Devil Woman	Cliff Richard	EMI 2458
33(3/ 4)	10(1/ 5)	9	Disco Connection	Isaac Hayes Movement	ABC 4100

UK TITLE

Position and date of entry	Highest position and date	Wks.	Title	Artist(s)	Cat. No.
34(18/ 9)	6(9/10)	9	Disco Duck	Rick Dees & His Cast of Idiots	RSO 2090 204
47(24/ 4)	25(8/ 5)	7	Disco Lady	Johnnie Taylor	CBS 4044
50(11/ 9)	21(16/10)	9	Disco Music (I Like It)	J.A.L.N. Band	Magnet MAG 73
26(1/11)	1(22/11)	10	D.I.V.O.R.C.E.	Billy Connolly	Polydor 2058 652
48(6/12)	18(24/ 1)	10	(Are You Ready) Do The Bus Stop	Fatback Band	Polydor 2066 637
50(6/11)	39(20/11)	4	Do You Feel Like We Do	Peter Frampton	A&M AMS 7260
46(24/ 7)	8(14/ 8)	9	Doctor Kiss-Kiss	5000 Volts	Philips 6006 533
46(4/12)	8(25/12)	4	*Dr. Love	Tina Charles	CBS 4779
37(25/12)	37(25/12)	1	*Don't Cry For Me Argentina	Julie Covington	MCA 260
37(18/12)	11(25/12)	2	*Don't Give Up On Us	David Soul	Private Stock PVT 84
49(3/ 7)	1(24/ 7)	14	Don't Go Breaking My Heart	Elton John & Kiki Dee	Rocket ROKN 512
36(13/11)	17(4/12)	7	*Don't Make Me Wait Too Long	Barry White	20th Century BTC 2309
43(20/ 3)	11(17/ 4)	8	Don't Stop It Now	Hot Chocolate	RAK 230
23(9/10)	4(13/11)	10	Don't Take Away The Music	Tavares	Capitol CL 15886
41(17/ 4)	41(17/ 4)	2	Doomsday	Evelyn Thomas	20th Century BTC 1017
48(20/12)	36(10/ 1)	6	Dreams Of You	Ralph McTell	Warner Bros K16648
44(17/ 1)	35(24/11)	4	Drive Safely Darling	Tony Christie	MCA 219
47(11/ 9)	29(9/10)	7	Every Nite's A Saturday Night With You	Drifters	Bell 1491
46(18/12)	35(25/12)	2	*Every Man Must Have A Dream	Liverpool Express	Warner Bros K16854
46(10/ 1)	10(31/ 1)	8	Evil Woman	Electric Light Orchestra	Jet 764
40(7/ 8)	7(4/ 9)	9	Extended Play (EP)	Bryan Ferry	Island 1 EP1
47(16/10)	13(25/12)	11	*Fairy Tale	Dana	GTO GT 66
39(17/ 4)	11(8/ 5)	7	Fallen Angel	Frankie Valli	Private Stock PVT 51
48(21/ 2)	9(27/ 3)	11	Falling Apart At The Seams	Marmalade	Target TGT 105
44(27/ 3)	1(8/ 5)	15	Fernando	Abba	Epic EPC 4036
42(10/ 7)	28(14/ 8)	9	Fifth of Beethoven, A	Walter Murphy Band	Private Stock PVT 59
47(10/ 1)	23(31/ 1)	7	50 Ways To Leave Your Lover	Paul Simon	CBS 3887
43(22/11)	16(20/12)	10	First Impressions	Impressions	Curtom K16638
47(15/ 5)	23(12/ 6)	10	Flasher, The	Mistura with Lloyd Michels	Route RT 30

Position and date of entry	Highest position and date	Wks.	Title	Artist(s)	Cat. No.
50(18/12)	41(25/12)	2	*Flip	Jesse Green	EMI 2564
45(15/11)	28(29/11)	8	Fly, Robin, Fly	Silver Convention	Magnet MAG 43
43(1/ 5)	6(5/ 6)	10	Fool To Cry	Rolling Stones	Rolling Stones RS 19121
50(15/ 5)	34(29/ 5)	4	Fooled Around and Fell In Love	Elvin Bishop	Capricorn 2089 024
39(17/ 1)	1(14/ 2)	9	Forever and Ever	Slik	Bell 1464
44(14/ 2)	10(6/ 3)	7	Funky Weekend	Stylistics	Avco 6015 044
43(16/10)	38(23/10)	3	Funny How Time Slips Away	Dorothy Moore	Contempo CS 2092
50(22/11)	38(6/12)	8	Gamblin' Bar Room Blues	Sensational Alex Harvey Band	Vertigo ALEX 002
49(3/ 4)	28(17/ 4)	5	Get Back	Beatles	Apple R5777
47(20/11)	11(11/12)	6	*Get Back	Rod Stewart	Riva 6
35(3/ 1)	21(17/ 1)	5	Get It Together	Crispy & Co.	Creole CR 114
45(3/ 4)	7(8/ 5)	11	Get Up And Boogie	Silver Convention	Magnet MAG 55
49(18/ 9)	22(9/10)	6	Get Up Offa That Thing	James Brown	Polydor 2066 687
46(4/ 9)	9(16/10)	12	Girl Of My Best Friend	Elvis Presley	RCA 2729
42(27/ 3)	7(24/ 4)	8	Girls, Girls, Girls	Sailor	Epic EPC 3858
44(6/12)	2(17/ 1)	12	Glass Of Champagne	Sailor	Epic EPC 3770
48(17/ 1)	41(24/ 1)	3	God's Gonna Punish You	Tymes	RCA 2626
39(29/11)	8(10/ 1)	10	Golden Years	David Bowie	RCA 2640
46(3/ 7)	18(24/ 7)	7	Good Vibrations	Beach Boys	Capitol CL 15875
48(4/12)	15(25/12)	4	*Grandma's Party (EP)	Paul Nicholas	RSO 2090 216
44(29/11)	29(13/12)	7	Green Green Grass Of Home	Elvis Presley	RCA 2635
46(11/12)	25(25/12)	3	*Haitian Divorce	Steely Dan	ABC 4152
48(14/ 2)	34(28/ 2)	4	(If Paradise Is) Half As Nice	Amen Corner	Immediate IMS 103
50(27/11)	32(4/12)	5	*Hang On Sloopy	Sandpipers	Satril SAT 114
44(22/11)	5(20/12)	10	Happy To Be On An Island In The Sun	Demis Roussos	Philips 6042 033
37(10/ 7)	10(7/ 8)	8	Harvest For The World	Isley Brothers	Epic EPC 4369
45(22/ 5)	6(19/ 6)	10	Heart On My Sleeve	Gallagher & Lyle	A&M AMS 7227
50(21/ 8)	25(4/ 9)	8	Heaven Is In The Back Seat Of My Cadillac	Hot Chocolate	RAK 240
39(10/ 7)	4(14/ 8)	11	Heaven Must Be Missing An Angel	Tavares	Capitol CL 15876
46(13/ 3)	12(3/ 4)	8	Hello Happiness	Drifters	Bell 1469
50(10/ 4)	37(17/ 4)	3	Help	Beatles	Parlophone R5305

16

Position and date of entry	Highest position and date	Wks.	Title	Artist(s)	Cat. No.
41(31/ 7)	10(21/ 8)	7	Here Comes The Sun	Steve Harley & Cockney Rebel	EMI 2505
49(14/ 8)	17(2/10)	10	Here I Go Again	Twiggy	Mercury 6007 100
50(6/ 3)	30(20/ 3)	6	Here There And Everywhere	Emmylou Harris	Reprise K14415
44(25/12)	44(25/12)	1	*Here's To Love	John Christie	EMI 2554
45(27/ 3)	12(17/ 4)	7	Hey Jude	Beatles	Apple R5722
43(28/ 2)	32(20/ 3)	5	Hey Miss Payne	Chequers	Creole CR 116
40(4/12)	31(11/12)	4	*Hey Mr. Dream Maker	Cliff Richard	EMI 2559
45(6/ 3)	16(3/ 4)	7	Hey Mr. Music Man	Peters & Lee	Philips 6006 502
46(16/10)	46(16/10)	2	Hold Tight	Liverpool Express	Warner Bros K16799
49(24/ 1)	33(7/ 2)	4	Honey I	George McCrae	Jayboy BOY 107
43(10/ 4)	21(1/ 5)	5	Honky Tonk Train Blues	Keith Emerson	Manticore K13513
43(13/11)	36(20/11)	5	Hot Valves (EP)	Be-Bop Deluxe	Harvest HAR 5117
50(17/ 1)	33(31/ 1)	4	How High The Moon	Gloria Gaynor	MGM 2006 558
45(25/ 9)	4(16/10)	10	Howzat	Sherbet	Epic EPC 4574
43(7/ 2)	43(7/ 2)	4	Hurricane	Bob Dylan	CBS 3879
40(2/10)	4(6/11)	11	Hurt	Manhattans	CBS 4562
50(1/ 5)	37(8/ 5)	5	Hurt	Elvis Presley	RCA 2674
23(11/ 9)	3(25/ 9)	9	I Am A Cider Drinker (Paloma Blanca)	Wurzels	EMI 2520
47(20/12)	34(10/ 1)	7	I Believe I'm Gonna Love You	Frank Sinatra	Reprise K14400
40(6/12)	2(3/ 1)	7	I Believe In Father Christmas	Greg Lake	Manticore K13511
			(I Believe) Love's A Prima Donna *see under* Love's		
46(21/ 8)	17(25/ 9)	8	I Can't Ask For Anymore Than You	Cliff Richard	EMI 2499
47(30/10)	37(13/11)	5	I Can't Live A Dream	Osmonds	Polydor 2066 726
50(12/ 6)	37(19/ 6)	4	I Don't Wanna Play House	Tammy Wynette	Epic EPC 4091
45(31/ 1)	13(6/ 3)	9	I Love Music	O'Jays	Philadelphia International PIR 3879
44(19/ 6)	13(17/ 7)	9	I Love To Boogie	T. Rex	EMI MARC 14
48(7/ 2)	1(6/ 3)	12	I Love To Love (But My Baby Loves To Dance)	Tina Charles	CBS 3937
49(28/ 8)	35(4/ 9)	5	I Need It	Johnny 'Guitar' Watson	DJM DJS 10694

Position and date of entry	Highest position and date	Wks.	Title	Artist(s)	Cat. No.
50(3/ 7)	36(10/ 7)	5	I Need To Be In Love	Carpenters	A&M AMS 7238
25(11/ 9)	4(25/ 9)	9	I Only Want To Be With You	Bay City Rollers	Bell 1493
42(19/ 6)	13(31/ 7)	10	I Recall A Gypsy Woman	Don Williams	ABC 4098
46(10/ 7)	32(31/ 7)	5	I Thought It Took A Little Time (But Today I Fell In Love)	Diana Ross	Tamla Motown TMG 1032
41(28/ 2)	6(3/ 4)	9	I Wanna Stay With You	Gallagher & Lyle	A&M AMS 7211
50(28/ 8)	26(9/10)	10	I Want More	Can	Virgin VS 153
29(18/12)	22(25/12)	2	*I Wish	Stevie Wonder	Tamla Motown TMG 1054
48(25/ 9)	26(16/10)	7	I'd Really Love To See You Tonight	England Dan & John Ford Coley	Atlantic K10810
50(6/12)	13(10/ 1)	8	If I Could (If Paradise Is) Half As Nice see under Half	David Essex	CBS 3776
46(30/10)	5(20/11)	9	*If Not You	Dr. Hook	Capitol CL 15885
41(14/ 8)	35(21/ 8)	4	If You Know What I Mean	Neil Diamond	CBS 4398
38(9/10)	1(13/11)	12	*If You Leave Me Now	Chicago	CBS 4603
45(20/ 3)	32(3/ 4)	4	If You Love Me	Mary Hopkin	Good Earth GD 2
42(24/ 4)	23(15/ 5)	8	I'll Go Where Your Music Takes Me	Jimmy James & the Vagabonds	Pye 7N 45585
50(25/ 9)	11(23/10)	9	I'll Meet You At Midnight	Smokie	RAK 241
31(20/ 3)	6(10/ 4)	9	I'm Mandy Fly Me	10cc	Mercury 6009 019
49(16/10)	41(30/10)	4	I'm Still Waiting	Diana Ross	Tamla Motown TMG 1041
46(24/ 4)	12(29/ 5)	10	I'm Your Puppet	James & Bobby Purify	Mercury 6167 324
43(1/11)	6(15/11)	11	Imagine	John Lennon	Apple R6009
42(20/12)	4(17/ 1)	10	In Dulci Jubilo/ On Horseback	Mike Oldfield	Virgin VS 131
27(22/11)	11(6/12)	8	In For A Penny	Slade	Polydor 2058 663
50(7/ 2)	46(14/ 2)	3	In The Mood	Sound 9418	UK 121
47(24/ 7)	4(21/ 8)	10	In Zaire	Johnny Wakelin	Pye 7N 45595
47(7/ 2)	39(28/ 2)	4	Inside America	Juggy Murray Jones	Contempo CS 2080
48(26/ 6)	9(24/ 7)	9	It Only Takes A Minute	100 Ton & A Feather	UK 135
47(24/ 1)	5(6/ 3)	11	It Should Have Been Me	Yvonne Fair	Tamla Motown TMG 1013
48(13/12)	4(3/ 1)	6	It's Gonna Be A Cold Cold Christmas	Dana	GTO GT 45

Position and date of entry	Highest position and date	Wks.	Title	Artist(s)	Cat. No.
50(14/ 8)	44(28/ 8)	4	It's So Nice (To Have You Home)	New Seekers	CBS 4391
50(24/ 7)	41(7/ 8)	4	It's Temptation	Sheer Elegance	Pye 7N 25715
45(13/12)	9(17/ 1)	11	Itchycoo Park	Small Faces	Immediate IMS 102
39(14/ 8)	31(21/ 8)	4	Jailbreak	Thin Lizzy	Vertigo 6059 150
46(9/10)	14(6/11)	9	Jaws	Lalo Schifrin	CTI CTSP 005
25(24/ 7)	3(7/ 8)	9	Jeans On	David Dundas	AIR CHS 2094
42(15/ 5)	9(26/ 6)	10	Jolene	Dolly Parton	RCA 2675
40(20/ 3)	3(1/ 5)	13	Jungle Rock	Hank Mizell	Charly CS 1005
49(31/ 1)	38(7/ 2)	4	Just One Look	Faith Hope & Charity	RCA 2632
49(11/12)	33(25/12)	3	*Keep It Comin' Love	KC & the Sunshine Band	Jayboy BOY 112
22(21/ 8)	2(18/ 9)	10	Killing of Georgie, The	Rod Stewart	Riva 4
44(13/12)	6(24/ 1)	12	King Of The Cops	Billy Howard	Penny Farthing PEN 892
43(19/ 6)	4(31/ 7)	11	Kiss And Say Goodbye	Manhattans	CBS 4317
49(13/ 3)	38(20/ 3)	3	La Booga Rooga	Surprise Sisters	Good Earth GD 1
47(2/10)	41(16/10)	4	Laser Love	T. Rex	EMI MARC 15
46(20/ 3)	39(3/ 4)	5	Lazy Sunday	Small Faces	Immediate IMS 106
48(5/ 6)	7(3/ 7)	11	Leader Of The Pack	Shangri-Las	Charly CS 1009
47(12/ 6)	7(3/ 7)	10	Leader Of The Pack	Shangri-Las	Contempo CS 9032

(both versions were given one chart position from 19/6 to the time they dropped out of the chart on 21/8)

Position and date of entry	Highest position and date	Wks.	Title	Artist(s)	Cat. No.
38(27/11)	7(18/12)	5	*Lean On Me	Mud	Private Stock PVT85
28(7/ 8)	2(28/ 8)	10	Let 'Em In	Wings	Parlophone R6015
48(31/ 1)	44(7/ 2)	3	Let Me Be The No. 1	Dooley Silverspoon	Sevile SEV 1020
43(3/ 1)	9(24/ 1)	7	Let The Music Play	Barry White	20th Century BTC2265
42(17/ 4)	7(5/ 6)	12	Let Your Love Flow	Bellamy Brothers	Warner Bros K16690
45(7/ 2)	11(28/ 2)	7	Let's Call It Quits	Slade	Polydor 2058 690
50(28/ 2)	20(13/ 3)	6	Let's Do The Latin Hustle	Eddie Drennon & BBS Unlimited	Pye 7N 25702
40(28/ 2)	16(27/ 3)	6	Let's Do The Latin Hustle	M & O Band	Creole CR 120
41(22/ 5)	30(5/ 6)	5	Let's Make A Baby	Billy Paul	Philadelphia International PIR 4144
34(12/ 6)	4(3/ 7)	10	Let's Stick Together	Bryan Ferry	Island WIP 6307
42(29/11)	5(3/ 1)	10	Let's Twist Again/The Twist	Chubby Checker	London HL-U10512
50(13/12)	34(3/ 1)	5	Let's Womble To The Party Tonight	Wombles	CBS 3794

Position and date of entry	Highest position and date	Wks.	Title	Artist(s)	Cat. No.
39(24/ 1)	35(31/ 1)	4	Lies In Your Eyes, The	Sweet	RCA 2641
42(3/ 4)	9(8/ 5)	9	Life Is Too Short Girl	Sheer Elegance	Pye 7N 25703
41(21/ 8)	4(18/ 9)	9	Light Of Experience (Doina De Jale)	Gheorghe Zamfir	Epic EPC4310
42(26/ 6)	2(24/ 7)	14	Little Bit More, A	Dr. Hook	Capitol CL 15871
50(20/11)	14(18/12)	6	*Little Does She Know	Kursaal Flyers	CBS 4689
46(11/ 9)	43(25/ 9)	5	Live At The Marquee (EP)	Eddie & the Hot Rods	Island 1 EP2
49(13/11)	4(18/12)	7	*Livin' Thing	Electric Light Orchestra	Jet Up 36184
38(4/12)	9(25/12)	4	*Living Next Door To Alice	Smokie	RAK 244
49(6/ 3)	40(13/ 3)	3	London Boys	T. Rex	EMI MARC 13
49(30/10)	9(27/11)	9	*Lost In France	Bonnie Tyler	RCA 2734
50(25/12)	50(25/12)	1	*Lost Without Your Love	Bread	Elektra K12241
39(16/10)	10(13/11)	9	Love And Affection	Joan Armatrading	A&M AMS 7249
45(24/ 4)	10(29/ 5)	10	Love Hangover	Diana Ross	Tamla Motown TMG 1024
48(25/10)	4(29/11)	11	Love Hurts	Jim Capaldi	Island WIP 6246
45(10/ 1)	3(7/ 2)	10	Love Machine	Miracles	Tamla Motown TMG 1015
43(6/11)	6(18/12)	8	*Love Me	Yvonne Elliman	RSO 2090 205
48(1/ 5)	28(22/ 5)	7	Love Me Like A Lover	Tina Charles	CBS 4237
20(10/ 4)	4(1/ 5)	6	Love Me Like I Love You	Bay City Rollers	Bell 1477
50(10/ 7)	19(7/ 8)	8	Love On Delivery	Billy Ocean	GTO GT 62
34(21/ 2)	2(27/ 3)	10	Love Really Hurts Without You	Billy Ocean	GTO GT 52
48(13/11)	41(20/11)	4	Love So Right	Bee Gees	RSO 2090 207
37(13/ 1)	4(7/ 2)	9	Love To Love You Baby	Donna Summer	GTO GT 17
48(6/11)	41(13/11)	4	(I Believe) Love's A Prima Donna	Steve Harley & Cockney Rebel	EMI 2539
45(11/ 9)	13(9/10)	8	Loving and Free/ Amoureuse	Kiki Dee	Rocket ROKN 515
39(21/ 8)	28(18/ 9)	9	Loving On The Losing Side	Tommy Hunt	Spark SRL 1146
38(24/ 1)	12(21/ 2)	7	Low Rider	War	Island WIP 6267
48(30/10)	28(13/11)	4	Lowdown	Boz Scaggs	CBS 4563
47(14/ 8)	42(21/ 8)	4	Lullaby Of Broadway	Winifred Shaw	United Artists UP 36131
47(4/12)	31(18/12)	4	*Maggie May	Rod Stewart	Mercury 6160 006

Position and date of entry	Highest position and date	Wks.	Title	Artist(s)	Cat. No.
47(13/12)	20(3/ 1)	6	Make A Daft Noise For Christmas	Goodies	Bradleys BRAD 7533
47(21/ 8)	35(28/ 8)	4	Make Yours A Happy Home	Gladys Knight & the Pips	Buddah BDS 3790
43(13/12)	1(31/ 1)	14	Mamma Mia	Abba	Epic EPC3790
47(26/ 6)	14(31/ 7)	8	Man To Man	Hot Chocolate	RAK 238
50(8/ 5)	50(8/ 5)	1	Manchester United	Manchester United Football Team	Decca F13633
50(26/ 6)	21(31/ 7)	7	Me And Baby Brother	War	Island WIP6303
46(3/ 1)	10(24/ 1)	9	Midnight Rider	Paul Davidson	Tropical ALO 56
48(8/*5)	10(5/ 6)	9	Midnight Train To Georgia	Gladys Knight & the Pips	Buddah BDS 44
43(20/12)	18(31/ 1)	10	Milkyway	Sheer Elegance	Pye 7N 25697
49(7/ 2)	15(27/ 3)	10	Miss You Nights	Cliff Richard	EMI 2376
48(28/ 8)	1(16/10)	18	*Mississippi	Pussycat	Sonet SON 2077
47(19/ 6)	5(7/ 8)	12	Misty Blue	Dorothy Moore	Contempo CS 2087
13(22/11)	3(6/12)	9	Money Honey	Bay City Rollers	Bell 1461
34(20/11)	3(11/12)	6	*Money, Money, Money	Abba	Epic EPC4713
45(24/ 1)	13(21/ 2)	8	Moonlight Serenade	Glenn Miller	RCA 2644
44(17/ 4)	5(15/ 5)	10	More, More, More	Andrea True Connection	Buddah BDS 442
46(7/ 8)	27(28/ 8)	6	Morning Glory	James & Bobby Purify	Mercury 6167 380
45(17/ 4)	24(8/ 5)	6	Movie Star	Harpo	DJM DJS 400
38(3/ 4)	23(17/ 4)	6	Movin'	Brass Construction	United Artists UP 36090
44(20/ 3)	3(10/ 4)	9	Music	John Miles	Decca F13627
46(8/ 5)	3(5/ 6)	9	My Resistance Is Low	Robin Sarstedt	Decca F13624
46(19/ 6)	30(3/ 7)	7	My Sweet Rosalie	Brotherhood Of Man	Pye 7N 45602
48(10/ 7)	11(14/ 8)	9	Mystery Song	Status Quo	Vertigo 6059 146
43(15/11)	5(13/12)	10	Na Na Is The Saddest Word	Stylistics	Avco 6105 041
42(6/ 3)	31(13/ 3)	4	Never Gonna Fall In Love Again	Dana	GTO GT 55
50(7/ 8)	17(4/ 9)	12	Nice And Slow	Jesse Green	EMI 2492
46(14/ 8)	38(21/ 8)	4	Night Fever	Fatback Band	Spring 2066 706
31(17/ 7)	24(31/ 7)	5	No Chance (No Charge)	Billy Connolly	Polydor 2058 748
50(24/ 4)	1(5/ 6)	11	No Charge	J.J. Barrie	Power Exchange PX 209
33(17/ 1)	7(14/ 2)	9	No Regrets	Walker Brothers	GTO GT 42
48(17/ 7)	5(14/ 8)	9	Now Is The Time	Jimmy James & the Vagabonds	Pye 7N 45606

Position and date of entry	Highest position and date	Wks.	Title	Artist(s)	Cat. No.
49(3/ 1)	33(24/ 1)	10	Old Rugged Cross, The	Ethna Campbell	Philips 6006 475
49(4/12)	44(11/12)	3	One Fine Morning	Tommy Hunt	Spark SRL 1148
43(3/ 7)	32(24/ 7)	7	One Piece At A Time	Johnny Cash & the Tennessee Three	CBS 4287
48(6/ 3)	42(13/ 3)	3	Other Side Of Me, The	Andy Williams	CBS 3905
46(27/ 3)	23(10/ 4)	5	Paperback Writer	Beatles	Apple R5452
50(29/ 5)	41(19/ 6)	4	Party Time	Fatback Band	Polydor 2066 682
37(28/ 2)	5(27/ 3)	9	People Like You And People Like Me	Glitter Band	Bell 1471
36(20/ 3)	7(3/ 4)	7	Pinball Wizard	Elton John	DJM DJS 652
34(9/10)	7(13/11)	11	Play That Funky Music	Wild Cherry	Epic EPC4593
39(27/11)	5(25/12)	5	*Portsmouth	Mike Oldfield	Virgin VS 163
50(9/10)	23(30/10)	7	Queen Of My Soul	Average White Band	Atlantic K10825
36(14/ 2)	7(6/ 3)	7	Rain	Status Quo	Vertigo 6059 133
48(17/ 4)	39(1/ 5)	4	Rain Forest	Biddu Orchestra	Epic EPC4084
47(10/ 4)	43(17/ 4)	4	Ram Goat Liver	Pluto Shervington	Trojan TR 7978
47(17/ 4)	17(29/ 5)	8	Reggae Like It Used To Be	Paul Nicholas	RSO 2090 185
50(16/10)	32(6/11)	5	Remember Yesterday	John Miles	Decca F13667
36(6/12)	10(3/ 1)	7	Renta Santa	Chris Hill	Philips 6006 491
45(8/ 5)	24(29/ 5)	9	Requiem	Slik	Bell 1478
50(20/ 3)	33(10/ 4)	5	Riders On The Storm	Doors	Elektra K12203
48(11/12)	28(25/12)	3	*Ring Out Solstice Bells (EP)	Jethro Tull	Chrysalis CXP 2
44(10/ 7)	36(24/ 7)	4	Rock And Roll Music	Beach Boys	Reprise K14440
50(23/10)	11(27/11)	9	Rock 'N' Me	Steve Miller Band	Mercury 6078 804
44(31/ 1)	3(28/ 2)	10	Rodrigo's Guitar Concerto De Aranjuez (Theme from 2nd Movement)	Manuel & the Music of the Mountains	EMI 2383
27(26/ 6)	1(17/ 7)	12	Roussos Phenomenon, The (EP)	Demis Roussos	Philips DEMIS 001
49(11/ 9)	16(30/10)	11	Rubber Band Man, The	Detroit Spinners	Atlantic K10807
50(4/ 9)	3(16/10)	17	*Sailing	Rod Stewart	Warner Bros K16600
50(20/12)	37(3/ 1)	4	Santa Claus Is Coming To Town	Carpenters	A&M AMS 7144

Position and date of entry	Highest position and date	Wks.	Title	Artist(s)	Cat. No.
48(21/ 8)	43(28/ 8)	3	Satin Sheets	Bellamy Brothers	Warner Bros K16775
14(13/ 3)	1(20/ 3)	16	Save Your Kisses For Me	Brotherhood of Man	Pye 7N 45569
47(13/11)	40(27/11)	4	Say You Love Me	Fleetwood Mac	Reprise K14447
47(6/ 3)	33(13/ 3)	4	Seagull	Rainbow Cottage	Penny Farthing PEN 906
49(20/11)	35(4/12)	4	Secrets	Sutherland Brothers & Quiver	CBS 4668
37(15/ 5)	12(5/ 6)	8	Shake It Down	Mud	Private Stock PVT65
49(17/ 7)	22(7/ 8)	8	(Shake Shake Shake) Shake Your Booty	KC & the Sunshine Band	Jayboy BOY 110
47(28/ 8)	32(4/ 9)	4	Shannon	Henry Gross	Lifesong ELS 45002
48(16/10)	42(23/10)	4	She's Gone	Daryl Hall & John Oates	Atlantic K10828
46(21/ 2)	23(27/ 3)	8	Ships In The Night	Be-Bop Deluxe	Harvest HAR 5104
49(1/ 5)	10(19/ 6)	12	Show Me The Way	Peter Frampton	A&M AMS 7218
26(29/11)	8(13/12)	8	Show Me You're A Woman	Mud	Private Stock PVT45
45(4/12)	23(25/12)	4	*Side Show	Barry Biggs	Dynamic DYN 118
50(17/ 7)	43(14/ 8)	5	Side Show	Chanter Sisters	Polydor 2058 735
29(15/ 5)	2(12/ 6)	11	Silly Love Songs	Wings	Parlophone R6014
27(24/ 4)	3(22/ 5)	9	Silver Star	Four Seasons	Warner Bros K16742
50(11/12)	34(25/12)	3	*Sing Me An Old Fashioned Song	Billie Jo Spears	United Artists UP 36179
43(7/ 8)	7(11/ 9)	9	Sixteen Bars	Stylistics	H&L 6105 059
48(1/11)	9(29/11)	11	Sky High	Jigsaw	Splash CPI 1
48(25/12)	48(25/12)	1	*Smile	Pussycat	Sonet SON 2096
45(6/11)	20(27/11)	8	*So Sad The Song	Gladys Knight & the Pips	Buddah BDS 448
50(5/ 6)	36(19/ 6)	4	Sold My Rock 'N' Roll (Gave It Up For Funky Soul)	Linda & the Funky Boys	Spark SRL 1139
4(27/11)	2(11/12)	5	*Somebody To Love	Queen	EMI 2565
43(31/ 1)	17(6/ 3)	8	Something's Been Making Me Blue	Smokie	RAK 227
44(13/11)	11(4/12)	7	*Sorry Seems To Be The Hardest Word	Elton John	Rocket ROKN 517
44(8/ 5)	13(26/ 6)	10	Soul City Walk	Archie Bell & the Drells	Philadelphia International PIR4250
44(9/10)	32(23/10)	5	Soul Dracula	Hot Blood	Creole CR 132
48(24/ 7)	42(31/ 7)	3	Soul Searchin' Time	Trammps	Atlantic K1079
39(21/ 2)	10(13/ 3)	7	Spanish Hustle	Fatback Band	Polydor 2066 256
47(20/ 3)	37(27/ 3)	4	Spanish Wine	Chris White	Charisma CB272
50(30/10)	21(4/12)	8	Spinning Rock Boogie	Hank C. Burnette	Sonet SON 2094
44(24/ 1)	10(28/ 2)	9	Squeeze Box	Who	Polydor 2121 275
41(10/ 4)	4(15/ 5)	10	S-S-S-Single Bed	Fox	GTO GT 57

Position and date of entry	Highest position and date	Wks.	Title	Artist(s)	Cat. No.
49(6/11)	38(13/11)	4	Stoney Ground	Guys 'n' Dolls	Magnet MAG76
50(13/11)	12(11/12)	7	*Stop Me (If You've Heard It All Before)	Billy Ocean	GTO GT 72
49(3/ 7)	38(10/ 7)	3	Strange Magic	Electric Light Orchestra	Jet 779
46(3/ 4)	32(10/ 4)	3	Strawberry Fields Forever	Beatles	Apple R5570
36(30/10)	7(20/11)	7	Substitute	Who	Polydor 2058 803
39(9/10)	7(23/10)	8	Summer Of My Life, The	Simon May	Pye 7N 45627
49(19/ 6)	49(19/ 6)	1	Sunday	Buster	RCA 2678
46(17/ 1)	17(31/ 1)	6	Sunshine Day	Osibisa	Bronze BRO 20
49(25/12)	49(25/12)	1	*Suspicion	Elvis Presley	RCA 2768
44(11/ 9)	31(25/ 9)	4	Sweet Home Alabama/Double Trouble/Free Bird	Lynyrd Skynyrd	MCA 251
44(6/ 3)	12(27/ 3)	7	Take It To The Limit	Eagles	Asylum K13029
50(2/10)	34(30/10)	6	Tears Of A Clown	Smokey Robinson & the Miracles	Tamla Motown TMG 1048
49(10/ 1)	35(17/ 1)	4	Tears On The Telephone	Claude Francois	Bradleys BRAD 7528
46(13/11)	35(27/11)	4	Teenage Depression	Eddie & the Hot Rods	Island WIP6354
50(13/ 3)	35(17/ 4)	8	That's Where The Happy People Go	Trammps	Atlantic K1079/7
25(3/ 4)	5(24/ 4)	8	Theme From Mahogany 'Do You Know Where You're Going To'	Diana Ross	Tamla Motown TMG 1010
50(27/ 3)	22(17/ 4)	6	There's A Kind Of Hush	Carpenters	A&M AMS 7219
37(11/12)	19(25/12)	3	*Things We Do For Love, The	10cc	Mercury 6008 022
47(29/11)	21(3/ 1)	8	Think Of Me (Wherever You Are)	Ken Dodd	EMI 2342
41(15/ 5)	9(12/ 6)	8	This Is It	Melba Moore	Buddah BDS 443
27(15/11)	4(6/12)	9	This Old Heart Of Mine	Rod Stewart	Riva 1
48(19/ 6)	41(3/ 7)	4	Tiger Baby/No, No, Joe	Silver Convention	Magnet MAG69
46(1/ 5)	36(8/ 5)	4	Toast Of Love	Three Degrees	Epic EPC4215
42(5/ 6)	5(26/ 6)	9	Tonight's The Night	Rod Stewart	Riva 2
49(8/ 5)	42(22/ 5)	3	Tracks Of My Tears, The	Linda Ronstadt	Asylum K13034
48(22/11)	2(20/12)	10	Trail Of The Lonesome Pine, The	Laurel & Hardy	United Artists UP 36026
49(29/ 5)	32(5/ 6)	3	Trocadero	Showaddywaddy	Bell 1476

Position and date of entry	Highest position and date	Wks.	Title	Artist(s)	Cat. No.
50(19/ 6)	41(10/ 7)	6	Tubular Bells	Champs Boys	Philips 6006 519
39(7/ 2)	24(21/ 2)	6	Tuxedo Junction	Manhattan Transfer	Atlantic K10670
44(22/ 5)	33(5/ 6)	4	TVC 15	David Bowie	RCA 2682
49(15/ 5)	46(29/ 5)	5	Two Of Us, The	Mac & Katie Kissoon	State STAT 21
47(25/ 9)	40(9/10)	3	Under One Roof	Rubettes	State STAT 27
36(6/11)	1(4/12)	8	*Under The Moon Of Love	Showaddywaddy	Bell 1495
50(18/ 9)	25(16/10)	7	Uptown, Uptempo Woman, The	Randy Edelman	20th Century BTC2225
47(28/ 2)	23(20/ 3)	7	Wake Up Everybody	Harold Melvin & the Blue Notes	Philadelphia International PIR 3866
42(17/ 1)	10(14/ 2)	8	Walk Away From Love	David Ruffin	Tamla Motown TMG 1017
49(22/ 5)	16(26/ 6)	9	Wanderer, The	Dion	Philips 6146 700
42(24/ 1)	28(7/ 2)	6	Way I Want To Touch You, The	Captain & Tennille	A&M AMS 7203
48(27/11)	34(4/12)	4	We Can Work It Out	Four Seasons	Warner Bros K16845
43(10/ 1)	5(7/ 2)	9	We Do It	R & J Stone	RCA 2616
48(24/ 1)	26(21/ 2)	7	Weak Spot (What A) Wonderful World *see under* Wonderful	Evelyn Thomas	20th Century BTC 1014
47(17/ 7)	4(4/ 9)	13	What I've Got In Mind	Billie Jo Spears	United Artists UP 36118
45(13/11)	1(25/12)	7	*When A Child Is Born (Soleado)	Johnny Mathis	CBS 4599
35(2/10)	2(23/10)	10	When Forever Has Gone	Demis Roussos	Philips 6042 186
49(20/12)	41(3/ 1)	4	White Christmas	Freddie Starr	Thunderbird THE 102
47(10/ 7)	43(24/ 7)	4	Who'd She Coo	Ohio Players	Mercury PLAY 001
48(8/11)	16(6/12)	9	Why Did You Do It	Stretch	Anchor ANCL 1021
43(6/12)	6(10/ 1)	10	Wide Eyed And Legless	Andy Fairweather Low	A&M AMS 7202
32(11/12)	17(25/12)	3	*Wild Side Of Life	Status Quo	Vertigo 6059 153
39(8/ 5)	35(15/ 5)	4	Winkle Man, The	Judge Dread	Cactus CT 90
45(25/12)	45(25/12)	1	*Winter Melody	Donna Summer	GTO GT76
45(16/10)	22(6/11)	8	Without You	Nilsson	RCA 2733
49(12/ 6)	25(3/ 7)	7	(What A) Wonderful World	Johnny Nash	Epic EPC4294
46(28/ 8)	38(4/ 9)	5	Work All Day	Barry Biggs	Dynamic DYN 101
30(28/ 8)	27(11/ 9)	4	Y Viva Suspenders/ Confessions Of A Bouncer	Judge Dread	Cactus CT 99

Position and date of entry	Highest position and date	Wks.	Title	Artist(s)	Cat. No.
41(13/ 3)	8(3/ 4)	7	Yesterday	Beatles	Apple R6013
43(26/ 6)	11(24/ 7)	9	You Are My Love	Liverpool Express	Warner Bros K16743
47(13/ 3)	40(27/ 3)	5	You Belong To Me	Gary Glitter	Bell 1473
45(31/ 7)	3(11/ 9)	11	You Don't Have To Go	Chi-Lites	Brunswick BR34
45(21/ 2)	5(20/ 3)	8	You Don't Have To Say You Love Me	Guy 'n' Dolls	Magnet MAG 50
44(29/ 5)	2(3/ 7)	11	You Just Might See Me Cry	Our Kid	Polydor 2058 729
30(30/10)	2(20/11)	9	*You Make Me Feel Like Dancing	Leo Sayer	Chrysalis CHS 2119
43(6/ 3)	2(3/ 4)	10	You See The Trouble With Me	Barry White	20th Century BTC 2277
47(3/ 4)	22(24/ 4)	6	You Sexy Sugar Plum (But I Like It)	Rodger Collins	Fantasy FTC 132
38(8/11)	2(29/11)	12	You Sexy Thing	Hot Chocolate	RAK 221
36(31/ 7)	6(28/ 8)	10	You Should Be Dancing	Bee Gees	RSO 2090 195
22(5/ 6)	1(26/ 6)	11	You To Me Are Everything	Real Thing	Pye 7N 25709
47(31/ 7)	10(11/ 9)	10	You'll Never Find Another Love Like Mine	Lou Rawls	Philadelphia International PIR4372
49(27/11)	24(18/12)	5	*You'll Never Get To Heaven (EP)	Stylistics	H&L STYL 001
47(29/ 5)	2(10/ 7)	13	Young Hearts Run Free	Candi Staton	Warner Bros K16730
37(7/ 2)	27(21/ 2)	6	Your Magic Put A Spell On Me	L.J. Johnson	Philips 6006 492
47(18/12)	32(25/12)	2	*You're More Than A Number In My Little Red Book	Drifters	Arista 78
24(3/ 7)	7(17/ 7)	8	You're My Best Friend	Queen	EMI 2494
49(23/10)	35(13/11)	6	You're My Best Friend	Don Williams	ABC 4144
41(29/ 5)	15(26/ 6)	7	You're My Everything	Lee Garrett	Chrysalis CHS 2087
36(1/ 5)	28(8/ 5)	4	You're The Reason Why	Rubettes	State STAT 20

Section 2

UK Artist Section

(*Music Week* Top 50 Singles Chart)

This section lists, under artist headings, the titles, writers and producers of all singles that made the *Music Week* Top 50 chart during 1976.

The tracks on double A sides and EPs are separated by obliques, to which writers' and producers' credits correspond. When a group is credited with writing a song, the names of the members of that group will be listed in brackets beneath the name of the group.

Artist(s)/Title	Writer(s)	Producer(s)
ABBA		
DANCING QUEEN	Benny Andersson Stig Anderson Bjorn Ulvaeus	Benny Andersson Bjorn Ulvaeus
FERNANDO	Benny Andersson Stig Anderson Bjorn Ulvaeus	Benny Andersson Bjorn Ulvaeus
MAMMA MIA	Benny Andersson Stig Anderson Bjorn Ulvaeus	Benny Andersson Bjorn Ulvaeus
MONEY, MONEY, MONEY	Benny Andersson Bjorn Ulvaeus	Benny Andersson Bjorn Ulvaeus
AMEN CORNER		
(If Paradise Is) HALF AS NICE	Lucio Battisti Jack Fishman	Andy Fairweather Low Shel Talmy
Joan ARMATRADING		
LOVE AND AFFECTION	Joan Armatrading	Glyn Johns
AVERAGE WHITE BAND		
QUEEN OF MY SOUL	Hamish Stuart	Arif Mardin
BAND OF THE BLACK WATCH		
DANCE OF THE CUCKOOS	Marvin Hatley	Barry Kingston
J.J. BARRIE		
NO CHARGE	Harlan Howard	Bill Amesbury
BAY CITY ROLLERS		
I ONLY WANT TO BE WITH YOU	Ivor Raymonde Mike Hawker	Jimmy Ienner
LOVE ME LIKE I LOVE YOU	Eric Faulkner Stuart 'Woody' Wood	Muff Winwood
MONEY HONEY	Eric Faulkner Stuart 'Woody' Wood	Phil Wainman
BEACH BOYS		
GOOD VIBRATIONS	Brian Wilson Mike Love	Brian Wilson
ROCK AND ROLL MUSIC	Chuck Berry	Brian Wilson
BEATLES		
BACK IN THE U.S.S.R.	John Lennon Paul McCartney	George Martin
GET BACK	John Lennon Paul McCartney	George Martin
HELP	John Lennon Paul McCartney	George Martin
HEY JUDE	John Lennon Paul McCartney	George Martin
PAPERBACK WRITER	John Lennon Paul McCartney	George Martin
STRAWBERRY FIELDS FOREVER	John Lennon Paul McCartney	George Martin
YESTERDAY	John Lennon Paul McCartney	George Martin

Artist(s)/Title	Writer(s)	Producer(s)
BE-BOP DELUXE		
HOT VALVES (EP)		
Maid In Heaven/	Bill Nelson	Roy Thomas Baker/
Bring Back The Spark/		John Leckie
Blazing Apostles/		Bill Nelson/
Jet Silver And The Dolls		John Leckie
Of Venus		Bill Nelson/
		Ian McLintock
SHIPS IN THE NIGHT	Bill Nelson	Bill Nelson
		John Leckie
BEE GEES		
LOVE SO RIGHT	Bee Gees	Bee Gees
		(Barry, Robin
		& Maurice Gibb)
YOU SHOULD BE DANCING	Bee Gees	Bee Gees
Archie BELL & THE DRELLS		
SOUL CITY WALK	John Whitehead	John Whitehead
	Gene McFadden	Gene McFadden
	Victor Carstarphen	Victor Carstarphen
BELLAMY BROTHERS		
LET YOUR LOVE FLOW	Larry E. Williams	Phil Gernhard
		Tony Scotti
SATIN SHEETS	Willis Alan Ramsey	Phil Gernhard
		Tony Scotti
BIDDU ORCHESTRA		
RAIN FOREST	Biddu	Biddu
Barry BIGGS		
SIDE SHOW	Vinny Barrett	Neville Hinds
	Bobby Eli	
WORK ALL DAY	Barry Biggs	Byron Lee
		Barry Biggs
Acker BILK, HIS CLARINET & STRINGS		
ARIA	Sergio Bardotti	Terry Brown
	Dario Baldan Bembo	
Elvin BISHOP		
FOOLED AROUND AND FELL IN LOVE	Elvin Bishop	Allan Blazek
		Bill Szymczyk
BONEY M		
DADDY COOL	Frank Farian	Frank Farian
	Antonio Reyam	
David BOWIE		
GOLDEN YEARS	David Bowie	David Bowie
		Harry Maslin
TVC 15	David Bowie	David Bowie
		Harry Maslin
BRASS CONSTRUCTION		
MOVIN'	Randy Muller	Jeff Lane
	Wade Williamson	
BREAD		
LOST WITHOUT YOUR LOVE	David Gates	David Gates

Artist(s)/Title	Writer(s)	Producer(s)
BROTHERHOOD OF MAN		
MY SWEET ROSALIE	Tony Hiller	Tony Hiller
	Lee Sheriden	
	Martin Lee	
SAVE YOUR KISSES FOR ME	Tony Hiller	Tony Hiller
	Lee Sheriden	
	Martin Lee	
James BROWN		
GET UP OFFA THAT THING	Deanna Brown	James Brown
	Deidra Brown	
	Yamma Brown	
Hank C. BURNETTE		
SPINNING ROCK BOOGIE	Hank C. Burnette	Sven Ake Hogberg
BUSTER		
SUNDAY	Ronnie Scott	David MacKay
	Steve Wolfe	Ronnie Scott
		Steve Wolfe
Ethna CAMPBELL		
THE OLD RUGGED CROSS	Traditional	Arthur Frewin
	arr. Tony Cliff	
	Dave Long	
CAN		
I WANT MORE	Can	Can
	Peter Gilmour	(Holger Czukay
		Michael Karoli
		Irmin Schmidt
		Jaki Liebezeit)
Jim CAPALDI		
LOVE HURTS	Boudleaux Bryant	Steve Smith
CAPTAIN & TENNILLE		
THE WAY I WANT TO TOUCH YOU	Toni Tennille	Morgan Cavett
Eric CARMEN		
ALL BY MYSELF	Eric Carmen	Jimmy Ienner
CARPENTERS		
I NEED TO BE IN LOVE	Richard Carpenter	Richard Carpenter
	John Bettis	
	Albert Hammond	
SANTA CLAUS IS COMING	Haven Gillespie	Jack Daugherty
TO TOWN	J. Fred Coots	Karen Carpenter
		Richard Carpenter
THERE'S A KIND OF HUSH	Les Reed	Richard Carpenter
	Geoff Stephens	
Johnny CASH &		
THE TENNESSEE THREE		
ONE PIECE AT A TIME	Wayne Kemp	Charlie Bragg
		Don Davis
CHAMPS BOYS		
TUBULAR BELLS	Mike Oldfield	Patrick Boceno
CHANTER SISTERS		
SIDE SHOW	Roger Cook	Roger Cook
	Herbie Flowers	Greg Jackman

Artist(s)/Title	Writer(s)	Producer(s)
Tina CHARLES		
DANCE LITTLE LADY DANCE	Biddu	Biddu
	Gerry Shury	
	Ron Roker	
DR. LOVE	Biddu	Biddu
I LOVE TO LOVE	Jack Robinson	Biddu
(But My Baby Loves To Dance)	James Bolden	
LOVE ME LIKE A LOVER	Jack Robinson	Biddu
	James Bolden	
Chubby CHECKER		
LET'S TWIST AGAIN/THE TWIST	Kal Mann	(Not listed)
	Dave Appell/	
	Hank Ballard	
CHEQUERS		
HEY MISS PAYNE	John Mathias	John Mathias
CHICAGO		
IF YOU LEAVE ME NOW	Peter Cetera	James William Guercio
CHI-LITES		
YOU DON'T HAVE TO GO	Eugene Record	Eugene Record
	Barbara Acklin	
John CHRISTIE		
HERE'S TO LOVE	Paul Curtis	Dave Clark
Tony CHRISTIE		
DRIVE SAFELY DARLING	Geoff Stephens	Geoff Stephens
	Barry Mason	
CLIMAX BLUES BAND		
COULDN'T GET IT RIGHT	Climax Blues Band	Climax Blues Band
		(Peter Haycock
		Colin Cooper
		Richard Jones
		Derek Holt
		John Kuffley)
Rodger COLLINS		
YOU SEXY SUGAR PLUM	Rodger Collins	Rodger Collins
(But I Like It)		
Billy CONNOLLY		
D.I.V.O.R.C.E.	Bobby Braddock	Phil Coulter
	Curly Putman	
	Sheb Wooley	
NO CHANCE (NO CHARGE)	Harlan Howard	Phil Coulter
Julie COVINGTON		
DON'T CRY FOR ME ARGENTINA	Andrew Lloyd-Webber	Andrew Lloyd-Webber
	Tim Rice	Tim Rice
CRISPY & CO.		
GET IT TOGETHER	Richard Edwyn	I.H.P. Productions
DANA		
FAIRY TALE	Paul Greedus	Barry Blue
IT'S GONNA BE A COLD COLD	Roger Greenaway	Geoff Stephens
CHRISTMAS	Geoff Stephens	
NEVER GONNA FALL IN LOVE AGAIN	Eric Carmen	Geoff Stephens

Artist(s)/Title	Writer(s)	Producer(s)
DANNY & THE JUNIORS		
AT THE HOP	John Madara	(Not listed)
	Arthur Singer	
	David White	
Paul DAVIDSON		
MIDNIGHT RIDER	Gregg Allman	Leighton Shervington
Kiki DEE		
LOVING AND FREE/AMOUREUSE	Kiki Dee/	Clive Franks
	Gary Osborne	Elton John
	Veronique Sanson	
(see also Elton JOHN & KIKI DEE)		
Rick DEES & HIS CAST OF IDIOTS		
DISCO DUCK	Rick Dees	Bobby Manuel
DETROIT SPINNERS		
(known as the SPINNERS in the U.S.)		
THE RUBBER BAND MAN	Thom Bell	Thom Bell
	Linda Creed	
Neil DIAMOND		
BEAUTIFUL NOISE	Neil Diamond	Robbie Robertson
IF YOU KNOW WHAT I MEAN	Neil Diamond	Robbie Robertson
Barbara DICKSON		
ANSWER ME	Gerhard Winkler	Junior Campbell
	Fred Rauch	
	Carl Sigman	
DION		
THE WANDERER	Ernest Maresca	Glen Stuart
DR. HOOK		
A LITTLE BIT MORE	Bobby Gosh	Ron Haffkine
IF NOT YOU	Dennis Locorriere	Ron Haffkine
Ken DODD		
THINK OF ME (Wherever You Are)	Pascal Auriat	Nick Ingman
	Pascal Sevran	
	Serge Lebrail	
	Bryan Blackburn	
Fats DOMINO		
BLUEBERRY HILL	Alan Lewis	(Not listed)
	Larry Stock	
	Vincent Rose	
DOORS		
RIDERS ON THE STORM	Doors	Bruce Botnick
		Doors
		(Jim Morrison
		Robbie Krieger
		Ray Manzarek
		John Densmore)
Eddie DRENNON & BBS UNLIMITED		
LET'S DO THE LATIN HUSTLE	Eddie Drennon	Eddie Drennon
DRIFTERS		
CAN I TAKE YOU HOME LITTLE GIRL	Roger Greenaway	Roger Greenaway
	Barry Mason	
EVERY NITE'S A SATURDAY	Geoff Stephens	Roger Greenaway
NIGHT WITH YOU	Roger Greenaway	

UK ARTIST

Artist(s)/Title	Writer(s)	Producer(s)
HELLO HAPPINESS	Les Reed	Roger Greenaway
	Roger Greenaway	
YOU'RE MORE THAN A NUMBER IN MY LITTLE RED BOOK	Roger Greenaway Tony Macaulay	Roger Greenaway
David DUNDAS		
JEANS ON	David Dundas	Roger Greenaway
	Roger Greenaway	
Bob DYLAN		
HURRICANE	Bob Dylan Jacques Levy	Don DeVito
EAGLES		
TAKE IT TO THE LIMIT	Randy Meisner Don Henley Glenn Frey	Bill Szymczyk
EDDIE & THE HOT RODS		
LIVE AT THE MARQUEE (EP)		Ed Hollis
96 Tears/	Rudy Martinez/	
Get Out Of Denver/	Bob Seger/	
Gloria/	Van Morrison/	
Satisfaction	Mick Jagger Keith Richard	
TEENAGE DEPRESSION	Dave Higgs	Ed Hollis Vic Maile
Randy EDELMAN		
CONCRETE AND CLAY	Tommy Moeller Brian Parker	Bill Schnee
THE UPTOWN, UPTEMPO WOMAN	Randy Edelman	Bill Schnee
ELECTRIC LIGHT ORCHESTRA		
EVIL WOMAN	Jeff Lynne	Jeff Lynne
LIVIN' THING	Jeff Lynne	Jeff Lynne
STRANGE MAGIC	Jeff Lynne	Jeff Lynne
Yvonne ELLIMAN		
LOVE ME	Barry & Robin Gibb	Freddie Perren
Keith EMERSON		
HONKY TONK TRAIN BLUES	Meade 'Lux' Lewis	Keith Emerson
ENGLAND DAN & JOHN FORD COLEY		
I'D REALLY LOVE TO SEE YOU TONIGHT	Parker McGee	Kyle Lehning
David ESSEX		
CITY LIGHTS	David Essex	Jeff Wayne
COMING HOME	David Essex	Jeff Wayne
IF I COULD	David Essex	Jeff Wayne
Yvonne FAIR		
IT SHOULD HAVE BEEN ME	Norman Whitfield William Stevenson	Norman Whitfield
Andy FAIRWEATHER LOW		
WIDE EYED AND LEGLESS	Andy Fairweather Low	Glyn Johns
FAITH HOPE & CHARITY		
JUST ONE LOOK	Gregory Carroll Doris Payne Rex Garvin	Van McCoy

Artist(s)/Title	Writer(s)	Producer(s)
FATBACK BAND		
(Are You Ready) DO THE BUS STOP	Bill Curtis Johnny Flippin	Fatback Band (Richard Cornwell Bill Curtis Johnny Flippin Johnny King Earl Shelton George Williams)
NIGHT FEVER	Gerry Thomas	Fatback Band
PARTY TIME	Douglas Gibson Gerry Thomas Larry Smith	Fatback Band
SPANISH HUSTLE	Gerry Thomas	Fatback Band
Bryan FERRY		
EXTENDED PLAY (EP)		Chris Thomas
The Price Of Love/	Don & Phil Everly/	Bryan Ferry
Shame Shame Shame/	Jimmy Reed/	
Heart On My Sleeve/	Benny Gallagher	
It's Only Love	Graham Lyle/ John Lennon Paul McCartney	
LET'S STICK TOGETHER	Wilbert Harrison	Chris Thomas Bryan Ferry
5000 VOLTS		
DOCTOR KISS-KISS	Tony Eyers	Tony Eyers
FLEETWOOD MAC		
SAY YOU LOVE ME	Christine McVie	Keith Olsen Fleetwood Mac (Christine McVie Stevie Nicks Lindsey Buckingham John McVie Mick Fleetwood)
FLINTLOCK		
DAWN	Mike Holoway Senior	Mike Holoway Senior
FOUR SEASONS		
DECEMBER, 1963	Bob Gaudio	Bob Gaudio
(Oh, What A Night)	Judy Parker	
SILVER STAR	Bob Gaudio Judy Parker	Bob Gaudio
WE CAN WORK IT OUT	John Lennon Paul McCartney	Bob Gaudio Lou Reizner
FOX		
S-S-S-SINGLE BED	Kenny Young	Kenny Young
Peter FRAMPTON		
BABY I LOVE YOUR WAY	Peter Frampton	Peter Frampton
DO YOU FEEL LIKE WE DO	Peter Frampton	Peter Frampton
SHOW ME THE WAY	Peter Frampton	Peter Frampton
Claude FRANCOIS		
TEARS ON THE TELEPHONE	Claude Francois Jean-Pierre Bourtayre Frank Thomas H.E.R. Barnes	Roger Greenaway

Artist(s)/Title	Writer(s)	Producer(s)
GALLAGHER & LYLE		
BREAKAWAY	Benny Gallagher Graham Lyle	David Kershenbaum
HEART ON MY SLEEVE	Benny Gallagher Graham Lyle	David Kershenbaum
I WANNA STAY WITH YOU	Benny Gallagher Graham Lyle	David Kershenbaum
Lee GARRETT		
YOU'RE MY EVERYTHING	Lee Garrett Robert Taylor	Eric Malamud Tom Sellers
Gloria GAYNOR		
HOW HIGH THE MOON	Morgan Lewis Nancy Hamilton	Meco Monardo Tony Bongiovi Jay Ellis
Gary GLITTER		
YOU BELONG TO ME	Gary Glitter Mike Leander	Mike Leander
GLITTER BAND		
PEOPLE LIKE YOU AND PEOPLE LIKE ME	Gerry Shephard John Springate	Mike Leander
GOODIES		
MAKE A DAFT NOISE FOR CHRISTMAS	Bill Oddie	Miki Antony
Jesse GREEN		
FLIP	Ken Gibson Carol Holness	Ken Gibson
NICE AND SLOW	Ken Gibson	Ken Gibson Dave Howman
Henry GROSS		
SHANNON	Henry Gross	Terry Cashman Tommy West
GUYS 'N' DOLLS		
STONEY GROUND	Steve Elson Dave Stephenson	Steve Elson Keith Rossiter
YOU DON'T HAVE TO SAY YOU LOVE ME	Giveseppe Donaggio Vinenzo Pallavacini Vicki Wickham Simon Napier-Bell	Chris Arnold David Martin Geoff Morrow
Daryl HALL & JOHN OATES		
SHE'S GONE	Daryl Hall John Oates	Arif Mardin
Steve HARLEY & COCKNEY REBEL		
HERE COMES THE SUN	George Harrison	Steve Harley
(I Believe) LOVE'S A PRIMA DONNA	Steve Harley	Steve Harley
HARPO		
MOVIE STAR	Harpo	Ben Palmers
Emmylou HARRIS		
HERE THERE AND EVERYWHERE	John Lennon Paul McCartney	Brian Ahern
Isaac HAYES MOVEMENT		
DISCO CONNECTION	Isaac Hayes	Isaac Hayes

Artist(s)/Title	Writer(s)	Producer(s)
Chris HILL		
BIONIC SANTA	Chris Hill	Chris Hill
	John Staines	John Staines
		Nigel Grainge
RENTA SANTA	Chris Hill	Chris Hill
	John Staines	John Staines
Mary HOPKIN		
IF YOU LOVE ME	Edith Piaf	Tony Visconti
	Marguerite Monnot	
	Geoffrey Parsons	
HOT BLOOD		
SOUL DRACULA	May Ambruster	Boona Music Prod.
	Peny Duc	
	Larry Melwing	
HOT CHOCOLATE		
DON'T STOP IT NOW	Errol Brown	Mickie Most
HEAVEN IS IN THE BACK SEAT		
OF MY CADILLAC	Errol Brown	Mickie Most
MAN TO MAN	Errol Brown	Mickie Most
YOU SEXY THING	Errol Brown	Mickie Most
	Tony Wilson	
Billy HOWARD		
KING OF THE COPS	Roger Miller	Billy Howard
Tommy HUNT		
LOVING ON THE LOSING SIDE	Eddie Adamberry	Barry Kingston
	Tony Craig	
ONE FINE MORNING	Eddie Adamberry	Barry Kingston
	Tony Craig	
IMPRESSIONS		
FIRST IMPRESSIONS	Ed Townsend	Ed Townsend
ISLEY BROTHERS		
HARVEST FOR THE WORLD	Isley Brothers	Isley Brothers
		(Ernie Isley
		Marvin Isley
		Ronald Isley
		Chris Jasper
		Rudolph Isley
		O'Kelly Isley)
J.A.L.N. BAND		
DISCO MUSIC (I Like It)	Roy G. Hemmings	Mike Finesilver
		Peter Whitehouse
Jimmy JAMES & THE VAGABONDS		
I'LL GO WHERE YOUR MUSIC	Biddu	Biddu
TAKES ME		
NOW IS THE TIME	Biddu	Biddu
JETHRO TULL		
RING OUT, SOLSTICE BELLS/ (EP)	Ian Anderson	Ian Anderson
MARCH, THE MAD SCIENTIST/		
CHRISTMAS SONG/		
PAN DANCE		
JIGSAW		
SKY HIGH	Clive Scott	Chas Peate
	Des Dyer	

Artist(s)/Title	Writer(s)	Producer(s)
Elton JOHN		
BENNY AND THE JETS	Elton John	Gus Dudgeon
	Bernie Taupin	
PINBALL WIZARD	Pete Townsend	Gus Dudgeon
SORRY SEEMS TO BE THE	Elton John	Gus Dudgeon
HARDEST WORD	Bernie Taupin	
Elton JOHN & KIKI DEE		
DON'T GO BREAKING MY HEART	Ann Orson	Gus Dudgeon
(see also KIKI DEE)	Carte Blanche	
L.J. JOHNSON		
YOUR MAGIC PUT A SPELL ON ME	Ian Levine	Ian Levine
	Danny Leake	Danny Leake
Juggy Murray JONES		
INSIDE AMERICA	Juggy Jones	Juggy Murray
	Ken Waymon	
JUDGE DREAD		
CHRISTMAS IN DREADLAND/	Ted Lemon	Ted Lemon
COME OUTSIDE	Alex Hughes/	Alex Hughes
	Charles Blackwell	
THE WINKLE MAN	Ted Lemon	Ted Lemon
	Alex Hughes	Alex Hughes
Y VIVA SUSPENDERS/	Leo Rozenstraten	Ted Lemon
CONFESSIONS OF A BOUNCER	Leo Caerts	Alex Hughes
	Ted Lemon	
	Alex Hughes/	
	Ted Lemon	
	Alex Hughes	
KC & THE SUNSHINE BAND		
KEEP IT COMIN' LOVE	Harry Wayne Casey	Harry Wayne Casey
	Richard Finch	Richard Finch
(Shake Shake Shake)	Harry Wayne Casey	Harry Wayne Casey
SHAKE YOUR BOOTY	Richard Finch	Richard Finch
Mac & Katie KISSOON		
THE TWO OF US	Wayne Bickerton	Wayne Bickerton
	Tony Waddington	Tony Waddington
Gladys KNIGHT & THE PIPS		
MAKE YOURS A HAPPY HOME	Richard Tufo	Curtis Mayfield
MIDNIGHT TRAIN TO GEORGIA	Jim Weatherly	Tony Camillo
SO SAD THE SONG	Michael Masser	Michael Masser
	Gerry Goffin	
KURSAAL FLYERS		
LITTLE DOES SHE KNOW	Will Birch	Mike Batt
	Graeme Douglas	
	Paul Shuttleworth	
Greg LAKE		
I BELIEVE IN FATHER CHRISTMAS	Greg Lake	Greg Lake
	Pete Sinfield	Pete Sinfield
LAUREL & HARDY		
THE TRAIL OF THE LONESOME PINE	Ballard MacDonald	(Not listed)
	Harry Carroll	

Artist(s)/Title	Writer(s)	Producer(s)
John LENNON		
IMAGINE	John Lennon	John Lennon
Linda LEWIS		
BABY I'M YOURS	Van McCoy	Tony Silvester
		Bert DeCoteaux
LINDA & THE FUNKY BOYS		
SOLD MY ROCK 'N' ROLL	Detlef Petersen	Detlef Petersen
(Gave It Up For Funky Soul)	James Hopkins	
Laurie LINGO & THE DIPSTICKS		
CONVOY GB	Chip Davis	Wayne Bickerton
	Bill Fries	Tony Waddington
	C.W. McCall	
LITTLE ANTHONY & THE IMPERIALS		
BETTER USE YOUR HEAD	Teddy Randazzo	Teddy Randazzo
	Victoria Pike	
LIVERPOOL EXPRESS		
EVERY MAN MUST HAVE A DREAM	Roger Craig	Hal Carter
	Billy Kinsley	Peter Swettenham
HOLD TIGHT	Roger Craig	Hal Carter
	Billy Kinsley	Peter Swettenham
YOU ARE MY LOVE	Roger Craig	Hal Carter
	Billy Kinsley	Peter Swettenham
LYNYRD SKYNYRD		
SWEET HOME ALABAMA/	Ed King	Al Kooper/
DOUBLE TROUBLE/	Gary Rossington	Al Kooper/
FREE BIRD	Ronnie Van Zant/	Tom Dowd
	Allen Collins	
	Ronnie Van Zant/	
	Allen Collins	
	Ronnie Van Zant	
M & O BAND		
LET'S DO THE LATIN HUSTLE	Eddie Drennon	Muff Mufin
		Colin Owen
MANCHESTER UNITED FOOTBALL TEAM		
MANCHESTER UNITED	Tony & Keith Hiller	Tony Hiller
MANHATTAN TRANSFER		
TUXEDO JUNCTION	Buddy Feyne	Ahmet Ertegun
	William Johnson	Tim Hauser
	Erskine Hawkins	
	Julian Dash	
MANHATTANS		
HURT	Al Jacobs	Bobby Martin
	Jimmie Crane	Manhattans
		(Wilfred Lovett
		Gerald Austin
		Sonny Bivins
		Kenny Kelly
		Richard Taylor)
KISS AND SAY GOODBYE	Wilfred Lovett	Bobby Martin
		Manhattans

Artist(s)/Title	Writer(s)	Producer(s)
Manfred MANN'S EARTHBAND		
BLINDED BY THE LIGHT	Bruce Springsteen	Manfred Mann Earthband (Dave Flett Chris Hamlet Thompson Colin Pattenden Chris Slade)
MANUEL & THE MUSIC OF THE MOUNTAINS		
RODRIGO'S GUITAR CONCERTO DE ARANJUEZ (Theme from 2nd Movement)	Joaquin Rodrigo-Vidre	Norman Newell
MARMALADE		
FALLING APART AT THE SEAMS	Tony Macaulay	Tony Macaulay
Johnny MATHIS		
WHEN A CHILD IS BORN (Soleado)	Fred Jay Zacar	Jack Gold
Simon MAY		
THE SUMMER OF MY LIFE	Simon May	Barry Leng
C.W. McCALL		
CONVOY	Chip Davis Bill Fries C.W. McCall	Don Sears Chip Davis
George McCRAE		
HONEY I	Harry Wayne Casey Richard Finch	Harry Wayne Casey Richard Finch
Maureen McGOVERN		
THE CONTINENTAL	Con Conrade Herb Magidson	Carl Maduri
Ralph McTELL		
DREAMS OF YOU	J.S. Bach Ralph McTell	Stephen Allen
Harold MELVIN & THE BLUE NOTES		
WAKE UP EVERYBODY	John Whitehead Victor Carstarphen Gene McFadden	Kenny Gamble Leon Huff
John MILES		
MUSIC	John Miles	Alan Parsons
REMEMBER YESTERDAY	John Miles Bob Marshall	Rupert Holmes
Glenn MILLER		
MOONLIGHT SERENADE	Glenn Miller Mitchell Parish	(Not Listed)
Steve MILLER BAND		
ROCK 'N' ME	Steve Miller	Steve Miller
MIRACLES		
LOVE MACHINE	Warren 'Pete' Moore William Griffin	Freddie Perren
MISTURA with LLOYD MICHELS		
THE FLASHER	Lloyd Michels Richard Hurwitz	Lloyd Michels Richard Hurwitz
Willie MITCHELL		
THE CHAMPION	Willie Mitchell	Willie Mitchell

Artist(s)/Title	Writer(s)	Producer(s)
Hank MIZELL		
JUNGLE ROCK	Hank Mizell	Hank Mizell
	Jim Bobo	
	Bill Collins	
	Ralph Simonton	
Dorothy MOORE		
FUNNY HOW TIME SLIPS AWAY	Willie Nelson	Tommy Couch
		James Stroud
		Wolf Stephenson
MISTY BLUE	Bob Montgomery	Tom Couch
		James Stroud
Melba MOORE		
THIS IS IT	Van McCoy	Van McCoy
MUD		
LEAN ON ME	Bill Withers	Pip Williams
SHAKE IT DOWN	Rob Davies	Pip Williams
	Ray Stiles	
SHOW ME YOU'RE A WOMAN	Phil Wainman	Phil Wainman
	Johnny Goodison	
Walter MURPHY BAND		
A FIFTH OF BEETHOVEN	Walter Murphy	Thomas J. Valentino
Johnny NASH		
(What A) WONDERFUL WORLD	Herb Alpert	Sonny Limbo
	Lou Adler	Micky Buckins
	Sam Cooke	
NEW SEEKERS		
IT'S SO NICE (To Have You Home)	Bill Martin	Ron Richards
	Phil Coulter	
Paul NICHOLAS		
DANCING WITH THE CAPTAIN	Dominic Bugatti	Christopher Neil
	Frank Musker	
GRANDMA'S PARTY/(EP)	Dominic Bugatti	Christopher Neil
FLAT FOOT FLOYD/	Frank Musker/	
MR. SAX AND THE GIRL/	Christopher Neil	
SHUFFLIN' SHOES	Paul Nicholas/	
	Dominic Bugatti	
	Frank Musker/	
	Christopher Neil	
	Paul Nicholas	
REGGAE LIKE IT USED TO BE	Dominic Bugatti	Christopher Neil
	Frank Musker	
NILSSON		
WITHOUT YOU	Pete Ham	Richard Perry
	Tom Evans	
Billy OCEAN		
LOVE ON DELIVERY	Ben Findon	Ben Findon
	Les Charles	
LOVE REALLY HURTS WITHOUT YOU	Ben Findon	Ben Findon
	Les Charles	
STOP ME (If You've Heard It	Ben Findon	Ben Findon
All Before)	Les Charles	
	Mike Myers	

UK ARTIST

Artist(s)/Title	Writer(s)	Producer(s)
OHIO PLAYERS		
WHO'D SHE COO	William Beck James Williams Marshall Jones Marvin Pierce	Ohio Players (William Beck James Williams Marshall Jones Marvin Pierce Clarence Satchell Ralph Middlebrooks Leroy Bonner)
O'JAYS		
I LOVE MUSIC	Kenny Gamble Leon Huff	Kenny Gamble Leon Huff
Mike OLDFIELD		
IN DULCI JUBILO/ ON HORSEBACK	J.S. Bach Mike Oldfield/ William Murray Mike Oldfield	Mike Oldfield
PORTSMOUTH	Traditional	Mike Oldfield
100 TON & A FEATHER		
IT ONLY TAKES A MINUTE	Dennis Lambert Brian Potter	Jonathan King
OSIBISA		
DANCE THE BODY MUSIC	Teddy Osei Mac Tontoh Sol Amarfio Kiki Gyan	Gerry Bron
SUNSHINE DAY	Teddy Osei Mac Tontoh Sol Amarfio	Gerry Bron
Donny & Marie OSMOND		
DEEP PURPLE	Peter DeRose Mitchell Parish	Mike Curb
OSMONDS		
I CAN'T LIVE A DREAM	Arnold Capitanelli	Mike Curb Michael Lloyd
OUR KID		
YOU JUST MIGHT SEE ME CRY	Barry Mason Roger Greenaway	Tony Sadler
Dolly PARTON		
JOLENE	Dolly Parton	Bob Ferguson
Billy PAUL		
LET'S MAKE A BABY	Kenny Gamble Leon Huff	Kenny Gamble Leon Huff
PETERS & LEE		
HEY MR. MUSIC MAN	Gunther-Eric Thoner Bryan Blackburn	John Franz
Elvis PRESLEY		
GIRL OF MY BEST FRIEND	Beverley Ross Sam Bobrick	(Not listed)
GREEN GREEN GRASS OF HOME	Claude Putman Jr.	(Not listed)
HURT	Jimmie Crane Al Jacobs	(Not listed)

Artist(s)/Title	Writer(s)	Producer(s)
SUSPICION	Doc Pomus Mort Shuman	(Not listed)
James & Bobby PURIFY I'M YOUR PUPPET	Spooner Oldham Dan Penn	Papadon Productions
MORNING GLORY	Mac Gayden	Papadon Productions
PUSSYCAT MISSISSIPPI	Werner Theunissen	Eddy Hilberts
SMILE	Werner Theunissen	Eddy Hilberts
QUEEN BOHEMIAN RHAPSODY	Freddie Mercury	Roy Thomas Baker Queen (Freddie Mercury Brian May Roger Taylor John Deacon)
SOMEBODY TO LOVE	Freddie Mercury	Queen
YOU'RE MY BEST FRIEND	John Deacon	Roy Thomas Baker Queen
RAINBOW COTTAGE SEAGULL	Brian Gibbs	Larry Page
Lou RAWLS YOU'LL NEVER FIND ANOTHER LOVE LIKE MINE	Kenny Gamble Leon Huff	Kenny Gamble Leon Huff
REAL THING CAN'T GET BY WITHOUT YOU	Ken Gold Micky Denne	Ken Gold
YOU TO ME ARE EVERYTHING	Ken Gold Micky Denne	Ken Gold
Cliff RICHARD DEVIL WOMAN	Christine Authors Terry Britten	Bruce Welch
HEY MR. DREAM MAKER	Bruce Welch Alan Tarney	Bruce Welch
I CAN'T ASK FOR ANYMORE THAN YOU	Ken Gold Micky Denne	Bruce Welch
MISS YOU NIGHTS	Dave Townsend	Bruce Welch
RITCHIE FAMILY THE BEST DISCO IN TOWN	Jacques Morali Ritchie Rome Henri Belolo Philip Hurtt	Jacques Morali Ritchie Rome
Smokey ROBINSON & THE MIRACLES TEARS OF A CLOWN	Hank Cosby William Robinson Stevie Wonder	Hank Cosby Smokey Robinson
ROLLING STONES FOOL TO CRY	Keith Richard Mick Jagger	The Glimmer Twins

UK ARTIST

Artist(s)/Title	Writer(s)	Producer(s)
Linda RONSTADT		
THE TRACKS OF MY TEARS	William Robinson	Peter Asher
	Marv Tarplin	
	Warren 'Pete' Moore	
ROSE ROYCE		
CAR WASH	Norman Whitfield	Norman Whitfield
Diana ROSS		
I THOUGHT IT TOOK A LITTLE TIME	Pam Sawyer	Michael Masser
(But Today I Fell In Love)	Michael Masser	
I'M STILL WAITING	Deke Richards	Deke Richards
LOVE HANGOVER	Pam Sawyer	Hal Davis
	Marilyn McLeod	
THEME FROM MAHOGANY	Gerry Goffin	Michael Masser
'DO YOU KNOW WHERE YOU'RE	Michael Masser	
GOING TO'		
Demis ROUSSOS		
CAN'T SAY HOW MUCH I LOVE YOU	Robert Costandinos	Demis Roussos
HAPPY TO BE ON AN ISLAND IN	David Lewis	Georges Petsilas
THE SUN		
THE ROUSSOS PHENOMENON (EP)	Stylianos Vlavianos	Demis Roussos
Forever And Ever/	Robert Costandinos/	
Sing An Ode To Love/	Harry Chalkitis	
So Dreamy/	Stylianos Vlavianos	
My Friend The Wind	Robert Costandinos/	
	Lucky Vlaviano	
	Robert Rupen/	
	Stylianos Vlavianos	
	Robert Costandinos	
WHEN FOREVER HAS GONE	Barry Mason	Peter Sullivan
	Stylianos Vlavianos	
ROXY MUSIC		
BOTH ENDS BURNING	Bryan Ferry	Chris Thomas
		Bryan Ferry
RUBETTES		
UNDER ONE ROOF	John Richardson	Rubettes
	Alan Williams	(John Richardson
		Alan Williams
		Tony Thorpe
		Mike Clarke)
YOU'RE THE REASON WHY	John Richardson	Alan Blakley
	Alan Williams	Rubettes
David RUFFIN		Alan Blakley
WALK AWAY FROM LOVE	Charles Kipps	Van McCoy
SAILOR		
GIRLS, GIRLS, GIRLS	Georg Kajanus	Jeffrey Lesser
GLASS OF CHAMPAGNE	Georg Kajanus	Jeffrey Lesser
ST. ANDREW'S CHORALE		
CLOUD 99	Zacar	(Not listed)

44

Artist(s)/Title	Writer(s)	Producer(s)
SANDPIPERS		
HANG ON SLOOPY	Bert Russell	Henry Hadaway
	Wes Farrell	Sandpipers
		(James Brady
		Gary Duckworth
		Richard Shoff)
Robin SARSTEDT		
MY RESISTANCE IS LOW	Hoagy Carmichael	Ray Singer
	Harold Adamson	
Leo SAYER		
YOU MAKE ME FEEL LIKE DANCING	Leo Sayer	Richard Perry
	Vini Poncia	
Boz SCAGGS		
LOWDOWN	Boz Scaggs	Joe Wissert
	David Paich	
Lalo SCHIFRIN		
JAWS	John Williams	Lalo Schifrin
SENSATIONAL ALEX HARVEY BAND		
THE BOSTON TEA PARTY	Harvey McKenna	David Batchelor
GAMBLIN' BAR ROOM BLUES	Jimmie Rodgers	David Batchelor
	Shelley Lee Allen	
SEX PISTOLS		
ANARCHY IN THE U.K.	Sex Pistols	Chris Thomas
	(Paul Cook	
	Steve Jones	
	Glen Matlock	
	Johnny Rotten)	
SHANGRI-LAS		
LEADER OF THE PACK	Ellie Greenwich	George 'Shadow' Morton
	Jeff Barry	
	Shadow Morton	
Winifred SHAW		
LULLABY OF BROADWAY	Harry Warren	Alan Warner
	Al Dubin	
SHEER ELEGANCE		
IT'S TEMPTATION	Bev Gordon	Paul Lynton
		Paul Grade
LIFE IS TOO SHORT GIRL	Herbie Watkins	Paul Lynton
		Paul Grade
MILKYWAY	Herbie Watkins	Paul Lynton
		Paul Grade
SHERBET		
HOWZAT	Garth Porter	Richard Lush
	Tony Mitchell	Sherbet
		(Garth Porter
		Tony Mitchell
		Harvey James
		Alan Sandow
		Daryl Braithwaite)
Pluto SHERVINGTON		
DAT	Leighton Shervington	Paul Khouri
RAM GOAT LIVER	Leighton Shervington	Paul Khouri

Artist(s)/Title	Writer(s)	Producer(s)
SHOWADDYWADDY		
TROCADERO	Showaddywaddy (Malcolm Allured Dave Bartram Romeo Challenger Rod Deas Russ Field Buddy Gask Al James Trevor Oakes)	Mike Hurst
UNDER THE MOON OF LOVE	Tommy Boyce Curtis Lee	Mike Hurst
SILVER CONVENTION		
FLY, ROBIN, FLY	Sylvester Levay Stephan Prager	Michael Kunze
GET UP AND BOOGIE	Sylvester Levay Stephan Prager	Michael Kunze
TIGER BABY/NO, NO, JOE	Sylvester Levay Stephan Prager	Michael Kunze
Dooley SILVERSPOON		
LET ME BE THE NO. 1	Sonny Casella	Sonny Casella
Paul SIMON		
50 WAYS TO LEAVE YOUR LOVER	Paul Simon	Paul Simon Phil Ramone
Frank SINATRA		
I BELIEVE I'M GONNA LOVE YOU	Gloria Sklerov Harry Lloyd	Snuff Garrett
SLADE		
IN FOR A PENNY	Neville Holder James Lea	Chas Chandler
LET'S CALL IT QUITS	Neville Holder James Lea	Chas Chandler
SLIK		
FOREVER AND EVER	Bill Martin Phil Coulter	Bill Martin Phil Coulter
REQUIEM	Bill Martin Phil Coulter	Bill Martin Phil Coulter
SMALL FACES		
ITCHYCOO PARK	Steve Marriott Ronnie Lane	Steve Marriott Ronnie Lane
LAZY SUNDAY	Steve Marriott Ronnie Lane	Steve Marriott Ronnie Lane
SMOKIE		
I'LL MEET YOU AT MIDNIGHT	Michael Chapman Nicky Chinn	Michael Chapman Nicky Chinn
LIVING NEXT DOOR TO ALICE	Michael Chapman Nicky Chinn	Michael Chapman Nicky Chinn
SOMETHING'S BEEN MAKING ME BLUE	Michael Chapman Nicky Chinn	Michael Chapman Nicky Chinn
David SOUL		
DON'T GIVE UP ON US	Tony Macaulay	Tony Macaulay

Artist(s)/Title	Writer(s)	Producer(s)
SOUND 9418		
IN THE MOOD	Joe Garland	Jonathan King
	Andy Razaf	
Billie Jo SPEARS		
SING ME AN OLD FASHIONED SONG	Larry Henley	Larry Butler
	Johnny Slate	
WHAT I'VE GOT IN MIND	Kenny O'Dell	Larry Butler
STARLAND VOCAL BAND		
AFTERNOON DELIGHT	Bill Danoff	Milton Okun
Freddie STARR		
WHITE CHRISTMAS	Irving Berlin	Mick Green
Candi STATON		
DESTINY	Dave Crawford	Dave Crawford
YOUNG HEARTS RUN FREE	Dave Crawford	Dave Crawford
STATUS QUO		
MYSTERY SONG	Rick Parfitt	Status Quo
	Bob Young	(John Coghlan
		Alan Lancaster
		Rick Parfitt
		Francis Rossi)
RAIN	Rick Parfitt	Status Quo
WILD SIDE OF LIFE	Arlie Carter	Roger Glover
	William Warren	
STEELEYE SPAN		
ALL AROUND MY HAT	Traditional	Mike Batt
	arr. Steeleye Span	
	(Tim Hart	
	Robert Johnson	
	Rick Kemp	
	Peter Knight	
	Nigel Pegrum	
	Maddy Prior)	
STEELY DAN		
HAITIAN DIVORCE	Walter Becker	Gary Katz
	Donald Fagen	
STEVENSON'S ROCKET		
ALRIGHT BABY	Pete Smith	Peter Shelley
	Pete Waterman	Pete Waterman
Rod STEWART		
GET BACK	John Lennon	Lou Reizner
	Paul McCartney	Rod Stewart
THE KILLING OF GEORGIE	Rod Stewart	Tom Dowd
MAGGIE MAY	Martin Quittenton	Rod Stewart
	Rod Stewart	
SAILING	Gavin Sutherland	Tom Dowd
THIS OLD HEART OF MINE	Eddie Holland	Tom Dowd
	Lamont Dozier	
	Brian Holland	
TONIGHT'S THE NIGHT	Rod Stewart	Tom Dowd
R & J STONE		
WE DO IT	Russell Stone	Phil Swern

Artist(s)/Title	Writer(s)	Producer(s)
STRETCH		
WHY DID YOU DO IT	Kirby	Hot Wax Productions Ltd.
STYLISTICS		
CAN'T HELP FALLING IN LOVE	Hugo & Luigi George David Weiss	Hugo & Luigi
FUNKY WEEKEND	Hugo & Luigi George David Weiss	Hugo & Luigi
NA NA IS THE SADDEST WORD	Hugo & Luigi George David Weiss	Hugo & Luigi
SIXTEEN BARS	Hugo & Luigi George David Weiss	Hugo & Luigi
YOU'LL NEVER GET TO HEAVEN (If You Break My Heart)/(EP) THE MIRACLE/ COUNTRY LIVING/ YOU ARE BEAUTIFUL/	Burt Bacharach Hal David/ Hugo & Luigi George David Weiss/ Thom Bell Linda Creed/ Hugo & Luigi George David Weiss	Thom Bell/ Hugo & Luigi/ Thom Bell/ Hugo & Luigi
Donna SUMMER		
COULD IT BE MAGIC	Adrienne Anderson Barry Manilow	Pete Bellotte Giorgio Moroder
LOVE TO LOVE YOU BABY	Pete Bellotte Giorgio Moroder Donna Summer	Pete Bellotte
WINTER MELODY	Pete Bellotte Giorgio Moroder Donna Summer	Pete Bellotte Giorgio Moroder
SURPRISE SISTERS		
LA BOOGA ROOGA	Andy Fairweather Low	Tony Visconti
SUTHERLAND BROTHERS & QUIVER		
ARMS OF MARY	Iain Sutherland	Ron & Howard Albert
SECRETS	Iain Sutherland	Ron & Howard Albert
SWEET		
THE LIES IN YOUR EYES	Sweet	Sweet (Brian Connolly Steve Priest Mike Tucker Andy Scott)
TAVARES		
DON'T TAKE AWAY THE MUSIC	Keni St. Lewis Freddie Perren Christine Yarian	Freddie Perren
HEAVEN MUST BE MISSING AN ANGEL	Keni St. Lewis Freddie Perren	Freddie Perren
Johnnie TAYLOR		
DISCO LADY	Al Vance Don Davis Harvey Scales	Don Davis

Artist(s)/Title	Writer(s)	Producer(s)
10cc		
ART FOR ART'S SAKE	Eric Stewart Graham Gouldman	10cc (Eric Stewart Graham Gouldman Lol Creme Kevin Godley)
I'M MANDY FLY ME	Eric Stewart Graham Gouldman Lol Creme	10cc
THE THINGS WE DO FOR LOVE	Graham Gouldman Eric Stewart	10cc
THIN LIZZY		
THE BOYS ARE BACK IN TOWN	Phil Lynott	John Alcock
JAILBREAK	Phil Lynott	John Alcock
Evelyn THOMAS		
DOOMSDAY	Ian Levine Danny Leake	Ian Levine Danny Leake
WEAK SPOT	Ian Levine Paul Wilson	Ian Levine Danny Leake
THREE DEGREES		
TOAST OF LOVE	Sheila Ferguson Tatsushi Umegaki	Richard Barrett
TRAMMPS		
SOUL SEARCHIN' TIME	Leroy Green Norman Harris	Ronnie Baker Norman Harris Earl Young
THAT'S WHERE THE HAPPY PEOPLE GO	Ronnie Baker	Ronnie Baker Norman Harris Earl Young
T. REX		
I LOVE TO BOOGIE	Marc Bolan	Marc Bolan
LASER LOVE	Marc Bolan	Marc Bolan
LONDON BOYS	Marc Bolan	Marc Bolan
Andrea TRUE CONNECTION		
MORE, MORE, MORE	Gregg Diamond	Gregg Diamond
TWIGGY		
HERE I GO AGAIN	Country Joe McDonald	Tony Eyers
Bonnie TYLER		
LOST IN FRANCE	Ronnie Scott Steve Wolfe	Dave MacKay
TYMES		
GOD'S GONNA PUNISH YOU	Billy Jackson Alfonso Thornton	Billy Jackson
Frankie VALLI		
FALLEN ANGEL	Doug Flett Guy Fletcher	Bob Gaudio
Johnny WAKELIN		
IN ZAIRE	Johnny Wakelin	Steve Elson Keith Rossiter
WALKER BROTHERS		
NO REGRETS	Tom Rush	Scott Walker

UK ARTIST

Artist(s)/Title	Writer(s)	Producer(s)
WAR		
LOW RIDER	Jerry Goldstein War (Papa Dee Allen Harold Brown B.B. Dickerson Lonnie Jordan Charles Miller Lee Oskar Howard Scott)	Jerry Goldstein
ME AND BABY BROTHER	War	Jerry Goldstein
Johnny 'Guitar' WATSON		
I NEED IT	Johnny 'Guitar' Watson	Johnny 'Guitar' Watson
Barry WHITE		
BABY, WE BETTER TRY AND GET IT TOGETHER	Barry White	Barry White
DON'T MAKE ME WAIT TOO LONG	Barry White	Barry White
LET THE MUSIC PLAY	Barry White	Barry White
YOU SEE THE TROUBLE WITH ME	Barry White Ray Parker	Barry White
Chris WHITE		
SPANISH WINE	Chris White	Shel Talmy
WHO		
SQUEEZE BOX	Pete Townshend	Glyn Johns
SUBSTITUTE	Pete Townshend	Who (Pete Townshend Roger Daltrey John Entwistle Keith Moon)
WILD CHERRY		
PLAY THAT FUNKY MUSIC	Richard Parissi	Richard Parissi
Andy WILLIAMS		
THE OTHER SIDE OF ME	Neil Sedaka Howard Greenfield	Jack Gold
Don WILLIAMS		
I RECALL A GYPSY WOMAN	Allen Reynolds	Allen Reynolds Don Williams
YOU'RE MY BEST FRIEND	Wayland Holyfield	Don Williams
WING & A PRAYER FIFE & DRUM CORPS		
BABY FACE	Benny Davis Harry Akst	Harold Wheeler Stephen Y. Scheaffer
WINGS		
LET 'EM IN	Paul McCartney	Paul McCartney
SILLY LOVE SONGS	Paul McCartney	Paul McCartney
WOMBLES		
LET'S WOMBLE TO THE PARTY TONIGHT	Mike Batt	Mike Batt
Stevie WONDER		
I WISH	Stevie Wonder	Stevie Wonder
WURZELS		
THE COMBINE HARVESTER (BRAND NEW KEY)	Melanie Safka	Bob Barratt

Artist(s)/Title	Writer(s)	Producer(s)
I AM A CIDER DRINKER (PALOMA BLANCA)	Wurzels (Tommy Banner Tony Baylis Pete Budd) Johannes Bouwens	Bob Barratt
Tammy WYNETTE I DON'T WANNA PLAY HOUSE	Billy Sherrill Glenn Sutton	Billy Sherrill
Gheorghe ZAMFIR LIGHT OF EXPERIENCE (DOINA DE JALE)	Traditional	Gheorghe Zamfir

Section 3

UK Label Section

(*Music Week* Top 50 Singles Chart)

This section lists all singles that made the *Music Week* Top 50 chart during 1976, under catalogue numbers and their respective record labels in alphabetical and numerical order. The figures in brackets next to the record labels denote the number of chart singles each label had.

Listing under record companies instead of record labels was decided against, as some labels are owned by companies where others might just be distributed, and in some cases those distribution ties might change during the year.

A&M (12)
AMS 7144 Santa Claus Is Coming To Town—Carpenters
AMS 7202 Wide Eyed And Legless—Andy Fairweather Low
AMS 7203 The Way I Want To Touch You—Captain & Tennille
AMS 7211 I Wanna Stay With You—Gallagher & Lyle
AMS 7218 Show Me The Way—Peter Frampton
AMS 7219 There's A Kind Of Hush—Carpenters
AMS 7227 Heart On My Sleeve—Gallagher & Lyle
AMS 7238 I Need To Be In Love—Carpenters
AMS 7245 Breakaway—Gallagher & Lyle
AMS 7246 Baby I Love Your Way—Peter Frampton
AMS 7249 Love And Affection—Joan Armatrading
AMS 7260 Do You Feel Like We Do—Peter Frampton

ABC (5)
4098 I Recall A Gypsy Woman—Don Williams
4100 Disco Connection—Isaac Hayes Movement
4123 At The Hop—Danny & the Juniors
4144 You're My Best Friend—Don Williams
4152 Haitian Divorce—Steely Dan

AIR (1)
CHS 2094 Jeans On—David Dundas

ANCHOR (1)
ANCL 1021 Why Did You Do It—Stretch

APPLE (6)
R 5452 Paperback Writer—Beatles
R 5570 Strawberry Fields Forever—Beatles
R 5722 Hey Jude—Beatles
R 5777 Get Back—Beatles
R 6009 Imagine—John Lennon
R 6013 Yesterday—Beatles

ARISTA (3)
42 All By Myself—Eric Carmen
43 Baby I'm Yours—Linda Lewis
78 You're More Than A Number In My Little Red Book—Drifters

ASYLUM (2)
K 13029 Take It To The Limit—Eagles
K 13034 The Tracks Of My Tears—Linda Ronstadt

ATLANTIC (9)
K 10670 Tuxedo Junction—Manhattan Transfer
K 10703 That's Where The Happy People Go—Trammps
K 10705 Baby Face—Wing & A Prayer Fife & Drum Corps
K 10797 Soul Searchin' Time—Trammps
K 10807 The Rubber Band Man—Detroit Spinners
K 10810 I'd Really Love To See You Tonight—England Dan & John Ford Coley
K 10825 Queen Of My Soul—Average White Band
K 10827 Daddy Cool—Boney M
K 10828 She's Gone—Daryl Hall & John Oates

AVCO (3)
6105 041 Na Na Is The Saddest Word—Stylistics
6105 044 Funky Weekend—Stylistics
6105 050 Can't Help Falling In Love—Stylistics

BELL (12)
1461 Money Honey—Bay City Rollers
1462 Can I Take You Home Little Girl—Drifters
1464 Forever And Ever—Slik
1469 Hello Happiness—Drifters
1471 People Like You And People Like Me—Glitter Band
1473 You Belong To Me—Gary Glitter
1476 Trocadero—Showaddywaddy
1477 Love Me Like I Love You—Bay City Rollers
1478 Requiem—Slik
1491 Every Nite's A Saturday Night With You—Drifters
1493 I Only Want To Be With You—Bay City Rollers
1495 Under The Moon Of Love—Showaddywaddy

BRADLEYS (2)
BRAD 7528 Tears On The Telephone—Claude Francois
BRAD 7533 Make A Daft Noise For Christmas—Goodies

BRONZE (3)
BRO 20 Sunshine Day—Osibisa
BRO 26 Dance The Body Music—Osibisa
BRO 29 Blinded By The Light—Manfred Mann's Earthband

BRUNSWICK (1)
BR 34 You Don't Have To Go—Chi-Lites

BTM (1)
SBT 105 Couldn't Get It Right—Climax Blues Band

BUDDAH (5)
BDS 442 More, More, More—Andrea True Connection
BDS 443 This Is It—Melba Moore
BDS 444 Midnight Train To Georgia—Gladys Knight & the Pips
BDS 448 So Sad The Song—Gladys Knight & the Pips
BDS 3790 Make Yours A Happy Home—Gladys Knight & the Pips

CACTUS (3)
CT 80 Christmas In Dreadland/Come Outside—Judge Dread
CT 90 The Winkle Man—Judge Dread
CT 99 Y Viva Suspenders/Confessions Of A Bouncer—Judge Dread

CAPITOL (5)
CL 15871 A Little Bit More—Dr. Hook
CL 15875 Good Vibrations—Beach Boys
CL 15876 Heaven Must Be Missing An Angel—Tavares
CL 15885 If Not You—Dr. Hook
CL 15886 Don't Take Away The Music—Tavares

CAPRICORN (1)
2089 024 Fooled Around And Fell In Love—Elvin Bishop

CBS (24)
3776 If I Could—David Essex
3794 Let's Womble To The Party Tonight—Wombles

3879 Hurricane—Bob Dylan
3887 50 Ways To Leave Your Lover—Paul Simon
3903 The Other Side Of Me—Andy Williams
3937 I Love To Love (But My Baby Loves To Dance)—Tina Charles
4001 Arms Of Mary—Sutherland Brothers & Quiver
4044 Disco Lady—Johnnie Taylor
4050 City Lights—David Essex
4237 Love Me Like A Lover—Tina Charles
4287 One Piece At A Time—Johnny Cash & the Tennessee Three
4317 Kiss And Say Goodbye—Manhattans
4391 It's So Nice (To Have You Home)—New Seekers
4398 If You Know What I Mean—Neil Diamond
4480 Dance Little Lady Dance—Tina Charles
4486 Coming Home—David Essex
4562 Hurt—Manhattans
4563 Lowdown—Boz Scaggs
4599 When A Child Is Born (Soleado)—Johnny Mathis
4601 Beautiful Noise—Neil Diamond
4603 If You Leave Me Now—Chicago
4668 Secrets—Sutherland Brothers & Quiver
4689 Little Does She Know—Kursaal Flyers
4779 Dr. Love—Tina Charles

CHARISMA (1)
CB 272 Spanish Wine—Chris White

CHARLY (2)
CS 1005 Jungle Rock—Hank Mizell
CS 1009 Leader Of The Pack—Shangri-Las

CHRYSALIS (4)
CHS 2078 All Around My Hat—Steeleye Span
CHS 2087 You're My Everything—Lee Garrett
CHS 2119 You Make Me Feel Like Dancing—Leo Sayer
CXP 2 Ring Out Solstice Bells (EP)—Jethro Tull

CONTEMPO (4)
CS 2080 Inside America—Juggy Murray Jones
CS 2087 Misty Blue—Dorothy Moore
CS 2092 Funny How Time Slips Away—Dorothy Moore
CS 9032 Leader Of The Pack—Shangri-Las

CREOLE (4)
CR 114 Get It Together—Crispy & Co.
CR 116 Hey Miss Payne—Chequers
CR 120 Let's Do The Latin Hustle—M & O Band
CR 132 Soul Dracula—Hot Blood

CTI (1)
CTSP 005 Jaws—Lalo Schifrin

CURTOM (1)
K 16638 First Impressions—Impressions

DECCA (5)
F 13617 Cloud 99—St. Andrew's Chorale
F 13624 My Resistance Is Low—Robin Sarstedt
F 13627 Music—John Miles

F 13633 **Manchester United**—Manchester United Football Team
F 13667 **Remember Yesterday**—John Miles

DJM (4)
DJS 400   **Movie Star**—Harpo
DJS 652   **Pinball Wizard**—Elton John
DJS 10694 **I Need It**—Johnny 'Guitar' Watson
DJS 10705 **Benny And The Jets**—Elton John

DYNAMIC (2)
DYN 101 **Work All Day**—Barry Biggs
DYN 118 **Side Show**—Barry Biggs

ELEKTRA (2)
K 12203 **Riders On A Storm**—Doors
K 12241 **Lost Without Your Love**—Bread

EMI (20)
2342 **Think Of Me (Wherever You Are)**—Ken Dodd
2375 **Bohemian Rhapsody**—Queen
2376 **Miss You Nights**—Cliff Richard
2383 **Rodrigo's Guitar Concerto De Aranjuez (Theme from 2nd Movement)**—Manuel and the
    Music of the Mountains
2450 **The Combine Harvester (Brand New Key)**—Wurzels
2458 **Devil Woman**—Cliff Richard
2492 **Nice And Slow**—Jesse Green
2494 **You're My Best Friend**—Queen
2499 **I Can't Ask For Anymore Than You**—Cliff Richard
2505 **Here Comes The Sun**—Steve Harley & Cockney Rebel
2520 **I Am A Cider Drinker (Paloma Blanca)**—Wurzels
2539 **(I Believe) Love's A Prima Donna**—Steve Harley & Cockney Rebel
2554 **Here's To Love**—John Christie
2559 **Hey Mr. Dream Maker**—Cliff Richard
2564 **Flip**—Jesse Green
2565 **Somebody To Love**—Queen
2566 **Anarchy In The U.K.**—Sex Pistols
MARC 13 **London Boys**—T. Rex
MARC 14 **I Love To Boogie**—T. Rex
MARC 15 **Laser Love**—T. Rex

EPIC (14)
EPC 3770 **Glass Of Champagne**—Sailor
EPC 3790 **Mamma Mia**—Abba
EPC 3858 **Girls, Girls, Girls**—Sailor
EPC 4036 **Fernando**—Abba
EPC 4084 **Rain Forest**—Biddu
EPC 4091 **I Don't Wanna Play House**—Tammy Wynette
EPC 4215 **Toast Of Love**—Three Degrees
EPC 4294 **(What A) Wonderful World**—Johnny Nash
EPC 4310 **Light Of Experience (Doina De Jale)**—Gheorghe Zamfir
EPC 4369 **Harvest For The World**—Isley Brothers
EPC 4499 **Dancing Queen**—Abba
EPC 4574 **Howzat**—Sherbet
EPC 4593 **Play That Funky Music**—Wild Cherry
EPC 4713 **Money, Money, Money**—Abba

FANTASY (1)
FTC 132 **You Sexy Sugar Plum (But I Like It)**—Rodger Collins

GOOD EARTH (2)
GD 1 **La Booga Rooga**—Surprise Sisters
GD 2 **If You Love Me**—Mary Hopkin

GTO (11)
GT 17 **Love To Love You Baby**—Donna Summer
GT 42 **No Regrets**—Walker Brothers
GT 45 **It's Gonna Be A Cold Cold Christmas**—Dana
GT 52 **Love Really Hurts Without You**—Billy Ocean
GT 55 **Never Gonna Fall In Love Again**—Dana
GT 57 **S-S-S- Single Bed**—Fox
GT 60 **Could It Be Magic**—Donna Summer
GT 62 **Love On Delivery**—Billy Ocean
GT 66 **Fairy Tale**—Dana
GT 72 **Stop Me (If You've Heard It All Before)**—Billy Ocean
GT 76 **Winter Melody**—Donna Summer

H & L (2)
6105 059 **Sixteen Bars**—Stylistics
STYL 001 **You'll Never Get To Heaven (EP)**—Stylistics

HARVEST (2)
HAR 5104 **Ships In The Night**—Be-Bop DeLuxe
HAR 5117 **Hot Valves (EP)**—Be-Bop DeLuxe

IMMEDIATE (3)
IMS 102 **Itchycoo Park**—Small Faces
IMS 103 **(If Paradise Is) Half As Nice**—Amen Corner
IMS 106 **Lazy Sunday**—Small Faces

ISLAND (8)
WIP 6246 **Love Hurts**—Jim Capaldi
WIP 6262 **Both Ends Burning**—Roxy Music
WIP 6267 **Low Rider**—War
WIP 6303 **Me And Baby Brother**—War
WIP 6307 **Let's Stick Together**—Bryan Ferry
WIP 6354 **Teenage Depression**—Eddie & the Hot Rods
1 EP1 **Extended Play (EP)**—Bryan Ferry
1 EP2 **Live At The Marquee (EP)**—Eddie & the Hot Rods

JAYBOY (3)
BOY 107 **Honey I**—George McCrae
BOY 110 **(Shake Shake Shake) Shake Your Booty**—KC & the Sunshine Band
BOY 112 **Keep It Comin' Love**—KC & the Sunshine Band

JET (3)
764 **Evil Woman**—Electric Light Orchestra
779 **Strange Magic**—Electric Light Orchestra
UP 36184 **Livin' Thing**—Electric Light Orchestra

LIFESONG (1)
ELS 45002 **Shannon**—Henry Gross

LONDON (2)
HL-U 10512 **Let's Twist Again/The Twist**—Chubby Checker
HL-U 10545 **The Champion**—Willie Mitchell

UK LABEL 59

MAGNET (7)
MAG 43 Fly, Robin, Fly—Silver Convention
MAG 47 Alright Baby—Stevenson's Rocket
MAG 50 You Don't Have To Say You Love Me—Guys 'n' Dolls
MAG 55 Get Up And Boogie—Silver Convention
MAG 69 Tiger Baby/No, No, Joe—Silver Convention
MAG 73 Disco Music (I Like It)—J.A.L.N. Band
MAG 76 Stoney Ground—Guys 'n' Dolls

MANTICORE (2)
K 13511 I Believe In Father Christmas—Greg Lake
K 13513 Honky Tonk Train Blues—Keith Emerson

MCA (4)
219 Drive Safely Darling—Tony Christie
251 Sweet Home Alabama/Double Trouble/Free Bird—Lynyrd Skynyrd
260 Don't Cry For Me Argentina—Julie Covington
267 Car Wash—Rose Royce

MERCURY (9)
6007 100 Here I Go Again—Twiggy
6008 017 Art For Art's Sake—10cc
6008 022 The Things We Do For Love—10cc
6009 019 I'm Mandy Fly Me—10cc
6078 804 Rock 'n' Me—Steve Miller Band
6160 006 Maggie May—Rod Stewart
6167 324 I'm Your Puppet—James & Bobby Purify
6167 380 Morning Glory—James & Bobby Purify
PLAY 001 Who'd She Coo—Ohio Players

MGM (3)
2006 558 How High The Moon—Gloria Gaynor
2006 560 Convoy—C.W. McCall
2006 561 Deep Purple—Donny & Marie Osmond

MOUNTAIN (1)
TOP 12 The Boston Tea Party—Sensational Alex Harvey Band

OPAL (1)
PAL 5 Dat—Pluto Shervington

PARLOPHONE (4)
R 5305 Help—Beatles
R 6014 Silly Love Songs—Wings
R 6015 Let 'Em In—Wings
R 6016 Back In The U.S.S.R.—Beatles

PENNY FARTHING (2)
PEN 892 King Of The Cops—Billy Howard
PEN 906 Seagull—Rainbow Cottage

PHILADELPHIA INTERNATIONAL (5)
PIR 3866 Wake Up Everybody—Harold Melvin & the Blue Notes
PIR 3879 I Love Music—O'Jays
PIR 4144 Let's Make A Baby—Billy Paul
PIR 4250 Soul City Walk—Archie Bell & the Drells
PIR 4372 You'll Never Find Another Love Like Mine—Lou Rawls

60   UK LABEL

PHILIPS (12)
6006 475 The Old Rugged Cross—Ethna Campbell
6006 491 Renta Santa—Chris Hill
6006 492 Your Magic Put A Spell On Me—L.J. Johnson
6006 502 Hey Mr. Music Man—Peters & Lee
6006 519 Tubular Bells—Champs Boys
6006 533 Dr. Kiss-Kiss—5000 Volts
6006 551 Bionic Santa—Chris Hill
6042 033 Happy To Be On An Island In The Sun—Demis Roussos
6042 114 Can't Say How Much I Love You—Demis Roussos
6042 186 When Forever Has Gone—Demis Roussos
6146 700 The Wanderer—Dion
DEMIS 001 The Roussos Phenomenon (EP)—Demis Roussos

PINNACLE (1)
P-8419 Dawn—Flintlock

POLYDOR (14)
2058 652 D.I.V.O.R.C.E.—Billy Connolly
2058 663 In For A Penny—Slade
2058 690 Let's Call It Quits—Slade
2058 729 You Just Might See Me Cry—Our Kid
2058 735 Side Show—Chanter Sisters
2058 748 No Chance (No Charge)—Billy Connolly
2058 777 The Best Disco In Town—Ritchie Family
2058 803 Substitute—Who
2066 256 Spanish Hustle—Fatback Band
2066 637 (Are You Ready) Do The Bus Stop—Fatback Band
2066 682 Party Time—Fatback Band
2066 687 Get Up Offa That Thing—James Brown
2066 726 I Can't Live A Dream—Osmonds
2121 275 Squeeze Box—Who

POWER EXCHANGE (1)
PX 209 No Charge—J.J. Barrie

PRIVATE STOCK (6)
PVT 45 Show Me You're A Woman—Mud
PVT 51 Fallen Angel—Frankie Valli
PVT 59 A Fifth Of Beethoven—Walter Murphy Band
PVT 65 Shake It Down—Mud
PVT 84 Don't Give Up On Us—David Soul
PVT 85 Lean On Me—Mud

PYE (13)
7N 25697 Milkyway—Sheer Elegance
7N 25702 Let's Do The Latin Hustle—Eddie Drennon & BBS Unlimited
7N 25703 Life Is Too Short Girl—Sheer Elegance
7N 25709 You To Me Are Everything—Real Thing
7N 25715 It's Temptation—Sheer Elegance
7N 45569 Save Your Kisses For Me—Brotherhood of Man
7N 45585 I'll Go Where Your Music Takes Me—Jimmy James & the Vagabonds
7N 45595 In Zaire—Johnny Wakelin
7N 45602 My Sweet Rosalie—Brotherhood of Man
7N 45606 Now Is The Time—Jimmy James & the Vagabonds
7N 45607 Aria—Acker Bilk, His Clarinet & Strings

7N 45618 Can't Get By Without You—Real Thing
7N 45627 The Summer Of My Life—Simon May

RAK (7)
221 You Sexy Thing—Hot Chocolate
227 Something's Been Making Me Blue—Smokie
230 Don't Stop It Now—Hot Chocolate
238 Man To Man—Hot Chocolate
240 Heaven Is In The Back Seat Of My Cadillac—Hot Chocolate
241 I'll Meet You At Midnight—Smokie
244 Living Next Door To Alice—Smokie

RCA (16)
2616 We Do It—R & J Stone
2626 God's Gonna Punish You—Tymes
2632 Just One Look—Faith Hope & Charity
2635 Green Green Grass Of Home—Elvis Presley
2640 Golden Years—David Bowie
2641 The Lies In Your Eyes—Sweet
2644 Moonlight Serenade—Glenn Miller
2674 Hurt—Elvis Presley
2675 Jolene—Dolly Parton
2678 Sunday—Buster
2682 TVC 15—David Bowie
2716 Afternoon Delight—Starland Vocal Band
2729 Girl Of My Best Friend—Elvis Presley
2733 Without You—Nilsson
2734 Lost In France—Bonnie Tyler
2768 Suspicion—Elvis Presley

REPRISE (4)
K 14400 I Believe I'm Gonna Love You—Frank Sinatra
K 14415 Here There And Everywhere—Emmylou Harris
K 14440 Rock And Roll Music—Beach Boys
K 14447 Say You Love Me—Fleetwood Mac

RIVA (4)
1 This Old Heart Of Mine—Rod Stewart
2 Tonight's The Night—Rod Stewart
4 The Killing Of Georgie—Rod Stewart
6 Get Back—Rod Stewart

ROCKET (3)
ROKN 512 Don't Go Breaking My Heart—Elton John & Kiki Dee
ROKN 515 Loving And Free/Amoureuse—Kiki Dee
ROKN 517 Sorry Seems To Be The Hardest Word—Elton John

ROLLING STONES (1)
RS 19121 Fool To Cry—Rolling Stones

ROUTE (1)
RT 30 The Flasher—Mistura with Lloyd Michels

RSO (8)
2090 174 Answer Me—Barbara Dickson
2090 185 Reggae Like It Used To Be—Paul Nicholas
2090 195 You Should Be Dancing—Bee Gees
2090 204 Disco Duck—Rick Dees & His Cast of Idiots

2090 205 **Love Me**—Yvonne Elliman
2090 206 **Dancing With The Captain**—Paul Nicholas
2090 207 **Love So Right**—Bee Gees
2090 216 **Grandma's Party (EP)**—Paul Nicholas

SATRIL (1)
SAT 114 **Hang On Sloopy**—Sandpipers

SEVILE (1)
SEV 1020 **Let Me Be The No. 1**—Dooley Silverspoon

SONET (3)
SON 2077 **Mississippi**—Pussycat
SON 2094 **Spinning Rock Boogie**—Hank C. Burnette
SON 2096 **Smile**—Pussycat

SPARK (4)
SRL 1135 **Dance Of The Cuckoos**—Band of the Black Watch
SRL 1139 **Sold My Rock 'n' Roll (Gave It Up For Funky Soul)**—Linda & the Funky Boys
SRL 1146 **Loving On The Easy Side**—Tommy Hunt
SRL 1148 **One Fine Morning**—Tommy Hunt

SPLASH (1)
CPI 1 **Sky High**—Jigsaw

SPRING (1)
2066 706 **Night Fever**—Fatback Band

STATE (4)
STAT 20 **You're The Reason Why**—Rubettes
STAT 21 **The Two Of Us**—Mac & Katie Kissoon
STAT 23 **Convoy GB**—Laurie Lingo & the Dipsticks
STAT 27 **Under One Roof**—Rubettes

TAMLA MOTOWN (9)
TMG 1010 **Theme From Mahogany 'Do You Know Where You're Going To'**—Diana Ross
TMG 1013 **It Should Have Been Me**—Yvonne Fair
TMG 1015 **Love Machine**—Miracles
TMG 1017 **Walk Away From Love**—David Ruffin
TMG 1024 **Love Hangover**—Diana Ross
TMG 1032 **I Thought It Took A Little Time (But Today I Fell In Love)**—Diana Ross
TMG 1041 **I'm Still Waiting**—Diana Ross
TMG 1048 **Tears Of A Clown**—Smokey Robinson & the Miracles
TMG 1054 **I Wish**—Stevie Wonder

TARGET (1)
TGT 105 **Falling Apart At The Seams**—Marmalade

THUNDERBIRD (1)
THE 102 **White Christmas**—Freddie Starr

TROJAN (1)
TR 7978 **Ram Goat Liver**—Pluto Shervington

TROPICAL (1)
ALO 56 **Midnight Rider**—Paul Davidson

20th CENTURY (9)
BTC 1014 **Weak Spot**—Evelyn Thomas
BTC 1017 **Doomsday**—Evelyn Thomas

BTC 2222 The Continental—Maureen McGovern
BTC 2225 The Uptown, Uptempo Woman—Randy Edelman
BTC 2261 Concrete And Clay—Randy Edelman
BTC 2265 Let The Music Play—Barry White
BTC 2277 You See The Trouble With Me—Barry White
BTC 2298 Baby, We Better Try And Get It Together—Barry White
BTC 2309 Don't Make Me Wait Too Long—Barry White

UNITED ARTISTS (7)
UP 35797 Blueberry Hill—Fats Domino
UP 36026 The Trail Of The Lonesome Pine—Laurel & Hardy
UP 36090 Movin'—Brass Construction
UP 36118 What I've Got In Mind—Billie Jo Spears
UP 36131 Lullaby Of Broadway—Winifred Shaw
UP 36141 Better Use Your Head—Little Anthony & the Imperials
UP 36179 Sing Me An Old Fashioned Song—Billie Jo Spears

UK (2)
121 In The Mood—Sound 9418
135 It Only Takes A Minute—100 Ton & A Feather

VERTIGO (6)
6059 133 Rain—Status Quo
6059 139 The Boys Are Back In Town—Thin Lizzy
6059 146 Mystery Song—Status Quo
6059 150 Jailbreak—Thin Lizzy
6059 153 Wild Side Of Life—Status Quo
ALEX 002 Gamblin' Bar Room Blues—Sensational Alex Harvey Band

VIRGIN (3)
VS 131 In Dulci Jubilo/On Horseback—Mike Oldfield
VS 153 I Want More—Can
VS 163 Portsmouth—Mike Oldfield

WARNER BROS (12)
K 16600 Sailing—Rod Stewart
K 16648 Dreams Of You—Ralph McTell
K 16688 December, 1963 (Oh, What A Night)—Four Seasons
K 16690 Let Your Love Flow—Bellamy Brothers
K 16730 Young Hearts Run Free—Candi Staton
K 16742 Silver Star—Four Seasons
K 16743 You Are My Love—Liverpool Express
K 16775 Satin Sheets—Bellamy Brothers
K 16799 Hold Tight—Liverpool Express
K 16806 Destiny—Candi Staton
K 16845 We Can Work It Out—Four Seasons
K 16854 Every Man Must Have A Dream—Liverpool Express

Section 4

UK Writer Section

(*Music Week* Top 50 Singles Chart)

This section lists the writers, cross-referenced with co-writers, of all singles that made the *Music Week* Top 50 chart during 1976.

All writers are listed in alphabetical order, with the names of the co-writers bracketed beneath them, followed by the title of the song and the artist below that.

Certain writers credit themselves twice—once by their real name and again by their pseudonym (i.e. C.W. McCall and Bill Fries).

When a group is credited with writing a song, all the members of that group are listed in brackets under the group's name. The individual members are also cross-referenced with the name of the group.

There are cases where credits will not correspond with the information found on the record (i.e. Faith Hope & Charity's *Just One Look,* which was in fact written by three people, but usually only credited to two).

Barbara ACKLIN
(w.Eugene Record)
You Don't Have To Go—Chi-Lites

Eddie ADAMBERRY
(w.Tony Craig)
Loving On The Losing Side—Tommy Hunt
One Fine Morning—Tommy Hunt

Harold ADAMSON
(w.Hoagy Carmichael)
My Resistance Is Low—Robin Sarstedt

Lou ADLER
(w.Herb Alpert/Sam Cooke)
(What A) Wonderful World—Johnny Nash

Harry AKST
(w.Benny Davis)
Baby Face—Wing & A Prayer Fife & Drum Corps

Papa Dee/Sylvester ALLEN
(see WAR)

Shelley Lee ALLEN
(w.Jimmie Rodgers)
Gamblin' Bar Room Blues—Sensational Alex Harvey Band

Gregg ALLMAN
Midnight Rider—Paul Davidson

Malcolm ALLURED
(see SHOWADDYWADDY)

Herb ALPERT
(w.Lou Adler/Sam Cooke)
(What A) Wonderful World—Johnny Nash

Sol AMARFIO
(w.Teddy Osei/Mac Tontoh)
Sunshine Day—Osibisa
(w.Kiki Gyan/Teddy Osei/Mac Tontoh)
Dance The Body Music—Osibisa

May AMBRUSTER
(w. Peny Duc/Larry Melwing)
Soul Dracula—Hot Blood

Adrienne ANDERSON
(w.Barry Manilow)
Could It Be Magic—Donna Summer

Ian ANDERSON
Ring Out, Solstice Bells (EP)—Jethro Tull
March, The Mad Scientist—Christmas Song—Pan Dance

Stig ANDERSON
(w.Benny Andersson/Bjorn Ulvaeus)
Dancing Queen—Abba
Fernando—Abba
Mamma Mia—Abba

Benny ANDERSSON
(w.Bjorn Ulvaeus)
Money, Money, Money—Abba
(w.Stig Anderson/Bjorn Ulvaeus)
Dancing Queen—Abba
Fernando—Abba
Mamma Mia—Abba

Dave APPELL
(w.Kal Mann)
Let's Twist Again—Chubby Checker

Joan ARMATRADING
Love And Affection—Joan Armatrading

Pascal AURIAT
(w.Bryan Blackburn/Serge Lebrail/Pascal Sevran)
Think Of Me (Wherever You Are)—
Ken Dodd

Christine AUTHORS
(w.Terry Britten)
Devil Woman—Cliff Richard
(the US version credits her as Christine
HODGSON, which is Ms.Author's maiden
name)

J.S./Johann Sebastian BACH
(w.Ralph McTell)
Dreams Of You—Ralph McTell
(w.Mike Oldfield)
In Dulci Jubilo—Mike Oldfield

Burt BACHARACH
(w.Hal David)
**You'll Never Get To Heaven (If You Break
My Heart)**—Stylistics (from the EP of the
same name)

Ronnie/Ron BAKER
That's Where The Happy People Go—
Trammps

Dario BALDAN BEMBO
(w.Sergio Bardotti)
Aria—Acker Bilk, His Clarinet & Strings

Hank BALLARD
The Twist—Chubby Checker

Tommy BANNER
(see The WURZELS)

Sergio BARDOTTI
(w.Dario Baldan Bembo)
Aria—Acker Bilk, His Clarinet & Strings

H.E.R. BARNES
(w.Jean-Pierre Bourtayre/Claude
Francois/Frank Thomas)
Tears On The Telephone—Claude
Francois

Vinny BARRETT
(w.Bobby Eli)
Side Show—Barry Biggs

Jeff BARRY
(w.Ellie Greenwich/George Morton)
Leader Of The Pack—Shangri-Las

Dave BARTRAM
(see SHOWADDYWADDY)

Mike BATT
Let's Womble To The Party Tonight—
Wombles

Lucio BATTISTI
(w.Jack Fishman)
(If Paradise Is) Half As Nice—Amen
Corner

Tony BAYLIS
(see The WURZELS)

William BECK
(w.Marshall Jones/Marvin Pierce/
James Williams)
Who'd She Coo—Ohio Players

Walter BECKER
(w.Donald Fagen)
Haitian Divorce—Steely Dan

BEE GEES
(Barry, Maurice & Robin Gibb)
Love So Right—Bee Gees
You Should Be Dancing—Bee Gees
(also see Barry & Robin Gibb)

Thom BELL
(w.Linda Creed)
Country Living—Stylistics (from **You'll
Never Get To Heaven** (EP))
The Rubber Band Man—Detroit Spinners

Pete BELLOTTE
(w.Giorgio Moroder/Donna Summer)
Love To Love You Baby—Donna Summer
Winter Melody—Donna Summer

Hank BELOLO
(w.Phil Hurtt/Jacques Morali/Ritchie
Rome)
The Best Disco In Town—Ritchie Family

Irving BERLIN
White Christmas—Freddie Starr

Bert BERNS
(see Bert RUSSELL)

Chuck BERRY
Rock And Roll Music—Beach Boys

John BETTIS
(w.Richard Carpenter/Albert Hammond)
I Need To Be In Love—Carpenters

Wayne BICKERTON
(w.Tony WADDINGTON)
The Two Of Us—Mac & Katie Kissoon

BIDDU
Dr. Love—Tina Charles
I'll Go Where Your Music Takes Me—
Jimmy James & the Vagabonds
Now Is The Time—Jimmy James & the
Vagabonds
Rain Forest—Biddu Orchestra
(w.Gerry Shury/Ron Roker)
Dance Little Lady Dance/Tina Charles

Barry BIGGS
Work All Day—Barry Biggs

Will BIRCH
(w.Graeme Douglas/Paul Shuttleworth)
Little Does She Know—Kursaal Flyers

Elvin BISHOP
Fooled Around And Fell In Love—Elvin
Bishop

Bryan BLACKBURN
(w.Gunter-Eric Thoner)
Hey Mr. Music Man—Peters & Lee
(w.Pascal Auriat/Serge Lebrail/Pascal
Sevran)
Think Of Me (Wherever You Are)—
Ken Dodd

Charles BLACKWELL
Come Outside—Judge Dread

Carte BLANCHE
(see Elton John/Bernie Taupin)

Jim BOBO
(w.Bill Collins/Hank Mizell/Ralph Simonton)
Jungle Rock—Hank Mizell

Sam BOBRICK
(w.Beverley Ross)
Girl Of My Best Friend—Elvis Presley

Marc BOLAN
I Love To Boogie—T. Rex
Laser Love—T. Rex
London Boys—T. Rex

James BOLDEN
(w.Jack Robinson)
I Love To Love (But My Baby Loves To Dance)—Tina Charles
Love Me Like A Lover—Tina Charles

Jean-Pierre BOURTAYRE
(w.H.E.R. Barnes/Claude Francois/Frank Thomas)
Tears On The Telephone—Claude Francois

Johannes BOUWENS
(w.The Wurzels)
I Am A Cider Drinker (Paloma Blanca)—Wurzels

David BOWIE
Golden Years—David Bowie
TVC 15—David Bowie

Tommy BOYCE
(w.Curtis Lee)
Under The Moon Of Love—Showaddywaddy

Bobby BRADDOCK
(w.Curly Putman/Sheb Wooley)
D.I.V.O.R.C.E.—Billy Connolly

Terry BRITTEN
(w.Christine Authors)
Devil Woman—Cliff Richard

Deanna BROWN
(w.Deidra Brown/Yamma Brown)
Get Up Offa That Thing—James Brown

Deidra BROWN
(w.Deanna Brown/Yamma Brown)
Get Up Offa That Thing—James Brown

Errol BROWN
Don't Stop It Now—Hot Chocolate
Heaven Is In The Back Seat Of My Cadillac—Hot Chocolate
Man To Man—Hot Chocolate
(w.Tony Wilson)
You Sexy Thing—Hot Chocolate

Harold BROWN
(see WAR)

Yamma BROWN
(w.Deanna Brown/Deidra Brown)
Get Up Offa That Thing—James Brown

Boudleaux BRYANT
Love Hurts—Jim Capaldi

Pete BUDD
(see The WURZELS)

Dominic BUGATTI
(w. Frank Musker)
Dancing With The Captain—Paul Nicholas
Grandma's Party (EP)—Paul Nicholas
Mr. Sax And The Girl—Paul Nicholas
(from Grandma's Party (EP))
Reggae Like It Used To Be—Paul Nicholas

Hank C. BURNETTE
Spinning Rock Boogie—Hank C. Burnette

Leo CAERTS
(w.Alex Hughes/Ted Lemon/Leo Rozenstraten)
Y Viva Suspenders—Judge Dread

CAN
(Michael Karoli, Holger Czukay, Jaki Liebezeit & Irmin Schmidt)
(w.Peter Gilmour)
I Want More—Can

Arnold CAPITANELLI
I Can't Live A Dream—Osmonds

Eric CARMEN
All By Myself—Eric Carmen
Never Gonna Fall In Love Again—Dana

Hoagy CARMICHAEL
(w.Harold Adamson)
My Resistance Is Low—Robin Sarstedt

Richard CARPENTER
(w.John Bettis/Albert Hammond)
I Need To Be In Love—Carpenters

Gregory CARROLL
(w.Rex Garvin/Doris Payne)
Just One Look—Faith Hope & Charity

Harry CARROLL
(w.Ballard MacDonald)
The Trail Of The Lonesome Pine—Laurel
& Hardy

Victor CARSTARPHEN
(w.Gene McFadden/John Whitehead)
Soul City Walk—Archie Bell & the Drells
Wake Up Everybody—Harold Melvin &
the Blue Notes

Arlie CARTER
(w.William Warren)
Wild Side Of Life—Status Quo

Sonny CASELLA
Let Me Be The No. 1—Dooley Silverspoon

Harry WAYNE CASEY (aka KC)
(w.Richard Finch)
Honey I—George McCrae
Keep It Comin' Love—KC & the Sunshine
Band
(Shake Shake Shake) Shake Your Booty
—KC & the Sunshine Band

Peter CETERA
If You Leave Me Now—Chicago

Harry CHALKITIS
(w.Robert Costandinos/Stylianos
Vlavianos)
Sing An Ode To Love—Demis Roussos
(from **The Roussos Phenomenon** (EP))

Romeo CHALLENGER
(see SHOWADDYWADDY)

Michael/Mike CHAPMAN
(w.Nicky Chinn)
I'll Meet You At Midnight—Smokie
Living Next Door To Alice—Smokie
Something's Been Making Me Blue—
Smokie

Les CHARLES
(w.Ben Findon)
Love On Delivery—Billy Ocean
Love Really Hurts Without You—Billy
Ocean
(w.Ben Findon/Mike Myers)
Stop Me (If You've Heard It All Before)—
Billy Ocean

Nicky CHINN
(w.Michael Chapman)
I'll Meet You At Midnight—Smokie

Living Next Door To Alice—Smokie
Something's Been Making Me Blue—
Smokie

Di Damicco CIRO
(see ZACAR)

Tony CLIFF (real name—Arthur Frewin)
Arrangement of **The Old Rugged Cross**—
Ethna Campbell

CLIMAX BLUES BAND
(Colin Cooper, Peter Haycock, Derek Holt,
Richard Jones & John Kuffley)
Couldn't Get It Right—Climax Blues Band

Allen COLLINS
(w.Ronnie Van Zant)
Double Trouble—Lynyrd Skynyrd
Free Bird—Lynyrd Skynyrd

Bill COLLINS
(w.Jim Bobo/Hank Mizell/Ralph
Simonton)
Jungle Rock—Hank Mizell

Rodger COLLINS
You Sexy Sugar Plum (But I Like It)—
Rodger Collins

Brian CONNOLLY
(see SWEET)

Robert COSTANDINOS (aka Robert RUPEN)
(real name—Alexandre KOUYOUMDJIAN)
Can't Say How Much I Love You—
Demis Roussos
(w.Stylianos Vlavianos)
Forever And Ever
My Friend The Wind
Sing An Ode To Love
(all from The Roussos Phenomenon (EP))

Con CONRADE
(w.Herb Magidson)
The Continental—Maureen McGovern

Paul COOK
(see SEX PISTOLS)

Roger COOK
(w.Herbie Flowers)
Side Show—Chanter Sisters

Sam COOKE
(w.Lou Adler/Herb Alpert)
(What A) Wonderful World—Johnny Nash

Colin COOPER
(see CLIMAX BLUES BAND)

J. Fred COOTS
(w.Haven Gillespie)
Santa Claus Is Coming To Town—
Carpenters

Hank COSBY
(w.William Robinson/Stevie Wonder)
Tears Of A Clown—Smokey Robinson &
the Miracles

Phil COULTER
(w.Bill Martin)
Forever and And Ever—Slik
It's So Nice (To Have You Home)—New
Seekers
Requiem—Slik

Roger CRAIG
(w.Billy Kinsley)
Every Man Must Have A Dream—
Liverpool Express
Hold Tight—Liverpool Express
You Are My Love—Liverpool Express

Tony CRAIG
(w.Eddie Adamberry)
Loving On The Losing Side—Tommy Hunt
One Fine Morning—Tommy Hunt

Jimmie CRANE
(w.Al Jacobs)
Hurt—Manhattans
Hurt—Elvis Presley

Dave CRAWFORD
Destiny—Candi Staton
Young Hearts Run Free—Candi Staton

Linda CREED
(w.Thom Bell)
Country Living—Stylistics (from **You'll
Never Get To Heaven (EP)**)
The Rubber Band Man—Detroit
Spinners

Lol CREME
(w.Graham Gouldman/Eric Stewart)
I'm Mandy Fly Me—10cc

Bill CURTIS
(w.Johnny Flippin)
(Are You Ready) Do The Bus Stop—
Fatback Band

Paul CURTIS
Here's To Love—John Christie

Holger CZUKAY
(see CAN)

Bill DANOFF
Afternoon Delight—Starland Vocal Band

Julian DASH
(w.Buddy Feyne/Erskine Hawkins/
William Johnson)
Tuxedo Junction—Manhattan Transfer

Hal DAVID
(w.Burt Bacharach)
**You'll Never Get To Heaven (If You
Break My Heart) (EP)—**Stylistics (from the
EP of the same name)

Rob DAVIES
(w.Ray Stiles)
Shake It Down—Mud

Benny DAVIS
(w.Harry Akst)
Baby Face—Wing & A Prayer Fife & Drum
Corps

Chip DAVIS
(w.Bill Fries/C.W. McCall)
Convoy—C.W. McCall
Convoy GB—Laurie Lingo & the
Dipsticks

Don DAVIS
(w.Harvey Scales/Al Vance)
Disco Lady—Johnnie Taylor

John DEACON
You're My Best Friend—Queen

Rod DEAS
(see SHOWADDYWADDY)

Kiki DEE
Loving And Free—Kiki Dee

Rick DEES
Disco Duck—Rick Dees & His Cast of
Idiots

Micky DENNE
(w.Ken Gold)
Can't Get By Without You—Real Thing
I Can't Ask For Anymore Than You—
Cliff Richard
You To Me Are Everything—Real Thing

John DENSMORE
(see DOORS)

Peter DeROSE
(w.Mitchell Parish)
Deep Purple—Donny & Marie Osmond

Gregg DIAMOND
  More, More, More—Andrea True
  Connection

Neil DIAMOND
  Beautiful Noise—Neil Diamond
  If You Know What I Mean—Neil Diamond

B.B./Morris DICKERSON
  (see WAR)

Giveseppe DONAGGIO
  (w.Simon Napier-Bell/Vinenzo Pallavacini/
  Vicki Wickham)
  You Don't Have To Say You Love Me—
  Guys 'n' Dolls

DOORS
  (John Densmore, Robbie Krieger, Ray
  Manzarek & Jim Morrison)
  Riders On A Storm—Doors

Graeme DOUGLAS
  (w.Will Birch/Paul Shuttleworth)
  Little Does She Know

Lamont DOZIER
  (w.Brian & Eddie Holland)
  This Old Heart Of Mine—Rod Stewart

Eddie DRENNON
  Let's Do The Latin Hustle—Eddie
  Drennon & BBS Unlimited
  Let's Do The Latin Hustle—M & O Band

Al DUBIN
  (w.Harry Warren)
  Lullaby Of Broadway—Winifred Shaw

Perry DUC
  (w.May Ambruster/Larry Melwing)
  Soul Dracula—Hot Blood

David DUNDAS
  (w.Roger Greenaway)
  Jeans On—David Dundas

Des DYER
  (w.Clive Scott)
  Sky High—Jigsaw

Bob DYLAN
  (w.Jacques Levy)
  Hurricane—Bob Dylan

Randy EDELMAN
  The Uptown, Uptempo Woman—Randy
  Edelman

Richard EDWYN
  Get It Together—Crispy & Co.

Bobby ELI
  (w.Vinny Barrett)
  Side Show—Barry Biggs

Steve ELSON
  (w.Dave Stephenson)
  Stoney Ground—Guys 'n' Dolls

David ESSEX
  City Lights—David Essex
  Coming Home—David Essex
  If I Could—David Essex

Tom EVANS
  (w.Pete Ham)
  Without You—Nilsson

Don EVERLY
  (w.Phil EVERLY)
  The Price Of Love—Bryan Ferry (from
  Extended Play (EP))

Phil EVERLY
  (w.Don Everly)
  The Price Of Love—Bryan Ferry (from
  Extended Play (EP))

Tony EYERS
  Doctor Kiss-Kiss—5000 Volts

Donald FAGEN
  (w.Walter Becker)
  Haitian Divorce—Steely Dan

Andy FAIRWEATHER LOW
  La Booga Rooga—Surprise Sisters
  Wide Eyed And Legless—Andy
  Fairweather Low

Frank FARIAN
  (w. Antonio Reyam)
  Daddy Cool—Boney M

Wes FARRELL
  (w.Bert Russell)
  Hang On Sloopy—Sandpipers

Eric FAULKNER
  (w.Stuart 'Woody' Wood)
  Love Me Like I Love You—Bay City Rollers
  Money Honey—Bay City Rollers

Sheila FERGUSON
  (w.Tatshushi Umegaki)
  Toast Of Love—Three Degrees

Bryan FERRY
Both Ends Burning—Roxy Music

Buddy FEYNE
(w.Julian Dash/Erskine Hawkins/William Johnson)
Tuxedo Junction—Manhattan Transfer

Russ FIELD
(see SHOWADDYWADDY)

Richard FINCH
(w.Harry Wayne Casey)
Honey I—George McCrae
Keep It Comin' Love—KC & the Sunshine Band
(Shake Shake Shake) Shake Your Booty—KC & the Sunshine Band

Ben FINDON
(w.Les Charles)
Love On Delivery—Billy Ocean
Love Really Hurts Without You—Billy Ocean
(w.Les Charles/Mike Myers)
Stop Me (If You've Heard It All Before)—Billy Ocean

Jack FISHMAN
(w.Lucio Battisti)
(If Paradise Is) Half As Nice—Amen Corner

Guy FLETCHER
(w.Doug Flett)
Fallen Angel—Frankie Valli

Doug FLETT
(w.Guy Fletcher)
Fallen Angel—Frankie Valli

Johnny FLIPPIN
(w.Bill Curtis)
(Are You Ready) Do The Bus Stop—Fatback Band

Herbie FLOWERS
(w.Roger Cook)
Side Show—Chanter Sisters

Peter FRAMPTON
Baby I Love Your Way—Peter Frampton
Do You Feel Like We Do—Peter Frampton
Show Me The Way—Peter Frampton

Claude FRANCOIS
(H.E.R. Barnes/Jean-Pierre Bourtayre/Frank Thomas)
Tears On The Telephone—Claude Francois

Arthur FREWIN
(see Tony CLIFF)

Glen FREY
(w.Don Henley/Randy Meisner)
Take It To The Limit—Eagles

Bill FRIES (aka C.W. McCall)
(w.Chip Davis/C.W. McCall)
Convoy—C.W. McCall
Convoy GB—Laurie Lingo & the Dipsticks

Benny GALLAGHER
(w.Graham Lyle)
Breakaway—Gallagher & Lyle
Heart On My Sleeve—Bryan Ferry (from **Extended Play (EP)**)
Heart On My Sleeve—Gallagher & Lyle
I Wanna Stay With You—Gallagher & Lyle

Kenny GAMBLE
(w.Leon Huff)
Let's Make A Baby—Billy Paul
You'll Never Find Another Love Like Mine—Lou Rawls
I Love Music—O'Jays

Joe GARLAND
(w.Andy Razaf)
In The Mood—Sound 9418

Lee GARRETT
(w.Robert Taylor)
You're My Everything—Lee Garrett

Rex GARVIN
(w.Gregory Carroll/Doris Payne)
Just One Look—Faith Hope & Charity

Buddy GASK
(see SHOWADDYWADDY)

David GATES
Lost Without Your Love—Bread

Bob GAUDIO
(w.Judy Parker)
December, 1963 (Oh, What A Night)—Four Seasons
Silver Star—Four Seasons

Mac GAYDEN
Morning Glory—James & Bobby Purify

Barry GIBB
(w.Robin Gibb)
Love Me—Yvonne Elliman
(also see Bee Gees)

Maurice GIBB
(see BEE GEES)

Robin GIBB
(w.Barry Gibb)
Love Me—Yvonne Elliman
(also see Bee Gees)

Brian GIBBS
Seagull—Rainbow Cottage

Ken GIBSON
Nice And Slow—Jesse Green
(w.Carol Holness)
Flip—Jesse Green

Douglas GIBSON
(w.Larry Smith/Gerry Thomas)
Party Time—Fatback Band

Haven GILLESPIE
(w.J. Fred Coots)
Santa Claus Is Coming To Town—
Carpenters

Peter GILMOUR
(w.Can)
I Want More—Can

Gary GLITTER
(w.Mike Leander)
You Belong To Me—Gary Glitter

Gerry GOFFIN
(w.Michael Masser)
**Theme From Mahogany 'Do You Know
Where You're Going To'**—Diana Ross
So Sad The Song—Gladys Knight
& the Pips

Ken GOLD
(w.Micky Denne)
Can't Get By Without You—Real Thing
I Can't Ask For Anymore Than You—
Cliff Richard
You To Me Are Everything—Real Thing

Jerry GOLDSTEIN
(w.War)
Low Rider—War

Johnny GOODISON
(w.Phil Wainman)
Show Me You're A Woman—Mud

Bev GORDON
It's Temptation—Sheer Elegance

Bobby GOSH
A Little Bit More—Dr. Hook

Graham GOULDMAN
(w.Eric Stewart)
Art For Art's Sake—10cc
The Things We Do For Love—10cc
(w.Lol Creme/Eric Stewart)
I'm Mandy Fly Me—10cc

Paul GREEDUS
Fairy Tale—Dana

Leroy GREEN
(w.Norman Harris)
Soul Searchin' Time—Trammps

Roger GREENAWAY
(w.David Dundas)
Jeans On—David Dundas
(w.Tony Macaulay)
**You're More Than A Number In My
Little Red Book**—Drifters
(w.Barry Mason)
Can I Take You Home Little Girl—
Drifters
You Just Might See Me Cry—Our Kid
(w.Les Reed)
Hello Happiness—Drifters
(w.Geoff Stephens)
Every Nite's A Saturday Night With You
—Drifters
It's Gonna Be A Cold Cold Christmas—
Dana

Howard/Howie GREENFIELD
(w.Neil Sedaka)
The Other Side Of Me—Andy Williams

Ellie GREENWICH
(w.Jeff Barry/George Morton)
Leader Of The Pack—Shangri-Las

William GRIFFIN
(w.Warren 'Pete' Moore)
Love Machine—Miracles

Henry GROSS
Shannon—Henry Gross

Kiki GYAN
(w.Sol Amarfio/Teddy Osei/Mac Tontoh)
Dance The Body Music—Osibisa

Daryl HALL
(w.John Oates)
She's Gone—Daryl Hall & John Oates

Pete HAM
(w.Tom Evans)
Without You—Nilsson

74

Nancy HAMILTON
(w.Morgan Lewis)
How High The Moon—Gloria Gaynor

Albert HAMMOND
(w.John Bettis/Richard Carpenter)
I Need To Be In Love—Carpenters

Steve HARLEY
(I Believe) Love's A Prima Donna—
Steve Harley & Cockney Rebel

HARPO
Movie Star—Harpo

Norman HARRIS
(w.Leroy Green)
Soul Searchin' Time—Trammps

George HARRISON
Here Comes The Sun—Steve Harley
& Cockney Rebel

Wilbert HARRISON
Let's Stick Together—Bryan Ferry

Tim HART
(see STEELEYE SPAN)

Marvin HATLEY
Dance Of The Cuckoos—Band of the
Black Watch

Mike HAWKER
(w.Ivor Raymonde)
I Only Want To Be With You—Bay City
Rollers

Erskine HAWKINS
(w.Julian Dash/Buddy Feyne/William
Johnson)
Tuxedo Junction—Manhattan Transfer

Peter HAYCOCK
(see CLIMAX BLUES BAND)

Isaac HAYES
Disco Connection—Isaac Hayes
Movement

Roy G. HEMMINGS
Disco Music (I Like It)—J.A.L.N. Band

Don HENLEY
(w.Glenn Frey/Randy Meisner)
Take It To The Limit—Eagles

Larry HENLEY
(w.Johnny Slate)
Sing Me An Old Fashioned Song—
Billie Jo Spears

Dave HIGGS
Teenage Depression—Eddie & the
Hot Rods

Chris HILL
(w.John Staines)
Bionic Santa—Chris Hill
Renta Santa—Chris Hill

Keith HILLER
(w.Tony Hiller)
Manchester United—Manchester United
Football Team

Tony HILLER
(w.Keith Hiller)
Manchester United—Manchester United
Football Team
(w.Lee Sheriden/Martin Lee)
My Sweet Rosalie—Brotherhood of Man
Save Your Kisses For Me—Brotherhood
of Man

Noddy/Neville HOLDER
(w.Jim Lea)
In For A Penny—Slade
Let's Call It Quits—Slade

Brian HOLLAND
(w.Lamont Dozier/Eddie Holland)
This Old Heart Of Mine—Rod Stewart

Eddie HOLLAND
(w.Lamont Dozier/Brian Holland)
This Old Heart Of Mine—Rod Stewart

Carol HOLNESS
(w.Ken Gibson)
Flip—Jesse Green

Mike HOLOWAY Senior
Dawn—Flintlock

Derek HOLT
(see CLIMAX BLUES BAND)

Wayland HOLYFIELD
You're My Best Friend—Don Williams

James HOPKINS
(w.Detlef Petersen)
Sold My Rock 'N' Roll (Gave It Up For
Funky Soul)—Linda & the Funky Boys

Harlan HOWARD
No Chance (No Charge)—Billy Connolly
No Charge—J.J. Barrie

Leon HUFF
(w.Kenny Gamble)
Let's Make A Baby—Billy Paul
**You'll Never Find Another Love Like
Mine**—Lou Rawls
I Love Music—O'Jays

Alex HUGHES (aka Judge Dread)
(w.Ted Lemon)
Christmas In Dreadland—Judge Dread
Confessions Of A Bouncer—Judge Dread
The Winkle Man—Judge Dread
(w.Leo Caerts/Ted Lemon/Leo
Rozenstraten)
Y Viva Suspenders—Judge Dread

HUGO (aka Hugo Peretti)
(w.George David Weiss/Luigi)
Can't Help Falling In Love—Stylistics
Funky Weekend—Stylistics
The Miracle—Stylistics (from **You'll Never
Get To Heaven** (EP))
Na Na Is The Saddest Word—Stylistics
Sixteen Bars—Stylistics
You Are Beautiful—Stylistics (from **You'll
Never Get To Heaven** (EP))

Phil HURTT
(w.Hank Belolo/Jacques Morali/
Ritchie Rome)
The Best Disco In Town—Richie Family

Richard HURWITZ
(w.Lloyd Michels)
The Flasher—Mistura with Lloyd Michels

Ernie ISLEY
Marvin ISLEY
O'Kelly ISLEY
Ronald ISLEY
Rudolph ISLEY
(see ISLEY BROTHERS)

ISLEY BROTHERS
(Ernie, Marvin, O'Kelly, Ronald & Rudolph
Isley, Chris Jasper)
Harvest For The World—Isley Brothers

Billy JACKSON
(w.Alfonso Thornton)
God's Gonna Punish You—Tymes

Al JACOBS
(w.Jimmie Crane)
Hurt—Manhattans
Hurt—Elvis Presley

Mick JAGGER
(w.Keith Richard)
Fool To Cry—Rolling Stones
Satisfaction—Eddie & the Hot Rods (from
Live At The Marquee (EP))

Al JAMES
(see SHOWADDYWADDY)

Chris JASPER
(see ISLEY BROTHERS)

Fred JAY
(w.Zacar)
When A Child Is Born (Soleado)—Johnny
Mathis

Elton JOHN
(w.Bernie Taupin)
Benny And The Jets—Elton John
Sorry Seems To Be The Hardest Word—
Elton John
Don't Go Breaking My Heart—Elton John
& Kiki Dee (written under the names of
Ann Orson & Carte Blanche)

Robert JOHNSON
(see STEELEYE SPAN)

William JOHNSON
(w.Julian Dash/Buddy Feyne/Erskine
Hawkins)
Tuxedo Junction—Manhattan Transfer

Juggy JONES
(w.Ken Waymon)
Inside America—Juggy Murray Jones
(The Producer of this single—Juggy
Murray—is the same person)

Marshall JONES
(w.William Beck/Marvin Pierce/James
Williams)
Who'd She Coo—Ohio Players

Richard JONES
(see CLIMAX BLUES BAND)

Steve JONES
(see SEX PISTOLS)

Lonnie JORDAN
(see WAR)

Georg KAJANUS
Girls, Girls, Girls—Sailor
Glass Of Champagne—Sailor

Michael KAROLI
(see CAN)

Rick KEMP
(see STEELEYE SPAN)

Wayne KEMP
One Piece At A Time—Johnny Cash &
the Tennessee Three

Ed KING
(w.Gary Rossington/Ronnie Van Zant)
Sweet Home Alabama—Lynyrd Skynyrd

Billy KINSLEY
(w.Roger Craig)
Every Man Must Have A Dream—
Liverpool Express
Hold Tight—Liverpool Express
You Are My Love—Liverpool Express

Charles KIPPS
Walk Away From Love—David Ruffin

KIRBY
Why Did You Do It—Stretch

Peter KNIGHT
(see STEELEYE SPAN)

Alexandre KOUYOUMDJIAN
(see Robert COSTANDINOS/Robert
RUPEN)

Robbie KRIEGER
(see DOORS)

John KUFFLEY
(see CLIMAX BLUES BAND)

Greg LAKE
(w.Pete Sinfield)
I Believe In Father Christmas—Greg Lake

Dennis LAMBERT
(w.Brian Potter)
It Only Takes A Minute—100 Ton & A
Feather

Ronnie LANE
(w.Steve Marriott)
Itchycoo Park—Small Faces
Lazy Sunday—Small Faces

Jim/James LEA
(w.Noddy Holder)
In For A Penny—Slade
Let's Call It Quits—Slade

Danny LEAKE
(w.Ian Levine)
Doomsday—Evelyn Thomas
Your Magic Put A Spell On Me—
L.J. Johnson

Mike LEANDER
(w.Gary Glitter)
You Belong To Me—Gary Glitter

Serge LEBRAIL
(w.Pascal Auriat/Bryan Blackburn/
Pascal Sevran)
Think Of Me (Wherever You Are)—
Ken Dodd

Curtis LEE
(w.Tommy Boyce)
Under The Moon Of Love—
Showaddywaddy

Martin LEE
(w.Tony Hiller/Lee Sheriden)
My Sweet Rosalie—Brotherhood of Man
Save Your Kisses For Me—Brotherhood
of Man

Ted LEMON
(w.Alex Hughes)
Christmas In Dreadland—Judge Dread
Confessions Of A Bouncer—Judge Dread
The Winkle Man—Judge Dread
(w.Leo Caerts/Alex Hughes/Leo
Rozenstraten)
Y Viva Suspenders—Judge Dread

John LENNON
Imagine—John Lennon
(w.Paul McCartney)
Back In The U.S.S.R.—Beatles
Get Back—Beatles
Get Back—Rod Stewart
Help—Beatles
Here There And Everywhere—Emmylou
Harris
Hey Jude—Beatles
It's Only Love—Bryan Ferry (from
Extended Play (EP))
Paperback Writer—Beatles
Strawberry Fields Forever—Beatles
We Can Work It Out—Four Seasons
Yesterday—Beatles

Sylvester LEVAY
(w.Stephan Prager)
Fly, Robin, Fly—Silver Convention
Get Up And Boogie—Silver Convention
Tiger Baby/No, No, Joe—Silver
Convention

Ian LEVINE
(w.Danny Leake)
Doomsday—Evelyn Thomas

Your Magic Put A Spell On Me—
L.J. Johnson
(w.Paul Wilson)
Weak Spot—Evelyn Thomas

Jacques LEVY
(w.Bob Dylan)
Hurricane—Bob Dylan

Alan LEWIS
(w.Vincent Rose/Larry Stock)
Blueberry Hill—Fats Domino

David LEWIS
Happy To Be On An Island In The Sun—
Demis Roussos

Meade 'Lux' LEWIS
Honky Tonk Train Blues—Keith Emerson

Morgan LEWIS
(w.Nancy Hamilton)
How High The Moon—Gloria Gaynor

Jaki LIEBEZEIT
(see CAN)

Harry LLOYD
(w.Gloria Sklerov)
I Believe I'm Gonna Love You—Frank
Sinatra

Andrew LLOYD WEBBER
(w.Tim Rice)
Don't Cry For Me Argentina—Julie
Covington

Dennis LOCORRIERE
If Not You—Dr. Hook

Dave LONG (real name—Cy PAYNE)
Arrangement of The Old Rugged Cross—
Ethna Campbell

Mike LOVE
(w.Brian Wilson)
Good Vibrations—Beach Boys

Wilfred LOVETT
Kiss And Say Goodbye—Manhattans

LUIGI
(aka Luigi CREATORE)
(w.Hugo/George David Weiss)
Can't Help Falling In Love—Stylistics
Funky Weekend—Stylistics
The Miracle—Stylistics (from **You'll
Never Get To Heaven (EP)**)
Na Na Is The Saddest Word—Stylistics
Sixteen Bars—Stylistics

You Are Beautiful—Stylistics (from **You'll
Never Get To Heaven (EP)**)

Graham LYLE
(w.Benny Gallagher)
Breakaway—Gallagher & Lyle
Heart On My Sleeve—Bryan Ferry
(from **Extended Play (EP)**)
Heart On My Sleeve—Gallagher & Lyle
I Wanna Stay With You—Gallagher &
Lyle

Jeff LYNNE
Evil Woman—Electric Light Orchestra
Livin' Thing—Electric Light Orchestra
Strange Magic—Electric Light Orchestra

Phil LYNOTT
The Boys Are Back In Town—Thin Lizzy
Jailbreak—Thin Lizzy

Tony MACAULAY
Don't Give Up On Us—David Soul
Falling Apart At The Seams—Marmalade
(w.Roger Greenaway)
**You're More Than A Number In My Little
Red Book—**Drifters

Ballard MacDONALD
(w.Harry Carroll)
The Trail Of The Lonesome Pine—Laurel
& Hardy

John MADARA
(w.Arthur Singer/David White)
At The Hop—Danny & the Juniors

Herb MAGIDSON
(w.Con Conrade)
The Continental—Maureen McGovern

Barry MANILOW
(w.Adrienne Anderson)
Could It Be Magic—Donna Summer

Kal MANN
(w.Dave Appell)
Let's Twist Again—Chubby Checker

Ray MANZAREK
(see DOORS)

Ernest MARESCA
The Wanderer—Dion

Steve MARRIOTT
(w.Ronnie Lane)
Itchycoo Park—Small Faces
Lazy Sunday—Small Faces

Bob MARSHALL
(w.John Miles)
Remember Yesterday—John Miles

Bill MARTIN
(w.Phil Coulter)
Forever And Ever—Slik
It's So Nice (To Have You Home)—New Seekers
Requiem—Slik

Rudy MARTINEZ
96 Tears—Eddie & the Hot Rods (from **Live At The Marquee (EP)**)

Barry MASON
(w.Roger Greenaway)
Can I Take You Home Little Girl—Drifters
You Just Might See Me Cry—Our Kid
(w.Geoff Stephens)
Drive Safely Darling—Tony Christie
(w.Stylianos Vlavianos)
When Forever Has Gone—Demis Roussos

Michael MASSER
(w.Gerry Goffin)
Theme From Maghogany 'Do You Know Where You're Going To'—Diana Ross
So Sad The Song—Gladys Knight & the Pips
(w.Pam Sawyer)
I Thought It Took A Little Time (But Today I Fell In Love)—Diana Ross

John MATHIAS
Hey Miss Payne—Chequers

Glen MATLOCK
(see SEX PISTOLS)

Simon MAY
The Summer Of My Life—Simon May

C.W. McCALL (real name—Bill FRIES)
(w.Chip Davis/Bill Fries)
Convoy—C.W. McCall
Convoy—Laurie Lingo & the Dipsticks

Paul McCARTNEY
Let 'Em In—Wings
Silly Love Songs—Wings
(w.John Lennon)
Back In The U.S.S.R.—Beatles
Get Back—Beatles
Get Back—Rod Stewart
Help—Beatles
Here There And Everywhere—Emmylou Harris

Hey Jude—Beatles
It's Only Love—Bryan Ferry
(from **Extended Play (EP)**)
Paperback Writer—Beatles
Strawberry Fields Forever—Beatles
We Can Work It Out—Four Seasons
Yesterday—Beatles

Van McCOY
Baby I'm Yours—Linda Lewis
This Is It—Melba Moore

Country Joe McDONALD
Here I Go Again—Twiggy

Gene McFADDEN
(w.Victor Carstarphen/John Whitehead)
Soul City Walk—Archie Bell & the Drells
Wake Up Everybody—Harold Melvin & the Blue Notes

Parker McGEE
I'd Really Love To See You Tonight—England Dan & John Ford Coley

Harvey McKENNA
The Boston Tea Party—Sensational Alex Harvey Band

Marilyn McLEOD
(w.Pam Sawyer)
Love Hangover—Diana Ross

Ralph McTELL
(w.J.S. Bach)
Dreams Of You—Ralph McTell

Christine McVIE
Say You Love Me—Fleetwood Mac

Larry MELWING
(w.May Ambruster/Peny Duc)
Soul Dracula—Hot Blood

Randy MEISNER
(w.Glenn Frey/Don Henley)
Take It To The Limit—Eagles

Freddie MERCURY
Bohemian Rhapsody—Queen
Somebody To Love—Queen

Lloyd MICHELS
(w.Richard Hurwitz)
The Flasher—Mistura with Lloyd Michels

John MILES
Music—John Miles
(w.Bob Marshall)
Remember Yesterday—John Miles

Charles MILLER
(see WAR)

Glenn MILLER
(w.Mitchell Parish)
Moonlight Serenade—Glenn Miller

Roger MILLER
King Of The Cops—Billy Howard

Steve MILLER
Rock 'N' Me—Steve Miller Band

Tony MITCHELL
(w.Garth Porter)
Howzat—Sherbet

Willie MITCHELL
The Champion—Willie Mitchell

Hank MIZELL
(w.Jim Bobo/Bill Collins/Ralph
Simonton)
Jungle Rock—Hank Mizell

Tommy MOELLER
(w.Brian Parker)
Concrete And Clay—Randy Edelman

Marguerite MONNOT
(w.Geoffrey Parsons/Edith Piaf)
If You Love Me—Mary Hopkin

Bob MONTGOMERY
Misty Blue—Dorothy Moore

Warren 'Pete' MOORE
(w.William Griffin)
Love Machine—Miracles
(w.William Robinson/Marv Tarplin)
The Tracks Of My Tears—Linda Ronstadt

Jacques MORALI
(w.Hank Belolo/Phil Hurtt/Ritchie Rome)
The Best Disco In Town—Ritchie Family

Giorgio MORODER
(w.Pete Bellotte/Donna Summer)
Love To Love You Baby—Donna Summer
Winter Melody—Donna Summer

Jim MORRISON
(see DOORS)

Van MORRISON
Gloria—Eddie & the Hot Rods (from
Live At The Marquee (EP))

George 'Shadow' MORTON
(w.Jeff Barry/Ellie Greenwich)
Leader Of The Pack—Shangri-Las

Randy MULLER
(w.Wade Williamson)
Movin'—Brass Construction

Walter MURPHY
A Fifth Of Beethoven—Walter Murphy
Band

William MURRAY
(w.Mike Oldfield)
On Horseback—Mike Oldfield

Frank MUSKER
(w.Dominic Bugatti)
Dancing With The Captain—Paul
Nicholas
Grandma's Party (EP)—Paul Nicholas
(from the EP of the same name)
Mr. Sax And The Girl—Paul Nicholas
(from **Grandma's Party (EP)**)
Reggae Like It Used To Be—Paul Nicholas

Mike MYERS
(w.Les Charles/Ben Findon)
Stop Me (If You've Heard It All Before)—
Billy Ocean

Simon NAPIER-BELL
(w.Giveseppe Donaggio/Vinenzo
Pallavacini/Vicki Wickham)
You Don't Have To Say You Love Me—
Guys 'n' Dolls

Christopher NEIL
(w.Paul Nicholas)
Flat Foot Floyd—Paul Nicholas
Shufflin' Shoes—Paul Nicholas
(both from **Grandma's Party (EP)**)

Bill NELSON
Hot Valves (EP)—Be Bop DeLuxe
Maid In Heaven
Bring Back The Spark
Blazing Apostles
Jet Silver and the Dolls of Venus
Ships In The Night—Be Bop DeLuxe

Willie NELSON
Funny How Time Slips Away—Dorothy
Moore

Paul NICHOLAS
(w.Christopher Neil)
Flat Foot Floyd—Paul Nicholas
Shufflin' Shoes—Paul Nicholas
(both from **Grandma's Party (EP)**)

Trevor OAKES
(see SHOWADDYWADDY)

John OATES
(w.Daryl Hall)
She's Gone—Daryl Hall & John Oates

Bill ODDIE
Make A Daft Noise For Christmas—
Goodies

Kenny O'DELL
What I've Got In Mind—Billie Jo Spears

Mike OLDFIELD
Tubular Bells—Champs Boys
(w.J.S. Bach)
In Dulci Jubilo—Mike Oldfield
(w.William Murray)
On Horseback—Mike Oldfield

Spooner OLDHAM
(w.Dan Penn)
I'm Your Puppet—James & Bobby Purify

Ann ORSON
(see Elton John/Bernie Taupin)

Gary OSBORNE
(w.Veronique Sanson)
Amoureuse—Kiki Dee

Teddy OSEI
(w.Sol Amarfio/Mac Tontoh)
Sunshine Day—Osibisa
(w.Sol Amarfio/Kiki Gyan/Mac Tontoh)
Dance The Body Music—Osibisa

Lee OSKAR
(see WAR)

David PAICH
(w.Boz Scaggs)
Lowdown—Boz Scaggs

Vinenzo PALLAVACINI
(w.Giveseppe Donaggio/Simon
Napier-Bell/Vicki Wickham)
You Don't Have To Say You Love Me—
Guys 'n' Dolls

Rick PARFITT
Rain—Status Quo
(w.Bob Young)
Mystery Song—Status Quo

Mitchell PARISH
(w.Peter DeRose)
Deep Purple—Donny & Marie Osmond
(w.Glenn Miller)
Moonlight Serenade—Glenn Miller

Richard PARISSI
Play That Funky Music—Wild Cherry

Brian PARKER
(w.Tommy Moeller)
Concrete And Clay—Randy Edelman

Judy PARKER
(w.Bob Gaudio)
December, 1963 (Oh, What A Night)—
Four Seasons
Silver Star—Four Seasons

Ray PARKER
(w.Barry White)
You See The Trouble With Me—Barry
White

Geoffrey PARSONS
(w.Marguerite Monnot/Edith Piaf)
If You Love Me—Mary Hopkin

Dolly PARTON
Jolene—Dolly Parton

Cy PAYNE
(see Dave LONG)

Doris PAYNE
(w.Gregory Carroll/Rex Garvin)
Just One Look—Faith Hope & Charity

Nigel PEGRUM
(see STEELEYE SPAN)

Dan PENN
(w.Spooner Oldham)
I'm Your Puppet—James & Bobby Purify

Freddie PERREN
(w.Keni St. Lewis)
Heaven Must Be Missing An Angel—
Tavares
(w.Keni St. Lewis/Christine Yarian)
Don't Take Away The Music—Tavares

Detlef PETERSEN
(w.James Hopkins)
**Sold My Rock 'n' Roll (Gave It Up For
Funky Soul)**—Linda & the Funky Boys

Edith PIAF
(w.Marguerite Monnot/Geoffrey Parsons)
If You Love Me—Mary Hopkin

Marvin PIERCE
(w.William Beck/Marshall Jones/
James Williams)
Who'd She Coo—Ohio Players

Victoria PIKE
(w.Teddy Randazzo)
Better Use Your Head—Little Anthony &
the Imperials

Doc/Jerome POMUS
(w.Mort Shuman)
Suspicion—Elvis Presley

Vini PONCIA
(w. Leo Sayer)
You Make Me Feel Like Dancing—
Leo Sayer

Garth PORTER
(w.Tony Mitchell)
Howzat—Sherbet

Brian POTTER
(w.Dennis Lambert)
It Only Takes A Minute—100 Ton & A
Feather

Stephan PRAGER
(w.Sylvester Levay)
Fly, Robin, Fly—Silver Convention
Get Up And Boogie—Silver Convention
Tiger Baby/No, No, Joe—Silver
Convention

Steve PRIEST
(see SWEET)

Maddy PRIOR
(see STEELEYE SPAN)

Claude/'Curly' PUTMAN (Jr.)
Green Green Grass Of Home—Elvis
Presley
(w.Bobby Braddock/Sheb Wooley)
D.I.V.O.R.C.E.—Billy Connolly

Martin QUITTENTON
(w.Rod Stewart)
Maggie May—Rod Stewart

Willis Alan RAMSEY
Satin Sheets—Bellamy Brothers

Teddy RANDAZZO
(w.Victoria Pike)
Better Use Your Head—Little Anthony &
the Imperials

Fred RAUCH
(w.Carl Sigman/Gerhard Winkler)
Answer Me—Barbara Dickson

Ivor RAYMONDE
(w.Mike Hawker)
I Only Want To Be With You—Bay City
Rollers

Andy RAZAF
(w.Joe Garland)
In The Mood—Sound 9418

Eugene RECORD
(w. Barbara Acklin)
You Don't Have To Go—Chi-Lites

Jimmy REED
Shame Shame Shame—Bryan Ferry
(from **Extended Play (EP)**)

Les REED
(w.Geoff Stephens)
There's A Kind Of Hush—Carpenters
(w.Roger Greenaway)
Hello Happiness—Drifters

Antonio REYAM
(w.Frank Farian)
Daddy Cool—Boney M

Allen REYNOLDS
I Recall A Gypsy Woman—Don Williams

Tim RICE
(w.Andrew Lloyd-Webber)
Don't Cry For Me Argentina—
Julie Covington

Keith RICHARD
(w.Mick Jagger)
Fool To Cry—Rolling Stones
Satisfaction—Eddie & the Hot Rods
(from **Live At The Marquee (EP)**)

Deke RICHARDS
I'm Still Waiting—Diana Ross

John RICHARDSON
(w.Alan Williams)
Under One Roof—Rubettes
You're The Reason Why—Rubettes

Jack ROBINSON
(w.James Bolden)
**I Love To Love (But My Baby Loves To
Dance)**—Tina Charles
Love Me Like A Lover—Tina Charles

William/'Smokey' ROBINSON
(w.Hank Cosby/Stevie Wonder)
Tears Of A Clown—Smokey Robinson &
the Miracles

(w.Warren 'Pete' Moore/Marv Tarplin)
The Tracks Of My Tears—Linda Ronstadt

Jimmie RODGERS
(w.Shelley Lee Allen)
Gamblin' Bar Room Blues—Sensational
Alex Harvey Band

Joaquin RODRIGO-VIDRE
**Rodrigo's Guitar Concerto De Aranjuez
(Theme from 2nd Movement)**—Manuel
& the Music of the Mountains

Ron ROKER
(w.Biddu/Gerry Shury)
Dance Little Lady Dance—Tina Charles

Ritchie ROME
(w.Hank Belolo/Phil Hurtt/Jacques
Morali)
The Best Disco In Town—Ritchie Family

Vincent ROSE
(w.Alan Lewis/Larry Stock)
Blueberry Hill—Fats Domino

Beverley ROSS
(w.Sam Bobrick)
Girl Of My Best Friend—Elvis Presley

Gary ROSSINGTON
(w.Ed King/Ronnie Van Zant)
Sweet Home Alabama—Lynyrd Skynyrd

Johnny ROTTEN
(see SEX PISTOLS)

Leo ROZENSTRATEN
(w.Leo Caerts/Alex Hughes/Ted Lemon)
Y Viva Suspenders—Judge Dread

Robert RUPEN (aka Robert COSTANDINOS)
(real name—Alexandre Kouyoumdjian)
(w.Stylianios Vlavianos)
So Dreamy—Demis Roussos
(from **The Roussos Phenomenon (EP)**)

Tom RUSH
No Regrets—Walker Brothers

Bert RUSSELL (aka Bert BERNS)
(w.Wes Farrell)
Hang On Sloopy—Sandpipers

Melanie SAFKA
**The Combine Harvester (Brand New
Key)**—Wurzels

Keni ST. LEWIS
(w.Freddie Perren)
Heaven Must Be Missing An Angel—
Tavares
(w.Freddie Perren/Christine Yarian)
Don't Take Away The Music—Tavares

Veronique SANSON
(w.Gary Osborne)
Amoureuse—Kiki Dee

Pam SAWYER
(w.Michael Masser)
**I Thought It Took A Little Time (But
Today I Fell In Love)**—Diana Ross
(w.Marilyn McLeod)
Love Hangover—Diana Ross

Leo SAYER
(w.Vini Poncia)
You Make Me Feel Like Dancing—
Leo Sayer

Boz SCAGGS
(w.David Paich)
Lowdown—Boz Scaggs

Harvey SCALES
(w.Don Davis/Al Vance)
Disco Lady—Johnnie Taylor

Irmin SCHMIDT
(see CAN)

Andy SCOTT
(see SWEET)

Clive SCOTT
(w.Des Dyer)
Sky High—Jigsaw

Howard SCOTT
(see WAR)

Ronnie SCOTT
(w.Steve Wolfe)
Lost In France—Bonnie Tyler
Sunday—Buster

Neil SEDAKA
(w.Howard Greenfield)
The Other Side Of Me—Andy Williams

Bob SEGER
Get Out Of Denver—Eddie & the Hot Rods
(from **Live At The Marquee (EP)**)

Pascal SEVRAN
(w.Pascal Auriat/Bryan Blackburn/
Serge Lebrail)
Think Of Me (Wherever You Are)—
Ken Dodd

SEX PISTOLS
(Paul Cook, Steve Jones, Glen Matlock &
Johnny Rotten)
Anarchy In The U.K.—Sex Pistols

Gerry SHEPHARD
(w.John Springate)
People Like You And People Like Me—
Glitter Band

Lee SHERIDEN
(w.Tony Hiller/Martin Lee)
My Sweet Rosalie—Brotherhood of Man
Save Your Kisses For Me—Brotherhood
of Man

Billy SHERRILL
(w.Glenn Sutton)
I Don't Wanna Play House—Tammy
Wynette

Leighton/Pluto SHERVINGTON
Dat—Pluto Shervington
Ram Goat Liver—Pluto Shervington

SHOWADDYWADDY
(Malcolm Allured, Dave Bartram, Romeo
Challenger, Rod Deas, Russ Field, Buddy
Gask, Al James & Trevor Oakes)
Trocadero—Showaddywaddy

Mort SHUMAN
(w.Doc Pomus)
Suspicion—Elvis Presley

Gerry SHURY
(w.Biddu/Ron Roker)
Dance Little Lady Dance—Tina Charles

Paul SHUTTLEWORTH
(w.Will Birch/Graeme Douglas)
Little Does She Know—Kursaal Flyers

Carl SIGMAN
(w.Fred Rauch/Gerhard Winkler)
Answer Me—Barbara Dickson

Paul SIMON
50 Ways To Leave Your Lover—Paul
Simon

Ralph SIMONTON
(w.Jim Bobo/Bill Collins/Hank Mizell)
Jungle Rock—Hank Mizell

Pete SINFIELD
(w.Greg Lake)
I Believe In Father Christmas—Greg Lake

Arthur SINGER
(w.John Madara/David White)
At The Hop—Danny & the Juniors

Gloria SKLEROV
(w.Harry Lloyd)
I Believe I'm Gonna Love You—Frank
Sinatra

Johnny SLATE
(w.Larry Henley)
Sing Me An Old Fashioned Song—
Billie Jo Spears

Larry SMITH
(w.Douglas Gibson/Gerry Thomas)
Party Time—Fatback Band

Pete SMITH
(w.Pete Waterman)
Alright Baby—Stevenson's Rocket

John SPRINGATE
(w.Gerry Shephard)
People Like You And People Like Me—
Glitter Band

Bruce SPRINGSTEEN
Blinded By The Light—Manfred Mann's
Earthband

John STAINES
(w.Chris Hill)
Bionic Santa—Chris Hill
Renta Santa—Chris Hill

STEELEYE SPAN
(Tim Hart, Robert Johnson, Rick Kemp,
Peter Knight, Nigel Pegrum & Maddy Prior)
Arrangement of All Around My Hat—
Steeleye Span

Geoff STEPHENS
(w.Roger Greenaway)
Every Nite's A Saturday Night With You
—Drifters
It's Gonna Be A Cold Cold Christmas—
Dana
(w.Barry Mason)
Drive Safely Darling—Tony Christie
(w.Les Reed)
There's A Kind Of Hush—Carpenters

Dave STEPHENSON
(w.Steve Elson)
Stoney Ground—Guys 'n' Dolls

William STEVENSON
(w.Norman Whitfield)
It Should Have Been Me—Yvonne Fair

Eric STEWART
(w.Graham Gouldman)
Art For Art's Sake—10cc
The Things We Do For Love—10cc
(w.Lol Creme/Graham Gouldman)
I'm Mandy Fly Me—10cc

Rod STEWART
The Killing Of Georgie—Rod Stewart
Tonight's The Night—Rod Stewart
(w.Martin Quittenton)
Maggie May—Rod Stewart

Ray STILES
(w.Rob Davies)
Shake It Down—Mud

Larry STOCK
(w.Alan Lewis/Vincent Rose)
Blueberry Hill—Fats Domino

Russell STONE
We Do It—R & J Stone

Hamish STUART
Queen Of My Soul—Average White Band

Donna SUMMER
(w.Pete Bellotte/Giorgio Moroder)
Love To Love You Baby—Donna Summer
Winter Melody—Donna Summer

Gavin SUTHERLAND
Sailing—Rod Stewart

Iain SUTHERLAND
Arms Of Mary—Sutherland Brothers & Quiver
Secrets—Sutherland Brothers & Quiver

Glenn SUTTON
(w.Billy Sherrill)
I Don't Wanna Play House—Tammy Wynette

SWEET
(Brian Connolly, Steve Priest, Andy Scott & Mike Tucker)
The Lies In Your Eyes—Sweet

Alan TARNEY
(w.Bruce Welch)
Hey Mr. Dream Maker—Cliff Richard

Marv TARPLIN
(w.Warren 'Pete' Moore/William Robinson)
The Tracks Of My Tears—Linda Ronstadt

Bernie TAUPIN
(w.Elton John)
Benny And The Jets—Elton John
Sorry Seems To Be The Hardest Word—Elton John
Don't Go Breaking My Heart—Elton John & Kiki Dee (written under the names of Ann Orson & Carte Blanche)

Robert TAYLOR
(w.Lee Garrett)
You're My Everything—Lee Garrett

Toni TENNILLE
The Way I Want To Touch You—Captain & Tennille

Werner THEUNISSEN
Mississippi—Pussycat
Smile—Pussycat

Frank THOMAS
(w.H.E.R. Barnes/Jean-Pierre Bourtayre/Claude Francois)
Tears On The Telephone—Claude Francois

Gerry THOMAS
Night Fever—Fatback Band
Spanish Hustle—Fatback Band
(w.Douglas Gibson/Larry Smith)
Party Time—Fatback Band

Gunther-Eric THONER
(w.Bryan Blackburn)
Hey Mr. Music Man—Peters & Lee

Alfonso THORNTON
(w.Billy Jackson)
God's Gonna Punish You—Tymes

Mac TONTOH
(w.Sol Amarfio/Teddy Osei)
Sunshine Day—Osibisa
(w.Sol Amarfio/Kiki Gyan/Teddy Osei)
Dance The Body Music—Osibisa

Pete TOWNSHEND
Pinball Wizard—Elton John

Squeeze Box—Who
Substitute—Who

Dave TOWNSEND
Miss You Nights—Cliff Richard

Ed TOWNSEND
First Impressions—Impressions

TRADITIONAL
All Around My Hat—Steeleye Span
Light Of Experience (Doina De Jale)—
Gheorghe Zamfir
The Old Rugged Cross—Ethna Campbell
Portsmouth—Mike Oldfield

Mike TUCKER
(see SWEET)

Richard TUFO
Make Yours A Happy Home—Gladys
Knight & the Pips

Bjorn ULVAEUS
(w.Benny Andersson)
Money, Money, Money—Abba
(w.Stig Anderson/Benny Andersson)
Dancing Queen—Abba
Fernando—Abba
Mamma Mia—Abba

Tatsushi UMEGAKI
(w.Sheila Ferguson)
Toast Of Love—Three Degrees

Ronnie VAN ZANT
(w.Allen Collins)
Double Trouble—Lynyrd Skynyrd
Free Bird—Lynyrd Skynyrd
(w.Ed King/Gary Rossington)
Sweet Home Alabama—Lynyrd Skynyrd

Al VANCE
(w.Don Davis/Harvey Scales)
Disco Lady—Johnnie Taylor

Lucky VLAVIANO (real name—Stylianos
Vlavianos)
(w.Robert Rupen)
So Dreamy—Demis Roussos (from
The Roussos Phenomenon (EP))

Stylianos VLAVIANOS (aka Lucky
VLAVIANO)
(w.Robert Costandinos)
Forever And Ever—Demis Roussos
My Friend The Wind—Demis Roussos
(both from **The Roussos Phenomenon
(EP)**)

(w.Harry Chalkitis/Robert Costandinos)
Sing An Ode To Love—Demis Roussos
(from **The Roussos Phenomenon (EP)**)
(w.Barry Mason)
When Forever Has Gone—Demis Roussos

Tony WADDINGTON
(w.Wayne Bickerton)
The Two Of Us—Mac & Katie Kissoon

Phil WAINMAN
(w.Johnny Goodison)
Show Me You're A Woman—Mud

Johnny WAKELIN
In Zaire—Johnny Wakelin

WAR
(Papa Dee Allen, Harold Brown,
B.B. Dickerson, Lonnie Jordan, Charles
Miller, Lee Oskar & Howard Scott)
Me And Baby Brother—War
(w.Jerry Goldstein)
Low Rider—War

Harry WARREN
(w.Al Dubin)
Lullaby Of Broadway—Winifred Shaw

William WARREN
(w.Arlie Carter)
Wild Side Of Life—Status Quo

Peter WATERMAN
(w.Pete Smith)
Alright Baby—Stevenson's Rocket

Herbie WATKINS
Life Is Too Short Girl—Sheer Elegance
Milky Way—Sheer Elegance

Johnny 'Guitar' WATSON
I Need It—Johnny 'Guitar' Watson

Ken WAYMON
(w.Juggy Jones)
Inside America—Juggy Murray Jones

Jim WEATHERLY
Midnight Train To Georgia—Gladys
Knight & the Pips

George David WEISS
(w.Hugo & Luigi)
Can't Help Falling In Love—Stylistics
Funky Weekend—Stylistics
The Mircale—Stylistics (from **You'll Never
Get To Heaven (EP)**)
Na Na Is The Saddest Word—Stylistics

Sixteen Bars—Stylistics
You Are Beautiful—Stylistics (from
You'll Never Get To Heaven (EP)

Bruce WELCH
(w.Alan Tarney)
Hey Mr. Dream Maker—Cliff Richard

Barry WHITE
Baby, We Better Try And Get It Together
—Barry White
Don't Make Me Wait Too Long—
Barry White
Let The Music Play—Barry White
(w.Ray Parker)
You See The Trouble With Me—
Barry White

Chris WHITE
Spanish Wine—Chris White

David WHITE
(w.John Madara/Arthur Singer)
At The Hop—Danny & the Juniors

John WHITEHEAD
(w.Victor Carstarphen/Gene McFadden)
Soul City Walk—Archie Bell & the Drells
Wake Up Everybody—Harold Melvin &
the Blue Notes

Norman WHITFIELD
Car Wash—Rose Royce
(w.William Stevenson)
It Should Have Been Me—Yvonne Fair

Vicki WICKHAM
(w.Giveseppe Donaggio/Simon
Napier-Bell/Vinenzo Pallavacini)
You Don't Have To Say You Love Me—
Guys 'n' Dolls

Alan WILLIAMS
(w.John Richardson)
Under One Roof—Rubettes
You're The Reason Why—Rubettes

James WILLIAMS
(w.William Beck/Marshall Jones/Marvin
Pierce)
Who'd She Coo—Ohio Players

John WILLIAMS
Jaws—Lalo Schifrin

Larry E. WILLIAMS
Let Your Love Flow—Bellamy Brothers

Wade WILLIAMSON
(w.Randy Muller)
Movin'—Brass Construction

Brian WILSON
(w.Mike Love)
Good Vibrations

Paul WILSON
(w.Ian Levine)
Weak Spot—Evelyn Thomas

Tony WILSON
(w.Errol Brown)
You Sexy Thing—Hot Chocolate

Gerhard WINKLER
(w.Fred Rauch/Carl Sigman)
Answer Me—Barbara Dickson

Bill WITHERS
Lean On Me—Mud

Steve WOLFE
(w.Ronnie Scott)
Lost In France—Bonnie Tyler
Sunday—Buster

Stevie WONDER
I Wish—Stevie Wonder
(w.Hank Cosby/William Robinson)
Tears Of A Clown—Smokey Robinson &
the Miracles

Stuart 'Woody' WOOD
(w.Eric Faulkner)
Love Me Like I Love You—Bay City Rollers
Money Honey—Bay City Rollers

Sheb WOOLEY
(w.Bobby Braddock/Curly Putman)
D.I.V.O.R.C.E.—Billy Connolly

WURZELS
(Tommy Banner, Tony Baylis & Pete Budd)
(w.Johannes Bouwens)
I Am A Cider Drinker (Paloma Blanca)—
Wurzels

Christine YARIAN
(w.Freddie Perren/Keni St. Lewis)
Don't Take Away The Music—Tavares

Kenny YOUNG
S-S-S-Single Bed—Fox

Bob YOUNG
(w.Rick Parfitt)
Mystery Song—Status Quo

ZACAR
   (real name—Di Damicco CIRO)
   Cloud 99—St. Andrew's Chorale
   (w.Fred Jay)
   When A Child Is Born (Soleado)—Johnny
   Mathis

Section 5

UK Album Section

(*Music Week* Top 50 Album Chart)

This section lists the position and week of entry, highest chart position and week, weeks on chart, artist, title, producers and catalogue number of all albums that made the *Music Week* Top 50 album chart during 1976.

These charts are based on the *Music Week*/British Market Research Bureau figures. The sales are based on the previous fortnight's chart to that printed—i.e. the chart published in *Music Week* on July 24, 1976, will be for the sales of Saturday, July 3 to Friday, July 9. (The singles chart differs—see Section 1). *Music Week* is not published during Christmas week, therefore an additional week's chart placing is added to all those albums that were on the chart the previous week. Over the years, there have been occasions where more than one week has not been published, in addition to which there was a period in time when only the Top 15 was published and on occasion the Top 20 and Top 30. Therefore the weeks on chart column has, in some cases, been estimated from the relevant data. *denotes record still in chart on January 1, 1977. All names in brackets denote the members of groups. For all other information about producers' credits see Section 6. There is not a cross-referenced label section for albums, as in many cases records have been in the charts for several years (i.e. the Beatles 'Sgt. Pepper', which originally charted in 1967). The reason behind listing label credits was to assess each companies' chart performance during the year, with what was basically new product.

Position and date of entry	Highest position and date	Wks.	Artist(s) Title Producer(s)	Cat. No.
			ABBA	
42(17/ 1/76)	13(31/ 1/76)	10	**Abba**	(Epic EPC 80835)
			Bjorn Ulvaeus	
			Benny Andersson	
6(13/11/76)	2(27/11/76)	7*	**Arrival**	(Epic EPC 86018)
			Bjorn Ulvaeus	
			Benny Andersson	
38(27/ 3/76)	1(24/ 4/76)	40*	**Greatest Hits**	(Epic EPC 69218)
			Bjorn Ulvaeus	
			Benny Andersson	
			Cliff ADAMS SINGERS	
42(6/11/76)	23(20/11/76)	8*	**Sing Something Simple 76**	(Warwick
			John Browell	WW 5016/7)
			Jon ANDERSON	
11(10/ 7/76)	8(17/ 7/76)	10	**Olias Of Sunhillow**	(Atlantic K50261)
			(Not listed)	
			Joan ARMATRADING	
34(21/ 8/76)	12(9/10/76)	18*	**Joan Armatrading**	(A&M
			Glyn Johns	AMLH 64588)
			Pam AYERS	
33(4/12/76)	23(18/12/76)	4*	**Some More Of Me Poems And Songs**	(Galaxy GAL 6010)
			Dick Rowe	
48(20/ 3/76)	13(1/ 5/76)	20*	**Some Of Me Poems And Songs**	(Galaxy GAL 6003)
			Dick Rowe	
			BAD COMPANY	
4(7/ 2/76)	4(7/ 2/76)	10	**Run With The Pack**	(Island ILPS 9346)
			Bad Company	
			(Boz Burrell	
			Simon Kirke	
			Mick Ralphs	
			Paul Rodgers)	
			BAND OF THE BLACK WATCH	
45(31/ 1/76)	11(6/ 3/76)	10	**Scotch On The Rocks**	(Spark SRLM 503)
			Barry Kingston	
			BARCLAY JAMES HARVEST	
30(9/10/76)	19(16/10/76)	3	**Octoberon**	(Polydor 2442 144)
			Barclay James Harvest	
			(Les Holroyd	
			John Lees	
			Mel Pritchard	
			Stuart 'Wooly' Wolstenholme)	
			Shirley BASSEY	
18(1/ 5/76)	13(8/ 5/76)	5	**Love, Life And Feelings**	(United Artists UAS 29944)
			Martin Davis	

Position and date of entry	Highest position and date	Wks.	Artist(s) Title Producer(s)	Cat. No.
24(20/11/76)	15(27/11/76)	6*	**Thoughts Of Love** George Butler Tony Colton Martin Davis Johnny Harris Kenneth Hume Noel Rogers	(United Artists UAS 30011)
			BAY CITY ROLLERS	
32(11/ 9/76)	4(25/ 9/76)	9	**Dedication** Colin Frechter Jimmy Ienner Phil Wainman	(Bell SYBEL 8005)
1(19/ 4/75)	1(19/ 4/75)	38	**Once Upon A Star** Phil Wainman	(Bell SYBEL 8001)
1(28/ 9/74)	1(28/ 9/74)	58	**Rollin'** Phil Coulter Bill Martin	(Bell BELLS 244)
5(28/11/75)	3(27/12/75)	11	**Wouldn't You Like It** Phil Wainman	(Bell SYBEL 8002)
			BEACH BOYS	
31(10/ 7/76)	31(10/ 7/76)	3	**15 Big Ones** Brian Wilson	(Reprise/Brother K54079)
21(26/ 6/76)	1(10/ 7/76)	27*	**20 Golden Greats** Beach Boys (Al Jardine Mike Love Brian Wilson Carl Wilson Dennis Wilson) Nikolas Venet Brian Wilson	(Capitol EMTV 1)
			BEATLES	
6(21/ 4/73)	3(27/ 4/73)	107	**The Beatles 1962-1966** George Martin	(Apple PCSP 717)
5(21/ 4/73)	2(27/ 4/73)	95	**The Beatles 1967-1970** George Martin	(Apple PCSP 718)
45(7/ 8/76)	45(7/ 8/76)	1	**Beatles Tapes** Music Produced by Martin Ford	(Polydor 2683 068)
25(12/ 6/76)	11(19/ 6/76)	14	**Rock 'N' Roll Music** George Martin	(Parlophone PCSP 719)
8(1/ 6/67)	1(8/ 6/67)	112	**Sgt. Pepper's Lonely Hearts Club Band** George Martin	(Parlophone PCSP 7027)
			BE-BOP DELUXE	
35(11/ 9/76)	12(25/ 9/76)	6	**Modern Music** John Leckie Bill Nelson	(Harvest SHSP 4058)
35(17/ 1/76)	17(31/ 1/76)	11	**Sunburst Finish** John Leckie Bill Nelson	(Harvest SHSP 4053)

Position and date of entry	Highest position and date	Wks.	Artist(s) Title Producer(s)	Cat. No.
38(10/ 7/76)	38(10/ 7/76)	2	Jeff BECK **Wired** George Martin	(Epic EPC 86012)
32(5/ 6/76)	21(19/ 6/76)	6	BELLAMY BROTHERS **Bellamy Brothers Featuring 'Let Your Love Flow'** Phil Gernhard Tony Scotti	(Warner Bros K56242)
45(9/10/76)	22(30/10/76)	6	BEVERLEY-PHILLIPS ORCHESTRA **Gold On Silver** Brian Matthew	(Warwick WW 5018)
38(25/ 9/76)	38(25/ 9/76)	3	Acker BILK, HIS CLARINET & STRINGS **The One For Me** Terry Brown	(Pye NSPLX 41052)
13(23/10/76)	13(23/10/76)	4	BLACK SABBATH **Technical Ecstasy** Black Sabbath (Terry 'Geezer' Butler Tony Iommi Ozzy Osbourne Bill Ward	(Vertigo 9102 750)
35(31/ 1/76)	35(31/ 1/76)	3	**We Sold Our Soul For Rock 'N' Roll** Roger Bain Black Sabbath Mike Butcher Patrick Meehan	(Nems 6641 335)
50(22/ 5/76)	11(29/ 5/76)	18	BLACKMORE'S RAINBOW **Rainbow Rising** Martin Birch	(Polydor 2490 137)
49(19/ 6/76)	26(3/ 7/76)	8	BLUE OYSTER CULT **Agents Of Fortune** Murray Krugman David Lucas Sandy Pearlman	(CBS 81385)
16(10/ 4/76)	16(10/ 4/76)	7	Pat BOONE **Pat Boone Originals** (Not listed)	(ABC ABSD 301)
9(29/ 5/76)	2(10/ 7/76)	20	David BOWIE **Changesonebowie** David Bowie Gus Dudgeon Harry Maslin Ken Scott Tony Visconti	(RCA RS 1055)
13(24/ 1/76)	5(31/ 1/76)	14	**Station To Station** David Bowie Harry Maslin	(RCA APL1-1327)

Position and date of entry	Highest position and date	Wks.	Artist(s) Title Producer(s)	Cat. No.
			Max BOYCE	
10(6/11/76)	9(13/11/76)	8*	**The Incredible Plan** Bob Barratt	(EMI MB 102)
35(21/ 6/75)	21(27/ 9/75)	20	**'Live' At Treorchy** Bob Barratt	(One-Up OU 2033)
9(18/10/75)	1(1/11/75)	16	**We All Had Doctors' Papers** Bob Barratt	(EMI MB 101)
			BRASS CONSTRUCTION	
11(13/ 3/76)	9(20/ 3/76)	9	**Brass Construction** Jeff Lane	(United Artists UAS 29923)
			BREAD	
18(14/10/72)	7(28/10/72)	129	**The Best Of Bread** David Gates James Griffin Robb Royer	(Elektra K42115)
			Nigel BROOKS SINGERS	
44(22/ 5/76)	44(22/ 5/76)	1	**20 All Time Eurovision Favourites** Jeff Jarratt Don Reedman	(K-Tel NE 712)
37(15/11/75)	5(6/12/75)	15	**20 Songs Of Joy** (Not listed)	(K-Tel NE 706)
			BROTHERHOOD OF MAN	
25(10/ 4/76)	20(8/ 5/76)	8	**Love And Kiss From** Tony Hiller	(Pye NSPL 18490)
			Jackson BROWNE	
27(20/11/76)	26(27/11/76)	3	**The Pretender** Jon Landau	(Asylum K53048)
			Max BYGRAVES	
5(30/10/76)	3(13/11/76)	9*	**100 Golden Greats** Gordon Smith	(Ronco RTDX 2019)
			CAMEL	
15(3/ 4/76)	15(3/ 4/76)	4	**Moon Madness** Rhett Davies Camel (Peter Bardens Doug Ferguson Andy Latimer Andy Ward)	(Decca TXR-S 115)
			Glen CAMPBELL	
38(13/11/71)	8(4/12/71)	111	**Glen Campbell's Greatest Hits** Al DeLory Kelly Gordon Neely Plumb	(Capitol ST21885)

Position and date of entry	Highest position and date	Wks.	Artist(s) Title Producer(s)	Cat. No.
5(6/11/76)	1(13/11/76)	8*	**20 Golden Greats** Jimmy Bowen Al DeLory Kelly Gordon Dennis Lambert Brian Potter	(Capitol EMTV 2)
			CARPENTERS	
5(14/ 6/75)	1(21/ 6/75)	29	**Horizon** Richard Carpenter	(A&M AMLK 64530)
10(19/ 6/76)	3(26/ 6/76)	14	**A Kind Of Hush** Richard Carpenter	(A&M AMLK 64581)
28(18/12/76)	28(18/12/76)	2*	**Live At The Palladium** Richard Carpenter	(A&M AMLS 68403)
20(12/ 1/74)	1(19/ 1/74)	109	**The Singles 1969-1973** Karen Carpenter Richard Carpenter Jack Daugherty	(A&M AMLH 63601)
			Johnny CASH	
48(25/ 9/76)	48(25/ 9/76)	1	**Best Of Johnny Cash** (Not listed)	(CBS 10000)
			Johnny CASH & THE TENNESSEE THREE	
49(31/ 7/76)	49(31/ 7/76)	1	**One Piece At A Time** Charlie Bragg Don Davis	(CBS 81416)
			CHICAGO	
30(30/10/76)	21(20/11/76)	7	**Chicago X** James William Guercio	(CBS 86010)
			Tony CHRISTIE	
28(23/10/76)	28(23/10/76)	3	**Best Of Tony Christie** Peter Callander Snuff Garrett Mitch Murray Geoff Stephens Peter Sullivan	(MCA MCF 2769)
			Eric CLAPTON	
11(28/ 8/76)	8(4/ 9/76)	6	**No Reason To Cry** Rob Fraboni	(RSO 2479 179)
			Perry COMO	
15(18/10/75)	1(8/11/75)	25	**40 Greatest** (Not listed)	(K-Tel NE 700)
			Billy CONNOLLY	
22(4/12/76)	22(4/12/76)	4*	**Atlantic Bridge** Phil Coulter	(Polydor 2383 419)
6(22/11/75)	6(22/11/75)	13	**Get Right Intae Him** Phil Coulter	(Polydor 2383 368)
			Peter COOK & DUDLEY MOORE	
31(11/ 9/76)	12(18/ 9/76)	14	**Derek And Clive Live** Peter Cook & Dudley Moore	(Island ILPS 9434)

Position and date of entry	Highest position and date	Wks.	Artist(s) Title Producer(s)	Cat. No.
			Alice COOPER	
28(10/ 7/76)	23(31/ 7/76)	6	**Alice Cooper Goes To Hell** Bob Ezrin	(Warner Bros K56171)
			DEEP PURPLE	
12(13/11/76)	12(13/11/76)	4	**Deep Purple Made In Europe** Deep Purple (Ritchie Blackmore Jon Lord David Coverdale Ian Paice Glenn Hughes) Martin Birch	(Purple TPSA 7517)
			John DENVER	
32(16/ 3/74)	9(13/ 3/76)	60	**Back Home Again** Milton Okun	(RCA APL1-0548)
32(16/ 3/74)	13(28/ 9/74)	55	**The Best Of John Denver** Milton Okun	(RCA APL1-0374)
23(1/ 5/76)	2(15/ 5/76)	28	**Live In London** Milton Okun	(RCA RS 1050)
18(28/ 8/76)	9(11/ 9/76)	9	**Spirit** Milton Okun	(RCA APL1-1694)
43(27/ 9/75)	14(20/ 3/76)	19	**Windsong** Milton Okun	(RCA APL1-1183)
			Sydney DEVINE	
49(27/11/76)	49(27/11/76)	1	**Devine Time** Tommy Scott	(Philips 6308 283)
28(27/ 3/76)	14(24/ 4/76)	9	**Doubly Devine** Tommy Scott	(Philips 6625 019)
			Neil DIAMOND	
23(26?/ 6/76)	10(3/ 7/76)	23	**Beautiful Noise** Robbie Robertson	(CBS 86004)
			DR. FEELGOOD	
8(18/ 9/76)	1(25/ 9/76)	8	**Stupidity** Dr. Feelgood (Lee Brilleaux Wilko Johnson John B. Sparks The Big Figure)	(United Artists UAS 29990)
			DR. HOOK	
38(12/ 6/76)	5(31/ 7/76)	29*	**A Little Bit More** Ron Haffkine Waylon Jennings	(Capitol E-ST 23795)
			DOOBIE BROTHERS	
42(3/ 4/76)	42(3/ 4/76)	1	**Takin' It To The Streets** Ted Templeman	(Warner Bros K56196)
			DRIFTERS	
28(25/10/76)	2(10/ 1/76)	29	**24 Original Hits** (Not listed)	(Atlantic K60106)

Position and date of entry	Highest position and date	Wks.	Artist(s) Title Producer(s)	Cat. No.
			Bob DYLAN	
4(17/ 1/76)	3(24/ 1/76)	32	**Desire** Don DeVito	(CBS 86003)
16(25/ 9/76)	3(2/10/76)	6	**Hard Rain** Bob Dylan Don DeVito	(CBS 86016)
			EAGLES	
39(28/ 6/75)	39(28/ 6/75)	9	**Desperado** Glyn Johns	(Asylum K53008)
5(11/12/76)	5(11/12/76)	3*	**Hotel California** Bill Szymczyk	(Asylum K53051)
9(28/ 6/75)	8(5/ 7/75)	40	**One Of These Nights** Bill Szymczyk	(Asylum K53014)
27(21/ 2/76)	2(6/ 3/76)	44*	**Their Greatest Hits 1971-1975** Glyn Johns Bill Szymczyk	(Asylum K53017)
			EDDIE & THE HOT RODS	
43(4/12/76)	43(4/12/76)	1	**Teenage Depression** Ed Hollis Vic Maile	(Island ILPS 9457)
			ELECTRIC LIGHT ORCHESTRA	
10(27/11/76)	9(4/12/76)	5*	**A New World Record** Jeff Lynne	(United Artists UAG 30017)
			David ESSEX	
8(13/ 9/75)	3(27/ 9/75)	20	**All The Fun Of The Fair** Jeff Wayne	(CBS 69160)
41(16/10/76)	31(23/10/76)	5	**Out On The Street** Jeff Wayne	(CBS 86017)
			Don ESTELLE & WINDSOR DAVIES	
10(17/ 1/76)	10(17/ 1/76)	5	**Sing Lofty** Walter J. Ridley	(EMI EMC 3102)
			EVERLY BROTHERS	
38 (21/ 2/76)	10(20/ 3/76)	6	**Walk Right Back With The Everlys** (Not listed)	(Warner Bros K56168)
			FATBACK BAND	
26(21/ 2/76)	19(6/ 3/76)	6	**Raising Hell** Fatback Band (Richard Cornwell Bill Curtis Johnny Flippin Johnny King Earl Shelton George Williams)	(Polydor 2391 203)

Position and date of entry	Highest position and date	Wks.	Artist(s) Title Producer(s)	Cat. No.
			Bryan FERRY	
31(18/ 9/76)	19(25/ 9/76)	5	**Let's Stick Together** Bryan Ferry Chris Thomas	(Island ILPS 9367)
			FIVEPENNY PIECE	
27(19/ 6/76)	9(26/ 6/76)	4	**King Cotton** Fivepenny Piece (Eddie Crotty John Meeks Lynda Meeks Colin Radcliffe George Radcliffe)	(EMI EMC 3129)
			FLEETWOOD MAC	
49(23/10/76)	23(30/10/76)	5	**Fleetwood Mac** Keith Olsen Fleetwood Mac (Lindsey Buckingham Mick Fleetwood Christine McVie John McVie Stevie Nicks)	(Reprise K54043)
			FOUR SEASONS	
35(21/ 2/76)	20(28/ 2/76)	7	**The Four Seasons Story** Bob Crewe	(Private Stock DAPS 1001)
41(28/ 2/76)	16(17/ 4/76)	15	**Who Loves You** Bob Gaudio (see also Frankie VALLI & THE FOUR SEASONS)	(Warner Bros K56179)
			Peter FRAMPTON	
31(15/ 5/76)	6(12/ 6/76)	33*	**Frampton Comes Alive!** Peter Frampton	(A&M AMLM 63703)
			Rory GALLAGHER	
32(16/10/76)	32(16/10/76)	1	**Calling Card** Roger Glover	(Chrysalis CHR 1124)
			GALLAGHER & LYLE	
45(14/ 2/76)	6(13/ 3/76)	34	**Breakaway** David Kershenbaum	(A&M AMLH 68348)
			Art GARFUNKEL	
8(18/10/75)	7(25/10/75)	17	**Breakaway** Richard Perry Paul Simon Art Garfunkel Phil Ramone	(CBS 86002)
			Marvin GAYE	
22(1/ 5/76)	22(1/ 5/76)	5	**I Want You** Leon Ware	(Tamla Motown STML 12025)

Position and date of entry	Highest position and date	Wks.	Artist(s) Title Producer(s)	Cat. No.
			GENESIS	
5(14/ 2/76)	3(28/ 2/76)	30	**A Trick Of The Tail**	(Charisma
			David Hentschel	CDS 4001)
			Genesis	
			(Mike Rutherford	
			Tony Banks	
			Phil Collins	
			Steve Hackett)	
			Gary GLITTER	
41(20/ 3/76)	33(17/ 4/76)	2	**Gary Glitter's Greatest Hits**	(Bell
			Mike Leander	BELLS 262)
			Bert DeCoteaux	
			Tony Silvester	
			GRATEFUL DEAD	
42(21/ 8/76)	42(21/ 8/76)	1	**Steal Your Face**	(United Artists
			Grateful Dead	UAD 60131/2)
			(Jerry Garcia	
			Donna Godchaux	
			Keith Godchaux	
			Mickey Hart	
			Bill Kreutzmann	
			Phil Lesh	
			Bob Weir)	
			Daryl HALL & JOHN OATES	
27(4/ 9/76)	25(18/ 9/76)	5	**Bigger Than Both Of Us**	(RCA
			Christopher Bond	APL1-1467)
			Mike HARDING	
19(3/ 7/76)	19(3/ 7/76)	8	**One Man Show**	(Philips
			Mike Harding	6625 022)
			Steve HARLEY & COCKNEY REBEL	
37(13/11/76)	28(20/11/76)	3	**Love's A Prima Donna**	(EMI
			Steve Harley	EMC 3156)
23(31/ 1/76)	18(14/ 2/76)	5	**Timeless Flight**	(EMI
			Steve Harley	EMA 775)
			Emmylou HARRIS	
44(31/ 1/76)	17(21/ 2/76)	8	**Elite Hotel**	(Reprise
			Brian Ahern	K54060)
			George HARRISON	
35(4/12/76)	35(4/12/76)	2	**Thirty Three And ⅓**	(Dark Horse
			George Harrison	K56319)
			HAWKWIND	
38(4/ 9/76)	33(11/ 9/76)	3	**Astonishing Sounds, Amazing Music**	(Charisma
				CDS 4004)
			Hawkwind	
			(Dave Brock	
			Bob Calvert	
			Simon House	
			Simon King	
			Paul Rudolph	
			Nik Turner)	

Position and date of entry	Highest position and date	Wks.	Artist(s) Title Producer(s)	Cat. No.
34(10/ 4/76)	34(10/ 4/76)	3	**Road Hawks** Doug Bennett Dick Taylor Doctor Technical Hawkwind (Dave Brock Bob Calvert Del Dettmar John Harrison Simon House Simon King Lemmy Huw Lloyd-Langton Dik Mik Terry Ollis Allan Powell Nik Turner)	(United Artists UAK 29919)
			Steve HILLAGE	
11(2/10/76)	10(23/10/76)	10	**L** Todd Rundgren	(Virgin V 2066)
			HOT CHOCOLATE	
21(6/11/76)	6(20/11/76)	8*	**XIV Greatest Hits** Mickie Most	(RAK SRAK 524)
32(24/ 7/76)	32(24/ 7/76)	4	**Man To Man** Mickie Most	(RAK SRAK 522)
			Ian HUNTER	
47(15/ 5/76)	29(22/ 5/76)	3	**All American Alien Boy** Ian Hunter	(CBS 81310)
			ISLEY BROTHERS	
50(14/ 8/76)	50(14/ 8/76)	1	**Harvest For The World** Isley Brothers (Ernie Isley Marvin Isley Chris Jasper O'Kelly Isley Ronald Isley Rudolph Isley)	(Epic EPC 81268)
			JEFFERSON STARSHIP	
30(17/ 7/76)	30(17/ 7/76)	1	**Spitfire** Larry Cox Jefferson Starship (Marty Balin John Barbata Craig Chaquico David Freiberg Paul Kantner Pete Sears Grace Slick)	(Grunt BFL 1557)

Position and date of entry	Highest position and date	Wks.	Artist(s) Title Producer(s)	Cat. No.
			JETHRO TULL	
45(17/ 1/76)	44(24/ 1/76)	3	**M.U. The Best Of Jethro Tull** Ian Anderson Terry Ellis	(Chrysalis CHR 1078)
46(1/ 5/76)	25(15/ 5/76)	6	**Too Old To Rock 'N' Roll Too Young To Die** Ian Anderson	(Chrysalis CHR 1111)
			Elton JOHN	
21(23/10/76)	3(30/10/76)	10*	**Blue Moves** Gus Dudgeon	(Rocket ROSP 1)
1(9/11/74)	1(9/11/74)	70	**Greatest Hits** Gus Dudgeon	(DJM DJLPH 442)
17(1/ 5/76)	6(8/ 5/76)	6	**Here And There** Gus Dudgeon	(DJM DJLPH 473)
			JUDGE DREAD	
26(22/11/75)	26(22/11/75)	10	**Bedtime Stories** Alex Hughes Ted Lemon	(Cactus CTLP 113)
			KISS	
49(12/ 6/76)	49(12/ 6/76)	1	**Alive!** Eddie Kramer	(Casablanca CBSP 401)
37(15/ 5/76)	22(22/ 5/76)	5	**Destroyer** Bob Ezrin	(Casablanca CBSP 4008)
			Gladys KNIGHT & THE PIPS	
22(14/ 2/76)	6(5/ 6/76)	38	**The Best Of Gladys Knight & The Pips** Tony Camillo Kenny Kerner Ralph Moss Curtis Mayfield Richie Wise	(Buddah BDLH 5013)
			James LAST	
19(8/11/76)	3(22/11/76)	17	**Make The Party Last** James Last	(Polydor 2371 612)
			LED ZEPPELIN	
47(31/ 5/75)	42(9/ 8/75)	8	**Four Symbols** Jimmy Page	(Atlantic K50008)
1(10/ 4/76)	1(10/ 4/76)	13	**Presence** Jimmy Page	(Swan Song SSK59402)
5(23/10/76)	1(30/10/76)	10*	**The Soundtrack From The Film The Song Remains The Same** Jimmy Page	(Swan Song SSK89402)
			John LENNON/ PLASTIC ONO BAND	
19(1/11/75)	8(22/11/75)	14	**Shaved Fish** John Lennon Yoko Ono Phil Spector	(Apple PCS 7173)

Position and date of entry	Highest position and date	Wks.	Artist(s) Title Producer(s)	Cat. No.
			Nils LOFGREN	
8(3/ 4/76)	8(3/ 4/76)	10	**Cry Tough** Al Kooper David Briggs	(A&M AMLH 64573)
			LONDON PHILHARMONIC CHOIR/JOHN ALLDIS/ NATIONAL PHILHARMONIC ORCHESTRA	
27(30/10/76)	10(20/11/76)	9*	**Sounds Of Glory** Irving Martin	(Arcade ADE P25)
			LONE STAR	
47(18/ 9/76)	47(18/ 9/76)	1	**Lone Star** Roy Thomas Baker	(Epic EPC 81545)
			LYNYRD SKYNYRD	
34(14/ 2/76)	34(14/ 2/76)	4	**Gimme Back My Bullets** Tom Dowd	(MCA MCF 2744)
17(23/10/76)	17(23/10/76)	3	**One More From The Road** Tom Dowd	(MCA MCSP 279)
			MAN	
40(3/ 4/76)	40(3/ 4/76)	1	**The Welsh Connection** Man (Micky Jones Deke Leonard John McKenzie Phil Ryan Terry Williams)	(MCA MCF 2753)
			Henry MANCINI	
47(30/10/76)	26(6/11/76)	3	**40 Greatest** Joe Reisman & others not listed	(Arcade ADE P24)
			MANHATTANS	
45(31/ 7/76)	37(14/ 8/76)	2	**The Manhattans** Bert DeCoteaux Bobby Martin Manhattans (Gerald Austin Sonny Bivins Kenny Kelly Wilfred 'Blue' Lovett Richard Taylor)	(CBS 81513)
			Manfred MANN'S EARTHBAND	
32(4/ 9/76)	10(25/ 9/76)	9	**The Roaring Silence** Manfred Mann's Earthband (Manfred Mann Dave Flett Chris Hamlet Thompson Colin Pattenden Chris Slade)	(Bronze ILPS 9357)

Position and date of entry	Highest position and date	Wks.	Artist(s) / Title / Producer(s)	Cat. No.
			MANUEL & THE MUSIC OF THE MOUNTAINS	
50(17/ 1/76)	3(6/ 3/76)	16	**Carnival**	(Studio Two
			Norman Newell	TWO 337)
			Bob MARLEY & THE WAILERS	
30(24/ 4/76)	15(1/ 5/76)	9	**Rastaman Vibration**	(Island
			Bob Marley & the Wailers	ILPS 9383)
			(Aston 'Family Man' Barrett	
			Carlton Barrett	
			Tyrone Downie	
			Donald Kinsey	
			Alvin 'Seeco' Patterson	
			Earl 'Chinna' Smith	
			Al Anderson)	
			Lena MARTELL	
42(18/12/76)	42(18/12/76)	2*	**The Best Of Lena Martell**	(Pye
			George Elrick	NSPL 18506)
			Dean MARTIN	
7(6/11/76)	7(6/11/76)	8*	**20 Original Dean Martin Hits**	(Reprise
			(Not listed)	K54066)
			Johnny MATHIS	
14(19/ 6/76)	14(19/ 6/76)	6*	**I Only Have Eyes For You**	(CBS 81329)
			Jack Gold	
			Paul McCARTNEY & WINGS	
45(1/12/73)	1(13/ 7/74)	109	**Band On The Run**	(Apple
			Paul McCartney	PAS 10007)
			(see also WINGS)	
			John MILES	
30(13/ 3/76)	9(10/ 4/76)	9	**Rebel**	(Decca
			Alan Parsons	SKL 5231)
			Glenn MILLER	
42(21/ 2/76)	20(6/ 3/76)	6	**Glenn Miller — A Memorial 1944-1969**	(RCA GM1)
			(Not listed)	
			Glenn MILLER AND HIS ORCHESTRA	
41(21/ 2/76)	41(21/ 2/76)	1	**A Legendary Performer**	(RCA DPM 2065)
			David MacKay	
			George T. Simon	
			Steve MILLER BAND	
23(29/ 5/76)	11(5/ 6/76)	8	**Fly Like An Eagle**	(Mercury
			Steve Miller	9286 177)
			Spike MILLIGAN/THE LONDON SYMPHONY ORCHESTRA	
49(4/12/76)	49(4/12/76)	1	**The Snow Goose**	(RCA RS 1088)
			Ed Welch	
			Stuart Taylor	
			Joni MITCHELL	
39(27/11/76)	11(4/12/76)	5*	**Hejira**	(Asylum K53053)
			(Not listed)	

Position and date of entry	Highest position and date	Wks.	Artist(s) Title Producer(s)	Cat. No.
22(10/ 1/76)	14(24/ 1/76)	6	**The Hissing Of Summer Lawns** (Not listed)	(Asylum SYLA 8763)
25(5/ 6/76)	25(5/ 6/76)	3	Tony MONOPOLY **Tony Monopoly** Paul Murphy	(Buk BULP 2000)
37(27/ 3/76)	22(1/ 5/76)	7	Patrick MORAZ **Patrick Moraz** Patrick Moraz	(Charisma CDS 4002)
27(26/ 6/76)	3(31/ 7/76)	15	Nana MOUSKOURI **Passport** Andre Chapelle Roger Cook Snuff Garrett	(Philips 9101 061)
37(13/12/75)	33(27/12/75)	4	MUD **Use Your Imagination** Phil Wainman	(Private Stock PVLP 1003)
50(15/ 5/76)	49(29/ 5/76)	2	Olivia NEWTON-JOHN **Come On Over** John Farrar	(EMI EMC 3124)
40(16/10/76)	33(23/10/76)	2	Ted NUGENT **Free For All** Cliff Davies Lew Futterman Tom Werman	(Epic EPC 81397)
44(6/11/76)	24(18/12/76)	7*	Mike OLDFIELD **Boxed** David Bedford Peter Jenner Mike Oldfield	(Virgin VBOX 1)
12(1/11/75)	4(8/11/75)	21	**Ommadawn** Mike Oldfield	(Virgin V2043)
31(30/ 6/73)	1(21/ 9/74)	179*	**Tubular Bells** (Not listed)	(Virgin V2001)
47(27/12/75)	1(17/ 1/76)	17	Roy ORBISON **The Best Of Roy Orbison** (Not listed)	(Arcade ADE P19)
48(15/ 5/76)	48(15/ 5/76)	2	Donny & Marie OSMOND **Deep Purple** Mike Curb	(Polydor 2391 220)
30(4/12/76)	13(11/12/76)	4*	Gilbert O'SULLIVAN **Greatest Hits** Gordon Mills	(MAM MAMA 2003)
46(23/10/76)	46(23/10/76)	1	Robert PALMER **Some People Can Do** **What They Like** Steve Smith	(Island ILPS 9420)

Position and date of entry	Highest position and date	Wks.	Artist(s) Title Producer(s)	Cat. No.
			PETERS & LEE	
7(20/ 9/75)	2(18/10/75)	29	**Favourites** John Franz	(Philips 9109 205)
44(4/12/76)	44(4/12/76)	4*	**Invitation** John Franz	(Philips 9109 217)
			PINK FLOYD	
2(17/ 3/73)	2(17/ 3/73)	182	**The Dark Side Of The Moon** Pink Floyd (David Gilmour Nick Mason Roger Waters Richard Wright)	(Harvest SHVL 804)
3(13/ 9/75)	1(20/ 9/75)	43	**Wish You Were Here** Pink Floyd	(Harvest SHVL 814)
			Gene PITNEY	
46(18/ 9/76)	6(16/10/76)	13	**His 20 Greatest** (Not listed)	(Arcade ADE P22)
			Elvis PRESLEY	
25(21/ 6/75)	17(27/12/75)	24	**Elvis' 40 Greatest** (Not listed)	(Arcade ADEP 12)
36(5/ 6/76)	29(12/ 6/76)	4	**From Elvis Presley Boulevard, Memphis, Tennessee** (Not listed)	(RCA RS 1060)
			QUEEN	
8(11/12/76)	1(18/12/76)	3*	**A Day At The Races** Queen (John Deacon Brian May Freddie Mercury Roger Taylor)	(EMI EMC 104)
2(29/11/75)	1(13/12/75)	40	**A Night At The Opera** Roy Thomas Baker Queen	(EMI EMTC 103)
47(16/ 3/74)	24(24/ 1/76)	25	**Queen** John Anthony Roy Thomas Baker Queen	(EMI EMC 3006)
35(9/ 3/74)	5(23/ 3/74)	44	**Queen 2** Roy Thomas Baker Queen	(EMI EMA 767)
6(9/11/74)	2(16/11/74)	41	**Sheer Heart Attack** Roy Thomas Baker	(EMI EMC 3061)
			REAL THING	
34(23/10/76)	34(23/10/76)	2	**Real Thing** Ken Gold Jerome Rimson	(Pye NSPL 18507)

Position and date of entry	Highest position and date	Wks.	Artist(s) Title Producer(s)	Cat. No.
			Helen REDDY	
14(31/ 1/76)	5(21/ 2/76)	15	**The Best Of Helen Reddy** Tom Catalano Jay Senter Joe Wissert	(Capitol E-ST 11467)
			Jim REEVES	
19(6/ 9/75)	1(11/10/75)	23	**40 Golden Greats** (Not listed)	(Arcade ADEP 16)
			Cliff RICHARD	
24(15/ 5/76)	5(29/ 5/76)	20	**I'm Nearly Famous** Bruce Welch	(EMI EMC 3122)
			RICHMOND STRINGS/ MIKE SAMMES SINGERS	
45(5/ 6/76)	18(12/ 6/76)	7	**Music Of America** Gordon Smith	(Ronco RTD 2016)
			ROLLING STONES	
4(24/ 4/76)	2(1/ 5/76)	12	**Black And Blue** The Glimmer Twins	(Rolling Stones COC 59106)
7(22/11/75)	7(22/11/75)	37	**Rolled Gold** Eric Easton Jimmy Miller Andrew Loog Oldham Rolling Stones (Mick Jagger Brian Jones Keith Richard Charlie Watts Bill Wyman)	(Decca ROST 1/2)
			Linda RONSTADT	
37(11/12/76)	37(11/12/76)	3*	**Greatest Hits** Peter Asher John Boylan Elliot F. Mazer John David Souther Nikolas Venet	(Asylum K53055)
32(21/ 8/76)	32(21/ 8/76)	6	**Hasten Down The Wind** Peter Asher	(Asylum K53045)
			Diana ROSS	
14(31/ 7/76)	2(28/ 8/76)	20*	**Greatest Hits/2** Tom Baird Hal Davis Mel Larson Jerry Marcellino Michael Masser Michael Randall Diana Ross	(Tamla Motown STML 12036)

Position and date of entry	Highest position and date	Wks.	Artist(s) Title Producer(s)	Cat. No.
12(13/ 3/76)	4(20/ 3/76)	25	**Diana Ross** Gil Askey Lawrence Brown Don Costa Hal Davis Berry Gordy Michael Masser Diana Ross	(Tamla Motown STML 12022)
			Demis ROUSSOS	
16(12/ 6/76)	2(24/ 7/76)	29*	**Forever And Ever** Demis Roussos	(Philips 6325 021)
33(10/ 4/76)	4(19/ 6/76)	30	**Happy To Be** Georges Petsilas Demis Roussos	(Philips 9101 027)
45 (19/ 6/76)	39(3/ 7/76)	4	**My Only Fascination** Mike Curb Leo Leandros Demis Roussos	(Philips 6325 094)
50(5/ 4/76)	25(19/ 6/76)	15	**Souvenirs** Leo Leandros Demis Roussos	(Philips 6325 201)
			ROXY MUSIC	
4(25/10/75)	4(25/10/75)	17	**Siren** Chris Thomas	(Island ILPS 9344)
13(17/ 7/76)	6(31/ 7/76)	12	**Viva! Roxy Music** Chris Thomas	(Island ILPS 9400)
			SAILOR	
45(3/ 4/76)	45(3/ 4/76)	3	**Trouble** Jeffrey Lesser	(Epic EPC 69192)
			SANTANA	
23(27/ 3/76)	13(3/ 4/76)	8	**Amigos** David Rubinson & Friends, Inc.	(CBS 86005)
			Leo SAYER	
44(13/11/76)	18(20/11/76)	5	**Endless Flight** Richard Perry	(Chrysalis CHR 1125)
			Neil SEDAKA	
14(26/ 6/76)	2(17/ 7/76)	22	**Laughter & Tears.** **The Best Of Neil Sedaka Today** Neil Sedaka Robert Appere Malcolm Jones 10cc (Graham Gouldman Eric Stewart Lol Creme Kevin Godley)	(Polydor 2383 399)

Position and date of entry	Highest position and date	Wks.	Artist(s) Title Producer(s)	Cat. No.
			SENSATIONAL ALEX HARVEY BAND	
20(27/ 3/76)	14(10/ 4/76)	6	**Penthouse Tapes** David Batchelor	(Vertigo 9102 007)
21(17/ 7/76)	11(31/ 7/76)	9	**Sahb Stories** David Batchelor	(Mountain TOPS 112)
			SHOWADDYWADDY	
15(11/12/76)	4(18/12/76)	3*	**Greatest Hits** Mike Hurst	(Arista ARTY 145)
41(15/ 5/76)	41(15/ 5/76)	1	**Trocadero** Mike Hurst	(Bell SYBEL 8003)
			Paul SIMON	
11(18/10/75)	11(18/10/75)	27	**Still Crazy After All These Years** Paul Simon Phil Ramone Art Garfunkel	(CBS 86001)
			SIMON & GARFUNKEL	
1(7/ 2/70)	1(7/ 2/70)	291	**Bridge Over Trouble Water** Paul Simon Arthur Garfunkel Roy Halee	(CBS 63699)
4(8/ 7/72)	2(15/ 7/72)	220	**Simon & Garfunkel's Greatest Hits** Paul Simon Arthur Garfunkel Roy Halee	(CBS 69003)
			SLADE	
14(13/ 3/76)	14(13/ 3/76)	3	**Nobody's Fools** Chas Chandler	(Polydor 2383 377)
			David SOUL	
43(13/11/76)	13(27/11/76)	7*	**David Soul** Elliot F. Mazer	(Private Stock PVLP 1012)
			SOUNDTRACKS/ORIGINAL CAST RECORDINGS	
23(13/11/76)	23(13/11/76)	5*	**All This And World War II** Lou Reizner & other not listed	(Riva RVLP 2)
1(27/ 3/76)	1(27/ 3/76)	13	**Rock Follies** Andy Mackay	(Island ILPS 9362)
			Billie Jo SPEARS	
47(28/ 8/76)	47(28/ 8/76)	1	**What I've Got In Mind** Larry Butler	(United Artists UAS 29955)
			Candi STATON	
34(17/ 7/76)	34(17/ 7/76)	1	**Young Hearts Run Free** Dave Crawford	(Warner Bros K56259)

Position and date of entry	Highest position and date	Wks.	Artist(s) Title Producer(s)	Cat. No.
			STATUS QUO	
1(6/ 3/76)	1(6/ 3/76)	19	**Blue For You** Status Quo (Francis Rossi Rick Parfitt Alan Lancaster John Coghlan)	(Vertigo 9102 006)
			STEELEYE SPAN	
38(11/10/75)	7(15/11/75)	19	**All Around My Hat** Mike Batt	(Chrysalis CHR 1091)
41(9/10/76)	41(9/10/76)	1	**Rocket Cottage** Mike Batt	(Chrysalis CHR 1123)
			STEELY DAN	
11(8/ 5/76)	11(8/ 5/76)	10	**The Royal Scam** Gary Katz	(ABC ABCL 5161)
			Cat STEVENS	
17(5/ 7/75)	2(13/ 9/75)	22	**Greatest Hits** Paul Samwell-Smith Cat Stevens	(Island ILPS 9310)
			Rod STEWART	
2(19/ 6/76)	1(26/ 6/76)	28*	**A Night On The Town** Tom Dowd	(Riva RVLP 1)
1(16/ 8/75)	1(16/ 8/75)	58	**Atlantic Crossing** Tom Dowd	(Warner Bros K56151)
			STILLS-YOUNG BAND	
15(25/ 9/76)	12(2/10/76)	5	**Long May You Run** Stephen Stills Neil Young Don Gehman	(Reprise K54081)
			STREETWALKERS	
16(29/ 5/76)	16(29/ 5/76)	6	**Red Card** Streetwalkers (Roger Chapman Charlie Witney Bob Tench Nicko Jon Plotel)	(Vertigo 9102 010)
			STYLISTICS	
19(22/ 3/75)	1(5/ 4/75)	53	**The Best Of The Stylistics** Hugo & Luigi Thom Bell Marty Bryant Bill Perry	(Avco 9109 003)
40(4/ 9/76)	1(18/ 9/76)	17*	**The Best Of The Stylistics Vol. 2** Hugo & Luigi	(H&L 9109 010)
39(29/ 5/76)	21(5/ 6/76)	5	**Fabulous** Hugo & Luigi	(Avco 9109 008)
44(22/11/75)	26(29/11/75)	8	**You Are Beautiful** Hugo & Luigi	(Avco 9109 006)

Position and date of entry	Highest position and date	Wks.	Artist(s) Title Producer(s)	Cat. No.
			Donna SUMMER	
43(17/ 1/76)	16(31/ 1/76)	8	**Love To Love You Baby** Pete Bellotte	(GTO GTLP 008)
41(11/ 9/76)	41(11/ 9/76)	4	**A Love Trilogy** Giorgio Moroder Pete Bellotte	(GTO GTLP 010)
			SUPERTRAMP	
20(22/11/75)	20(22/11/75)	13	**Crisis? What Crisis?** Ken Scott Supertramp (Roger Hodgson Bob C. Benberg Dougie Thomson John Anthony Helliwell Richard Davies)	(A&M AMLH 68347)
			SUTHERLAND BROTHERS & QUIVER	
45(1/ 5/76)	26(15/ 5/76)	6	**Reach For The Sky** Ron & Howard Albert	(CBS 69191)
49(25/ 9/76)	49(25/ 9/76)	2	**Slipstream** Ron & Howard Albert	(CBS 81593)
			TANGERINE DREAM	
46(30/10/76)	39(13/11/76)	4	**Stratosfear** Tangerine Dream (Chris Franke Edgar Froese Peter Baumann)	(Virgin V 2068)
			TAVARES	
30(14/ 8/76)	22(23/10/76)	9	**Sky High** Freddie Perren	(Capitol E-ST 11533)
			10cc	
5(17/ 1/76)	5(17/ 1/76)	28	**How Dare You** 10cc (Lol Creme Kevin Godley Graham Gouldman Eric Stewart)	(Mercury 9102 501)
6(8/ 3/75)	3(3/ 5/75)	37	**The Original Soundtrack** 10cc	(Mercury 9102 500)
			THIN LIZZY	
25(3/ 4/76)	10(21/ 8/76)	31	**Jailbreak** John Alcock	(Vertigo 9102 008)
11(23/10/76)	11(23/10/76)	7	**Johnny The Fox** John Alcock	(Vertigo 9102 012)
			T. REX	
50(7/ 2/76)	50(7/ 2/76)	1	**Futuristic Dragon** Marc Bolan	(EMI BLN 5004)
			Robin TROWER	
29(28/ 2/76)	15(13/ 3/76)	6	**Live** (Not listed)	(Chrysalis CHR 1089)

Position and date of entry	Highest position and date	Wks.	Artist(s) Title Producer(s)	Cat. No.
31(16/10/76)	31(16/10/76)	1	**Long Misty Days** Robin Trower Geoff Emerick	(Chrysalis CHR 1107)
			TWIGGY	
46(7/ 8/76)	33(28/ 8/76)	5	**Twiggy** Tony Eyers	(Mercury 9102 600)
			Frankie VALLI & THE FOUR SEASONS	
35(6/11/76)	4(27/11/76)	8*	**The Greatest Hits Of** **Frankie Valli & The** **Four Seasons** Bob Crewe Bob Gaudio Hank Medress Dave Appell (see also FOUR SEASONS)	(K-Tel NE 942)
			VANGELIS	
30(25/ 9/76)	18(9/10/76)	5	**Albedo 0.39** Vangelis	(RCA RS 1080)
31(24/ 1/76)	31(24/ 1/76)	1	**Heaven And Hell** Vangelis	(RCA RS 1025)
			VARIOUS	
42(2/10/76)	21(9/10/76)	4	**Armchair Melodies** (Not listed)	(K-Tel NE 927)
32(20/ 3/76)	17(27/ 3/76)	4	**By Invitation Only** (Not listed)	(Atlantic K60112)
26(2/10/76)	8(16/10/76)	8	**Country Comfort** (Not listed)	(K-Tel NE 924)
30(1/11/75)	30(1/11/75)	11	**Disco Hit '75** (Not listed)	(Arcade ADE P18)
41(20/11/76)	3(4/12/76)	6*	**Disco Rocket** (Not listed)	(K-Tel NE 948)
47(23/10/76)	21(13/11/76)	6	**Forty Mania** Gordon Smith	(Ronco RTD 2018)
28(29/11/75)	11(6/12/75)	7	**40 Super Greats** (Not listed)	(K-Tel NE 708)
41(27/11/76)	14(4/12/76)	5*	**44 Superstars** (Not listed)	(K-Tel NE 939)
45(26/ 6/76)	45(26/ 6/76)	1	**Golden Fiddle Awards** (Not listed)	(Mountain TOPC 5002)
41(3/ 4/76)	17(25/ 9/76)	12	**Great Italian Love Songs** (Not listed)	(K-Tel NE 303)
19(29/11/75)	11(20/12/75)	9*	**Greatest Hits Of Walt Disney** (Not listed)	(Ronco RTD 2013)
33(29/ 5/76)	15(5/ 6/76)	3	**Hamilton's Hot Shots** (Not listed)	(Warwick WW 5014)
29(1/ 5/76)	4(15/ 5/76)	10	**Hit Machine** (Not listed)	(K-Tel TE 713)

Position and date of entry	Highest position and date	Wks.	Artist(s) Title Producer(s)	Cat. No.
24(3/ 4/76)	3(24/ 4/76)	24*	**Instrumental Gold** Brian Matthew	(Warwick WW 5012)
6(27/ 3/76)	3(3/ 4/76)	13	**Juke Box Jive** (Not listed)	(K-Tel NE 709)
39(18/10/75)	15(1/11/75)	30	**Motown Gold** (Not listed)	(Tamla Motown STML 12003)
25(17/ 1/76)	3(31/ 1/76)	9	**Music Express** (Not listed)	(K-Tel TE 702)
31(18/12/76)	31(18/12/76)	2*	**Songs Of Praise** Brian Matthew	(Warwick WW 5020)
27(2/10/76)	1(16/10/76)	13*	**Soul Motion** (Not listed)	(K-Tel NE 930)
24(10/ 1/76)	9(17/ 1/76)	5	**Star Trackin' '76** (Not listed)	(Ronco RTL 2014)
30(18/ 9/76)	30(18/ 9/76)	1	**Summer Cruisin'** (Not listed)	(K-Tel NE 918)
19(8/ 5/76)	7(22/ 5/76)	6	**A Touch Of Country** (Not listed)	(Topaz TOC/R 1976)
			Rick WAKEMAN	
12(10/ 4/76)	9(1/ 5/76)	8	**No Earthly Connection** Rick Wakeman	(A&M AMLK 64583)
			WALKER BROTHERS	
49(7/ 2/76)	49(7/ 2/76)	1	**No Regrets** Scott Walker	(GTO GTLP 007)
			Joe WALSH	
28(3/ 4/76)	28(3/ 4/76)	2	**You Can't Argue With A Sick Mind** Joe Walsh	(Anchor ABCL 5156)
			Bert WEEDON	
14(16/10/76)	1(6/11/76)	11*	**Bert Weedon's 22 Golden Guitar Greats** Chris Harding Brian Matthew	(Warwick WW5019)
			Alan WHITE	
50(28/ 2/76)	41(6/ 3/76)	3	**Ramshackled** Alan White Bob Potter	(Atlantic K50217)
			Barry WHITE	
23(8/11/75)	11(10/ 1/76)	27	**Greatest Hits** Barry White	(20th Century BTH 8000)
32(14/ 2/76)	22(10/ 4/75)	11	**Let The Music Play** Barry White	(20th Century BT 502)
			Slim WHITMAN	
1(24/ 1/76)	1(24/ 1/76)	16	**The Very Best Of Slim Whitman** Scott Turner Biff Collie Kelso Herston Herb Shucher Tommy Allsup	(United Artists UAS 29898)

Position and date of entry	Highest position and date	Wks.	Artist(s) Title Producer(s)	Cat. No.
			Roger WHITTAKER	
27(8/ 5/76)	27(8/ 5/76)	5	**The Second Album Of The Very Best Of Roger Whittaker** Denis Preston	(EMI EMC 3117)
15(23/ 8/75)	5(13/ 9/75)	33	**The Very Best Of Roger Whittaker** Denis Preston	(Columbia SCX 6560)
			WHO	
26(25/ 9/76)	2(9/10/76)	14*	**The Story Of The Who** Kit Lambert Glyn Johns The Who (Roger Daltrey John Entwistle Keith Moon Peter Townshend)	(Polydor 2683 069)
			Don WILLIAMS	
47(3/ 7/76)	29(10/ 7/76)	8	**Greatest Hits Vol. 1** Allen Reynolds Don Williams	(ABC ABCL 5147)
			John WILLIAMS & DANIEL BARENBOIM	
33(21/ 2/76)	20(20/ 3/76)	6	**Rodrigo: Concierto De Aranjuez** Villa-Lobos: **Concerto** Paul Myers	(CBS 76369)
			WINGS	
3(7/ 6/75)	1(14/ 6/75)	26	**Venus And Mars** Paul McCartney	(Capitol PCTC 254)
2(3/ 4/76)	2(3/ 4/76)	32	**Wings At The Speed Of Sound** Paul McCartney (see also Paul McCartney & Wings)	(Parlophone PAS 10010)
			WISHBONE ASH	
36(20/ 3/76)	36(20/ 3/76)	2	**Locked In** Tom Dowd	(MCA MCF 2750)
22(13/11/76)	22(13/11/76)	2	**New England** Ron & Howard Albert	(MCA MCG 3523)
			WOMBLES	
29(18/12/76)	29(18/12/76)	2*	**The Best Of The Wombles — 20 Wombling Greats** Mike Batt	(Warwick PR 5022)
			Stevie WONDER	
18(2/10/76)	2(16/10/76)	13*	**Songs In The Key Of Life** Stevie Wonder	(Tamla Motown TMSP 6002)
			WURZELS	
50(19/ 6/76)	15(10/ 7/76)	18	**The Combine Harvester** Bob Barratt	(One Up OU 2138)

Section 6

UK Producer Section

(*Music Week* Top 50 UK Singles and Albums Charts)

This section lists the producers of all singles and albums that made the *Music Week* Top 50 UK singles and albums charts during 1976.

Albums are denoted by (LP) after the title. Many records are credited as co-productions, as associate productions, with assistant producers, or in association with etc., so that only those actually listed as producer are credited, except in the very few cases where it is well established who the producers are (i.e. Nicky Chinn produced in association with Mike Chapman). As very few records have co-production credits, this section (unlike the writer section) is not cross-referenced to other producers. A producer will be credited even though he might have only been responsible for one track on the album (i.e. Simon & Garfunkel's *My Little Town,* which appeared on both artists' solo albums and was the only track produced by the two on those respective albums). In some cases a producer's name appears in place of a production company, and the only time that a company's name does appear is when it has been impossible to find out the name of the actual producer.

Brian AHERN
Here There And Everywhere—Emmylou
Harris
Elite Hotel (LP)—Emmylou Harris

Ron & Howard ALBERT
Arms Of Mary—Sutherland Brothers &
Quiver
Secrets—Sutherland Brothers & Quiver
New England (LP)—Wishbone Ash
Reach For The Sky (LP)—Sutherland
Brothers & Quiver
Slipstream (LP)—Sutherland Brothers &
Quiver

John ALCOCK
The Boys Are Back In Town—Thin Lizzy
Jailbreak—Thin Lizzy
Jailbreak (LP)—Thin Lizzy
Johnny The Fox (LP)—Thin Lizzy

Stephen ALLEN
Dreams Of You—Ralph McTell

Tommy ALLSUP
The Very Best Of Slim Whitman (LP)—
Slim Whitman

Bill AMESBURY
No Charge—J.J. Barrie

Al ANDERSON
(see Bob MARLEY & THE WAILERS)

Ian ANDERSON
Ring Out Solstice Bells (EP)—Jethro Tull
M.U. The Best Of Jethro Tull (LP)—
Jethro Tull
**Too Old To Rock 'N' Roll Too Young To
Die (LP)**—Jethro Tull

Benny ANDERSSON
Dancing Queen—Abba
Fernando—Abba
Mamma Mia—Abba
Money, Money, Money—Abba
Abba (LP)—Abba
Arrival (LP)—Abba
Greatest Hits (LP)—Abba

John ANTHONY
Queen (LP)—Queen

Miki ANTONY
Make A Daft Noise For Christmas—
Goodies

Dave APPELL
**The Greatest Hits Of Frankie Valli & The
Four Seasons (LP)**—Frankie Valli & The
Four Seasons

Robert APPERE
**Laughter & Tears. The Best Of Neil
Sedaka Today (LP)**—Neil Sedaka

Chris ARNOLD
You Don't Have To Say You Love Me—
Guys 'n' Dolls

Peter ASHER
The Tracks Of My Tears—Linda Ronstadt
Greatest Hits (LP)—Linda Ronstadt
Hasten Down The Wind (LP)—Linda
Ronstadt

Gil ASKEY
Diana Ross (LP)—Diana Ross

Gerald AUSTIN
(see The MANHATTANS)

BAD COMPANY
(Boz Burrell, Simon Kirke, Mick Ralphs &
Paul Rodgers)
Run With The Pack (LP)—Bad Company

Roger BAIN
We Sold Our Soul For Rock 'n' Roll (LP)
—Black Sabbath

Tom BAIRD
Greatest Hits/2 (LP)—Diana Ross

Ronnie/Ron BAKER
Soul Searchin' Time—Trammps
That's Where The Happy People Go—
Trammps

Roy Thomas BAKER
Bohemian Rhapsody—Queen
Maid Of Heaven—Be-Bop DeLuxe
(from Hot Valves EP)
You're My Best Friend—Queen
Lone Star (LP)—Lone Star
A Night At The Opera (LP)—Queen
Queen (LP)—Queen
Queen 2 (LP)—Queen
Sheer Heart Attack (LP)—Queen

Marty BALIN
(see JEFFERSON STARSHIP)

Tony BANKS
(see GENESIS)

UK PRODUCER

John BARBATA
(see JEFFERSON STARSHIP)

BARCLAY JAMES HARVEST
(Les Holroyd, John Lees, Mel Pritchard &
Stuart 'Wooly' Wolstenholme)
Octoberon (LP)—Barclay James Harvest

Peter BARDENS
(see CAMEL)

Bob BARRATT
The Combine Harvester (Brand New Key)
—Wurzels
I Am A Cider Drinker (Paloma Blanca)—
Wurzels
The Combine Harvester (LP)—Wurzels
The Incredible Plan (LP)—Max Boyce
'Live' At Treorchy (LP)—Max Boyce
We All Had Doctors' Papers (LP)—
Max Boyce

Aston 'Family Man' BARRETT
(see Bob MARLEY & THE WAILERS)

Carlton BARRETT
(see Bob MARLEY & THE WAILERS)

Richard BARRETT
Toast Of Love—Three Degrees

David BATCHELOR
The Boston Tea Party—Sensational
Alex Harvey Band
Gamblin' Bar Room Blues—Sensational
Alex Harvey Band
Penthouse Tapes (LP)—Sensational
Alex Harvey Band
SAHB Stories (LP)—Sensational Alex
Harvey Band)

Mike BATT
All Around My Hat—Steeleye Span
Let's Womble To The Party Tonight—
Wombles
Little Does She Know—Kursaal Flyers
All Around My Hat (LP)—Steeleye Span
Rocket Cottage (LP)—Steeleye Span
The Best Of The Wombles—
20 Wombling Greats (LP)—Wombles

Peter BAUMANN
(see TANGERINE DREAM)

BEACH BOYS
(Al Jardine, Mike Love, Brian Wilson,
Carl Wilson & Dennis Wilson)
20 Golden Greats (LP)—Beach Boys

William BECK
(see OHIO PLAYERS)

David BEDFORD
Boxed (LP)—Mike Oldfield

BEE GEES
(Barry, Maurice & Robin Gibb)
Love So Right—Bee Gees
You Should Be Dancing—Bee Gees

Thom BELL
Country Living—Stylistics (from **You'll
Never Get To Heaven** (EP))
The Rubber Band Man—Detroit Spinners
You'll Never Get To Heaven—Stylistics
(from the EP of the same name)
The Best Of The Stylistics (LP)—
Stylistics

Pete BELLOTTE
Could It Be Magic—Donna Summer
Love To Love You Baby—Donna Summer
Winter Melody—Donna Summer
Love To Love You Baby (LP)—Donna
Summer
A Love Trilogy (LP)—Donna Summer

Bob C. BENBERG
(see SUPERTRAMP)

Doug BENNETT
Road Hawks (LP)—Hawkwind

Wayne BICKERTON
The Two Of Us—Mac & Katie Kissoon
Convoy GB—Laurie Lingo & the Dipsticks

BIDDU
Rain Forest—Biddu
Dance Little Lady Dance—Tina Charles
Dr. Love—Tina Charles
**I Love To Love (But My Baby Loves To
Dance)**—Tina Charles
Love Me Like A Lover—Tina Charles
I'll Go Where Your Music Takes Me—
Jimmy James & the Vagabonds
Now Is The Time—Jimmy James & the
Vagabonds

The BIG FIGURE
(see DR. FEELGOOD)

Barry BIGGS
Work All Day—Barry Biggs

Martin BIRCH
Rainbow Rising (LP)—Blackmore's
Rainbow
Deep Purple Made In Europe (LP)—
Deep Purple

Sonny BIVINS
(see MANHATTANS)

BLACK SABBATH
(Terry 'Geezer' Butler, Tony Iommi, Ozzy
Osbourne & Bill Ward)
Technical Ecstasy (LP)—Black Sabbath
We Sold Our Soul For Rock 'n' Roll (LP)
—Black Sabbath

Ritchie BLACKMORE
(see DEEP PURPLE)

Alan BLAKLEY
You're The Reason Why—Rubettes
Under One Roof—Rubettes

Allan BLAZEK
Fooled Around And Fell In Love—
Elvin Bishop

Barry BLUE
Fairy Tale—Dana

Patrick BOCENO
Tubular Bells—Champs Boys

Marc BOLAN
I Love To Boogie—T. Rex
Laser Love—T. Rex
London Boys—T. Rex
Futuristic Dragon (LP)—T. Rex

Christopher BOND
Bigger Than Both Of Us (LP)—Daryl
Hall & John Oates

Tony BONGIOVI
How High The Moon—Gloria Gaynor

Leroy BONNER
(see OHIO PLAYERS)

BOONA MUSIC PRODUCTIONS
Soul Dracula—Hot Blood

Bruce BOTNICK
Riders On The Storm—Doors

Jimmy BOWEN
20 Golden Greats (LP)—Glen Campbell

David BOWIE
Golden Years—David Bowie
TVC 15—David Bowie
Changesonebowie (LP)—David Bowie
Station To Station (LP)—David Bowie

John BOYLAN
Greatest Hits (LP)—Linda Ronstadt

James BRADY
(see SANDPIPERS)

Charlie BRAGG
One Piece At A Time—Johnny Cash &
the Tennessee Three
One Piece At A Time (LP)—Johnny Cash
& the Tennessee Three

Daryl BRAITHWAITE
(see SHERBET)

David BRIGGS
Cry Tough (LP)—Nils Lofgren

Lee BRILLEAUX
(see DR. FEELGOOD)

Dave BROCK
(see HAWKWIND)

Gerry BRON
Dance The Body Music—Osibisa
Sunshine Day—Osibisa

John BROWELL
Sing Something Simple 76 (LP)—Cliff
Adams Singers

James BROWN
Get Up Offa That Thing—James Brown

Lawrence BROWN
Diana Ross (LP)—Diana Ross

Terry BROWN
Aria—Acker Bilk, His Clarinet & Strings
The One For Me (LP)—Acker Bilk, His
Clarinet & Strings

Marty BRYANT
The Best Of The Stylistics (LP)—
Stylistics

Lindsey BUCKINGHAM
(see FLEETWOOD MAC)

Micky BUCKINS
(What A) Wonderful World—Johnny Nash

Boz BURRELL
(see BAD COMPANY)

Mike BUTCHER
We Sold Our Soul For Rock 'n' Roll (LP)
—Black Sabbath

George BUTLER
Thoughts Of Love (LP)—Shirley Bassey

Larry BUTLER
Sing Me An Old Fashioned Song—Billie Jo Spears
What I've Got In Mind—Billie Jo Spears
What I've Got In Mind (LP)—Billie Jo Spears

Terry 'Geezer' BUTLER
(see BLACK SABBATH)

Pete CALLANDER
Best Of Tony Christie (LP)—Tony Christie

Bob CALVERT
(see HAWKWIND)

CAMEL
(Peter Bardens, Doug Ferguson, Andy Latimer & Andy Ward)
Moon Madness (LP)—Camel

Tony CAMILLO
Midnight Train To Georgia—Gladys Knight & the Pips
The Best Of Gladys Knight & The Pips (LP)—Gladys Knight & the Pips

Junior CAMPBELL
Answer Me—Barbara Dickson

CAN
(Michael Karoli, Holger Czukay, Jaki Liebezeit & Irmin Schmidt)
I Want More—Can

Karen CARPENTER
Santa Claus Is Coming To Town—Carpenters
The Singles 1969-1973 (LP)—Carpenters

Richard CARPENTER
Santa Claus Is Coming To Town—Carpenters
I Need To Be In Love—Carpenters
There's A Kind Of Hush—Carpenters
Horizon (LP)—Carpenters
A Kind Of Hush (LP)—Carpenters
Live At The Palladium (LP)—Carpenters
The Singles 1969-1973 (LP)—Carpenters

Victor CARSTARPHEN
Soul City Walk—Archie Bell & the Drells

Hal CARTER
Every Man Must Have A Dream—Liverpool Express
Hold Tight—Liverpool Express
You Are My Love—Liverpool Express

Sonny CASELLA
Let Me Be The No. 1—Dooley Silverspoon

Harry Wayne CASEY (aka KC)
Honey I—George McCrae
Keep It Comin' Love—KC & the Sunshine Band
(Shake Shake Shake) Shake Your Booty—KC & the Sunshine Band

Terry CASHMAN
Shannon—Henry Gross

Tom CATALANO
The Best Of Helen Reddy (LP)—Helen Reddy

Morgan CAVETT
The Way I Want To Touch You—Captain & Tennille

Chas CHANDLER
In For A Penny—Slade
Let's Call It Quits—Slade
Nobody's Fools (LP)—Slade

Andre CHAPELLE
Passport (LP)—Nana Mouskouri

Michael CHAPMAN
I'll Meet You At Midnight—Smokie
Living Next Door To Alice—Smokie
Something's Been Making Me Blue—Smokie

Roger CHAPMAN
(see STREETWALKERS)

Craig CHAQUICO
(see JEFFERSON STARSHIP)

Nicky CHINN
I'll Meet You At Midnight—Smokie
Living Next Door To Alice—Smokie
Something's Been Making Me Blue—Smokie

Dave CLARK
Here's To Love—John Christie

Mike CLARKE
(see RUBETTES)

CLIMAX BLUES BAND
(Colin Cooper, Peter Haycock, Derek Holt,
Richard Jones & John Kuffley)
Couldn't Get It Right—Climax Blues Band

John COGHLAN
(see STATUS QUO)

Biff COLLIE
The Very Best Of Slim Whitman (LP)—
Slim Whitman

Phil COLLINS
(see GENESIS)

Rodger COLLINS
You Sexy Sugar Plum (But I Like It)—
Rodger Collins

Tony COLTON
Thoughts Of Love (LP)—Shirley Bassey

Brian CONNOLLY
(see SWEET)

Peter COOK
Derek And Clive Live (LP)—Peter Cook &
Dudley Moore

Roger COOK
Side Show—Chanter Sisters
Passport (LP)—Nana Mouskouri

Colin COOPER
(see CLIMAX BLUES BAND)

Richard CORNWELL
(see FATBACK BAND)

Hank COSBY
Tears Of A Clown—Smokey Robinson &
the Miracles

Don COSTA
Diana Ross (LP)—Diana Ross

Tom/Tommy COUCH
Funny How Time Slips Away—Dorothy
Moore
Misty Blue—Dorothy Moore

Phil COULTER
D.I.V.O.C.E.—Billy Connolly
Forever And Ever—Slik
No Chance (No Charge)—Billy Connolly
Requiem—Slik
Atlantic Bridge (LP)—Billy Connolly
Get Right Intae Him (LP)—Billy Connolly
Rollin' (LP)—Bay City Rollers

David COVERDALE
(see DEEP PURPLE)

Larry COX
Spitfire (LP)—Jefferson Starship

Dave CRAWFORD
Destiny—Candi Staton
Young Hearts Run Free—Candi Staton
Young Hearts Run Free (LP)—Candi
Staton

Lol CREME
(see 10cc)

Bob CREWE
The Four Seasons Story (LP)—Four
Seasons
**The Greatest Hits Of Frankie Valli & The
Four Seasons (LP)**—Frankie Valli & The
Four Seasons

Eddie CROTTY
(see FIVEPENNY PIECE)

Mike CURB
Deep Purple—Donny & Marie Osmond
I Can't Live A Dream—Osmonds
Deep Purple (LP)—Donny & Marie
Osmond
My Only Fascination (LP)—Demis
Roussos

Bill CURTIS
(see FATBACK BAND)

Holger CZUKAY
(see CAN)

Roger DALTREY
(see WHO)

Jack DAUGHERTY
Santa Claus Is Coming To Town—
Carpenters
The Singles 1969-1973 (LP)—Carpenters

Cliff DAVIES
Free For All (LP)—Ted Nugent

Rhett DAVIES
Moon Madness (LP)—Camel

Richard DAVIES
(see SUPERTRAMP)

Chip DAVIS
Convoy—C.W. McCall

Don DAVIS
One Piece At A Time—Johnny Cash & the
Tennessee Three
One Piece At A Time(LP)—Johnny Cash &
the Tennessee Three

Don DAVIS
Disco Lady—Johnnie Taylor

Hal DAVIS
Love Hangover—Diana Ross
Diana Ross (LP)—Diana Ross
Greatest Hits/2 (LP)—Diana Ross

Martin DAVIS
Love, Life And Feelings (LP)—Shirley Bassey
Thoughts Of Love (LP)—Shirley Bassey

John DEACON
(see QUEEN)

Bert DeCOTEAUX
Baby I'm Yours—Linda Lewis
Gary Glitter's Greatest Hits (LP)—Gary Glitter
The Manhattans (LP)—Manhattans

DEEP PURPLE
(Ritchie Blackmore, Jon Lord, David Coverdale, Ian Paice & Glenn Hughes)
Deep Purple Made In Europe (LP)—Deep Purple

Al DeLORY
Glen Campbell's Greatest Hits (LP)—Glen Campbell
20 Golden Greats (LP)—Glen Campbell

John DENSMORE
(see DOORS)

Del DETTMAR
(see HAWKWIND)

Don DeVITO
Hurricane—Bob Dylan
Desire (LP)—Bob Dylan
Hard Rain (LP)—Bob Dylan

Gregg DIAMOND
More, More, More—Andrea True Connection

DR. FEELGOOD
(Lee Brilleaux, Wilko Johnson, John B. Sparks & The Big Figure)
Stupidity (LP)—Dr. Feelgood

DOORS
(John Densmore, Robbie Krieger, Ray Manzarek & Jim Morrison)
Riders On The Storm—Doors

Tom DOWD
Free Bird—Lynyrd Skynyrd
The Killing Of Georgie—Rod Stewart
Sailing—Rod Stewart
This Old Heart Of Mine—Rod Stewart
Tonight's The Night—Rod Stewart
Gimme Back My Bullets (LP)—Lynyrd Skynyrd
One More For From The Road (LP)—Lynyrd Skynyrd
A Night On The Town (LP)—Rod Stewart
Atlantic Crossing (LP)—Rod Stewart
Locked In (LP)—Wishbone Ash

Tyrone DOWNIE
(see Bob MARLEY & THE WAILERS)

Eddie DRENNON
Let's Do The Latin Hustle—Eddie Drennon & BBS Unlimited

Gary DUCKWORTH
(see SANDPIPERS)

Gus DUDGEON
Benny And The Jets—Elton John
Pinball Wizard—Elton John
Sorry Seems To Be The Hardest Word—Elton John
Don't Go Breaking My Heart—Elton John & Kiki Dee
Changesonebowie (LP)—David Bowie
Blue Moves (LP)—Elton John
Greatest Hits (LP)—Elton John
Here And There (LP)—Elton John

Bob DYLAN
Hard Rain (LP)—Bob Dylan

EARTHBAND
(see Manfred MANN'S EARTHBAND)

Eric EASTON
Rolled Gold (LP)—Rolling Stones

Jay ELLIS
How High The Moon—Gloria Gaynor

Terry ELLIS
M.U. The Best Of Jethro Tull (LP)—Jethro Tull

George ELRICK
The Best Of Lena Martell (LP)—Lena Martell

Steve ELSON
Stoney Ground—Guys 'n' Dolls
In Zaire—Johnny Wakelin

Geoff EMERICK
Long Misty Days (LP)—Robin Trower

Keith EMERSON
Honky Tonk Train Blues—Keith Emerson

John ENTWISTLE
(see WHO)

Ahmet ERTEGUN
Tuxedo Junction—Manhattan Transfer

Tony EYERS
Doctor Kiss-Kiss—5000 Volts
Here I Go Again—Twiggy
Twiggy (LP)—Twiggy

Bob EZRIN
Alice Cooper Goes To Hell (LP)—Alice
Cooper
Destroyer (LP)—Kiss

Andy FAIRWEATHER LOW
(If Paradise Is) Half As Nice—Amen
Corner

Frank FARIAN
Daddy Cool—Boney M

John FARRAR
Come On Over (LP)—Olivia Newton-John

FATBACK BAND
(Richard Cornwell, Bill Curtis, Johnny
Flippin, Johnny King, Earl Shelton &
George Williams)
(Are You Ready) Do The Bus Stop—
Fatback Band
Night Fever—Fatback Band
Party Time—Fatback Band
Spanish Hustle—Fatback Band
Raising Hell (LP)—Fatback Band

Bob FERGUSON
Jolene—Dolly Parton

Doug FERGUSON
(see CAMEL)

Bryan FERRY
Extended Play (EP)—Bryan Ferry
Let's Stick Together—Bryan Ferry
Both Ends Burning—Roxy Music
Let's Stick Together (LP)—Bryan Ferry

Richard FINCH
Honey I—George McCrae
Keep It Comin' Love—KC & the Sunshine
Band
(Shake Shake Shake) Shake Your Booty—
KC & the Sunshine Band

Ben FINDON
Love On Delivery—Billy Ocean
Love Really Hurts Without You—Billy
Ocean
Stop Me (If You've Heard It All Before)—
Billy Ocean

Mike FINESILVER
Disco Music (I Like It)—J.A.L.N. Band

FIVEPENNY PIECE
(Eddie Crotty, John Meeks, Lynda Meeks,
Colin Radcliffe & George Radcliffe)
King Cotton (LP)—Fivepenny Piece

Mick FLEETWOOD
(see FLEETWOOD MAC)

FLEETWOOD MAC
(Lindsey Buckingham, Mick Fleetwood,
Christine McVie, John McVie &
Stevie Nicks)
Say You Love Me—Fleetwood Mac
Fleetwood Mac (LP)—Fleetwood Mac

Dave FLETT
(see Manfred MANN'S EARTHBAND)

Johnny FLIPPIN
(see FATBACK BAND)

Martin FORD (Music only)
Beatles Tapes (LP)—Beatles

Rob FRABONI
No Reason To Cry (LP)—Eric Clapton

Peter FRAMPTON
Baby I Love Your Way—Peter Frampton
Do You Feel Like We Do—Peter Frampton
Show Me The Way—Peter Frampton
Frampton Comes Alive! (LP)—Peter
Frampton

Chris FRANKE
(see TANGERINE DREAM)

Clive FRANKS
Loving And Free/Amoureuse—Kiki Dee

John FRANZ
Hey Mr. Music Man—Peters & Lee
Favourites (LP)—Peters & Lee
Invitation (LP)—Peters & Lee

Colin FRECHTER
Dedication (LP)—Bay City Rollers

David FREIBERG
(see JEFFERSON STARSHIP)

Arthur FREWIN
   The Old Rugged Cross—Ethna Campbell

Edgar FROESE
   (see TANGERINE DREAM)

Lew FUTTERMAN
   Free For All (LP)—Ted Nugent

Kenny GAMBLE
   Wake Up Everybody—Harold Melvin & the
   Blue Notes
   I Love Music—O'Jays
   Let's Make A Baby—Billy Paul
   You'll Never Find Another Love Like Mine
   —Lou Rawls

Jerry GARCIA
   (see GRATEFUL DEAD)

Art/Arthur GARFUNKEL
   Breakaway (LP)—Art Garfunkel
   Still Crazy After All These Years (LP)—
   Paul Simon
   Bridge Over Troubled Water (LP)—Simon
   & Garfunkel
   Simon & Garfunkel's Greatest Hits (LP)—
   Simon & Garfunkel

Snuff/Tommy GARRETT
   I Believe I'm Gonna Love You—Frank
   Sinatra
   Best Of Tony Christie (LP)—Tony Christie
   Passport (LP)—Nana Mouskouri

David GATES
   Lost Without Your Love—Bread
   The Best Of Bread (LP)—Bread

Bob GAUDIO
   We Can Work It Out—Four Seasons
   December, 1963 (Oh, What A Night)—
   Four Seasons
   Silver Star—Four Seasons
   Fallen Angel—Frankie Valli
   Who Loves You (LP)—Four Seasons
   The Greatest Hits Of Frankie Valli &
   The Four Seasons (LP)—Frankie Valli &
   the Four Seasons

Don GEHMAN
   Long May You Run (LP)—Stills-Young
   Band

GENESIS
   (Tony Banks, Phil Collins, Steve Hackett &
   Mike Rutherford)
   A Trick Of The Tail (LP)—Genesis

Phil GERNHARD
   Let Your Love Flow—Bellamy Brothers
   Satin Sheets—Bellamy Brothers
   Bellamy Brothers Featuring 'Let Your
   Love Flow' (LP)—Bellamy Brothers

Barry GIBB
   (see BEE GEES)

Maurice GIBB
   (see BEE GEES)

Robin GIBB
   (see BEE GEES)

Ken GIBSON
   Flip—Jesse Green
   Nice And Slow—Jesse Green

David GILMOUR
   (see PINK FLOYD)

THE GLIMMER TWINS (aka Mick Jagger/
   Keith Richard)
   Fool To Cry—Rolling Stones
   Black And Blue (LP)—Rolling Stones
   (see also ROLLING STONES)

Roger GLOVER
   Wild Side Of Life—Status Quo
   Calling Card (LP)—Rory Gallagher

Donna GODCHAUX
   (see GRATEFUL DEAD)

Keith GODCHAUX
   (see GRATEFUL DEAD)

Kevin GODLEY
   (see 10cc)

Jack GOLD
   When A Child Is Born (Soleado)—Johnny
   Mathis
   The Other Side Of Me—Andy Williams
   I Only Have Eyes For You (LP)—Johnny
   Mathis

Ken GOLD
   Can't Get By Without You—Real Thing
   You To Me Are Everything—Real Thing
   Real Thing (LP)—Real Thing

Jerry GOLDSTEIN
   Low Rider—War
   Me And Baby Brother—War

Kelly GORDON
   Glen Campbell's Greatest Hits (LP)—
   Glen Campbell
   20 Golden Greats (LP)—Glen Campbell

Berry GORDY
  Diana Ross (LP)—Diana Ross

Graham GOULDMAN
  (see 10cc)

Paul GRADE
  It's Temptation—Sheer Elegance
  Life's Too Short Girl—Sheer Elegance
  Milkyway—Sheer Elegance

Nigel GRAINGE
  Bionic Santa—Chris Hill

GRATEFUL DEAD
  (Jerry Garcia, Donna Godchaux, Keith
  Godchaux, Mickey Hart, Bill Kreutzmann,
  Phil Lesh & Bob Weir)
  Steal Your Face (LP)—Grateful Dead

Mick GREEN
  White Christmas—Freddie Starr

Roger GREENAWAY
  Can I Take You Home Little Girl—Drifters
  Every Nite's A Saturday Night With You—
  Drifters
  Hello Happiness—Drifters
  You're More Than A Number In My Little
  Red Book—Drifters
  Jeans On—David Dundas
  Tears On The Telephone—Claude Francois

James GRIFFIN
  The Best Of Bread (LP)—Bread

James William GUERCIO
  If You Leave Me Now—Chicago
  Chicago X (LP)—Chicago

Steve HACKETT
  (see GENESIS)

Henry HADAWAY
  Hang On Sloopy—Sandpipers

Ron HAFFKINE
  If Not You—Dr. Hook
  A Little Bit More—Dr. Hook
  A Little Bit More (LP)—Dr. Hook

Roy HALEE
  Bridge Over Troubled Water (LP)—
  Simon & Garfunkel
  Simon & Garfunkel's Greatest Hits (LP)—
  Simon & Garfunkel

Chris HARDING
  Bert Weedon's 22 Golden Guitar Greats
  (LP)—Bert Weedon

Mike HARDING
  One Man Show (LP)—Mike Harding

Steve HARLEY
  Here Comes The Sun—Steve Harley &
  Cockney Rebel
  (I Believe) Love's A Prima Donna—Steve
  Harley & Cockney Rebel
  Love's A Prima Donna (LP)—Steve Harley
  & Cockney Rebel
  Timeless Flight (LP)—Steve Harley &
  Cockney Rebel

Johnny HARRIS
  Thoughts Of Love (LP)—Shirley Bassey

Norman HARRIS
  Soul Searchin' Time—Trammps
  That's Where The Happy People Go—
  Trammps

George HARRISON
  Thirty Three and ⅓ (LP)—George Harrison

John HARRISON
  (see HAWKWIND)

Mickey HART
  (see GRATEFUL DEAD)

Tim HAUSER
  Tuxedo Junction—Manhattan Transfer

HAWKWIND
  (Dave Brock, Bob Calvert, Simon House,
  Simon King, Paul Rudolph & Nik Turner)
  Astonishing Sounds, Amazing Music
  (LP)—Hawkwind
  (Dave Brock, Bob Calvert, Del Dettmar,
  John Harrison, Simon House, Simon King,
  Lemmy, Huw Lloyd-Langton, Dik Mik,
  Terry Ollis, Allan Powell & Nik Turner)
  Road Hawks (LP)—Hawkwind

Peter HAYCOCK
  (see CLIMAX BLUES BAND)

Isaac HAYES
  Disco Connection—Isaac Hayes
  Movement

John Anthony HELLIWELL
  (see SUPERTRAMP)

David HENTSCHEL
  A Trick Of The Tail (LP)—Genesis

Kelso HERSTON
  The Very Best Of Slim Whitman (LP)—
  Slim Whitman

Eddy HILBERTS
Mississippi—Pussycat
Smile—Pussycat

Chris HILL
Bionic Santa—Chris Hill
Renta Santa—Chris Hill

Tony HILLER
My Sweet Rosalie—Brotherhood of Man
Save Your Kisses For Me—Brotherhood of Man
Manchester United—Manchester United Football Team
Love And Kisses From (LP)—Brotherhood of Man

Neville HINDS
Side Show—Barry Biggs

Roger HODGSON
(see SUPERTRAMP)

Sven Ake HOGBERG
Spinning Rock Boogie—Hank C. Burnette

Ed HOLLIS
Live At The Marquee (EP)—Eddie & the Hot Rods
Teenage Depression—Eddie & the Hot Rods
Teenage Depression (LP)—Eddie & the Hot Rods

Rupert HOLMES
Remember Yesterday—John Miles

Mike HOLOWAY Senior
Dawn—Flintlock

Les HOLROYD
(see BARCLAY JAMES HARVEST)

Derek HOLT
(see CLIMAX BLUES BAND)

HOT WAX PRODUCTIONS LTD.
Why Did You Do It—Stretch

Simon HOUSE
(see HAWKWIND)

Billy HOWARD
King Of The Cops—Billy Howard

Dave HOWMAN
Nice And Slow—Jesse Green

Leon HUFF
Wake Up Everybody—Harold Melvin & the Blue Notes
I Love Music—O'Jays
Let's Make A Baby—Billy Paul
You'll Never Find Another Love Like Mine—Lou Rawls

Alex HUGHES
Christmas In Dreadland/Come Outside—Judge Dread
The Winkle Man—Judge Dread
Y Viva Suspenders/Confessions Of A Bouncer—Judge Dread
Bedtime Stories (LP)—Judge Dread

Glenn HUGHES
(see DEEP PURPLE)

HUGO (aka Hugo Peretti)
Can't Help Falling In Love—Stylistics
Funky Weekend—Stylistics
Na Na Is The Saddest Word—Stylistics
Sixteen Bars—Stylistics
The Miracle & You Are Beautiful (from You'll Never Get To Heaven (If You Break My Heart) (EP))—Stylistics
The Best Of The Stylistics (LP)—Stylistics
The Best Of The Stylistics Vol. 2 (LP)—Stylistics
Fabulous (LP)—Stylistics
You Are Beautiful (LP)—Stylistics

Kenneth HUME
Thoughts Of Love (LP)—Shirley Bassey

Ian HUNTER
All American Alien Boy (LP)—Ian Hunter

Mike HURST
Trocadero—Showaddywaddy
Under The Moon Of Love—Showaddywaddy
Greatest Hits (LP)—Showaddywaddy
Trocadero (LP)—Showaddywaddy

Richard HURWITZ
The Flasher—Mistura with Lloyd Michels

Jimmy IENNER
I Only Want To Be With You—Bay City Rollers
All By Myself—Eric Carmen
Dedication (LP)—Bay City Rollers

I.H.P. PRODUCTIONS
Get It Together—Crispy & Co.

Nick INGMAN
Think Of Me (Wherever You Are)—
Ken Dodd

Tony IOMMI
(see BLACK SABBATH)

Ernie ISLEY
Marvin ISLEY
O'Kelly ISLEY
Ronald ISLEY
Rudolph ISLEY
(see ISLEY BROTHERS)

ISLEY BROTHERS
(Ernie, Marvin, O'Kelly, Ronald,
Rudolph Isley & Chris Jasper)
Harvest For The World—Isley Brothers

Greg JACKMAN
Side Show—Chanter Sisters

Billy JACKSON
God's Gonna Punish You—Tymes

Mick JAGGER
(see ROLLING STONES: GLIMMER TWINS)

Harvey JAMES
(see SHERBET)

Al JARDINE
(see BEACH BOYS)

Jeff JARRATT
20 All Time Eurovision Favourites (LP)—
Nigel Brooks Singers

Chris JASPER
(see ISLEY BROTHERS)

JEFFERSON STARSHIP
(Marty Balin, John Barbata, Craig
Chaquico, David Freiberg, Paul Kantner,
Pete Sears & Grace Slick)
Spitfire (LP)—Jefferson Starship

Peter JENNER
Boxed (LP)—Mike Oldfield

Waylon JENNINGS
A Little Bit More (LP)—Dr. Hook

Elton JOHN
Loving And Free/Amoureuse—Kiki Dee

Glyn JOHNS
Love And Affection—Joan Armatrading
Wide Eyed And Legless—Andy
Fairweather Low
Squeeze Box—Who

Joan Armatrading (LP)—Joan
Armatrading
Desperado (LP)—Eagles
Their Greatest Hits 1971-1975 (LP)—
Eagles
The Story Of The Who (LP)—Who

Wilko JOHNSON
(see DR. FEELGOOD)

Brian JONES
(see ROLLING STONES)

Malcolm JONES
**Laughter & Tears. The Best Of Neil
Sedaka Today (LP)**—Neil Sedaka

Marshall JONES
(see OHIO PLAYERS)

Micky JONES
(see MAN)

Richard JONES
(see CLIMAX BLUES BAND)

Paul KANTNER
(see JEFFERSON STARSHIP)

Michael KAROLI
(see CAN)

Gary KATZ
Haitian Divorce—Steely Dan
The Royal Scam (LP)—Steely Dan

Kenny KELLY
(see MANHATTANS)

Kenny KERNER
**The Best Of Gladys Knight & The Pips
(LP)**—Gladys Knight & the Pips

David KERSHENBAUM
Breakaway—Gallagher & Lyle
Heart On My Sleeve—Gallagher & Lyle
I Wanna Stay With You—Gallagher &
Lyle
Breakaway (LP)—Gallagher & Lyle

Paul KHOURI
Dat—Pluto Shervington
Ram Goat Liver—Pluto Shervington

Johnny KING
(see FATBACK BAND)

Jonathan KING
It Only Takes A Minute—100 Ton & A
Feather
In The Mood—Sound 9418

UK PRODUCER

Simon KING
(see HAWKWIND)

Barry KINGSTON
Dance Of The Cuckoos—Band of the
Black Watch
Loving On The Losing Side—Tommy Hunt
One Fine Morning—Tommy Hunt
Scotch On The Rocks (LP)—Band of the
Black Watch

Donald KINSEY
(see Bob MARLEY & THE WAILERS)

Simon KIRKE
(see BAD COMPANY)

Al KOOPER
Double Trouble—Lynyrd Skynyrd
Sweet Home Alabama—Lynyrd Skynyrd
Cry Tough (LP)—Nils Lofgren

Eddie KRAMER
Alive!—Kiss

Bill KREUTZMANN
(see GRATEFUL DEAD)

Robbie KRIEGER
(see DOORS)

Murray KRUGMAN
Agents Of Fortune (LP)—Blue Oyster Cult

John KUFFLEY
(see CLIMAX BLUES BAND)

Michael KUNZE
Fly, Robin, Fly—Silver Convention
Get Up And Boogie—Silver Convention
Tiger Baby/No, No, Joe—Silver
Convention

Greg LAKE
I Believe In Father Christmas—Greg Lake

Dennis LAMBERT
20 Golden Greats (LP)—Glen Campbell

Kit LAMBERT
The Story Of The Who (LP)—Who

Alan LANCASTER
(see STATUS QUO)

Jon LANDAU
The Pretender (LP)—Jackson Browne

Jeff LANE
Movin'—Brass Construction
Brass Construction (LP)—Brass
Construction

Ronnie LANE
Itchycoo Park—Small Faces
Lazy Sunday—Small Faces

Mel LARSON
Greatest Hits/2 (LP)—Diana Ross

James LAST
Make The Party Last (LP)—James Last

Andy LATIMER
(see CAMEL)

Danny LEAKE
Your Magic Put A Spell On Me—
L.J. Johnson
Doomsday—Evelyn Thomas
Weak Spot—Evelyn Thomas

Mike LEANDER
You Belong To Me—Gary Glitter
People Like You And People Like Me—
Glitter Band
Gary Glitter's Greatest Hits (LP)—Gary
Glitter

Leo LEANDROS
My Only Fascination (LP)—Demis
Roussos
Souvenirs (LP)—Demis Roussos

John LECKIE
**Bring Back The Spark & Blazing
Apostles**—Be Bop DeLuxe (from Hot
Valves (EP))
Ships In The Night—Be Bop DeLuxe
Modern Music (LP)—Be Bop DeLuxe
Sunburst Finish (LP)—Be Bop DeLuxe

Byron LEE
Work All Day—Barry Biggs

John LEES
(see BARCLAY JAMES HARVEST)

Kyle LEHNING
I'd Really Love To See You Tonight—
England Dan & John Ford Coley

LEMMY
(see HAWKWIND)

Ted LEMON
Christmas In Dreadland/Come Outside
—Judge Dread
The Winkle Man—Judge Dread
**Y Viva Suspenders/Confessions Of A
Bouncer**—Judge Dread
Bedtime Stories (LP)—Judge Dread

Barry LENG
  The Summer Of My Life—Simon May

John LENNON
  Imagine—John Lennon
  Shaved Fish (LP)—John Lennon/Plastic
  Ono Band

Deke LEONARD
  (see MAN)

Phil LESH
  (see GRATEFUL DEAD)

Jeffrey LESSER
  Girls, Girls, Girls—Sailor
  Glass Of Champagne—Sailor
  Trouble (LP)—Sailor

Ian LEVINE
  Your Magic Put A Spell On Me—
  L.J. Johnson
  Doomsday—Evelyn Thomas
  Weak Spot—Evelyn Thomas

Jaki LIEBEZEIT
  (see CAN)

Sonny LIMBO
  (What A) Wonderful World—Johnny Nash

Michael LLOYD
  I Can't Live A Dream—Osmonds

Huw LLOYD-LANGTON
  (see HAWKWIND)

Andrew LLOYD-WEBBER
  Don't Cry For Me Argentina—Julie
  Covington

Jon LORD
  (see DEEP PURPLE)

Mike LOVE
  (see BEACH BOYS)

Wilfred LOVETT
  (see MANHATTANS)

David LUCAS
  Agents Of Fortune (LP)—Blue Oyster Cult

LUIGI (aka Luigi CREATORE)
  Can't Help Falling In Love—Stylistics
  Funky Weekend—Stylistics
  Na Na Is The Saddest Word—Stylistics
  Sixteen Bars—Stylistics
  The Miracle & You Are Beautiful—
  Stylistics (from You'll Never Get To
  Heaven (If You Break My Heart) (EP))

The Best Of The Stylistics (LP)—
Stylistics
The Best Of The Stylistics Vol. 2 (LP)—
Stylistics
Fabulous (LP)—Stylistics
You Are Beautiful (LP)—Stylistics

Richard LUSH
  Howzat—Sherbet

Jeff LYNNE
  Evil Woman—Electric Light Orchestra
  Livin' Thing—Electric Light Orchestra
  Strange Magic—Electric Light Orchestra
  A New World Record (LP)—Electric Light
  Orchestra

Paul LYNTON
  It's Temptation—Sheer Elegance
  Life's Too Short Girl—Sheer Elegance
  Milkyway—Sheer Elegance

Tony MACAULAY
  Falling Apart At The Seams—Marmalade
  Don't Give Up On Us—David Soul

Andy MACKAY
  Rock Follies (LP)—Soundtrack

David MACKAY
  A Legendary Performer (LP)—Glenn
  Miller & His Orchestra

David/Dave MACKAY
  Sunday—Buster
  Lost In France—Bonnie Tyler

Carl MADURI
  The Continental—Maureen McGovern

Vic MAILE
  Teenage Depression—Eddie & the Hot
  Rods
  Teenage Depression (LP)—Eddie & the
  Hot Rods

Eric MALAMUD
  You're My Everything—Lee Garrett

MAN
  (Micky Jones, Deke Leonard, John
  McKenzie, Phil Ryan & Terry Williams)
  The Welsh Connection (LP)—Man

MANHATTANS
  (Gerald Austin, Sonny Bivins, Kenny Kelly,
  Wilfred Lovett & Richard Taylor)
  Hurt—Manhattans
  Kiss And Say Goodbye—Manhattans
  The Manhattans (LP)—Manhattans

Manfred MANN
(see Manfred MANN'S EARTHBAND)

Manfred MANN's EARTHBAND
(Manfred Mann, Dave Flett, Chris Hamlet
Thompson, Colin Pattenden & Chris Slade)
Blinded By The Light—Manfred Mann's
Earthband
The Roaring Silence (LP)—Manfred
Mann's Earthband

Bobby MANUEL
Disco Duck—Rick Dees & His Cast Of
Idiots

Ray MANZAREK
(see DOORS)

Jerry MARCELLINO
Greatest Hits/2 (LP)—Diana Ross

Arif MARDIN
Queen Of My Soul—Average White Band
She's Gone—Daryl Hall & John Oates

Bob MARLEY
(see Bob MARLEY & THE WAILERS)

Bob MARLEY & THE WAILERS
(Bob Marley, Aston 'Family Man' Barrett,
Carlton Barrett, Tyrone Downie, Donald
Kinsey, Alvin 'Seeco' Patterson, Earl
'Chinna' Smith & Al Anderson)
Rastaman Vibration (LP)—Bob Marley &
the Wailers

Steve MARRIOTT
Itchycoo Park—Small Faces
Lazy Sunday—Small Faces

Bill MARTIN
Forever And Ever—Slik
Requiem—Slik
Rollin' (LP)—Bay City Rollers

Bobby MARTIN
Hurt—Manhattans
Kiss And Say Goodbye—Manhattans
The Manhattans (LP)—Manhattans

David MARTIN
You Don't Have To Say You Love Me—
Guys 'n' Dolls

George MARTIN
Back In The U.S.S.R.—Beatles
Get Back—Beatles
Help—Beatles
Hey Jude—Beatles
Paperback Writer—Beatles

Strawberry Fields Forever—Beatles
Yesterday—Beatles
The Beatles 1962-1966 (LP)—Beatles
The Beatles 1967-1970 (LP)—Beatles
Rock 'n' Roll Music (LP)—Beatles
**Sgt. Pepper's Lonely Hearts Club Band
(LP)**—Beatles
Wired (LP)—Jeff Beck

Irving MARTIN
Sounds Of Glory (LP)—London
Philharmonic Choir/John Alldis/National
Philharmonic Orchestra

Harry MASLIN
Golden Years—David Bowie
TVC 15—David Bowie
Changesonebowie (LP)—David Bowie
Station To Station (LP)—David Bowie

Nick MASON
(see PINK FLOYD)

Michael MASSER
So Sad The Song—Gladys Knight &
the Pips
**I Thought It Took A Little Time (But
Today I Fell In Love)**—Diana Ross
**Theme From Mahogany 'Do You Know
Where You're Going To'**—Diana Ross
Greatest Hits/2 (LP)—Diana Ross
Diana Ross (LP)—Diana Ross

John MATHIAS
Hey Miss Payne—Chequers

Brian MATTHEW
Instrumental Gold (LP)—Various
Songs Of Praise (LP)—Various
**Bert Weedon's 22 Golden Guitar Greats
(LP)**—Bert Weedon
Gold On Silver (LP)—Beverley-Phillips
Orchestra

Brian MAY
(see QUEEN)

Curtis MAYFIELD
Make Yours A Happy Home—Gladys
Knight & the Pips
Car Wash—Rose Royce
**The Best Of Gladys Knight & The Pips
(LP)**—Gladys Knight & the Pips

Elliot F. MAZER
Greatest Hits (LP)—Linda Ronstadt
David Soul (LP)—David Soul

Paul McCARTNEY
Let 'Em In—Wings
Silly Love Songs—Wings
Band On The Run (LP)—Paul McCartney
& Wings
Venus And Mars (LP)—Wings
Wings At The Speed Of Sound (LP)—
Wings

Van McCOY
Just One Look—Faith Hope & Charity
This Is It—Melba Moore
Walk Away From Love—David Ruffin

Gene McFADDEN
Soul City Walk—Archie Bell & the Drells

John McKENZIE
(see MAN)

Ian McLINTOCK
Jet Silver And The Dolls Of Venus—
Be Bop DeLuxe (from **Hot Valves (EP)**)

Christine McVIE
(see FLEETWOOD MAC)

John McVIE
(see FLEETWOOD MAC)

Hank MEDRESS
**The Greatest Hits Of Frankie Valli &
The Four Seasons (LP)**—Frankie Valli &
the Four Seasons

John MEEKS
(see FIVEPENNY PIECE)

Lynda MEEKS
(see FIVEPENNY PIECE)

Patrick MEEHAN
We Sold Our Soul For Rock 'n' Roll (LP)
—Black Sabbath

Freddie MERCURY
(see QUEEN)

Lloyd MICHELS
The Flasher—Mistura with Lloyd Michels

Ralph MIDDLEBROOKS
(see OHIO PLAYERS)

Dik MIK
(see HAWKWIND)

Jimmy MILLER
Rolled Gold (LP)—Rolling Stones

Steve MILLER
Rock 'n' Me—Steve Miller Band
Fly Like An Eagle (LP)—Steve Miller Band

Gordon MILLS
Greatest Hits (LP)—Gilbert O'Sullivan

Tony MITCHELL
(see SHERBET)

Willie MITCHELL
The Champion—Willie Mitchell

Hank MIZELL
Jungle Rock—Hank Mizell

Meco MONARDO
How High The Moon—Gloria Gaynor

Keith MOON
(see WHO)

Dudley MOORE
Derek And Clive Live (LP)—Peter Cook &
Dudley Moore

Jacques MORALI
The Best Disco In Town—Ritchie Family

Patrick MORAZ
Patrick Moraz (LP)—Patrick Moraz

Giorgio MORODER
Could It Be Magic—Donna Summer
Winter Melody—Donna Summer
A Love Trilogy (LP)—Donna Summer

Jim MORRISON
(see DOORS)

Geoff MORROW
You Don't Have To Say You Love Me—
Guys 'n' Dolls

George/'Shadow' MORTON
Leader Of The Pack—Shangri-Las

Ralph MOSS
**The Best Of Gladys Knight & The Pips
(LP)**—Gladys Knight & the Pips

Mickie MOST
Don't Stop It Now—Hot Chocolate
**Heaven Is In The Back Seat Of My
Cadillac**—Hot Chocolate
Man To Man—Hot Chocolate
You Sexy Thing—Hot Chocolate
XIV Greatest Hits (LP)—Hot Chocolate
Man To Man (LP)—Hot Chocolate

Muff MUFIN
Let's Do The Latin Hustle—M & O Band

Paul MURPHY
Tony Monopoly (LP)—Tony Monopoly

Juggy MURRAY
Inside America—Juggy Murray Jones
(The co-writer of this single—Juggy
Murray Jones—is the same person)

Mitch MURRAY
Best Of Tony Christie (LP)—Tony Christie

Paul MYERS
**Rodrigo: Concierto De Aranjuez
Villa-Lobos: Concerto (LP)**—John
Williams & Daniel Barenboim

Christopher NEIL
Dancing With The Captain—Paul
Nicholas
Grandma's Party (EP)—Paul Nicholas
Reggae Like It Used To Be—Paul Nicholas

Bill NELSON
Bring Back The Spark & Blazing Apostles
(from Hot Valves (EP))—Be Bop DeLuxe
Ships In The Night—Be Bop DeLuxe
Modern Music (LP)—Be Bop DeLuxe
Sunburst Finish (LP)—Be Bop DeLuxe

Norman NEWELL
**Rodrigo's Guitar Concerto De
Aranjuez (Theme from 2nd Movement)**—
Manuel & the Music of the Mountains
Carnival (LP)—Manuel & the Music of the
Mountains

NICKO
(see STREETWALKERS)

Stevie NICKS
(see FLEETWOOD MAC)

OHIO PLAYERS
(William Beck, James Williams, Marshall
Jones, Marvin Pierce, Clarence Satchell,
Ralph Middlebrooks & Leroy Bonner)
Who'd She Coo—Ohio Players

Milton OKUN
Afternoon Delight—Starland Vocal Band
Back Home Again (LP)—John Denver
The Best Of John Denver (LP)—John
Denver
Live In London (LP)—John Denver
Spirit (LP)—John Denver
Windsong (LP)—John Denver

Mike OLDFIELD
In Dulci Jubilo/On Horseback—Mike
Oldfield
Portsmouth—Mike Oldfield
Boxed (LP)—Mike Oldfield
Ommadawn (LP)—Mike Oldfield

Andrew Loog OLDHAM
Rolled Gold (LP)—Rolling Stones

Terry OLLIS
(see HAWKWIND)

Keith OLSEN
Say You Love Me—Fleetwood Mac
Fleetwood Mac (LP)—Fleetwood Mac

Yoko ONO
Shaved Fish (LP)—John Lennon/Plastic
Ono Band

Ozzy OSBOURNE
(see BLACK SABBATH)

Colin OWEN
Let's Do The Latin Hustle—M & O Band

Jimmy PAGE
Four Symbols (LP)—Led Zeppelin
Presence (LP)—Led Zeppelin
**The Soundtrack From The Film The Song
Remains The Same (LP)**—Led Zeppelin

Larry PAGE
Seagull—Rainbow Cottage

Ian PAICE
(see DEEP PURPLE)

Ben PALMERS
Movie Star—Harpo

PAPADON PRODUCTIONS
I'm Your Puppet—James & Bobby Purify
Morning Glory—James & Bobby Purify

Rick PARFITT
(see STATUS QUO)

Richard PARISSI
Play That Funky Music—Wild Cherry

Alan PARSONS
Music—John Miles
Rebel (LP)—John Miles

Colin PATTENDEN
(see Manfred MANN'S EARTHBAND)

Alvin 'Seeco' PATTERSON
(see Bob MARLEY & THE WAILERS)

Sandy PEARLMAN
  Agents Of Fortune (LP)—Blue Oyster Cult

Chas PEATE
  Sky High—Jigsaw

Freddie PERREN
  Love Me—Yvonne Elliman
  Love Machine—Miracles
  Don't Take Away The Music—Tavares
  Heaven Must Be Missing An Angel—
  Tavares
  Sky High (LP)—Tavares

Bill PERRY
  The Best Of The Stylistics (LP)—
  Stylistics

Richard PERRY
  Without You—Nilsson
  You Make Me Feel Like Dancing—
  Leo Sayer
  Breakaway (LP)—Art Garfunkel
  Endless Flight (LP)—Leo Sayer

Detlef PETERSEN
  Sold My Rock 'n' Roll (Gave It Up For
  Funky Soul)—Linda & the Funky Boys

Georges PETSILAS
  Happy To Be On An Island In The Sun—
  Demis Roussos
  Happy To Be (LP)—Demis Roussos

Marvin PIERCE
  (see OHIO PLAYERS)

PINK FLOYD
  (David Gilmour, Nick Mason, Roger
  Waters & Richard Wright)
  The Dark Side Of The Moon (LP)—Pink
  Floyd
  Wish You Were Here (LP)—Pink Floyd

Jon PLOTEL
  (see STREETWALKERS)

Neely PLUMB
  Glen Campbell's Greatest Hits (LP)—
  Glen Campbell

Garth PORTER
  (see SHERBET)

Bob POTTER
  Ramshackled (LP)—Alan White

Brian POTTER
  20 Golden Greats (LP)—Glen Campbell

Allan POWELL
  (see HAWKWIND)

Denis PRESTON
  The Second Album Of The Very Best Of
  Roger Whittaker (LP)—Roger Whittaker
  The Very Best Of Roger Whittaker (LP)—
  Roger Whittaker

Steve PRIEST
  (see SWEET)

Mel PRITCHARD
  (see BARCLAY JAMES HARVEST)

QUEEN
  (John Deacon, Brian May, Freddie Mercury
  & Roger Taylor)
  Bohemian Rhapsody—Queen
  Somebody To Love—Queen
  You're My Best Friend—Queen
  A Day At The Races (LP)—Queen
  A Night At The Opera (LP)—Queen
  Queen (LP)—Queen
  Queen 2 (LP)—Queen
  Sheer Heart Attack (LP)—Queen

Colin RADCLIFFE
  (see FIVEPENNY PIECE)

George RADCLIFFE
  (see FIVEPENNY PIECE)

Mick RALPHS
  (see BAD COMPANY)

Phil RAMONE
  50 Ways To Leave Your Lover—Paul
  Simon
  Still Crazy After All These Years (LP)—
  Paul Simon
  Breakaway (LP)—Art Garfunkel

Michael RANDALL
  Greatest Hits/2 (LP)—Diana Ross

Teddy RANDAZZO
  Better Use Your Head—Little Anthony &
  the Imperials

Eugene RECORD
  You Don't Have To Go—Chi-Lites

Don REEDMAN
  20 All Time Eurovision Favourites (LP)—
  Nigel Brooks Singers

Joe REISMAN
  40 Greatest (LP)—Henry Mancini

Lou REIZNER
We Can Work It Out—Four Seasons
Get Back—Rod Stewart
All This And World War II (LP)—
Soundtrack

Allen REYNOLDS
I Recall A Gypsy Woman—Don Williams
Greatest Hits Vol. 1 (LP)—Don Williams

Tim RICE
Don't Cry For Me Argentina—Julie
Covington

Keith RICHARD
(see ROLLING STONES: GLIMMER TWINS)

Deke RICHARDS
I'm Still Waiting—Diana Ross

Ron RICHARDS
It's So Nice (To Have You Home)—
New Seekers

John RICHARDSON
(see RUBETTES)

Walter J. RIDLEY
Sing Lofty (LP)—Don Estelle & Windsor
Davies

Jerome RIMSON
Real Thing (LP)—Real Thing

Robbie ROBERTSON
Beautiful Noise—Neil Diamond
If You Know What I Mean—Neil Diamond
Beautiful Noise (LP)—Neil Diamond

William/'Smokey' ROBINSON
Tears Of A Clown—Smokey Robinson &
the Miracles

Paul RODGERS
(see BAD COMPANY)

Noel ROGERS
Thoughts Of Love (LP)—Shirley Bassey

ROLLING STONES
(Mick Jagger, Brian Jones, Keith Richard,
Charlie Watts & Bill Wyman)
Rolled Gold (LP)—Rolling Stones
(see also GLIMMER TWINS)

Ritchie ROME
The Best Disco In Town—Ritchie Family

Diana ROSS
Greatest Hits/2 (LP)—Diana Ross
Diana Ross (LP)—Diana Ross

Francis ROSSI
(see STATUS QUO)

Keith ROSSITER
Stoney Ground—Guys 'n' Dolls
In Zaire—Johnny Wakelin

Demis ROUSSOS
Can't Say How Much I Love You—
Demis Roussos
The Roussos Phenomenon (EP)—
Demis Roussos
Forever And Ever (LP)—Demis Roussos
Happly To Be (LP)—Demis Roussos
My Only Fascination (LP)—Demis
Roussos
Souvenirs (LP)—Demis Roussos

Dick ROWE
**Some More Of Me Poems And Songs
(LP)**—Pam Ayres
Some Of Me Poems And Songs (LP)—
Pam Ayres

Robb ROYER
The Best Of Bread (LP)—Bread

RUBETTES
(Mike Clarke, John Richardson, Tony
Thorpe & Alan Williams)
Under One Roof—Rubettes
You're The Reason Why—Rubettes

David RUBINSON & FRIENDS, INC.
Amigos (LP)—Santana

Paul RUDOLPH
(see HAWKWIND)

Todd RUNDGREN
L (LP)—Steve Hillage

Mike RUTHERFORD
(see GENESIS)

Phil RYAN
(see MAN)

Tony SADLER
You Just Might See Me Cry—Our Kid

Paul SAMWELL-SMITH
Greatest Hits (LP)—Cat Stevens

Alan SANDOW
(see SHERBET)

SANDPIPERS
(James Brady, Gary Duckworth,
Richard Shoff)
Hang On Sloopy—Sandpipers

134

Clarence SATCHELL
(see OHIO PLAYERS)

Stephen Y. SCHEAFFER
Baby Face—Wing & A Prayer Fife & Drum Corps

Lalo SCHIFRIN
Jaws—Lalo Schifrin

Irmin SCHMIDT
(see CAN)

Bill SCHNEE
Concrete And Clay—Randy Edelman
The Uptown, Uptempo Woman—Randy Edelman

Andy SCOTT
(see SWEET)

Ken SCOTT
Changesonebowie (LP)—David Bowie
Crisis? What Crisis? (LP)—Supertramp

Ronnie SCOTT
Sunday—Buster

Tommy SCOTT
Devine Time (LP)—Sydney Devine
Doubly Devine (LP)—Sydney Devine

Tony SCOTTI
Let Your Love Flow—Bellamy Brothers
Satin Sheets—Bellamy Brothers
Bellamy Brothers Featuring 'Let Your Love Flow' (LP)—Bellamy Brothers

Don SEARS
Convoy—C.W. McCall

Pete SEARS
(see JEFFERSON STARSHIP)

Neil SEDAKA
Laughter & Tears. The Best Of Neil Sedaka Today (LP)—Neil Sedaka

Tom SELLERS
You're My Everything—Lee Garrett

Jay SENTER
The Best Of Helen Reddy (LP)—Helen Reddy

Peter SHELLEY
Alright Baby—Stevenson's Rocket

Earl SHELTON
(see FATBACK BAND)

SHERBET
(Daryl Braithwaite, Harvey James, Tony Mitchell, Garth Porter & Alan Sandow)
Howzat—Sherbet

Billy SHERRILL
I Don't Wanna Play House—Tammy Wynette

Leighton/Pluto SHERVINGTON
Midnight Rider—Paul Davidson

Richard SHOFF
(see SANDPIPERS)

Herb SHUCHER
The Very Best Of Slim Whitman (LP)—Slim Whitman

Tony SILVESTER
Baby I'm Yours—Linda Lewis
Gary Glitter's Greatest Hits (LP)—Gary Glitter

George T. SIMON
A Legendary Performer (LP)— Glenn Miller and His Orchestra

Paul SIMON
50 Ways To Leave Your Lover—Paul Simon
Breakaway (LP)—Art Garfunkel
Still Crazy After All These Years (LP)—Paul Simon
Bridge Over Troubled Water (LP)—Simon & Garfunkel
Simon & Garfunkel's Greatest Hits (LP)—Simon & Garfunkel

Pete SINFIELD
I Believe In Father Christmas—Greg Lake

Ray SINGER
My Resistance Is Low—Robin Sarstedt

Chris SLADE
(see Manfred MANN'S EARTHBAND)

Grace SLICK
(see JEFFERSON STARSHIP)

Earl 'Chinna' SMITH
(see Bob MARLEY & THE WAILERS)

Gordon SMITH
100 Golden Greats (LP)—Max Bygraves
Music Of America (LP)—Richmond Strings/Mike Sammes Singers
Forty Mania (LP)—Various

Steve Smith
Love Hurts—Jim Capaldi
Some People Can Do What They Like (LP)—Robert Palmer

John David SOUTHER
Greatest Hits (LP)—Linda Ronstadt

John B. SPARKS
(see DR. FEELGOOD)

Phil SPECTOR
Shaved Fish (LP)—John Lennon/Plastic Ono Band

John STAINES
Bionic Santa—Chris Hill
Renta Santa—Chris Hill

STATUS QUO
(John Coghlan, Alan Lancaster, Rick Parfitt & Francis Rossi)
Mystery Song—Status Quo
Rain—Status Quo
Blue For You (LP)—Status Quo

Geoff STEPHENS
Drive Safely Darling—Tony Christie
It's Gonna Be A Cold Cold Christmas—Dana
Never Gonna Fall In Love Again—Dana
Best Of Tony Christie (LP)—Tony Christie

Wolf STEPHENSON
Funny How Time Slips Away—Dorothy Moore

Cat STEVENS
Greatest Hits (LP)—Cat Stevens

Eric STEWART
(see 10cc)

Rod STEWART
Get Back—Rod Stewart
Maggie May—Rod Stewart

Stephen STILLS
Long May You Run (LP)—Stills-Young Band

STREETWALKERS
(Roger Chapman, Nicko, Jon Plotel, Bob Tench & Charlie Witney)
Red Card (LP)—Streetwalkers

James STROUD
Funny How Time Slips Away—Dorothy Moore
Misty Blue—Dorothy Moore

Glen STUART
The Wanderer—Dion

Peter SULLIVAN
When Forever Has Gone—Demis Roussos
Best Of Tony Christie (LP)—Tony Christie

SUPERTRAMP
(Bob C. Benberg, Richard Davies, John Anthony Helliwell, Roger Hodgson & Dougie Thomson)
Crisis? What Crisis? (LP)—Supertramp

SWEET
(Brian Connolly, Steve Priest, Andy Scott & Mike Tucker)
The Lies In Your Eyes—Sweet

Phil SWERN
We Do It—R & J Stone

Peter SWETTENHAM
Every Man Must Have A Dream—Liverpool Express
Hold Tight—Liverpool Express
You Are My Love—Liverpool Express

Bill SZYMCZYK
Fooled Around And Fell In Love—Elvin Bishop
Take It To The Limit—Eagles
Hotel California (LP)—Eagles
One Of These Nights (LP)—Eagles
Their Greatest Hits 1971-1975 (LP)—Eagles

Shel TALMY
Spanish Wine—Chris White
(If Paradise Is) Half As Nice—Amen Corner

TANGERINE DREAM
(Peter Baumann, Chris Franke & Edgar Froese)
Stratosfear (LP)—Tangerine Dream

Dick TAYLOR
Road Hawks (LP)—Hawkwind

Richard TAYLOR
(see MANHATTANS)

Roger TAYLOR
(see QUEEN)

Stuart TAYLOR
The Snow Goose (LP)—Spike Milligan/The London Symphony Orchestra

Doctor TECHNICAL
Road Hawks (LP)—Hawkwind

Ted TEMPLEMAN
Takin' It To The Streets (LP)—Doobie Brothers

10cc
(Lol Creme, Kevin Godley, Graham Gouldman & Eric Stewart)
Art For Art's Sake—10cc
I'm Mandy Fly Me—10cc
The Things We Do For Love—10cc
The Laughter & Tears. The Best Of Neil Sedaka Today (LP)—Neil Sedaka
How Dare You (LP)—10cc
The Original Soundtrack (LP)—10cc

Bob TENCH
(see STREETWALKERS)

Chris THOMAS
Extended Play (EP)—Bryan Ferry
Let's Stick Together—Bryan Ferry
Both Ends Burning—Roxy Music
Anarchy In The U.K.—Sex Pistols
Let's Stick Together (LP)—Bryan Ferry
Siren (LP)—Roxy Music
Viva! Roxy Music (LP)—Roxy Music

Chris Hamlet THOMPSON
(see Manfred MANN'S EARTHBAND)

Dougie THOMSON
(see SUPERTRAMP)

Tony THORPE
(see RUBETTES)

Pete TOWNSHEND
(see WHO)

Ed TOWNSEND
First Impressions—Impressions

Robin TROWER
Long Misty Days (LP)—Robin Trower

Mike TUCKER
(see SWEET)

Nik TURNER
(see HAWKWIND)

Scott TURNER
The Very Best Of Slim Whitman (LP)—Slim Whitman

Bjorn ULVAEUS
Dancing Queen—Abba
Fernando—Abba
Mamma Mia—Abba
Money, Money, Money—Abba

Abba (LP)—Abba
Arrival (LP)—Abba
Greatest Hits (LP)—Abba

Thomas J. VALENTINO
A Fifth Of Beethoven—Walter Murphy Band

VANGELIS
Albedo 0.39 (LP)—Vangelis
Heaven And Hell (LP)—Vangelis

Nikolas VENET
20 Golden Greats (LP)—Beach Boys
Greatest Hits (LP)—Linda Ronstadt

Tony VISCONTI
If You Love Me—Mary Hopkin
La Booga Rooga—Surprise Sisters
Changesonebowie (LP)—David Bowie

Tony WADDINGTON
The Two Of Us—Mac & Katie Kissoon
Convoy GB—Laurie Lingo & the Dipsticks

WAILERS
(see Bob MARLEY & THE WAILERS)

Phil WAINMAN
Money Honey—Bay City Rollers
Show Me You're A Woman—Mud
Dedication (LP)—Bay City Rollers
Once Upon A Star (LP)—Bay City Rollers
Wouldn't You Like It (LP)—Bay City Rollers
Use Your Imagination (LP)—Mud

Rick WAKEMAN
No Earthly Connection (LP)—Rick Wakeman

Scott WALKER
No Regrets—Walker Brothers
No Regrets (LP)—Walker Brothers

Joe WALSH
You Can't Argue With A Sick Mind (LP)—Joe Walsh

Andy WARD
(see CAMEL)

Bill WARD
(see BLACK SABBATH)

Leon WARE
I Want You (LP)—Marvin Gaye

Alan WARNER
Lullaby Of Broadway—Winifred Shaw

Pete WATERMAN
   Alright Baby—Stevenson's Rocket

Roger WATERS
   (see PINK FLOYD)

Johnny 'Guitar' WATSON
   I Need It—Johnny 'Guitar' Watson

Charlie WATTS
   (see ROLLING STONES)

Jeff WAYNE
   City Lights—David Essex
   Coming Home—David Essex
   If I Could—David Essex
   All The Fun Of The Fair (LP)—David Essex
   Out On The Street (LP)—David Essex

Bob WEIR
   (see GRATEFUL DEAD)

Bruce WELCH
   Devil Woman—Cliff Richard
   Hey Mr. Dream Maker—Cliff Richard
   I Can't Ask For Anymore Than You—
   Cliff Richard
   Miss You Nights—Cliff Richard
   I'm Nearly Famous (LP)—Cliff Richard

Ed WELCH
   The Snow Goose (LP)—Spike Milligan/
   The London Symphony Orchestra

Tom WERMAN
   Free For All (LP)—Ted Nugent

Tommy WEST
   Shannon—Henry Gross

Harold WHEELER
   Baby Face—Wing & A Prayer Fife & Drum
   Corps

Alan WHITE
   Ramshackled (LP)—Alan White

Barry WHITE
   Baby, We Better Try And Get It Together
   —Barry White
   Don't Make Me Wait Too Long—Barry
   White
   Let The Music Play—Barry White
   You See The Trouble With Me—Barry
   White
   Greatest Hits (LP)—Barry White
   Let The Music Play (LP)—Barry White

John WHITEHEAD
   Soul City Walk—Archie Bell & the Drells

Peter WHITEHOUSE
   Disco Music (I Like It)—J.A.L.N. Band

Norman WHITFIELD
   It Should Have Been Me—Yvonne Fair
   Car Wash—Norman Whitfield

WHO
   (Roger Daltrey, John Entwistle, Keith
   Moon & Pete Townshend)
   Substitute—Who
   The Story Of The Who (LP)—Who

Alan WILLIAMS
   (see RUBETTES)

Don WILLIAMS
   I Recall A Gypsy Woman—Don Williams
   You're My Best Friend—Don Williams
   Greatest Hits Vol. 1 (LP)—Don Williams

George WILLIAMS
   (see FATBACK BAND)

James WILLIAMS
   (see OHIO PLAYERS)

Pip WILLIAMS
   Lean On Me—Mud
   Shake It Down—Mud

Terry WILLIAMS
   (see MAN)

Brian WILSON
   Good Vibrations—Beach Boys
   Rock And Roll Music—Beach Boys
   15 Big Ones (LP)—Beach Boys
   20 Golden Greats (LP)—Beach Boys
   (see also BEACH BOYS)

Carl WILSON
   (see BEACH BOYS)

Dennis WILSON
   (see BEACH BOYS)

Muff WINWOOD
   Love Me Like I Love You—Bay City Rollers

Richie WISE
   The Best Of Gladys Knight & The Pips
   (LP)—Gladys Knight & the Pips

Joe WISSERT
   Lowdown—Boz Scaggs
   The Best Of Helen Reddy (LP)—Helen
   Reddy

Charlie WITNEY
   (see STREETWALKERS)

Steve WOLFE
    Sunday—Buster

Stuart 'Wooly' WOLSTENHOLME
    (see BARCLAY JAMES HARVEST)

Stevie WONDER
    I Wish—Stevie Wonder
    Songs In The Key Of Life (LP)—Stevie
    Wonder

Richard WRIGHT
    (see PINK FLOYD)

Bill WYMAN
    (see ROLLING STONES)

Earl YOUNG
    Soul Searchin' Time—Trammps
    That's Where The Happy People Go—
    Trammps

Kenny YOUNG
    S-S-S-Single Bed—Fox

Neil YOUNG
    Long May You Run (LP)—Stills-Young
    Band

Gheorghe ZAMFIR
    Light Of Experience (Doina De Jale)—
    Gheorghe Zamfir

Part Two

Section 7

US Title Section

(*Billboard* Top 100 Singles Chart)

This section lists the position and week of entry, highest placing and week, duration on chart, title, artist and catalogue number of all singles that made the *Billboard* Top 100 chart during 1976.

These charts are based on *Billboard's* figures. They are not as accurate as their UK counterpart, and are very much an assessment. Similarly they don't refer exactly to a particular week of sales, so although *Billboard* is published on a Monday, the chart refers to the end of the previous week. *denotes record still in chart on January 1, 1977.

For details of how to find your way about this part of the book, refer to the introduction to Part 1, Section 1.

Position and date of entry	Highest position and date	Wks.	Title	Artist(s)	Cat. No.
100(7/ 2)	98(14/ 2)	2	Abyssinia Jones	Edwin Starr	Granite G 532
80(14/ 2)	20(17/ 4)	14	Action	Sweet	Capitol P-4220
87(14/ 8)	74(28/ 8)	5	After The Dance	Marvin Gaye	Tamla T-54273F
85(23/10)	10(25/12)	10	*After The Lovin'	Engelbert Humperdinck	Epic 8-50270
87(8/ 5)	1(10/ 7)	20	Afternoon Delight	Starland Vocal Band	Windsong CB 10588
71(27/11)	37(25/12)	5	*Ain't Nothing Like The Real Thing	Donny & Marie Osmond	Kolob PD 14363
85(20/12)	2(6/ 3)	19	All By Myself	Eric Carmen	Arista AS 0165
100(4/12)	97(18/12)	3	All Roads (Lead Back To You)	Donny Most	United Artists UA-XW871-Y
98(20/12)	72(7/ 2)	8	Amazing Grace (Used To Be Her Favorite Song)	Amazing Rhythm Aces	ABC 12142
86(21/ 8)	75(11/ 9)	4	Amber Cascades	America	Warner Bros WBS 8238
75(26/ 6)	32(7/ 8)	9	Another Rainy Day In New York City	Chicago	Columbia 3-10360
91(4/ 9)	37(6/11)	12	Anything You Want	John Valenti	Ariola America P-7625
77(3/ 4)	33(15/ 5)	9	Anytime (I'll Be There)	Paul Anka	United Artists UA-XW789-Y
97(10/ 4)	81(1/ 5)	5	Arms Of Mary	Sutherland Brothers & Quiver	Columbia 3-10284
97(29/11)	83(27/12)	6	Art For Art's Sake	10cc	Mercury 73725
82(27/11)	79(4/12)	2	Baby, Baby I Love You	Terry Cashman	Lifesong LS 45015
88(30/10)	60(18/12)	9	*Baby Boy	Mary Kay Place (as Loretta Haggers)	Columbia 3-10422
86(15/11)	14(6/ 3)	20	Baby Face	Wing & A Prayer Fife & Drum Corps	Wing & A Prayer 103
77(26/ 6)	12(28/ 8)	16	Baby I Love Your Way	Peter Frampton	A&M AM 1832
84(20/11)	58(18/12)	6	*Baby, I'll Give It To You	Seals & Crofts	Warner Bros WBS 8277
92(24/ 7)	92(24/ 7)	2	Baby, We Better Try And Get It Together	Barry White	20th Century TC 2298
79(25/12)	79(25/12)	1	*Baby, You Look Good To Me Tonight	John Denver	RCA PB 10854
73(3/ 1)	53(31/ 1)	5	Back To The Island	Leon Russell	Shelter SRL 40483
99(10/ 1)	94(31/ 1)	4	Bad Luck	Atlanta Disco Band	Ariola America P-7611
61(7/ 2)	41(6/ 3)	6	Banapple Gas	Cat Stevens	A&M AM 1785
76(10/ 4)	20(12/ 6)	13	Baretta's Theme (Keep Your Eyes On The Sparrow)	Rhythm Heritage	ABC 12177
81(28/ 8)	17(27/11)	18	*Best Disco In Town, The	Ritchie Family	Marlin MAR 3306

Position and date of entry	Highest position and date	Wks.	Title	Artist(s)	Cat. No.
79(4/ 9)	7(4/12)	17	*Beth/Detroit Rock City	Kiss	Casablanca NB 863
89(1/ 5)	71(22/ 5)	5	Better Days	Melissa Manchester	Arista AS 0183
90(26/ 6)	86(10/ 7)	3	Better Place To Be, A	Harry Chapin	Elektra E-45327
83(8/ 5)	57(5/ 6)	5	Bigfoot	Bro Smith	Big Tree BT 16061
82(6/12)	58(27/12)	5	Blind Man In The Bleachers, The	Kenny Starr	MCA 40474
95(20/11)	32(25/12)	6	*Blinded By The Light	Manfred Mann's Earthband	Warner Bros WBS 8252
79(26/ 6)	59(24/ 7)	6	BLT	Lee Oskar	United Artists UA-XW807-Y
99(13/12)	94(10/ 1)	5	Blue Guitar	Justin Hayward & John Lodge	Threshold THS 67021
81(3/ 1)	9(24/ 4)	24	Bohemian Rhapsody	Queen	Elektra E-45297
84(14/ 2)	1(15/ 5)	21	Boogie Fever	Sylvers	Capitol P-4179
84(15/ 5)	12(24/ 7)	17	Boys Are Back In Town, The	Thin Lizzy	Mercury 73786
95(21/ 8)	81(4/ 9)	3	Brand New Love Affair	Jigsaw	Chelsea CH 3043
81(27/12)	39(31/ 1)	11	Breakaway	Art Garfunkel	Columbia 3-10273
94(4/ 7)	94(4/ 7)	2	Breaker-Breaker	Outlaws	Arista AS 0188
99(29/11)	92(10/ 1)	7	Breakfast For Two	Country Joe McDonald	Fantasy F-758
79(13/12)	8(21/ 2)	14	Breaking Up Is Hard To Do	Neil Sedaka	Rocket PIG 40500
90(16/10)	63(13/11)	6	Breezin'	George Benson	Warner Bros WBS 8268
98(4/12)	83(25/12)	4	*Caledonia	Robin Trower	Chrysalis CHS 2122
81(16/10)	66(30/10)	3	California Day	Starland Vocal Band	Windsong CB 10785
100(21/2)	91(13/ 3)	5	Call, The	Anne Murray	Capitol P-4207
66(7/ 2)	56(14/ 2)	4	Can The Can	Suzi Quatro	Big Tree BT-16053
82(14/ 8)	45(18/ 9)	7	Can You Do It	Grand Funk Railroad	MCA 40590
99(24/ 7)	91(7/ 8)	3	Can't Change My Heart	Cate Bros	Asylum E-45326
86(27/ 3)	39(24/ 4)	9	Can't Hide Love	Earth Wind & Fire	Columbia 3-10309
69(5/ 6)	52(19/ 6)	4	Can't Stop Groovin' Now, Wanna Do It Some More	B.T. Express	Columbia 3-10346
97(9/10)	97(9/10)	1	Can't You See	Waylon Jennings	RCA PB 10721
86(23/10)	9(25/12)	10	*Car Wash	Rose Royce	MCA 40615
87(25/12)	87(25/12)	1	*Carry On Wayward Son	Kansas	Kirshner ZS8 4267
84(30/10)	71(4/12)	6	Catfish	Four Tops	ABC 12214
96(6/11)	94(13/11)	2	Ca-the-Drals	D.C. LaRue	Pyramid PD 8007
89(25/12)	89(25/12)	1	*C.B. Savage	Rod Hart	Plantation PL 144

Position and date of entry	Highest position and date	Wks.	Title	Artist(s)	Cat. No.
87(3/ 1)	63(7/ 2)	9	Chain Gang Medley	Jim Croce	Lifesong LS 45001
84(13/12)	58(3/ 1)	4	Christmas For Cowboys	John Denver	RCA PB 10464
90(24/ 1)	82(14/ 2)	4	Close To You	B.T. Express	Roadshow RDJ 7005
81(5/ 6)	38(31/ 7)	11	C'mon Marianne	Donny Osmond	Kolob PD 14320
83(13/ 3)	23(8/ 5)	12	Come On Over	Olivia Newton John	MCA 40525
82(6/12)	1(10/ 1)	16	Convoy	C.W. McCall	MGM M-14839
89(26/ 6)	59(31/ 7)	7	Cotton Candy	Sylvers	Capitol P-4255
85(1/ 5)	52(22/ 5)	5	Could It Be Magic	Donna Summer	Oasis OC 405
86(8/11)	11(17/ 1)	14	Country Boy (You Got Your Feet In L.A.)	Glen Campbell	Capitol P-4155
93(18/ 9)	77(30/10)	8	Cowboy Song	Thin Lizzy	Mercury 73841
86(17/ 4)	35(5/ 6)	13	Crazy On You	Heart	Mushroom M-7021
62(7/ 2)	22(20/ 3)	9	Cupid	Tony Orlando & Dawn	Elektra E-45302
83(6/11)	81(13/11)	3	(One More Year Of) Daddy's Little Girl	Ray Sawyer	Capitol P-4344
90(1/ 5)	39(12/ 6)	8	Dance Wit Me	Rufus featuring Chaka Khan	ABC 12179
93(3/ 7)	60(31/ 7)	9	Dancin' Kid	Disco Tex & the Sex-o-lettes	Chelsea CH 3045
86(11/12)	66(25/12)	3	*Dancing Queen	Abba	Atlantic 45-3372
100(3/ 1)	91(14/ 2)	8	Daydreamer	C.C. & Company	Westbound W-5016
90(2/10)	63(6/11)	7	Daylight	Vicki Sue Robinson	RCA PB 10775
90(23/10)	8(25/12)	10	*Dazz	Brick	Bang BDJ 727
85(27/12)	1(13/ 3)	27	December, 1963 (Oh, What A Night)	Four Seasons	Warner Bros WBS 8168
89(13/12)	17(10/ 4)	23	Deep Purple	Donny & Marie Osmond	Kolob PD 14840
87(17/ 7)	71(31/ 7)	4	Devil With The Blue Dress	Pratt & McClain with Brotherlove	Reprise RPS 1361
87(3/ 7)	6(25/ 9)	22	Devil Woman	Cliff Richard	Rocket PIG 40574
87(28/ 8)	29(30/10)	14	Did You Boogie With Your Baby (In The Back Row Of The Movie Show)	Flash Cadillac And The Continental Kids	Private Stock PS 45079
89(14/ 8)	1(16/10)	20	*Disco Duck	Rick Dees & His Cast Of Idiots	RSO RS 857
87(7/ 2)	1(3/ 4)	19	Disco Lady	Johnnie Taylor	Columbia 3-10281
93(17/ 1)	92(7/ 2)	4	Disco Sax/For The Love Of You	Houston Person	Westbound W-5015
77(27/11)	50(25/12)	5	*Do It To My Mind	Johnny Bristol	Atlantic 45-3360
97(20/ 3)	94(3/ 4)	3	Do It With Feeling	Michael Zager's Moon Band featuring Peabo Bryson	Bang BDJ 720

Position and date of entry	Highest position and date	Wks.	Title	Artist(s)	Cat. No.
75(30/10)	39(25/12)	9	*Do What You Want, Be What You Are	Daryl Hall & John Oates	RCA PB 10808
77(18/ 9)	10(13/11)	15	*Do You Feel Like We Do	Peter Frampton	A&M AM 1867
86(24/ 7)	37(18/ 9)	10	(The System Of) Doctor Tarr & Professor Fether	Alan Parsons Project	20th Century TC 2297
91(27/11)	91(27/11)	2	Dog Eat Dog	Ted Nugent	Epic 8-50301
100(20/12)	63(31/ 1)	7	Don't Cry Joni	Conway Twitty	MCA 40407
			(Don't Fear) The Reaper see under Reaper		
91(30/10)	72(18/12)	8	Don't Fight The Hands (That Need You)	Hamilton, Joe Frank & Dennison	Playboy P-6088
66(3/ 7)	1(7/ 8)	20	Don't Go Breaking My Heart	Elton John & Kiki Dee	Rocket PIG 40585
85(18/12)	75(25/12)	2	*Don't Leave Me This Way	Thelma Houston	Tamla T-54278F
87(27/ 3)	27(8/ 5)	10	Don't Pull Your Love/Then You Can Tell Me Goodbye	Glen Campbell	Capitol P-4245
80(7/ 8)	33(18/ 9)	9	Don't Stop Believin'	Olivia Newton-John	MCA 40600
80(17/ 4)	42(15/ 5)	6	Don't Stop It Now	Hot Chocolate	Big Tree BT 16060
83(30/10)	34(18/12)	9	*Don't Take Away The Music	Tavares	Capitol P-4348
82(11/ 9)	43(2/10)	8	Don't Think... Feel	Neil Diamond	Columbia 3-10405
80(4/ 7)	61(14/ 8)	7	Don't Touch Me There	Tubes	A&M AM 1826
58(2/10)	26(6/11)	9	Dose Of Rock And Roll, A	Ringo Starr	Atlantic 45-3361
90(20/ 3)	80(27/ 3)	3	Double Trouble	Lynyrd Skynyrd	MCA 40532
95(23/10)	47(4/12)	9	Down To Love Town	Originals	Soul 35119
83(6/12)	43(3/ 1)	7	Down To The Line	Bachman-Turner Overdrive	Mercury 73724
81(10/ 1)	6(10/ 4)	20	Dream On	Aerosmith	Columbia 3-10278
98(3/ 1)	2(10/ 4)	20	Dream Weaver	Gary Wright	Warner Bros WBS 8167
82(18/12)	72(25/12)	2	*Dreamboat Annie	Heart	Mushroom M-7023
75(27/11)	40(25/12)	5	*Drivin' Wheel	Foghat	Bearsville BBS 0313
88(13/12)	54(24/ 1)	8	Easy As Pie	Billy 'Crash' Craddock	ABC/Dot DOA 17584
95(6/ 3)	72(10/ 4)	6	Eh! Cumpari	Gaylord & Holiday	Prodigal PLP 0622

US TITLE

Position and date of entry	Highest position and date	Wks.	Title	Artist(s)	Cat. No.
94(18/ 9)	42(6/11)	10	**End Is Not In Sight (The Cowboy Tune), The**	Amazing Rhythm Aces	ABC 12202
82(13/11)	21(25/12)	7	***Enjoy Yourself**	Jacksons	Epic 8-50289
100(6/12)	83(17/ 1)	8	**Every Beat Of My Heart**	Crown Heights Affair	De-Lite DEP 1575
76(6/11)	55(18/12)	8	***Every Face Tells A Story**	Olivia Newton-John	MCA 40642
88(3/ 4)	62(8/ 5)	7	**Everyday Without You**	Hamilton, Joe Frank & Reynolds	Playboy P-6068
81(21/ 5)	66(5/ 6)	3	**Everything That 'Cha Do (Will Come Back To You)**	Wet Willie	Capricorn CPS 0254
84(12/ 6)	49(31/ 7)	9	**Everything's Coming Up Love**	David Ruffin	Motown M-1393F
87(15/11)	10(14/ 2)	17	**Evil Woman**	Electric Light Orchestra	United Artists UA-XW729-Y
81(3/ 4)	36(8/ 5)	8	**Fallen Angel**	Frankie Valli	Private Stock PS 45074
98(25/12)	98(25/12)	1	***(She's Just A) Fallen Angel**	Starz	Capitol P-4343
99(27/ 3)	49(15/ 5)	9	**Falling Apart At The Seams**	Marmalade	Ariola America P-7619
73(27/12)	12(20/ 3)	16	**Fanny (Be Tender With My Love)**	Bee Gees	RSO RS 519
98(21/ 6)	6(25/10)	32	**Feelings**	Morris Albert	RCA PB-10279
95(25/12)	95(25/12)	1	***Feelings**	Walter Jackson	Chi-Sound CH-XW908-Y
77(4/ 9)	13(20/11)	16	**Fernando**	Abba	Atlantic 45-3346
89(25/ 9)	59(16/10)	5	**Fez, The**	Steely Dan	ABC 12222
80(29/ 5)	1(9/10)	28	**Fifth Of Beethoven, A**	Walter Murphy & the Big Apple Band	Private Stock PS 45073
74(20/12)	1(7/ 2)	17	**50 Ways To Leave Your Lover**	Paul Simon	Columbia 3-10270
94(23/10)	94(23/10)	2	**Find 'Em, Fool 'Em And Forget 'Em**	Dobie Gray	Capricorn CPS 0259
94(4/ 9)	93(11/ 9)	2	**Fire**	Mother's Finest	Epic 8-50269
95(18/10)	38(27/12)	13	**Fire On The Mountain**	Marshall Tucker Band	Capricorn CPS 0244
82(5/ 6)	74(19/ 6)	3	**Flaming Youth**	Kiss	Casablanca NB 858
83(13/11)	44(18/12)	7	***Flight '76**	Walter Murphy Band	Private Stock PS 45123
93(9/10)	87(30/10)	4	**Flowers**	Emotions	Columbia 3-10347
			(the B side of this single— I DON'T WANNA LOSE YOUR LOVE— replaced it the week after this dropped out of the chart—see under I)		
58(6/12)	13(24/ 1)	12	**Fly Away**	John Denver	RCA PB-10517
73(18/12)	52(25/12)	2	***Fly Like An Eagle**	Steve Miller Band	Capitol P-4372

US TITLE

Position and date of entry	Highest position and date	Wks.	Title	Artist(s)	Cat. No.
87(11/10)	1(29/11)	17	Fly, Robin, Fly	Silver Convention	Midland International MB-10339
99(10/ 4)	91(15/ 5)	6	Fonz Song, The	Heyettes	London 5N-232
85(5/ 6)	45(3/ 7)	7	Fool For The City	Foghat	Bearsville BSS 0307
63(24/ 4)	10(5/ 6)	9	Fool To Cry	Rolling Stones	Rolling Stones RS 19304
			(this was subsequently re-marketed as the B side of HOT STUFF which also charted — see under H)		
88(6/ 3)	3(22/ 5)	17	Fooled Around And Fell In Love	Elvin Bishop	Capricorn CPS 0252
86(21/ 2)	30(17/ 4)	11	Fopp	Ohio Players	Mercury 73775
100(29/11)	63(17/ 1)	8	For A Dancer	Prelude	Pye 71045
58(15/11)	22(20/12)	12	For The Love Of You	Isley Brothers	T-Neck ZS8-2259
88(10/ 4)	76(8/ 5)	5	Forever Lovers	Mac Davis	Columbia 3-10304
47(15/11)	5(17/ 1)	16	Fox On The Run	Sweet	Capitol P-4157
89(22/ 5)	49(24/ 7)	12	Foxy Lady	Crown Heights Affair	De-Lite DEP 1581
82(12/ 6)	41(3/ 7)	8	Framed	Cheech & Chong	Ode ODE-66124
88(11/12)	74(25/12)	3	*Free	Deniece Williams	Columbia 3-10429
83(4/12)	43(25/12)	4	*Free Bird	Lynyrd Skynyrd	MCA 40665
86(6/12)	52(3/ 1)	6	Free Ride	Tavares	Capitol P-4184
94(21/ 8)	85(4/ 9)	3	Free Spirit	Atlanta Rhythm Section	Polydor PD 14339
89(8/11)	28(27/12)	11	Full Of Fire	Al Green	Hi 5N 2300
97(23/10)	91(13/11)	4	Full Time Thing (Between Dusk & Dawn)	Whirlwind	Roulette 7195
96(6/12)	76(31/ 1)	9	Funky Weekend	Stylistics	Avco AV 4661
87(24/ 7)	58(18/ 9)	11	Funny How Time Slips Away	Dorothy Moore	Malaco 1033
90(28/ 2)	79(13/ 3)	4	Game Is Over (What's The Matter With You), The	Brown Sugar	Capitol P-4198
82(17/ 4)	9(21/ 8)	26	Get Closer	Seals & Crofts	Warner Bros WBS 8190
83(14/ 8)	30(9/10)	15	Get The Funk Out Ma Face	Brothers Johnson	A&M AM 1851
84(13/ 3)	2(12/ 6)	20	Get Up And Boogie	Silver Convention	Midland International MB 10571
69(14/ 8)	45(11/ 9)	7	Get Up Offa That Thing	James Brown	Polydor PD 14326
79(17/ 7)	12(9/10)	19	Getaway	Earth Wind & Fire	Columbia 3-10373
90(18/ 9)	70(2/10)	5	Gimme Your Money Please	Bachman-Turner Overdrive	Mercury 73843

Position and date of entry	Highest position and date	Wks.	Title	Artist(s)	Cat. No.
78(25/ 9)	38(13/11)	11	Give It Up (Turn It Loose) (Give Up The Funk) Tear The Roof Off The Sucker see under Tear	Tyrone Davis	Columbia 3-10388
87(22/11)	61(27/12)	7	Going Down Slowly	Pointer Sisters	ABC/Blue Thumb BTA 268
82(13/12)	10(10/ 4)	21	Golden Years	David Bowie	RCA PB-10441
64(7/ 2)	48(10/ 4)	12	Good Hearted Woman	Waylon & Willie	RCA PB-10529
71(5/ 6)	34(10/ 7)	8	Good Vibrations	Todd Rundgren	Bearsville BBS 0309
89(4/ 9)	56(25/ 9)	5	Goofus	Carpenters	A&M AM 1859
54(12/ 6)	7(24/ 7)	16	Got To Get You Into My Life	Beatles	Capitol P-4274
78(17/ 7)	53(14/ 8)	8	Gotta Be The One	Maxine Nightingale	United Artists UA XW820-Y
95(28/ 8)	95(28/ 8)	2	Grasshopper	Spin	Ariola America P-7632
88(16/10)	64(6/11)	5	Groovy People	Lou Rawls	Philadelphia International ZS8 3604
55(24/ 1)	14(28/ 2)	11	Grow Some Funk Of Your Own/I Feel Like A Bullet (In The Gun Of Robert Ford)	Elton John	MCA 40505
81(24/ 1)	67(21/ 2)	6	Growin' Up	Dan Hill	20th Century TC 2254
90(25/12)	90(25/12)	1	*Ha Cha Cha (Funktion)	Brass Construction	United Artists UA XW921-Y
86(18/12)	76(25/12)	2	*Happier	Paul Anka	United Artists UA XW911-Y
97(11/10)	66(20/12)	13	Happy	Eddie Kendricks	Tamla T-54263F
89(3/ 4)	5(5/ 6)	14	Happy Days	Pratt & McClain with Brotherlove	Reprise RPS 1351
98(19/ 6)	94(26/ 6)	2	Happy Man	Impact	Atco 45-7049
97(6/ 3)	19(22/ 5)	13	Happy Music	Blackbyrds	Fantasy F-762
74(18/12)	62(25/12)	2	*Hard Luck Woman	Kiss	Casablanca NB 873
93(26/ 6)	46(28/ 8)	12	Hard Work	John Handy	ABC/Impulse IMP 31005
92(21/ 8)	63(2/10)	11	Harvest For The World	Isley Brothers	T.Neck ZS8 2261
90(11/12)	86(25/12)	3	*Heart On My Sleeve	Bryan Ferry	Atlantic 45-3364
93(21/ 8)	67(11/12)	8	Heart On My Sleeve	Gallagher & Lyle	A&M AM 1850
86(5/ 6)	15(4/ 9)	21	Heaven Must Be Missing An Angel	Tavares	Capitol P-4270

Position and date of entry	Highest position and date	Wks.	Title	Artist(s)	Cat. No.
87(20/ 3)	47(24/ 4)	7	Heavy Love	David Ruffin	Motown M-1388F
84(17/ 7)	70(24/ 7)	3	Hell Cat	Bellamy Brothers	Warner Bros WBS 8220
70(16/10)	24(11/12)	11	*Hello Old Friend	Eric Clapton	RSO RS 861
86(6/11)	70(27/11)	5	Help Wanted	Hudson Brothers	Arista AS 0208
95(13/ 3)	65(10/ 4)	5	Here There And Everywhere	Emmylou Harris	Reprise RPS 1346
95(2/10)	82(16/10)	5	Here's Some Love	Tanya Tucker	MCA 40598
81(14/ 2)	49(1/ 5)	12	He's A Friend	Eddie Kendricks	Tamla T-54266F
96(25/12)	96(25/12)	1	*Hey Baby	J.J. Cale	Shelter SRL 62002
91(27/ 3)	72(24/ 4)	5	Hey Baby	Ted Nugent	Epic 8-50197
91(17/ 7)	48(4/ 9)	9	Hey Shirley (This Is Squirrely)	Shirley & Squirrely	Casino GRT 054
96(31/ 7)	95(7/ 8)	2	Hideaway	John Sebastian	Reprise RPS 1355
99(14/ 2)	68(20/ 3)	10	High Fly	John Miles	London 5N 20084
86(22/ 5)	76(29/ 5)	3	High Out Of Time	Carole King	Ode ODE-66123
79(28/ 2)	40(10/ 4)	8	Hit The Road Jack	Stampeders	Quality QA 501
90(17/ 1)	35(6/ 3)	10	Hold Back The Night	Trammps	Buddah BDA 507
90(19/ 6)	47(14/ 8)	10	Hold On	Sons Of Champlin	Ariola America P-7627
96(13/12)	90(27/12)	4	Hollywood Hot	Eleventh Hour	20th Century TC 2215
86(25/ 9)	71(16/10)	4	Home Tonight	Aerosmith	Columbia 3-10407
86(20/12)	41(21/ 2)	13	Homecoming, The	Hagood Hardy	Capitol P-4156
89(10/ 7)	59(7/ 8)	6	Honey Child	Bad Company	Swan Song SS-70109
80(10/ 1)	65(7/ 2)	5	Honey I	George McCrae	TK 1016
86(9/10)	12(25/12)	12	*Hot Line	Sylvers	Capitol P-4336
63(26/ 6)	49(17/ 7)	6	Hot Stuff/Fool To Cry	Rolling Stones	Rolling Stones RS 19304
			(Fool To Cry was the original A side, and its chart placings can be found under F)		
85(21/ 8)	61(18/ 9)	8	Howzat	Sherbet	MCA 40610
90(29/ 5)	82(19/ 6)	4	Hungry Years, The	Wayne Newton	Chelsea CH 3041
86(29/11)	33(10/ 1)	11	Hurricane	Bob Dylan	Columbia 3-10245
85(27/ 3)	28(29/ 5)	11	Hurt/For The Heart	Elvis Presley	RCA PB-10601
97(21/ 2)	94(6/ 3)	3	I Am Somebody	Jimmy James & the Vagabonds	Pye 71057
99(20/12)	95(3/ 1)	3	I Believe In Father Christmas	Greg Lake	Atlantic 45-3305
84(18/12)	80(25/12)	2	*I Can't Ask For Anymore Than You	Cliff Richard	Rocket PIG 40652
78(7/ 8)	29(11/ 9)	9	I Can't Hear You No More	Helen Reddy	Capitol P-4312
98(2/10)	46(13/11)	9	I Can't Live A Dream	Osmonds	Polydor PD 14348

Position and date of entry	Highest position and date	Wks.	Title	Artist(s)	Cat. No.
86(27/12)	60(17/ 1)	4	I Cheat The Hangman	Doobie Brothers	Warner Bros WBS 8161
86(10/ 1)	72(31/ 1)	4	I Could Have Danced All Night/ Jump For Joy	Biddu Orchestra	Epic 8-50173
86(14/ 2)	15(1/ 5)	15	I Do, I Do, I Do, I Do, I Do	Abba	Atlantic 45-3310
78(6/11)	51(4/12)	6	I Don't Wanna Lose Your Love	Emotions	Columbia 3-10347
			this is the B side of FLOWERS, which charted previously. For its chart placings see under F		
100(24/1)	100(24/1)	1	I Don't Want To Leave You	Debbie Taylor	Arista AS 0144
83(11/ 9)	43(23/10)	7	I Got To Know	Starbuck	Private Stock PS 45104
90(31/ 1)	43(20/ 3)	8	I Heard It Through The Grapevine	Creedence Clearwater Revival	Fantasy F-759
98(27/ 3)	91(26/ 6)	8	I Hope We Get To Love In Time	Marilyn McCoo & Billy Davis Jr.	ABC 12170
81(30/10)	46(11/12)	8	I Kinda Miss You	Manhattans	Columbia 3-10430
89(6/11)	30(25/12)	8	*I Like Dreamin'	Kenny Nolan	20th Century TC 2287
82(4/12)	47(25/12)	4	*I Like To Do It	KC & the Sunshine Band	TK 1020
70(1/11)	5(24/ 1)	17	I Love Music	O'Jays	Philadelphia International ZS8-3577
55(12/ 6)	25(24/ 7)	11	I Need To Be In Love	Carpenters	A&M AM 1828
86(3/ 7)	13(18/12)	20	*I Never Cry	Alice Cooper	Warner Bros WBS 8228
83(15/ 5)	35(22/ 5)	4	I.O.U.	Jimmy Dean	Casino GRT 052
83(4/ 9)	12(23/10)	16	I Only Want To Be With You	Bay City Rollers	Arista AS 0205
59(20/ 3)	47(3/ 4)	7	I Thought It Took A Little Time (But Today I Fell In Love)	Diana Ross	Motown M-1387F
100(10/4)	49(3/ 7)	14	I Wanna Stay With You	Gallagher & Lyle	A&M AM 1778
64(24/ 4)	15(26/ 6)	13	I Want You	Marvin Gaye	Tamla T-54264F
40(4/12)	7(25/12)	4	*I Wish	Stevie Wonder	Tamla T-54272F
48(15/11)	1(17/ 1)	20	I Write The Songs	Barry Manilow	Arista AS 0157
89(12/ 6)	2(25/ 9)	24	I'd Really Love To See You Tonight	England Dan & John Ford Coley	Big Tree BT 16069
84(16/10)	74(30/10)	4	If I Only Could	Rowans	Asylum E-45347
88(17/ 1)	65(28/ 2)	7	If I Only Knew	Ozark Mountain Daredevils	A&M AM 1772
100(14/2)	78(20/ 3)	7	If Love Must Go	Dobie Gray	Capricorn CPS 0249
85(27/11)	55(25/12)	5	*If Not You	Dr. Hook	Capitol P-4364

Position and date of entry	Highest position and date	Wks.	Title	Artist(s)	Cat. No.
55(19/ 6)	11(7/ 8)	12	If You Know What I Mean	Neil Diamond	Columbia 3-10366
60(14/ 8)	1(23/10)	20	*If You Leave Me Now	Chicago	Columbia 3-10390
90(21/ 2)	48(27/ 3)	7	If You Only Believe (Jesus For Tonight	Michel Polnareff	Atlantic 45-3314
88(1/ 5)	3(10/ 7)	17	I'll Be Good To You	Brothers Johnson	A&M AM 1806
83(12/ 6)	71(10/ 7)	6	I'll Get Over You	Crystal Gayle	United Artists UA XW781-Y
97(25/ 9)	80(9/10)	3	I'll Play The Fool	Dr. Buzzard's Original Savannah Band	RCA PB-10762
89(·8/ 5)	17(7/ 8)	19	I'm Easy	Keith Carradine	ABC 12117
98(29/ 5)	40(7/ 8)	14	I'm Gonna Let My Heart Do The Walking	Supremes	Motown M-1391F
85(10/ 4)	60(24/ 4)	4	I'm Mandy Fly Me	10cc	Mercury 73779
99(6/ 3)	91(3/ 4)	5	I'm So Lonesome I Could Cry	Terry Bradshaw	Mercury 73760
77(7/ 2)	66(14/ 2)	4	In France They Kiss On Main Street	Joni Mitchell	Asylum E-45298
86(13/12)	32(27/ 3)	17	Inseparable	Natalie Cole	Capitol P-4193
49(11/10)	1(1/11)	15	Island Girl	Elton John	MCA 40461
87(13/11)	49(25/12)	7	*It Keeps You Runnin'	Doobie Brothers	Warner Bros WBS 8282
81(19/ 6)	46(17/ 7)	8	It Keeps You Runnin'	Carly Simon	Elektra E-45323
80(8/ 5)	60(22/ 5)	4	It Makes Me Giggle	John Denver	RCA PB-10687
98(24/ 4)	85(22/ 5)	5	It Should Have Been Me	Yvonne Fair	Motown M-1323F
89(18/ 9)	28(4/12)	15	*It's A Long Way There	Little River Band	Harvest P-4318
86(8/ 5)	68(29/ 5)	4	It's Cool	Tymes	RCA PB-10561
87(21/ 8)	29(2/10)	10	It's O.K.	Beach Boys	Brother/ Reprise RPS 1368
88(11/ 9)	44(13/11)	11	It's Only Love	Z Z Top	London 5N-241
86(10/ 4)	38(29/ 5)	10	It's Over	Boz Scaggs	Columbia 3-10319
90(4/ 7)	81(7/ 8)	5	I've Been Lovin' You	Easy Street	Capricorn CPS 0255
88(27/ 3)	29(15/ 5)	10	I've Got A Feelin' (We'll Be Seeing Each Other Again)	Al Wilson	Playboy P-6062
83(21/ 2)	63(20/ 3)	6	Jam, The	Graham Central Station	Warner Bros WBS 8175
99(31/ 1)	87(28/ 2)	6	January	Pilot	EMI 4202
90(3/ 4)	69(1/ 5)	6	Jasper	Jim Stafford	Polydor PD-14309

Position and date of entry	Highest position and date	Wks.	Title	Artist(s)	Cat. No.
87(10/ 4)	73(1/ 5)	4	Jealousy	Major Harris	Atlantic 45-3321
90(9/10)	24(25/12)	10	*Jeans On	David Dundas	Chrysalis CHS 2094
88(5/ 6)	72(26/ 6)	4	Johnny Cool	Steve Gibbons Band	MCA 40551
90(5/ 6)	82(26/ 6)	4	Jukin'	Atlanta Rhythm Section	Polydor PD-14323
84(2/10)	72(23/10)	5	Jump	Aretha Franklin	Atlantic 45-3358
68(10/ 1)	9(20/ 3)	15	Junk Food Junkie	Larry Groce	Warner Bros WBS 8165
85(18/ 9)	7(27/11)	15	*Just To Be Close To You	Commodores	Motown M-1402F
67(7/ 2)	27(13/ 3)	9	Just You And I	Melissa Manchester	Arista AS 0168
84(7/ 2)	54(28/ 2)	6	Keep Holding On	Temptations	Gordy G-7146F
87(23/10)	38(25/12)	10	*Keep Me Cryin'	Al Green	Hi 5N-2319
93(24/ 4)	85(15/ 5)	4	Kentucky Moonrunner	Cledus Maggard & the Citizen's Band	Mercury 73789
87(10/ 7)	82(17/ 7)	3	Kid Charlemagne	Steely Dan	ABC 12195
99(17/ 4)	1(24/ 7)	26	Kiss And Say Goodbye	Manhattans	Columbia 3-10310
80(3/ 1)	48(14/ 2)	10	Lady Bump	Penny McLean	Atlantic 45-7038
99(27/11)	91(18/12)	4	Laid Back Love	Major Harris	WMOT WM-4002
52(12/ 6)	21(7/ 8)	15	Last Child	Aerosmith	Columbia 3-10359
44(15/11)	18(20/12)	8	Last Game Of The Season (A Blind Man In The Bleachers), The	David Geddes	Big Tree BT 16052
59(3/ 7)	3(14/ 8)	16	Let 'Em In	Wings	Capitol P-4293
98(1/ 5)	10(24/ 7)	20	Let Her In	John Travolta	Midland International MB-10623
77(22/ 5)	77(22/ 5)	3	Let It Shine	Santana	Columbia 3-10336
75(6/12)	30(17/ 1)	9	Let It Shine/ He Ain't Heavy — He's My Brother	Olivia Newton-John	MCA 40495
85(30/10)	80(13/11)	4	Let Me Down Easy	American Flyer	United Artists UA-XW874-Y
86(28/ 8)	86(28/ 8)	2	Let Me In	Derringer	Blue Sky ZS8-2765
70(27/12)	32(14/ 2)	9	Let The Music Play	Barry White	20th Century TC 2265
88(31/ 1)	1(1/ 5)	19	Let Your Love Flow	Bellamy Brothers	Warner Bros WBS 8169
100(18/9)	55(11/12)	13	Let's Be Young Tonight	Jermaine Jackson	Motown M-1401F
68(25/10)	1(27/12)	15	Let's Do It Again	Staple Singers	Curtom CMS 0109
83(23/10)	61(11/12)	8	Let's Get It Together	El Coco	AVIS 115
98(27/ 9)	35(10/ 1)	14	Let's Live Together	Road Apples	Polydor PD-14285

Position and date of entry	Highest position and date	Wks.	Title	Artist(s)	Cat. No.
90(10/ 4)	83(24/ 4)	4	Let's Make A Baby	Billy Paul	Philadelphia International ZS8 3584
97(28/ 8)	92(11/ 9)	3	Let's Rock	Ellison Chase	Big Tree BT 16072
89(17/ 7)	67(14/ 8)	5	Light Up The World With Sunshine	Hamilton, Joe Frank & Dennison	Playboy P-6077
74(11/ 9)	36(2/10)	7	Like A Sad Song	John Denver	RCA PB-10774
83(29/ 5)	61(26/ 6)	7	Lipstick	Michel Polnareff	Atlantic 45-3330
99(14/ 8)	96(28/ 8)	3	Listen To The Buddah	Ozo	DJM DJUS-1012
83(19/ 6)	11(9/10)	24	Little Bit More, A	Dr. Hook	Capitol P-4280
95(10/ 1)	95(10/ 1)	1	Little Drummer Boy, The	Moonlion	PIP 6513
83(5/ 6)	42(10/ 7)	8	Livin' Ain't Livin'	Firefall	Atlantic 45-3333
79(6/ 3)	20(24/ 4)	12	Livin' For The Weekend	O'Jays	Philadelphia International ZS8 3587
88(23/10)	15(25/12)	10	*Livin' Thing	Electric Light Orchestra	United Artists UA-XW888-Y
86(30/10)	72(13/11)	4	Livin' It Down	Freddy Fender	ABC/Dot DOA 17652
84(4/12)	53(25/12)	4	*Living Next Door To Alice	Smokie	RSO RS 860
88(14/ 2)	62(20/ 3)	8	Locomotive Breath	Jethro Tull	Chrysalis CHS 2110
69(24/ 1)	3(10/ 4)	18	Lonely Night (Angel Face)	Captain & Tennille	A&M AM 1782
94(29/ 5)	75(10/ 7)	8	Lonely One, The	Special Delivery featuring Terry Huff	Mainstream MRL 5581
82(22/ 5)	62(12/ 6)	4	Lonely Teardrops	Narvel Felts	ABC/Dot DOA 17620
84(24/ 4)	65(15/ 5)	6	Lookin' Out For #1	Bachman-Turner Overdrive	Mercury 73784
61(6/ 3)	29(10/ 4)	8	Looking For Space	John Denver	RCA PB-10586
90(14/ 2)	27(24/ 4)	14	Lorelei	Styx	A&M AM 1786
47(27/11)	22(25/12)	5	*Lost Without Your Love	Bread	Elektra E-45365
100(20/3)	77(8/ 5)	8	Love And Understanding (Come Together)	Kool & the Gang	DeLite DEP 1579
77(2/10)	20(11/12)	13	*Love Ballad	L.T.D.	A&M AM 1847
100(11/12)	94(25/12)	3	*Love Bug	Bumble Bee Unlimited	Mercury 73864
89(7/ 2)	30(10/ 4)	11	Love Fire	Jigsaw	Chelsea CH 3037
95(3/ 4)	80(24/ 4)	4	Love Hangover	5th Dimension	ABC 12181
78(3/ 4)	1(29/ 5)	18	Love Hangover	Diana Ross	Motown M-1392F
95(22/11)	8(13/ 3)	23	Love Hurts	Nazareth	A&M AM 1671
84(10/ 4)	16(29/ 5)	11	Love In The Shadows	Neil Sedaka	Rocket PIG 40543
83(17/ 4)	2(31/ 7)	27	Love Is Alive	Gary Wright	Warner Bros WBS 8143

154

Position and date of entry	Highest position and date	Wks.	Title	Artist(s)	Cat. No.
89(27/12)	30(20/ 3)	14	Love Is The Drug	Roxy Music	Atco 45-7042
100(13/3)	97(27/ 3)	3	Love Lifted Me	Kenny Rogers	United Artists UA-XW746-Y
90(25/10)	1(6/ 3)	28	Love Machine	Miracles	Tamla T-54262F
85(2/10)	14(25/12)	13	*Love Me	Yvonne Elliman	RSO RS 858
86(7/ 2)	56(28/ 2)	6	Love Me Tonight	Head East	A&M AM 1784
89(11/ 9)	64(9/10)	8	Love Of My Life	Gino Vannelli	A&M AM 1861
77(27/12)	36(7/ 2)	8	Love Or Leave	Spinners	Atlantic 45-3309
85(3/ 4)	22(22/ 5)	11	Love Really Hurts Without You	Billy Ocean	Ariola America/ GTO 7621
51(15/11)	1(31/ 1)	16	Love Rollercoaster	Ohio Players	Mercury 73734
70(18/ 9)	3(20/11)	15	*Love So Right	Bee Gees	RSO RS 859
72(11/12)	51(25/12)	3	*Love Theme From 'A Star Is Born' (Evergreen)	Barbra Streisand	Columbia 3-10450
55(6/12)	2(7/ 2)	18	Love To Love You Baby	Donna Summer	Oasis OC 401
82(3/ 7)	3(9/10)	22	Lowdown	Boz Scaggs	Columbia 3-10367
83(18/12)	73(25/12)	2	*Lucky Man	Starbuck	Private Stock PS 45125
92(18/ 9)	79(9/10)	5	Made To Love You	Gary Wright	Warner Bros WBS 8250
79(13/11)	36(25/12)	7	*Mademoiselle	Styx	A&M AM 1877
85(17/ 7)	9(6/11)	23	Magic Man	Heart	Mushroom M-7011
96(20/12)	76(7/ 2)	8	Make Love To Your Mind	Bill Withers	Columbia 3-10255
99(28/ 2)	96(13/ 3)	3	Make Me Smile (Come Up And See Me)	Steve Harley & Cockney Rebel	EMI 4201
97(6/11)	91(11/12)	6	Make You Blind	Glitter Band	Arista AS 0207
90(8/ 5)	25(3/ 7)	12	Making Our Dreams Come True (Theme from 'Laverne & Shirley')	Cyndi Greco	Private Stock PS 45086
83(22/ 5)	32(3/ 7)	9	Mamma Mia	Abba	Atlantic 45-3315
89(4/12)	65(25/12)	4	*Man Smart, Woman Smarter	Robert Palmer	Island IS 075
92(17/ 7)	79(31/ 7)	4	Mary Hartman, Mary Hartman (Theme)	Deadly Nightshade	Phantom HB 10709
81(11/ 9)	49(16/10)	9	Message In Our Music	O'Jays	Philadelphia International ZS8-3601
91(21/ 2)	69(27/ 3)	10	Mighty High	Mighty Clouds of Joy	ABC 12164
86(11/ 9)	49(30/10)	12	Mr. Melody	Natalie Cole	Capitol P-4328
69(20/ 3)	3(12/ 6)	22	Misty Blue	Dorothy Moore	Malaco 1029
51(7/ 2)	16(10/ 4)	15	Money Honey	Bay City Rollers	Arista AS 0170

Position and date of entry	Highest position and date	Wks.	Title	Artist(s)	Cat. No.
82(25/12)	82(25/12)	1	*Moody Blue/ She Thinks I Still Care	Elvis Presley	RCA PB-10857
90(17/ 4)	3(31/ 7)	22	Moonlight Feels Right	Starbuck	Private Stock PS 45039
99(1/ 5)	97(8/ 5)	2	Moonlight Serenade	Bobby Vinton	ABC 12178
98(13/ 3)	4(17/ 7)	25	More, More, More	Andrea True Connection	Buddah BDA 515
86(18/ 9)	5(25/12)	15	*More Than A Feeling	Boston	Epic 8-50266
90(31/ 7)	62(2/10)	12	More You Do It (The More I Like It Done To Me), The	Ronnie Dyson	Columbia 3-10356
84(3/ 4)	14(26/ 6)	16	Movin'	Brass Construction	United Artists UA-XW775-Y
74(13/ 3)	54(10/ 4)	5	Mozambique	Bob Dylan	Columbia 3-10298
90(15/ 5)	88(29/ 5)	3	Music	John Miles	London 5N-20086
68(25/ 9)	4(20/11)	14	*Muskrat Love	Captain & Tennille	A&M AM 1870
81(18/10)	9(13/12)	14	My Little Town	Simon & Garfunkel	Columbia 3-10230
95(11/ 9)	48(13/11)	11	My Sweet Summer Suite	Love Unlimited Orchestra	20th Century TC 2301
88(28/ 8)	8(11/12)	18	*Nadia's Theme (The Young & The Restless)	Barry DeVorzon & Perry Botkin Jr.	A&M AM 1856
78(1/ 5)	11(3/ 7)	15	Never Gonna Fall In Love	Eric Carmen	Arista AS 0184
48(18/12)	20(25/12)	2	*New Kid In Town	Eagles	Asylum E-45373
88(28/ 2)	70(27/ 3)	6	New Orleans	Staple Singers	Curtom CMS 0113
87(18/ 9)	30(13/11)	14	Nice 'N' Naasty	Salsoul Orchestra	Salsoul SZ-2011
85(11/12)	59(25/12)	3	*Night Moves	Bob Seger & the Silver Bullet Band	Capitol P-4369
97(29/ 5)	96(5/ 6)	2	Night Walk	Van McCoy	H&L 4667
76(9/10)	10(11/12)	12	*Nights Are Forever Without You	England Dan & John Ford Coley	Big Tree BT 16079
82(4/10)	7(13/12)	16	Nights On Broadway	Bee Gees	RSO RS 515
93(20/11)	54(25/12)	6	*9,999,999 Tears	Dickey Lee	RCA PB-10764
67(7/ 8)	60(28/ 8)	6	No, No, Joe	Silver Convention	Midland International MB-10723
97(5/ 6)	84(26/ 6)	5	Norma Jean Wants To Be A Movie Star	Sundown Company	Polydor PD 14312
98(7/ 2)	93(21/ 2)	3	Nursery Rhymes	People's Choice	TSOP ZS8 4773

Position and date of entry	Highest position and date	Wks.	Title	Artist(s)	Cat. No.
83(5/ 6)	69(19/ 6)	4	Nutbush City Limits	Bob Seger & the Silver Bullet Band	Capitol P-4269
79(20/11)	49(11/12)	6	*Ob-La-Di, Ob-La-Da	Beatles	Capitol P-4347
88(17/ 7)	54(14/ 8)	6	Ode To Billy Joe	Bobbie Gentry	Capitol P-4294
81(31/ 7)	65(14/ 8)	4	Ode To Billy Joe	Bobbie Gentry	Warner Bros WBS 8210

The Capitol version was originally released in 1967. The Warner Bros. came from the soundtrack of the film of the same name, released during 1976.

Position and date of entry	Highest position and date	Wks.	Title	Artist(s)	Cat. No.
90(6/ 3)	82(27/ 3)	4	Once A Fool	Kiki Dee	Rocket PIG 40506
93(10/ 1)	79(7/ 2)	5	Once You Hit The Road	Dionne Warwick	Warner Bros WBS 8154
94(17/ 1)	93(24/ 1)	4	One Fine Day	Julie	Tom Cat YB 10454
98(28/ 8)	88(18/ 9)	10	One For The Money	Whispers	Soul Train SB-10700
58(7/ 8)	25(2/10)	12	One Love In My Lifetime	Diana Ross	Motown M-1398F
			(One More Year Of) Daddy's Little Girl see under D		
71(17/ 4)	29(29/ 5)	10	One Piece At A Time	Johnny Cash & the Tennessee Three	Columbia 3-10321
77(14/ 2)	28(10/ 4)	11	Only Love Is Real	Carole King	Ode ODE 66119
85(3/ 1)	6(17/ 4)	22	Only Sixteen	Dr. Hook	Capitol P-4174
100(8/ 5)	81(3/ 7)	9	Open	Smokey Robinson	Tamla T-54267F
95(6/11)	77(25/12)	8	*Open Sesame	Kool & the Gang	De-Lite DEP 1586
82(20/ 3)	66(10/ 4)	4	Ophelia	Band	Capitol P-4230
85(18/10)	11(20/12)	12	Our Day Will Come	Frankie Valli	Private Stock PS 45043
93(7/ 8)	89(21/ 8)	3	Out Of The Darkness	David Crosby/ Graham Nash	ABC 12199
91(8/11)	20(17/ 1)	14	Over My Head	Fleetwood Mac	Reprise RPS 1339
90(29/11)	26(31/ 1)	15	Paloma Blanca	George Baker Selection	Warner Bros WBS 8115
74(8/11)	22(27/12)	11	Part Time Love	Gladys Knight & the Pips	Buddah BDA 513
78(14/ 8)	69(11/ 9)	5	Party	Van McCoy	H&L 4670
92(7/ 8)	80(28/ 8)	4	Party Line	Andrea True Connection	Buddah BDA 538
98(23/10)	84(27/11)	6	Peter Gunn	Deodato	MCA 40631
75(13/12)	49(10/ 1)	6	Play On Love	Jefferson Starship	Grunt FB-10456
96(19/ 6)	1(18/ 9)	25	Play That Funky Music	Wild Cherry	Epic 8-50225
87(7/ 8)	43(18/ 9)	8	Popsicle Toes	Michael Franks	Reprise RPS 1360
93(14/ 8)	78(18/ 9)	6	Princess And The Punk, The	Barry Mann	Arista AS 0194

Position and date of entry	Highest position and date	Wks.	Title	Artist(s)	Cat. No.
93(25/12)	93(25/12)	1	*Prisoner (Captured By Your Eyes)	L.A. Jets	RCA PB-10826
85(13/ 3)	66(10/ 4)	5	Queen Of Clubs	KC & the Sunshine Band	TK 1005
82(4/ 9)	40(16/10)	8	Queen Of My Soul	Average White Band	Atlantic 45-3354
86(17/ 1)	61(21/ 2)	7	Quiet Storm	Smokey Robinson	Tamla T-54265F
93(29/ 5)	76(26/ 6)	7	Rain, Oh Rain	Fools Gold	Morning Glory MS 700
87(19/ 6)	52(4/ 9)	12	Rainbow In Your Eyes	Leon & Mary Russell	Paradise PDS 8208
96(21/ 2)	90(13/ 3)	4	Rattlesnake	Ohio Players	Westbound W 5018
87(16/10)	80(30/10)	3	Raven, The	Alan Parsons Project	20th Century TC 2308
83(31/ 7)	12(6/11)	20	(Don't Fear) The Reaper	Blue Oyster Cult	Columbia 3-10384
85(10/ 1)	67(28/ 2)	8	Remember Me	Willie Nelson	Columbia 3-10275
72(24/ 1)	39(21/ 2)	7	Renegade	Michael Murphey	Epic 8-50184
90(7/ 8)	78(21/ 8)	3	Rescue Me	Melissa Manchester	Arista AS 0196
89(6/ 3)	11(5/ 6)	18	Rhiannon (Will You Ever Win)	Fleetwood Mac	Reprise RPS 1345
95(14/ 2)	2(1/ 5)	20	Right Back Where We Started From	Maxine Nightingale	United Artists UA-XW752-Y
56(15/11)	12(24/ 1)	14	Rock And Roll All Nite (Live Version)	Kiss	Casablanca NB 850
67(1/ 5)	28(12/ 6)	9	Rock And Roll Love Letter	Bay City Rollers	Arista AS 1085
75(5/ 6)	5(14/ 8)	17	Rock And Roll Music	Beach Boys	Brother/Reprise RPS 1354
96(17/ 7)	93(31/ 7)	3	Rock Creek Park	Blackbyrds	Fantasy F-771
85(14/ 8)	1(6/11)	18	Rock 'N' Me	Steve Miller Band	Capitol P-4323
83(24/ 7)	76(11/ 9)	8	Rocky Mountain Music	Eddie Rabbitt	Elektra E-45315
73(4/ 7)	51(17/ 7)	6	Roots, Rock, Reggae	Bob Marley & the Wailers	Island IS 060
94(14/ 8)	94(14/ 8)	1	Rose Of Cimarron	Poco	ABC 12204
90(21/ 8)	90(21/ 8)	2	Roxy Roller	Sweeney Todd	London 5N-240
99(18/ 9)	99(18/ 9)	1	Roxy Roller	Sweeney Todd featuring Brian Guy Adams	London 5N-244
			(the first version was withdrawn owing to some legal problems, followed by the second version which was the same backing track with a new lead vocalist)		
84(11/ 9)	2(4/12)	16	*Rubber Band Man, The	Spinners	Atlantic 45-3355

Position and date of entry	Highest position and date	Wks.	Title	Artist(s)	Cat. No.
81(4/12)	64(25/12)	4	*St. Charles	Jefferson Starship	Grunt FB-10791
89(20/ 3)	69(10/ 4)	4	Sally	Grand Funk Railroad	Capitol P-4235
91(31/ 1)	4(26/ 6)	28	Sara Smile	Daryl Hall & John Oates	RCA PB-10530
80(11/ 9)	73(25/ 9)	3	Satin Sheets	Bellamy Brothers	Warner Bros WBS 8248
85(11/10)	1(3/ 1)	17	Saturday Night	Bay City Rollers	Arista AS 0149
78(20/11)	26(25/12)	6	*Saturday Nite	Earth Wind & Fire	Columbia 3-10439
87(11/12)	67(25/12)	3	*Save It For A Rainy Day	Stephen Bishop	ABC 12232
98(8/ 5)	27(10/ 7)	11	Save Your Kisses For Me	Brotherhood of Man	Pye 71066
85(29/ 5)	75(12/ 6)	3	Save Your Kisses For Me	Bobby Vinton	ABC 12186
74(3/ 7)	11(18/ 9)	19	Say You Love Me	Fleetwood Mac	Reprise RPS 1356
100(3/ 7)	98(10/ 7)	2	Say You Love Me	D.J. Rogers	RCA PB-10568
81(29/11)	33(27/12)	7	School Boy Crush	Average White Band	Atlantic 45-3304
98(31/ 1)	75(27/ 3)	9	Scotch On The Rocks	Band of the Black Watch	Private Stock PS 45055
79(10/ 7)	1(11/ 9)	21	(Shake Shake Shake) Shake Your Booty	KC & the Sunshine Band	TK 1019
85(16/10)	25(25/12)	11	*Shake Your Rump To The Funk	Bar Kays	Mercury 73833
84(28/ 2)	6(5/ 6)	20	Shannon	Henry Gross	Lifesong LS 45002
90(13/11)	84(11/12)	5	Sherry	Keane Brothers	20th Century TC 2302
73(24/ 7)	7(30/10)	20	She's Gone	Daryl Hall & John Oates	Atlantic 45-3332
			(She's Just A) Fallen Angel see under Fallen		
62(1/ 5)	4(10/ 7)	16	Shop Around	Captain & Tennille	A&M AM 1817
81(20/ 3)	31(1/ 5)	10	Shout It Out Loud	Kiss	Casablanca NB 854
88(21/ 2)	6(8/ 5)	18	Show Me The Way	Peter Frampton	A&M AM 1693
84(7/ 8)	59(28/ 8)	7	Showdown	Electric Light Orchestra	United Artists UA XW842-Y
83(3/ 7)	22(18/ 9)	16	Shower The People	James Taylor	Warner Bros WBS 8222
58(10/ 4)	1(22/ 5)	19	Silly Love Songs	Wings	Capitol P-4256
97(11/12)	95(18/12)	2	Silver Heels	Blaze	Epic 8-50292
82(29/ 5)	38(10/ 7)	8	Silver Star	Four Seasons	Warner Bros WBS 8203
86(24/ 1)	71(28/ 2)	6	Since I Fell For You	Charlie Rich	Epic 8-50182
73(22/11)	5(7/ 2)	17	Sing A Song	Earth Wind & Fire	Columbia 3-10251
90(27/11)	65(18/12)	4	Sixteen Reasons	Laverne & Shirley	Atlantic 45-3367

US TITLE

159

Position and date of entry	Highest position and date	Wks.	Title	Artist(s)	Cat. No.
99(24/ 4)	47(12/ 6)	9	Sixteen Tons	Don Harrison Band	Atlantic 45-3323
88(30/ 8)	3(6/12)	21	Sky High	Jigsaw	Chelsea CH-3022
93(6/11)	63(25/12)	8	*Slow Dancing	Funky Kings	Arista AS 0209
77(13/12)	20(13/ 3)	17	Slow Ride	Foghat	Bearsville BBS 0306
89(9/10)	47(6/11)	8	So Sad The Song	Gladys Knight & the Pips	Buddah BDA 544
100(24/7)	100(24/7)	1	Solitary Man	T.G. Sheppard	Hitsville H-6032F
45(27/11)	19(25/12)	5	*Somebody To Love	Queen	Elektra E-45362
61(5/ 6)	33(4/ 7)	7	Somebody's Gettin' It	Johnnie Taylor	Columbia 3-10334
89(30/10)	85(13/11)	3	Someday	Henry Gross	Lifesong LS 45014
78(4/12)	46(25/12)	4	*Someone To Lay Down Beside Me	Linda Ronstadt	Asylum E-45361
81(12/ 6)	28(14/ 8)	12	Something He Can Feel	Aretha Franklin	Atlantic 45-3326
85(6/12)	19(14/ 2)	14	Somewhere In The Night	Helen Reddy	Capitol P-4192
89(29/ 5)	25(7/ 8)	16	Sophisticated Lady (She's A Different Lady)	Natalie Cole	Capitol P-4259
54(13/11)	6(25/12)	7	*Sorry Seems To Be The Hardest Word	Elton John	Rocket PIG 40645
89(6/12)	75(3/ 1)	5	Soul Train '75'	Soul Train Gang	Soul Train SB-10400
97(25/12)	97(25/12)	1	*Spend Some Time	Elvin Bishop	Capricorn CPS 0266
100(3/4)	97(17/ 4)	3	Spirit In The Night	Manfred Mann's Earthband	Warner Bros WBS 8152
80(18/12)	70(25/12)	2	*Spring Affair	Donna Summer	Casablanca NB 872
85(10/ 7)	37(21/ 8)	10	Springtime Mama	Henry Gross	Lifesong LS 45008
89(29/11)	16(14/ 2)	16	Squeeze Box	Who	MCA 40475
74(9/10)	11(25/12)	12	*Stand Tall	Burton Cummings	Portrait 6-7001
67(26/ 6)	36(31/ 7)	9	Steppin' Out	Neil Sedaka	Rocket PIG 40582
75(1/ 5)	40(29/ 5)	7	Still Crazy After All These Years	Paul Simon	Columbia 3-10332
69(31/ 7)	5(23/10)	18	Still The One	Orleans	Asylum E-45336
71(13/ 3)	14(22/ 5)	14	Strange Magic	Electric Light Orchestra	United Artists UA XW770-Y
90(17/ 7)	27(18/ 9)	12	Street Singin'	Lady Flash	RSO RS 852
84(6/ 3)	56(3/ 4)	6	Street Talk	B.C. Generation	20th Century TC 2271
89(10/ 1)	89(10/ 1)	2	Strong Enough To Be Gentle	Black Oak Arkansas	MCA 40496
85(24/ 7)	68(14/ 8)	4	Struttin' My Stuff	Elvin Bishop	Capricorn CPS 0256
80(10/ 7)	7(25/ 9)	16	Summer	War	United Artists UA XW834-Y
98(11/ 9)	96(25/ 9)	3	Sun...Sun...Sun	Ja kki	Pyramid PD 8004
86(14/ 8)	34(2/10)	10	Sunrise	Eric Carmen	Arista AS 0200
88(7/ 8)	35(25/ 9)	9	Superstar	Paul Davis	Bang BDJ 726
82(27/12)	5(24/ 4)	23	Sweet Love	Commodores	Motown M-1381F
93(7/ 2)	93(7/ 2)	2	Sweet Loving Man	Morris Albert	RCA PB-10437
97(4/ 9)	94(2/10)	6	Sweet Summer Music	Attitudes	Dark Horse DH-10011

Position and date of entry	Highest position and date	Wks.	Title	Artist(s)	Cat. No.
82(3/ 1)	5(3/ 4)	21	**Sweet Thing**	Rufus featuring Chaka Khan	ABC 12149
			(The System Of) Doctor Tarr & Professor Fether *see under* **Doctor**		
83(21/ 8)	41(2/10)	9	**Take A Hand**	Rick Springfield	Chelsea CH-3051
60(7/ 2)	33(13/ 3)	7	**Take It Like A Man**	Bachman-Turner Overdrive	Mercury 73766
80(20/12)	*4(13/ 3)*	22	**Take It To The Limit**	Eagles	Asylum E-45293
73(24/ 1)	53(7/ 2)	5	**Take Me**	Grand Funk Railroad	Capitol P-4199
85(8/ 5)	11(24/ 7)	16	**Take The Money And Run**	Steve Miller Band	Capitol P-4260
72(17/ 4)	13(26/ 6)	14	**Takin' It To The Streets**	Doobie Brothers	Warner Bros WBS 8196
70(24/ 1)	25(10/ 4)	13	**Tangerine**	Salsoul Orchestra	Salsoul SZ 2004
86(15/ 5)	15(31/ 7)	17	**(Give Up The Funk) Tear The Roof Off The Sucker**	Parliament	Casablanca NB 856
67(24/ 7)	40(28/ 8)	9	**Teddy Bear**	Red Sovine	Starday SD-142
90(4/ 9)	66(2/10)	6	**Teddy Bear's Last Ride**	Diana Williams	Capitol P-4317
99(17/ 1)	72(14/ 2)	6	**Tell It Like It Is**	Andy Williams	Columbia 3-10263
96(17/ 4)	94(24/ 4)	2	**Tell The World How I Feel About 'Cha Baby**	Harold Melvin & the Blue Notes	Philadelphia International ZS8 3588
88(19/ 6)	54(7/ 8)	9	**Ten Percent**	Double Exposure	Salsoul SZ 2008
91(24/ 1)	83(7/ 2)	3	**Tenth Avenue Freeze-Out**	Bruce Springsteen	Columbia 3-10274
99(7/ 2)	91(28/ 2)	4	**Texas**	Charlie Daniels Band	Kama Sutra KA 607
71(21/ 8)	11(23/10)	16	**That'll Be The Day**	Linda Ronstadt	Asylum E-45340
50(25/10)	*1(22/11)*	16	**That's The Way (I Like It)**	KC & the Sunshine Band	TK 1015
96(10/ 4)	27(26/ 6)	15	**That's Where The Happy People Go**	Trammps	Atlantic 45-3306
84(3/ 1)	68(24/ 1)	5	**That's Why I Love You**	Andrew Gold	Asylum E-45286
89(1/11)	*1(24/ 1)*	17	**Theme From Mahogany 'Do You Know Where You're Going To'**	Diana Ross	Motown M-1377F
90(25/11)	1(28/ 2)	24	**Theme From S.W.A.T.**	Rhythm Heritage	ABC 12135
75(28/ 2)	12(24/ 4)	13	**There's A Kind Of Hush**	Carpenters	A&M AM 1800

Position and date of entry	Highest position and date	Wks.	Title	Artist(s)	Cat. No.
90(27/ 3)	73(17/ 4)	4	There Won't Be No Country Music (There Won't Be No Rock 'N' Roll)	C.W. McCall	Polydor PD 14301
90(30/10)	89(13/11)	3	Things	Anne Murray	Capitol P-4329
90(24/ 4)	45(12/ 6)	9	Thinking Of You	Paul Davis	Bang BDJ 724
100(24/4)	91(22/ 5)	5	This Is It	Melba Moore	Buddah BDA 519
87(12/ 6)	10(28/ 8)	19	This Masquerade	George Benson	Warner Bros WBS 8209
90(10/ 1)	83(31/ 1)	4	This Old Heart Of Mine	Rod Stewart	Warner Bros WBS 8170
99(22/11)	*48(27/12*	*8*	This Old Man	Purple Reign	Private Stock PS 45052
82(18/ 9)	29(30/10)	10	This One's For You	Barry Manilow	Arista AS 0206
82(20/11)	27(25/12)	6	*This Song	George Harrison	Dark Horse DH 8294
100(1/ 5)	84(22/ 5)	5	'Til I Can Make It On My Own	Tammy Wynette	Epic 8-50196
79(10/ 1)	44(28/ 2)	9	'Til It's Time To Say Goodbye	Jonathan Cain	October OCT 1001
57(15/11)	*7(7/ 2)*	*20*	Times Of Your Life	Paul Anka	United Artists UA XW737-Y
81(15/ 5)	23(10/ 7)	12	Today's The Day	America	Warner Bros WBS 8212
100(10/1)	99(24/ 1)	4	Tonight's The Night	S.S.O.	Shadybrook 45019
81(2/10)	1(13/11)	13	*Tonight's The Night	Rod Stewart	Warner Bros WBS 8262
87(20/11)	29(25/12)	6	*Torn Between Two Lovers	Mary MacGregor	Ariola America P-7638
100(5/ 6)	98(12/ 6)	2	Touch & Go	Ecstasy, Passion & Pain	Roulette 7182
83(20/12)	*25(28/ 2)*	*13*	The Tracks Of My Tears	Linda Ronstadt	Asylum E-45295
98(28/ 2)	86(13/ 3)	4	Train Called Freedom	South Shore Commission	Wand WND 11294
88(10/ 7)	80(24/ 7)	4	Try Me, I Know We Can Make It	Donna Summer	Oasis OC-406
67(20/ 3)	10(22/ 5)	15	Tryin' To Get The Feeling Again	Barry Manilow	Arista AS 0172
100(29/5)	98(5/ 6)	2	Tubular Bells	Champs' Boys	Janus J-259
93(10/ 4)	10(14/ 8)	25	Turn The Beat Around	Vicki Sue Robinson	RCA PB-10562
79(22/ 5)	64(5/ 6)	5	TVC 15	David Bowie	RCA PB-10664
97(7/ 2)	24(22/ 5)	20	Union Man	Cate Bros	Asylum E-45294
95(17/ 7)	94(31/ 7)	3	Up The Creek (Without A Paddle)	Temptations	Gordy G-7150F
83(6/ 3)	80(20/ 3)	3	Uptown & Country	Tom Scott	Ode ODE 66118
99(3/ 1)	97(10/ 1)	3	Valentine Love	Norman Connors	Buddah BDA 499

Position and date of entry	Highest position and date	Wks.	Title	Artist(s)	Cat. No.
87(29/ 5)	59(26/ 6)	6	**Vaya Con Dios**	Freddy Fender	ABC/Dot DOA 17627
98(24/ 1)	46(6/ 3)	8	**Venus**	Frankie Avalon	DeLite DEP 1578
94(1/11)	33(20/12)	10	**Volare**	Al Martino	Capitol P-4134
82(22/11)	12(28/ 2)	17	**Wake Up Everybody**	Harold Melvin & the Blue Notes	Philadelphia International ZS8 3579
83(17/ 7)	56(7/ 8)	5	**Wake Up Susan**	Spinners	Atlantic 45-3341
90(8/11)	9(24/ 1)	15	**Walk Away From Love**	David Ruffin	Motown M-1376F
90(20/11)	28(25/12)	6	***Walk This Way**	Aerosmith	Columbia 3-10449
93(25/ 9)	76(23/10)	6	**Wanna Make Love (Come Flick My BIC)**	Sun	Capitol P-4254
80(27/ 9)	4(29/11)	17	**Way I Want To Touch You, The**	Captain & Tennille	A&M AM 1725
83(14/ 2)	36(10/ 4)	10	**We Can't Hide It Anymore**	Larry Santos	Casablanca NB 844
78(27/11)	35(25/12)	5	***Weekend In New England**	Barry Manilow	Arista AS 0212
84(27/ 3)	1(8/ 5)	14	**Welcome Back**	John Sebastian	Reprise RPS 1349
90(14/ 8)	78(28/ 8)	3	**We're All Alone**	Frankie Valli	Private Stock PS 45098
96(10/ 1)	94(24/ 1)	4	**We're On The Right Track**	South Shore Commission	Wand WN 11291
97(19/ 6)	16(2/10)	21	**Wham Bam (Shang-A-Lang)**	Silver	Arista AS 0189
85(20/11)	42(25/12)	6	***What Can I Say**	Boz Scaggs	Columbia 3-10440
78(24/ 1)	69(7/ 2)	4	**What's The Name Of This Funk (Spider Man)**	Ramsey Lewis	Columbia 3-10235
92(28/ 8)	87(4/ 9)	2	**Wheels Of Fortune**	Doobie Brothers	Warner Bros WBS 8233
61(10/ 4)	41(1/ 5)	6	**When Love Has Gone Away**	Richard Cocciante	20th Century TC 2275
88(25/12)	88(25/12)	1	***When Love Is New**	Arthur Prysock	Old Town 1000
70(30/10)	38(4/12)	6	**Whenever I'm Away From You**	John Travolta	Midland International MB-10780
81(17/ 4)	68(1/ 5)	6	**Where Did Our Love Go**	J. Geils Band	Atlantic 45-3320
98(6/11)	33(25/12)	8	***Whispering/ Cherchez La Femme/Se Si Bon**	Dr. Buzzard's Original Savannah Band	RCA PB-10827
96(11/12)	91(25/12)	3	***White Bird**	David LaFlamme	Amherst 717
87(27/12)	19(13/ 3)	15	**White Knight, The**	Cledus Maggard & the Citizen's Band	Mercury 73751
88(23/ 8)	3(15/11)	20	**Who Loves You**	Four Seasons	Warner Bros WBS 8122

Position and date of entry	Highest position and date	Wks.	Title	Artist(s)	Cat. No.
86(29/ 5)	47(19/ 6)	7	Who Loves You Better	Isley Brothers	T-Neck ZS8-2260
81(26/ 6)	18(18/ 9)	17	Who'd She Coo	Ohio Players	Mercury 73814
99(19/ 6)	95(4/ 7)	4	Will You Love Me Tomorrow	Dana Valery	Phantom JB-10566
87(8/11)	21(24/ 1)	15	Winners And Losers	Hamilton, Joe Frank & Reynolds	Playboy P-6054
69(24/ 7)	12(18/ 9)	17	With Your Love	Jefferson Starship	Grunt FB-10746
81(28/ 2)	42(3/ 4)	7	Without Your Love (Mr. Jordan)	Charlie Ross	Big Tree BT 16056
87(29/11)	44(17/ 1)	9	Woman Tonight	America	Warner Bros WBS 8157
93(27/ 3)	87(24/ 4)	6	Words (Are Impossible)	Donny Gerrard	Greedy G 101
100(6/ 3)	95(20/ 3)	3	Wow	Andre Gagnon	London 5N-230
70(28/ 8)	2(20/11)	18	*Wreck Of The Edmund Fitzgerald, The	Gordon Lightfoot	Reprise RPS 1369
98(11/12)	84(25/12)	3	*Year Of The Cat	Al Stewart	Janus J-266
84(8/ 5)	46(12/ 6)	10	Yes, Yes, Yes	Bill Cosby	Capitol P-4258
77(11/12)	56(25/12)	3	*Yesterday's Hero	Bay City Rollers	Arista AS 0216
100(13/12)	42(24/ 1)	9	Yesterday's Hero	John Paul Young	Ariola America P-7607
94(13/ 3)	79(17/ 4)	7	You Are Beautiful	Stylistics	Avco AV 4664
83(28/ 8)	27(6/11)	16	You Are My Starship	Norman Connors	Buddah BDA 542
82(21/ 8)	9(11/12)	19	*You Are The Woman	Firefall	Atlantic 45-3335
90(11/ 9)	2(25/12)	16	*You Don't Have To Be A Star (To Be In My Show)	Marilyn McCoo & Billy Davis Jr.	ABC 12208
96(1/ 5)	87(22/ 5)	4	You Got The Magic	John Fogerty	Elektra E-45309
77(25/ 9)	53(16/10)	5	You Gotta Make Your Own Sunshine	Neil Sedaka	Rocket PIG 40614
68(23/10)	4(25/12)	10	*You Make Me Feel Like Dancing	Leo Sayer	Warner Bros WBS 8283
86(16/10)	68(27/11)	8	You Ought To Be Havin' Fun	Tower Of Power	Columbia 3-10409
86(1/11)	3(7/ 2)	21	You Sexy Thing	Hot Chocolate	Big Tree BT 10647
67(3/ 7)	1(4/ 9)	20	You Should Be Dancing	Bee Gees	RSO RS 853
94(17/ 7)	86(7/ 8)	4	You To Me Are Everything	Broadway	Granite G 540
93(17/ 7)	64(28/ 8)	8	You To Me Are Everything	Real Thing	United Artists UA XW833-Y
99(31/ 7)	98(7/ 8)	2	You To Me Are Everything	Revelation	RSO RS 854
85(14/ 2)	32(10/ 4)	10	You'll Lose A Good Thing	Freddy Fender	ABC/Dot DOA 17607

Position and date of entry	Highest position and date	Wks.	Title	Artist(s)	Cat. No.
79(5/ 6)	2(4/ 9)	21	You'll Never Find Another Love Like Mine	Lou Rawls	Philadelphia International ZS8-3593
72(20/ 3)	20(22/ 5)	13	Young Blood	Bad Company	Swan Song SS 70108
73(29/ 5)	20(14/ 8)	16	Young Hearts Run Free	Candi Staton	Warner Bros WBS 8181
97(24/ 1)	93(31/ 1)	2	Young Love	Ray Stevens	Barnaby B-618
87(17/ 1)	87(17/ 1)	3	You're Fooling You	Dramatics	ABC 12150
95(29/ 5)	88(26/ 6)	5	You're Just The Right Size	Salsoul Orchestra	Salsoul SZ 2007
78(22/ 5)	16(31/ 7)	16	You're My Best Friend	Queen	Elektra E-45318
93(4/12)	85(25/12)	4	*You're My Driving Wheel	Supremes	Motown M-1407F
80(22/ 5)	58(26/ 6)	6	You're My Everything	Lee Garrett	Chrysalis CHS 2112
90(4/12)	60(25/12)	4	*You've Got Me Runnin'	Gene Cotton	ABC 12227
96(29/11)	91(13/12)	6	Zip, The	MFSB	Philadelphia International ZS8-3578

Section 8

US Artist Section

(Billboard Top 100 Singles Chart)

This section lists, under artist headings, the titles, writers and producers of all singles that made the *Billboard* Top 100 chart during 1976.

The tracks on double A sides are separated by obliques, to which writers' and producers' credits correspond.

When a group is credited with writing a song, the names of the members of that group will be listed in brackets beneath the name of the group. There are certain cases where an individual group member will be credited with writing a song as well as the group (i.e. Lionel Richie and the Commodores). Presumably this is when the group write the music and the individual writes the lyrics—or vice versa.

Artist(s)/Title	Writer(s)	Producer(s)
ABBA		
Dancing Queen	Benny Andersson	Benny Andersson
	Stig Anderson	Bjorn Ulvaeus
	Bjorn Ulvaeus	
Fernando	Benny Andersson	Benny Andersson
	Stig Anderson	Bjorn Ulvaeus
	Bjorn Ulvaeus	
I Do, I Do, I Do, I Do, I Do	Benny Andersson	Benny Andersson
	Stig Anderson	Bjorn Ulvaeus
	Bjorn Ulvaeus	
Mamma Mia	Benny Andersson	Benny Andersson
	Stig Anderson	Bjorn Ulvaeus
	Bjorn Ulvaeus	
AEROSMITH		
Dream On	Steven Tyler	Adrian Barber
Home Tonight	Steven Tyler	Jack Douglas
		Aerosmith
		(Tom Hamilton
		Joey Kramer
		Joe Perry
		Steven Tyler
		Brad Whitford)
Last Child	Steven Tyler	Jack Douglas
	Brad Whitford	
Walk This Way	Steven Tyler	Jack Douglas
	Joe Perry	
Morris **ALBERT**		
Feelings	Morris Albert	Morris Albert
Sweet Loving Man	Morris Albert	Morris Albert
AMAZING RHYTHM ACES		
Amazing Grace (Used To Be Her Favorite Song)	H. Russell Smith	Barry 'Byrd' Burton
The End Is Not In Sight (The Cowboy Tune)	H. Russell Smith	Barry 'Byrd' Burton
AMERICA		
Amber Cascades	Dewey Bunnell	George Martin
Today's The Day	Dan Peek	George Martin
Woman Tonight	Dan Peek	George Martin
AMERICAN FLYER		
Let Me Down Easy	Eric Kaz	George Martin
	Craig Fuller	
Paul **ANKA**		
Anytime (I'll Be There)	Paul Anka	Denny Diante
Happier	Paul Anka	Denny Diante
Times Of Your Life	Roger Nichols	Bob Skaff
	Bill Lane	
ATLANTA DISCO BAND		
Bad Luck	John Whitehead	Dave Crawford
	Gene McFadden	
	Victor Carstarphen	

Artist(s)/Title	Writer(s)	Producer(s)
ATLANTA RHYTHM SECTION		
Free Spirit	Buddy Buie Robert Nix Ronnie Hammond	Buddy Buie
Jukin'	Buddy Buie Robert Nix	Buddy Buie
ATTITUDES		
Sweet Summer Music	Paul Stallworth Chuck Higgins Jr. Gilbert Bottiglier	Attitudes (Jim Keltner Paul Stallworth Danny Kootch David Foster)
Frankie AVALON		
Venus	Ed Marshall	Billy Terrell
AVERAGE WHITE BAND		
Queen Of My Soul	Hamish Stuart	Arif Mardin
School Boy Crush	Hamish Stuart Steve Ferrone Alan Gorrie	Arif Mardin
BACHMAN-TURNER OVERDRIVE		
Down To The Line	Randy Bachman	Randy Bachman
Gimme Your Money Please	C.F. Turner	Randy Bachman
Lookin' Out For # 1	Randy Bachman	Randy Bachman
Take It Like A Man	C.F. Turner Blair Thornton	Randy Bachman
BAD COMPANY		
Honey Child	Bad Company	Bad Company (Mick Ralphs Paul Rodgers Simon Kirke Boz Burrell)
Young Blood	Jerry Leiber Mike Stoller Doc Pomus	Bad Company
George BAKER SELECTION		
Paloma Blanca	Johannes Bouwens	Hans Bouwens
BAND		
Ophelia	Robbie Robertson	The Band (Robbie Robertson Garth Hudson Rick Danko Richard Manuel Levon Helm)
BAND OF THE BLACK WATCH		
Scotch On The Rocks	Bill Bates	Barry Kingston

Artist(s)/Title	Writer(s)	Producer(s)
BAR-KAYS		
Shake Your Rump To The Funk	Bar Kays	Allen Jones
	(James Alexander	
	Charles Allen	
	Michael Beard	
	Larry Dodson	
	Harvey Henderson	
	Lloyd Smith	
	Winston Stewart	
	Frank Thompson)	
BAY CITY ROLLERS		
I Only Want To Be With You	Mike Hawker	Jimmy Ienner
	Ivor Raymonde	
Money Honey	Eric Faulkner	Phil Wainman
	Stuart 'Woody' Wood	
Rock And Roll Love Letter	Tim Moore	Colin Frechter
Saturday Night	Bill Martin	Bill Martin
	Phil Coulter	Phil Coulter
Yesterday's Hero	Harry Vanda	Jimmy Ienner
	George Young	
B.C. GENERATION		
Street Talk	Bob Crewe	Bob Crewe
	Cindy Bullens	
BEACH BOYS		
It's O.K.	Brian Wilson	Brian Wilson
	Mike Love	
Rock And Roll Music	Chuck Berry	Brian Wilson
BEATLES		
Got To Get You Into My Life	John Lennon	George Martin
	Paul McCartney	
Ob-La-Di, Ob-La-Da	John Lennon	George Martin
	Paul McCartney	
BEE GEES		
Fanny (Be Tender With My Love)	Bee Gees	Arif Mardin
	(Barry, Robin	
	& Maurice Gibb)	
Love So Right	Bee Gees	Bee Gees
Nights On Broadway	Bee Gees	Arif Mardin
You Should Be Dancing	Bee Gees	Bee Gees
BELLAMY BROTHERS		
Hell Cat	David Bellamy	Phil Gernhard
		Tony Scotti
Let Your Love Flow	Larry E. Williams	Phil Gernhard
		Tony Scotti
Satin Sheets	Willis Alan Ramsey	Phil Gernhard
		Tony Scotti
George BENSON		
Breezin'	Bobby Womack	Tommy LiPuma
This Masquerade	Leon Russell	Tommy LiPuma

US ARTIST

Artist(s)/Title	Writer(s)	Producer(s)
BIDDU ORCHESTRA		
I Could Have Danced All Night/ Jump For Joy	Alan Jay Lerner Frederick Loewe/ Lee Vanderbilt Biddu	Biddu
Elvin **BISHOP**		
Fooled Around And Fell In Love	Elvin Bishop	Allan Blazek Bill Szymczyk
Spend Some Time	Elvin Bishop	Allan Blazek
Struttin' My Stuff	Elvin Bishop Phil Aaberg	Allan Blazek Bill Szymczyk
Stephen **BISHOP**		
Save It For A Rainy Day	Stephen Bishop	Henry Lewy Stephen Bishop
BLACK OAK ARKANSAS		
Strong Enough To Be Gentle	Black Oak Arkansas (Tommy Aldridge Jim Dandy Pat Daugherty 'Little' Jimmy Henderson Rickie Lee Reynolds)	Richard Podolor
BLACKBYRDS		
Happy Music	Donald Byrd	Donald Byrd
Rock Creek Park	Blackbyrds (Stephen Johnson Orville Saunders Kevin Toney Joe Hall Keith Killgo)	Donald Byrd
BLAZE		
Silver Heels	Robert Welch	Stan Hertzman Blaze (Richy Ceccolini Crunchy Kosta Tom Mackno Paul Sanchez Sam Wuhrer)
BLUE OYSTER CULT		
(Don't Fear) The Reaper	Donald Roeser	Murray Krugman Sandy Pearlman David Lucas
BOSTON		
More Than A Feeling	Tom Scholz	John Boylan Tom Scholz
David **BOWIE**		
Golden Years	David Bowie	David Bowie Harry Maslin
TVC 15	David Bowie	David Bowie Harry Maslin
Terry **BRADSHAW**		
I'm So Lonesome I Could Cry	Hank Williams	Jerry Kennedy

Artist(s)/Title	Writer(s)	Producer(s)
BRASS CONSTRUCTION		
Ha Cha Cha (Funktion)	Randy Muller	Jeff Lane
Movin'	Randy Muller	Jeff Lane
	Wade Williamson	
BREAD		
Lost Without Your Love	David Gates	David Gates
BRICK		
Dazz	Regi Hargis	Jim Healy
	Eddie Irons	Johnny Duncan
	Ray Ransom	Robert E. Lee
		Brick
		(Jimmy 'Lord' Brown
		Regi Hargis
		Eddie Irons
		Don Nevins
		Ray Ransom)
Johnny BRISTOL		
Do It To My Mind	Johnny Bristol	Johnny Bristol
BROADWAY		
You To Me Are Everything	Ken Gold	Tony Silvester
	Micky Denne	
BROTHERHOOD OF MAN		
Save Your Kisses For Me	Tony Hiller	Tony Hiller
	Lee Sheriden	
	Martin Lee	
BROTHERS JOHNSON		
Get The Funk Out Ma Face	Quincy Jones	Quincy Jones
	George Johnson	
	Louis Johnson	
I'll Be Good To You	George Johnson	Quincy Jones
	Louis Johnson	
	Senora Sam	
James BROWN		
Get Up Offa That Thing	Deanna Brown	James Brown
	Deidra Brown	
	Yamma Brown	
BROWN SUGAR		
The Game Is Over (What The Matter With You)	Ronnie B. Walker	
	Vince Montana Jr.	Vince Montana Jr.
B.T. EXPRESS		
Can't Stop Groovin' Now, Wanna Do It Some More	Billy Nichols	Jeff Lane
Close To You	Burt Bacharach	Jeff Lane
	Hal David	
BUMBLE BEE UNLIMITED		
Love Bug	Patrick Adams	Greg Carmichael
		Patrick Adams
Jonathan CAIN		
'Til It's Time To Say Goodbye	Jonathan Cain	J.C. Phillips
J.J. CALE		
Hey Baby	J.J. Cale	Audie Ashworth

Artist(s)/Title	Writer(s)	Producer(s)
Glen CAMPBELL		
Country Boy (You Got Your Feet In L.A.)	Dennis Lambert Brian Potter	Dennis Lambert Brian Potter
Don't Pull Your Love/Then You Can Tell Me Goodbye	Dennis Lambert Brian Potter/ John D. Loudermilk	Dennis Lambert Brian Potter
CAPTAIN & TENNILLE		
Lonely Night (Angel Face)	Neil Sedaka	The Captain (Daryl Dragon) Toni Tennille
Muskrat Love	Willis Alan Ramsey	The Captain Toni Tennille
Shop Around	William Robinson Berry Gordy	The Captain Toni Tennille
The Way I Want To Touch You	Toni Tennille	Morgan Cavett
Eric CARMEN		
All By Myself	Eric Carmen	Jimmy Ienner
Never Gonna Fall In Love Again	Eric Carmen	Jimmy Ienner
Sunrise	Eric Carmen	Jimmy Ienner
CARPENTERS		
Goofus	Wayne King William Harold Gus Kahn	Richard Carpenter
I Need To Be In Love	Richard Carpenter John Bettis Albert Hammond	Richard Carpenter
There's A Kind Of Hush	Les Reed Geoff Stephens	Richard Carpenter
Keith CARRADINE		
I'm Easy	Keith Carradine	Richard Baskin
Johnny CASH		
One Piece At A Time	Wayne Kemp	Charlie Bragg Don Davis
Terry CASHMAN		
Baby, Baby I Love You	Terry Cashman Tommy West	Terry Cashman Tommy West
CATE BROS		
Can't Change My Heart	Earl & Ernie Cate	Steve Cropper
Union Man	Earl & Ernie Cate Steve Cropper	Steve Cropper
C.C. & COMPANY		
Daydreamer	Terry Dempsey	Mike Theodore Dennis Coffey
CHAMPS BOYS		
Tubular Bells	Mike Oldfield	Patrick Boceno
Harry CHAPIN		
Better Place To Be, A	Harry Chapin	Fred Kewley
Ellison CHASE		
Let's Rock	Ellison Chase Gary Askeras	Jeff Kasenetz Jerry Katz Ritchie Cordell

Artist(s)/Title	Writer(s)	Producer(s)
CHEECH & CHONG		
Framed	Jerry Leiber	Lou Adler
	Mike Stoller	
	Thomas Chong	
	Richard Marin	
CHICAGO		
Another Rainy Day In New York City	Robert Lamm	James William Guercio
If You Leave Me Now	Peter Cetera	James William Guercio
Eric CLAPTON		
Hello Old Friend	Eric Clapton	Rob Fraboni
Richard COCCIANTE		
When Love Has Gone Away	Richard Cocciante	Catherine Arnoul
	Marco Luberti	
	Danielle Rouby	
Natalie COLE		
Inseparable	Chuck Jackson	Chuck Jackson
	Marvin Yancy	Marvin Yancy
Mr. Melody	Chuck Jackson	Chuck Jackson
	Marvin Yancy	Marvin Yancy
Sophisticated Lady (She's A Different Lady)	Chuck Jackson	Chuck Jackon
	Marvin Yancy	Marvin Yancy
	Natalie Cole	Gene Barge
		Richard Evans
COMMODORES		
Just To Be Close To You	Lionel Richie	James Carmichael
	Commodores	Commodores
		(William King
		Ronald LaPraed
		Tom McClary
		Walter Orange
		Lionel Richie
		Milan Williams)
Sweet Love	Lionel Richie	James Carmichael
	Commodores	Commodores
Norman CONNORS		
Valentine Love	Michael Henderson	Skip Drinkwater
You Are My Starship	Michael Henderson	Skip Drinkwater
		Jerry Schoenbaum
Alice COOPER		
I Never Cry	Alice Cooper	Bob Ezrin
	Dick Wagner	
Bill COSBY		
Yes, Yes, Yes	Stu Gardner	Stu Gardner
	Bill Cosby	
Gene COTTON		
You've Got Me Runnin'	Parker McGee	Steve Gibson
Billy 'Crash' CRADDOCK		
Easy As Pie	Rory Bourke	Ron Chancey
	Johnny Wilson	
	Gene Dobbins	

Artist(s)/Title	Writer(s)	Producer(s)
CREEDENCE CLEARWATER REVIVAL		
I Heard It Through The Grapevine	Norman Whitfield	John C. Fogerty
	Barrett Strong	
Jim CROCE		
Chain Gang Medley	Sam Cooke	Terry Cashman
	Jerry Butler	Tommy West
	Calvin Carter	
	Curtis Mayfield	
	Jerry Leiber	
	Mike Stoller	
David CROSBY/Graham NASH		
Out Of The Darkness	Craig Degree	David Crosby
	David Crosby	Graham Nash
	Graham Nash	
CROWN HEIGHTS AFFAIR		
Every Beat Of My Heart	Freida Nerangis	Freida Nerangis
	Britt Britton	Britt Britton
Foxy Lady	Freida Nerangis	Freida Nerangis
	Britt Britton	Britt Britton
Burton CUMMINGS		
Stand Tall	Burton Cummings	Richard Perry
Charlie DANIELS BAND		
Texas	Charlie Daniels	Paul Hornsby
Mac DAVIS		
Forever Lovers	Sterling Whipple	Rick Hall
Paul DAVIS		
Superstar	Paul Davis	Paul Davis
Thinking Of You	Paul Davis	Paul Davis
Tyrone DAVIS		
Give It Up (Turn It Loose)	Leo Graham	Leo Graham
DEADLY NIGHTSHADE		
Mary Hartman, Mary Hartman (Theme)	Barry White	Michael Manieri
Jimmy DEAN		
I.O.U.	Larry Markes	Jack Wiedemann
	Jimmy Dean	
Kiki DEE		
Once A Fool	Dennis Lambert	Robert Appere
	Brian Potter	
(see also Elton JOHN & Kiki DEE)		
Rick DEES & HIS CAST OF IDIOTS		
Disco Duck	Rick Dees	Bobby Manuel
John DENVER		
Baby, You Look Good To Me Tonight	Bill Danoff	Milton Okun
Christmas For Cowboys	Steve Weisberg	Milton Okun
Fly Away	John Denver	Milton Okun
It Makes Me Giggle	John Denver	Milton Okun
Like A Sad Song	John Denver	Milton Okun
Looking For Space	John Denver	Milton Okun

Artist(s)/Title	Writer(s)	Producer(s)
DEODATO		
Peter Gunn	Henry Mancini	Eumir Deodato
DERRINGER		
Let Me In	Rick Derringer	Rick Derringer
	Cynthia Weil	
Barry DeVORZON & Perry		
BOTKIN Jr.		
Nadia's Theme (The Young & The		
Restless)	Barry DeVorzon	Barry DeVorzon
	Perry Botkin Jr.	Perry Botkin Jr.
Neil DIAMOND		
Don't Think . . . Feel	Neil Diamond	Robbie Robertson
If You Know What I Mean	Neil Diamond	Robbie Robertson
DISCO TEX & THE		
SEX-O-LETTES		
Dancin' Kid	Kenny Nolan	Kenny Nolan
DR. BUZZARD's ORIGINAL		
'SAVANNAH' BAND		
I'll Play The Fool	Stony Browder Jr.	Sander Linzer
	August Darnell	
Whispering/Cherchez La Femme/		
Se Si Bon	John Schonberger	Sandy Linzer
	Richard Coburn	
	Vincent Rose/	
	Stony Browder Jr.	
	August Darnell/	
	Stony Browder Jr.	
	August Darnell	
DR. HOOK		
If Not You	Dennis Locorriere	Ron Haffkine
A Little Bit More	Bobby Gosh	Ron Haffkine
Only Sixteen	Sam Cooke	Ron Haffkine
DOOBIE BROTHERS		
I Cheat The Hangman	Pat Simmons	Ted Templeman
It Keeps You Runnin'	Michael McDonald	Ted Templeman
Takin' It To The Streets	Michael McDonald	Ted Templeman
Wheels Of Fortune	Pat Simmons	Ted Templeman
	Jeff Baxter	
	John Hartman	
DOUBLE EXPOSURE		
Ten Percent	Allan Felder	Ronnie Baker
	T.G. Conway	Norman Harris
		Earl Young
DRAMATICS		
You're Fooling You	Tony Hester	Tony Hester
David DUNDAS		
Jeans On	David Dundas	Roger Greenaway
	Roger Greenaway	
Bob DYLAN		
Hurricane	Bob Dylan	Don DeVito
	Jacques Levy	
Mozambique	Bob Dylan	Don DeVito
	Jacques Levy	

US ARTIST

Artist(s)/Title	Writer(s)	Producer(s)
Ronnie DYSON		
The More You Do It (The More I Like It Done To Me)	Marvin Yancy Chuck Jackson	Marvin Yancy Chuck Jackson
EAGLES		
New Kid In Town	John David Souther Don Henley Glenn Frey	Bill Szymczyk
Take It To The Limit	Randy Meisner Don Henley Glenn Frey	Bill Szymczyk
EARTH WIND & FIRE		
Can't Hide Love	Skip Scarborough	Maurice White Charles Stepney
Getaway	Beloyd Taylor Peter Cor	Maurice White Charles Stepney
Saturday Nite	Maurice White Al McKay Philip Bailey	Maurice White Charles Stepney
Sing A Song	Maurice White Al McKay	Maurice White Charles Stepney
EASY STREET		
I've Been Lovin' You	Easy Street Pete Zorn	Dennis Weinreich Easy Street (Richard Burgess Peter Marsh Ken Nicol)
ECSTASY PASSION & PAIN		
Touch & Go	Norman Harris Allan Felder Bunny Sigler	Bobby Martin
EL COCO		
Let's Get It Together	Merria Ross	Lauren Render Michael Lewis
ELECTRIC LIGHT ORCHESTRA		
Evil Woman	Jeff Lynne	Jeff Lynne
Livin' Thing	Jeff Lynne	Jeff Lynne
Showdown	Jeff Lynne	Jeff Lynne
Strange Magic	Jeff Lynne	Jeff Lynee
ELEVENTH HOUR		
Hollywood Hot	Bob Crewe Cindy Bullens	Bob Crewe
Yvonne ELLIMAN		
Love Me	Barry & Robin Gibb	Freddie Perren
EMOTIONS		
Flowers	Maurice White Al McKay	Maurice White
I Don't Wanna Lose Your Love	Jean & Wanda Hutchingson	Maurice White Charles Stepney
ENGLAND DAN & JOHN FORD COLEY		
I'd Really Love To See You Tonight	Parker McGee	Kyle Lehning
Nights Are Forever	Parker McGee	Kyle Lehning

Artist(s)/Title	Writer(s)	Producer(s)
Yvonne FAIR		
It Should Have Been Me	Norman Whitfield William Stevenson	Norman Whitfield
Narvel FELTS		
Lonely Teardrops	Berry Gordy Jr. Gwendolyn Gordy Tyran Carlo	Johnny Morris
Freddy FENDER		
Livin' It Down	Ben Peters	Huey P. Meaux
Vaya Con Dios	Larry Russell Buddy Pepper Inez James	Huey P. Meaux
You'll Lose A Good Thing	Barbara Lynn Ozen	Huey P. Meaux
Bryan FERRY		
Heart On My Sleeve	Benny Gallagher Graham Lyle	Chris Thomas Bryan Ferry
5th DIMENSION		
Love Hangover	Pam Sawyer Marilyn McLeod	Marc Gordon
FIREFALL		
Livin' Ain't Livin'	Rick Roberts	Jim Mason
You Are The Woman	Rick Roberts	Jim Mason
FLASH CADILLAC AND THE CONTINENTAL KIDS		
Did You Boogie With Your Baby (In The Back Row Of The Movie Show)	Rod McQueen	Joe Renzetti
FLEETWOOD MAC		
Over My Head	Christine McVie	Keith Olsen Fleetwood Mac (Christine McVie Mick Fleetwood Lindsey Buckingham Stevie Nicks John McVie)
Rhiannon (Will You Ever Win)	Stevie Nicks	Keith Olsen Fleetwood Mac
Say You Love Me	Christine McVie	Keith Olsen Fleetwood Mac
John FOGERTY		
You Got The Magic	John Fogerty	John Fogerty
FOGHAT		
Drivin' Wheel	Dave Peverett Rod Price	Don Hartman
Fool For The City	Dave Peverett	Nick Jameson
Slow Ride	Dave Peverett	Nick Jameson
FOOLS GOLD		
Rain, Oh Rain	Denny Henson	Glenn Frey
FOUR SEASONS		
December, 1963 (Oh, What A Night)	Bob Gaudio Judy Parker	Bob Gaudio
Silver Star	Bob Gaudio Judy Parker	Bob Gaudio

Artist(s)/Title	Writer(s)	Producer(s)
Who Loves You	Bob Gaudio Judy Parker	Bob Gaudio
FOUR TOPS Catfish	Lawrence Payton Fred Bridges Mikki Farrow	Lawrence Payton
Peter FRAMPTON Baby I Love Your Way Do You Feel Like We Do Show Me The Way	Peter Frampton Peter Frampton Peter Frampton	Peter Frampton Peter Frampton Peter Frampton
Aretha FRANKLIN Jump Something He Can Feel	Curtis Mayfield Curtis Mayfield	Curtis Mayfield Curtis Mayfield
Michael FRANKS Popsicle Toes	Michael Franks	Tommy LiPuma
FUNKY KINGS Slow Dancing	Jack Tempchin	Paul A. Rothchild
Andre GAGNON Wow	Andre Gagnon	Andre Gagnon Peter Tessier
GALLAGHER & LYLE Heart On My Sleeve	Benny Gallagher Graham Lyle	David Kershenbaum
I Wanna Stay With You	Benny Gallagher Graham Lyle	David Kershenbaum
Art GARFUNKEL Breakaway	Benny Gallagher Graham Lyle	Richard Perry
Lee GARRETT You're My Everything	Lee Garrett Robert Taylor	Eric Malamud Tom Sellers
Marvin GAYE After The Dance	Marvin Gaye Leon Ware	Leon Ware
I Want You	Leon Ware T-Boy Ross	Leon Ware T-Boy Ross
Crystal GAYLE I'll Get Over You	Richard Leigh	Allen Reynolds
GAYLORD & HOLIDAY Eh! Cumpari	Public Domain	Sam Locricchio
David GEDDES The Last Game Of The Season (A Blind Man In The Bleachers)	Sterling Whipple	Paul Vance
J. GEILS BAND Where Did Our Love Go	Eddie Holland Lamont Dozier Brian Holland	Ahmet Ertegun
Bobbie GENTRY Ode To Billy Joe	Bobbie Gentry	Kelly Gordon Bobby Paris
Ode To Billy Joe	Bobbie Gentry	Marshall Lieb

Artist(s)/Title	Writer(s)	Producer(s)
Donny GERRARD		
Words (Are Impossible)	Luigi Albertelli	Henry Grumpo Marx
	Bobby Hart	Robbie Buchanan
	Danny Janssen	
	Enrico Riccardi	
Steve GIBBONS BAND		
Johnny Cool	Steve Gibbons	Ken Laguna
GLITTER BAND		
Makes You Blind	Mike Leander	Mike Leander
	Peter Phipps	
	Gerry Shephard	
Andrew GOLD		
That's Why I Love You	Andrew Gold	Charles Plotkin
	Gene Garfin	
GRAHAM CENTRAL STATION		
The Jam	Larry Graham	Larry Graham
GRAND FUNK RAILROAD		
Can You Do It	Thelma Gordy	Frank Zappa
	Richard Street	
Sally	Mark Farner	Jimmy Ienner
Take Me	Don Brewer	Jimmy Ienner
	Craig Frost	
Dobie GRAY		
Find 'Em, Fool 'Em & Forget 'Em	George Jackson	Rick Hall
	Roe Hall	
If Love Must Go	Will Jennings	Troy Seals
		Dobie Gray
Cyndi GRECO		
Making Our Dreams Come True		
(Theme from 'Laverne & Shirley')	Charles Fox	Charles Fox
	Norman Gimbel	Janna Merlyn Feliciano
Al GREEN		
Full Of Fire	Willie Mitchell	Willie Mitchell
	Al Green	
	Mabon Hughes	
Keep Me Cryin'	Willie Mitchell	Willie Mitchell
	Al Green	Al Green
Larry GROCE		
Junkfood Junkie	Larry Groce	Randolph Nauert
Henry GROSS		
Shannon	Henry Gross	Terry Cashman
		Tommy West
Someday	Henry Gross	Terry Cashman
		Tommy West
Springtime Mama	Henry Gross	Terry Cashman
		Tommy West
Daryl HALL & John OATES		
Do What You Want, Be What You Are	Daryl Hall	Christopher Bond
	John Oates	

Artist(s)/Title	Writer(s)	Producer(s)
Sara Smile	Daryl Hall John Oates	Christopher Bond Daryl Hall John Oates
She's Gone	Daryl Hall John Oates	Arif Mardin
HAMILTON, JOE, FRANK & DENNISON		
Don't Fight The Hands (That Need You)	Jimmy George Robert Caldwell	John D'Andrea
Light Up The World With Sunshine	Ben Findon Geoff Wilkens	John D'Andrea
HAMILTON, JOE, FRANK & REYNOLDS		
Everyday Without You	Dan Hamilton	Dan Hamilton Joe Frank Carollo Alan Dennison
Winners And Losers	Dan & Ann Hamilton	Dan Hamilton Joe Frank Carollo Alan Dennison
John HANDY		
Hard Work	John Handy	Esmond Edwards
Hagood HARDY		
The Homecoming	Hagood Hardy	Peter Anastasoff
Steve HARLEY & COCKNEY REBEL		
Make Me Smile (Come Up And See Me)	Steve Harley	Steve Harley Alan Parsons
Emmylou HARRIS		
Here There And Everywhere	John Lennon Paul McCartney	Brian Ahern
Rod HART		
C.B. Savage	Rod Hart	Rod Hart
Major HARRIS		
Jealousy	Joseph Jefferson Charles Simmons	Ron Kersey Major Harris
Laid Back Love	Bobby Eli Len Barry	Bobby Eli
Don HARRISON BAND		
Sixteen Tons	Merle Travis	Don Harrison Band (Doug Clifford Stu Cook Russell Da Shiell Don Harrison)
George HARRISON		
This Song	George Harrison	George Harrison
Justin HAYWARD & John LODGE		
Blue Guitar	Justin Hayward	Tony Clarke 10cc (Lol Creme Kevin Godley Graham Gouldman Eric Stewart)

Artist(s)/Title	Writer(s)	Producer(s)
HEAD EAST		
Love Me Tonight	Michael Somerville	Roger Boyd
HEART		
Crazy On You	Ann & Nancy Wilson	Mike Flicker
Dreamboat Annie	Ann & Nancy Wilson	Mike Flicker
Magic Man	Ann & Nancy Wilson	Mike Flicker
HEYETTES		
The Fonz Song	Michael S. Fein	Jackie Mills
Dan HILL		
Growin' Up	Dan Hill	Matthew McCauley
		Fred Mollin
HOT CHOCOLATE		
Don't Stop It Now	Errol Brown	Mickie Most
You Sexy Thing	Errol Brown	Mickie Most
	Tony Wilson	
Thelma HOUSTON		
Don't Leave Me This Way	Kenny Gamble	Hal Davis
	Leon Huff	
	Cary Gilbert	
HUDSON BROTHERS		
Help Wanted	Chris Bond	Dennis Lambert
		Brian Potter
Engelbert HUMPERDINCK		
After The Lovin'	Richie Adams	Joel Diamond
	Alan Bernstein	Charlie Calello
IMPACT		
Happy Man	Bobby Eli	Bobby Eli
	Charles Kelly	
ISLEY BROTHERS		
For The Love Of You	Isley Brothers	Isley Brothers
		(Ernie Isley
		Marvin Isley
		Chris Jasper
		Ronald Isley
		O'Kelly Isley
		Rudolph Isley)
Harvest For The World	Isley Brothers	Isley Brothers
Who Loves You Better	Isley Brothers	Isley Brothers
Jermaine JACKSON		
Let's Be Young Tonight	Michael L. Smith	Michael L. Smith
	Don Daniels	
Walter JACKSON		
Feelings	Morris Albert	Carl Davis
JACKSONS		
Enjoy Yourself	Kenny Gamble	Kenny Gamble
	Leon Huff	Leon Huff
JA KKI		
Sun Sun Sun	Johnnymelfi	Johnnymelfi
Jimmy JAMES & THE VAGABONDS		
I Am Somebody	Biddu	Biddu

US ARTIST

Artist(s)/Title	Writer(s)	Producer(s)
JEFFERSON STARSHIP		
Play On Love	Grace Slick Pete Sears	Larry Cox Jefferson Starship (Marty Balin Grace Slick Paul Kantner Pete Sears Craig Chaquico Papa John Creach David Freiberg John Barbata)
St. Charles	Paul Kantner Martin Balin Thunderhawk Craig Chaquico Jesse Barish	Larry Cox Jefferson Starship (minus Papa John Creach)
With Your Love	Marty Balin Joey Covington Victor Smith	Larry Cox Jefferson Starship (minus Papa John Creach)
Waylon JENNINGS		
Can't You See (see also: WAYLON & WILLIE)	Toy Caldwell	Waylon Jennings Ken Mansfield
JETHRO TULL		
Locomotive Breath	Ian Anderson	Ian Anderson Terry Ellis
JIGSAW		
Brand New Love Affair	Charles Graham Iris May	Chas Peate
Love Fire	Des Dyer Clive Scott	Chas Peate
Sky High	Des Dyer Clive Scott	Chas Peate
Elton JOHN		
Grow Some Funk Of Your Own/ I Feel Like A Bullet (In The Gun Of Robert Ford)	Elton John Bernie Taupin Davey Johnstone/ Elton John- Bernie Taupin	Gus Dudgeon
Island Girl	Elton John Bernie Taupin	Gus Dudgeon
Sorry Seems To Be The Hardest Word	Elton John Bernie Taupin	Gus Dudgeon
Elton JOHN & Kiki DEE		
Don't Go Breaking My Heart	Ann Orson Carte Blanche	Gus Dudgeon
JULIE		
One Fine Day	Gerry Goffin Carole King	Herb Bernstein

Artist(s)/Title	Writer(s)	Producer(s)
KANSAS		
Carry On Wayward Son	Kerry Livgren	Jeff Glixman
KC & THE SUNSHINE BAND		
I Like To Do It	Harry Wayne Casey	Harry Wayne Casey
	Richard Finch	Richard Finch
Queen Of Clubs	Harry Wayne Casey	Richard Finch
	Willie Clarke	
(Shake Shake Shake) Shake Your Booty	Harry Wayne Casey	Harry Wayne Casey
	Richard Finch	Richard Finch
That's The Way I Like It	Harry Wayne Casey	Harry Wayne Casey
	Richard Finch	Richard Finch
KEANE BROTHERS		
Sherry	Dwayn Ford	David Foster
Eddie KENDRICKS		
Happy	Leonard Caston	Frank Wilson
	Kathy Wakefield	Leonard Caston
He's A Friend	Allan Felder	Norman Harris
	Bruce Gray	
	T.G. Conway	
Carole KING		
High Out Of Time	Gerry Goffin	Lou Adler
	Carole King	
Only Love Is Real	Carole King	Lou Adler
KISS		
Beth/Detroit Rock City	Peter Criss	Bob Ezrin
	Stan Penridge	
	Bob Ezrin/	
	Paul Stanley	
	Bob Ezrin	
Flaming Youth	Ace Frehley	Bob Ezrin
	Paul Stanley	
	Gene Simmons	
Hard Luck Woman	Paul Stanley	Eddie Kramer
Rock And Roll All Nite (Live Version)	Paul Stanley	Eddie Kramer
	Gene Simmons	
Shout It Out Loud	Gene Simmons	Bob Ezrin
	Paul Stanley	
	Bob Ezrin	
Gladys KNIGHT & THE PIPS		
Part Time Love	David Gates	Kenny Kerner
		Richie Wise
So Sad The Song	Michael Masser	Michael Masser
	Gerry Goffin	

Artist(s)/Title	Writer(s)	Producer(s)
KOOL & THE GANG		
Love And Understanding (Come Together)	Claydes Smith Ronald Bell Kool & the Gang	Kool & the Gang (Ronald Bell Claydes Smith George M. Brown Dennis Thomas Spike Mickens Ricky West Otha Nash Larry Gittens Robert 'Kool' Bell)
Open Sesame	Ronald Bell Kool & the Gang	Kool & the Gang
LADY FLASH		
Street Singin'	Barry Manilow Adrienne Anderson	Barry Manilow Ron Dante
David LaFLAMME		
White Bird	David & Linda LaFlamme	David LaFlamme
L.A. JETS		
Prisoner (Captured By Your Eyes)	Karen Lawrence John DeSautels	Gary Klein
Greg LAKE		
I Believe In Father Christmas	Greg Lake Pete Sinfield	Greg Lake Pete Sinfield
D.C. LaRUE		
Ca-the-drals	D.C. LaRue Aram Schefrin	Aram Schefrin D.C. LaRue
LAVERNE & SHIRLEY		
Sixteen Reasons	Bill & Doree Post	Sidney Sharp Jimmie Haskell
Dickey LEE		
9,999,999 Tears	Razzy Bailey	Roy Dea Dickey Lee
Ramsey LEWIS		
What's The Name Of This Funk (Spider Man)	Charles Stepney Morris Stewart Derf Reklaw Raheem	Charles Stepney Ramsey Lewis
Gordon LIGHTFOOT		
The Wreck Of The Edmund Fitzgerald	Gordon Lightfoot	Lenny Waronker Gordon Lightfoot
LITTLE RIVER BAND		
It's A Long Way There	Graham Goble	Glenn Wheatley Beeb Birtles Graham Goble Glenn Shorrock
LOVE UNLIMITED ORCHESTRA		
My Sweet Summer Suite	Barry White	Barry White

Artist(s)/Title	Writer(s)	Producer(s)
L.T.D.		
Love Ballad	Skip Scarborough	Larry & Fonce Mizell
		Chuck Davis
LYNYRD SKYNYRD		
Double Trouble	Allen Collins	Tom Dowd
	Ronnie Van Zant	
Free Bird	Allen Collins	Tom Dowd
	Ronnie Van Zant	
Cledus MAGGARD & THE CITIZEN'S BAND		
Kentucky Moonrunner	Jay Huguely	Jerry Kennedy
	Jerry Kennedy	
The White Knight	Jay Huguely	Jerry Kennedy
	Jerry Kennedy	
Melissa MANCHESTER		
Better Days	Melissa Manchester	Vini Poncia
	Carole Bayer Sager	
Just You And I	Melissa Manchester	Vini Poncia
	Carole Bayer Sager	
Rescue Me	Carl Smith	Vini Poncia
	Raynard Miner	
MANHATTANS		
I Kinda Miss You	Wilfred Lovett	Bobby Martin
		Manhattans
		(Gerald Austin
		Sonny Bivins
		Kenny Kelly
		Wilfred Lovett
		Richard Taylor)
Kiss And Say Goodbye	Wilfred Lovett	Bobby Martin
		Manhattans
Barry MANILOW		
I Write The Songs	Bruce Johnston	Ron Dante
		Barry Manilow
This One's For You	Barry Manilow	Ron Dante
	Marty Panzer	Barry Manilow
Tryin' To Get The Feeling Again	David Pomeranz	Ron Dante
		Barry Manilow
Weekend In New England	Randy Edelman	Ron Dante
		Barry Manilow
Barry MANN		
The Princess And The Punk	Barry Mann	Dennis Lambert
	Cynthia Weil	Brian Potter
Manfred MANN'S EARTHBAND		
Blinded By The Light	Bruce Springsteen	Manfred Mann's
		Earth Band
		(Dave Flett
		Manfred Mann
		Chris Hamlet
		Thompson
		Colin Pattenden
		Chris Slade)

Artist(s)/Title	Writer(s)	Producer(s)
Spirit In The Night	Bruce Springsteen	Manfred Mann's Earthband
Bob MARLEY & THE WAILERS		
Roots, Rock, Reggae	Vincent Ford	Bob Marley & the Wailers (Aston 'Family' Man Barrett Carlton Barrett Tyrone Downie Alvin 'Seeco' Patterson Earl 'Chinna' Smith Donald Kinsey Al Anderson)
MARMALADE		
Falling Apart At The Seams	Tony Macaulay	Tony Macaulay
MARSHALL TUCKER BAND		
Fire On The Mountain	George McCorkle	Paul Hornsby
Al MARTINO		
Volare	Domenico Modugno Franco Migliacci Mitchell Parish	Mike Curb
MARY MacGREGOR		
Torn Between Two Lovers	Peter Yarrow Phil Jarrell	Peter Yarrow Barry Beckett
C.W. McCALL		
Convoy	C.W. McCall Bill Fries Chip Davis	Don Sears Chip Davis
There Won't Be No Country Music (There Won't Be No Rock 'n' Roll)	C.W. McCall Bill Fries Chip Davis	Don Sears Chip Davis
Marilyn McCOO & BILLY DAVIS		
I Hope We Get To Love In Time	James Dean John Glover	Don Davis
You Don't Have To Be A Star (To Be In My Show)	James Dean John Glover	Don Davis
Van McCOY		
Night Walk	Van McCoy	Van McCoy
Party	Van McCoy	Van McCoy
George McCRAE		
Honey I	Harry Wayne Casey Richard Finch	Harry Wayne Casey Richard Finch
Country Joe McDONALD		
Breakfast For Two	Country Joe McDonald	Jim Stern
Penny McLEAN		
Lady Bump	Sylvester Levay Stephan Prager	Michael Kunze
Harold MELVIN & THE BLUE NOTES		
Tell The World How I Feel About 'Cha Baby	John Whitehead Gene McFadden Victor Carstarphen	Kenny Gamble Leon Huff

Artist(s)/Title	Writer(s)	Producer(s)
Wake Up Everybody	John Whitehead	Kenny Gamble
	Gene McFadden	Leon Huff
	Victor Carstarphen	
MFSB		
The Zip	Kenneth Gamble	Kenneth Gamble
	Leon Huff	Leon Huff
		Jack Faith
MIGHTY CLOUDS OF JOY		
Mighty High	Dave Crawford	Dave Crawford
	Richard Downing	
John MILES		
High Fly	John Miles	Alan Parsons
	Bob Marshall	
Music	John Miles	Alan Parsons
Steve MILLER BAND		
Fly Like An Eagle	Steve Miller	Steve Miller
Rock 'N' Me	Steve Miller	Steve Miller
Take The Money And Run	Steve Miller	Steve Miller
MIRACLES		
Love Machine	Warren 'Pete' Moore	Freddie Perren
	William Griffin	
Joni MITCHELL		
In France They Kiss On Main Street	Joni Mitchell	(Not listed)
MOONLION		
Little Drummer Boy	Katherine Davis	Rick Bleiweiss
	Harry Simeone	Bill Stahl
	Henry Onorati	
Dorothy MOORE		
Funny How Time Slips Away	Willie Nelson	Tom Couch
		James Stroud
		Wolf Stephenson
Misty Blue	Bob Montgomery	Tommy Couch
		James Stroud
Melba MOORE		
This Is It	Van McCoy	Van McCoy
Donny MOST		
All Roads (Lead Back To You)	Jeffrey Marmelzat	Danny Jordan
	Spencer Proffer	Dick Smedler
MOTHER'S FINEST		
Fire	Sanford 'Pepe' Daniel	Tom Werman
	Jerry 'Wizzard' Seay	
	Joyce Kennedy	
	Glenn Murdock	
	Gary 'Mo' Moore	
	Michael Keck	
Michael MURPHEY		
Renegade	Michael Murphey	Bob Johnston
Walter MURPHY BAND		
Flight '76	Walter Murphy	Thomas J. Valentino
Walter MURPHY &		
THE BIG APPLE BAND		
A Fifth Of Beethoven	Walter Murphy	Thomas J. Valentino

US ARTIST

Artist(s)/Title	Writer(s)	Producer(s)
Anne MURRAY		
The Call	Gene MacLellan	Tom Catalano
Things	Bobby Darin	Tom Catalano
NAZARETH		
Love Hurts	Boudleaux Bryant	Manny Charlton
Willie NELSON		
Remember Me	T.T. Tyler	Willie Nelson
(see also: WAYLON & WILLIE)		
Wayne NEWTON		
Hungry Years	Neil Sedaka	John Madara
	Howard Greenfield	
Olivia NEWTON-JOHN		
Come On Over	Barry & Robin Gibb	John Farrar
Don't Stop Believin'	John Farrar	John Farrar
Every Face Tells A Story	Mike Allison	John Farrar
	Donald Black	
	Peter Sills	
Let It Shine/He Ain't Heavy—	Linda Hargrove/	John Farrar
He's My Brother	Bobby Russell	
	Bobby Scott	
Maxine NIGHTINGALE		
Gotta Be The One	Pierre Tubbs	Pierre Tubbs
Right Back Where We Started From	Pierre Tubbs	Pierre Tubbs
	Vince Edwards	
Kenny NOLAN		
I Like Dreamin'	Kenny Nolan	Kenny Nolan
		Charles Calello
Ted NUGENT		
Dog Eat Dog	Ted Nugent	Tom Werman
		Cliff Davies
		Lew Futterman
Hey Baby	Derek St. Holmes	Lew Futterman
		Tom Werman
Billy OCEAN		
Love Really Hurts Without You	Ben Findon	Ben Findon
	Les Charles	
OHIO PLAYERS		
Fopp	Ohio Players	Ohio Players
		(James Williams
		Clarence Satchell
		Leroy Bonner
		Marshall Jones
		Ralph Middlebrooks
		Marvin Pierce
		William Beck)
Love Rollercoaster	Ohio Players	Ohio Players
Rattlesnake	Belda Baine	(Not listed)
	Louise Crane	

Artist(s)/Title	Writer(s)	Producer(s)
Who'd She Coo	William Beck	Ohio Players
	James Williams	
	Marshall Jones	
	Marvin Pierce	
O'JAYS		
I Love Music	Kenny Gamble	Kenny Gamble
	Leon Huff	Leon Huff
Livin' For The Weekend	Kenny Gamble	Kenny Gamble
	Leon Huff	Leon Huff
	Cary Gilbert	
Message In Our Music	Kenny Gamble	Kenny Gamble
	Leon Huff	Leon Huff
ORIGINALS		
Down To Love Town	Don Daniels	Frank Wilson
	Michael B. Sutton	Michael Sutton
	Kathy Wakefield	
Tony ORLANDO & DAWN		
Cupid	Sam Cooke	Hank Medress
		Dave Appell
ORLEANS		
Still The One	John & Johanna Hall	Charles Plotkin
Lee OSKAR		
BLT	Greg Errico	Greg Errico
	Lee Oskar	Jerry Goldstein
Donny OSMOND		
C'mon Marianne	Larry Russell Brown	Mike Curb
	Raymond Bloodworth	
Donny & Marie OSMOND		
Ain't Nothing Like The Real Thing	Nickolas Ashford	Mike Curb
	Valerie Simpson	Michael Lloyd
Deep Purple	Peter DeRose	Mike Curb
	Mitchell Parish	
OSMONDS		
I Can't Live A Dream	Arnold Capitanelli	Mike Curb
		Michael Lloyd
OUTLAWS		
Breaker-Breaker	Huey Thomasson	Paul A. Rothchild
OZARK MOUNTAIN DAREDEVILS		
If I Only Knew	Larry Lee	David Anderle
	Steve Cash	
OZO		
Listen To The Buddah	Kenny George	Kaplan Kaye
Robert PALMER		
Man Smart, Woman Smarter	Joseph Kuhm	Steve Smith
PARLIAMENT		
(Give Up The Funk)	George Clinton	George Clinton
Tear The Roof Off The Sucker	Bootsy Collins	
	Jerome Brailey	
Alan PARSONS PROJECT		
(The System of) Doctor Tarr	Eric Woolfson	Alan Parsons
& Professor Fether	Alan Parsons	

US ARTIST

Artist(s)/Title	Writer(s)	Producer(s)
The Raven	Eric Woolfson Alan Parsons	Alan Parsons
Billy PAUL Let's Make A Baby	Kenny Gamble Leon Huff	Kenny Gamble Leon Huff
PEOPLE'S CHOICE Nursery Rhymes	Leon Huff Cary Gilbert	Kenny Gamble Leon Huff
Houston PERSON Disco Sax/For The Love Of You	Jimmy Roach/ Isley Brothers (Ernie Isley Marvin Isley Ronald Isley Chris Jasper Kelly Isley Rudolph Isley)	Bernard Mendelson Jimmy Roach Houston Person
PILOT January	David Paton	Alan Parsons
Mary Kay PLACE (as Loretta Haggers) Baby Boy	Mary Kay Place	Brian Ahern
POCO Rose Of Cimarron	Rusty Young	Mark Harman Poco (Rusty Young Timothy B. Schmit Paul Cotton George Grantham)
POINTER SISTERS Going Down Slowly	Allen Toussaint	David Rubinson & Friends, Inc.
Michel POLNAREFF If You Only Believe (Jesus For Tonight)	Michel Polnareff George Clinton Jacob Brackman	Michel Polnareff
Lipstick	Michel Polnareff	Michel Polnareff
PRATT & McCLAIN with BROTHERLOVE Devil With The Blue Dress	Frederick Long William Stevenson	Steve Barri Michael Omartian
Happy Days	Norman Gimbel Charles Fox	Steve Barri Michael Omartian
PRELUDE For A Dancer	Jackson Browne	Micky Sweeney Prelude (Brian Hume Irene Hume Ian Vardy)
Elvis PRESLEY Hurt/For The Heart	Jimmie Crane Al Jacobs/ Dennis Linde	(Not listed)

Artist(s)/Title	Writer(s)	Producer(s)
Moody Blue/	Mark James	Felton Jarvis
She Thinks I Still Care	Steve Duffy	Elvis Presley
Arthur PRYSOCK	Dave L. Lipscomb	
When Love Is New	Kenny Gamble	Sam Weiss
	Leon Huff	John Davis
PURPLE REIGN		
This Old Man	Public Domain	Mike Natale
Suzi QUATRO		
Can The Can	Nicky Chinn	Nicky Chinn
	Mike Chapman	Mike Chapman
QUEEN		
Bohemian Rhapsody	Freddie Mercury	Roy Thomas Baker
		Queen
		(Freddie Mercury
		Brain May
		John Deacon
		Roger Taylor)
Somebody To Love	Freddie Mercury	Queen
You're My Best Friend	John Deacon	Roy Thomas Baker
		Queen
Eddie RABBITT		
Rocky Mountain Music	Eddie Rabbitt	David Malloy
Lou RAWLS		
Groovy People	Kenny Gamble	Kenny Gamble
	Leon Huff	Leon Huff
You'll Never Find Another	Kenny Gamble	Kenny Gamble
Love Like Mine	Leon Huff	Leon Huff
REAL THING		
You To Me Are Everything	Ken Gold	Ken Gold
	Micky Denne	
Helen REDDY		
I Can't Hear You No More	Carole King	Joe Wissert
	Gerry Goffin	
Somewhere In The Night	Richard Kerr	Joe Wissert
	Will Jennings	
REVELATION		
You To Me Are Everything	Ken Gold	Freddie Perren
	Micky Denne	
RHYTHM HERITAGE		
Baretta's Theme	Morgan Ames	Steve Barri
(Keep Your Eyes On The Sparrow)	Dave Grusin	Michael Omartian
Theme From S.W.A.T.	Barry DeVorzon	Steve Barri
		Michael Omartian
Charlie RICH		
Since I Fell For You	Buddy Johnson	Billy Sherrill
Cliff RICHARD		
Devil Woman	Christine Hodgson	Bruce Welch
	Terry Britten	
I Can't Ask For Anymore Than You	Ken Gold	Bruce Welch
	Micky Denne	

Artist(s)/Title	Writer(s)	Producer(s)
RITCHIE FAMILY		
The Best Disco In Town	Jacques Morali	Jacques Morali
	Ritchie Rome	Ritchie Rome
	Henri Belolo	
	Philip Hurtt	
ROAD APPLES		
Let's Live Together	Fin Finnerty	David Kershenbaum
Smokey ROBINSON		
Open	William Robinson	Smokey Robinson
	Marv Tarplin	
	Pamela Moffett	
Quiet Storm	William Robinson	Smokey Robinson
	Rose Ella Jones	
Vicki Sue ROBINSON		
Daylight	Harold T. Payne	Warren Schatz
	Bobby Womack	
Turn The Beat Around	Pete & Gerald Jackson	Warren Schatz
D.J. ROGERS		
Say You Love Me	D.J. Rogers	D.J. Rogers
Kenny ROGERS		
Love Lifted Me	James Rowe	Larry Butler
	Howard Smith	
ROLLING STONES		
Fool To Cry	Keith Richard	The Glimmer Twins
	Mick Jagger	
Hot Stuff/Fool To Cry	Keith Richard	The Glimmer Twins
	Mick Jagger	
Linda RONSTADT		
Someone To Lay Down Beside Me	Karla Bonoff	Peter Asher
That'll Be The Day	Jerry Allison	Peter Asher
	Buddy Holly	
	Norman Petty	
The Tracks Of My Tears	William Robinson	Peter Asher
	Marv Tarplin	
	Warren 'Pete' Moore	
ROSE ROYCE		
Car Wash	Norman Whitfield	Norman Whitfield
Charlie ROSS		
Without Your Love (Mr. Jordan)	Paul Vance	Paul Vance
	Perry Cone	
Diana ROSS		
I Thought It Took A Little Time	Michael Masser	Michael Masser
(But Today I Fell In Love)	Pam Sawyer	
Love Hangover	Pam Sawyer	Hal Davis
	Marilyn McLeod	
One Love In My Lifetime	Terri McFaddin	Lawrence Brown
	Lawrence Brown	
	Leonard Perry	
Theme From Mahogany	Michael Masser	Michael Masser
'Do You Know Where You're	Gerry Goffin	
Going To'		
ROWANS		
If I Only Could	Chris Rowan	Bill Wolf

Artist(s)/Title	Writer(s)	Producer(s)
ROXY MUSIC		
Love Is The Drug	Bryan Ferry Andy MacKay	Chris Thomas
David RUFFIN		
Everything's Coming Up Love	Van McCoy	Van McCoy
Heavy Love	Van McCoy Joe Cobb	Van McCoy
Walk Away From Love	Charles Kipps	Van McCoy
RUFUS featuring Chaka Khan		
Dance Wit Me	Gavin Christopher	Rufus (Andre Fischer Chaka Khan Tony Maiden Kevin Murphy Bobby Watson)
Sweet Thing	Tony Maiden Chaka Khan	Rufus
Todd RUNDGREN		
Good Vibrations	Brian Wilson Mike Love	Todd Rundgren
Leon RUSSELL		
Back To The Island	Leon Russell	Leon Russell Denny Cordell
Leon & Mary RUSSELL		
Rainbow In Your Eyes	Leon Russell	Leon & Mary Russell
SALSOUL ORCHESTRA		
Nice 'N' Naasty	Vincent Montana Jr.	Vincent Montana Jr.
Tangerine	Johnny Mercer Victor Schertzinger	Vincent Montana Jr.
You're Just The Right Size	Vincent Montana Jr.	Vincent Montana Jr.
SANTANA		
Let It Shine	David Brown Ray Gardner	David Rubinson & Friends, Inc.
Larry SANTOS		
We Can't Hide It Anymore	Barry Murphy	Don Davis
Ray SAWYER		
(One More Year Of) Daddy's Little Girl	Hazel Smith	Ron Haffkine
Leo SAYER		
You Make Me Feel Like Dancing	Leo Sayer Vini Poncia	Richard Perry
Boz SCAGGS		
It's Over	Boz Scaggs	Joe Wissert
Lowdown	Boz Scaggs David Paich	Joe Wissert
What Can I Say	Boz Scaggs David Paich	Joe Wissert
Tom SCOTT		
Uptown & Country	Tom Scott	Tom Scott Hank Cicalo

Artist(s)/Title	Writer(s)	Producer(s)
SEALS & CROFTS		
Baby, I'll Give It To You	Lana Bogan Jimmy Seals	Louie Shelton
Get Closer	Jimmy Seals Dash Crofts	Louie Shelton
John SEBASTIAN		
Hideaway	John Sebastian	Steve Barri John Sebastian
Welcome Back	John Sebastian	Steve Barri John Sebastian
Neil SEDAKA		
Breaking Up Is Hard To Do	Neil Sedaka Howard Greenfield	Neil Sedaka Robert Appere
Love In The Shadows	Neil Sedaka Phil Cody	Neil Sedaka Robert Appere
Steppin' Out	Neil Sedaka Phil Cody	Neil Sedaka Robert Appere
You Gotta Make Your Own Sunshine	Neil Sedaka Howard Greenfield	Neil Sedaka Robert Appere
Bob SEGER & THE SILVER BULLET BAND		
Night Moves	Bob Seger	Bob Seger Punch Andrews
Nutbush City Limits	Tina Turner	Bob Seger Punch Andrews
T.G. SHEPPARD		
Solitary Man	Neil Diamond	Jack Gilmer Bill Browder
SHERBET		
Howzat	Garth Porter Tony Mitchell	Richard Lush Sherbet (Garth Porter Tony Mitchell Harvey James Alan Sandow Daryl Braithwaite)
SHIRLEY & SQUIRRELY		
Hey Shirley (This Is Squirrely)	James Green Jr. Danny Wolfe	Bob Millsap
SILVER		
Wham Bam (Shang-A-Lang)	Rick Geils	Tom Sellers Clive Davis
SILVER CONVENTION		
Fly, Robin, Fly	Sylvester Levay Stephan Prager	Michael Kunze
Get Up And Boogie	Sylvester Levay Stephan Prager	Michael Kunze
No, No, Joe	Sylvester Levay Stephan Prager	Michael Kunze Sylvester Levay
Carly SIMON		
It Keeps You Runnin'	Michael McDonald	Ted Templeman

196

US ARTIST

Artist(s)/Title	Writer(s)	Producer(s)
Paul SIMON		
50 Ways To Leave Your Lover	Paul Simon	Paul Simon
		Phil Ramone
Still Crazy After All These Years	Paul Simon	Paul Simon
		Phil Ramone
SIMON & GARFUNKEL		
My Little Town	Paul Simon	Paul Simon
		Art Garfunkel
		Phil Ramone
Bro SMITH		
Bigfoot	Johnny Cash	JCPI
SMOKIE		
Living Next Door To Alice	Nicky Chinn	Nicky Chinn
	Mike Chapman	Mike Chapman
SONS OF CHAMPLIN		
Hold On	Bill Champlin	Keith Olsen
	Laura Allan	
SOUL TRAIN GANG		
Soul Train '75'	Dick Griffey	Don Cornelius
	Don Cornelius	Dick Griffey
SOUTH SHORE COMMISSION		
Train Called Freedom	Bunny Sigler	Bunny Sigler
	Ronnie Tyson	
We're On The Right Track	Norman Harris	Stan Watson
	Allan Felder	Norman Harris
Red SOVINE		
Teddy Bear	Dale Royal	Tommy Hill
	Billy Joe Burnette	
	Tommy Hill	
	Red Sovine	
SPECIAL DELIVERY featuring Terry Huff		
The Lonely One	Terry Huff	Bob Shad
	Adrian Clements	
SPIN		
Grasshopper	Hans Jansen	John Sonneveld
	Jan Vennik	Spin
		(Rein Van Der Broek
		Hans Hollestelle
		Jan Hollestelle
		Hans Jansen
		Cees Kranenberg
		Jan Vennik)
SPINNERS (known as the DETROIT SPINNERS in the UK)		
Love Or Leave	Charles Simmons	Thom Bell
	Bruce Hawes	
	Joseph Jefferson	
The Rubber Band Man	Linda Creed	Thom Bell
	Thom Bell	
Wake Up Susan	Sherman Marshall	Thom Bell
	Thom Bell	

Artist(s)/Title	Writer(s)	Producer(s)
Rick SPRINGFIELD		
Take A Hand	Rick Springfield	Mark K. Smith
Bruce SPRINGSTEEN		
Tenth Avenue Freeze-Out	Bruce Springsteen	Bruce Springsteen
		Jon Landau
		Mike Appel
S.S.O.		
Tonight's The Night	Francis Weyer	Roland Kruger
	Donald Lucas	
Jim STAFFORD		
Jasper	Jim Stafford	Phil Gernhard
	Dave Loggins	
STAMPEDERS		
Hit The Road Jack	Percy Mayfield	Mel Shaw
STAPLE SINGERS		
Let's Do It Again	Curtis Mayfield	Curtis Mayfield
New Orleans	Curtis Mayfield	Curtis Mayfield
STARBUCK		
I Got To Know	Bruce Blackman	Bruce Blackman
		Mike Clark
Lucky Man	Bruce Blackman	Bruce Blackman
		Mike Clark
Moonlight Feels Right	Bruce Blackman	Bruce Blackman
		Mike Clark
STARLAND VOCAL BAND		
Afternoon Delight	Bill Danoff	Milton Okun
California Day	Bill Danoff	Milton Okun
Edwin STARR		
Abyssinia Jones	Edwin Starr	Edwin Starr
Kenny STARR		
The Blind Man In The Bleachers	Sterling Whipple	Snuffy Miller
Ringo STARR		
A Dose Of Rock And Roll	Carl Grossman	Arif Mardin
STARZ		
(She's Just A) Fallen Angel	Sean DeLaney	Jack Douglas
	Joe Grob	
	Brenden Harkin	
	Richie Ranno	
	Michael Lee Smith	
	Peter Sweval	
Candi STATON		
Young Hearts Run Free	Dave Crawford	Dave Crawford
STEELY DAN		
The Fez	Donald Fagen	Gary Katz
	Walter Becker	
	Paul L. Griffin	
Kid Charlemagne	Donald Fagen	Gary Katz
	Walter Becker	
Cat STEVENS		
Banapple Gas	Cat Stevens	Cat Stevens
Ray STEVENS		
Young Love	Carole Joyner	Ray Stevens
	Ric Cartey	

Artist(s)/Title	Writer(s)	Producer(s)
Al STEWART		
Year Of The Cat	Al Stewart Peter Wood	Alan Parsons
Rod STEWART		
This Old Heart Of Mine	Eddie Holland Lamont Dozier Brian Holland	Tom Dowd
Tonight's The Night	Rod Stewart	Tom Dowd
Barbra STREISAND		
Love Theme From 'A Star Is Born' (Evergreen)	Barbra Streisand Paul Williams	Barbra Streisand Phil Ramone
STYLISTICS		
Funky Weekend	Hugo & Luigi George David Weiss	Hugo & Luigi
Your Are Beautiful	Hugo & Luigi George David Weiss	Hugo & Luigi
STYX		
Lorelei	Dennis DeYoung James Young	Styx (Dennis DeYoung Chuck Panozzo John Panozzo John Curulewski James Young)
Mademoiselle	Dennis DeYoung Tommy Shaw	Styx (Dennis DeYoung Chuck Panozzo John Panozzo Tommy Shaw James Young)
Donna SUMMER		
Could It Be Magic	Barry Manilow Adrienne Anderson	Giorgio Moroder Pete Bellotte
Love To Love You Baby	Giorgio Moroder Pete Bellotte Donna Summer	Pete Bellotte
Spring Affair	Donna Summer Giorgio Moroder Pete Bellotte	Giorgio Moroder Pete Bellotte
Try Me, I Know We Can Make It	Giorgio Moroder Pete Bellotte Donna Summer	Pete Bellotte
SUN		
Wanna Make Love (Come Flick My BIC)	Byron Byrd	Beau Ray Fleming Byron Byrd
SUNDOWN COMPANY		
Norma Jean Wants To Be A Movie Star	Johnny Cunningham	Joe Beck
SUPREMES		
I'm Gonna Let My Heart Do The Walking	Harold Beatty Eddie & Brian Holland	Brian Holland

Artist(s)/Title	Writer(s)	Producer(s)
You're My Driving Wheel	Floyd Stafford Reginald Brown Brian Holland Harold Beatty	Brian Holland
SUTHERLAND BROTHERS & QUIVER Arms Of Mary	Iain Sutherland	Ron & Howard Albert
SWEENEY TODD Roxy Roller	James McCulloch Nick Gilder	Martin Schaer
SWEENEY TODD featuring Brian Guy ADAMS Roxy Roller	James McCulloch Nick Gilder	Martin Schaer
SWEET Action	Sweet (Brian Connolly Andy Scott Steve Priest Mike Tucker)	Mike Chapman Nicky Chinn
Fox On The Run	Sweet	Mike Chapman Nicky Chinn
SYLVERS Boogie Fever	Keni St. Lewis Freddie Perren	Freddie Perren
Cotton Candy	Keni St. Lewis Freddie Perren	Freddie Perren
Hot Line	Keni St. Lewis Freddie Perren	Freddie Perren
TAVARES Don't Take Away The Music	Keni St. Lewis Freddie Perren Christine Yarian	Freddie Perren
Free Ride	Dan Hartman	Dennis Lambert Brian Potter
Heaven Must Be Missing An Angel	Keni St. Lewis Freddie Perren	Freddie Perren
Debbie TAYLOR I Don't Want To Leave You	David Jordan Andrew Smith	David Jordan
James TAYLOR Shower The People	James Taylor	Lenny Waronker Russ Titelman
Johnnie TAYLOR Disco Lady	Harvey Scales Al Vance Don Davis	Don Davis
Somebody's Gettin' It	Clarence Colter Chico Jones Don Davis	Don Davis
TEMPTATIONS Keep Holding On	Eddie & Brian Holland	Brian Holland

Artist(s)/Title	Writer(s)	Producer(s)
Up The Creek (Without A Paddle)	Jeffrey Bowen Jimmy Ford Truman Thomas	Jeffrey Bowen
10cc Art For Art's Sake	Graham Gouldman Eric Stewart	10cc (Graham Gouldman Eric Stewart Lol Creme Kevin Godley)
I'm Mandy Fly Me	Eric Stewart Graham Gouldman Lol Creme	10cc
THIN LIZZY The Boys Are Back In Town Cowboy Song	Phil Lynott Phil Lynott Brian Downey	John Alcock John Alcock
TOWER OF POWER You Ought To Be Havin' Fun	Hubert Tubbs Emilio Castillo Steve Kupka	Emilio Castillo
TRAMMPS Hold Back The Night	Ronnie Baker Earl Young Allan Felder Norman Harris	Ronnie Baker Norman Harris Earl Young
That's Where The Happy People Go	Ronnie Baker	Ronnie Baker Norman Harris Earl Young
John TRAVOLTA Let Her In Whenever I'm Away From You	Gary Benson Gary Benson Dave Mindel	Bob Reno Bob Reno John Davis
Robin TROWER Caledonia	Robin Trower James Dewar	Geoff Emerick Robin Trower
Andrea TRUE CONNECTION More, More, More Party Line	Gregg Diamond Gregg Diamond	Gregg Diamond Gregg Diamond
TUBES Don't Touch Me There	Ron Nagle Dorknocker	Ken Scott
Tanya TUCKER Here's Some Love	Jack Roberts Richard Mainegra	Jerry Crutchfield
Conway TWITTY Don't Cry Joni	Conway Twitty	(Not listed)
TYMES It's Cool	Marvin Yancy Chuck Jackson	Billy Jackson
John VALENTI Anything You Want	John Valenti Joey Spinazola	Bob Cullen

US ARTIST

Artist(s)/Title	Writer(s)	Producer(s)
Dana VALERY		
Will You Love Me Tomorrow	Carole King	John D'Andrea
	Gerry Goffin	
Frankie VALLI		
Fallen Angel	Guy Flett	Bob Gaudio
	Doug Fletcher	
Our Day Will Come	Bob Hilliard	Dave Appell
	Mort Garson	Hank Medress
We're All Alone	Boz Scaggs	Bob Gaudio
Gino VANNELLI		
Love Of My Life	Gino Vannelli	Gino Vannelli
		Joe Vannelli
		Geoff Emerick
Bobby VINTON		
Moonlight Serenade	Mitchell Parish	Bob Morgan
	Glenn Miller	
Save Your Kisses For Me	Tony Hiller	Bob Morgan
	Lee Sheriden	
	Martin Lee	
WAR		
Summer	War	Jerry Goldstein
	(Papa Dee Allen	
	Harold Brown	
	B.B. Dickerson	
	Lonnie Jordan	
	Charles Miller	
	Lee Oskar	
	Howard Scott)	
	Jerry Goldstein	
Dionne WARWICK		
Once You Hit The Road	Joseph Jefferson	Thom Bell
	Charles Simmons	
WAYLON & WILLIE		
Good Hearted Woman	Waylon Jennings	Ray Pennington
(see also: Waylon JENNINGS:	Willie Nelson	Waylon Jennings
Willie NELSON)		
WET WILLIE		
Everything That 'Cha Do		
(Will Come Back To You)	Ricky Hirsch	Paul Hornsby
WHIRLWIND		
Full Time Thing (Between		
Dusk & Dawn)	Mystro & Lyric	Aram Schefrin
WHISPERS		
One For The Money	Jerry Akines	Norman Harris
	John Simmons	
	Victor Drayton	
	Reginald 'Buddy' Turner	
Barry WHITE		
Baby, We Better Try To Get It		
Together	Barry White	Barry White
Let The Music Play	Barry White	Barry White

Artist(s)/Title	Writer(s)	Producer(s)
WHO		
Squeeze Box	Pete Townshend	Glyn Johns
WILD CHERRY		
Play That Funky Music	Robert Parissi	Robert Parissi
Andy WILLIAMS		
Tell It Like It Is	George Davis Lee Diamond	Rick Hall
Deniece WILLIAMS		
Free	Deniece Williams Susaye Greene Hank Redd Nathan Watts	Maurice White Charles Stepney
Diana WILLIAMS		
Teddy Bear's Last Ride	Dale Royal Billy Joe Burnette	Bill Denny
Al WILSON		
I've Got A Feeling (We'll Be Seeing Each Other Again)	Carl Hampton Homer Banks	Marc Gordon
WINGS		
Let 'Em In	Paul McCartney	Paul McCartney
Silly Love Songs	Paul McCartney	Paul McCartney
Bill WITHERS		
Make Love To You Mind	Bill Withers	Bill Withers Larry Nash
WING & A PRAYER FIFE & DRUM CORPS		
Baby Face	Harry Akst Benny Davis	Harold Wheeler Stephen Y. Scheaffer
Stevie WONDER		
I Wish	Stevie Wonder	Stevie Wonder
Gary WRIGHT		
Dream Weaver	Gary Wright	Gary Wright
Love Is Alive	Gary Wright	Gary Wright
Made Love To You	Gary Wright	Gary Wright
Tammy WYNETTE		
'Til I Can Make It On My Own	Tammy Wynette Billy Sherrill George Richey	Billy Sherrill
John Paul YOUNG		
Yesterday's Hero	Harry Vanda George Young	Harry Vanda George Young
Michael ZAGER'S MOON BAND featuring Peabo BRYSON		
Do It With Feeling	Paul Davis Michael Zager	Michael Zager Jerry Love
Z Z TOP		
It's Only Love	Z Z Top (Billy Gibbons Dusty Hill Frank Beard)	Bill Ham

Section 9

US Label Section

(*Billboard* Top 100 Singles Chart)

This section lists all singles that made the *Billboard* Top 100 chart during 1976, under catalogue numbers and their respective record labels in alphabetical and numerical order.

The figures in brackets next to the record labels denote the number of chart singles each label had.

Listing under record companies instead of record labels was decided against, as some labels are owned by companies where others might just be distributed, and in some cases those distribution ties might change during the year.

A&M (24)

AM 1671 **Love Hurts**—Nazareth
1693 **Show Me The Way**—Peter Frampton
1725 **The Way I Want To Touch You**—Captain & Tennille
1772 **If I Only Knew**—Ozark Mountain Daredevils
1778 **I Wanna Stay With You**—Gallagher & Lyle
1782 **Lonely Night (Angel Face)**—Captain & Tennille
1784 **Love Me Tonight**—Head East
1785 **Banapple Gas**—Cat Stevens
1786 **Lorelei**—Styx
1800 **There's A Kind Of Hush**—Carpenters
1806 **I'll Be Good To You**—Brothers Johnson
1817 **Shop Around**—Captain & Tennille
1826 **Don't Touch Me There**—Tubes
1828 **I Need To Be In Love**—Carpenters
1832 **Baby I Love Your Way**—Peter Frampton
1847 **Love Ballad**—L.T.D.
1850 **Heart On My Sleeve**—Gallagher & Lyle
1851 **Get The Funk Out Ma Face**—Brothers Johnson
1856 **Nadia's Theme (The Young & the Restless)**—Barry DeVorzon & Perry Botkin Jr.
1859 **Goofus**—Carpenters
1861 **Love Of My Life**—Gino Vannelli
1867 **Do You Feel Like We Do**—Peter Frampton
1870 **Muskrat Love**—Captain & Tennille
1877 **Mademoiselle**—Styx

ABC (21)

12117 **I'm Easy**—David Carradine
12135 **Theme From S.W.A.T.**—Rhythm Heritage
12142 **Amazing Grace (Used To Be Her Favorite Song)**—Amazing Rhythm Aces
12149 **Sweet Thing**—Rufus featuring Chaka Khan
12150 **You're Fooling You**—Dramatics
12164 **Mighty High**—Mighty Clouds of Joy
12170 **I Hope We Get To Love In Time**—Marilyn McCoo & Billy Davis Jr.
12177 **Baretta's Theme (Keep Your Eyes On The Sparrow)**—Rhythm Heritage
12178 **Moonlight Serenade**—Bobby Vinton
12179 **Dance Wit Me**—Rufus featuring Chaka Khan
12181 **Love Hangover**—5th Dimension
12186 **Save Your Kisses For Me**—Bobby Vinton
12195 **Kid Charlemagne**—Steely Dan
12199 **Out Of The Darkness**—David Crosby/Graham Nash
12202 **The End Is Not In Sight (The Cowboy Tune)**—Amazing Rhythm Aces
12204 **Rose Of Cimarron**—Poco
12208 **You Don't Have To Be A Star (To Be In My Show)**—Marilyn McCoo & Billy Davis Jr.
12214 **Catfish**—Four Tops
12222 **The Fez**—Steely Dan
12227 **You've Got Me Runnin'**—Gene Cotton
12232 **Save It For A Rainy Day**—Stephen Bishop

ABC/BLUE THUMB (1)
BTA 268 **Going Down Slowly**—Pointer Sisters

US LABEL

ABC/DOT (5)
DOA 17584 Easy As Pie—Billy 'Crash' Craddock
17607 You'll Lose A Good Thing—Freddy Fender
17620 Lonely Teardrops—Narvel Felts
17627 Vaya Con Dios—Freddy Fender
17652 Livin' It Down—Freddy Fender

ABC/IMPULSE (1)
IMP 31005 Hard Work—John Handy

AMHERST(1)
717 White Bird—David La Flamme

ARIOLA AMERICA (8)
P 7607 Yesterday's Hero—John Paul Young
7611 Bad Luck—Atlanta Disco Band
7619 Falling Apart At The Seams—Marmalade
7621 Love Really Hurts Without You—Billy Ocean
7625 Anything You Want—John Valenti
7627 Hold On—Sons of Champlin
7632 Grasshopper—Spin
7638 Torn Between Two Lovers—Mary MacGregor

ARISTA (22)
AS 0144 I Don't Want To Leave You—Debbie Taylor
0149 Saturday Night—Bay City Rollers
0157 I Write The Songs—Barry Manilow
0165 All By Myself—Eric Carmen
0168 Just You And I—Melissa Manchester
0170 Money Honey—Bay City Rollers
0172 Tryin' To Get The Feeling Again—Barry Manilow
0183 Better Days—Melissa Manchester
0184 Never Gonna Fall In Love Again—Eric Carmen
0185 Rock And Roll Love Letter—Bay City Rollers
0188 Breaker-Breaker—Outlaws
0189 Wham Bam (Shang-A-Lang)—Silver
0194 The Princess And The Punk—Barry Mann
0196 Rescue Me—Melissa Manchester
0200 Sunrise—Eric Carmen
0205 I Only Want To Be With You—Bay City Rollers
0206 This One's For You—Barry Manilow
0207 Makes You Blind—Glitter Band
0208 Help Wanted—Hudson Brothers
0209 Slow Dancing—Funky Kings
0212 Weekend In New England—Barry Manilow
0216 Yesterday's Hero—Bay City Rollers

ASYLUM (11)
E 45286 That's Why I Love You—Andrew Gold
45293 Take It To The Limit—Eagles
45294 Union Man—Cate Bros
45295 The Tracks Of My Tears—Linda Ronstadt
45298 In France They Kiss On Main Street—Joni Mitchell
45326 Can't Change My Heart—Cate Bros
45336 Still The One—Orleans
45340 That'll Be The Day—Linda Ronstadt

45347 If I Only Could—Rowans
45361 Someone To Lay Down Beside Me—Linda Ronstadt
45373 New Kid In Town—Eagles

ATCO (2)
45-7042 Love Is The Drug—Roxy Music
7049 Happy Man—Impact

ATLANTIC (26)
45-3304 School Boy Crush—Average White Band
3305 I Believe In Father Christmas—Greg Lake
3306 That's Where The Happy People Go—Trammps
3309 Love Or Leave—Spinners
3310 I Do, I Do, I Do, I Do, I Do—Abba
3314 If You Only Believe (Jesus For Tonight)—Michel Polnareff
3315 Mamma Mia—Abba
3320 Where Did Our Love Go—J. Geils Band
3321 Jealousy—Major Harris
3323 Sixteen Tons—Don Harrison Band
3326 Something He Can Feel—Aretha Franklin
3330 Lipstick—Michel Polnareff
3332 She's Gone—Daryl Hall & John Oates
3333 Livin' Ain't Livin'—Firefall
3335 You Are The Woman—Firefall
3341 Wake Up Susan—Spinners
3346 Fernando—Abba
3354 Queen Of My Soul—Average White Band
3355 The Rubber Band Man—Spinners
3358 Jump—Aretha Franklin
3360 Do It To My Mind—Johnny Bristol
3361 A Dose Of Rock And Roll—Ringo Starr
3364 Heart On My Sleeve—Bryan Ferry
3367 Sixteen Reasons—Laverne & Shirley
3372 Dancing Queen—Abba
7038 Lady Bump—Penny McLean

AVCO (2)
AV 4661 Funky Weekend—Stylistics
4664 You Are Beautiful—Stylistics

AVI (1)
AVIS 115 Let's Get It Together—El Coco

BANG (4)
BDJ 720 Do It With Feeling—Michael Zager's Moon Band featuring Peabo Bryson
724 Thinking Of You—Paul Davis
726 Superstar—Paul Davis
727 Dazz—Brick

BARNABY (1)
B-618 Young Love—Ray Stevens

BEARSVILLE (4)
BBS 0306 Slow Ride—Foghat
0307 Fool For The City—Foghat
0309 Good Vibrations—Todd Rundgren
0313 Drivin' Wheel—Foghat

BIG TREE (9)
BT 16047 You Sexy Thing—Hot Chocolate
16052 The Last Game Of The Season (A Blind Man In The Bleachers)—David Geddes
16053 Can The Can—Suzi Quatro
16056 Without Your Love (Mr. Jordan)—Charlie Ross
16060 Don't Stop It Now—Hot Chocolate
16061 Bigfoot—Bro Smith
16069 I'd Really Love To See You Tonight—England Dan & John Ford Coley
16072 Let's Rock—Ellison Chase
16079 Nights Are Forever—England Dan & John Ford Coley

BLUE SKY (1)
ZS8-2765 Let Me In—Derringer

BUDDAH (8)
BDA 499 Valentine Love—Norman Connors
507 Hold Back The Night—Trammps
513 Part Time Love—Gladys Knight & the Pips
515 More, More, More—Andrea True Connection
519 This Is It—Melba Moore
538 Party Line—Andrea True Connection
542 You Are My Starship—Norman Connors
544 So Sad The Song—Gladys Knight & the Pips

CAPITOL (41)
P 4134 Volare—Al Martino
4155 Country Boy (You Got Your Feet In L.A.)—Glen Campbell
4156 The Homecoming—Hagood Hardy
4157 Fox On The Run—Sweet
4174 Only Sixteen—Dr. Hook
4179 Boogie Fever—Sylvers
4184 Free Ride—Tavares
4192 Somewhere In The Night—Helen Reddy
4193 Inseparable—Natalie Cole
4198 The Game Is Over (What's The Matter With You)—Brown Sugar
4199 Take Me—Grand Funk Railroad
4207 The Call—Anne Murray
4220 Action—Sweet
4230 Ophelia—Band
4235 Sally—Grand Funk Railroad
4245 Don't Pull Your Love/Then You Can Tell Me Goodbye—Glen Campbell
4254 Wanna Make Love (Come Flick My BIC)—Sun
4255 Cotton Candy—Sylvers
4256 Silly Love Songs—Wings
4258 Yes, Yes, Yes—Bill Cosby
4259 Sophisticated Lady (She's A Different Lady)—Natalie Cole
4260 Take The Money And Run—Steve Miller Band
4269 Nutbush City Limits—Bob Seger & the Silver Bullet Band
4270 Heaven Must Be Missing An Angel—Tavares
4274 Got To Get You Into My Life—Beatles
4280 A Little Bit More—Dr. Hook
4293 Let 'Em In—Wings
4294 Ode To Billy Joe—Bobbie Gentry
4312 I Can't Hear You No More—Helen Reddy
4317 Teddy Bear's Last Ride—Diana Williams

210   US LABEL

4323 **Rock 'n' Me**—Steve Miller Band
4328 **Mr. Melody**—Natalie Cole
4329 **Things**—Anne Murray
4344 **(One More Year Of) Daddy's Little Girl**—Ray Sawyer
4336 **Hot Line**—Sylvers
4343 **(She's Just A) Fallen Angel**—Starz
4347 **Ob-La-Di, Ob-La-Da**—Beatles
4348 **Don't Take Away The Music**—Tavares
4364 **If Not You**—Dr. Hook
4369 **Night Moves**—Bob Seger & the Silver Band
4372 **Fly Like An Eagle**—Steve Miller Band

CAPRICORN (8)
CPS 0244 **Fire On The Mountain**—Marshall Tucker Band
0249 **If Love Must Go**—Dobie Gray
0252 **Fooled Around And Fell In Love**—Elvin Bishop
0254 **Everything That 'Cha Do (Will Come Back To You)**—Wet Willie
0255 **I've Been Loving You**—Easy Street
0256 **Struttin' My Stuff**—Elvin Bishop
0259 **Find 'Em, Fool 'Em, Forget 'Em**—Dobie Gray
0266 **Spend Some Time**—Elvin Bishop

CASABLANCA (8)
NB 844 **We Can't Hide It Anymore**—Larry Santos
850 **Rock And Roll All Nite (Live Version)**—Kiss
854 **Shout It Out Loud**—Kiss
856 **(Give Up The Funk) Tear The Roof Off The Sucker**—Parliament
858 **Flaming Youth**—Kiss
863 **Beth/Detroit Rock City**—Kiss
872 **Spring Affair**—Donna Summer
873 **Hard Luck Woman**—Kiss

CASINO (2)
GRT 052 **I.O.U.**—Jimmy Dean
054 **Hey Shirley (This Is Squirrely)**—Shirley & Squirrely

CHELSEA (6)
CH 3022 **Sky High**—Jigsaw
3037 **Love Fire**—Jigsaw
3041 **The Hungry Years**—Wayne Newton
3043 **Brand New Love Affair**—Jigsaw
3045 **Dancin' Kid**—Disco Tex & the Sex-o-lettes
3051 **Take A Hand**—Rick Springfield

CHI-SOUND (1)
CH-XW 908-Y **Feelings**—Walter Jackson

CHRYSALIS (4)
CHS 2094 **Jeans On**—David Dundas
2110 **Locomotive Breath**—Jethro Tull
2112 **You're My Everything**—Lee Garrett
2122 **Caledonia**—Robin Trower

COLUMBIA (43)
3-10230 **My Little Town**—Simon & Garfunkel
10235 **What's The Name Of This Funk (Spider Man)**—Ramsey Lewis
10245 **Hurricane**—Bob Dylan

10251 **Sing A Song**—Earth Wind & Fire
10255 **Make Love To Your Mind**—Bill Withers
10263 **Tell It Like It Is**—Andy Williams
10270 **50 Ways To Leave Your Lover**—Paul Simon
10273 **Breakaway**—Art Garfunkel
10274 **Tenth Avenue Freeze-Out**—Bruce Springsteen
10275 **Remember Me**—Willie Nelson
10278 **Dream On**—Aerosmith
10281 **Disco Lady**—Johnnie Taylor
10284 **Arms Of Mary**—Sutherland Brothers & Quiver
10298 **Mozambique**—Bob Dylan
10304 **Forever Lovers**—Mac Davis
10309 **Can't Hide Love**—Earth Wind & Fire
10310 **Kiss And Say Goodbye**—Manhattans
10319 **It's Over**—Boz Scaggs
10321 **One Piece At A Time**—Johnny Cash & the Tennessee Three
10332 **Still Crazy After All These Years**—Paul Simon
10334 **Somebody's Gettin' It**—Johnnie Taylor
10336 **Let It Shine**—Santana
10346 **Can't Stop Groovin' Now, Wanna Do It Some More**—B.T. Express
10347 **Flowers/I Don't Wanna Lose Your Love**—Emotions
10356 **The More You Do It (The More I Like It Done To Me)**—Ronnie Dyson
10359 **Last Child**—Aerosmith
10360 **Another Rainy Day In New York City**—Chicago
10366 **If You Know What I Mean**—Neil Diamond
10367 **Lowdown**—Boz Scaggs
10373 **Getaway**—Earth Wind & Fire
10384 **(Don't Fear) The Reaper**—Blue Oyster Cult
10388 **Give It Up (Turn It Loose)**—Tyrone Davis
10390 **If You Leave Me Now**—Chicago
10405 **Don't Think . . . Feel**—Neil Diamond
10407 **Home Tonight**—Aerosmith
10409 **You Ought To Be Havin' Fun**—Tower of Power
10422 **Baby Boy**—Mary Kay Place (as Loretta Haggers)
10429 **Free**—Deniece Williams
10430 **I Kinda Miss You**—Manhattans
10439 **Saturday Nite**—Earth Wind & Fire
10440 **What Can I Say**—Boz Scaggs
10449 **Walk This Way**—Aerosmith
10450 **Love Theme From 'A Star Is Born' (Evergreen)**—Barbra Streisand

CURTOM (2)
CMS 0109 **Let's Do It**—Staple Singers
     0113 **New Orleans**—Staple Singers

DARK HORSE (2)
DH   8294 **This Song**—George Harrison
     10011 **Sweet Summer Music**—Attitudes

DE-LITE (5)
DEP 1575 **Every Beat Of My Heart**—Crown Heights Affair
     1578 **Venus**—Frankie Avalon
     1579 **Love And Understanding (Come Together)**—Kool & the Gang
     1581 **Foxy Lady**—Crown Heights Affair
     1586 **Open Sesame**—Kool & the Gang

212   **US LABEL**

DJM (1)
DJUS 1012 Listen To The Buddah—Ozo

ELEKTRA (9)
E 45297 Bohemian Rhapsody—Queen
45302 Cupid—Tony Orlando & Dawn
45309 You Got The Magic—John Fogerty
45315 Rocky Mountain Music—Eddie Rabbitt
45318 You're My Best Friend—Queen
45323 It Keeps You Runnin'—Carly Simon
45327 A Better Place To Be—Harry Chapin
45362 Somebody To Love—Queen
45365 Lost Without Your Love—Bread

EMI (2)
4201 Make Me Smile (Come Up And See Me)—Steve Harley & Cockney Rebel
4202 January—Pilot

EPIC (12)
8-50173 I Could Have Danced All Night/Jump For Joy—Biddu Orchestra
50182 Since I Fell For You—Charlie Rich
50184 Renegade—Michael Murphey
50196 'Til I Can Make It On My Own—Tammy Wynette
50197 Hey Baby—Ted Nugent
50225 Play That Funky Music—Wild Cherry
50266 More Than A Feeling—Boston
50269 Fire—Mother's Finest
50270 After The Lovin'—Engelbert Humperdinck
50289 Enjoy Yourself—Jacksons
50292 Silver Heels—Blaze
50301 Dog Eat Dog—Ted Nugent

FANTASY (4)
F 758 Breakfast For Two—Country Joe McDonald
759 I Heard It Through The Grapevine—Creedence Clearwater Revival
762 Happy Music—Blackbyrds
771 Rock Creek Park—Blackbyrds

GORDY (2)
G 7146 Keep Holding On—Temptations
7150 Up The Creek (Without A Paddle)—Temptations

GRANITE (2)
G 532 Abyssinia Jones—Edwin Starr
540 You To Me Are Everything—Broadway

GREEDY (1)
G 101 Words (Are Impossible)—Donny Gerrard

GRUNT (3)
FB 10456 Play On Love—Jefferson Starship
10746 With Your Love—Jefferson Starship
10791 St. Charles—Jefferson Starship

H&L (2)
4667 Night Walk—Van McCoy
4670 Party—Van McCoy

US LABEL

213

HARVEST (1)
P 4318 It's A Long Way There—Little River Band

HI (2)
5N 2300 Full Of Fire—Al Green
2319 Keep Me Cryin'—Al Green

HITSVILLE (1)
H-6032F Solitary Man—T.G. Sheppard

ISLAND (2)
IS 060 Roots, Rock, Reggae—Bob Marley & the Wailers
075 Man Smart, Woman Smarter—Robert Palmer

JANUS (2)
J 259 Tubular Bells—Champs Boys
266 Year Of The Cat—Al Stewart

KAMA SUTRA (1)
KA 607 Texas—Charlie Daniels Band

KIRSHNER (1)
ZS8-4267 Carry On Wayward Son—Kansas

KOLOB (3)
PD 14320 C'mon Marianne—Donny Osmond
14363 Ain't Nothin' Like The Real Thing—Donny & Marie Osmond
14840 Deep Purple—Donny & Marie Osmond

LIFESONG (5)
LS 45001 Chain Gang Medley—Jim Croce
45002 Shannon—Henry Gross
45008 Springtime Mama—Henry Gross
45014 Someday—Henry Gross
45015 Baby. Baby I Love You—Terry Cashman

LONDON (7)
5N 230 Wow—Andre Gagnon
232 The Fonz Song—Heyettes
240 Roxy Roller—Sweeney Todd
241 It's Only Love—Z Z Top
244 Roxy Roller—Sweeney Todd featuring Brian Guy Adams
20084 High Fly—John Miles
20086 Music—John Miles

MAINSTREAM (1)
MRL 5581 The Lonely One—Special Delivery featuring Terry Huff

MALACO (2)
1029 Misty Blue—Dorothy Moore
1033 Funny How Time Slips Away—Dorothy Moore

MARLIN (1)
3306 The Best Disco In Town—Ritchie Family

MCA (18)
40407 Don't Cry Joni—Conway Twitty
40461 Island Girl—Elton John
40474 The Blind Man In The Bleachers—Kenny Starr
40475 Squeeze Box—Who

214

40495 Let It Shine/He Ain't Heavy—He's My Brother—Olivia Newton-John
40496 Strong Enough To Be Gentle—Black Oak Arkansas
40505 Grow Some Funk Of Your Own/I Feel Like A Bullet (In The Gun Of Robert Ford)—Elton John
40525 Come On Over—Olivia Newton-John
40532 Double Trouble—Lynyrd Skynyrd
40551 Johnny Cool—Steve Gibbons Band
40590 Can You Do It—Grand Funk Railroad
40598 Here's Some Love—Tanya Tucker
40600 Don't Stop Believin'—Olivia Newton-John
40610 Howzat—Sherbet
40615 Car Wash—Rose Royce
40631 Peter Gunn—Deodato
40642 Every Face Tells A Story—Olivia Newton-John
40665 Free Bird—Lynyrd Skynyrd

MERCURY (16)
73724 Down To The Line—Bahcman-Turner Overdrive
73725 Art For Art's Sake—10cc
73734 Love Rollercoaster—Ohio Players
73751 The White Knight—Cledus Maggard & the Citizen's Band
73760 I'm So Lonesome I Could Cry—Terry Bradshaw
73766 Take It Like A Man—Bachman-Turner Overdrive
73775 Fopp—Ohio Players
73779 I'm Mandy Fly Me—10cc
73784 Lookin' Out For # 1—Bachman-Turner Overdrive
73786 The Boys Are Back In Town—Thin Lizzy
73789 Kentucky Moonrunner—Cledus Maggard & the Citizen's Band
73814 Who'd She Coo—Ohio Players
73833 Shake Your Rump To The Funk—Bar-Kays
73841 Cowboy Song—Thin Lizzy
73843 Gimme Your Money Please—Bachman-Turner Overdrive
73864 Love Bug—Bumble Bee Unlimited

MGM (1)
M 14839 Convoy—C.W. McCall

MIDLAND INTERNATIONAL (5)
MB 10339 Fly, Robin, Fly—Silver Convention
10571 Get Up And Boogie—Silver Convention
10623 Let Her In—John Travolta
10723 No, No, Joe—Silver Convention
10780 Whenever I'm Away From You—John Travolta

MORNING GLORY (1)
MS 700 Rain, Oh Rain—Fools Gold

MOTOWN (13)
M-1323F It Should Have Been Me—Yvonne Fair
1376 Walk Away From Love—David Ruffin
1377 Theme From Mahogany 'Do You Know Where You're Going To'—Diana Ross
1381 Sweet Love—Commodores
1387 I Thought It Took A Little Time (But Today I Fell In Love)—Diana Ross
1388 Heavy Love—David Ruffin
1391 I'm Gonna Let My Heart Do The Walking—Supremes
1392 Love Hangover—Diana Ross

1393 **Everything's Comin' Up Love**—David Ruffin
1398 **One Love In My Lifetime**—Diana Ross
1401 **Let's Be Young Tonight**—Jermaine Jackson
1402 **Just To Be Close To You**—Commodores
1407 **You're My Driving Wheel**—Supremes

MUSHROOM (3)
M-7011 **Magic Man**—Heart
7021 **Dreamboat Annie**—Heart
7023 **Crazy On You**—Heart

OASIS (3)
OC-401 **Love To Love You Baby**—Donna Summer
405 **Could It Be Magic**—Donna Summer
406 **Try Me, I Know We Can Make It**—Donna Summer

OCTOBER (1)
OCT 1001 **'Til It's Time To Say Goodbye**—Jonathan Cain

ODE (4)
ODE-66118-S **Uptown & Country**—Tom Scott
66119 **Only Love Is Real**—Carole King
66123 **High Out Of Time**—Carole King
66124 **Framed**—Cheech & Chong

OLD TOWN (1)
OT 1000 **When Love Is New**—Arthur Prysock

PARADISE (1)
PDS 8208 **Rainbow In Your Eyes**—Leon & Mary Russell

PHANTOM (2)
HB 10566 **Will You Love Me Tomorrow**—Dana Valery
10709 **Mary Hartman, Mary Hartman Theme**—Deadly Nightshade

PHILADELPHIA INTERNATIONAL (9)
ZS8-3577 **I Love Music**—O'Jays
3578 **The Zip**—MFSB
3579 **Wake Up Everybody**—Harold Melvin & the Blue Notes
3584 **Let's Make A Baby**—Billy Paul
3587 **Livin' For The Weekend**—O'Jays
3588 **Tell The World How I Feel About 'Cha Baby**—Harold Melvin & the Blue Notes
3593 **You'll Never Find Another Love Like Mine**—Lou Rawls
3601 **Message In Our Music**—O'Jays
3604 **Groovy People**—Lou Rawls

PIP (1)
PIP 6513 **The Little Drummer Boy**—Moonlion

PLANTATION (1)
PL 144 **C.B. Savage**—Rod Hart

PLAYBOY (5)
P-6054 **Winners And Losers**—Hamilton, Joe Frank & Reynolds
6062 **I've Got A Feeling (We'll Be Seeing Each Other Again)**—Al Wilson
6068 **Everyday Without You**—Hamilton, Joe Frank & Reynolds
6077 **Light Up The World With Sunshine**—Hamilton, Joe Frank & Dennison
6088 **Don't Fight The Hands (That Need You)**—Hamilton, Joe Frank & Dennison

POLYDOR (8)
PD 14285 Let's Live Together—Road Apples
  14301 There Won't Be No Country Music (There Won't Be No Rock 'N' Roll)—C.W. McCall
  14309 Jasper—Jim Stafford
  14312 Norma Jean Wants To Be A Movie Star—Sundown Company
  14323 Jukin'—Atlanta Rhythm Section
  14326 Get Up Offa That Thing—James Brown
  14339 Free Spirit—Atlanta Rhythm Section
  14348 I Can't Live A Dream—Osmonds

PORTRAIT (1)
6-7001 Stand Tall—Burton Cummings

PRIVATE STOCK (12)
PS 45039 Moonlight Feels Right—Starbuck
  45043 Our Day Will Come—Frankie Valli
  45052 This Old Man—Purple Reign
  45055 Scotch On The Rocks—Band of the Black Watch
  45073 A Fifth Of Beethoven—Walter Murphy & the Big Apple Band
  45074 Fallen Angel—Frankie Valli
  45079 Did You Boogie With Your Baby (In The Back Row Of The Movie Show)—
       Flash Cadillac & the Continental Kids
  45086 Making Our Dreams Come True (Theme From 'Laverne & Shirley')—Cyndi Greco
  45098 We're All Alone—Frankie Valli
  45104 I Got To Know—Starbuck
  45123 Flight '76—Walter Murphy Band
  45125 Lucky Man—Starbuck

PRODIGAL (1)
PLP 6022 Eh! Cumpari—Gaylord & Holiday

PYE (3)
71045 For A Dancer—Prelude
71057 I Am Somebody—Jimmy James & the Vagabonds
71066 Save Your Kisses For Me—Brotherhood of Man

PYRAMID (2)
PD 8004 Sun...Sun...Sun—Ja kki
   8007 Ca-the-Drals—D.C. LaRue

QUALITY (1)
QA 501 Hit The Road Jack—Stampeders

RCA (24)
PB 10279 Feelings—Morris Albert
  10437 Sweet Loving Man—Morris Albert
  10441 Golden Years—David Bowie
  10464 Christmas For Cowboys—John Denver
  10517 Fly Away—John Denver
  10529 Good Hearted Woman—Waylon & Willie
  10530 Sara Smile—Daryl Hall & John Oates
  10561 It's Cool—Tymes
  10562 Turn The Beat Around—Vicki Sue Robinson
  10568 Say You Love Me—D.J. Rogers
  10586 Looking For Space—John Denver
  10601 Hurt/For The Heart—Elvis Presley
  10664 TVC 15—David Bowie

10687 **It Makes Me Giggle**—John Denver
10721 **Can't You See**—Waylon Jennings
10762 **I'll Play The Fool**—Dr. Buzzard's Original Savannah Band
10764 **9,999,999 Tears**—Dickey Lee
10774 **Like A Sad Song**—John Denver
10775 **Daylight**—Vicki Sue Robinson
10808 **Do What You Want, Be What You Are**—Daryl Hall & John Oates
10826 **Prisoner (Captured By Your Eyes)**—L.A. Jets
10827 **Whispering/Cherchez La Femme/Se Si Bon**—Dr. Buzzard's Original Savannah Band
10854 **Baby You Look Good To Me Tonight**—John Denver
10857 **Moody Blue/She Thinks I Still Care**—Elvis Presley

REPRISE (12)
RPS 1339 **Over My Head**—Fleetwood Mac
1345 **Rhiannon (Will You Ever Win)**—Fleetwood Mac
1346 **Here There And Everywhere**—Emmylou Harris
1349 **Welcome Back**—John Sebastian
1351 **Happy Days**—Pratt & McClain with Brotherlove
1355 **Hideaway**—John Sebastian
1356 **Say You Love Me**—Fleetwood Mac
1360 **Popsicle**—Michael Franks
1361 **Devil With The Blue Dress**—Pratt & McClain
1369 **The Wreck Of The Edmund Fitzgerald**—Gordon Lightfoot
Brother/Reprise RPS 1354 **Rock And Roll Music**—Beach Boys
Brother/Reprise RPS 1368 **It's OK**—Beach Boys

ROADSHOW (1)
RDJ 7005 **Close To You**—B.T. Express

ROCKET (9)
PIG 40500 **Breaking Up Is Hard To Do**—Neil Sedaka
40506 **Once A Fool**—Kiki Dee
40543 **Love In The Shadows**—Neil Sedaka
40574 **Devil Woman**—Cliff Richard
40582 **Steppin' Out**—Neil Sedaka
40585 **Don't Go Breaking My Heart**—Elton John/Kiki Dee
40614 **You Gotta Make Your Own Sunshine**—Neil Sedaka
40645 **Sorry Seems To Be The Hardest Word**—Elton John
40652 **I Can't Ask For Anymore Than You**—Cliff Richard

ROLLING STONES (1)
RS 19304 **Fool To Cry/Hot Stuff**—Rolling Stones

ROULETTE (2)
7182 **Touch & Go**—Ecstasy Passion & Pain
7195 **Full Time Thing (Between Dusk & Dawn)**—Whirlwind

RSO (10)
RS 515 **Nights On Broadway**—Bee Gees
519 **Fanny (Be Tender With My Love)**—Bee Gees
852 **Street Singin'**—Lady Flash
853 **You Should Be Dancing**—Bee Gees
854 **You To Me Are Everything**—Revelation
857 **Disco Duck**—Rick Dees & His Cast Of Idiots
858 **Love Me**—Yvonne Elliman
859 **Love So Right**—Bee Gees
860 **Living Next Door To Alice**—Smokie
861 **Hello Old Friend**—Eric Clapton

US LABEL

SALSOUL (4)
SZ-2004 Tangerine—Salsoul Orchestra
     2007 You're Just The Right Size—Salsoul Orchestra
     2008 Ten Percent—Double Exposure
     2011 Nice 'n' Naasty—Salsoul Orchestra

SHADYBROOK (1)
45019 Tonight's The Night—S.S.O.

SHELTER (2)
SRL 40483 Back To The Island—Leon Russell
    62002 Hey Baby—J.J. Cale

SOUL (1)
35119 Down To Love Town—Originals

SOUL TRAIN (2)
SB 10400 Soul Train '75'—Soul Train Gang
    10700 One For The Money—Whispers

STARDAY (1)
SD-142 Teddy Bear—Red Sovine

SWANSONG (2)
SS 70108 Young Blood—Bad Company
    70109 Honey Child—Bad Company

TAMLA (9)
T-54262F Love Machine—Miracles
    54263 Happy—Eddie Kendricks
    54264 I Want You—Marvin Gaye
    54265 Quiet Storm—Smokey Robinson
    54266 He's A Friend—Eddie Kendricks
    54267 Open—Smokey Robinson
    54272 I Wish—Stevie Wonder
    54273 After The Dance—Marvin Gaye
    54278 Don't Leave Me This Way—Thelma Houston

THRESHOLD (1)
THS 67021 Blue Guitar—Justin Hayward & John Lodge

TK (5)
1005 Queen Of Clubs—KC & the Sunshine Band
1015 That's The Way I Like It—KC & the Sunshine Band
1016 Honey I—George McCrae
1019 (Shake Shake Shake) Shake Your Booty—KC & the Sunshine Band
1020 I Like To Do It—KC & the Sunshine Band

T-NECK (3)
ZS8 2259 For The Love Of You—Isley Brothers
    2260 Who Loves You Better—Isley Brothers
    2261 Harvest For The World—Isley Brothers

TOM CAT (1)
YB 10454 One Fine Day—Julie

TSOP (1)
ZS8-4773 Nursery Rhymes—People's Choice

US LABEL

219

20TH CENTURY (11)

TC 2215 Hollywood Hot—Eleventh Hour
    2254 Growin' Up—Dan Hill
    2265 Let The Music Play—Barry White
    2271 Street Talk—B.C. Generation
    2275 When Love Has Gone Away—Richard Cocciante
    2287 I Like Dreamin'—Kenny Nolan
    2297 (The System Of) Doctor Tarr & Professor Fether—Alan Parsons Project
    2298 Baby, We Better Try And Get It Together—Barry White
    2301 My Sweet Summer Suite—Love Unlimited Orchestra
    2302 Sherry—Keane Brothers
    2308 The Raven—Alan Parsons Project

UNITED ARTISTS (18)

UA-XW729-Y Evil Woman—Electric Light Orchestra
    737   Times Of Your Life—Paul Anka
    746   Love Lifted Me—Kenny Rogers
    752   Right Back Where We Started From—Maxine Nightingale
    770   Strange Magic—Electric Light Orchestra
    775   Movin'—Brass Construction
    781   I'll Get Over You—Crystal Gayle
    789   Anytime (I'll Be There)—Paul Anka
    807   BLT—Lee Oskar
    820   Gotta Be The One—Maxine Nightingale
    833   You To Me Are Everything—Real Thing
    834   Summer—War
    842   Showdown—Electric Light Orchestra
    871   All Roads (Lead Back To You)—Donny Most
    874   Let Me Down Easy—American Flyer
    888   Livin' Thing—Electric Light Orchestra
    911   Happier—Paul Anka
    921   Ha Cha Cha (Funktion)—Brass Construction

WAND (2)

WND 11291 We're On The Right Track—South Shore Commission
    11294 Train Called Freedom—South Shore Commission

WARNER BROS (33)

WBS 8115 Paloma Blanca—George Baker Selection
    8122 Who Loves You—Four Seasons
    8143 Love Is Alive—Gary Wright
    8152 Spirit In The Night—Manfred Mann's Earthband
    8154 Once You Hit The Road—Dionne Warwick
    8157 Woman Tonight—America
    8161 I Cheat The Hangman—Doobie Brothers
    8165 Junkfood Junkie—Larry Groce
    8167 Dream Weaver—Gary Wright
    8168 December, 1963 (Oh, What A Night)—Four Seasons
    8169 Let Your Love Flow—Bellamy Brothers
    8170 This Old Heart Of Mine—Rod Stewart
    8175 The Jam—Graham Central Station
    8181 Young Hearts Run Free—Candi Staton
    8190 Get Closer—Seals & Crofts
    8196 Takin' It To The Streets—Doobie Brothers
    8203 Silver Star—Four Seasons

8209 **This Masquerade**—George Benson
8210 **Ode To Billy Joe**—Bobbie Gentry
8212 **Today's The Day**—America
8220 **Hell Cat**—Bellamy Brothers
8222 **Shower The People**—James Taylor
8228 **I Never Cry**—Alice Cooper
8233 **Wheels Of Fortune**—Doobie Brothers
8238 **Amber Cascades**—America
8248 **Satin Sheets**—Bellamy Brothers
8250 **Made To Love You**—Gary Wright
8252 **Blinded By The Light**—Manfred Mann's Earthband
8262 **Tonight's The Night**—Rod Stewart
8268 **Breezin'**—George Benson
8277 **Baby, I'll Give It To You**—Seals & Crofts
8282 **It Keeps You Runnin'**—Doobie Brothers
8283 **You Make Me Feel Like Dancing**—Leo Sayer

WESTBOUND (3)
W 5015 **Disco Sax/For The Love Of You**—Houston Person
5016 **Daydreamer**—C.C. & Company
5018 **Rattlesnake**—Ohio Players

WINDSONG (2)
CB 10588 **Afternoon Delight**—Starland Vocal Band
10785 **California Day**—Starland Vocal Band

WING & A PRAYER (1)
103 **Baby Face**—Wing & A Prayer Fife & Drum Corps

WMOT (1)
WM-4002 **Laid Back Love**—Major Harris

Section 10

US Writer Section

(*Billboard* Top 100 Singles Chart)

This section lists the writers, cross-referenced with co-writers, of all singles that made the *Billboard* Top 100 chart during 1976.

All writers are listed in alphabetical order, with the name of the co-writers bracketed beneath them, followed by the title of the song and the artist below that.

Certain writers credit themselves twice—once by their real name and again by their pseudonym (i.e. C.W. McCall and Bill Fries). When a group is credited with writing a song, all the members of that group are listed in brackets under the group's name. The individual members are also cross-referenced with the name of the group.

There are cases where credits will not correspond with the information found on the record (i.e. Vicki Sue Robinson's *Daylight,* credited to Bobby Womack, but also written by Harold T. Payne).

Phil AABERG
(w.Elvin Bishop)
Struttin' My Stuff—Elvin Bishop

Patrick ADAMS
Love Bug—Bumble Bee Unlimited

Richie ADAMS
(w.Alan Bernstein)
After The Lovin'—Engelbert Humperdinck

Jerry AKINES
(w.John Bellmon/Victor Drayton/Buddy
Turner)
One For The Money—Whispers

Harry AKST
(w.Benny Davis)
Baby Face—Wing & A Prayer Fife & Drum
Corps

Morris ALBERT
Feelings—Morris Albert
Feelings—Walter Jackson
Sweet Loving Man—Morris Albert

Luigi ALBERTELLI
(w.Bobby Hart/Danny Janssen/
Enrico Riccardi)
Words (Are Impossible)—Donny Gerrard

Tommy ALDRIDGE
(see BLACK OAK ARKANSAS)

James ALEXANDER
(see BAR-KAYS)

Laura ALLAN
(w.Bill Champlin)
Hold On—Sons of Champlin

Charles ALLEN
(see BAR-KAYS)

Papa Dee/Sylvester ALLEN
(see WAR)

Jerry ALLISON
(w.Buddy Holly/Norman Petty)
That'll Be The Day—Linda Ronstadt

Mike ALLISON
(w.Donald Black/Peter Sills)
Every Face Tells A Story—Olivia
Newton-John

Morgan AMES
(w.Dave Grusin)
**Baretta's Theme (Keep Your Eyes On
The Sparrow)**—Rhythm Heritage

Adrienne ANDERSON
(w.Barry Manilow)
Could It Be Magic—Donna Summer
Street Singin'—Lady Flash

Ian ANDERSON
Locomotive Breath—Jethro Tull

Stig ANDERSON
(w.Benny Andersson/Bjorn Ulvaeus)
Dancing Queen—Abba
Fernando—Abba
I Do, I Do, I Do, I Do, I Do—Abba
Mamma Mia—Abba

Benny ANDERSSON
(w.Stig Anderson/Bjorn Ulvaeus)
Dancing Queen—Abba
Fernando—Abba
I Do, I Do, I Do, I Do, I Do—Abba
Mamma Mia—Abba

Paul ANKA
Anytime (I'll Be There)—Paul Anka
Happier—Paul Anka

Biddu APPIAN
(see BIDDU)

Nickolas ASHFORD
(w.Valerie Simpson)
Ain't Nothing Like The Real Thing—
Donny & Marie Osmond

Gary ASKERAS
(w.Ellison Chase)
Let's Rock—Ellison Chase

Burt BACHARACH
(w.Hal David)
Close To You—B.T. Express

Randy BACHMAN
Down To The Line—Bachman-Turner
Overdrive
Lookin' Out For #1—Bachman-Turner
Overdrive

BAD COMPANY
(Boz Burrell/Simon Kirke/Mick Ralphs/
Paul Rodgers)
Honey Child—Bad Company

Philip BAILEY
(w.Maurice White/Al McKay)
Saturday Nite—Earth Wind & Fire

Razzy BAILEY
9,999,999 Tears—Dickey Lee

Belda BAINE
(w.Louise Crane)
Rattlesnake—Ohio Players

Ronnie/Ron BAKER
That's Where The Happy People Go—
Trammps
(w.Allan Felder/Norman Harris/Earl
Young)
Hold Back The Night—Trammps

Marty BALIN
(w.Joey Covington/Victor Smith)
With Your Love—Jefferson Starship
(w.Jesse Barish/Craig Chaquico/Paul
Kantner/Thunderhawk)
St. Charles—Jefferson Starship

Homer BANKS
(w.Carl Hampton)
**I've Got A Feeling (We'll Be Seeing Each
Other Again)**—Al Wilson

Jesse BARISH
(w.Marty Balin/Craig Chaquico/Paul
Kantner/Thunderhawk)
St. Charles—Jefferson Starship

BAR-KAYS
(James Alexander/Charles Allen/
Michael Beard/Larry Dodson/Harvey
Henderson/Lloyd Smith/Winston
Stewart/Frank Thompson)
Shake Your Rump To The Funk—
Bar-Kays

Len BARRY
(w.Bobby Eli)
Laid Back Love—Major Harris

Bill BATES
Scotch On The Rocks—Band of the
Black Watch

Jeff BAXTER
(w.John Hartman/Pat Simmons)
Wheels Of Fortune—Doobie Brothers

Frank BEARD
(see Z Z Top)

Michael BEARD
(see BAR-KAYS)

Harold BEATTY
(w.Brian & Eddie Holland)
**I'm Gonna Let My Heart Do The
Walking**—Supremes
(w.Reginald Brown/Brian Holland/Floyd
Stafford)
You're My Driving Wheel—Supremes

William BECK
(w.Marshall Jones/Marvin Pierce/James
Williams)
Who'd She Coo—Ohio Players
(see also OHIO PLAYERS)

Walter BECKER
(w.Donald Fagen)
Kid Charlemagne—Steely Dan
(w.Donald Fagen/Paul L. Griffin)
The Fez—Steely Dan

BEE GEES
(Barry, Maurice & Robin Gibb)
Fanny (Be Tender With My Love)—
Bee Gees
Love So Right—Bee Gees
Nights On Broadway—Bee Gees
You Should Be Dancing—Bee Gees
(see also Barry & Robin GIBB)

Ronald BELL
(w.Kool & the Gang)
Open Sesame—Kool & the Gang
(w.Kool & the Gang/Claydes Smith)
**Love And Understanding (Come
Together)**—Kool & the Gang

Thom BELL
(w.Linda Creed)
The Rubber Band Man—Spinners
(w.Sherman Marshall)
Wake Up Susan—Spinners

David BELLAMY
Hell Cat—Bellamy Brothers

John BELLMON
(w.Jerry Akines/Victor Drayton/Buddy
Turner)
One For The Money—Whispers

Pete BELLOTTE
(w.Giorgio Moroder/Donna Summer)
Love To Love You Baby—Donna Summer
Spring Affair—Donna Summer
Try Me, I Know We Can Make It—Donna
Summer

Henri BELOLO
  (w.Phil Hurtt/Jacques Morali/Ritchie Rome)
  The Best Disco In Town—Ritchie Family

Gary BENSON
  Let Her In—John Travolta
  (w.Dave Mindel)
  Whenever I'm Away From You—John Travolta

Alan BERNSTEIN
  (w.Richie Adams)
  After The Lovin'—Engelbert Humperdinck

Chuck BERRY
  Rock And Roll Music—Beach Boys

John BETTIS
  (w.Richard Carpenter/Albert Hammond)
  I Need To Be In Love—Carpenters

BIDDU (aka Biddu APPIAN)
  I Am Somebody—Jimmy James & the Vagabonds
  (w.Lee Vanderbilt)
  Jump For Joy—Biddu Orchestra

Elvin BISHOP
  Fooled Around And Fell In Love—Elvin Bishop
  Spend Some Time—Elvin Bishop
  (w.Phil Aaberg)
  Struttin' My Stuff—Elvin Bishop

Stephen BISHOP
  Save It For A Rainy Day—Stephen Bishop

Donald BLACK
  (w.Mike Allison/Peter Sills)
  Every Face Tells A Story—Olivia Newton-John

BLACK OAK ARKANSAS
  (Tommy Aldridge, Jim Dandy, Pat Daugherty, 'Little' Jimmy Henderson & Rickie Lee Reynolds)
  Strong Enough To Be Gentle—Black Oak Arkansas

BLACKBYRDS
  (Joe Hall/Stephen Johnson/Keith Killgo/Orville Saunders/Kevin Toney)
  Rock Creek Park—Blackbyrds

Bruce BLACKMAN
  I Got To Know—Starbuck
  Lucky Man—Starbuck
  Moonlight Feels Right—Starbuck

Carte BLANCHE
  (see Elton John/Bernie Taupin)

Raymond BLOODWORTH
  (w.Larry Russell Brown)
  C'mon Marianne—Donny Osmond

Lana BOGAN
  (w.Jimmy Seals)
  Baby, I'll Give It To You—Seals & Crofts

Chris BOND
  Help Wanted—Hudson Brothers

Leroy BONNER
  (see OHIO PLAYERS)

Karla BONOFF
  Someone To Lay Down Beside Me—Linda Ronstadt

Perry BOTKIN Jr.
  (w.Barry DeVorzon)
  Nadia's Theme (The Young & The Restless)—Barry DeVorzon & Perry Botkin Jr.

Gilbert BOTTIGLIER
  (w.Chuck Higgins Jr./Paul Stallworth)
  Sweet Summer Music—Attitudes

Rory BOURKE
  (w.Gene Dobbins/Johnny Wilson)
  Easy As Pie—Billy 'Crash' Craddock

Johannes BOUWENS
  Paloma Blanca—George Baker Selection

Jeffrey BOWEN
  (w.Jimmy Ford/Truman Thomas)
  Up The Creek (Without A Paddle)—Temptations

David BOWIE
  Golden Years—David Bowie
  TVC 15—David Bowie

Jacob BRACKMAN
  (w.George Clinton/Michel Polnareff)
  If You Only Believe (Jesus For Tonight)—Michel Polnareff

Jerome BRAILEY
  (w.George Clinton/Bootsy Collins)
  (Give Up The Funk) Tear The Roof Off The Sucker—Parliament

Don BREWER
  (w.Craig Frost)
  Take Me—Grand Funk Railroad

Fred BRIDGES
(w.Mikki Farrow/Lawrence Payton)
Catfish—Four Tops

Johnny BRISTOL
Do It To My Mind—Johnny Bristol

Terry BRITTEN
(w.Christine Hodgson)
Devil Woman—Cliff Richard

Britt BRITTON
(w.Freida Nerangis)
Every Beat Of My Heart—Crown Heights
Affair
Foxy Lady—Crown Heights Affair

Stony BROWDER Jr.
(w.August Darnell)
I'll Play The Fool—Dr. Buzzard's Original
Savannah Band
Se Si Bon—Dr. Buzzard's Original
Savannah Band
Cherchez La Femme—Dr. Buzzard's
Original Savannah Band

David BROWN
(w.Ray Gardner)
Let It Shine—Santana

Deanna BROWN
(w.Deidra Brown/Yamma Brown)
Get Up Offa That Thing—James Brown

Deidra BROWN
(w.Deanna Brown/Yamma Brown)
Get Up Offa That Thing—James Brown

Errol BROWN
Don't Stop It Now—Hot Chocolate
(w.Tony Wilson)
You Sexy Thing—Hot Chocolate

George M. BROWN
(see KOOL & THE GANG)

Harold BROWN
(see WAR)

Larry Russell BROWN
(w.Raymond Bloodworth)
C'mon Marianne—Donny Osmond

Lawrence BROWN
(w.Terri McFaddin/Leonard Perry)
One Love In My Lifetime—Supremes

Reginald BROWN
(w.Harold Beatty/Brian Holland/
Floyd Stafford)
You're My Driving Wheel—Supremes

Yamma BROWN
(w.Deanna Brown/Deidra Brown)
Get Up Offa That Thing—James Brown

Jackson BROWNE
For A Dancer—Prelude

Boudleaux BRYANT
Love Hurts—Nazareth

Buddy BUIE
(w.Robert Nix)
Jukin'—Atlanta Rhythm Section
(w.Ronnie Hammond/Robert Nix)
Free Spirit—Atlanta Rhythm Section

Cindy BULLENS
(w.Bob Crewe)
Hollywood Hot—Eleventh Hour
Street Talk—B.C. Generation

Dewey BUNNELL
Amber Cascades—America

Richard BURGESS
(see EASY STREET)

Billy Joe BURNETTE
(w.Dale Royal)
Teddy Bear's Last Ride—Diana Williams
(w.Tommy Hill/Dale Royal/Red Sovine)
Teddy Bear—Red Sovine

Boz BURRELL
(see BAD COMPANY

Jerry BUTLER
(w.Calvin Carter/Sam Cooke/Jerry
Leiber/Curtis Mayfield/Mike Stoller)
Chain Gang Medley—Jim Croce

Byron BYRD
Wanna Make Love (Come Flick My BIC)
—Sun

Donald BYRD
Happy Music—Blackbyrds

Jonathan CAIN
'Til It's Time To Say Goodbye—Jonathan
Cain

Robert CALDWELL
(w.Jimmy George)
Don't Fight The Hands (That Need You)
—Hamilton, Joe Frank & Dennison

Toy CALDWELL
Can't You See—Waylon Jennings

J.J. CALE
Hey Baby—J.J. Cale

Arnold CAPITANELLI
  I Can't Live A Dream—Osmonds

Tyran CARLO
  (Berry Gordy/Gwendolyn Gordy)
  Lonely Teardrops—Narvel Felts

Eric CARMEN
  All By Myself—Eric Carmen
  Never Gonna Fall In Love Again—Eric
  Carmen
  Sunrise—Eric Carmen

Richard CARPENTER
  (w.John Bettis/Albert Hammond)
  I Need To Be In Love—Carpenters

Keith CARRADINE
  I'm Easy—Keith Carradine

Calvin CARTER
  (w.Jerry Butler/Sam Cooke/Jerry
  Leiber/Curtis Mayfield/Mike Stoller)
  Chain Gang Medley—Jim Croce

Ric CARTEY
  (w.Carole Joyner)
  Young Love—Ray Stevens

Victor CARSTARPHEN
  (w.Gene McFadden/John Whitehead)
  Bad Luck—Atlanta Disco Band
  Tell The World How I Feel About 'Cha
  Baby—Harold Melvin & the Blue Notes
  Wake Up Everybody—Harold Melvin &
  the Blue Notes

Harry Wayne CASEY (aka KC)
  (w.Willie Clarke)
  Queen Of Clubs—KC & the Sunshine
  Band
  (w.Richard Finch)
  Honey I—George McCrae
  I Like To Do It—KC & the Sunshine Band
  (Shake Shake Shake) Shake Your Booty
  —KC & the Sunshine Band
  That's The Way I Like It—KC & the
  Sunshine Band

Johnny CASH
  Bigfoot—Bro Smith

Steve CASH
  (w.Larry Lee)
  If I Only Knew—Ozark Mountain
  Daredevils

Terry CASHMAN
  (w.Tommy West)
  Baby, Baby I Love You—Terry Cashman

Emilio CASTILLO
  (w.Steve Kupka/Hubert Tubbs)
  You Ought To Be Havin' Fun—Tower of
  Power

Leonard CASTON
  (w.Kathy Wakefield)
  Happy—Eddie Kendricks

Earl CATE
  (w.Ernie Cate)
  Can't Change My Heart—Cate Bros
  (w.Ernie Cate/Steve Cropper)
  Union Man—Cate Bros

Ernie CATE
  (w.Earl Cate)
  Can't Change My Heart—Cate Bros
  (w.Earl Cate/Steve Cropper)
  Union Man—Cate Bros

Peter CETERA
  If You Leave Me Now—Chicago

Bill CHAMPLIN
  (w.Laura Allan)
  Hold On—Sons of Champlin

Harry CHAPIN
  A Better Place To Be—Harry Chapin

Michael/Mike CHAPMAN
  (w.Nicky Chinn)
  Can The Can—Suzi Quatro
  Living Next Door To Alice—Smokie

Craig CHAQUICO
  (w.Marty Balin/Paul Kantner/Jesse
  Barish/Thunderhawk)
  St. Charles—Jefferson Starship

Les CHARLES
  (w.Ben Findon)
  Love Really Hurts Without You—
  Billy Ocean

Ellison CHASE
  (w.Gary Askeras)
  Let's Rock—Ellison Chase

Nicky CHINN
  (w.Mike Chapman)
  Can The Can—Suzi Quatro
  Living Next Door To Alice—Smokie

Thomas CHONG
  (w.Jerry Leiber/Richard Marin/Mike
  Stoller)
  Framed—Cheech & Chong

Gavin CHRISTOPHER
Dance Wit Me—Rufus featuring Chaka Khan

Eric CLAPTON
Hello Old Friend—Eric Clapton

Willie CLARKE
(w.Harry Wayne Casey)
Queen Of Clubs—KC & the Sunshine Band

Adrian CLEMENTS
(w.Terry Huff)
The Lonely One—Special Delivery featuring Terry Huff

George CLINTON
(w.Jacob Brackman/Michel Polnareff)
If You Only Believe (Jesus For Tonight)—Michel Polnareff

George CLINTON
(w.Jerome Brailey/Bootsy Collins)
(Give Up The Funk) Tear The Roof Off The Sucker—Parliament

Joe COBB
(w.Van McCoy)
Heavy Love—David Ruffin

Richard COBURN
(w.Vincent Rose/John Schonberger)
Whispering—Dr. Buzzard's Original Savannah Band

Richard COCCIANTE
(w.Marco Luberti/Danielle Rouby)
When Love Has Gone Away—Richard Cocciante

Phil CODY
(w.Neil Sedaka)
Love In The Shadows—Neil Sedaka
Steppin' Out—Neil Sedaka

Natalie COLE
(w.Chuck Jackson/Marvin Yancy)
Sophisticated Lady (She's A Different Lady)—Natalie Cole

Allen COLLINS
(w.Ronnie Van Zant)
Double Trouble—Lynyrd Skynyrd
Free Bird—Lynyrd Skynyrd

William/'Bootsy' COLLINS
(w.Jerome Brailey/George Clinton)
(Give Up The Funk) Tear The Roof Off The Sucker—Parliament

Clarence COLTER
(w.Don Davis/Chico Jones)
Somebody's Gettin' It—Johnnie Taylor

COMMODORES
(William King, Ronald LaPraed, Tom McClary, Walter Orange, Lionel Richie & Milan Williams)
(w.Lionel Richie)
Just To Be Close To You—Commodores
Sweet Love—Commodores

Perry CONE
(w.Paul Vance)
Without Your Love (Mr. Jordan)—Charlie Ross

Brian CONNOLLY
(see SWEET)

T.G. (Talmadge) CONWAY
(w.Allan Felder)
Ten Percent—Double Exposure
(w.Allan Felder/Bruce Gray)
He's A Friend—Eddie Kendricks

Sam COOKE
Cupid—Tony Orlando & Dawn
Only Sixteen—Dr. Hook
(w.Jerry Butler/Calvin Carter/Jerry Leiber/Curtis Mayfield/Mike Stoller)
Chain Gang Medley—Jim Croce

Alice COOPER
(w.Dick Wagner)
I Never Cry—Alice Cooper

Peter COR
(w.Beloyd Taylor)
Getaway—Earth Wind & Fire

Don CORNELIUS
(w.Dick Griffey)
Soul Train '75'—Soul Train Gang

Bill COSBY
(w.Stu Gardner)
Yes, Yes, Yes—Bill Cosby

Phil COULTER
(w.Bill Martin)
Saturday Night—Bay City Rollers

Joey COVINGTON
(w.Marty Balin/Victor Smith)
With Your Love—Jefferson Starship

Jimmie CRANE
(w.Al Jacobs)
Hurt—Elvis Presley

Louise CRANE
  (w.Belda Baine)
  Rattlesnake—Ohio Players

Dave CRAWFORD
  Young Hearts Run Free—Candi Staton
  (w.Richard Downing)
  Mighty Clouds Of Joy—Mighty High

Luigi CREATORE
  (see LUIGI)

Linda CREED
  (w.Thom Bell)
  The Rubber Band Man—Spinners

Lol CREME
  (w.Graham Gouldman/Eric Stewart)
  I'm Mandy Fly Me—10nc

Bob CREWE
  (w.Cindy Bullens)
  Hollywood Hot—Eleventh Hour
  Street Talk—B.C. Generation

Peter CRISS
  (w.Bob Ezrin/Stan Penridge)
  Beth—Kiss

Dash CROFTS
  (w.Jimmy Seals)
  Get Closer—Seals & Crofts

Steve CROPPER
  (w.Earl & Ernie Cate)
  Union Man—Cate Bros

David CROSBY
  (w.Craig Degree/Graham Nash)
  Out Of The Darkness—David Crosby/
  Graham Nash

Burton CUMMINGS
  Stand Tall—Burton Cummings

Johnny CUNNINGHAM
  Norma Jean Wants To Be A Movie Star—
  Sundown Company

Jim DANDY
  (see BLACK OAK ARKANSAS)

Sanford 'Pepe' DANIEL
  (w.Michael Keck, Joyce Kennedy, Gary
  'Mo' Moore, Glenn Murdock & Jerry
  'Wizzard' Seay).
  Fire—Mother's Finest

Charlie DANIELS
  Texas—Charlie Daniels Band

Don DANIELS
  (w.Michael L. Smith)
  Let's Be Young Tonight—Jermaine
  Jackson
  (w.Michael B. Sutton/Kathy Wakefield)
  Down To Love Town—Originals

Bill DANOFF
  Baby, You Look Good To Me Tonight
  —John Denver
  Afternoon Delight—Starland Vocal Band
  California Day—Starland Vocal Band

Bobby DARIN
  Things—Anne Murray

August DARNELL
  (w.Stony Browder Jr.)
  I'll Play The Fool—Dr. Buzzard's Original
  Savannah Band
  Se Si Bon—Dr. Buzzard's Original
  Savannah Band
  Cherchez La Femme—Dr. Buzzard's
  Original Savannah Band

Pat DAUGHERTY
  (see BLACK OAK ARKANSAS)

Hal DAVID
  (w.Burt Bacharach)
  Close To You—B.T. Express

Benny DAVIS
  (w.Harry Akst)
  Baby Face—Wing & A Prayer Fife & Drum
  Corps

Chip DAVIS
  (w.Bill Fries/C.W. McCall)
  Convoy—C.W. McCall
  **There Won't Be No Country Music (There
  Won't Be No Rock 'n' Roll)**—C.W. McCall

Don DAVIS
  (w.Harvey Scales/Al Vance)
  Disco Lady—Johnnie Taylor
  (w.Clarence Colter/Chico Jones)
  Somebody's Gettin' It—Johnnie Taylor

George DAVIS
  (w.Lee Diamond)
  Tell It Like It Is—Andy Williams

Katherine DAVIS
  (w.Henry Onorati/Harry Simeone)
  Little Drummer Boy—Moonlion

Paul DAVIS
  Superstar—Paul Davis
  Thinking Of You—Paul Davis

Paul DAVIS
(w.Michael Zager)
Do It With Feeling—Michael Zager's
Moon Band featuring Peabo Bryson

John DEACON
You're My Best Friend—Queen

James DEAN
(w.John Glover)
I Hope We Get To Love In Time—Marilyn
McCoo & Billy Davis Jr.
You Don't Have To Be A Star (To Be In
My Show)—Marilyn McCoo & Billy
Davis Jr.

Jimmy DEAN
(w.Larry Markes)
I.O.U.—Jimmy Dean)

Rick DEES
Disco Duck—Rick Dees & His Cast Of
Idiots

Craig DEGREE (aka Craig DOERGE)
(w.David Crosby/Graham Nash)
Out Of The Darkness—David Crosby/
Graham Nash

Sean DELANEY
(w.Dube Grob/Brenden Harkin/
Richie Ranno/Michael Lee Smith/Peter
Sweval)
(She's Just A) Fallen Angel—Starz

Terry DEMPSEY
Daydreamer—C.C. & Company

Micky DENNE
(w.Ken Gold)
I Can't Ask For Anymore Than You—
Cliff Richard
You To Me Are Everything—Broadway
You To Me Are Everything—Real Thing
You To Me Are Everything—Revelation

John DENVER
Fly Away—John Denver
It Makes Me Giggle—John Denver
Like A Sad Song—John Denver
Looking For Space—John Denver

Peter DeROSE
(w.Mitchell Parish)
Deep Purple—Donny & Marie Osmond

Rick DERRINGER
(w.Cynthia Weil)
Let Me In—Derringer

John DeSAUTELS
(w.Karen Lawrence)
Prisoner (Captured By Your Eyes)—
L.A. Jets

Barry DeVORZON
Theme From S.W.A.T.—Rhythm Heritage
(w.Perry Botkin Jr.)
Nadia's Theme (The Young & The
Restless)—Barry DeVorzon & Perry
Botkin Jr.

James DEWAR
(w.Robin Trower)
Caledonia—Robin Trower

Dennis DeYOUNG
(w.James Young)
Lorelei—Styx
(w.Tommy Shaw)
Mademoiselle—Styx

Gregg DIAMOND
More, More, More—Andrea True
Connection
Party Line—Andrea True Connection

Lee DIAMOND
(w.George Davis)
Tell It Like It Is—Andy Williams

Neil DIAMOND
Don't Think . . . Feel—Neil Diamond
If You Know What I Mean—Neil Diamond
Solitary Man—T.G. Sheppard

B.B./Morris DICKERSON
(see WAR)

Gene DOBBINS
(w.Rory Bourke/Johnny Wilson)
Easy As Pie—Billy 'Crash' Craddock

Larry DODSON
(see BAR-KAYS)

Craig DOERGE
(see Craig DEGREE)

DORKNOCKER (aka Leila T. Snake)
(w.Ron Nagle)
Don't Touch Me There—Tubes

Brian DOWNEY
(w.Phil Lynott)
Cowboy Song—Thin Lizzy

Richard DOWNING
(w.Dave Crawford)
Mighty High—Mighty Clouds of Joy

Lamont DOZIER
(w.Brian Holland/Eddie Holland)
Where Did Our Love Go—J. Geils Band
This Old Heart Of Mine—Rod Stewart

Victor DRAYTON
(w.Jerry Akines/John Bellmon/
Buddy Turner)
One For The Money—Whispers

Steve DUFFY
(w.Dave L. Lipscomb)
She Thinks I Still Care—Elvis Presley
(usually credited to Dickey Lee who bought
the song from the two composers)

David DUNDAS
(w.Roger Greenaway)
Jeans On—David Dundas

Des DYER
(w.Clive Scott)
Love Fire—Jigsaw
Sky High—Jigsaw

Bob DYLAN
(w.Jacques Levy)
Hurricane—Bob Dylan
Mozambique—Bob Dylan

EASY STREET
(Richard Burgess, Peter Marsh & Ken
Nicol)
(w.Pete Zorn)
I've Been Lovin' You—Easy Street

Randy EDELMAN
Weekend In New England—Barry
Manilow

Vince EDWARDS
(w.Pierre Tubbs)
Gotta Be The One—Maxine Nightingale

Bobby ELI
(w.Len Barry)
Laid Back Love—Major Harris
(w.Charles Kelly)
Happy Man—Impact

Greg ERRICO
(w.Lee Oskar)
BLT—Lee Oskar

Bob EZRIN
(w.Peter Criss/Stan Penridge)
Beth—Kiss
(w.Paul Stanley)

Detroit ROCK CITY—Kiss
(w.Gene Simmons/Paul Stanley)
Shout It Out Loud—Kiss

Donald FAGEN
(w.Walter Becker)
Kid Charlemagne—Steely Dan
(w.Walter Becker/Paul L. Griffin)
The Fez—Steely Dan

Mark FARNER
Sally—Grand Funk Railroad

John FARRAR
Don't Stop Believin'—Olivia
Newton-John

Mikki FARROW
(w.Fred Bridges/Lawrence Payton)
Catfish—Four Tops

Eric FAULKNER
(w.Stuart 'Woody' Wood)
Money Honey—Bay City Rollers

Michael S. FEIN
The Fonz Song—Heyettes

Allan FELDER
(w.T.G. Conway)
Ten Percent—Double Exposure
(w.Norman Harris)
We're On The Right Track—South Shore
Commission
(w.Norman Harris/Bunny Sigler)
Touch & Go—Ecstasy, Passion & Pain
(w.Bruce Gray/T.G. Conway)
He's A Friend—Eddie Kendricks
(w.Ronnie Baker/Norman Harris/
Earl Young)
Hold Back The Night—Trammps

Steve FERRONE
(w.Alan Gorrie/Hamish Stuart)
School Boy Crush—Average White Band

Bryan FERRY
(w.Andy MacKay)
Love Is The Drug—Roxy Music

Richard FINCH
(w.Harry Wayne Casey)
I Like To Do It—KC & the Sunshine Band
(Shake Shake Shake) Shake Your Booty
—KC & the Sunshine Band
Honey I—George McCrae
That's The Way I Like It—KC & the
Sunshine Band

Ben FINDON
(w.Geoff Wilkens)
Light Up The World With Sunshine—
Hamilton, Joe Frank & Dennison
(w.Les Charles)
Love Really Hurts Without You—Billy
Ocean

Fin FINNERTY
Let's Live Together—Road Apples

Doug FLETCHER
(w.Guy Flett)
Fallen Angel—Frankie Valli

Guy FLETT
(w.Doug Fletcher)
Fallen Angel—Frankie Valli

John FOGERTY
You Got The Magic—John Fogerty

Dwayn FORD
Sherry—Keane Brothers

Jimmy FORD
(w.Jeffrey Bowen/Truman Thomas)
Up The Creek (Without A Paddle)—
Temptations

Vincent FORD
Roots, Rock, Reggae—Bob Marley &
the Wailers

Charles FOX
(w.Norman Gimbel)
**Making Our Dreams Come True (Theme
from 'Laverne & Shirley')**—Cyndi Greco
Happy Days—Pratt & McClain with
Brotherlove

Peter FRAMPTON
Baby I Love Your Way—Peter Frampton
Do You Feel Like We Do—Peter Frampton
Show Me The Way—Peter Frampton

Michael FRANKS
Popsicle Toes—Michael Franks

Ace FREHLEY
(w.Gene Simmons/Paul Stanley)
Flaming Youth—Kiss

Glenn FREY
(w.Don Henley/John David Souther)
New Kid In Town—Eagles
(w.Don Henley/Randy Meisner)
Take It To The Limit—Eagles

Bill FRIES (aka C.W. McCALL)
(w.Chip Davis/C.W. McCall)
Convoy—C.W. McCall
**There Won't Be No Country Music (There
Won't Be No Rock 'n' Roll)**—C.W. McCall

Craig FROST
(w.Don Brewer)
Take Me—Grand Funk Railroad

Craig FULLER
(w.Eric Kaz)
Let Me Down Easy—American Flyer

Andre GAGNON
Wow—Andre Gagnon

Benny GALLAGHER
(w.Graham Lyle)
Heart On My Sleeve—Bryan Ferry
Heart On My Sleeve—Gallagher & Lyle
I Wanna Stay With You—Gallagher &
Lyle
Breakaway—Art Garfunkel

Kenny GAMBLE
(w.Leon Huff)
Enjoy Yourself—Jacksons
The Zip—MFSB
I Love Music—O'Jays
Message In Our Music—O'Jays
Let's Make A Baby—Billy Paul
When Love Is New—Arthur Prysock
Groovy—Lou Rawls
**You'll Never Find Another Love Like
Mine**—Lou Rawls
(w.Cary Gilbert)
Don't Leave Me This Way—Thelma
Houston
Livin' For The Weekend—O'Jays

Ray GARDNER
(w.David Brown)
Let It Shine—Santana

Stu GARDNER
(w.Bill Cosby)
Yes, Yes, Yes—Bill Cosby

Gene GARFIN
(w.Andrew Gold)
That's Why I Love You—Andrew Gold

Lee GARRETT
(w.Robert Taylor)
You're My Everything—Lee Garrett

Mort GARSON
(w.Bob Hilliard)
Our Day Will Come—Frankie Valli

David GATES
Lost Without Your Love—Bread
Part Time Love—Gladys Knight & the Pips

Bob GAUDIO
(w.Judy Parker)
December, 1963 (Oh, What A Night)—
Four Seasons
Silver Star—Four Seasons
Who Loves You—Four Seasons

Marvin GAYE
(w.Leon Ware)
After The Dance—Marvin Gaye

Rick GEILS .
Wham Bam (Shang-A-Lang)—Silver

Bobbie GENTRY
Ode To Billy Joe—Bobbie Gentry

Jimmy GEORGE
(w.Robert Caldwell)
Don't Fight The Hands (That Need You)
—Hamilton, Joe Frank & Dennison

Kenny GEORGE
Listen To The Buddah—Ozo

Barry GIBB
(w.Robin Gibb)
Love Me—Yvonne Elliman
Come On Over—Olivia Newton-John
(see also BEE GEES)

Maurice GIBB
(see BEE GEES)

Robin GIBB
(w.Barry Gibb)
Love Me—Yvonne Elliman
Come On Over—Olivia Newton-John
(see also BEE GEES)

Billy GIBBONS
(see Z Z Top)

Steve GIBBONS
Johnny Cool—Steve Gibbons Band

Cary GILBERT
(w.Kenny Gamble/Leon Huff)
Don't Leave Me This Way—Thelma
Houston
Livin' For The Weekend—O'Jays
(w.Leon Huff)
Nursery Rhymes—People's Choice

Nick GILDER
(w.James McCulloch)
Roxy Roller—Sweeney Todd
Roxy Roller—Sweeney Todd featuring
Brian Guy Adams

Norman GIMBEL
(w.Charles Fox)
**Making Our Dreams Come True (Theme
from 'Laverne & Shirley')**—Cyndi Greco
Happy Days—Pratt & McClain with
Brotherlove

Larry GITTENS
(see KOOL & THE GANG)

John GLOVER
(w.James Dean)
I Hope We Get To Love In Time—
Marilyn McCoo & Billy Davis Jr.
**You Don't Have To Be A Star (To Be
In My Show)**—Marilyn McCoo & Billy
Davis Jr.

Graham GOBLE
It's A Long Way There—Little River Band

Gerry GOFFIN
(w.Carole King)
One Fine Day—Julie
High Out Of Time—Carole King
I Can't Hear You No More—Helen Reddy
Will You Love Me Tomorrow—Dana
Valery
(w.Michael Masser)
So Sad The Song—Gladys Knight & the
Pips
**Theme From Mahogany 'Do You Know
Where You're Going To'**—Diana Ross

Andrew GOLD
(w.Gene Garfin)
That's Why I Love You—Andrew Gold

Ken GOLD
(w.Micky Denne)
I Can't Ask For Anymore Than You—
Cliff Richard
You To Me Are Everything—Broadway
You To Me Are Everything—Real Thing
You To Me Are Everything—Revelation

Jerry GOLDSTEIN
(w.War)
Summer—War

Berry GORDY (Jr.)
(w.William Robinson)
Shop Around—Captain & Tennille
(w.Tyran Carlo/Gwendolyn Gordy)
Lonely Teardrops—Narvel Felts

Gwendolyn GORDY
(w.Tyran Carlo/Berry Gordy)
Lonely Teardrops—Narvel Felts

Thelma GORDY
(w.Richard Street)
Can You Do It—Grand Funk Railroad

Alan GORRIE
(w.Steve Ferrone/Hamish Stuart)
School Boy Crush—Average White Band

Bobby GOSH
A Little Bit More—Dr. Hook

Graham GOULDMAN
(w.Eric Stewart)
Art For Art's Sake—10cc
(w.Lol Creme/Eric Stewart)
I'm Mandy Fly Me—10cc

Charles GRAHAM
(w.Iris May)
Brand New Love Affair—Jigsaw

Larry GRAHAM
The Jam—Graham Central Station

Leo GRAHAM
Give It Up (Turn It Loose)—Tyrone Davis

Bruce GRAY
(w.T.G. Conway/Allan Felder)
He's A Friend—Eddie Kendricks

Al GREEN
(w.Willie Mitchell)
Keep Me Cryin'—Al Green
(w.Mabon Hughes/Willie Mitchell)
Full Of Fire—Al Green

Jimmy GREEN Jr.
(w.Danny Wolfe)
Hey Shirley (This Is Squirrely)—Shirley
& Squirrely

Roger GREENAWAY
(w.David Dundas)
Jeans On—David Dundas

Susaye GREENE
(w.Hank Redd/Nathan Watts/
Deniece Williams)
Free—Deniece Williams

Howard GREENFIELD
(w.Neil Sedaka)
The Hungry Years—Wayne Newton
Breaking Up Is Hard To Do—Neil Sedaka
You Gotta Make Your Own Sunshine—
Neil Sedaka

Dick GRIFFEY
(w.Don Cornelius)
Soul Train '75'—Soul Train Gang

Paul L. GRIFFIN
(w.Walter Becker/Donald Fagen)
The Fez—Steely Dan

William GRIFFIN
(w.Warren 'Pete' Moore)
Love Machine—Miracles

Joe X./Dube GROB
(w.Sean Delaney/Brenden Harkin)
Richie Ranno/Michael Lee Smith/
Peter Sweval)
(She's Just A) Fallen Angel—Starz

Larry GROCE
Junkfood Junkie—Larry Groce

Henry GROSS
Shannon—Henry Gross
Someday—Henry Gross
Springtime Mama—Henry Gross

Carl GROSSMAN
A Dose Of Rock And Roll—Ringo Starr

Dave GRUSIN
(w.Morgan Ames)
Baretta's Theme (Keep Your Eyes On The
Sparrow)—Rhythm Heritage

Daryl HALL
(w.John Oates)
Do What You Want, Be What You Are—
Daryl Hall & John Oates
Sara Smile—Daryl Hall & John Oates
She's Gone—Daryl Hall & John Oates

Joe HALL
(see BLACKBYRDS)

Johanna HALL
(w.John Hall)
Still The One—Orleans

John HALL
(w.Johanna Hall)
Still The One—Orleans

Roe HALL
(w.George Jackson)
Find 'Em, Fool 'Em, Forget 'Em—Dobie
Gray

Ann HAMILTON
(w.Dan Hamilton)
Winners And Losers—Hamilton, Joe Frank
& Reynolds

Dan HAMILTON
Everyday Without You—Hamilton, Joe
Frank & Reynolds
(w.Ann Hamilton)
Winners And Losers—Hamilton, Joe Frank
& Reynolds

Albert HAMMOND
(w.John Bettis/Richard Carpenter)
I Need To Be In Love—Carpenters

Ronnie HAMMOND
(w.Buddy Buie/Robert Nix)
Free Spirit—Atlanta Rhythm Section

Carl HAMPTON
(w.Homer Banks)
**I've Got A Feeling (We'll Be Seeing Each
Other Again)**—Al Wilson

John HANDY
Hard Work—John Handy

Hagood HARDY
The Homecoming—Hagood Hardy

Regi HARGIS
(w.Eddie Irons/Ray Ransom)
Dazz—Brick

Linda HARGROVE
Let It Shine—Olivia Newton-John

Brenden HARKIN
(w.Sean Delaney/Dube Grob/Richie
Ranno/Michael Lee Smith/Peter Sweval)
(She's Just A) Fallen Angel—Starz

Steve HARLEY
Make Me Smile (Come Up And See Me)
—Steve Harley & Cockney Rebel

William HAROLD
(w.Gus Kahn/Wayne King)
Goofus—Carpenters

Norman HARRIS
(w.Allan Felder)
We're On The Right Track—South Shore
Commission
(w.Allan Felder/Bunny Sigler)

Touch & Go—Ecstasy Passion & Pain
(w.Ronnie Baker/Allan Felder/Earl
Young)
Hold Back The Night—Trammps

George HARRISON
This Song—George Harrison

Bobby HART
(w.Luigi Alberteili/Danny Janssen/
Enrico Riccardi)
Words (Are Impossible)—Donny Gerrard

Rod HART
C.B. Savage—Rod Hart

Dan HARTMAN
Free Ride—Tavares

John HARTMAN
(w.Jeff Baxter/Pat Simmons)
Wheels Of Fortune—Doobie Brothers

Bruce HAWES
(w.Joseph Jefferson/Charles Simmons)
Love Or Leave—Spinners

Mike HAWKER
(w.Ivor Raymonde)
I Only Want To Be With You—Bay City
Rollers

Justin HAYWARD
Blue Guitar—Justin Hayward & John
Lodge

Harvey HENDERSON
(see BAR-KAYS)

'Little Jimmy' HENDERSON
(see BLACK OAK ARKANSAS)

Michael HENDERSON
Valentine Love—Norman Connors
You Are My Starship—Norman Connors

Don HENLEY
(w.Glenn Frey/John David Souther)
New Kid In Town—Eagles
(w.Glenn Frey/Randy Meisner)
Take It To The Limit—Eagles

Denny HENSON
Rain, Oh Rain—Fools Gold

Tony HESTER
You're Fooling You—Dramatics

Chuck HIGGINS Jr.
(w.Gilbert Bottiglier/Paul Stallworth)
Sweet Summer Music—Attitudes

Dan HILL
   Growin' Up—Dan Hill

Dusty HILL
   (see Z Z Top)

Tommy HILL
   (w.Billy Joe Burnette/Dale Royal/Red
   Sovine)
   Teddy Bear—Red Sovine

Tony HILLER
   (w.Martin Lee/Lee Sheriden)
   Save Your Kisses For Me—Brotherhood
   of Man
   Save Your Kisses For Me—Bobby Vinton

Bob HILLIARD
   (w.Mort Garson)
   Our Day Will Come—Frankie Valli

Ricky HIRSCH
   **Everything That 'Cha Do (Will Come
   Back To You)**—Wet Willie

Christine HODGSON
   (w.Terry Britten)
   Devil Woman—Cliff Richard
   (the UK version credits Ms. Hodgson by
   her married name Christine AUTHORS)

Brian HOLLAND
   (w.Eddie Holland)
   Keep Holding On—Temptations
   (w.Lamont Dozier/Eddie Holland)
   Where Did Our Love Go—J. Geils Band
   This Old Heart Of Mine—Rod Stewart
   (w.Harold Beatty/Eddie Holland)
   I'm Gonna Let My Heart Do The Walking
   —Supremes
   (w.Harold Beatty/Reginald Brown/Floyd
   Stafford)
   You're My Driving Wheel—Supremes

Eddie HOLLAND
   (w.Brian Holland)
   Keep Holding On—Temptations
   (w.Lamont Dozier/Brian Holland)
   Where Did Our Love Go—J. Geils Band
   This Old Heart Of Mine—Rod Stewart
   (w.Harold Beatty/Brian Holland)
   I'm Gonna Let My Heart Do The Walking
   —Supremes

Buddy HOLLY
   (w.Jerry Allison/Norman Petty)
   That'll Be The Day—Linda Ronstadt

Leon HUFF
   (w.Kenny Gamble)
   Enjoy Yourself—Jacksons
   The Zip—MFSB
   I Love Music—O'Jays
   Message In Our Music—O'Jays
   Let's Make A Baby—Billy Paul
   When Love Is New—Arthur Prysock
   Groovy—Lou Rawls
   **You'll Never Find Another Love Like
   Mine**—Lou Rawls
   (w.Kenny Gamble/Cary Gilbert)
   Don't Leave Me This Way—Thelma
   Houston
   Livin' For The Weekend—O'Jays
   (w.Cary Gilbert)
   Nursery Rhymes—People's Choice

Terry HUFF
   (w.Adrian Clements)
   The Lonely One—Special Delivery
   featuring Terry Huff

Mabon HUGHES
   (w.Al Green/Willie Mitchell)
   Full Of Fire—Al Green

HUGO (aka Hugo PERETTI)
   (w.Luigi/George David Weiss)
   Funky Weekend—Stylistics
   You Are Beautiful—Stylistics

Jay HUGUELY (aka Cledus MAGGARD)
   (w.Jerry Kennedy)
   Kentucky Moonrunner—Cledus Maggard
   & the Citizen's Band
   The White Knight—Cledus Maggard &
   the Citizen's Band

Phil HURTT
   (w.Henri Belolo/Jacques Morali/Ritchie
   Rome)
   The Best Disco In Town—Ritchie Family

Jean HUTCHINGSON
   (w. Wanda Hutchingson)
   I Don't Wanna Lose Your Love—Emotions

Wanda HUTCHINGSON
   (w.Jean Hutchingson)
   I Don't Wanna Lose Your Love—Emotions

Eddie IRONS
   (w.Regi Hargis/Ray Ransom)
   Dazz—Brick

Ernie ISLEY
Marvin ISLEY
O'Kelly ISLEY
Ronald ISLEY
Rudolph ISLEY
(see ISLEY BROTHERS)

ISLEY BROTHERS
(Ernie, Marvin, O'Kelly, Ronald & Rudolph
Isley & Chris Jasper)
For The Love Of You—Isley Brothers
Harvest For The World—Isley Brothers
Who Loves You Better—Isley Brothers
For The Love Of You—Houston Person

Chuck JACKSON
(w.Marvin Yancy)
Inseparable—Natalie Cole
Mr. Melody—Natalie Cole
The More You Do It (The More I Like
It Done To Me)—Ronnie Dyson
It's Cool—Tymes
(w.Natalie Cole/Marvin Yancy)
Sophisticated Lady (She's A Different
Lady)—Natalie Cole

George JACKSON
(w.Roe Hall)
Find 'Em, Fool 'Em, Forget 'Em—
Dobie Gray

Gerald JACKSON
(w.Pete Jackson)
Turn The Beat Around—Vicki Sue
Robinson

Pete JACKSON
(w.Gerald Jackson)
Turn The Beat Around—Vicki Sue
Robinson

Al JACOBS
(w.Jimmie Crane)
Hurt—Elvis Presley

Mick JAGGER
(w.Keith Richard)
Fool To Cry—Rolling Stones
Hot Stuff—Rolling Stones

Inez JAMES
(w.Buddy Pepper/Larry Russell)
Vaya Con Dios—Freddy Fender

Mark JAMES
Moody Blue—Elvis Presley

Hans JANSEN
(w.Jan Vennik)
Grasshopper—Spin

Danny JANSSEN
(w.Luigi Albertelli/Bobby Hart/Enrico
Riccardi)
Words (Are Impossible)—Donny Gerrard

Phil JARRELL
(w.Peter Yarrow)
Torn Between Two Lovers—Mary
MacGregor

Chris JASPER
(see ISLEY BROTHERS)

Joseph JEFFERSON
(w.Charles Simmons)
Jealousy—Major Harris
Once You Hit The Road—Dionne
Warwick
(w.Bruce Hawes/Charles Simmons)
Love Or Leave—Spinners

Waylon JENNINGS
(w.Willie Nelson)
Good Hearted Woman—Waylon & Willie

Will JENNINGS
If Love Must Go—Dobie Gray
(w.Richard Kerr)
Somewhere In The Night—Helen Reddy

Elton JOHN
(w.Bernie Taupin)
I Feel Like A Bullet (In The Gun Of
Robert Ford)—Elton John
Island Girl—Elton John
Sorry Seems To Be The Hardest Word—
Elton John
Don't Go Breaking My Heart—Elton John
& Kiki Dee (written under the names of
Ann Orson & Carte Blanche)
(w.Davey Johnstone/Bernie Taupin)
Grow Some Funk Of Your Own—Elton
John

JOHNNYMELFI
Sun ... Sun ... Sun—Ja kki

Buddy JOHNSON
Since I Fell For You—Charlie Rich

George JOHNSON
(w.Louis Johnson/Quincy Jones)
Get The Funk Out Ma Face—Brothers
Johnson
(w.Louis Johnson/Senora Sam)
I'll Be Good To You—Brothers Johnson

Louis JOHNSON
(w.George Johnson/Quincy Jones)
Get The Funk Out Ma Face—Brothers
Johnson
(w.George Johnson/Senora Sam)
I'll Be Good To You—Brothers Johnson

Stephen JOHNSON
(see BLACKBYRDS)

Bruce JOHNSTON
I Write The Songs—Barry Manilow

Davey JOHNSTONE
(w.Elton John/Bernie Taupin)
Grow Some Funk Of Your Own—
Elton John

Chico JONES
(w.Clarence Cotter/Don Davis)
Somebody's Gettin' It—Johnnie Taylor

Marshall JONES
(w.William Beck/Marvin Pierce/James
Williams)
Who'd She Coo—Ohio Players
(see also OHIO PLAYERS)

Quincy JONES
(w.George Johnson/Louis Johnson)
Get The Funk Out Ma Face—Brothers
Johnson

Rose Ella JONES
(w.William Robinson)
Quiet Storm—Smokey Robinson

David JORDAN
(w.Andrew Smith)
I Don't Want To Leave You—Debbie
Taylor

Lonnie JORDAN
(see WAR)

Carole JOYNER
(w.Ric Cartey)
Young Love—Ray Stevens

Gus KAHN
(w.William Harold/Wayne King)
Goofus—Carpenters

Paul KANTNER
(w.Marty Balin/Craig Chaquico/
Jesse Barish/Thunderhawk)
St. Charles—Jefferson Starship

Eric KAZ
(w.Craig Fuller)
Let Me Down Easy—American Flyer

Michael KECK
(w.Sanford 'Pepe' Daniel, Joyce Kennedy,
Gary 'Mo' Moore, Glenn Murdock & Jerry
'Wizzard' Seay)
Fire—Mother's Finest

Charles KELLY
(w.Bobby Eli)
Happy Man—Impact

Wayne KEMP
One Piece At A Time—Johnny Cash
& the Tennessee Three

Jerry KENNEDY
(w.Jay Huguely)
Kentucky Moonrunner—Cledus Maggard
& the Citizen's Band
The White Knight—Cledus Maggard &
the Citizen's Band

Joyce KENNEDY
(w.Sanford 'Pepe' Daniel, Michael Keck,
Gary 'Mo' Moore, Glenn Murdock &
Jerry 'Wizzard' Seay)
Fire—Mother's Finest

Richard KERR
(w.Will Jennings)
Somewhere In The Night—Helen Reddy

Chaka KHAN
(w.Tony Maiden)
Sweet Thing—Rufus featuring Chaka
Khan

Keith KILLGO
(see BLACKBYRDS)

Carole KING
Only Love Is Real—Carole King
(w.Gerry Goffin)
One Fine Day—Julie
I Can't Hear You No More—Helen Reddy
High Out Of Time—Carole King
Will You Love Me Tomorrow—Dana
Valery

Wayne KING
(w.William Harold/Gus Kahn)
Goofus—Carpenters

William KING
(see COMMODORES)

Charles KIPPS
Walk Away From Love—David Ruffin

Simon KIRKE
(see BAD COMPANY)

KOOL & THE GANG
(Robert 'Kool' Bell, Ronald Bell, George
M. Brown, Larry Gittens, Spike Mickens,
Otha Nash, Claydes Smith, Dennis Thomas
& Ricky West)
(w.Ronald Bell)
Open Sesame—Kool & the Gang
(w.Ronald Bell/Claydes Smith)
**Love And Understanding (Come
Together)**—Kool & the Gang

Joseph KUHM
Man Smart,Woman Smarter—Robert
Palmer

Steve KUPKA
(w.Emilio Castillo/Hubert Tubbs)
You Ought To Be Havin' Fun—Tower of
Power

David LaFLAMME
(w.Linda LaFlamme)
White Bird—David LaFlamme

Linda LaFLAMME
(w.David LaFlamme)
White Bird—David LaFlamme

Greg LAKE
(w.Pete Sinfield)
I Believe In Father Christmas—Greg Lake

Dennis LAMBERT
(w.Brian Potter)
**Country Boy (You Got Your Feet In
L.A.)**—Glen Campbell
Don't Pull Your Love—Glen Campbell
Once A Fool—Kiki Dee

Robert LAMM
Another Rainy Day In New York City—
Chicago

Bill LANE
(w.Roger Nichols)
Times Of Your Life—Paul Anka

Ronald LaPRAED
(see COMMODORES)

D.C. LaRUE
(w.Aram Schefrin)
Ca-the-drals—D.C. LaRue

Karen LAWRENCE
(w.John DeSautels)
Prisoner (Captured By Your Eyes)—
L.A. Jets

Mike LEANDER
(w.Peter Phipps/Gerry Shephard)
Makes You Blind—Glitter Band

Larry LEE
(w.Steve Cash)
If I Only Knew—Ozark Mountain
Daredevils

Martin LEE
(w.Tony Hiller/Lee Sheriden)
Save Your Kisses For Me—Brotherhood
of Man
Save Your Kisses For Me—Bobby Vinton

Jerry LEIBER
(w.Mike Stoller/Doc Pomus)
Young Blood—Bad Company
(w.Thomas Chong/Richard Marin/Mike
Stoller)
Framed—Cheech & Chong
(w.Jerry Butler/Calvin Carter/Sam
Cooke/Curtis Mayfield/Mike Stoller)
Chain Gang Medley—Jim Croce

Richard LEIGH
I'll Get Over You—Crystal Gayle

John LENNON
(w.Paul McCartney)
Got To Get You Into My Life—Beatles
Ob-La-Di, Ob-La-Da—Beatles
Here There And Everywhere—Emmylou
Harris

Alan Jay LERNER
(w.Frederick Loewe)
I Could Have Danced All Night—Biddu
Orchestra

Sylvester LEVAY
(w.Stephan Prager)
Lady Bump—Penny McLean
Fly, Robin, Fly—Silver Convention
Get Up And Boogie—Silver Convention
No, No, Joe—Silver Convention

Jacques LEVY
(w.Bob Dylan)
Hurricane—Bob Dylan
Mozambique—Bob Dylan

Gordon LIGHTFOOT
The Wreck Of The Edmund Fitzgerald—
Gordon Lightfoot

Dennis LINDE
For The Heart—Elvis Presley

Dave L. LIPSCOMB
(w.Steve Duffy)
She Thinks I Still Care—Elvis Presley
(usually credited to Dickey Lee who
bought the song from the two composers.)

Kerry LIVGREN
Carry On Wayward Son—Kansas

Dennis LOCORRIERE
If Not You—Dr. Hook

Frederick LOEWE
(w.Alan Jay Lerner)
I Could Have Danced All Night—Biddu
Orchestra

Dave LOGGINS
(w.Jim Stafford)
Jasper—Jim Stafford

Frederick LONG
(w.William Stevenson)
Devil With The Blue Dress—Pratt &
McClain with Brotherlove

John D. LOUDERMILK
Then You Can Tell Me Goodbye—Glen
Campbell

Mike LOVE
(w.Brian Wilson)
It's O.K.—Beach Boys
Good Vibrations—Todd Rundgren

Wilfred LOVETT
I Kinda Miss You—Manhattans
Kiss And Say Goodbye—Manhattans

Marco LUBERTI
(w.Richard Cocciante/Danielle Rouby)
When Love Has Gone Away—Richard
Cocciante

Donald LUCAS
(w.Francis Weyer)
Tonight's The Night—S.S.O.

LUIGI (aka Luigi CREATORE)
(w.Hugo/George David Weiss)
Funky Weekend—Stylistics
You Are Beautiful—Stylistics

Graham LYLE
(w.Benny Gallagher)
Heart On My Sleeve—Bryan Ferry
Heart On My Sleeve—Gallagher & Lyle
I Wanna Stay With You—Gallagher &
Lyle
Breakaway—Art Garfunkel

Jeff LYNNE
Evil Woman—Electric Light Orchestra
Livin' Thing—Electric Light Orchestra
Showdown—Electric Light Orchestra
Strange Magic—Electric Light Orchestra

Phil LYNOTT
The Boys Are Back In Town—Thin Lizzy
(w.Brian Downey)
Cowboy Song—Thin Lizzy

LYRIC
(see MYSTRO & LYRIC)

Tony MACAULAY
Fallin Apart At The Seams—Marmalade

Andy MACKAY
(w.Bryan Ferry)
Love Is The Drug—Roxy Music

Gene MACLELLAN
The Call—Anne Murray

Tony MAIDEN
(w.Chaka Khan)
Sweet Thing—Rufus featuring Chaka
Khan

Richard MAINEGRA
(w.Jack Roberts)
Here's Some Love—Tanya Tucker

Melissa MANCHESTER
(w.Carole Bayer Sager)
Better Days—Melissa Manchester
Just You And I—Melissa Manchester

Henry MANCINI
Peter Gunn—Deodato

Barry MANILOW
(w.Adrienne Anderson)
Street Singin'—Lady Flash
Could It Be Magic—Donna Summer
(w.Marty Panzer)
This One's For You—Barry Manilow

Barry MANN
(w.Cynthia Weil)
The Princess And The Punk—Barry Mann

Richard MARIN
(w.Thomas Chong/Jerry Leiber/Mike
Stoller)
Framed—Cheech and Chong

Larry MARKES
(w.Jimmy Dean)
I.O.U.—Jimmy Dean

Bob MARLEY
  Roots, Rock, Reggae—Bob Marley &
  the Wailers

Jeffrey MARMELZAT
  (w.Spencer Proffer)
  All Roads (Lead Back To You)—Donny
  Most

Peter MARSH
  (see EASY STREET)

Bob MARSHALL
  (w.John Miles)
  High Fly—John Miles

Ed MARSHALL
  Venus—Frankie Avalon

Sherman MARSHALL
  (w.Thom Bell)
  Wake Up Susan—Spinners

Bill MARTIN
  (w.Phil Coulter)
  Saturday Night—Bay City Rollers

Michael MASSER
  (w.Gerry Goffin)
  So Sad The Song—Gladys Knight & the
  Pips
  Theme From Mahogany 'Do You Know
  Where You're Going To'—Diana Ross
  (w.Pam Sawyer)
  I Thought It Took A Little Time But
  Today I Fell In Love—Diana Ross

Iris MAY
  (w.Charles Graham)
  Brand New Love Affair—Jigsaw

Curtis MAYFIELD
  Jump—Aretha Franklin
  Something He Can Feel—Aretha
  Franklin
  Let's Do It Again—Staple Singers
  New Orleans—Staple Singers
  (w.Jerry Butler/Calvin Carter/Sam
  Cooke/Jerry Leiber/Mike Stoller)
  Chain Gang Medley—Jim Croce

Percy MAYFIELD
  Hit The Road Jack—Stampeders

C.W. McCALL
  (real name—Bill FRIES)
  (w.Chip Davis/Bill Fries)
  Convoy—C.W. McCall

There Won't Be No Country Music
(There Won't Be No Rock 'n' Roll)—
C.W. McCall

Paul McCARTNEY
  Let 'Em In—Wings
  Silly Love Songs—Wings
  (w.John Lennon)
  Got To Get You Into My Life—Beatles
  Ob-La-Di, Ob-La-Da—Beatles
  Here There And Everywhere—Emmylou
  Harris

Tom McCLARY
  (see COMMODORES)

George McCORKLE
  Fire On The Mountain—Marshall Tucker
  Band

Van McCOY
  Night Walk—Van McCoy
  Party—Van McCoy
  This Is It—Melba Moore
  Everything's Coming Up Love—David
  Ruffin
  (w.Joe Cobb)
  Heavy Love—David Ruffin

James McCULLOCH
  (w.Nick Gilder)
  Roxy Roller—Sweeney Todd
  Roxy Roller—Sweeney Todd featuring
  Brian Guy Adams

Country Joe McDONALD
  Breakfast For Two—Country Joe
  McDonald

Michael McDONALD
  It Keeps You Runnin'—Doobie Brothers
  Takin' It To The Streets—Doobie Brothers
  It Keeps You Runnin'—Carly Simon

Gene McFADDEN
  (w.Victor Carstarphen/John Whitehead)
  Bad Luck—Atlanta Disco Band
  Tell The World How I Feel About 'Cha
  Baby—Harold Melvin & the Blue Notes
  Wake Up Everybody—Harold Melvin &
  the Blue Notes

Terri McFADDIN
  (w.Lawrence Brown/Leonard Perry)
  One Love In My Lifetime—Diana Ross

Parker McGEE
You've Got Me Runnin'—Gene Cotton
I'd Really Love To See You Tonight—
England Dan & John Ford Coley
Nights Are Forever—England Dan &
John Ford Coley

Al McKAY
(w.Maurice White)
Flowers—Emotions
Sing A Song—Earth Wind & Fire
(w.Philip Bailey/Maurice White)
Saturday Nite—Earth Wind & Fire

Marilyn McLEOD
(w.Pam Sawyer)
Love Hangover—5th Dimension
Love Hangover—Diana Ross

Rod McQUEEN
Did You Boogie With Your Baby (In The
Back Row Of The Movie Show)—Flash
Cadillac & the Continental Kids

Christine McVIE
Over My Head—Fleetwood Mac
Say You Love Me—Fleetwood Mac

Randy MEISNER
(w.Glenn Frey/Don Henley)
Take It To The Limit—Eagles

Johnny MERCER
(w.Victor Schertzinger)
Tangerine—Salsoul Orchestra

Freddie MERCURY
Bohemian Rhapsody—Queen
Somebody To Love—Queen

Spike MICKENS
(see KOOL & THE GANG)

Ralph MIDDLEBROOKS
(see OHIO PLAYERS)

Franco MIGLIACCI
(w.Domenico Modugno/Mitchell Parish)
Volare—Al Martino

John MILES
Music—John Miles
(w.Bob Marshall)
High Fly—John Miles

Charles MILLER
(see WAR)

Glenn MILLER
(w.Mitchell Parish)
Moonlight Serenade—Bobby Vinton

Steve MILLER
Fly Like An Eagle—Steve Miller Band
Rock 'n' Me—Steve Miller Band
Take The Money And Run—Steve Miller
Band

Dave MINDEL
(w.Gary Benson)
Whenever I'm Away From You—John
Travolta

Raynard MINER
(w.Carl Smith)
Rescue Me—Melissa Manchester

Joni MITCHELL
In France They Kiss On Main Street—
Joni Mitchell

Tony MITCHELL
(w.Garth Porter)
Howzat—Sherbet

Willie MITCHELL
(w.Al Green)
Keep Me Cryin'—Al Green
(w.Al Green/Mabon Hughes)
Full Of Fire—Al Green

Domenico MODUGNO
(w.France Migliacci/Mitchell Parish)
Volare—Al Martino

Pamela MOFFETT
(w.William Robinson/Marv Tarplin)
Open—Smokey Robinson

Vincent/Vince MONTANA Jr.
Nice 'n' Naasty—Salsoul Orchestra
You're Just The Right Size—Salsoul
Orchestra
(w.Ronnie B. Walker)
The Game Is Over (What's The Matter
With You)—Brown Sugar

Bob MONTGOMERY
Misty Blue—Dorothy Moore

Gary 'Mo' MOORE
(w.Sanford 'Pepe' Daniel, Michael Keck,
Joyce Kennedy, Glenn Murdock & Jerry
'Wizzard' Seay)
Fire—Mother's Finest

Tim MOORE
Rock And Roll Love Letter—Bay City
Rollers

Warren 'Pete' MOORE
(w.William Griffin)
Love Machine—Miracles
(w.William Robinson/Marv Tarplin)
The Tracks Of My Tears—Linda Ronstadt

Jacques MORALI
(w.Henri Belolo/Phil Hurtt/Ritchie Rome)
The Best Disco In Town—Ritchie Family

Giorgio MORODER
(w.Pete Bellotte/Donna Summer)
Love To Love You Baby—Donna Summer
Spring Affair—Donna Summer
Try Me, I Know We Can Make It—Donna Summer

Randy MULLER
Ha Cha Cha (Funktion)—Brass Construction
(w.Wade Williamson)
Movin'—Brass Construction

Glenn MURDOCK
(w.Sanford 'Pepe' Daniel/Michael Keck/
Joyce Kennedy/Gary 'Mo' Moore/Jerry
'Wizzard' Seay)
Fire—Mother's Finest

Michael MURPHEY
Renegade—Michael Murphey

Barry MURPHY
We Can't Hide It Anymore—Larry Santos

Walter MURPHY
A Fifth Of Beethoven—Walter Murphy &
the Big Apple Band
Flight '76—Walter Murphy Band

MYSTRO & LYRIC
(real names—Melvin & Mervin STEALS)
Full Time Thing (Between Dusk & Dawn)
—Whirlwind

Ron NAGLE
(w.Dorknocker)
Don't Touch Me There—Tubes

Graham NASH
(w.David Crosby/Craig Degree)
Out Of The Darkness—David Crosby/
Graham Nash

Otha NASH
(see KOOL & THE GANG)

Willie NELSON
Funny How Time Slips Away—Dorothy Moore

(w.Waylon Jennings)
Good Hearted Woman—Waylon & Willie

Freida NERANGIS
(w.Britt Britton)
Every Beat Of My Heart—Crown Heights Affair
Foxy Lady—Crown Heights Affair

Ken NICOL
(see EASY STREET)

Billy NICHOLS
**Can't Stop Groovin' Now, Wanna Do It
Some More**—B.T. Express

Roger NICHOLS
(w.Bill Lane)
Times Of Your Life—Paul Anka

Stevie NICKS
Rhiannon (Will You Ever Win)—
Fleetwood Mac

Robert NIX
(w.Buddy Buie)
Jukin'—Atlanta Rhythm Section
(w.Buddy Buie/Ronnie Hammond)
Free Spirit—Atlanta Rhythm Section

Kenny NOLAN
Dancin' Kid—Disco Tex & the Sex-o-lettes
I Like Dreamin'—Kenny Nolan

Ted NUGENT
Dog Eat Dog—Ted Nugent

John OATES
(w Daryl Hall)
Do What You Want, Be What You Are—
Daryl Hall & John Oates
Sara Smile—Daryl Hall & John Oates
She's Gone—Daryl Hall & John Oates

OHIO PLAYERS
(William Beck, Leroy Bonner, Marshall
Jones, Ralph Middlebrooks, Marvin Pierce,
Clarence Satchell & James Williams)
Fopp—Ohio Players
Love Rollercoaster—Ohio Players

Mike OLDFIELD
Tubular Bells—Champs Boys

Henry ONORATI
(w.Katherine Davis/Harry Simeone)
Little Drummer Boy—Moonlion

Walter ORANGE
(see COMMODORES)

Ann ORSON
  (see Elton JOHN/Bernie TAUPIN)

Lee OSKAR
  (w.Greg Errico)
  BLT—Lee Oskar
  (see also WAR)

Barbara Lynn OZEN
  You'll Lose A Good Thing—Freddy
  Fender

David PAICH
  (w.Boz Scaggs)
  Lowdown—Boz Scaggs
  What Can I Say—Boz Scaggs

Marty PANZER
  (w.Barry Manilow)
  This One's For You—Barry Manilow

Mitchell PARISH
  (w.Franco Migliacci/Domenico Modugno)
  Volare—Al Martino
  (w.Glenn Miller)
  Moonlight Serenade—Bobby Vinton
  (w.Peter DeRose)
  Deep Purple—Donny & Marie Osmond

Richard PARISSI
  Play That Funky Music—Wild Cherry

Judy PARKER
  (w.Bob Gaudio)
  December, 1963 (Oh, What A Night)—
  Four Seasons
  Silver Star—Four Seasons
  Who Loves You—Four Seasons

Alan PARSONS
  (w.Eric Woolfson)
  (The System Of) Doctor Tarr & Professor
  Fether—Alan Parsons Project
  The Raven—Alan Parsons Project

David PATON
  January—Pilot

Harold T. PAYNE
  (w.Bobby Womack)
  Daylight—Vicki Sue Robinson

Lawrence PAYTON
  (w Fred Bridges/Mikki Farrow)
  Catfish—Four Tops

Dan PEEK
  Today's The Day—America
  Woman Tonight—America

Stan PENRIDGE
  (w.Peter Criss/Bob Ezrin)
  Beth—Kiss

Buddy PEPPER
  (w.Inez James/Larry Russell)
  Vaya Con Dios—Freddy Fender

Hugo PERETTI
  (see HUGO)

Freddie PERREN
  (w.Keni St. Lewis)
  Boogie Fever—Sylvers
  Cotton Candy—Sylvers
  Hot Line—Sylvers
  Heaven Must Be Missing An Angel—
  Tavares
  (w.Keni St. Lewis/Christine Yarian)
  Don't Take Away The Music—Tavares

Joe PERRY
  (w.Steven Tyler)
  Walk This Way—Aerosmith

Leonard PERRY
  (w.Lawrence Brown/Terri McFaddin)
  One Love In My Lifetime—Diana Ross

Ben PETERS
  Livin' It Down—Freddy Fender

Norman PETTY
  (w.Jerry Allison/Buddy Holly)
  That'll Be The Day

Dave PEVERETT (aka Lonesome Dave)
  Fool For The City—Foghat
  Slow Ride—Foghat
  (w.Rod Price)
  Drivin' Wheel—Foghat

Peter PHIPPS
  (w.Mike Leander/Gerry Shephard)
  Makes You Blind—Glitter Band

Marvin PIERCE
  (w.William Beck/Marshall Jones/James
  Williams)
  Who'd She Coo—Ohio Players
  (see also OHIO PLAYERS)

Mary Kay PLACE
  Baby Boy—Mary Kay Place (as Loretta
  Haggers)

Michel POLNAREFF
  Lipstick—Michel Polnareff
  (w.Jacob Brackman/George Clinton)
  If You Only Believe (Jesus For Tonight)
  —Michel Polnareff

David POMERANZ
Tryin' To Get The Feeling Again—Barry
Manilow

Doc/Jerome POMUS
(w.Jerry Leiber/Mike Stoller)
Young Blood—Bad Company

Vini PONCIA
(w.Leo Sayer)
You Make Me Feel Like Dancing—Leo
Sayer

Garth PORTER
(w.Tony Mitchell)
Howzat—Sherbet

Bill POST
(w.Doree Post)
Sixteen Reasons—Laverne & Shirley

Doree POST
(w.Bill Post)
Sixteen Reasons—Laverne & Shirley

Brian POTTER
(w.Dennis Lambert)
Country Boy (You Got Your Feet In
L.A.)—Glen Campbell
Don't Pull Your Love—Glen Campbell
Once A Fool—Kiki Dee

Stephan PRAGER
(w.Sylvester Levay)
Lady Bump—Penny McLean
Fly, Robin, Fly—Silver Convention
Get Up And Boogie—Silver Convention
No, No, Joe—Silver Convention

Rod PRICE
(w.Dave Peverett)
Drivin' Wheel—Foghat

Steve PRIEST
(see SWEET)

Spencer PROFFER
(w.Jeffrey Marmelzat)
All Roads (Lead Back To You)—Donny
Most

PUBLIC DOMAIN
Eh! Cumpari—Gaylord & Holiday
This Old Man—Purple Reign

Eddie RABBITT
Rocky Mountain Music—Eddie Rabbitt

Derf Reklaw RAHEEM
(w.Charles Stepney/Morris Stewart)
What's The Name Of This Funk (Spider
Man)—Ramsey Lewis

Mick RALPHS
(see BAD COMPANY)

Willis Alan RAMSEY
Satin Sheets—Bellamy Brothers
Muskrat Love—Captain & Tennille

Richie RANNO
(w.Sean Delaney/Dube Grob/
Brenden Harkin/Michael Lee Smith/
Peter Sweval)
(She's Just A) Fallen Angel—Starz

Ray RANSOM
(w.Regi Hargis/Eddie Irons)
Dazz—Brick

Ivor RAYMONDE
(w.Mike Hawker)
I Only Want To Be With You—Bay City
Rollers

Hank REDD
(w.Susaye Greene/Nathan Watts/
Deniece Williams)
Free—Deniece Williams

Les REED
(w.Geoff Stephens)
There's A Kind Of Hush—Carpenters

Rickie Lee REYNOLDS
(see BLACK OAK ARKANSAS)

Enrico RICCARDI
(w.Luigi Albertelli/Bobby Hart/
Danny Janssen)
Words (Are Impossible)—Donny Gerrard

Keith RICHARD
(w.Mick Jagger)
Fool To Cry—Rolling Stones
Hot Stuff—Rolling Stones

George RICHEY
(w.Billy Sherrill/Tammy Wynette)
'Til I Can Make It On My Own—Tammy
Wynette

Lionel RICHIE
(w.Commodores)
Just To Be Close To You—Commodores
Sweet Love—Commodores
(see also COMMODORES)

Jimmy ROACH
Disco Sax—Houston Person

Jack ROBERTS
(w.Richard Mainegra)
Here's Some Love—Tanya Tucker

Rick ROBERTS
Livin' Ain't Livin'—Firefall
You Are The Woman—Firefall

Robbie ROBERTSON
Ophelia—Band

William/Smokey ROBINSON
(w.Berry Gordy)
Shop Around—Captain & Tennille
(w.Rose Ella Jones)
Quiet Storm—Smokey Robinson
(w.Marv Tarplin/Pamela Moffett)
Open—Smokey Robinson
(w.Warren 'Pete' Moore/Marv Tarplin)
The Tracks Of My Tears—Linda Ronstadt

Paul RODGERS
(see BAD COMPANY)

Donald ROESER
(Don't Fear) The Reaper—Blue Oyster
Cult

D.J. ROGERS
Say You Love Me—D.J Rogers

Ritchie ROME
(w.Henri Belolo/Phil Hurtt/Jacques
Morali)
The Best Disco In Town—Ritchie Family

Vincent ROSE
(w.John Schonberger/Richard Coburn)
Whispering—Dr. Buzzard's Original
Savannah Band

Merria ROSS
Let's Get It Together—El Coco

T-Boy ROSS
(w Leon Ware)
I Want You—Marvin Gaye

Danielle ROUBY
(w.Richard Cocciante/Marco Luberti)
When Love Has Gone Away—Richard
Cocciante

Chris ROWAN
If I Only Could—Rowans

James ROWE
(w.Howard Smith)
Love Lifted Me—Kenny Rogers

Dale ROYAL
(w.Billy Joe Burnette)
Teddy Bear's Last Ride—Diana Williams
(w.Billy Joe Burnette/Tommy Hill/
Red Sovine)
Teddy Bear—Red Sovine

Bobby RUSSELL
(w.Bobby Scott)
He Ain't Heavy—He's My Brother—
Olivia Newton-John

Larry RUSSELL
(w.Inez James/Buddy Pepper)
Vaya Con Dios—Freddy Fender

Leon RUSSELL
This Masquerade—George Benson
Back To The Island—Leon Russell
Rainbow In Your Eyes—Leon & Mary
Russell

Carole Bayer SAGER
(w.Melissa Manchester)
Better Days—Melissa Manchester
Just You And I—Melissa Manchester

Derek ST. HOLMES
Hey Baby—Ted Nugent

Keni ST LEWIS
(w.Freddie Perren)
Boogie Fever—Sylvers
Cotton Candy—Sylvers
Hot Line—Sylvers
Heaven Must Be Missing An Angel—
Tavares
(w.Freddie Perren/Christine Yarian)
Don't Take Away The Music—Tavares

Senora SAM
(w.George Johnson/Louis Johnson)
I'll Be Good To You—Brothers Johnson

Clarence SATCHELL
(see OHIO PLAYERS)

Orville SAUNDERS
(see BLACKBYRDS)

Pam SAWYER
  (w.Marilyn McLeod)
  Love Hangover—5th Dimension
  Love Hangover—Diana Ross
  (w.Michael Masser)
  I Thought It Took A Little Time (But Today I Fell In Love)—Diana Ross

Leo SAYER
  (w.Vini Poncia)
  You Make Me Feel Like Dancing—Leo Sayer

Boz SCAGGS
  It's Over—Boz Scaggs
  We're All Alone—Frankie Valli
  (w.David Paich)
  Lowdown—Boz Scaggs
  What Can I Say—Boz Scaggs

Harvey SCALES
  (w.Don Davis/Al Vance)
  Disco Lady—Johnnie Taylor

Skip SCARBOROUGH
  Love Ballad—L.T.D.
  Can't Hide Love—Earth Wind & Fire

Aram SCHEFRIN
  (w.D.C. LaRue)
  Ca-the-drals—D.C. LaRue

Victor SCHERTZINGER
  (w.Johnny Mercer)
  Tangerine—Salsoul Orchestra

John SCHONBERGER
  (w.Richard Coburn/Vincent Rose)
  Whispering—Dr. Buzzard's Original Savannah Band

Tom SCHOLZ
  More Than A Feeling—Boston

Andy SCOTT
  (see SWEET)

Bobby SCOTT
  (w.Bobby Russell)
  He Ain't Heavy—He's My Brother—Oliva Newton-John

Clive SCOTT
  (w.Des Dyer)
  Love Fire—Jigsaw
  Sky High—Jigsaw

Howard SCOTT
  (see WAR)

Tom SCOTT
  Uptown & Country—Tom Scott

John SEBASTIAN
  Hideaway—John Sebastian
  Welcome Back—John Sebastian

Jimmy SEALS
  (w.Lana Bogan)
  Baby, I'll Give It To You—Seals & Crofts
  (w.Dash Crofts)
  Get Closer—Seals & Crofts

Pete SEARS
  (w.Grace Slick)
  Play On Love—Jefferson Starship

Jerry 'Wizzard' SEAY
  (w.Sanford 'Pepe' Daniel/Michael Keck/Joyce Kennedy/Gary 'Mo' Moore/Glenn Murdock)
  Fire—Mother's Finest

Neil SEDAKA
  Lonely Night (Angel Face)—Captain & Tennille
  (w.Howard Greenfield)
  The Hungry Years—Wayne Newton
  Breaking Up Is Hard To Do—Neil Sedaka
  You Gotta Make Your Own Sunshine—Neil Sedaka
  (w.Phil Cody)
  Love In The Shadows—Neil Sedaka
  Steppin' Out—Neil Sedaka

Bob SEGER
  Night Moves—Bob Seger & the Silver Bullet Band

Tommy SHAW
  (w.Dennis DeYoung)
  Mademoiselle—Styx

Gerry SHEPHARD
  (w.Mike Leander/Peter Phipps)
  Makes You Blind—Glitter Band

Lee SHERIDEN
  (w Tony Hiller/Martin Lee)
  Save Your Kisses For Me—Brotherhood of Man
  Save Your Kisses For Me—Bobby Vinton

Billy SHERRILL
  (w.George Richey/Tammy Wynette)
  'Til I Can Make It On My Own—Tammy Wynette

Bunny SIGLER
(w.Ronnie Tyson)
Train Called Freedom—South Shore
Commission
(w.Allan Felder)
Touch & Go—Ecstasy Passion & Pain

Peter SILLS
(w.Mike Allison/Donald Black)
Every Face Tells A Story—Olivia
Newton-John

Harry SIMEONE
(w.Katherine Davis/Henry Onorati)
Little Drummer Boy—Moonlion

Charles SIMMONS
(w.Joseph Jefferson)
Jealousy—Major Harris
Once You Hit The Road—Dionne
Warwick
(w.Bruce Hawes/Joseph Jefferson)
Love Or Leave—Spinners

Gene SIMMONS
(w.Paul Stanley)
Rock And Roll All Nite (Live Version)—
Kiss
(w.Bob Ezrin/Paul Stanley)
Shout It Out Loud—Kiss
(w.Ace Frehley/Paul Stanley)
Flaming Youth—Kiss

Pat SIMMONS
I Cheat The Hangman—Doobie Brothers
(w.Jeff Baxter/John Hartman)
Wheels Of Fortune—Doobie Brothers

Paul SIMON
50 Ways To Leave Your Lover—Paul
Simon
Still Crazy After All These Years—Paul
Simon
My Little Town—Simon & Garfunkel

Valerie SIMPSON
(w.Nickolas Ashford)
Ain't Nothing Like The Real Thing—
Donny & Marie Osmond

Pete SINFIELD
(w.Greg Lake)
I Believe In Father Christmas—Greg Lake

Grace SLICK
(w.Pete Sears)
Play On Love—Jefferson Starship

Andrew SMITH
(w.David Jordan)
I Don't Want To Leave You—Debbie
Taylor

Michael Lee SMITH
(w.Sean Delaney/Dube Grob/
Brenden Harkin/Richie Ranno/Peter
Sweval)
(She's Just A) Fallen Angel—Starz

Victor SMITH
(w.Marty Balin/Joey Covington)
With Your Love—Jefferson Starship

Carl SMITH
(w.Raynard Miner)
Rescue Me—Melissa Manchester

Claydes SMITH
(w.Ronald Bell/Kool & the Gang)
Love & Understanding (Come Together)
—Kool & the Gang

Hazel SMITH
(One More Year Of) Daddy's Little Girl—
Ray Sawyer

Howard SMITH
(w.James Rowe)
Love Lifted Me—Kenny Rogers

H. Russell SMITH
**Amazing Grace (Used To Be Her
Favorite Song**—Amazing Rhythm Aces
**The End Is Not In Sight (The Cowboy
Tune)**—Amazing Rhythm Aces

Lloyd SMITH
(see BAR-KAYS)

Michael L. SMITH
(w.Don Daniels)
Let's Be Young Tonight—Jermaine
Jackson

Leila T. SNAKE
(see DORKNOCKER)

Michael SOMERVILLE
Love Me Tonight—Head East

John David SOUTHER
(w.Glenn Frey/Don Henley)
New Kid In Town—Eagles

Red SOVINE
(w.Billy Joe Burnette/Tommy Hill/Dale
Royal)
Teddy Bear—Red Sovine

Joey SPINAZOLA
(w.John Valenti)
Anything You Want—John Valenti

Rick SPRINGFIELD
Take A Hand—Rick Springfield

Bruce SPRINGSTEEN
Blinded By The Light—Manfred Mann's
Earthband
Spirit In The Night—Manfred Mann's
Earthband
Tenth Avenue Freeze-Out—Bruce
Springsteen

Floyd STAFFORD
(w.Harold Beatty/Reginald Brown/
Brian Holland)
You're My Driving Wheel—Supremes

Jim STAFFORD
(w.Dave Loggins)
Jasper—Jim Stafford

Paul STALLWORTH
(w.Gilbert Bottiglier/Chuck Higgins Jr.)
Sweet Summer Music—Attitudes

Paul STANLEY
Hard Luck Woman—Kiss
(w.Bob Ezrin)
Detroit Rock City—Kiss
(w.Gene Simmons)
Rock And Roll All Nite (Live Version)—
Kiss
(w.Ace Frehley/Gene Simmons)
Flaming Youth—Kiss
(w.Bob Ezrin/Gene Simmons)
Shout It Out Loud—Kiss

Edwin STARR
Abyssinia Jones—Edwin Starr

Melvin and Mervin STEALS
(see MYSTRO* LYRIC)

Geoff STEPHENS
(w.Les Reed)
There's A Kind Of Hush—Carpenters

Charles STEPNEY
(w.Derf Reklaw Raheem/Morris Stewart)
**What's The Name Of This Funk (Spider
Man)**—Ramsey Lewis

Cat STEVENS
Banapple Gas—Cat Stevens

William STEVENSON
(w.Norman Whitfield)
It Should Have Been Me—Yvonne Fair
(w.Frederick Long)
Devil With The Blue Dress—Pratt &
McClain with Brotherlove

Al STEWART
(w.Peter Wood)
Year Of The Cat—Al Stewart

Eric STEWART
(w.Graham Gouldman)
Art For Art's Sake—10cc
(w.Lol Creme/Graham Gouldman)
I'm Mandy Fly Me—10cc

Morris STEWART
(w.Derf Reklaw Raheem/Charles Stepney)
**What's The Name Of This Funk (Spider
Man)**—Ramsey Lewis

Rod STEWART
Tonight's The Night—Rod Stewart

Winston STEWART
(see BAR-KAYS)

Mike STOLLER
(w.Jerry Leiber/Doc Pomus)
Young Blood—Bad Company
(w.Thomas Chong/Jerry Leiber/Richard
Marin)
Framed—Cheech & Chong
(w.Jerry Butler/Calvin Carter/Sam
Cooke/Jerry Leiber/Curtis Mayfield)
Chain Gang Medley—Jim Croce

Richard STREET
(w Thelma Gordy)
Can You Do It—Grand Funk Railroad

Barbra STREISAND
(w Paul Williams)
**Love Theme From 'A Star Is Born'
(Evergreen)**—Barbra Streisand

Barrett STRONG
(w.Norman Whitfield)
I Heard It Through The Grapevine—
Creedence Clearwater Revival

Hamish STUART
Queen Of My Soul—Average White Band
(w.Stuart Ferrone/Alan Gorrie)
School Boy Crush—Average White Band

Donna SUMMER
(w.Pete Bellotte/Giorgio Moroder)
Love To Love You Baby—Donna Summer
Spring Affair—Donna Summer
Try Me, I Know We Can Make It—Donna Summer

Iain SUTHERLAND
Arms Of Mary—Sutherland Brothers & Quiver

Michael B. SUTTON
(w.Don Daniels/Kathy Wakefield)
Down To Love Town—Originals

SWEET
(Brian Connolly, Steve Priest, Andy Scott & Mike Tucker)
Action—Sweet
Fox On The Run—Sweet

Peter SWEVAL
(w.Sean Delaney/Dube Grob/Brenden Harkin/Richie Ranno/Michael Lee Smith)
(She's Just A) Fallen Angel—Starz

Marv TARPLIN
(w.William Robinson/Pamela Moffett)
Open—Smokey Robinson
(w.Warren 'Pete' Moore/William Robinson)
The Tracks Of My Tears—Linda Ronstadt

Bernie TAUPIN
(w.Elton John)
I Feel Like A Bullet (In The Gun Of Robert Ford)—Elton John
Island Girl—Elton John
Sorry Seems To Be The Hardest Word—Elton John
Don't Go Breaking My Heart—Elton John & Kiki Dee (written under the names of Ann Orson & Carte Blanche)
(w.Elton John/Davey Johnstone)
Grow Some Funk Of Your Own—Elton John

Beloyd TAYLOR
(w.Peter Cor)
Getaway—Earth Wind & Fire

James TAYLOR
Shower The People—James Taylor

Robert TAYLOR
(w.Lee Garrett)
You're My Everything—Lee Garrett

Jack TEMPCHIN
Slow Dancing—Funky Kings

Toni TENNILLE
The Way I Want To Touch You—Captain & Tennille

Dennis THOMAS
(see KOOL & THE GANG)

Truman THOMAS
(w.Jeffrey Bowen/Jimmy Ford)
Up The Creek (Without A Paddle)—Temptations

Huey THOMASSON
Breaker-Breaker—Outlaws

Frank THOMPSON
(see BAR-KAYS)

Blair THORNTON
(w.C.F. Turner)
Take It Like A Man—Bachman-Turner Overdrive

THUNDERHAWK
(w.Marty Balin/Craig Chaquico/Paul Kantner/Jesse Barish)
St. Charles—Jefferson Starship

Kevin TONEY
(see BLACKBYRDS)

Allen TOUSSAINT
Going Down Slowly—Pointer Sisters

Pete TOWNSHEND
Squeeze Box—Who

Merle TRAVIS
Sixteen Tons—Don Harrison Band

Robin TROWER
(w.James Dewar)
Caledonia—Robin Trower

Hubert TUBBS
(w.Emilio Castillo/Steve Kupka)
You Ought To Be Havin' Fun—Tower of Power

Pierre TUBBS
Gotta Be The One—Maxine Nightingale
(w.Vince Edwards)
Right Back Where We Started From—Maxine Nightingale

Mike TUCKER
(see SWEET)

C.F. TURNER
Gimme Your Money Please—Bachman-
Turner Overdrive
(w.Blair Thornton)
Take It Like A Man—Bachman-Turner
Overdrive

Reginald/'Buddy' TURNER
(w.Jerry Akines/John Bellmon/Victor
Drayton)
One For The Money—Whispers

Tina TURNER
Nutbush City Limits—Bob Seger & the
Silver Bullet Band

Conway TWITTY
Don't Cry Joni—Conway Twitty

Steven TYLER
Dream On—Aerosmith
Home Tonight—Aerosmith
(w.Joe Perry)
Walk This Way—Aerosmith
(w.Brad Whitford)
Last Child—Aerosmith

T.T. TYLER
Remember Me—Willie Nelson

Ronnie TYSON
(w.Bunny Sigler)
Train Called Freedom—South Shore
Commission

Bjorn ULVAEUS
(w.Stig Anderson/Benny Andersson)
Dancing Queen—Abba
Fernando—Abba
I Do, I Do, I Do, I Do, I Do—Abba
Mamma Mia—Abba

John VALENTI
(w.Joey Spinazola)
Anything You Want—John Valenti

Ronnie VAN ZANT
(w.Allen Collins)
Double Trouble—Lynyrd Skynyrd
Free Bird—Lynyrd Skynyrd

Al VANCE
(w.Don Davis/Harvey Scales)
Disco Lady—Johnnie Taylor

Paul VANCE
(w.Perry Cone)
Without Your Love (Mr. Jordan)—
Charlie Ross

Harry VANDA
(w. George Young)
Yesterday's Hero—Bay City Rollers
Yesterday's Hero—John Paul Young

Lee VANDERBILT
(w.Biddu)
Jump For Joy—Biddu Orchestra

Gino VANNELLI
Love Of My Life—Gino Vannelli

Jan VENNIK
(w.Hans Jansen)
Grasshopper—Spin

Dick WAGNER
(w.Alice Cooper)
I Never Cry—Alice Cooper

Kathy WAKEFIELD
(w.Leonard Caston)
Happy—Eddie Kendricks
(w.Don Daniels/Michael B. Sutton)
Down To Love Town—Originals

Ronnie B. WALKER
(w.Vincent Montana Jr.)
**The Game Is Over (What's The Matter
With You)**—Brown Sugar

WAR
(Sylvester 'Papa Dee' Allen, Harold
Brown, Morris 'B.B.' Dickerson, Lonnie
Jordan, Charles Miller, Lee Oskar &
Howard Scott)
(w.Jerry Goldstein)
Summer—War

Leon WARE
(w.Marvin Gaye)
After The Dance—Marvin Gaye
(w.T-Boy Ross)
I Want You—Marvin Gaye

Nathan WATTS
(w.Susaye Greene/Hank Redd/
Deniece Williams)
Free—Deniece Williams

Cynthia WEIL
(w.Barry Mann)
The Princess And The Punk—Barry Mann
(w.Rick Derringer)
Let Me In—Derringer

Steve WEISBERG
Christmas For Cowboys—John Denver

George David WEISS
(w.Hugo & Luigi)
Funky Weekend—Stylistics
You Are Beautiful—Stylistics

Robert WELCH
Silver Heels—Blaze

Ricky WEST
(see KOOL & THE GANG)

Tommy WEST
(w.Terry Cashman)
Baby, Baby I Love You—Terry Cashman

Francis WEYER
(w.Donald Lucas)
Tonight's The Night—S.S.O.

Sterling WHIPPLE
Forever Lovers—Mac Davis
The Last Game Of The Season (A Blind Man In The Bleachers)—David Geddes
The Blind Man In The Bleachers—Kenny Starr

Barry WHITE
My Sweet Summer Suite—Love Unlimited Orchestra
Baby, We Better Try To Get It Together—Barry White
Let The Music Play—Barry White

Barry WHITE
Mary Hartman, Mary Hartman (Theme)—Deadly Nightshade

Maurice WHITE
(w.Al McKay)
Sing A Song—Earth Wind & Fire
Flowers—Emotions
(w.Philip Bailey/Al McKay)
Saturday Nite—Earth Wind & Fire

John WHITEHEAD
(w.Victor Carstarphen/Gene McFadden)
Bad Luck—Atlanta Disco Band
Tell The World How I Feel About 'Cha Baby—Harold Melvin & the Blue Notes
Wake Up Everybody—Harold Melvin & the Blue Notes

Norman WHITFIELD
Car Wash—Rose Royce
(w.Barrett Strong)
I Heard It Through The Grapevine—Creedence Clearwater Revival
(w.William Stevenson)
It Should Have Been Me—Yvonne Fair

Brad WHITFORD
(w.Steven Tyler)
Last Child—Aerosmith

Geoff WILKENS
(w.Ben Findon)
Light Up The World With Sunshine—Hamilton, Joe Frank & Dennison

Deniece WILLIAMS
(w.Susaye Greene/Hank Redd/Nathan Watts)
Free—Deniece Williams

Hank WILLIAMS
I'm So Lonesome I Could Cry—Terry Bradshaw

James WILLIAMS
(w.William Beck/Marshall Jones/Marvin Pierce)
Who'd She Coo—Ohio Players
(see also OHIO PLAYERS)

Larry E. WILLIAMS
Let Your Love Flow—Bellamy Brothers

Milan WILLIAMS
(see COMMODORES)

Paul WILLIAMS
(w.Barbra Streisand)
Love Theme From 'A Star Is Born' (Evergreen)—Barbra Streisand

Wade WILLIAMSON
(w.Randy Muller)
Movin'—Brass Construction

Ann WILSON
(w. Nancy Wilson)
Crazy On You—Heart
Dreamboat Annie—Heart
Magic Man—Heart

Brian WILSON
(w.Mike Love)
Good Vibrations—Todd Rundgren
It's O.K.—Beach Boys

Johnny WILSON
(w.Rory Bourke/Gene Dobbins)
Easy As Pie—Billy 'Crash' Craddock

Nancy WILSON
(w.Ann Wilson)
Crazy On You—Heart
Dreamboat Annie—Heart
Magic Man—Heart

Tony WILSON
(w.Errol Brown)
You Sexy Thing—Hot Chocolate

Bill WITHERS
Make Love To Your Mind—Bill Withers

Danny WOLFE
(w.Jimmy Green Jr.)
Hey Shirley (This Is Squirrely)—
Shirley & Squirrely

Bobby WOMACK
Breezin'—George Benson
(w.Harold T. Payne)
Daylight—Vicki Sue Robinson

Stevie WONDER
I Wish—Stevie Wonder

Peter WOOD
(w.Al Stewart)
Year Of The Cat—Al Stewart

Stuart 'Woody' WOOD
(w.Eric Faulkner)
Money Honey—Bay City Rollers

Eric WOOLFSON
(w.Alan Parsons)
**(The System Of) Doctor Tarr &
Professor Fether**—Alan Parsons Project
The Raven—Alan Parsons Project

Gary WRIGHT
Dream Weaver—Gary Wright
Love Is Alive—Gary Wright
Made Love To You—Gary Wright

Tammy WYNETTE
(w.George Richey/Billy Sherrill)
'Till I Can Make It On My Own—Tammy
Wynette

Marvin YANCY
(w.Chuck Jackson)
Inseparable—Natalie Cole
Mr. Melody—Natalie Cole
**The More You Do It (The More I Like
It Done To Me)**—Ronnie Dyson
It's Cool—Tymes
(w.Natalie Cole/Chuck Jackson)
**Sophisticated Lady (She's A Different
Lady)**—Natalie Cole

Christine YARIAN
(w.Freddie Perren/Keni St. Lewis)
Don't Take Away The Music—Tavares

Peter YARROW
(w.Phil Jarrell)
Torn Between Two Lovers—Mary
MacGregor

Earl YOUNG
(w.Ronnie Baker/Allan Felder/Norman
Harris)
Hold Back The Night—Trammps

George YOUNG
(w.Harry Vanda)
Yesterday's Hero—Bay City Rollers
Yesterday's Hero—John Paul Young

James YOUNG
(w.Dennis DeYoung)
Lorelei—Styx

Rusty YOUNG
Rose Of Cimarron—Poco

Michael ZAGER
(w.Paul Davis)
Do It With Feeling—Michael Zager's
Moon Band featuring Peabo Bryson

Pete ZORN
(w.Easy Street)
I've Been Lovin' You—Easy Street

Z Z TOP
(Frank Beard, Dusty Hill & Billy Gibbons)
It's Only Love—Z Z Top

Section 11

US Album Section

(*Billboard* Top 200 Album Chart)

This section lists the position and week of entry, highest chart position and week, weeks on chart, artist, title, producers and catalogue number of all albums that made the *Billboard* Top 200 album chart during 1976.

These charts are based on *Billboard's* figures. They are not as accurate as their UK counterpart, and are very much an assessment. Similarly they don't refer exactly to a particular week of sales, so although Billboard is published on Monday, the chart refers to the end of the previous week. *denotes record still in chart on January 1, 1977.

All names in brackets denote the members of groups. For all other information about producers' credits see Section 12. There is not a cross-referenced label section for albums, since in many cases records have been in the charts for several years (i.e. *The Sound of Music* Soundtrack, which originally charted in 1965). The reason behind listing label credits was to assess each companies' chart performance during the year, with what was basically new product.

Position and date of entry	Highest position and date	Wks.	Artist(s) Title Producer(s)	Cat. No.
			ABBA	
110(18/9/76)	48(27/11/76)	15*	**Greatest Hits** Benny Andersson Bjorn Ulvaeus	(Atlantic SD 18189)
			ACE	
188(27/12/75)	153(24/1/76)	6	**Time For Another** John Anthony	(Anchor ANCL 2013)
			AEROSMITH	
190(13/10/73)	21(3/ 4/76)	59	**Aerosmith** Adrian Barber	(Columbia KC32005)
193(6/4/74)	74(18/10/75)	86	**Get Your Wings** Jack Douglas Ray Colcord	(Columbia KC32847)
25(29/ 5/76)	3(26/ 6/76)	31*	**Rocks** Jack Douglas Aerosmith (Tom Hamilton Joey Kramer Joe Perry Steven Tyler Brad Whitford)	(Columbia PC34165)
160(26/4/75)	11(13/ 9/75)	86*	**Toys In The Attic** Jack Douglas	(Columbia PC33479)
			Morris **ALBERT**	
149(12/6/76)	135(26/6/76)	7	**Morris Albert** Antonio Carlos de Oliveira	(RCA APL1-1496)
183(6/9/75)	37(29/11/75)	19	**Feelings** Morris Albert	(RCA APL-1018)
			ALLMAN BROTHERS BAND	
113(13/12/75)	43(24/ 1/76)	14	**The Road Goes On Forever** Adrian Barber Tom Dowd Johnny Sandlin The Allman Brothers Band (Gregg Allman Richard Betts Jaimoe Chuck Leavell Berry Oakley Butch Trucks)	(Capricorn 2CP 0164)
146(4/12/76)	75(25/12/76)	4*	**Wipe The Windows . Check Oil . Dollar Gas** (Not listed)	(Capricorn 2 CXD 177)
			AMAZING RHYTHM ACES	
180(5/6/76)	157(10/7/76)	7	**Too Stuffed To Jump** Barry 'Byrd' Burton	(ABC ABCD 940)
			AMBROSIA	
160(18/9/76)	79(13/11/76)	15*	**Somewhere I've Never Travelled** Alan Parsons	(20th Century T510)

Position and date of entry	Highest position and date	Wks.	Artist(s) Title Producer(s)	Cat. No.
			AMERICA	
119(5/4/75)	4(14/ 6/75)	44	**Hearts** George Martin	(Warner Bros BS 2852)
79(1/ 5/76)	11(5/ 6/76)	22	**Hideaway** George Martin	(Warner Bros BS 2932)
116(22/11/75)	3(20/12/75)	58*	**History—America's Greatest Hits** George Martin Jeff Dexter Ian Samwell-Smith America (Gerry Beckley Dewey Bunnell Dan Peek)	(Warner Bros BS 2894
			AMERICAN FLYER	
120(4/9/76)	87(16/10/76)	10	**American Flyer** George Martin	(United Artists UA-LA650-G)
			Jon **ANDERSON**	
94(24/ 7/76)	47(11/ 9/76)	13	**Olias Of Sunhillow** (Not listed)	(Atlantic SD 18180)
			ANGEL	
183(20/12/75)	150(17/1/76)	6	**Angel** Derek Lawrence Big Jim Sullivan	(Casablanca NBLP 7021)
184(19/ 7/76)	155(24/7/76)	10	**Helluva Band** Derek Lawrence Big Jim Sullivan	(Casablanca NBLP 7028)
			Paul **ANKA**	
144(23/10/76)	88(25/12/76)	10*	**The Painter** Denny Diante	(United Artists UA-LA653-G)
96(13/12/75)	22(28/ 2/76)	25	**Times Of Your Life** Denny Diante Rick Hall Spencer Proffer Bob Skaff	(United Artists UA-LA569-G)
			ARMADA ORCHESTRA	
196(17/1/76)	196(17/1/76)	2	**Armada Orchestra** Within the Contempo Family	(Scepter SPS 5123)
			Joan **ARMATRADING**	
183(9/10/76)	177(23/10/76)	3	**Joan Armatrading** Glyn Johns	(A&M SP 4588)
			ASHFORD & SIMPSON	
192(8/5/76)	189(22/5/76)	4	**Come As You Are** Nickolas Ashford Valerie Simpson	(Warner Bros BS 2858)

Position and date of entry	Highest position and date	Wks.	Artist(s) Title Producer(s)	Cat. No.
			ASLEEP AT THE WHEEL	
189(18/9/76)	179(25/9/76)	3	**Wheelin' And Dealin'** Tommy Allsup Asleep At The Wheel (Chris O'Connell Ray Benson Link Davis Jr. Floyd Domino Tony Garnier Scott Hennige Danny Levin Bill Mabry Lucky Oceans Leroy Preston)	(Capitol ST 11546)
			Chet ATKINS & LES PAUL	
185(29/5/76)	172(12/6/76)	5	**Chester & Lester** Chet Atkins	(RCA APL1-1167)
			ATLANTA DISCO BAND	
198(17/1/76)	172(13/3/76)	9	**Bad Luck** Dave Crawford	(Ariola America ST 50004)
			ATLANTA RHYTHM SECTION	
181(5/6/76)	146(28/8/76)	15	**Red Tape** Buddy Buie	(Polydor PD-1-6060)
			Brian AUGER'S OBLIVION EXPRESS	
186(13/3/76)	169(3/4/76)	4	**Live Oblivion Vol. 2** Brian Auger	(2-RCA CPL2-1230)
			AUTOMATIC MAN	
146(2/10/76)	120(30/10/76)	7	**Automatic Man** Lou Casabianca Automatic Man (Michael Shrieve Bayete Pat Thrall Doni Harvey)	(Island ILPS 9397)
			AVERAGE WHITE BAND	
82(17/ 7/76)	9(28/ 8/76)	24*	**Soul Searching** Arif Mardin	(Atlantic SD 18179)
			Hoyt AXTON	
189(10/4/76)	171(1/5/76)	4	**Fearless** David Kershenbaum	(A&M SP 4571)
			Roy AYERS UBIQUITY	
130(14/8/76)	51(30/10/76)	17	**Everybody Loves The Sunshine** Roy Ayers	(Polydor PD-1-6070)
186(21/2/76)	90(15/ 5/76)	18	**Mystic Voyage** Roy Ayers	(Polydor PD-1-6057)
			AZTEC TWO-STEP	
191(25/12/76)	191(25/12/76)	1*	**Two's Company** Mark Abramson	(RCA APK1-1497)

Position and date of entry	Highest position and date	Wks.	Artist(s) Title Producer(s)	Cat. No.
			BACHMAN-TURNER OVERDRIVE	
81(14/ 8/76)	19(9/10/76)	15	**Best Of B.T.O. (So Far)** Randy Bachman	(Mercury SRM1-1101)
97(3/ 1/76)	23(6/ 3/76)	21	**Head On** Randy Bachman	(Mercury SRM1-1067)
			BACK STREET CRAWLER	
165(15/11/75)	111(20/12/75)	10	**The Band Plays On** Back Street Crawler (Tony Braunagel Paul Kossoff Mike Montgomery Terry Wilson Terry Wilson-Slesser)	(Atco SD 36-125)
167(14/8/76)	140(4/9/76)	5	**2nd Street** Back Street Crawler (Tony Braunagel John 'Rabbit' Bundrick Paul Kossoff Terry Wilson Terry Wilson-Slesser)	(Atco SD 36-138)
			BAD COMPANY	
84(14/ 2/76)	5(10/ 4/76)	28	**Run With The Pack** Bad Company (Boz Burrell Simon Kirke Mick Ralphs Paul Rodgers)	(Swansong SS 8415)
			Joan **BAEZ**	
144(17/5/75)	11(26/ 7/75)	46	**Diamonds & Rust** Joan Baez David Kershenbaum	(A&M SP 4527)
98(7/ 2/76)	34(20/ 3/76)	17	**From Every Stage** David Kershenbaum	(2A&M SP 3704)
122(6/11/76)	62(11/12/76)	8*	**Gulf Winds** David Kershenbaum	(A&M SP 4603)
			George **BAKER SELECTION**	
189(31/1/76)	153(28/2/76)	7	**Paloma Blanca** Hans Bouwens	(Warner Bros BS 2905)
			BAND	
126(4/9/76)	51(16/10/76)	14	**The Best Of The Band** The Band (Rick Danko Levon Helm Garth Hudson Richard Manuel Robbie Robertson)	(Capitol ST 11553)
94(13/12/75)	26(31/ 1/76)	19	**Northern Lights—Southern Cross** The Band	Capitol ST 11440)

Position and date of entry	Highest position and date	Wks.	Artist(s) Title Producer(s)	Cat. No.
			BAND OF THE BLACK WATCH	
189(20/3/76)	164(10/4/76)	4	**Scotch On The Rocks** Barry Kingston	(Private Stock PS 2007)
			Ron BANKS & THE DRAMATICS	
130(15/11/75)	93(13/12/75)	12	**Drama V** Ron Banks Don Davis Michael Henderson Tony Hester L.J. Reynolds (see also under DRAMATICS)	(ABC ABCD 916)
			Gato BARBIERI	
191(2/10/76)	106(11/12/76)	13*	**Caliente** Herb Alpert	(A&M SP 4597)
			BAR-KAYS	
157(13/11/76)	73(25/12/76)	7*	**Too Hot To Stop** Allen Jones	(Mercury SRM1-1099)
			Shirley BASSEY	
182(9/10/76)	149(13/11/76)	8	**Love, Life & Feelings** Martin Davis	(United Artists UA-LA605-G)
			BAY CITY ROLLERS	
178(27/9/75)	20(24/ 1/76)	35	**Bay City Rollers** Phil Coulter Bill Martin Phil Wainman	(Arista AL 4049)
93(18/ 9/76)	26(13/11/76)	15*	**Dedication** Colin Frechter Jimmy Ienner Phil Wainman	(Arista AL 4093)
94(20/ 3/76)	31(8/ 5/76)	16	**Rock 'n' Roll Love Letter** Colin Frechter Phil Wainman	(Arista AL 4071)
			BEACH BOYS	
128(8/12/73)	25(26/ 1/74)	24	**The Beach Boys In Concert** The Beach Boys (Blondie Chaplin Ricky Fataar Al Jardine Mike Love Carl Wilson Dennis Wilson)	(Brother/Reprise 2 RS 6484)
100(11/12/76)	76(25/12/76)	3*	**Beach Boys '69—The Beach Boys Live In London** (Not listed)	(Capitol ST 11584)
70(20/ 7/74)	1(5/10/74)	94*	**Endless Summer** The Beach Boys (Al Jardine Mike Love Brian, Carl & Dennis Wilson) Nikolas Venet Brian Wilson	(Capitol SVBB 11307)

Position and date of entry	Highest position and date	Wks.	Artist(s) Title Producer(s)	Cat. No.
76(17/ 7/76)	8(28/ 8/76)	24*	**15 Big Ones** Brian Wilson	(Brother/Reprise MS 2251)
76(19/ 7/75)	25(30/ 8/75)	23	**Good Vibrations—Best Of The Beach Boys** The Beach Boys	(Brother/Reprise MS 2223)
87(3/ 5/75)	8(28/ 6/75)	43	**Spirit Of America** The Beach Boys Nikolas Venet Brian Wilson	(Capitol SVBB 11384)
			BEATLES	
178(18/10/69)	1(1/11/69)	87	**Abbey Road** George Martin	(Capitol SO 383)
11(14/12/68)	1(28/12/68)	97*	**The Beatles (White Album)** George Martin	(Apple SWBO 101)
94(14/ 4/73)	3(19/ 5/73)	104	**The Beatles 1962-1966** George Martin	(Apple SKBO 3403)
97(14/ 4/73)	1(26/ 5/73)	107*	**The Beatles 1967-1970** George Martin	(Apple SKBO 3404)
8(26/ 6/76)	2(10/ 7/76)	27*	**Rock 'n' Roll Music** George Martin	(Capitol SKBO 11537)
8(24/ 6/67)	1(1/ 7/67)	119*	**Sgt. Pepper's Lonely Hearts Club Band** George Martin	(Capitol SMAS 2653)
			BE-BOP DELUXE	
169(16/10/76)	88(27/11/76)	8	**Modern Music** John Leckie Bill Nelson	(Harvest ST 11575)
190(7/2/76)	96(10/ 4/76)	17	**Sunburst Finish** John Leckie Bill Nelson	(Harvest ST 11478)
			Jeff BECK	
149(26/6/76)	16(7/ 8/76)	25	**Wired** George Martin	(Epic PE 33849)
			BEE GEES	
20(2/10/76)	8(13/11/76)	13*	**Children Of The World** The Bee Gees (Barry, Robin & Maurice Gibb)	(RSO RS-1-3003)
93(13/11/76)	56(18/12/76)	7*	**Gold, Vol. I** The Bee Gees Robert Stigwood	(RSO RS-1-3006)
171(21/6/75)	14(20/ 3/76)	75	**Main Course** Arif Mardin	(RSO SO 4807)
			Archie BELL & THE DRELLS	
187(10/1/76)	95(20/ 3/76)	20	**Dance Your Troubles Away** Victor Carstarphen Gene McFadden John Whitehead Kenny Gamble Leon Huff Bunny Sigler	(Philadelphia International PZ33844)

Position and date of entry	Highest position and date	Wks.	Artist(s) Title Producer(s)	Cat. No
			BELLAMY BROTHERS	
180(15/5/76)	69(12/ 6/76)	12	**Bellamy Brothers Featuring 'Let Your Love Flow'** Phil Gernhard Tony Scotti	(Warner Bros BS 2941)
			George BENSON	
149(17/4/76)	1(31/ 7/76)	37*	**Breezin'** Tommy LiPuma	(Warner Bros BS 2919)
187(26/6/76)	51(21/ 8/76)	16	**Good King Bad** Creed Taylor	(CTI 6062)
162(24/7/76)	125(4/9/76)	8	**The Other Side Of Abbey Road** Creed Taylor	(A&M SP 3028)
			George BENSON & JOE FARRELL	
167(30/10/76)	100(27/11/76)	8	**Benson & Farrell** Creed Taylor	(CTI 6069)
			BIDDU ORCHESTRA	
185(21/2/76)	170(6/3/76)	3	**Biddu Orchestra** Biddu	(Epic PE 33903)
			Elvin BISHOP	
123(20/11/76)	70(18/12/76)	6*	**Hometown Boy Makes Good** Allan Blazek	(Capricorn CP 0176)
186(24/1/76)	18(22/ 5/76)	34	**Struttin' My Stuff** Allan Blazek Bill Szymczyk	(Capricorn CP 0165)
			BLACK OAK ARKANSAS	
180(12/6/76)	176(10/7/76)	7	**Balls Of Fire** Black Oak Arkansas (Jim Dandy Pat Daugherty Tommy Aldridge 'Little' Jimmy Henderson Stanley Knight Rickie Lee Reynolds)	(MCA 2199)
195(28/2/76)	194(6/3/76)	2	**Live! Mutha** Black Oak Arkansas	(Atco SD 36-128)
187(18/10/75)	99(17/ 1/76)	17	**X Rated** Richard Podolor	(MCA 2155)
			BLACK SABBATH	
97(30/10/76)	51(27/11/76)	9*	**Technical Ecstasy** Black Sabbath (Terry 'Geezer' Butler Tommy Iommi Ozzy Osbourne Bill Ward)	(Warner Bros BS 2969)
105(28/2/76)	48(10/ 4/76)	10	**We Sold Our Soul For Rock 'n' Roll** Roger Bain Mike Butcher Patrick Meehan Black Sabbath	(2 Warner Bros BS 2923)

Position and date of entry	Highest position and date	Wks.	Artist(s) Title Producer(s)	Cat. No.
			BLACKBYRDS	
171(22/11/75)	16(22/ 5/76)	40	**City Life**	(Fantasy F 9490)
			Donald Byrd	
160(27/11/76)	71(25/12/76)	5*	**Unfinished Business**	(Fantasy F 9518)
			Donald Byrd	
			BLACKMORE'S RAINBOW	
128(5/6/76)	48(10/ 7/76)	17	**Rainbow Rising**	(Oyster
			Martin Birch	OY-1-1601)
			Bobby BLAND & B.B. KING	
128(17/7/76)	73(28/ 8/76)	14	**Together Again . . . Live**	(ABC/Impulse
			Esmond Edwards	ASD 9317)
			BLOOD SWEAT & TEARS	
165(7/8/76)	165(7/8/76)	3	**More Than Ever**	(Columbia
			Bob James	PC 34233)
			BLUE MAGIC	
186(25/9/76)	170(9/10/76)	5	**Mystic Dragons**	(Atco SD 36-140)
			Bobby Eli	
			BLUE OYSTER CULT	
97(19/ 6/76)	29(20/11/76)	28*	**Agents Of Fortune**	(Columbia
			Murray Krugman	PC 34164)
			David Lucas	
			Sandy Pearlman	
			Tommy BOLIN	
122(2/10/76)	98(23/10/76)	8	**Private Eyes**	Columbia
			Tommy Bolin	PC 34239)
			Dennis MacKay	
184(20/12/75)	96(7/ 2/76)	14	**Teaser**	(Nemperor
			Tommy Bolin	NE 436)
			Dennis MacKay	
			BOSTON	
124(25/9/76)	3(4/12/76)	14*	**Boston**	(Epic PE 34188)
			John Boylan	
			Tom Scholz	
			David BOWIE	
45(19/ 6/76)	10(17/ 7/76)	28*	**Changesonebowie**	(RCA APL1-1732)
			David Bowie	
			Gus Dudgeon	
			Harry Maslin	
			Ken Scott	
			Tony Visconti	
196(17/6/72)	75(7/ 4/73)	72	**The Rise & Fall Of Ziggy Stardust (Spiders From Mars)**	(RCA LSP 4702)
			David Bowie	
			Ken Scott	
88(7/ 2/76)	3(28/ 2/76)	32	**Station To Station**	(RCA APL1-1327)
			David Bowie	
			Harry Maslin	
141(22/ 3/75)	9(12/ 4/75)	51	**Young Americans**	(RCA APL1-0998)
			David Bowie	
			Harry Maslin	
			Tony Visconti	

Position and date of entry	Highest position and date	Wks.	Artist(s) Title Producer(s)	Cat. No.
			BRAND X	
193(13/11/76)	191(20/11/76)	3	**Unorthodox Behaviour** Brand X (Philip Collins John Goodsall Percy Jones Robin Lumley) Dennis MacKay	(Passport PPSD 98019)
			BRASS CONSTRUCTION	
133(7/2/76)	10(15/ 5/76)	35	**Brass Construction** Jeff Lane	(United Artists UA-LA545-G)
97(20/11/76)	26(25/12/76)	6*	**Brass Construction II** Jeff Lane	(United Artists UA-LA677-G)
			BRECKER BROTHERS	
139(28/2/76)	82(24/ 4/76)	16	**Back To Back** Randy & Michael Brecker	(Arista AL 4061)
			BRICK	
181(13/11/76)	40(25/12/76)	7*	**Good High** Johnny Duncan Jim Healy Robert E. Lee Brick (Jimmy 'Lord' Brown Regi Hargis Eddie Irons Don Nevins Ray Ransom)	(Bang BLP 408)
			Johnny BRISTOL	
189(11/12/76)	189(11/12/76)	3*	**Bristol's Creme** Johnny Bristol	(Atlantic SD 18197)
			David BROMBERG	
190(9/10/76)	104(27/11/76)	11	**How Late'll Ya Play 'Til ?** David Bromberg Steve Burgh	(Fantasy F 79007)
			BROTHERS JOHNSON	
189(6/3/76)	9(5/ 6/76)	38	**Look Out For # 1** Quincy Jones	(A&M SP 4567)
			James BROWN	
177(14/8/76)	147(11/9/76)	8	**Get Up Offa That Thing** James Brown	(Polydor PD-1-6071)
			Stanky BROWN GROUP	
194(15/5/76)	192(22/5/76)	3	**Our Pleasure To Serve You** Ron Frangipane Al Steckler	(Sire SASD 7516)
			Jackson BROWNE	
52(20/11/76)	5(18/12/76)	6*	**The Pretender** Jon Landau	(Asylum 7E-1079)
			Dave BRUBECK & PAUL DESMOND	
189(10/1/76)	167(7/2/76)	5	**1975: The Duets** John Snyder	(Horizon SP 703)

Position and date of entry	Highest position and date	Wks.	Artist(s) Title Producer(s)	Cat. No.
			B.T. EXPRESS	
83(29/ 5/76)	43(19/ 6/76)	12	**Energy To Burn** Jeff Lane	(Columbia PC 34178)
			Roy BUCHANAN	
183(15/5/76)	148(12/6/76)	7	**A Street Called Straight** Arif Mardin	(Atlantic SD 18170)
			Jimmy BUFFETT	
194(14/2/76)	65(27/ 3/76)	14	**Havana Daydreamin'** Don Gant	(ABC ABCD 914)
			Donald BYRD	
179(18/12/76)	169(25/12/76)	2*	**Donald Byrd's Best** Larry & Fonce Mizell	(Blue Note BN-LA700-G)
184(15/11/75)	49(24/ 1/76)	29	**Places And Spaces** Larry & Fonce Mizell	Blue Note BN-LA549-C)
			J.J. CALE	
168(25/9/76)	84(20/11/76)	13	**Troubadour** Audie Ashworth	(Shelter SRL 52002)
			CAMEL	
190(22/5/76)	118(3/7/76)	13	**Moonmadness** Rhett Davies Camel (Peter Bardens Doug Ferguson Andy Latimer Andy Ward)	(Janus JXS 7024)
			Glen CAMPBELL	
129(27/11/76)	116(11/12/76)	5*	**The Best Of Glen Campbell** Jimmy Bowen Al DeLory Kelly Gordon Dennis Lambert Brian Potter	(Capitol ST 11577)
97(1/ 5/76)	63(15/ 5/76)	9	**Bloodline** Dennis Lambert Brian Potter	(Capitol SW 11516)
174(9/8/75)	17(18/10/75)	30	**Rhinestone Cowboy** Dennis Lambert Brian Potter	(Capitol SW 11430)
			Jim CAPALDI	
197(14/2/76)	193(6/3/76)	4	**Short Cut Draw Blood** Chris Blackwell Jim Capaldi Steve Smith	(Island ILPS 9336)
			CAPTAIN & TENNILLE	
81(14/ 6/75)	2(2/ 8/75)	81*	**Love Will Keep Us Together** Morgan Cavett The Captain (Daryl Dragon)	(A&M SP 3505)
58(20/ 3/76)	9(1/ 5/76)	41*	**Song Of Joy** The Captain Toni Tennille	(A&M SP 4570)

Position and date of entry	Highest position and date	Wks.	Artist(s) Title Producer(s)	Cat. No.
			George CARLIN	
121(8/11/75)	34(3/ 1/76)	15	**An Evening With Wally Londo Featuring Bill Slaszo** Monte Kay Jack Lewis	(Little David LD 1008)
			Eric CARMEN	
190(15/11/75)	21(20/ 3/76)	51	**Eric Carmen** Jimmy Ienner	(Arista AL 4057)
			CARPENTERS	
68(10/ 7/76)	33(14/ 8/76)	16	**A Kind Of Hush** Richard Carpenter	(A&M SP 4581)
			Keith CARRADINE	
187(26/6/76)	61(18/ 9/76)	17	**I'm Easy** John Guerin	(Asylum 7E-1066)
			Johnny CASH & THE TENNESSEE THREE	
188(17/7/76)	185(24/7/76)	2	**One Piece At A Time** Charlie Bragg Don Davis	(Columbia KC 34193)
			Jimmy CASTOR BUNCH FEATURING THE EVERYTHING MAN	
158(25/9/76)	132(30/10/76)	9	**E-Man Groovin'** Jimmy Castor Johnnie Pruitt	(Atlantic SD 18186)
			CATE BROS	
186(7/2/76)	158(12/6/76)	9	**Cate Bros** Steve Cropper	(Asylum 7E-1050)
186(30/10/76)	182(6/11/76)	2	**In One Eye And Out The Other** Steve Cropper	(Asylum 7E-1080)
			Harry CHAPIN	
120(1/5/76)	48(29/ 5/76)	19	**Greatest Stories Live** Stephen Chapin Fred Kewley	(Elektra 7E-2009)
104(30/10/76)	87(20/11/76)	6	**On The Road To Kingdom Come** Stephen Chapin	(Elektra 7E-1082)
			Ray CHARLES & CLEO LAINE	
179(4/12/76)	138(25/12/76)	4*	**Porgy & Bess** Norman Granz	(RCA CPL2-1831)
			CHEECH AND CHONG	
88(26/ 6/76)	25(7/ 8/76)	13	**Sleeping Beauty (OD-40)** Lou Adler	(Ode SP 77040)
			CHICAGO	
14(29/11/75)	1(13/12/75)	52*	**Chicago IX—Greatest Hits** James William Guercio	(Columbia PC 33900)
12(3/ 7/76)	3(7/ 8/76)	26*	**Chicago X** James William Guercio	(Columbia PC 34200)
			CHIEFTAINS	
193(28/2/76)	187(20/3/76)	4	**5** Paddy Moloney	(Island ILPS 9334)

Position and date of entry	Highest position and date	Wks.	Artist(s) Title Producer(s)	Cat. No.
			CITY BOY	
190(28/8/76)	177(11/9/76)	3	**City Boy** Robert John Lange	(Mercury SRM1-1098)
			Eric CLAPTON	
26(16/10/76)	15(13/11/76)	11*	**No Reason To Cry** Rob Fraboni	(RSO RS-1-3004)
			Stanley CLARKE	
183(1/11/75)	34(6/12/75)	19	**Journey To Love** Stanley Clarke Ken Scott	(Nemperor NE 433)
101(25/9/76)	34(13/11/76)	14*	**School Days** Stanley Clarke Ken Scott	(Nemperor NE 439)
			CLIMAX BLUES BAND	
190(23/10/76)	125(11/12/76)	10*	**Gold Plated** Mike Vernon Climax Blues Band (Colin Cooper Peter Haycock Derek Holt Richard Jones John Kuffley)	(Sire SASD 7523)
			Billy COBHAM	
185(10/4/76)	128(29/5/76)	8	**Life & Times** Billy Cobham	(Atlantic SD 18166)
			Billy COBHAM/GEORGE DUKE BAND	
147(23/10/76)	99(20/11/76)	9	**'Live' On Tour In Europe** Billy Cobham George Duke	(Atlantic SD 18194)
			Joe COCKER	
116(15/5/76)	70(19/ 6/76)	10	**Stingray** Rob Fraboni	(A&M SP 4574)
			Commander CODY & HIS LOST PLANET AIRMEN	
184(31/7/76)	170(14/8/76)	3	**We've Got A Live One Here** Tom Anderson	(Warner Bros BS 2LS 2939)
			Dennis COFFEY	
186(17/1/76)	147(14/2/76)	7	**Finger Lickin' Good** Dennis Coffey Mike Theodore	(Westbound W 212)
			Natalie COLE	
190(30/ 8/75)	18(29/11/75)	56	**Inseparable** Chuck Jackson Marvin Yancy	(Capitol ST 11429)
43(29/ 5/76)	13(17/ 7/76)	30	**Natalie** Gene Barge Richard Evans Chuck Jackson Marvin Yancy	(Capitol ST 11517)

Position and date of entry	Highest position and date	Wks.	Artist(s) Title Producer(s)	Cat. No.
			Judy COLLINS	
101(11/9/76)	25(16/10/76)	16*	**Bread And Roses** Arif Mardin	(Elektra 7E-1076)
			William Bootsy COLLINS	
186(1/5/76)	59(17/ 7/76)	27	**Stretchin' Out In Bootsy's Rubber Band** George Clinton William Collins	(Warner Bros BS 2920)
			(this album has no artists' credit, so it could be William Bootsy Collins, Bootsy's Rubber Band, or the Rubber Band. The choice is yours)	
			Jessi COLTER	
118(7/8/76)	79(11/ 9/76)	8	**Diamond In The Rough** Waylon Jennings Ken Mansfield	(Capitol ST 11543)
150(7/2/76)	109(6/3/76)	8	**Jessi** Waylon Jennings Ken Mansfield (see also: Waylon Jennings)	(Capitol ST 11477)
			COMMODORES	
97(10/ 7/76)	12(2/10/76)	25*	**Hot On The Tracks** James Carmichael Commodores (William King Ronald LaPraed Tom McClary Walter Orange Lionel Richie Milan Williams)	(Motown M6-867S1)
139(8/11/75)	29(27/12/75)	32	**Movin' On** James Carmichael Commodores	(Motown M6-848S1)
			Perry COMO	
196(20/12/75)	142(31/1/76)	9	**Just Out Of Reach** Chet Atkins	(RCA APL1-0863)
			Norman CONNORS	
156(24/7/76)	39(9/10/76)	23*	**You Are My Starship** Skip Drinkwater Jerry Schoenbaum	(Buddah BDS 5655)
			Norman CONNORS PRESENTS AQUARIAN DREAM	
188(9/10/76)	154(13/11/76)	6	**Norman Connors Presents Aquarian Dream** Norman Connors	(Buddah BDS 5672)
			Ry COODER	
187(23/10/76)	177(13/11/76)	5	**Chicken Skin Music** Ry Cooder	(Reprise MS 2254)
			Rita COOLIDGE	
124(6/12/75)	85(10/ 1/76)	10	**It's Only Love** David Anderle	(A&M SP 4531)

Position and date of entry	Highest position and date	Wks.	Artist(s) Title Producer(s)	Cat. No
			Alice COOPER	
86(17/ 7/76)	27(18/12/76)	24*	**Alice Cooper Goes To Hell** Bob Ezrin	(Warner Bros BS 2896)
			Chick COREA	
124(6/3/76)	42(1/ 5/76)	15	**The Leprechaun** Chick Corea	(Polydor PD-1-6062)
			Bill COSBY	
143(5/6/76)	100(3/7/76)	12	**Bill Cosby Is Not Himself** **These Days Rat Own, Rat** **Own, Rat Own** Stu Gardner	(Capitol ST 11530)
			David COURTNEY	
200(21/2/76)	194(13/3/76)	4	**David Courtney's First Day** David Courtney Andrew Powell	(United Artists UA-LA553-G)
			CRACK THE SKY	
169(30/10/76)	142(27/11/76)	5	**Animal Notes** William Kirkland Terence P. Minogue Marty Nelson	(Lifesong LS 6005)
190(24/1/76)	161(21/2/76)	6	**Crack The Sky** William Kirkland Terence P Minogue Marty Nelson	(Lifesong LS 6000)
			Hank CRAWFORD	
184(17/4/76)	159(15/5/76)	7	**I Hear A Symphony** Creed Taylor	(Kudu KU 26 S1)
			CREEDENCE CLEARWATER REVIVAL	
144(6/3/76)	100(1/5/76)	14	**Chronicle** John Fogerty	(Fantasy CCR-2)
			Jim CROCE	
187(1/11/75)	87(24/ 1/76)	18	**The Faces I've Been** Terry Cashman Tommy West	(Lifesong LS 900)
48(5/10/74)	2(16/11/74)	46	**Photographs & Memories—** **His Greatest Hits** Terry Cashman Tommy West	(ABC ABCD 835)
			David CROSBY/GRAHAM NASH	
72(24/ 7/76)	26(18/ 9/76)	15	**Whistling Down The Wire** David Crosby Graham Nash	(ABC ABCD 956)
53(11/10/75)	6(29/11/75)	31	**Wind On The Water** David Crosby Graham Nash	(ABC ABCD 902)
			CROWN HEIGHTS AFFAIR	
186(4/10/75)	121(27/12/75)	17	**Dreaming A Dream** Britt Britton Freida Nerangis	(DeLite DEP 2017)

Position and date of entry	Highest position and date	Wks.	Artist(s) / Title / Producer(s)	Cat. No.
			CRUSADERS	
143(18/12/76)	132(25/12/76)	2*	The Best Of The Crusaders Stewart Levine	(ABC/Blue Thumb BTSY 6027/2)
172(22/5/76)	38(17/ 7/76)	18	Those Southern Knights Stewart Levine	(ABC/Blue Thumb BTSD 6024)
			Burton CUMMINGS	
90(6/11/76)	36(25/12/76)	8*	Burton Cummings Richard Perry	(Portrait PR 34261)
			Roger DALTREY	
70(9/ 8/75)	28(13/ 9/75)	23	Ride A Rock Horse Russ Ballard	(MCA 2147)
			Charlie DANIELS BAND	
106(4/12/76)	83(25/12/76)	4*	High Lonesome Paul Hornsby	(Epic PE 34377)
119(15/5/76)	35(3/ 7/76)	18	Saddle Tramp Paul Hornsby	(Epic PE 34150)
			Mac DAVIS	
190(10/4/76)	156(15/5/76)	9	Forever Lovers Rick Hall	(Columbia PC 34105)
			Miles DAVIS	
185(13/3/76)	168(3/4/76)	5	Agharta Teo Macero	(2-Columbia PG 33967)
			Tyrone DAVIS	
143(2/10/76)	89(13/11/76)	9	Love And Touch Leo Graham	(Columbia PC 34268)
			DEEP PURPLE	
84(6/12/75)	43(10/ 1/76)	14	Come Taste The Band Martin Birch Deep Purple (Jon Lord Tommy Bolin David Coverdale Glenn Hughes Ian Paice)	(Purple PR 2895)
163(27/11/76)	148(11/12/76)	5*	Made In Europe Martin Birch Deep Purple (Ritchie Blackmore David Coverdale Glenn Hughes Jon Lord Ian Paice)	(Purple PR 2995)
			Jon DENVER	
149(29/6/74)	1(10/ 8/74)	96	Back Home Again Milton Okun	(RCA CPL1-0548)
186(20/12/75)	138(24/1/76)	6	Denver Gift Box Milton Okun	(RCA APL2-1263)
21(8/ 3/75)	2(12/ 4/75)	50	An Evening With John Denver Milton Okun	(RCA CPL2-0764)

Position and date of entry	Highest position and date	Wks.	Artist(s) Title Producer(s)	Cat. No.
84(8/12/73)	1(30/ 3/74)	160*	**Greatest Hits** Milton Okun	(RCA CPL1-0374)
133(8/11/75)	14(27/12/75)	13*	**Rocky Mountain Christmas** Milton Okun	(RCA APL1-1201)
14(4/ 9/76)	7(25/ 9/76)	17*	**Spirit** Milton Okun	(RCA APL1-1694)
2(4/10/75)	1(18/10/75)	45	**Windsong** Milton Okun	(RCA APL1-1183)
			DEODATO	
181(9/10/76)	86(27/11/76)	11	**Very Together** Eumir Deodato	(MCA 2219)
			DERRINGER	
187(31/7/76)	154(28/8/76)	9	**Derringer** Rick Derringer	(Blue Sky PZ 34181)
			Barry DeVORZON	
181(6/11/76)	147(25/12/76)	8*	**Nadia's Theme** Barry DeVorzon	(Arista AL 4104)
			Barry DeVORZON & PERRY BOTKIN Jr.	
142(6/11/76)	53(25/12/76)	8*	**Nadia's Theme** Perry Botkin Jr. Barry DeVorzon	(A&M SP 3412)
			Neil DIAMOND	
22(3/ 7/76)	4(14/ 8/76)	26*	**Beautiful Noise** Robbie Robertson	(Columbia PC 33965)
124(9/10/76)	102(30/10/76)	5	**And The Singer Sings His Song** Tom Catalano Tommy Cogbill Neil Diamond Chips Moman Chip Taylor	(MCA 2227)
			Al DiMEOLA	
187(27/3/76)	129(15/5/76)	10	**Land Of The Midnight Sun** Al DiMeola	(Columbia PC 34074)
			DR. BUZZARD'S ORIGINAL SAVANNAH BAND	
190(21/8/76)	26(30/10/76)	19*	**Dr. Buzzard's Original Savannah Band** Sandy Linzer	(RCA APL1-1504)
			DR. HOOK	
188(5/7/75)	141(24/4/76)	16	**Bankrupt** Ron Haffkine	(Capitol ST 11397)
126(15/5/76)	62(30/10/76)	27*	**A Little Bit More** Ron Haffkine Waylon Jennings	(Capitol ST 11522)
			DONOVAN	
186(5/6/76)	174(19/6/76)	3	**Slow Down World** Donovan Leitch	(Epic PE 33945)

Position and date of entry	Highest position and date	Wks.	Artist(s) Title Producer(s)	Cat. No.
			DOOBIE BROTHERS	
68(20/11/76)	8(25/12/76)	6*	**The Best Of The Doobies** Ted Templeman	(Warner Bros. BS 2978)
89(3/ 4/76)	8(22/ 5/76)	39*	**Takin' It To The Streets** Ted Templeman	(Warner Bros BS 2899)
			DOUBLE EXPOSURE	
189(21/8/76)	129(23/10/76)	11	**Ten Percent** Ronnie Baker Bruce Hawes Norman Harris Vincent Montana Jr. Earl Young	(Salsoul SZS 5503)
			Carol DOUGLAS	
190(6/11/76)	188(13/11/76)	2	**Midnight Love Affair** Ed O'Loughlin	(Midland International BK1-1798)
			DRAMATICS	
144(30/10/76)	119(4/12/76)	9*	**Joy Ride** Ron Banks Don Davis Michael Henderson Tony Hester L.J. Reynolds Jimmy Roach	(ABC ABCD 955)
(see also under RON BANKS & THE DRAMATICS)				
			George DUKE	
198(24/1/76)	169(14/2/76)	6	**I Love The Blues She Heard My Cry** George Duke	(BASF/MPS MC 25671)
190(4/12/76)	190(4/12/76)	2	**Liberated Fantasy** George Duke	(BASF/MPS G 22835)
			Bob DYLAN	
23(24/ 1/76)	1(7/ 2/76)	35	**Desire** Don DeVito	(Columbia PC 33893)
72(2/10/76)	17(30/10/76)	12	**Hard Rain** Don DeVito Bob Dylan	(Columbia PC 34349)
			EAGLES	
145(5/5/73)	41(30/ 6/73)	70	**Desperado** Glyn Johns	(Asylum SD 5068)
4(25/12/76)	4(25/12/76)	1*	**Hotel California** Bill Szymczyk	(Asylum 7E-1084)
50(20/ 4/74)	17(1/ 6/74)	87	**On The Border** Glyn Johns Bill Szymczyk	(Asylum 7E-1004)
25(28/ 6/75)	1(26/ 7/75)	56	**One Of These Nights** Bill Szymczyk	(Asylum 7E-1039)
4(6/ 3/76)	1(13/ 3/76)	43*	**Their Greatest Hits 1971-1975** Glyn Johns Bill Szymczyk	(Asylum 7E-1052)

Position and date of entry	Highest position and date	Wks.	Artist(s) Title Producer(s)	Cat. No.
			Charles EARLAND	
171(3/4/76)	155(5/6/76)	11	Odyssey	(Mercury
			Charles Earland	SRM-1-1049)
			EARTH QUAKE	
178(4/9/76)	151(25/9/76)	4	8.5	(Beserkeley
			Matthew King Kaufman	BZ 0047)
			Glen Kolotkin	
			EARTH WIND & FIRE	
98(6/12/75)	2(20/12/75)	54	Gratitude	(Columbia
			Maurice White	PG 33694)
			Charles Stepney	
			Joe Wissert	
15(16/10/76)	2(30/10/76)	11*	Spirit	(Columbia
			Charles Stepney	PC 34241)
			Maurice White	
69(15/ 3/75)	1(17/ 5/75)	55	That's The Way Of The World	(Columbia
			Sig Shore	PC 33280)
			ELECTRIC LIGHT ORCHESTRA	
78(25/10/75)	8(21/ 2/76)	48	Face The Music	(United Artists
			Jeff Lynne	UA-LA546-G)
64(30/10/76)	6(25/12/76)	9*	A New World Record	(United Artists
			Jeff Lynne	UA-LA679-G)
69(3/ 7/76)	32(7/ 8/76)	26*	Ole Elo	(United Artists
			Jeff Lynne	UA-LA630-G)
			EMOTIONS	
198(28/8/76)	45(27/11/76)	18*	Flowers	(Columbia
			Charles Stepney	PC 34163)
			Maurice White	
			ENGLAND DAN & JOHN FORD COLEY	
97(21/ 8/76)	17(13/11/76)	19*	Nights Are Forever	(Big Tree
			Kyle Lehning	BT 89517)
			Coke ESCOVEDO	
197(13/3/76)	195(20/3/76)	2	Coke	(Mercury
			Pat Gleeson	SRM-1-1041)
190(29/5/76)	190(29/5/76	3	Comin' At Ya'	(Mercury
			Pat Gleeson	SRM-1-1085)
			FATBACK BAND	
195(28/8/76)	182(25/9/76)	5	Night Fever	(Spring
			Fatback Band	SP-1-6711)
			(Richard Cornwell	
			Bill Curtis	
			Johnny Flippin	
			Johnny King	
			Earl Shelton	
			George Williams)	
183(28/2/76)	158(10/4/76)	8	Raising Hell	(Event
			Fatback Band	EV-1-6905)

Position and date of entry	Highest position and date	Wks.	Artist(s) Title Producer(s)	Cat. No.
			Freddy FENDER	
169(18/10/75)	41(6/12/75)	18	Are You Ready For Freddy Huey P. Meaux	(ABC/Dot DOSD 2044)
144(19/4/75)	20(28/ 6/75)	43	Before The Next Teardrop Falls Huey P. Meaux	(ABC/Dot DOSD 2020)
175(6/11/76)	170(13/11/76)	3	If You're Ever In Texas Huey P. Meaux	(ABC/Dot DOSD 2061)
87(28/ 2/76)	59(20/ 3/76)	11	Rock 'n' Country Huey P. Meaux	(ABC/Dot DOSD 2050)
			Maynard FERGUSON	
137(17/4/76)	75(22/ 5/76)	14	Primal Scream Bob James	(Columbia PC 33953)
			Bryan FERRY	
183(16/10/76)	160(6/11/76)	5	Let's Stick Together Bryan Ferry Chris Thomas	(Atlantic SD 18187)
			FIREFALL	
144(8/5/76)	28(2/10/76)	34*	Firefall Jim Mason	(Atlantic SD 18174)
			FLAMIN'GROOVIES	
196(21/8/76)	142(2/10/76)	7	Shake Some Action Dave Edmunds	(Sire SASD 7521)
			FLEETWOOD MAC	
183(2/8/75)	1(4/ 9/76)	74*	Fleetwood Mac Keith Olsen Fleetwood Mac (Lindsey Buckingham Mick Fleetwood Christine McVie John McVie Stevie Nicks)	(Reprise MS 2225)
190(6/12/75)	118(24/1/76)	16	Fleetwood Mac In Chicago Marshall Chess Mike Vernon	(Sire SASH 3715-2)
			Dan FOGELBERG	
79(4/10/75)	23(22/11/75)	19	Captured Angel Dan Fogelberg	(Epic PE 33499)
			FOGHAT	
182(11/10/75)	23(3/ 4/76)	52	Fool For The City Nick Jameson	(Bearsville BR 6959)
113(20/11/76)	36(11/12/76)	6*	Night Shift Don Hartman	(Bearsville BR 6962)
169(28/2 76)	158(20/3/76)	4	Rock And Roll Outlaws Nick Jameson	(Bearsville BR 6956)
			FOOLS GOLD	
190(24/4/76)	100(19/6/76)	13	Fools Gold Glenn Frey Glyn Johns John Stronach Joe Walsh	(Morning Sky ML 5500)

Position and date of entry	Highest position and date	Wks.	Artist(s) Title Producer(s)	Cat. No.
			FOUR SEASONS	
95(13/12/75)	51(17/ 1/76)	17	**The Four Seasons Story** Bob Crewe	(Private Stock PS 7000)
140(29/11/75)	38(24/ 1/76)	31	**Who Loves You** Bob Gaudio	(Warner Bros BS 2900)
			FOUR TOPS	
167(13/11/76)	124(4/12/76)	7*	**Catfish** Lawrence Payton	(ABC ABCD 968)
			Redd FOXX	
171(3/1/76)	87(21/ 2/76)	13	**You Gotta Wash Your Ass** Redd Foxx	(Atlantic SD 18157)
			Peter FRAMPTON	
185(29/3/75)	32(17/ 5/75)	64	**Frampton** Peter Frampton	(A&M SP 4512)
143(31/1/76)	1(10/ 4/76)	48*	**Frampton Comes Alive!** Peter Frampton	(A&M SP 3703)
			Aretha FRANKLIN	
103(19/6/76)	18(7/ 8/76)	24	**Music From The Warner Bros. Motion Picture 'Sparkle'** Curtis Mayfield	(Atlantic SD 18176)
151(25/12/76)	151(25/12/76)	1*	**Ten Years Of Gold** Tom Dowd Aretha Franklin Quincy Jones Arif Mardin Curtis Mayfield Jerry Wexler	(Atlantic SD 18204)
129(15/11/75)	83(27/12/75)	11	**You** Aretha Franklin Jerry Wexler	(Atlantic SD 18151)
			Michael FRANKS	
198(31/7/76)	131(25/9/76)	13	**The Art Of Tea** Tommy LiPuma	(Reprise MS 2230)
			FUNKADELIC	
148(27/11/76)	96(18/12/76)	5*	**Hardcore Jollies** George Clinton	(Warner Bros BS 2973)
169(9/10/76)	103(6/11/76)	10	**Tales Of Kidd Funkadelic** George Clinton	(Westbound W 227)
			Richie FURAY BAND	
170(7/8/76)	130(18/9/76)	8	**I've Got A Reason** Michael Omartian Bill Schnee	(Asylum 7E-1067)
			Rory GALLAGHER	
157(29/11/75)	121(10/1/76)	13	**Against The Grain** Rory Gallagher	(Chrysalis CHR 1098)
188(30/10/76)	166(25/12/76)	8*	**Calling Card** Roger Glover	(Chrysalis CHR 1124)
			Jerry GARCIA	
196(14/2/76)	42(10/ 4/76)	14	**Reflections** (Not listed)	(Round RX-LA565-G)

Position and date of entry	Highest position and date	Wks.	Artist(s) Title Producer(s)	Cat. No.
			Art GARFUNKEL	
99(25/10/75)	7(29/11/75)	28	**Breakaway**	(Columbia
			Art Garfunkel	PC 33700)
			Richard Perry	
			Phil Ramone	
			Paul Simon	
			Marvin GAYE	
94(2/10/76)	44(30/10/76)	8	**Marvin Gaye's Greatest Hits**	(Tamla
			Lamont Dozier	T6-348S1)
			Marvin Gaye	
			Brian Holland	
			T-Boy Ross	
			Ed Townsend	
			Norman Whitfield	
			Leon Ware	
72(3/ 4/76)	4(5/ 6/76)	26	**I Want You**	(Tamla
			Leon Ware	T6-342S1)
			GAYLORD & HOLIDAY	
192(21/2/76)	180(10/4/76)	8	**Second Generation**	(Prodigal
			Sam Locricchio	P6-10009S1)
			Gloria GAYNOR	
180(11/10/75)	64(13/12/75)	21	**Experience**	(MGM M3G-4997)
			Tony Bongiovi	
			Jay Ellis	
			Meco Monardo	
185(14/8/76)	107(6/11/76)	14	**I've Got You**	(Polydor
			Tony Bongiovi	PD-1-6063)
			Jay Ellis	
			Meco Monardo	
			J. GEILS BAND	
76(22/ 5/76)	40(26/ 6/76)	11	**Live! Blow Your Face Out**	(Atlantic
			Allan Blazek	SD 2-507)
			Bill Szymczyk	
			J. Geils Band	
			(Stephen Jo Bladd	
			J. Geils	
			Seth Justman	
			Danny Klein	
			Magic Dick	
			Peter Wolf)	
			GENESIS	
173(20/3/76)	31(15/ 5/76)	19	**A Trick Of The Tail**	(Atco SD 36-129)
			David Hentschel	
			Genesis	
			(Tony Banks	
			Phil Collins	
			Steve Hackett	
			Mike Rutherford)	

Position and date of entry	Highest position and date	Wks.	Artist(s) Title Producer(s)	Cat. No.
			GENTLE GIANT	
149(29/5/76)	137(5/6/76)	5	**Interview** Gentle Giant (Gary Green Kerry Minnear Derek Shulman Ray Shulman John Weathers)	(Capitol ST 11532)
			Tompall GLASER (see: Waylon JENNINGS) Roger GLOVER & GUESTS	
187(24/1/76)	142(28/2/76)	8	**The Butterfly Ball & The Grasshopper's Feast** Roger Glover	(UK UKL 56000)
			Andrew GOLD	
190(10/1/76)	190(10/1/76)	2	**Andrew Gold** Charles Plotkin	(Asylum 7E-1047)
			GOLDEN EARRING	
162(28/2/76)	156(6/3/76)	4	**To The Hilt** Golden Earring (Rinus Gerritsen Barry Hay George Kooymans Robert Jan Stips Cesar Zuiderwijk)	(MCA 2183)
			Dickie GOODMAN	
186(6/12/75)	144(17/1/76)	8	**Mr. Jaws & Other Fables** Dickie Goodman Bill Ramal	(Cash CR 6000)
			Steve GOODMAN	
186(15/5/76)	175(5/6/76)	4	**Words We Can Dance To** Steve Goodman	(Asylum 7E-1061)
			GRAHAM CENTRAL STATION	
182(2/8/75)	22(4/10/75)	24	**Ain't No 'Bout-A-Doubt It** Larry Graham	(Warner Bros BS 2876)
141(26/6/76)	46(14/ 8/76)	16	**Mirror** Larry Graham	(Warner Bros BS 2937)
			GRAND FUNK RAILROAD	
120(31/1/76)	47(6/ 3/76)	11	**Born To Die** Jimmy Ienner	(Capitol ST 11482)
76(28/ 8/76)	52(18/ 9/76)	9	**Good Singin' Good Playin'** Frank Zappa	(MCA 2216)
155(20/11/76)	126(11/12/76)	5	**Grand Funk Hits** Jimmy Ienner Terry Knight Todd Rundgren	(Capitol ST 11579)

Position and date of entry	Highest position and date	Wks.	Artist(s) Title Producer(s)	Cat. No.
			GRATEFUL DEAD	
93(3/ 7/76)	56(31/ 7/76)	9	**Steal Your Face** Grateful Dead (Jerry Garcia Donna Godchaux Keith Godchaux Mickey Hart Bill Kreutzmann Phil Lesh Bob Weir)	(Grateful Dead GD-LA620-J2/ GD 104)
			Al GREEN	
101(20/ 3/76)	59(1/ 5/76)	16	**Full Of Fire** Al Green Willie Mitchell	(Hi SHL 32097)
90(13/9/75)	28(15/11/75)	23	**Al Green Is Love** Al Green Willie Mitchell	(Hi SHL 32092)
153(27/11/76)	103(25/12/76)	5*	**Have A Good Time** Al Green Willie Mitchell	(Hi SHL 32103)
			Larry GROCE	
189(27/3/76)	187(3/4/76)	2	**Junkfood Junkie** Randolph Nauert	(Warner Bros BS 2933)
			Henry GROSS	
183(14/2/76)	64(19/ 6/76)	28	**Release** Terry Cashman Tommy West	(Lifesong LS 6002)
			Arlo GUTHRIE	
167(2/ 10/76)	133(30/10/76)	6	**Amigo** John Pilla	(Reprise MS 2239)
			Steve HACKETT	
198(17/4/76)	191(8/5/76)	4	**Voyage Of The Acolyte** John Acock Steve Hackett	(Chrysalis CHR 1112)
			Daryl HALL & John OATES	
196(23/2/74)	33(20/11/76)	32*	**Abandoned Luncheonette** Arif Mardin	(Atlantic
120(28/8/76)	13(6/11/76)	18*	**Bigger Than Both Of Us** Christopher Bond	(RCA APL1-1467)
172(3/1/76)	17(26/ 6/76)	51*	**Daryl Hall & John Oates** Christopher Bond Daryl Hall John Oates	(RCA APL1-1144)
			HAMILTON JOE FRANK & REYNOLDS	
173(13/12/75)	82(21/ 2/76)	14	**Fallin' In Love** Joe Frank Carollo Alan Dennison Dan Hamilton	(Playboy PB 407)

Position and date of entry	Highest position and date	Wks.	Artist(s) Title Producer(s)	Cat. No.
			Herbie HANCOCK	
168(18/10/75)	21(29/11/75)	24	**Man-Child** Herbie Hancock David Rubinson & Friends, Inc.	(Columbia PC 33812)
91(11/ 9/76)	49(9/10/76)	16*	**Secrets** Herbie Hancock David Rubinson & Friends, Inc.	(Columbia PC 34280)
			John HANDY	
184(5/6/76)	43(18/ 9/76)	21	**Hard Work** Esmond Edwards	(ABC Impulse ASD 9314)
			Hagood HARDY	
200(3/1/76)	112(6/3/76)	14	**The Homecoming** Peter Anastasoff Hagood Hardy	(Capitol ST 11468)
			Emmylou HARRIS	
140(24/1/76)	25(20/ 3/76)	23	**Elite Hotel** Brian Ahern	(Reprise MS 2236)
			Major HARRIS	
186(28/2/76)	153(27/3/76)	6	**Jealousy** Bobby Eli Major Harris Ron Kersey Alan Rubens Steve Bernstein Norman Harris	(Atlantic SD 18160)
			Don HARRISON BAND	
179(1/5/76)	159(22/5/76)	6	**The Don Harrison Band** The Don Harrison Band (Doug Clifford Stu Cook Russell Da Shiell Don Harrison)	(Atlantic SD 18171)
			George HARRISON	
67(27/11/76)	31(25/12/76)	5*	**The Best Of George Harrison** George Harrison George Martin Phil Spector	(Capitol ST 11578)
69(11/12/76)	15(25/12/76)	3*	**Thirty Three & ⅓** George Harrison	(Dark Horse DH 3005)
			Ritchie HAVENS	
182(2/10/76)	157(23/10/76)	4	**The End Of The Beginning** David Kershenbaum	(A&M SP 4598)
			Isaac HAYES	
109(21/2/76)	45(3/ 4/76)	12	**Groove-A-Thon** Isaac Hayes	(Hot Buttered Soul ABCD 925)
163(24/7/76)	124(28/8/76)	7	**Juicy Fruit (Disco Freak)** Isaac Hayes	(Hot Buttered Soul ABCD 953)

Position and date of entry	Highest position and date	Wks.	Artist(s) Title Producer(s)	Cat. No.
			Isaac HAYES MOVEMENT	
176(17/1/76)	85(20/ 3/76)	17	**Disco Connection** Isaac Hayes	(Hot Buttered Soul ABCD 923)
			HEAD EAST	
186(22/5/76)	161(26/6/76)	6	**Get Yourself Up** Roger Boyd	(A&M SP 4579)
			HEART	
194(10/4/76)	7(30/10/76)	38*	**Dreamboat Annie** Mike Flicker	(Mushroom MRS 5005)
			Michael HENDERSON	
189(4/12/76)	187(11/12/76)	2	**Solid** Michael Henderson	(Buddah BDS 5662)
			Jimi HENDRIX	
96(29/11/75)	43(20/12/75)	11	**Midnight Lightning** Tony Bongiovi Alan Douglas	(Reprise MS 2229)
			Dan HILL	
180(6/12/75)	104(28/2/76)	17	**Dan Hill** Matthew McCauley Fred Mollin	(20th Century T 500)
			Chris HILLMAN	
185(19/6/76)	152(10/7/76)	6	**Slippin' Away** Ron & Howard Albert	(Asylum 7E-1062)
			Bob HOPE	
190(3/7/76)	175(24/7/76)	4	**America Is 200 Years Old ... And There's Still Hope!** Sid Kuller John Palladine	(Capitol ST 11538)
			HOT CHOCOLATE	
188(22/11/75)	41(14/ 2/76)	21	**Hot Chocolate** Mickie Most	(Big Tree BT 89512)
187(18/9/76)	172(2/10/76)	6	**Man To Man** Mickie Most	(Big Tree BT 89519)
			HOT TUNA	
160(20/11/76)	116(25/12/76)	6*	**Hoppkorv** Harry Maslin	(Grunt BFL1-1920)
121(29/11/75)	97(20/12/75)	9	**Yellow Fever** Hot Tuna (Jack Casady Jorma Kaukonen Bob Steeler) Mallory Earl	(Grunt BFL1-1238)
			Thelma HOUSTON	
187(25/12/76)	187(25/12/76)	1*	**Any Way You Like It** Hal Davis Clayton Ivey Harold Johnson Joe Porter Michael L. Smith Michael B. Sutton Terry Woodford	(Tamla T6-345S1)

Position and date of entry	Highest position and date	Wks.	Artist(s) Title Producer(s)	Cat. No.
			Steve HOWE	
110(20/12/75)	63(31/ 1/76)	11	Beginnings Steve Howe Eddie Offord	(Atlantic SD 18154)
			Freddie HUBBARD	
124(4/9/76)	05(25/ 9/76)	9	Windjammer Bob James	(Columbia PC 34166)
			HUDSON BROTHERS	
189(13/12/75)	165(10/1/76)	6	Ba-Fa Bernie Taupin	(Rocket
			Engelbert HUMPERDINCK	
122)27/11/76)	27(25/12/76)	5*	After The Lovin' Charlie Calello Joel Diamond Bobby Eli	(Epic PE 34381)
			Ian HUNTER	
198(22/5/76)	177(3/7/76)	7	All American Alien Boy Ian Hunter	(Columbia PC 34142)
			Willie HUTCH	
163(3/4/76)	163(3/4/76)	6	Concert In Blues Willie Hutch	(Motown M6-854S1)
			Leroy HUTSON	
192(6/3/76)	170(17/4/76)	8	Feel The Spirit Leroy Hutson	(Curtom CU 5010)
			Janis IAN	
71(24/ 1/76)	12(28/ 2/76)	19	Aftertones Brooks Arthur	(Columbia PC 33919)
184(22/3/75)	1(20/ 9/75)	64	Between The Lines Brooks Arthur	(Columbia PC 33394)
			IMPRESSIONS	
199(13/3/76)	195(27/3/76)	3	Loving Power Chuck Jackson Ed Townsend Rich Tufo Marvin Yancy	(Curtom CU 5009)
			ISLEY BROTHERS	
70(29/ 5/76)	9(3/ 7/76)	26	Harvest For The World Isley Brothers (Ernie Isley Marvin Isley Chris Jasper Ronald Isley O'Kelly Isley Rudolph Isley)	(T-Neck PZ 33809)
175(14/6/75)	1(13/ 9/75)	40	The Heat Is On Featuring Fight The Power Isley Brothers	(T-Neck PZ 33536)

Position and date of entry	Highest position and date	Wks.	Artist(s) Title Producer(s)	Cat. No.
			Jermaine JACKSON	
192(25/9/76)	164(6/11/76)	11	**My Name is Jermaine** Jeffrey Bowen Hal Davis Gwen Glenn Michael L. Smith Michael B. Sutton Gregory Wright	(Motown M6-842S1)
			Walter JACKSON	
174(9/10/76)	113(11/12/76)	12*	**Feeling Good** Carl Davis	(Chi-Sound CH-LA656-G)
			JACKSON 5IVE	
125(17/7/76)	84(21/ 8/76)	9	**Anthology** The Corporation Hal Davis Jerry Marcellino Mel Larson Brian Holland Johnny Bristol Sherlie Matthews Deke Richards Freddie Perren Fonce Mizell	(Motown M7-868R3)
			JACKSONS	
91(4/12/76)	65(25/12/76)	4*	**The Jacksons** Victor Carstarphen Kenny Gamble Leon Huff The Jacksons (Jackie, Marlon, Michael, Randy & Tito Jackson) Gene McFadden Dexter Wansel John Whitehead	(Epic PE 34229)
			Bob JAMES	
141(3/7/76)	49(18/ 9/76)	26*	**Three** Creed Taylor	(CTI 6063)
			Jimmy JAMES & THE VAGABONDS	
195(29/11/75)	139(6/3/76)	16	**You Don't Stand A Chance If You Can't Dance** Biddu	(Pye 12111)
			Al JARREAU	
176(28/8/76)	132(25/9/76)	11	**Glow** Tommy LiPuma Al Schmitt	(Reprise MS 2248)
			Keith JARRETT	
184(10/7/76)	179(24/7/76)	3	**Arbour Zena** Manfred Eicher	(ECM-1-1070)

Position and date of entry	Highest position and date	Wks.	Artist(s) / Title / Producer(s)	Cat. No.
195(13/3/76)	195(13/3/76)	1	**In The Light** Manfred Eicher Keith Jarrett	(ECM 1033/4)
189(17/7/76)	184(24/7/76)	2	**Mysteries** Esmond Edwards	(ABC Impulse ASD 9315)
			JEFFERSON STARSHIP	
190(18/10/75)	70(6/12/75)	14	**Dragon Fly** Larry Cox Jefferson Starship (Marty Balin John Barbata Craig Chaquico Papa John Creach David Freiberg Paul Kantner Pete Sears Grace Slick)	(Grunt BFL-0717)
90(19/ 7/75)	1(6/ 9/75)	76*	**Red Octopus** Larry Cox Jefferson Starship	(Grunt BFL1-0999)
72(10/ 7/76)	3(14/ 8/76)	25*	**Spitfire** Larry Cox Jefferson Starship (minus Papa John Creach)	(Grunt BFL1-1557)
			Waylon JENNINGS	
88(17/ 7/76)	34(28/ 8/76)	23*	**Are You Ready For The Country** Waylon Jennings Ken Mansfield	(RCA APL1-1816)
128(18/12/76)	98(25/12/76)	2*	**Waylon 'Live'** Waylon Jennings Ray Pennington	(RCA APL1-1108)
			Waylon JENNINGS, WILLIE NELSON, JESSI COLTER, TOMPALL GLASER	
54(7/ 2/76)	10(3/ 4/76)	38*	**The Outlaws** Chet Atkins Tompall Glaser Felton Jarvis Waylon Jennings Ronnie Light Willie Nelson Ray Pennington Shel Silverstein	(RCA APL1-1321)
			JETHRO TULL	
98(24/ 1/76)	13(6/ 3/76)	23	**M.U. The Best Of Jethro Tull** Ian Anderson Terry Ellis	(Chrysalis CHR 1078)
71(29/ 5/76)	14(3/ 7/76)	21	**Too Old To Rock 'n' Roll Too Young To Die** Ian Anderson	(Chrysalis CHR 1111)

Position and date of entry	Highest position and date	Wks.	Artist(s) Title Producer(s)	Cat. No.
			JIGSAW	
149(13/12/75)	55(14/ 2/76)	19	**Sky High** Chas Peate Des Dyer Clive Scott	(Chelsea CHL 509)
			Billy JOEL	
152(5/6/76)	122(3/7/76)	12	**Turnstiles** Billy Joel	(Columbia PC 33848)
			Elton JOHN	
3(13/11/76)	3(13/11/76)	7*	**Blue Moves** Gus Dudgeon	(Rocket 2-11004)
1(7/ 6/75)	1(7/ 6/75)	43	**Captain Fantastic & The Brown Dirt Cowboy** Gus Dudgeon	(MCA 2142)
47(23/11/74)	1(30/11/74)	91*	**Greatest Hits** Gus Dudgeon	(MCA 2128)
9(22/ 5/76)	4(12/ 6/76)	20	**Here And There** Gus Dudgeon	(MCA 2197)
1(8/11/75)	1(8/11/75)	26	**Rock Of The Westies** Gus Dudgeon	(MCA 2163)
			Quincy JONES	
95(2/10/76)	43(6/11/76)	13*	**I Heard That!** Quincy Jones	(A&M SP 3705)
93(23/ 8/75)	16(18/10/75)	30	**Mellow Madness** Quincy Jones	(A&M SP 4526)
			JOURNEY	
190(14/2/76)	100(10/4/76)	15	**Look Into The Future** Journey (Aynsley Dunbar Gregg Rolie Neal Schon Ross Valory)	(Columbia PC 33904)
			KANSAS	
96(6/11/76)	34(25/12/76)	8*	**Leftoverture** Jeff Glixman	(Kirshner PZ 34224)
176(27/12/75)	70(20/ 3/76)	20	**Masque** Jeff Glixman	(Kirshner PZ 33806)
			KAYAK	
200(17/1/76)	199(24/1/76)	2	**Royal Bed Bouncer** Gerrit Jan Leenders Kayak (Pim Koopman Tom Scherpenzeel Johan Slager Bert Veldkamp Max Werner)	(Janus JXS 5002)
			K.C. & THE SUNSHINE BAND	
144(2/8/75)	4(20/12/75)	47	**K.C. & The Sunshine Band** Harry Wayne Casey Richard Finch	(TK 603)

Position and date of entry	Highest position and date	Wks.	Artist(s) Title Producer(s)	Cat. No.
22(23/10/76)	13(27/11/76)	10*	**Part 3** Harry Wayne Casey Richard Finch	(TK 605)
			Eddie KENDRICKS	
187(9/10/76)	144(13/11/76)	7	**Goin' Up In Smoke** Norman Harris	(Tamla T6-346S1)
181(31/1/76)	38(24/ 4/76)	19	**He's A Friend** Norman Harris	(Tamal T6-343S1)
			KGB	
173(6/3/76)	124(3/4/76)	6	**KGB** Jim Price	(MCA 2166)
			Albert KING	
188(20/3/76)	166(24/4/76)	6	**Truckload Of Lovin'** Bert DeCoteaux Tony Silvester	(Utopia BUL1-1387)
			B.B. KING (see: Bobby BLAND)	
			Carole KING	
79(10/ 4/71)	1(19/ 6/71)	299*	**Tapestry** Lou Adler	(Ode SP 77009)
31(7/ 2/76)	3(27/ 3/76)	21	**Thoroughbred** Lou Adler	(Ode SP 77034)
			KINGFISH	
125(27/3/76)	50(8/ 5/76)	9	**Kingfish** Dan Healy Bob Weir	(Round RX-LA564-G/ RX 108)
			KINKS	
163(26/6/76)	144(17/7/76)	5	**The Kinks' Greatest— Celluloid Heroes** Raymond Douglas Davies	(RCA APL1-1743)
178(6/12/75)	45(24/ 1/76)	14	**The Kinks Present Schoolboys In Disgrace** Raymond Douglas Davies	(RCA LPL1-5102)
			KISS	
113(11/10/75)	9(13/12/75)	64*	**Alive!** Eddie Kramer	(2-Casablanca NBLP 7020)
81(3/ 4/76)	11(15/ 5/76)	33*	**Destroyer** Bob Ezrin	(Casablanca NBLP 7025)
182(19/4/75)	32(14/ 6/75)	20*	**Dressed To Kill** Neil Bogart Kiss Peter Criss Ace Frehley Gene Simmons & Paul Stanley)	(Casablanca NBLP 7016)
192(20/4/74)	87(8/ 6/74)	23	**Kiss** Kenny Kerner Richie Wise	(Casablanca NBLP 7001)

Position and date of entry	Highest position and date	Wks.	Artist(s) Title Producer(s)	Cat. No.
91(21/ 8/76)	36(25/ 9/76)	10	**The Originals** Neil Bogart Kiss Kenny Kerner Richie Wise	(Casablanca NBLP 7032)
32(20/11/76)	11(25/12/76)	6*	**Rock And Roll Over** Eddie Kramer	(Casablanca NBLP 7037)
			John KLEMMER	
125(18/9/76)	66(30/10/76)	15*	**Barefoot Ballet** Stephan Goldman John Klemmer	(ABC ABCD 950)
195(27/12/75)	90(8/ 5/76)	40	**Touch** Stephan Goldman John Klemmer	(ABC ABCD 922)
			Earl KLUGH	
143(10/7/76)	124(31/7/76)	6	**Earl Klugh** Dave Grusin Larry Rosen	(Blue Note BN-LA596-G)
191(11/12/76)	188(18/12/76)	2	**Living Inside Your Love** Dave Grusin Larry Rosen	(Blue Note BN-LA667-G)
			Gladys KNIGHT & THE PIPS	
160(7/2/76)	36(27/ 3/76)	15	**The Best Of Gladys Knight & The Pips** Tony Camillo Kenny Kerner Curtis Mayfield Ralph Moss Richie Wise	(Buddah BDS 5653)
171(27/11/76)	94(25/12/76)	5*	**The Original Motion Picture Soundtrack Performed By Gladys Knight & The Pips/ Gladys Knight In 'Pipe Dreams'** Dominic Frontiere Bubba Knight Michael Masser	(Buddah BDS 6576 ST)
173(18/10/75)	24(6/12/75)	16	**2nd Anniversary** Kenny Kerner Eugene McDaniels Richie Wise	(Buddah BDS 5639)
			KOKOMO	
196(17/4/76)	194(24/4/76)	2	**Rise And Shine** Brad Shapiro	(Columbia PC 34031)

Position and date of entry	Highest position and date	Wks.	Artist(s) Title Producer(s)	Cat. No.
			KOOL & THE GANG	
185(20/3/76)	68(29/ 5/76)	20	**Love & Understanding** Kool & the Gang (Ronald Bell George M. Brown Larry Gittens Spike Mickens Otha Nash Claydes Smith Dennis Thomas Ricky West Robert 'Kool' Bell)	(DeLite DEP 2018)
168(20/11/76)	114(25/12/76)	6*	**Open Sesame** Kool & the Gang	(DeLite DEP 2023)
			Leo KOTTKE	
173(27/11/76)	153(11/12/76)	4	**Leo Kottke 1971-1976 Did You Hear Me?** Denny Bruce	(Capitol ST 11576)
			KRAFTWERK	
185(13/12/75)	140(17/1/76)	8	**Radio-Activity** Ralf Hutter Florian Schneider	(Capitol ST 11457)
			Kris KRISTOFFERSON	
184(21/8/76)	180(28/8/76)	2	**Surreal Thing** David Anderle	(Monument PZ 34254)
183(6/12/75)	105(24/1/76)	11	**Who's To Bless And Who's To Blame** David Anderle	(Monument PZ 33379)
			LABELLE	
116(25/9/76)	94(30/10/76)	10	**Chameleon** David Rubinson & Friends, Inc.	(Epic PE 34789)
			L.A. EXPRESS	
190(6/3/76)	167(24/4/76)	8	**L.A. Express** L.A. Express (Max Bennett Victor Feldman Robben Ford John Guerin David Luell)	(Caribou PZ 33940)
			David LaFLAMME	
181(25/12/76)	181(25/12/76)	1*	**White Bird** David LaFlamme	(Amherst AMH 1007)
			Cleo LAINE	
170(7/2/76)	158(6/3/76)	10	**Born On A Friday** George Martin Rocky Thomas	(RCA LP1-5113)
			D.C. LaRUE	
195(26/6/76)	139(7/8/76)	13	**Ca-the-drals** D.C. LaRue Aram Schefrin	(Pyramid PY 9003)

Position and date of entry	Highest position and date	Wks.	Artist(s) Title Producer(s)	Cat. No.
			Hubert LAWS	
166(6/11/76)	139(27/11/76)	6	**Romeo & Juliet** Bob James	(Columbia PC 34330)
			Ronnie LAWS	
95(12/ 6/76)	46(10/ 7/76)	21	**Fever** Wayne Henderson	(Blue Note BN-LA628-G)
190(27/9/75)	73(6/12/75)	29	**Pressure Sensitive** Wayne Henderson	(Blue Note BN-LA452-G)
			LED ZEPPELIN	
36(27/11/71)	2(18/12/71)	201*	**IV** Jimmy Page	(Atlantic SD 7208)
2(24/ 4/76)	1(1/ 5/76)	25	**Presence** Jimmy Page	(Swansong SS 8416)
3(6/11/76)	2(13/11/76)	8*	**Soundtrack From The Film 'The Song Remains The Same'** Jimmy Page	(Swansong SS2-201)
			John LENNON/PLASTIC ONO BAND	
97(8/11/75)	12(13/12/75)	14	**Shaved Fish** John Lennon Yoko Ono Phil Spector	(Apple SW 3421)
			Ramsey LEWIS	
94(4/10/75)	46(22/11/75)	22	**Don't It Feel Good** Maurice White Charles Stepney	(Columbia PC 33800)
169(22/5/76)	77(19/ 6/76)	11	**Salongo** Maurice White Charles Stepney	(Columbia PC 34173)
			Gordon LIGHTFOOT	
186(22/11/75)	34(17/ 1/76)	20*	**Gord's Gold** Lenny Waronker Joe Wissert	(Reprise 2RS 2237)
94(26/ 6/76)	12(4/12/76)	27*	**Summertime Dream** Gordon Lightfoot Lenny Waronker	(Reprise MS 2246)
			LITTLE FEAT	
181(15/11/75)	36(13/12/75)	15	**The Last Record Album** Lowell George	(Warner Bros BS 2884)
			LITTLE RIVER BAND	
166(2/10/76)	80(11/12/76)	13*	**Little River Band** Beeb Birtles Graham Goble Glenn Shorrock Glenn Wheatley	(Capitol ST 11512)
			Nils LOFGREN	
91(17/ 4/76)	32(5/ 6/76)	16	**Cry Tough** David Briggs Al Kooper	(A&M SP 4573)

US ALBUM

291

Position and date of entry	Highest position and date	Wks.	Artist(s) Title Producer(s)	Cat. No.
			LOGGINS & MESSINA	
83(11/12/76)	63(25/12/76)	3*	The Best Of Friends	(Columbia
			Jim Messina	PC 34388)
87(31/ 1/76)	16(28/ 2/76)	17	Native Sons	(Columbia
			Jim Messina	PC 33578)
			LOVE UNLIMITED ORCHESTRA	
162(10/ 1/76)	92(14/ 2/76)	15	Music Maestro Please	(20th Century
			Barry White	T 480)
146(30/10/76)	123(27/11/76)	8	My Sweet Summer Suite	(20th Century
			Barry White	T 517)
			LOVIN' SPOONFUL	
187(24/4/76)	183(8/5/76)	3	The Best...Lovin' Spoonful	(Kama Sutra
			Erik Jacobsen	KSBS 2608-2)
			Joe Wissert	
			L.T.D.	
176(21/8/76)	52(11/12/76)	19*	Love To The World	(A&M SP 4589)
			Chuck Davis	
			Larry & Fonce Mizell	
			LYNYRD SKYNYRD	
104(21/2/76)	20(27/ 3/76)	16	Gimme Back My Bullets	(MCA 2170)
			Tom Dowd	
149(2/10/76)	9(13/11/76)	13*	One More For From The Road	(MCA 2-6001)
			Tom Dowd	
			Cledus MAGGARD & THE CITIZEN'S BAND	
180(13/3/76)	135(17/4/76)	8	The White Knight	(Mercury
			Jerry Kennedy	SRM1-1072)
			MAHAVISHNU ORCHESTRA/ JOHN McLAUGHLIN	
183(21/2/76)	118(13/3/76)	7	Inner Worlds	(Columbia
			John McLaughlin	PC 33908)
			MAHOGANY RUSH	
187(5/6/76)	175(19/6/76)	3	Mahogany Rush IV	(Columbia
			Frank Marino	PC 34190)
			MAIN INGREDIENT	
177(13/12/75)	158(24/1/76)	8	Shame On The World	(RCA APL1-1003)
			Cuba Gooding	
			Luther Simmons	
			Melissa MANCHESTER	
97(21/ 2/76)	24(27/ 3/76)	17	Better Days & Happy Endings	(Arista AL 4067)
			Vini Poncia	
133(20/11/76)	62(25/12/76)	6*	Help Is On The Way	(Arista AL 4095)
			Vini Poncia	
			Henry MANCINI	
181(18/9/76)	161(2/10/76)	4	A Legendary Performer	(RCA CPL1-1843)
			Ethel Gabriel	
			Henry MANCINI & HIS CONCERT ORCHESTRA	
189(14/2/76)	159(13/3/76)	6	Symphonic Soul	(RCA APL1-1025)
			Joe Reisman	

Position and date of entry	Highest position and date	Wks.	Artist(s) Title Producer(s)	Cat. No.
			MANDRILL	
188(7/2/76)	143(13/3/76)	8	**Beast From The East** Malcolm Cecil Mandrill (Brian Allsop Claude 'Coffee' Cave Andre Locke Tommy Trujillo Carlos Wilson Lou Wilson Ric Wilson Wilfredo 'Wolf' Wilson)	(United Artists UA-LA577-G)
			Chuck MANGIONE	
99(29/11/75)	68(3/ 1/76)	15	**Bellavia** Chuck Mangione	(A&M SP 4577)
174(6/12/75)	102(24/1/76)	20	**Encore—The Chuck Mangione Concerts** Chuck Mangione	(Mercury SRM-1-1050)
164(20/11/76)	106(25/12/76)	6*	**Main Squeeze** Chuck Mangione	(A&M SP 4612)
			MANHATTAN TRANSFER	
134(3/5/75)	33(19/7/75)	38	**Manhattan Transfer** Ahmet Ertegun Tim Hauser	(Atlantic SD 18133)
91(18/ 9/76)	48(16/10/76)	9	**Coming Out** Richard Perry	(Atlantic SD 18183)
			MANHATTANS	
181(1/5/76)	16(14/8/76)	27	**Manhattans** Bert DeCoteaux Manhattans (Gerald Austin Sonny Bivins Kenny Kelly Wilfred Lovett Richard Taylor) Bobby Martin	(Columbia PC 33820)
			Barry MANILOW	
134(2/8/75)	28(25/10/75)	33	**I** Ron Dante Barry Manilow	(Arista AL 4007)
160(23/11/74)	9(22/ 2/75)	34	**II** Ron Dante Barry Manilow	(Arista AL 4016)
34(21/ 8/76)	12(18/ 9/76)	19*	**This One's For You** Ron Dante Barry Manilow	(Arista AL 4090)
85(8/11/75)	5(7/ 2/76)	50	**Tryin' To Get The Feelin'** Ron Dante Barry M-	(Arista AL 4060)

Position and date of entry	Highest position and date	Wks.	Artist(s) Title Producer(s)	Cat. No.
			Herbie MANN featuring CISSY HOUSTON	
182(8/5/76)	178(15/5/76)	2	**Surprises** Herbie Mann	(Atlantic SD 1682)
			Manfred MANN'S EARTHBAND	
157(25/9/76)	117(30/10/76)	14*	**The Roaring Silence** Manfred Mann's Earthband (Manfred Mann Dave Flett Chris Hamlet Thompson Colin Pattenden Chris Slade)	(Warner Bros BS 2965)
			MARK—ALMOND	
167(31/7/76)	112(11/9/76)	14	**To The Heart** Roy Halee	(ABC ABCD 945)
			Bob MARLEY & THE WAILERS	
40(15/ 5/76)	8(3/ 7/76)	22	**Rastaman Vibration** Bob Marley The Wailers (Aston 'Family Man' Barrett Carlton Barrett Tyrone Downie Alvin 'Seeco' Patterson Earl 'Chinna' Smith Donald Kinsey Al Anderson)	(Island ILPS 9383)
128(23/10/76)	90(4/12/76)	9	**Live** Chris Blackwell Steve Smith	(Island ILPS 9376)
			MARSHALL TUCKER BAND	
82(26/ 6/76)	32(14/ 8/76)	20	**Long Hard Ride** Paul Hornsby	(Capricorn CP 0170)
111(13/9/75)	15(8/11/75)	34	**Searchin' For A Rainbow** Paul Hornsby	(Capricorn CP 0161)
			Dave MASON	
131(27/11/76)	79(25/12/76)	5*	**Certified Live** David Mason	(Columbia PG 34174)
129(18/10/75)	27(22/11/75)	17	**Split Coconut** Bruce Botnick Dave Mason	(Columbia PC 33698)
			Johnny MATHIS	
198(8/11/75)	97(24/ 1/76)	21	**Feelings** Jack Gold	(Columbia PC 33887)
112(26/6/76)	79(21/ 8/76)	15	**I Only Have Eyes For You** Jack Gold	(Columbia PC 34117)
			Curtis MAYFIELD	
189(3/7/76)	171(21/8/76)	8	**Give, Get, Take And Have** Curtis Mayfield	(Curtom CU 5007)

Position and date of entry	Highest position and date	Wks.	Artist(s) Title Producer(s)	Cat. No.
			C.W. McCALL	
165(29/11/75)	12(14/ 2/76)	19	**Black Bear Road** Chip Davis Don Sears	(MGM M3G-5008)
170(8/5/76)	143(22/5/76)	4	**Wilderness** Chip Davis Don Sears	(Polydor PD-1-6069)
			Paul McCARTNEY & WINGS	
33(22/12/73)	1(13/ 4/74)	106*	**Band On The Run** Paul McCartney (see also under WINGS)	(Capitol SO 3415)
			Marilyn McCOO & BILLY DAVIS Jr.	
133(18/9/76)	35(25/12/76)	15*	**I Hope We Get To Love In Time** Don Davis	(ABC ABCD 952)
			Van McCOY	
151(8/5/76)	106(26/6/76)	17	**The Real McCoy** Van McCoy	(H&L HL 69012)
			Country Joe McDONALD	
184(1/11/75)	124(3/1/76)	14	**Paradise With An Ocean View** Jim Stern	(Fantasy F 9495)
			Ralph McDONALD	
138(25/9/76)	114(30/10/76)	10	**Sound Of A Drum** Ralph McDonald William Salter	(Marlin 2202)
			McKENDREE SPRING	
197(27/3/76)	193(10/4/76)	3	**Too Young To Feel This Old** Mark London	(Pye 12124)
			Christine McVIE	
190(14/8/76)	104(2/10/76)	10	**The Legendary Christine Perfect Album** Christine Perfect Mike Vernon	(Sire SASD 7522)
			Harold MELVIN & THE BLUE NOTES	
91(3/ 7/76)	51(31/ 7/76)	14	**All Their Greatest Hits! Collectors' Item** Kenny Gamble Leon Huff Harold Melvin	(Philadelphia International PZ 34232)
52(13/12/75)	9(28/ 2/76)	24	**Wake Up Everybody** Kenny Gamble Leon Huff	(Philadelphia International PZ 33808)
			Sergio MENDES & BRASIL '77	
186(27/3/76)	180(3/4/76)	2	**Homecooking** Sergio Mendes	(Elektra 7E-1055)

Position and date of entry	Highest position and date	Wks.	Artist(s) Title Producer(s)	Cat. No.
			MFSB	
82(6/12/75)	**39**(17/ 1/76)	12	**Philadelphia Freedom** Roland Chambers Jack Faith Kenny Gamble Leon Huff Bobby Martin Dexter Wansel	(Philadelphia International PZ 33845)
127(10/7/76)	**106**(14/8/76)	9	**Summertime** Victor Carstarphen Kenneth Gamble Leon Huff Gene McFadden John Whitehead	(Philadelphia International PZ 34238)
			Bette MIDLER	
136(31/1/76)	**27**(28/ 2/76)	15	**Songs For The** **New Depression** Moogy Klingman	(Atlantic SD 18155)
			MIGHTY CLOUDS OF JOY	
197(24/1/76)	**168**(27/3/76)	6	**Kickin'** David Crawford	(ABC Peacock ABCD 899)
			John MILES	
185(22/5/76)	**171**(12/6/76)	4	**Rebel** Alan Parsons	(London PS 669)
			Steve MILLER BAND	
180(18/11/72)	**56**(10/ 2/73)	39	**Anthology** Glyn Johns Steve Miller Band (Tim Davis Steve Miller Jim Peterman Boz Scaggs Bob Winkelman)	(Capitol SVBB 11114)
69(29/ 5/76)	**3**(23/10/76)	31*	**Fly Like An Eagle** Steve Miller	(Capitol ST 11497)
			MIRACLES	
190(25/10/**75**)	**33**(7/ 2/76)	30	**City Of Angels** Freddie Perren	(Tamla T6-339S1)
190(16/10/76)	**178**(30/10/76)	3	**The Power Of Music** Warren 'Pete' Moore	(Tamla T6-344S1)
			Joni MITCHELL	
53(11/12/76)	**16**(25/12/76)	3*	**Hejira** (Not listed)	(Asylum 7E-1087)
130(6/12/75)	**4**(3/ 1/76)	17	**The Hissing Of Summer Lawns** (Not listed)	(Asylum 7E-1051)

Position and date of entry	Highest position and date	Wks.	Artist(s) Title Producer(s)	Cat. No.
			MONKEES	
125(7/8/76)	58(2/10/76)	16	**The Monkees Greatest Hits** Jeff Barry Tommy Boyce Chip Douglas Bobby Hart Douglas 'Farthing' Hatelid Jack Keller Monkees (Micky Dolenz David Jones Mike Nesmith Peter Tork)	(Arista AL 4089)
			MONTROSE	
181(25/9/76)	118(23/10/76)	7	**Jump On It** Jack Douglas	(Warner Bros BS 2963)
			MONTY PYTHON	
195(5/6/76)	186(19/6/76)	3	**Live At City Center** Nancy Lewis	(Arista AL 4073)
			Dorothy **MOORE**	
81(29/ 5/76)	29(17/ 7/76)	23	**Misty Blue** Tommy Couch Wolf Stephenson	(Malaco 6351)
			Melba **MOORE**	
188(25/12/76)	188(25/12/76)	1*	**Melba** Charles Kipps Van McCoy	(Buddah BDS 5677)
165(8/5/76)	145(22/5/76)	5	**This Is It** Van McCoy	(Buddah BDS 5657)
			Patrick **MORAZ**	
145(5/6/76)	132(26/6/76)	5	**i** Patrick Moraz	(Atlantic SD 18175)
			MOTHER'S FINEST	
187(11/9/76)	148(9/10/76)	8	**Mother's Finest** Tom Werman	(Epic PE 34179)
			Maria **MULDAUR**	
165(13/3/76)	53(10/4/76)	12	**Sweet Harmony** Joe Boyd Lenny Waronker	(Reprise MS 2235)
			Michael **MURPHEY**	
151(20/11/76)	130(11/12/76)	5	**Flowing Free Forever** Jeff Guercio Bob Johnston	(Epic PE 34220)
94(6/12/75)	44(17/ 1/76)	13	**Swans Against The Sun** Bob Johnston	(Epic PE 33851)
			Walter **MURPHY BAND**	
118(4/9/76)	15(30/10/76)	17*	**A Fifth Of Beethoven** Thomas J. Valentino	(Private Stock PS 2015)
			Anne **MURRAY**	
101(2/10/76)	96(9/10/76)	6	**Keeping In Touch** Tom Catalano	(Capitol ST 11559)

Position and date of entry	Highest position and date	Wks.	Artist(s) Title Producer(s)	Cat. No.
188(6/12/75)	142(24/1/76)	11	**Together** Tom Catalano	(Capitol ST 11433)
			MUSCLE SHOALS HORNS	
183(3/7/76)	154(24/7/76)	8	**Born To Get Down** Barry Beckett	(Bang BLP 403)
			NAZARETH	
32(8/ 5/76)	24(22/ 5/76)	14	**Close Enough For Rock 'N' Roll** Manny Charlton	(A&M SP 4562)
181(6/12/75)	17(27/ 3/76)	29	**Hair Of The Dog** Manny Charlton	(A&M SP 4511)
92(4/12/76)	75(18/12/76)	4*	**Play 'N' The Game** Manny Charlton	(A&M SP 4610)
			NEKTAR	
167(3/4/76)	89(29/ 5/76)	14	**Recycled** Peter Hauke Nektar (Roye Albrighton Mick Brockett 'Taff' Freeman Ron Howden 'Mo' Moore)	(Passport PPSD 98011)
152(18/9/76)	141(25/9/76)	4	**A Tab In The Ocean** Peter Hauke Nektar	(Passport PPSD 98017)
			Willie NELSON	
176(8/5/76)	149(22/5/76)	7	**Live** (Not listed)	(RCA APL1-1487)
197(5/6/76)	187(12/6/76)	3	**Phases And Stages** Jerry Wexler	(Atlantic SD 7291)
189(26/7/75)	28(29/11/75)	43	**Red Headed Stranger** Willie Nelson	(Columbia KC 33482)
150(20/3/76)	48(8/ 5/76)	15	**The Sound In Your Mind** Willie Nelson	(Columbia KC 34092)
91(16/10/76)	60(13/11/76)	7	**The Troublemaker** Arif Mardin (see also: Waylon JENNINGS)	(Lone Star KC 34112)
			NEW BIRTH	
183(28/8/76)	168(11/9/76)	4	**Love Potion** James Baker Melvin Wilson	(Warner Bros BS 2953)
			NEW RIDERS OF THE PURPLE SAGE	
188(12/6/76)	145(31/7/76)	8	**New Riders** Bob Johnston	(MCA 2196)
			Olivia NEWTON-JOHN	
49(11/10/75)	12(8/11/75)	22	**Clearly Love** John Farrar	(MCA 2148)
97(20/ 3/76)	13(15/ 5/76)	24	**Come On Over** John Farrar	(MCA 2186)

Position and date of entry	Highest position and date	Wks.	Artist(s) Title Producer(s)	Cat. No.
69(6/11/76)	30(11/12/76)	8*	**Don't Stop Believin'** John Farrar	(MCA 2223)
97(29/ 5/76)	65(26/ 6/76)	9	Maxine NIGHTINGALE **Right Back Where We Started From** Pierre Tubbs	(United Artists UA-LA626-G)
132(7/2/76)	111(21/2/76)	7	NILSSON **Sandman** Harry Nilsson	(RCA APL1-1031)
181(10/7/76)	158(14/8/76)	6	**That's The Way It Is** Trevor Lawrence	(RCA APL1-1119)
95(18/12/76)	85(25/12/76)	2*	NITTY GRITTY DIRT BAND **Dirt, Silver & Gold** William E. McEuen	(United Artists UA-LA670-L3)
80(2/10/76)	24(20/11/76)	13*	Ted NUGENT **Free For All** Cliff Davies Lew Futterman Tom Werman	(Epic PE 34121)
187(22/11/75)	28(10/ 4/76)	54	**Ted Nugent** Lew Futterman Tom Werman	(Epic PE 33692)
140(13/3/76)	60(10/ 4/76)	14	Laura NYRO **Smile** Charlie Calello Laura Nyro	(Columbia PC 33912)
83(12/ 6/76)	12(24/ 7/76)	20	OHIO PLAYERS **Contradiction** Ohio Players (William Beck Leroy Bonner Marshall Jones Ralph Middlebrooks Marvin Pierce Clarence Satchell James Williams)	(Mercury SRM-1-1088)
64(13/11/76)	31(11/12/76)	7*	**Gold** Ohio Players	(Mercury SRM-1-1122)
30(23/ 8/75)	2(27/ 9/75)	36	**Honey** Ohio Players	(Mercury SRM-1-1038)
158(20/12/75)	61(6/ 3/76)	14	**Rattlesnake** (Not listed)	(Westbound W 211)

Position and date of entry	Highest position and date	Wks.	Artist(s) Title Producer(s)	Cat. No.
			O'JAYS	
108(29/11/75)	7(24/ 1/76)	34	**Family Reunion** Kenny Gamble Leon Huff	(Philadelphia International PZ 33807)
81(2/10/76)	20(6/11/76)	13*	**Message In The Music** Victor Carstarphen Kenny Gamble Leon Huff Gene McFadden Bunny Sigler John Whitehead	(Philadelphia International PZ 34245)
			Mike OLDFIELD	
190(20/12/75)	146(31/1/76)	7	**Ommadawn** Mike Oldfield	(Virgin PZ 33913)
			Tony ORLANDO & DAWN	
92(28/ 6/75)	16(30/ 8/75)	32	**Greatest Hits** Dave Appell Hank Medress	(Arista AL 4045)
96(20/ 3/76)	94(27/ 3/76)	6	**To Be With You** Dave Appell Hank Medress	(Elektra 7E-1049)
			ORLEANS	
95(28/ 8/76)	30(16/10/76)	16	**Waking And Dreaming** Charles Plotkin	(Asylum 7E-1070)
			OSIBISA	
200(24/4/76)	200(24/4/76)	2	**Welcome Home** Gerry Bron	(Island ILPS 9355)
			Lee OSKAR	
188(3/4/76)	29(10/ 7/76)	24	**Lee Oskar** Greg Errico Jerry Goldstein	(United Artists UA-LA594-G)
			Donny OSMOND	
188(21/8/76)	145(2/10/76)	8	**Disco Train** Mike Curb Alan, Merrill & Wayne Osmond	(Kolob PD-1-6067)
			Donny & Marie OSMOND	
152(3/4/76)	60(29/ 5/76)	31*	**Donny & Marie Featuring Songs From Their Television Show** Mike Curb Michael Lloyd	(Kolob PD-1-6068)
190(27/11/76)	95(25/12/76)	5*	**New Season** Mike Curb Michael Lloyd Alan Osmond	(Kolob PD-1-6083)

Position and date of entry	Highest position and date	Wks.	Artist(s) Title Producer(s)	Cat. No.
			OSMONDS	
189(23/10/76)	145(20/11/76)	6	**Brainstorm** Mike Curb Michael Lloyd The Osmond Brothers (Alan, Donny, Jay, Merrill & Wayne Osmond)	(Kolob PD-1-6077)
187(20/12/75)	148(17/1/76)	8	**The Osmonds Around The World—Live In Concert** The Osmonds (Alan, Donny, Jay, Jimmy, Marie, Merrill & Wayne Osmond)	(Kolob M3JB 5012)
190(18/12/76)	170(25/12/76)	2*	**The Osmonds Christmas Album** Don Costa The Osmond Brothers	(Kolob PD-2-8001)
			OUTLAWS	
124(10/4/76)	36(15/ 5/76)	12	**Lady In Waiting** Paul A. Rothchild	(Arista AL 4070)
			OZARK MOUNTAIN DAREDEVILS	
125(8/11/75)	57(20/12/75)	16	**The Car Over The Lake Album** David Anderle	(A&M SP 4549)
107(2/10/76)	74(13/11/76)	10	**Men From Earth** David Anderle	(A&M SP 4601)
			PABLO CRUISE	
185(17/4/76)	179(8/5/76)	5	**Lifeline** Val Garay Pablo Cruise (Bud Cockrell David Jenkins Cory Lerios Stephen Price)	(A&M SP 4575)
			Robert **PALMER**	
158(22/11/75)	136(20/12/75)	8	**Pressure Drop** Steve Smith	(Island ILPS 9372)
183(23/10/76)	68(4/12/76)	10*	**Some People Can Do What They Like** Steve Smith	(Island ILPS 9420)
			PARIS	
181(11/9/76)	152(2/10/76)	6	**Big Towne 2061** Bob Hughes	(Capitol ST 11560)
139(7/2/76)	103(20/3/76)	9	**Paris** Jimmy Robinson	(Capitol ST 11464)
			PARLIAMENT	
69(16/10/76)	20(4/12/76)	11*	**The Clones Of Dr. Funkenstein** George Clinton	(Casablanca NBLP 7034)

Position and date of entry	Highest position and date	Wks.	Artist(s) Title Producer(s)	Cat. No.
187(21/2/76)	13(5/ 6/76)	37	**Mothership Connection** George Clinton	(Casablanca NBLP 7022)
			Alan PARSONS PROJECT	
121(15/5/76)	38(10/ 7/76)	28	**Tales of Mystery &** **Imagination . Edgar Allan Poe** Alan Parsons	(20th Century T 508)
			Gram PARSONS/FLYING BURRITO BROTHERS	
199(22/5/76)	185(12/6/76)	4	**Sleepless Nights** Jim Dickson Gram Parsons	(A&M SP 4578)
			Billy PAUL	
197(27/12/75)	139(17/4/76)	20	**When Love Is New** Kenny Gamble Leon Huff Billy Paul	(Philadelphia International PZ 33843)
			PEOPLE'S CHOICE	
188(26/6/76)	174(10/7/76)	3	**We Got The Rhythm** Kenny Gamble Leon Huff	(TSOP PZ 34124)
			Lydia PENSE AND COLD BLOOD	
196(13/3/76)	179(3/4/76)	4	**Lydia Pense And Cold Blood** Bob Monaco	(ABC ABCD 917)
			Esther PHILLIPS	
187(31/1/76)	170(21/2/76)	4	**Confessin' The Blues** King Curtis Nesuhi Ertegun	(Atlantic SD 1680)
			Michael PINDER	
182(1/5/76)	133(29/5/76)	8	**The Promise** Michael Pinder	(Threshold THS 18)
			PINK FLOYD	
95(17/ 3/73)	1(28/ 4/73)	134*	**The Dark Side Of The Moon** Pink Floyd (David Gilmour Nick Mason Roger Waters Richard Wright)	(Harvest SMAS 11163)
12(27/ 9/75)	1(4/10/75)	39	**Wish You Were Here** Pink Floyd	(Columbia PC 33453)
			PLEASURE	
181(28/8/76)	162(25/9/76)	5	**Accept No Substitutes** Wayne Henderson	(Fantasy F 9506)
			POCO	
184(3/4/76)	169(17/4/76)	4	**Live** Mark Harman Poco (Paul Cotton George Grantham Timothy B. Schmit Rusty Young)	(Epic PE 33336)

Position and date of entry	Highest position and date	Wks.	Artist(s) Title Producer(s)	Cat. No.
125(29/5/76)	89(26/ 6/76)	15	**Rose Of Cimarron** Mark Harman Poco	(ABC ABCD 946)
			POINT BLANK	
175(11/9/76)	175(11/9/76)	3	**Point Blank** Bill Ham	(Arista AL 4087)
			POINTER SISTERS	
183(4/12/76)	164(25/12/76)	4*	**The Best Of The Pointer Sisters** David Rubinson & Friends, Inc. Norman Whitfield	(ABC/Blue Thumb BTSY 6026/2)
			Michel POLNAREFF	
190(21/2/76)	117(10/4/76)	13	**Michel Polnareff** Bill Halverson Michel Polnareff Greg Prestopino Bill Schnee	(Atlantic SD 18153)
			Jean-Luc PONTY	
152(10/4/76)	123(19/6/76)	13	**Aurora** Jean-Luc Ponty	(Atlantic SD 18163)
155(4/12/76)	137(18/12/76)	4*	**Imaginary Voyage** Jean-Luc Ponty	(Atlantic SD 18195)
			Andy PRATT	
113(10/7/76)	104(28/8/76)	10	**Resolution** Arif Mardin	(Nemperor NE 438)
			PRATT & McCLAIN	
190(10/7/76)	190(10/7/76)	2	**Pratt & McClain Featuring 'Happy Days'** Steve Barri Michael Omartian	(Reprise MS 2250)
			PRELUDE	
199(22/11/75)	111(24/1/76)	14	**Owl Creek Incident** Micky Sweeney Prelude (Brian Hume Irene Hume Ian Vardy)	(Pye 12120)
			Elvis PRESLEY	
183(5/6/76)	41(17/7/76)	17	**From Elvis Presley Boulevard, Memphis, Tennessee** (Not Listed)	(RCA APL1-1506)
76(7/ 2/76)	46(6/ 3/76)	17	**Elvis, Vol. 2—A Legendary Performer** (Not listed)	(RCA CPL1-1349)
144(17/4/76)	76(29/ 5/76)	11	**The Sun Sessions** (Not listed)	(RCA APM1-1675)
			PRETTY THINGS	
182(21/2/76)	163(27/3/76)	6	**Savage Eye** Norman Smith	(Swansong SS 8414)

Position and date of entry	Highest position and date	Wks.	Artist(s) Title Producer(s)	Cat. No.
			Richard PRYOR	
78(9/10/76)	22(6/11/76)	12*	Bicentennial Nigger David Banks	(Warner Bros BS 2960)
90(23/ 8/75)	12(4/10/75)	25	Is It Something I Said? David Banks	(Reprise MS 2227)
120(29/11/75)	62(27/11/75)	10	That Nigger's Crazy David Banks	(Reprise MS 2241)
			PURE PRAIRIE LEAGUE	
146(20/11/76)	99(25/12/76)	6*	Dance Alan Abrahams	(RCA APL1-1924)
154(7/2/76)	33(27/ 3/76)	16	If The Shoe Fits John Boylan	(RCA APL1-1247)
			Flora PURIM	
168(16/10/76)	146(6/11/76)	5	500 Miles High At Montreux Orrin Keepnews	(Milestone M 9070)
200(13/3/76)	59(8/ 5/76)	15	Open Your Eyes You Can Fly Orrin Keepnews	(Milestone M 9065)
			QUEEN	
116(27/12/75)	4(17/ 4/76)	47	A Night At The Opera Roy Thomas Baker Queen (John Deacon Brian May Freddie Mercury Roger Taylor)	(Elektra 7E-1053)
			QUICKSILVER MESSENGER SERVICE	
132(15/11/75)	89(20/12/75)	12	Solid Silver Quicksilver Messenger Service (John Cipollina Gary Duncan Greg Elmore David Freiberg Dino Valenti) John Palladino	(Capitol ST 11462)
			RAMONES	
198(5/6/76)	111(18/9/76)	18	The Ramones Craig Leon	(Sire SASD 7520)
			Jean-Pierre RAMPAL & CLAUDE BOLLING	
188(31/1/76)	173(21/2/76)	4	Suite For Flute & Jazz Piano (Not listed)	(Columbia M 33233)
			Kenny RANKIN	
188(13/12/75)	81(21/ 2/76)	15	Inside Yvonne Rankin Michael Stewart	(Little David LD 1009)

Position and date of entry	Highest position and date	Wks.	Artist(s) Title Producer(s)	Cat. No.
			RASPBERRIES	
157(12/6/76)	138(3/7/76)	4	**Raspberries Best Featuring Eric Carmen** Jimmy Lenner	(Capitol ST 11524)
			Lou RAWLS	
188(5/6/76)	7(11/ 9/76)	30*	**All Things In Time** Jack Faith Kenny Gamble Leon Huff Bobby Martin Bunny Sigler Dexter Wansel	(Philadelphia International PZ 33957)
			Leon REDBONE	
156(31/7/76)	87(23/10/76)	15	**On The Track** Joel Dorn	(Warner Bros BS 2888)
			Helen REDDY	
134(6/12/75)	5(17/ 1/76)	50	**Helen Reddy's Greatest Hits** Tom Catalano Jay Senter Joe Wissert	(Capitol ST 11467)
31(14/ 8/76)	16(11/ 9/76)	13	**Music, Music** Joe Wissert	(Capitol ST 11547)
89(12/ 7/75)	11(27/ 9/75)	34	**No Way To Treat A Lady** Joe Wissert	(Capitol ST 11418)
			Lou REED	
65(7/ 2/76)	41(6/ 3/76)	14	**Coney Island Baby** Godfrey Diamond Lou Reed	(RCA APL1-0915)
153(13/11/76)	64(11/12/76)	7*	**Rock And Roll Heart** Lou Reed	(Arista AL 4100)
			RENAISSANCE	
158(5/6/76)	55(14/ 8/76)	20	**Live At Carnegie Hall** Renaissance (Jon Camp Michael Dunford Annie Haslam Terrence Sullivan John Tout)	(Sire SASY 3902-2)
			R.E.O.	
169(19/6/76)	159(10/7/76)	5	**R.E.O.** John Stronach	(Epic PE 34143)
			RETURN TO FOREVER	
170(3/4/76)	35(29/ 5/76)	15	**Romantic Warrior** Chick Corea	(Columbia PC 34076)
			REVERBERI	
195(21/2/76)	169(20/3/76)	7	**Reverberi** Gian Piero Reverberi	(Pausa PR 7003)
			RHYTHM HERITAGE	
100(6/3/76)	40(24/ 4/76)	17	**Disco-Fied** Steve Barri Michael Omartian	(ABC ABCD 934)

Position and date of entry	Highest position and date	Wks.	Artist(s) Title Producer(s)	Cat. No.
			Charlie RICH	
176(3/7/76)	148(31/7/76)	6	**Greatest Hits** Billy Sherrill	(Epic PE 34240)
186(3/4/76)	160(8/5/76)	6	**Silver Linings** Billy Sherrill	(Epic KE 33545)
			Cliff RICHARD	
189(7/8/76)	76(16/10/76)	15	**I'm Nearly Famous** Bruce Welch	(Rocket PIG 2210)
			RITCHIE FAMILY	
187(24/7/76)	30(13/11/76)	23*	**Arabian Nights** Jacques Morali Ritchie Rome	(Marlin 2201)
			Smokey ROBINSON	
174(19/4/75)	36(14/ 6/75)	42	**A Quiet Storm** Smokey Robinson	(Tamla T6-337S1)
150(6/3/76)	57(24/ 4/76)	15	**Smokey's Family Robinson** Smokey Robinson	(Tamla T6-341S1)
			Vicki Sue ROBINSON	
179(10/4/76)	49(26/ 6/76)	36	**Never Gonna Let You Go** Warren Schatz	(RCA APL1-1256)
163(23/10/76)	45(4/12/76)	9*	**Vicki Sue Robinson** Warren Schatz	(RCA APL1-1829)
			D.J. ROGERS	
188(18/9/76)	175(9/10/76)	5	**On The Road Again** D.J. Rogers	(RCA APL1-1697)
			ROLLING STONES	
8(8/ 5/76)	1(15/ 5/76)	24	**Black And Blue** The Glimmer Twins (Keith Richard/ Mick Jagger)	(Rolling Stones COC 79104)
			Linda RONSTADT	
15(18/12/76)	13(25/12/76)	2*	**Greatest Hits** Peter Asher John Boylan Elliot F. Mazer John David Souther Nikolas Venet	(Asylum 7E-1092)
49(28/ 8/76)	3(25/ 9/76)	18*	**Hasten Down The Wind** Peter Asher	(Asylum 7E-1072)
63(4/10/75)	4(8/11/75)	28	**Prisoner In Disguise** Peter Asher	(Asylum 7E-1045)
			Diana ROSS	
85(6/ 3/76)	5(26/ 6/76)	32	**Diana Ross** Gil Askey Lawrence Brown Don Costa Hal Davis Berry Gordy Michael Masser Diana Ross	(Motown M6-861S1)

Position and date of entry	Highest position and date	Wks.	Artist(s) Title Producer(s)	Cat. No.
61(7/ 8/76)	13(2/10/76)	21*	**Diana Ross' Greatest Hits** Tom Baird Hal Davis Mel Larson Jerry Marcellino Michael Masser Michael Randall Diana Ross	(Motown M6-869S1)
			ROXY MUSIC	
169(29/11/75)	50(14/ 2/76)	20	**Siren** Chris Thomas	(Atco SD 36-127)
114(7/8/76)	81(4/ 9/76)	7	**Viva! Roxy Music** Chris Thomas	(Atco SD 36-139)
			David RUFFIN	
94(12/ 6/76)	51(17/ 7/76)	12	**Everything's Coming Up Love** Van McCoy	(Motown M6-866S1)
171(15/11/75)	31(14/ 2/76)	27	**Who I Am** Van McCoy	(Motown M6-849S1)
			RUFUS featuring CHAKA KHAN	
32(6/12/75)	7(6/ 3/76)	32	**Rufus Featuring Chaka Khan** Rufus (Andre Fischer Chaka Khan Tony Maiden Kevin Murphy Bobby Watson)	(ABC ABCD 909)
			RUNAWAYS	
199(21/8/76)	194(28/8/76)	2	**The Runaways** Kim Fowley	(Mercury SRM-1-1090)
			Todd RUNDGREN	
184(15/5/76)	54(26/ 6/76)	15	**Faithful** Todd Rundgren	(Bearsville BR 6963)
			Todd RUNDGREN'S UTOPIA	
111(15/11/75)	66(20/12/75)	9	**Another Live** Todd Rundgren	(Bearsville BR 6961)
			RUSH	
195(2/10/76)	40(20/11/76)	13*	**All The World's A Stage** Rush (Alex Lifeson Geddy Lee Neil Peart) Terry Brown	(Mercury SRM-2-7508)
181(10/4/76)	61(29/ 5/76)	13	**2112** Terry Brown Rush	(Mercury SRM-1-1079)
			Tom RUSH	
185(7/2/76)	184(21/2/76)	3	**The Best Of Tom Rush** David Briggs Ed Freeman Tom Rush Mark Spector	(Columbia PC 33907)

Position and date of entry	Highest position and date	Wks.	Artist(s) Title Producer(s)	Cat. No
			Leon RUSSELL	
101(23/10/76)	40(4/12/76)	10*	Best Of Leon Denny Cordell Leon Russell	(Shelter SRL 52004)
70(3/ 5/75)	30(7/ 6/75)	40	Will O' The Wisp Denny Cordell Leon Russell	(Shelter SRL 52020)
			Leon & Mary RUSSELL	
144(1/5/76)	34(3/ 7/76)	28	Wedding Album Leon & Mary Russell Bobby Womack	(Paradise PA 2943)
			SALSOUL ORCHESTRA	
168(11/12/76)	93(25/12/76)	3*	Christmas Jollies Vincent Montana Jr.	(Salsoul SZS 5507)
124(23/10/76)	61(13/11/76)	10*	Nice 'N' Naasty Vincent Montana Jr.	(Salsoul SZS 5502)
190(29/11/75)	14(10/ 4/76)	45	The Salsoul Orchestra Vincent Montana Jr.	(Salsoul SZS 5501)
			David SANBORN	
172(28/8/76)	125(2/10/76)	8	Sanborn Phil Ramone	(Warner Bros BS 2957)
			SANTANA	
79(10/ 4/76)	10(5/ 6/76)	26	Amigos David Rubinson & Friends, Inc.	(Columbia PC 33576)
			Esther SATTERFIELD	
190(24/7/76)	180(14/8/76)	4	The Need To Be Chuck Mangione	(A&M SP 3411)
			SAVOY BROWN featuring KIM SIMMONDS	
184(22/11/75)	153(20/12/75)	7	Wire Fire Paul Raymond Kim Simmonds	(London PS 659)
			Leo SAYER	
147(27/11/76)	54(25/12/76)	5*	Endless Flight Richard Perry	(Warner Bros BS 2962)
			Boz SCAGGS	
191(13/7/74)	171(24/7/76)	5	Boz Scaggs Marlin Greene Boz Scaggs Jann Wenner	(Atlantic SD 8239)
113(20/3/76)	2(18/ 9/76)	41*	Silk Degrees Joe Wissert	(Columbia PC 33920)
			Tom SCOTT	
182(20/12/75)	42(13/ 3/76)	25	New York Connection Hank Cicalo Tom Scott	(Ode SP 77033)
			Tom SCOTT & THE L.A. EXPRESS	
198(14/2/76)	186(6/3/76)	4	Tom Cat Tom Scott	(Ode SP 77029)

Position and date of entry	Highest position and date	Wks.	Artist(s) Title Producer(s)	Cat. No.
			Gil SCOTT-HERON & BRIAN JACKSON	
182(13/11/76)	168(27/11/76)	5	**It's Your World** Brian Jackson Gil Scott-Heron	(Arista AL 5001)
			Earl SCRUGGS REVUE	
183(17/4/76)	161(1/5/76)	4	**Earl Scruggs Revue Volume II** Ron Bledsoe	(Columbia PC 34090)
			SEALS & CROFTS	
130(1/5/76)	37(25/9/76)	29	**Get Closer** Louie Shelton	(Warner Bros BS 2907)
69(15/11/75)	11(3/ 1/76)	54	**Greatest Hits** Louie Shelton	(Warner Bros BS 2886)
138(11/12/76)	77(25/12/76)	3*	**Sudan Village** Louie Shelton	(Warner Bros BS 2976)
			John SEBASTIAN	
182(15/5/76)	79(19/6/76)	10	**Welcome Back** Steve Barri John Sebastian	(Reprise MS 2249)
			Neil SEDAKA	
68(11/10/75)	16(27/12/75)	32	**The Hungry Years** Robert Appere Neil Sedaka	(Rocket PIG 2157)
168(7/12/74)	23(8/ 3/75)	62	**Sedaka's Back** Robert Appere Neil Sedaka	(MCA 463)
177(18/9/76)	159(9/10/76)	4	**Solitaire** Neil Sedaka	(RCA APL1-1790)
85(1/ 5/76)	26(12/ 6/76)	22	**Steppin' Out** Robert Appere Neil Sedaka	(Rocket PIG 2195)
			Bob SEGER & THE SILVER BULLET BAND	
178(1/5/76)	34(19/ 6/76)	35*	**Live Bullet** Punch Andrews Bob Seger	(2-Capitol SKBB 11523)
84(13/11/76)	45(25/12/76)	7*	**Night Moves** Punch Andrews Jack Richardson Bob Seger	(Capitol ST 11557)
			Doc SEVERINSEN	
195(17/4/76)	189(24/4/76)	4	**Night Journey** Doc Severinsen	(Epic PE 34078)
			SHAKTI with JOHN McLAUGHLIN	
194(12/6/76)	194(12/6/76)	2	**Shakti With John McLaughlin** John McLaughlin	(Columbia PC 34162)
			Beverly SILLS	
196(3/1/76)	113(17/1/76)	6	**The Music Of Victor Herbert** Christopher Bishop	(Angel SFO-37160)

Position and date of entry	Highest position and date	Wks.	Artist(s) Title Producer(s)	Cat. No.
			SILVER	
188(25/9/76)	142(23/10/76)	6	**Silver** Clive Davis Tom Sellers Silver (John Batdorf Greg Collier Tom Leadon Brent Mydland Harry Stinson)	(Arista AL 4076)
			SILVER CONVENTION	
101(13/11/76)	65(4/12/76)	7*	**Madhouse** Michael Kunze Sylvester Levay	(Midland International BKL1-1824)
182(13/9/75)	10(13/12/75)	25	**Save Me** Michael Kunze	(Midland International BKL1-1129)
58(10/ 4/76)	13(26/ 6/76)	24	**Silver Convention** Michael Kunze	(Midland International BKL1-1369)
			Carly **SIMON**	
70(26/ 6/76)	29(24/ 7/76)	13	**Another Passenger** Ted Templeman	(Elektra 7E-1064)
166(6/12/75)	17(17/ 1/76)	19	**The Best Of Carly Simon** Eddie Kramer Richard Perry Paul Samwell-Smith	(Elektra 7E-1048)
			Paul **SIMON**	
64(25/10/75)	1(6/12/75)	40	**Still Crazy After All These Years** Art Garfunkel Phil Ramone Paul Simon	(Columbia PC 33540)
			SIMON & GARFUNKEL	
110(1/7 72)	5(29/ 7/72)	126	**Simon & Garfunkel's Greatest Hits** Art Garfunkel Roy Halee Paul Simon	(Columbia PC 31350)
			Lonnie Liston **SMITH & THE COSMIC ECHOES**	
169(10/4/76)	75(29/ 5/76)	14	**Reflections Of A Golden Dream** Lonnie Liston Smith Bob Thiele	(Flying Dutchman BDL1-1460)
183(11/12/76)	140(25/12/76)	3*	**Renaissance** Lonnie Liston Smith Bob Thiele	(RCA APL1-1822)
185(18/10/75)	74(29/11/75)	15	**Visions Of A New World** Lonnie Liston Smith Bob Thiele	(Flying Dutchman BDL1-1196)

Position and date of entry	Highest position and date	Wks.	Artist(s) Title Producer(s)	Cat. No.
			Patti SMITH	
183(13/12/75)	47(7/ 2/76)	17	**Horses** John Cale	(Arista AL 4066)
			Patti SMITH GROUP	
161(27/11/76)	126(18/12/76)	5*	**Radio Ethiopia** Jack Douglas	(Arista AL 4097)
			Phoebe SNOW	
115(6/11/76)	29(18/12/76)	8*	**It Looks Like Snow** David Rubinson & Friends, Inc.	(Columbia PC 34387)
99(14/ 2/76)	13(27/ 3/76)	22	**Second Childhood** Phil Ramone	(Columbia PC 33952)
180(7/9/74)	4(15/ 3/75)	55*	**Phoebe Snow** Dino Airali	(Shelter SRL 52017)
			SONS OF CHAMPLIN	
196(5/6/76)	117(24/7/76)	10	**A Circle Filled With Love** Keith Olsen	(Ariola America ST 50007)
			SOUNDTRACKS/ORIGINAL CAST RECORDINGS	
80(27/11/76)	48(25/12/76)	5*	**All This And World War II** Lou Reizner	(20th Century 2T522)
199(14/2/76)	132(17/4/76)	15	**Barry Lyndon/Music From The Soundtrack** (Not listed)	(Warner Bros BS 2903)
179(16/8/75)	98(27/ 9/75)	25	**A Chorus Line** Goddard Lieberson	(Columbia PS 33581)
200(8/5/76)	200(8/5/76)	2	**Scott Joplin's Treemonisha** Thomas Mowery	(DGG 2707 083)
185(1/11/75)	20(3/ 1/76)	18	**Let's Do It Again —The Staple Singers— Music By Curtis Mayfield** Curtis Mayfield	(Curtom CU 5005)
163(9/10/76)	30(25/12/76)	12*	**Car Wash** Norman Whitfield	(MCA 2-6000)
200(17/4/76)	189(8/5/76)	4	**Mackintosh & T.J.** Richard Albright Waylon Jennings Arif Mardin Jerry Wexler	(RCA APL1-1520)
166(8/11/75)	19(24/ 1/76)	26	**Mahogany** Gil Askey Jermaine Jackson Michael Masser	(Motown M6-858S1)
124(25/12/76)	124(25/12/76)	1*	**NBC'S Saturday Night Live** Michael O'Donoghue	(Arista AL 4107)
199(17/4/76)	158(22/5/76)	7	**One Flew Over The Cuckoo's Nest** Jack Nitzsche	(Fantasy F-9500)
186(31/7/76)	183(14/8/76)	4	**Jonathan Livingston Seagull** Tom Catalano	(Columbia KS 32550)

Position and date of entry	Highest position and date	Wks.	Artist(s) Title Producer(s)	Cat. No.
109(20/3/65)	1(13/11/65)	233	**The Sound Of Music** Neely Plumb	(RCA LSOD 2005)
48(11/12/76)	38(25/12/76)	3*	**A Star Is Born** Phil Ramone Barbra Streisand	(Columbia JS 34403)
			John David SOUTHER	
140(8/5/76)	85(19/ 6/76)	11	**Black Rose** Peter Asher	(Asylum 7E-1059)
			SOUTHSIDE JOHNNY & THE ASBURY JUKES	
188(10/7/76)	125(21/8/76)	9	**I Don't Want To Go Home** Miami Steve Van Zandt	(Epic PE 34180)
			Red SOVINE	
141(11/9/76)	119(25/9/76)	6	**Teddy Bear** Tommy Hill	(Starday SD-968)
			SPARKS	
197(29/11/75)	169(3/1/76)	6	**Indiscreet** Tony Visconti	(Island ILPS 9345)
			SPIDERS FROM MARS	
200(3/4/76)	197(10/4/76)	2	**Spiders From Mars** Dennis McKay Spiders From Mars (Dave Black Trevor Bolder Pete McDonald Woody Woodmansey)	(Pye 12125)
			SPINNERS (known as the DETROIT SPINNERS in the UK)	
86(31/ 7/76)	25(4/ 9/76)	22*	**Happiness Is Being With The Spinners** Thom Bell	(Atlantic SD 18181)
97(13/12/75)	20(6/ 3/76)	21	**Live!** Thom Bell	(Atlantic SD 2-910)
122(9/8/75)	8(4/10/75)	26	**Pick Of The Litter** Thom Bell	(Atlantic SD 18141)
			SPIRIT	
190(31/7/76)	179(21/8/76)	4	**Farther Along** Al Schmitt	(Mercury SRM1-1094)
			Bruce SPRINGSTEEN	
84(13/ 9/75)	3(11/10/75)	29	**Born To Run** Mike Appel Jon Landau Bruce Springsteen	(Columbia PC 33795)
184(26/7/75)	60(18/10/75)	27	**Greetings From Asbury Park, N.J.** Mike Appel Jim Cretecos	(Columbia PC 31903)

Position and date of entry	Highest position and date	Wks.	Artist(s) / Title / Producer(s)	Cat. No.
181(26/7/75)	59(18/10/75)	29	**The Wild, The Innocent & The E-Street Shuffle** Mike Appel Jim Cretecos	(Columbia PC 32432)
			Chris SQUIRE	
189(24/1/76)	69(13/3/76)	12	**Fish Out Of Water** Chris Squire	(Atlantic SD 18159)
			STAPLES	
187(25/9/76)	155(16/10/76)	5	**Pass It On** Curtis Mayfield	(Warner Bros BS 2945)
			STARBUCK	
183(24/7/76)	78(28/8/76)	14	**Moonlight Feels Right** Bruce Blackman Mike Clark	(Private Stock PS 2013)
			STARCASTLE	
187(13/3/76)	95(22/5/76)	15	**Starcastle** Tommy Vicari	(Epic PE 33914)
			STARLAND VOCAL BAND	
152(29/5/76)	20(21/8/76)	25	**Starland Vocal Band** Milton Okun	(Windsong BHL1-1351)
			Ringo STARR	
176(6/12/75)	30(17/1/76)	11	**Blast From Your Past** Pete Drake George Harrison Richard Perry Ringo Starr	(Apple SW 3422)
57(16/10/76)	28(13/11/76)	9	**Ringo's Rotogravure** Arif Mardin	(Atlantic SD 18193)
			STARZ	
170(11/9/76)	123(23/10/76)	13	**Starz** Jack Douglas	(Capitol ST 11539)
			Candi STATON	
190(26/6/76)	129(14/8/76)	14	**Young Hearts Run Free** Dave Crawford	(Warner Bros BS 2948)
			STATUS QUO	
190(17/4/76)	148(15/5/76)	7	**Status Quo** Status Quo (John Coghlan Alan Lancaster Rick Parfitt Francis Rossi)	(Capitol ST 11509)
			STEELEYE SPAN	
157(6/12/75)	143(20/12/75)	6	**All Around My Hat** Mike Batt	(Chrysalis CHR 1091)
			STEELY DAN	
96(22/5/76)	15(10/7/76)	27	**The Royal Scam** Gary Katz	(ABC ABCD 931)
			Cat STEVENS	
66(12/7/75)	6(23/8/75)	35	**Greatest Hits** Paul Samwell-Smith Cat Stevens	(A&M SP 4519)

Position and date of entry	Highest position and date	Wks.	Artist(s) Title Producer(s)	Cat. No
29(13/12/75)	13(24/ 1/76)	19	**Numbers** Cat Stevens Ray STEVENS	(A&M SP 4555)
196(27/12/75)	173(17/1/76)	4	**The Very Best Of Ray Stevens** Ray Stevens Al STEWART	(Barnaby BR 6018)
176(20/11/76)	147(11/12/76)	6*	**Modern Times** Alan Parsons	(Janus JXS 7012)
189(9/10/76)	25(25/12/76)	12*	**Year Of The Cat** Alan Parsons Rod STEWART	(Janus JXS 7022)
76(6/ 9/75)	9(1/11/75)	27*	**Atlantic Crossing** Tom Dowd	(Warner Bros BS 2875)
143(15/5/76)	90(19/ 6/76)	17*	**The Best Of Rod Stewart** Lou Reizner Rod Stewart Ron Wood	(Mercury SRM2-7507)
84(17/ 7/76)	2(4/12/76)	24*	**A Night On The Town** Tom Dowd Stephen STILLS	(Warner Bros BS 2938)
102(15/5/76)	31(3/ 7/76)	15	**Illegal Stills** Don Gehman Stephen Stills	(Columbia PC 34148)
131(27/12/75)	42(14/ 2/76)	11	**Live** Michael John Bowen Don Gehman Tom Dowd Bill Halverson STILLS-YOUNG BAND	(Atlantic SD 18156)
183(30/10/76)	26(27/11/76)	12*	**Long May You Run** Don Gehman Stephen Stills Neil Young Sly STONE	(Reprise MS 2253)
114(8/11/75)	45(13/12/75)	10	**High On You** (Not listed) STRAWBS	(Epic PE 33835)
183(30/10/76)	144(27/11/76)	5	**Deep Cuts** Rupert Holmes Jeffrey Lesser Barbra STREISAND	(Oyster OY-1-1603)
99(6/ 3/76)	46(3/ 4/76)	14	**Classical Barbra** Claus Ogerman	(Columbia M 33452)
107(1/11/75)	12(20/12/75)	20	**Lazy Afternoon** Rupert Holmes Jeffrey Lesser STUFF	(Columbia PC 33815)
170(27/11/76)	163(11/12/76)	3	**Stuff** Tommy LiPuma Herb Lovelle	(Warner Bros BS 2968)

Position and date of entry	Highest position and date	Wks.	Artist(s) Title Producer(s)	Cat. No.
			STYLISTICS	
138(19/6/76)	117(3/7/76)	6	**Fabulous** Hugo & Luigi	(H&L HL 69013)
181(8/11/75)	99(20/12/75)	11	**You Are Beautiful** Hugo & Luigi	(Avco AV 69010)
			STYX	
93(30/10/76)	66(27/11/76)	9*	**Crystal Ball** Styx (Dennis DeYoung Chuck Panozzo John Panozzo Tommy Shaw James Young)	(A&M SP 4604)
124(20/12/75)	58(27/ 3/76)	26	**Equinox** Styx (John Curulewski Dennis DeYoung Chuck Panozzo John Panozzo James Young)	(A&M SP 4559)
			Donna **SUMMER**	
56(6/11/76)	29(11/12/76)	8*	**Four Seasons Of Love** Giorgio Moroder Pete Bellotte	(Oasis OCLP 7038)
190(1/11/75)	11(14/ 2/76)	30	**Love To Love You Baby** Pete Bellotte	(Oasis OCLP 5003)
181(27/3/76)	21(5/ 6/76)	27	**A Love Trilogy** Giorgio Moroder Pete Bellotte	(Oasis OCLP 5004)
			SUPERTRAMP	
131(13/12/75)	44(31/ 1/76)	17	**Crisis? What Crisis?** Ken Scott Supertramp (Bob C. Benberg Richard Davies John Anthony Helliwell Roger Hodgson Dougie Thomson)	(A&M SP 4560)
			SUPREMES	
78(22/ 5/76)	42(19/ 6/76)	15	**High Energy** Brian Holland	(Motown M6-863-S1)
			SUTHERLAND BROTHERS & QUIVER	
197(8/5/76)	195(15/5/76)	2	**Reach For The Sky** Ron & Howard Albert	(Columbia PC 33982)
			SWEET	
132(26/7/75)	25(25/10/75)	44	**Desolation Boulevard** Mike Chapman Nicky Chinn	(Capitol ST 11395)

Position and date of entry	Highest position and date	Wks.	Artist(s) Title Producer(s)	Cat. No.
60(6/ 3/76)	27(17/ 4/76)	13	'Give Us A Wink!' Sweet (Brian Connolly Steve Priest Andy Scott Mike Tucker)	(Capitol ST 11496)
			SYLVERS	
200(14/2/76)	58(29/ 5/76)	25	Showcase Freddie Perren	(Capitol ST 11465)
157(20/11/76)	80(25/12/76)	6*	Something Special! Freddie Perren	(Capitol ST 11580)
			SYNERGY	
192(26/6/76)	144(7/8/76)	11	Sequencer Marty Scott	(Passport PPSD 98014)
			TAVARES	
100(12/6/76)	24(18/ 9/76)	29*	Sky High Freddie Perren	(Capitol ST 11533)
			James TAYLOR	
89(3/ 7/76)	16(21/ 8/76)	24	In The Pocket Russ Titelman Lenny Waronker	(Warner Bros BS 2912)
150(4/12/76)	28(25/12/76)	4*	James Taylor's Greatest Hits Peter Asher David Spinozza Russ Titelman Lenny Waronker	(Warner Bros BS 2979)
			Johnnie TAYLOR	
167(13/3/76)	5(24/ 4/76)	28	Eargasm Don Davis	(Columbia PC 33951)
			TEMPTATIONS	
101(29/11/75)	40(20/12/75)	20	House Party James Carmichael Steve Cropper Suzee Ikeda Clayton Ivey Brian Holland Temptations (Dennis Edwards Melvin Franklin Glenn Leonard Richard Street Otis Williams) Terry Woodford	(Gordy G6-973S1)
97(11/ 9/76)	53(23/10/76)	14	The Temptations Do The Temptations Suzee Ikeda Michael L. Smith Tall 'T' Productions	(Gordy G6-975S1)
99(3/ 4/76)	29(5/ 6/76)	20	Wings Of Love Jeffrey Bowen Berry Gordy	(Gordy G6-971S1)

Position and date of entry	Highest position and date	Wks.	Artist(s) Title Producer(s)	Cat. No.
			10cc	
187(14/ 2/76)	47(27/ 3/76)	13	**How Dare You** 10cc (Lol Creme Kevin Godley Graham Gouldman Eric Stewart)	(Mercury SRM-1-1061)
			THIN LIZZY	
189(17/4/76)	18(24/ 7/76)	28	**Jailbreak** John Alcock	(Mercury SRM-1-1081)
68(13/11/76)	52(27/11/76)	7*	**Johnny The Fox** John Alcock	(Mercury SRM-1-1119)
			Marlo THOMAS & FRIENDS	
177(20/12/75)	152(10/1/76)	5	**Free To Be...You And Me** Bruce Hart Carole Hart Stephen Lawrence	(Arista AL 4003)
			Ray THOMAS	
169(14/8/76)	147(28/8/76)	5	**Hopes Wishes & Dreams** Ray Thomas Derek Varnals	(Threshold THS 17)
			THREE DEGREES	
199(17/1/76)	199(17/1/76)	1	**Live** Bobby Martin	(Philadelphia International PZ 33840)
			THREE DOG NIGHT	
161(24/4/76)	123(15/5/76)	6	**American Pastime** Bob Monaco	(ABC ABCD 928)
			Isao TOMITA	
106(14/2/76)	71(20/ 3/76)	12	**Firebird** Plasma Music, Inc.	(RCA ARL1-1312)
			TOOTS & THE MAYTALS	
196(1/11/75)	168(7/2/76)	13	**Funky Kingston** Chris Blackwell Dave Bloxham Warrick Lynn	(Island ILPS 9330)
187(17/7/76)	157(14/8/76)	5	**Reggae Got Soul** Chris Blackwell Joe Boyd Warrick Lynn	(Island ILPS 9374)
			Peter TOSH	
200(31/7/76)	199(7/8/76)	2	**Legalize It** Peter Tosh	(Columbia PC 34253)

Position and date of entry	Highest position and date	Wks.	Artist(s) Title Producer(s)	Cat. No.
			TOWER OF POWER	
106(11/9/76)	42(9/10/76)	16*	**Ain't Nothin' Stoppin' Us Now** Emilio Castillo Tower Of Power (Greg Adams Ronnie Beck Emilio Castillo Bruce Conte Mic Gillette Steve Kupka Edward McGee Lenny Pickett Francis Rocco Prestia Chester Thompson)	(Columbia PC 34202)
184(22/5/76)	99(19/ 6/76)	8	**Live And In Living Color** Emilio Castillo Tower Of Power (Greg Adams Emilio Castillo Bruce Conte David Garibaldi Mic Gillette Steve Kupka Lenny Pickett Francis Rocco Prestia Chester Thompson Hubert Tubbs)	(Warner Bros BS 2924)
			TRAMMPS	
104(15/5/76)	50(26/ 6/76)	24	**Where The Happy People Go** Ron Baker Norman Harris Earl Young	(Atlantic SD 18172)
			John TRAVOLTA	
162(22/5/76)	39(31/ 7/76)	22	**John Travolta** Bob Reno	(Midland International BKL1-1563)
			TRIUMVIRAT	
119(7/8/76)	85(28/ 8/76)	8	**Old Loves Die Hard** Jorgen Fritz	(Capitol ST 11551)
			TROPEA	
164(20/3/76)	138(10/4/76)	7	**Tropea** John Tropea	(Marlin 2200)
			Robin TROWER	
99(27/ 3/76)	10(1/ 5/76)	20	**Live!** (Not listed)	(Chrysalis CHR 1089)
47(9/10/76)	24(13/11/76)	12*	**Long Misty Days** Geoff Emerick Robin Trower	(Chrysalis CHR 1107)
			Andrea TRUE CONNECTION	
101(19/6/76)	47(7/ 8/76)	17	**More, More, More** Gregg Diamond	(Buddah BDS 5670)

Position and date of entry	Highest position and date	Wks.	Artist(s) Title Producer(s)	Cat. No.
			TUBES	
109(15/5/76)	46(3/ 7/76)	15	**Young And Rich** Ken Scott	(A&M SP 4580)
			Stanley TURRENTINE	
151(12/6/76)	100(14/8/76)	14	**Everybody Come On Out** Orrin Keepnews Stanley Turrentine	(Fantasy F 9508)
194(1/11/75)	76(13/12/75)	16	**Have You Ever Seen The Rain** Gene & Billy Page Stanley Turrentine	(Fantasy F 9493)
152(27/11/76)	110(25/12/76)	5*	**The Man With The Sad Face** Stanley Turrentine	(Fantasy F 9519)
			Dwight TWILLEY BAND	
185(31/7/76)	138(9/10/76)	14	**Sincerely** Robin Cable Oister Bob Schaper	(Shelter SRL 52001)
			McCoy TYNER	
178(12/6/76)	128(24/7/76)	11	**Fly With The Wind** Orrin Keepnews	(Milestone M 9067)
198(3/1/76)	198(3/1/76)	2	**Trident** Orrin Keepnews	(Milestone M 9063)
			UFO	
190(19/6/76)	169(10/7/76)	4	**No Heavy Pettin'** Leo Lyons	(Chrysalis CHR 1103)
			URIAH HEEP	
177(20/3/76)	145(10/4/76)	6	**The Best Of Uriah Heep** Gerry Bron	(Mercury SRM1-1070)
182(26/6/76)	161(10/7/76)	3	**High And Mighty** Uriah Heep (Mick Box David Byron Ken Hensley Lee Kerslake John Wetton)	(Bronze BS 2949)
			Frankie VALLI	
189(20/12/75)	132(24/1/76)	8	**Gold** Bob Crewe	(Private Stock PS 2001)
187(13/12/75)	107(10/1/76)	8	**Our Day Will Come** Dave Appell Hank Medress	(Private Stock PS 2006)
			Gino VANNELLI	
97(14/ 8/76)	32(2/10/76)	19*	**The Gist Of Gemini** Geoff Emerick Gino & Joe Vannelli	(A&M SP 4596)
			VARIOUS—	
190(22/11/75)	145(10/1/76)	10	**History Of British Rock Volume III** (Not listed)	(Sire SASH 3712-2)

Position and date of entry	Highest position and date	Wks.	Artist(s) Title Producer(s)	Cat. No.
200(27/12/75)	192(10/1/76)	3	**Threads Of Glory — 200 Years Of America In Words & Music** Si Alpert Tony D'Amato	(London 6SP 14000)
189(24/7/76)	153(21/8/76)	6	**Volunteer Jam** Paul Hornsby	(Capricorn CP 0172)
177(10/4/76)	177(10/4/76)	2	**Hustle Hits** (Not listed)	(DeLite DEP 2019)
			Martha VELEZ	
198(15/5/76)	153(10/7/76)	17	**Escape From Babylon** Craig Leon Bob Marley Lee Perry	(Sire SASD 7515)
			Bobby VINTON	
194(27/12/75)	161(24/1/76)	7	**The Bobby Vinton Show** Bob Morgan	(ABC ABCD 924)
			Loudon WAINWRIGHT III	
193(19/6/76)	188(3/7/76)	4	**T-Shirt** Loudon Wainwright III	(Arista AL 4068)
			Tom WAITS	
185(29/11/75)	164(27/12/75)	6	**Nighthawks At The Diner** Bones Howe	(Asylum 7E-2008)
105(6/11/76)	89(27/11/76)	5	**Small Change** Bones Howe	(Asylum 7E-1078)
			Rick WAKEMAN	
100(15/5/76)	67(12/ 6/76)	8	**No Earthly Connection** Rick Wakeman	(A&M SP 4583)
			David T. WALKER	
181(4/9/76)	166(18/9/76)	5	**On Love** David T. Walker	(Ode SP 77035)
			Jerry Jeff WALKER	
120(3/7/76)	84(14/ 8/76)	10	**It's A Good Night For Singin'** Michael Brovsky	(MCA 2202)
			Joe WALSH	
47(10/ 4/76)	20(29/ 5/76)	18	**You Can't Argue With A Sick Mind** Joe Walsh	(ABC ABCD 932)
			WAR	
19(4/ 9/76)	6(25/ 9/76)	17*	**Greatest Hits** Jerry Goldstein	(United Artists UA-LA648-G)
46(5/ 7/75)	8(30/ 8/75)	31	**Why Can't We Be Friends?** Jerry Goldstein	(United Artists UA-LA441-G)
			WAR featuring ERIC BURDON	
150(25/12/76)	150(25/12/76)	1*	**Love Is All Around** Jerry Goldstein	(ABC ABCD 988)
			Dionne WARWICK	
189(6/12/75)	137(31/1/76)	15	**Track Of The Cat** Thom Bell	(Warner Bros BS 2893)

Position and date of entry	Highest position and date	Wks.	Artist(s) Title Producer(s)	Cat. No.
			Grover WASHINGTON Jr.	
83(15/11/75)	10(20/12/75)	30	**Feels So Good** Creed Taylor	(Kudu KU24S1)
			Johnny 'Guitar' WATSON	
130(7/8/76)	52(16/10/76)	21*	**Ain't That A Bitch** Johnny 'Guitar' Watson	(DJM DJLPA-3)
			WEATHER REPORT	
90(17/ 4/76)	42(29/ 5/76)	12	**Black Market** Joe Zawinul	(Columbia PC 34099)
			Tim WEISBERG	
181(2/10/76)	148(6/11/76)	7	**Live At Last** Lynn Blessing Tim Weisberg	(A&M SP 4600)
			WET WILLIE	
151(3/4/76)	133(1/5/76)	7	**The Wetter The Better** Paul Hornsby	(Capricorn CP 0166)
			WHISPERS	
196(28/8/76)	189(25/9/76)	6	**One For The Money** Norman Harris	(Soul Train BVL1-1450)
			Barry WHITE	
110(15/11/75)	23(13/12/75)	25	**Greatest Hits** Barry White	(20th Century T 493)
149(27/11/76)	125(18/12/76)	5*	**Is This Whatcha Wont?** Barry White	(20th Century T 516)
186(14/2/76)	42(3/ 4/76)	15	**Let The Music Play** Barry White	(20th Century T 502)
			Lenny WHITE	
183(31/1/76)	177(7/2/76)	3	**Venusian Summer** Lenny White	(Nemperor NE 435)
			WHO	
79(25/10/75)	8(29/11/75)	25	**The Who By Numbers** Glyn Johns	(MCA 2161)
			Rusty WIER	
187(17/1/76)	131(6/3/76)	9	**Rusty Wier** Glen Spreen	(20th Century T 495)
			WILD CHERRY	
100(24/7/76)	5(25/ 9/76)	23*	**Wild Cherry** Richard Parissi	(Epic PE 34195)
			Deniece WILLIAMS	
190(30/10/76)	92(25/12/76)	9*	**This Is Niecy** Maurice White Charles Stepney	(Columbia PC 34242)
			Paul WILLIAMS	
184(13/12/75)	146(10/1/76)	6	**Ordinary Fool** Paul Williams	(A&M SP 4550)
			Al WILSON	
185(10/7/76)	185(10/7/76)	2	**I've Got A Feeling** Marc Gordon Hal Davis	(Playboy PB 410)

Position and date of entry	Highest position and date	Wks.	Artist(s) Title Producer(s)	Cat. No.
			Nancy WILSON	
183(1/5/76)	126(12/6/76)	13	**This Mother's Daughter** Eugene McDaniels	(Capitol ST 11518)
			WING & A PRAYER FIFE & DRUM CORPS	
166(14/2/76)	47(17/ 4/76)	16	**Baby Face** Harold Wheeler Stephen Y. Scheaffer	(Wing HS 3025)
			Pete WINGFIELD	
182(6/12/76)	165(20/12/75)	5	**Breakfast Special** Pete Wingfield Barry Hammond	(Island ILPS 9333)
			WINGS	
25(14/ 6/75)	1(19/ 7/75)	71	**Venus And Mars** Paul McCartney	(Capitol SMAS 11419)
32(10/ 4/76)	1(24/ 4/76)	38*	**Wings At The Speed Of Sound** Paul McCartney	(Capitol SW 11525)
7(25/12/76)	7(25/12/76)	1*	**Wings Over America** Paul McCartney	(Capitol SWCO 11593)
			(see also Paul McCARTNEY & WINGS)	
			Johnny WINTER	
155(6/3/76)	93(17/ 4/76)	12	**Captured Live** Johnny Winter	(Blue Sky PZ 33944)
			Johnny & Edgar WINTER	
119(19/6/76)	89(17/ 7/76)	9	**Together** Johnny & Edgar Winter	(Blue Sky PZ 34033)
			WISHBONE ASH	
182(27/3/76)	136(15/5/76)	9	**Locked In** Tom Dowd	(Atlantic SD 18164)
185(18/12/76)	175(25/12/76)	2*	**New England** Ron & Howard Albert	(Atlantic SD 18200)
			Bill WITHERS	
185(8/11/75)	81(3/ 1/76)	15	**Making Music** Bill Withers Larry Nash	(Columbia PC 33704)
187(6/11/76)	169(20/11/76)	4	**Naked & Warm** Bill Withers	(Columbia PC 34327)
			Bobby WOMACK	
189(17/1/76)	147(28/2/76)	11	**Safety Zone** David Rubinson & Friends, Inc.	(United Artists UA-LA544-G)
			Stevie WONDER	
79(10/ 8/74)	1(14/ 9/74)	60*	**Fulfillingness' First Finale** Stevie Wonder	(Tamla T6-332S1)
85(18/ 8/73)	4(22/ 9/73)	83*	**Innervisions** Stevie Wonder	(Tamla T6-326S1)
1(16/10/76)	1(16/10/76)	11*	**Songs In The Key Of Life** Stevie Wonder	(Tamla T13-340C2)
			Gary WRIGHT	
192(23/8/75)	7(10/ 4/76)	70	**The Dream Weaver** Gary Wright	(Warner Bros BS 2868)

Position and date of entry	Highest position and date	Wks.	Artist(s) / Title / Producer(s)	Cat. No.
			Gary WRIGHT . SPOOKY TOOTH	
186(24/4/76)	172(8/5/76)	4	**That Was Only Yesterday** Chris Blackwell Jimmy Miller Chris Stainton Gary Wright	(A&M SPSP 3528)
			Bill WYMAN	
185(27/3/76)	166(17/4/76)	5	**Stone Alone** Bill Wyman	(Rolling Stones COC 79103)
			Stomu YAMASHTA/Steve WINWOOD/Michael SHRIEVE	
123(21/8/76)	60(2/10/76)	12	**Go** Paul Buckmaster Dennis McKay Stomu Yamashta	(Island ILPS 9387)
			Jesse Colin YOUNG	
160(27/3/76)	34(15/ 5/76)	15	**On The Road** Jesse Colin Young	(Warner Bros BS 2913)
			Neil YOUNG with CRAZY HORSE	
90(29/11/75)	25(10/ 1/76)	21	**Zuma** David Briggs Tim Mulligan Neil Young	(Reprise MS 2242)
			Frank ZAPPA	
188(27/11/76)	61(18/12/76)	5*	**Zoot Allures** Frank Zappa	(Warner Bros BS 2970)
			Warren ZEVON	
189(28/8/76)	189(28/8/76)	2	**Warren Zevon** Jackson Browne	(Asylum 7E-1060)
			Z Z TOP	
99(17/ 3/75)	10(13/11/75)	47	**Fandango** Bill Ham	(London PS 656)

Section 12

US Producer Section

(*Billboard* Top 100 singles and Top 200 albums chart)

This section lists the producers of all singles and albums that made the *Billboard* Top 100 singles and Top 200 albums chart during 1976.

Albums are denoted by (LP) after the title. Many records are credited as co-productions, as associate productions, with assistant producers, or in association with etc., so that only those actually listed as producer are credited, except in the very few cases where it is well established who the producers are (i.e. Nicky Chinn produced in association with Mike Chapman). As very few records have co-production credits, this section (unlike the writer section) is not cross-referenced to other producers. A producer will be credited even though he might have only been responsible for one track on the album (i.e. Simon & Garfunkel's *My Little Town,* which appeared on both artists' solo albums and was the only track produced by the two on those respective albums). In some cases a producer's name appears in place of a production company, and the only time that a company's name does appear is when it has been impossible to find out the name of the actual producer.

Alan ABRAHAMS
  Dance (LP)—Pure Prairie League

Mark ABRAMSON
  Two's Company (LP)—Aztec Two-Step

John ACOCK
  Voyage (LP)—Steve Hackett

Greg ADAMS
  (see TOWER OF POWER)

Patrick ADAMS
  Love Bug—Bumble Bee Unlimited

Lou ADLER
  Framed—Cheech & Chong
  High Out Of Time—Carole King
  Only Love Is Real—Carole King
  Sleeping Beauty (OD-40) (LP)—
  Cheech & Chong
  Tapestry (LP)—Carole King
  Thoroughbred (LP)—Carole King

AEROSMITH
  (Tom Hamilton, Joey Kramer, Joe Perry,
  Steven Tyler & Brad Whitford)
  Home Tonight—Aerosmith
  Rocks (LP)—Aerosmith

Brian AHERN
  Baby Boy—Mary Kay Place (as Loretta
  Haggers)
  Here There And Everywhere—Emmylou
  Harris
  Elite Hotel (LP)—Emmylou Harris

Dino AIRALI
  Phoebe Snow (LP)—Phoebe Snow

Howard ALBERT
  Arms Of Mary—Sutherland Brothers &
  Quiver
  Slippin' Away (LP)—Chris Hillman
  Reach For The Sky (LP)—Sutherland
  Brothers & Quiver
  New England (LP)—Wishbone Ash

Morris ALBERT
  Feelings—Morris Albert
  Sweet Loving Man—Morris Albert
  Feelings (LP)—Morris Albert

Ron ALBERT
  Arms Of Mary—Sutherland Brothers &
  Quiver
  Slippin' Away (LP)—Chris Hillman
  Reach For The Sky (LP)—Sutherland
  Brothers & Quiver
  New England (LP)—Wishbone Ash

Richard ALBRIGHT
  Mackintosh And T.J. (LP)—Soundtrack

Roye ALBRIGHTON
  (see NEKTAR)

John ALCOCK
  The Boys Are Back In Town—Thin Lizzy
  Cowboy Song—Thin Lizzy
  Jailbreak (LP)—Thin Lizzy
  Johnny The Fox (LP)—Thin Lizzy

Tommy ALDRIDGE
  (see BLACK OAK ARKANSAS)

Gregg ALLMAN
  (see ALLMAN BROTHERS BAND)

ALLMAN BROTHERS BAND
  (Gregg Allman, Richard Betts, Jaimoe,
  Chuck Leavell, Berry Oakley &
  Butch Trucks)
  The Road Goes On Forever (LP)—
  Allman Brothers Band

Brain ALLSOP
  (see MANDRILL)

Tommy ALLSUP
  Wheelin' And Dealin'—Asleep At The
  Wheel

Herb ALPERT
  Caliente (LP)—Gato Barbieri

Si ALPERT
  Threads Of Glory—200 Years Of
  America In Words & Music (LP)—Various

AMERICA
  (Gerry Beckley, Dewey Bunnell &
  Dan Peek)
  History—America's Greatest Hits (LP)—
  America

Peter ANASTASOFF
  The Homecoming—Hagood Hardy
  The Homecoming (LP)—Hagood Hardy

David ANDERLE
  If I Only Knew—Ozark Mountain
  Daredevils
  It's Only Love (LP)—Rita Coolidge
  Surreal Thing (LP)—Kris Kristofferson
  Who's To Bless And Who's To Blame
  (LP)—Kris Kristofferson
  The Car Over The Lake Album (LP)—
  Ozark Mountain Daredevils
  Men From Earth (LP)—Ozark Mountain
  Daredevils

Al ANDERSON
(see Bob MARLEY & THE WAILERS)

Ian ANDERSON
Locomotive Breath—Jethro Tull
M.U. The Best Of Jethro Tull (LP)—
Jethro Tull
**Too Old To Rock 'N' Roll Too Young To
Die (LP)**—Jethro Tull

Tom ANDERSON
We've Got A Live One Here (LP)—
Commander Cody & His Lost Planet
Airmen

Benny ANDERSSON
Dancing Queen—Abba
Fernando—Abba
I Do, I Do, I Do, I Do, I Do—Abba
Mamma Mia—Abba
Greatest Hits (LP)—Abba

Punch ANDREWS
Night Moves—Bob Seger & the
Silver Bullet Band
Nutbush City Limits—Bob Seger & the
Silver Bullet Band
Live Bullet (LP)—Bob Seger & the
Silver Bullet Band
Night Moves (LP)—Bob Seger & the
Silver Bullet Band

John ANTHONY
Time For Another (LP)—Ace

Mike APPEL
Tenth Avenue Freeze-Out—
Bruce Springsteen
Born To Run (LP)—Bruce Springsteen
Greetings From Asbury Park, N.J. (LP)-
Bruce Springsteen
**The Wild, The Innocent & The E-Street
Shuffle (LP)**—Bruce Springsteen

Dave APPELL
Cupid—Tony Orlando & Dawn
Our Day Will Come—Frankie Valli
Greatest Hits (LP)—Tony Orlando & Dawn
To Be With You (LP)—Tony Orlando &
Dawn
Our Day Will Come (LP)—Frankie Valli

Robert APPERE
Once A Fool—Kiki Dee
Breaking Up Is Hard To Do—Neil Sedaka
Love In The Shadows—Neil Sedaka
Steppin' Out—Neil Sedaka

You Gotta Make Your Own Sunshine—
Neil Sedaka
The Hungry Years (LP)—Neil Sedaka
Sedaka's Back (LP)—Neil Sedaka
Steppin' Out (LP)—Neil Sedaka

Catherine ARNOUL
When Love Has Gone Away—
Richard Cocciante

Brooks ARTHUR
Aftertones (LP)—Janis Ian
Between The Lines (LP)—Janis Ian

Peter ASHER
Someone To Lay Down Beside Me—
Linda Ronstadt
That'll Be The Day—Linda Ronstadt
The Tracks Of My Tears—Linda Ronstadt
Greatest Hits (LP)—Linda Ronstadt
Hasten Down The Wind (LP)—
Linda Ronstadt
Prisoner In Disguise (LP)—
Linda Ronstadt
Black Rose (LP)—John David Souther
James Taylor's Greatest Hits (LP)—
James Taylor

Nickolas ASHFORD
Come As You Are (LP)—Ashford &
Simpson

Audie ASHWORTH
Hey Baby—J.J. Cale
Troubadour (LP)—J.J. Cale

Gil ASKEY
Diana Ross (LP)—Diana Ross
Mahogany (LP)—Soundtrack

ASLEEP AT THE WHEEL
(Ray Benson, Link Davis Jr.,
Floyd Domino, Tony Garnier,
Scott Hennige, Danny Levin, Bill Mabry,
Lucky Oceans, Chris O'Connell &
Leroy Preston)
Wheelin' And Dealin' (LP)—Asleep At
The Wheel

Chet ATKINS
Chester & Lester (LP)—Chet Atkins &
Les Paul
Just Out Of Reach (LP)—Perry Como
The Outlaws (LP)—Waylon Jennings,
Willie Nelson, Jessi Colter,
Tompall Glaser

ATTITUDES
(David Foster, Jim Keltner, Danny Kootch
& Paul Stallworth)
Sweet Summer Music—Attitudes
(see also: David FOSTER)

Brian AUGER
Live Oblivion—Vol. 2—Brian Auger's
Oblivion Express

Gerald AUSTIN
(see MANHATTANS)

AUTOMATIC MAN
(Bayete, Doni Harvey, Michael Shrieve &
Pat Thrall)
Automatic Man (LP)—Automatic Man

Roy AYERS
Everybody Loves The Sunshine (LP)—
Roy Ayers
Mystic Voyage (LP)—Roy Ayers

Randy BACHMAN
Down To The Line—Bachman-Turner
Overdrive
Gimme Your Money Please—Bachman-
Turner Overdrive
Lookin' Out For #1—Bachman-Turner
Overdrive
Take It Like A Man—Bachman-Turner
Overdrive
Best Of B.T.O. (So Far) (LP)—Bachman-
Turner Overdrive
Head On (LP)—Bachman-Turner
Overdrive

BACK STREET CRAWLER
(Tony Braunagel, Paul Kossoff,
Mike Montgomery, Terry Wilson &
Terry Wilson-Slesser)
The Band Plays On (LP)—Back Street
Crawler
(Tony Braunagel, John 'Rabbit' Bundrick,
Paul Kossoff, Terry Wilson &
Terry Wilson-Slesser)
2nd Street (LP)—Back Street Crawler

BAD COMPANY
(Boz Burrell, Simon Kirke, Mick Ralphs &
Paul Rodgers)
Honey Child—Bad Company
Young Blood—Bad Company
Run With The Pack (LP)—Bad Company

Joan BAEZ
Diamonds & Rust (LP)—Joan Baez

Roger BAIN
We Sold Our Soul For Rock 'N' Roll (LP)
—Black Sabbath

Tom BAIRD
Diana Ross (LP)—Diana Ross

James BAKER
Love Potion (LP)—New Birth

Ronnie/Ron BAKER
Ten Percent—Double Exposure
Hold Back The Night—Trammps
That's Where The Happy People Go—
Trammps
Ten Percent (LP)—Double Exposure
Where The Happy People Go (LP)—
Trammps

Roy Thomas BAKER
Bohemian Rhapsody—Queen
You're My Best Friend—Queen
A Night At The Opera (LP)—Queen

Marty BALIN
(see JEFFERSON STARSHIP)

Russ BALLARD
Ride A Rock Horse (LP)—Roger Daltrey

BAND
(Rick Danko, Levon Helm, Garth Hudson,
Richard Manuel & Robbie Robertson)
Ophelia—Band
The Best Of The Band (LP)—Band
Northern Lights—Southern Cross (LP)—
Band
(see also Robbie ROBERTSON)

David BANKS
Bicenntenial Nigger (LP)—Richard Pryor
Is It Something I Said? (LP)—
Richard Pryor
That Nigger's Crazy (LP)—Richard Pryor

Ron BANKS
Drama V (LP)—Ron Banks & the
Dramatics
Joy Ride (LP)—Dramatics

Tony BANKS
(see GENESIS)

John BARBATA
(see JEFFERSON STARSHIP)

Adrian BARBER
Dream On—Aerosmith
The Road Goes On Forever (LP)—
Allman Brothers Band

Peter BARDENS
(see CAMEL)

Gene BARGE
Sophisticated Lady (She's A Different Lady)—Natalie Cole
Natalie (LP)—Natalie Cole

Aston 'Family Man' BARRETT
(see Bob MARLEY & THE WAILERS)

Carlton BARRETT
(see Bob MARLEY & THE WAILERS)

Steve BARRI
Devil With The Blue Dress—Pratt & McClain with Brotherlove
Happy Days—Pratt & McClain with Brotherlove
Baretta's Theme (Keep Your Eyes On The Sparrow)—Rhythm Heritage
Theme From S.W.A.T.—Rhythm Heritage
Hideaway—John Sebastian
Welcome Back—John Sebastian
Pratt & McClain Featuring 'Happy Days' (LP)—Pratt & McClain
Disco-Fied (LP)—Rhythm Heritage
Welcome Back (LP)—John Sebastian

Jeff BARRY
The Monkees Greatest Hits (LP)—Monkees

Richard BASKIN
I'm Easy—Keith Carradine

John BATDORF
(see SILVER)

Mike BATT
All Around My Hat (LP)—Steeleye Span

BAYETE
(see AUTOMATIC MAN)

BEACH BOYS
(Blondie Chaplin, Ricky Fataar, Al Jardine, Mike Love, Carl Wilson & Dennis Wilson)
The Beach Boys In Concert (LP)—Beach Boys
(Al Jardine, Mike Love, Brian Wilson, Carl Wilson & Dennis Wilson)
Endless Summer (LP)—Beach Boys
Good Vibrations—Best Of The Beach Boys (LP)—Beach Boys
Spirit Of America (LP)—Beach Boys
(see also Brian WILSON)

Joe BECK
Norma Jean Wants To Be A Movie Star—Sundown Company

Ronnie BECK
(see TOWER OF POWER)

William BECK
(see OHIO PLAYERS)

Barry BECKETT
Torn Between Two Lovers—Mary MacGregor
Born To Get Down (LP)—Muscle Shoals Horns

Gerry Beckley
(see AMERICA)

BEE GEES
(Barry, Maurice & Robin Gibb)
Love So Right—Bee Gees
You Should Be Dancing—Bee Gees
Children Of The World (LP)—Bee Gees
Gold Vol. 1 (LP)—Bee Gees

Robert 'Kool' BELL
(see KOOL & THE GANG)

Ronald BELL
(see KOOL & THE GANG)

Thom BELL
Love Or Leave—Spinners
The Rubber Band Man—Spinners
Wake Up Susan—Spinners
Once You Hit The Road—Dionne Warwick
Happiness Is Being With The Spinners (LP)—Spinners
Live! (LP)—Spinners
Pick Of The Litter (LP)—Spinners
Track Of The Cat (LP)—Dionne Warwick

Pete BELLOTTE
Could It Be Magic—Donna Summer
Love To Love You Baby—Donna Summer
Spring Affair—Donna Summer
Try Me, I Know We Can Make It—Donna Summer
Four Seasons Of Love (LP)—Donna Summer
Love To Love You Baby (LP)—Donna Summer
A Love Trilogy (LP)—Donna Summer

Bob C. BENBERG
(see SUPERTRAMP)

Max BENNETT
(see L.A. EXPRESS)

Ray BENSON
(see ASLEEP AT THE WHEEL)

Herb BERNSTEIN
One Fine Day—Julie

Steve BERNSTEIN
Jealousy (LP)—Major Harris

Richard BETTS
(see ALLMAN BROTHERS BAND)

BIDDU
I Could Have Danced All Night/Jump
For Joy—Biddu Orchestra
I Am Somebody—Jimmy James & the
Vagabonds
Biddu Orchestra (LP)—Biddu Orchestra
You Don't Stand A Chance If You
Can't Dance (LP)—Jimmy James &
the Vagabonds

Martin BIRCH
Rainbow Rising (LP)—Blackmore's
Rainbow
Come Taste The Band (LP)—Deep Purple
Made In Europe (LP)—Deep Purple

Beeb BIRTLES
Little River Band (LP)—Little River
Band

Christoper BISHOP
The Music Of Victor Herbert (LP)—
Beverly Sills

Stephen BISHOP
Save It For A Rainy Day—
Stephen Bishop

Sonny BIVINS
(see MANHATTANS)

Dave BLACK
(see SPIDERS FROM MARS)

BLACK OAK ARKANSAS
(Tommy Aldridge, Jim Dandy,
Pat Daugherty, 'Little' Jimmy Henderson,
Stanley Knight & Rickie Lee Reynolds)
Balls Of Fire (LP)—Black Oak Arkansas
Live! Mutha (LP)—Black Oak Arkansas

BLACK SABBATH
(Terry 'Geezer' Butler, Tommy Iommi,
Ozzy Osbourne & Bill Ward)
Technical Ecstasy (LP)—Black Sabbath

We Sold Our Soul For Rock 'N' Roll (LP)
—Black Sabbath

Bruce BLACKMAN
I Got To Know—Starbuck
Lucky Man—Starbuck
Moonlight Feels Right—Starbuck
Moonlight Feels Right (LP)—Starbuck

Ritchie BLACKMORE
(see DEEP PURPLE)

Chris BLACKWELL
Short Cut Draw Blood (LP)—
Jim Capaldi
Live (LP)—Bob Marley & the Wailers
Funky Kingston (LP)—Toots & the
Maytals
Reggae Got Soul (LP)—Toots & the
Maytals
That Was Only Yesterday (LP)—
Gary Wright: Spooky Tooth

Stephen Jo BLADD
(see J. GEILS BAND)

BLAZE
(Richy Ceccolini, Crunchy, Kosta,
Tom Mackno, Paul Sanchez &
Sam Wuhrer)
Silver Heels—Blaze

Allan BLAZEK
Fooled Around And Fell In Love—
Elvin Bishop
Spend Some Time—Elvin Bishop
Struttin' My Stuff—Elvin Bishop
Hometown Boy Makes Good (LP)—
Elvin Bishop
Struttin' My Stuff (LP)—Elvin Bishop
Live! Blow Your Face Out (LP)—
J. Geils Band

Ron BLEDSOE
Earl Scruggs Revue Volume II (LP)—
Earl Scruggs Revue

Rick BLEIWEISS
Little Drummer Boy—Moonlion

Lynn BLESSING
Live At Last (LP)—Tim Weisberg

Dave BLOXHAM
Funky Kingston (LP)—Toots & the
Maytals

Patrick BOCENO
Tubular Bells—Champs Boys

Neil BOGART
Dressed To Kill (LP)—Kiss
The Originals (LP)—Kiss

Trevor BOLDER
(see SPIDERS FROM MARS)

Tommy BOLIN
Private Eyes (LP)—Tommy Bolin
Teaser (LP)—Tommy Bolin
(see also DEEP PURPLE)

Christopher BOND
Do What You Want, Be What You Are—
Daryl Hall & John Oates
Sara Smile—Daryl Hall & John Oates
Bigger Than Both Of Us (LP)—Daryl Hall
& John Oates
Daryl Hall & John Oates (LP)—Daryl Hall
& John Oates

Tony BONGIOVI
Experience (LP)—Gloria Gaynor
I've Got You (LP)—Gloria Gaynor
Midnight Lightning (LP)—Gloria Gaynor

Leroy BONNER
(see OHIO PLAYERS)

Perry BOTKIN Jr.
**Nadia's Theme (The Young & The
Restless)**—Barry DeVorzon &
Perry Botkin Jr.
Nadia's Theme (LP)—Barry DeVorzon &
Perry Botkin Jr.

Bruce BOTNICK
Split Coconut (LP)—Dave Mason

Hans BOUWENS
Paloma Blanca—George Baker Selection
Paloma Blanca (LP)—George Baker
Selection

Jeffrey BOWEN
Up The Creek (Without A Paddle)—
Temptations
My Name Is Jermaine (LP)—Jermaine
Jackson
Wings Of Love (LP)—Temptations

Jimmy BOWEN
The Best Of Glen Campbell (LP)—
Glen Campbell

Michael John BOWEN
Live (LP)—Stephen Stills

David BOWIE
Golden Years—David Bowie
TVC 15—David Bowie
Changesonebowie (LP)—David Bowie
**The Rise And Fall Of Ziggy Stardust
(Spiders From Mars) (LP)**—David Bowie
Station To Station (LP)—David Bowie
Young Americans (LP)—David Bowie

Mick BOX
(see URIAH HEEP)

Tommy BOYCE
The Monkees Greatest Hits (LP)—
Monkees

Joe BOYD
Sweet Harmony (LP)—Maria Muldaur
Reggae Got Soul (LP)—Toots & the
Maytals

Roger BOYD
Love Me Tonight—Head East
Get Yourself Up (LP)—Head East

John BOYLAN
More Than A Feeling—Boston
Boston (LP)—Boston
If The Shoe Fits (LP)—Pure Prairie
League
Greatest Hits (LP)—Linda Ronstadt

Charlie BRAGG
One Piece At A Time—Johnny Cash &
the Tenessee Three
One Piece At A Time (LP)—Johnny Cash
& the Tennessee Three

BRAND X
(Philip Collins, John Goodsall,
Percy Jones & Robin Lumley)
Unorthodox Behaviour (LP)—Brand X

Daryl BRAITHWAITE
(see SHERBET)

Tony BRAUNAGEL
(see BACK STREET CRAWLER)

Michael BRECKER
Back To Back (LP)—Brecker Brothers

Randy BRECKER
Back To Back (LP)—Brecker Brothers

BRICK
(Jimmy 'Lord' Brown, Regi Hargis,
Eddie Irons, Don Nevins & Ray Ransom)
Dazz—Brick
Good High (LP)—Brick

David BRIGGS*
Cry Tough (LP)—Nils Lofgren
The Best Of Tom Rush (LP)—Tom Rush
Zuma (LP)—Neil Young with Crazy Horse

Johnny BRISTOL
Do It To My Mind—Johnny Bristol
Bristol's Creme (LP)—Johnny Bristol
Anthology (LP)—Jackson 5ive

Britt BRITTON
Every Beat Of My Heart—Crown Heights Affair
Foxy Lady—Crown Heights Affair
Dreaming A Dream (LP)—Crown Heights Affair

Mick BROCKETT
(see NEKTAR)

David BROMBERG
How Late'll Ya Play 'Til? (LP)—David Bromberg

Gerry BRON
Welcome Home (LP)—Osibisa
The Best Of Uriah Heep (LP)—Uriah Heep

Michael BROVSKY
It's A Good Night For Singin' (LP)—Jerry Jeff Walker

Bill BROWDER
Solitary Man—T.G. Sheppard

George M. BROWN
(see KOOL & THE GANG)

James BROWN
Get Up Offa That Thing—James Brown
Get Up Offa That Thing (LP)—James Brown

Jimmy 'Lord' BROWN
(see BRICK)

Lawrence BROWN
One Love In My Lifetime—Diana Ross
Diana Ross (LP)—Diana Ross

Terry BROWN
2112 (LP)—Rush
All The World's A Stage (LP)—Rush

Jackson BROWNE
Warren Zevon (LP)—Warren Zevon

Denny BRUCE
Leo Kottke 1971-1976 Did You Hear Me? (LP)—Leo Kottke

Robbie BUCHANAN
Words (Are Impossible)—Donny Gerrard

Lindsey BUCKINGHAM
(see FLEETWOOD MAC)

Buddy BUIE
Free Spirit—Atlanta Rhythm Section
Jukin'—Atlanta Rhythm Section
Red Tape (LP)—Atlanta Rhythm Section

Paul BUCKMASTER
Go (LP)—Stomu Yamashta/Steve Winwood/Michael Shrieve

John 'Rabbit' BUNDRICK
(see BACK STREET CRAWLER)

Dewey BUNNELL
(see AMERICA)

Richard BURGESS
(see EASY STREET)

Steve BURGH
How Late'll Ya Play 'Til? (LP)—David Bromberg

Boz BURRELL
(see BAD COMPANY)

Barry 'Byrd' BURTON
Amazing Grace (Used To Be Her Favorite Song)—Amazing Rhythm Aces
The End Is Not In Sight (The Cowboy Tune)—Amazing Rhythm Aces
Too Stuffed To Jump (LP)—Amazing Rhythm Aces

Mike BUTCHER
We Sold Our Soul For Rock 'N' Roll (LP)—Black Sabbath

Larry BUTLER
Love Lifted Me—Kenny Rogers

Terry 'Geezer' BUTLER
(see BLACK SABBATH)

Byron BYRD
Wanna Make Love (Come Flick My BIC)—Sun

Donald BYRD
Happy Music—Blackbyrds
Rock Creek Park—Blackbyrds
City Life (LP)—Blackbyrds
Unfinished Business (LP)—Blackbyrds

David BYRON
(see URIAH HEEP)

Robin CABLE
  Sincerely (LP)—Dwight Twilley Band

John CALE
  Horses (LP)—Patti Smith

Charlie CALELLO
  After The Lovin'—Engelbert Humperdinck
  I Like Dreamin'—Kenny Nolan
  After The Lovin' (LP)—
  Engelbert Humperdinck
  Smile (LP)—Laura Nyro

CAMEL
  (Peter Bardens, Doug Ferguson,
  Andy Latimer & Andy Ward)
  Moon Madness (LP)—Camel

Tony CAMILLO
  The Best Of Gladys Knight & The Pips
  (LP)—Gladys Knight & the Pips

Jon CAMP
  (see RENAISSANCE)

Jim CAPALDI
  Short Cut Draw Blood (LP)—
  Jim Capaldi

The CAPTAIN (aka Daryl Dragon)
  Lonely Night (Angel Face)—Captain &
  Tennille
  Muskrat Love—Captain & Tennille
  Shop Around—Captain & Tennille
  Love Will Keep Us Together (LP)—
  Captain & Tennille
  Song Of Joy (LP)—Captain & Tennille

Greg CARMICHAEL
  Love Bug—Bumble Bee Unlimited

James CARMICHAEL
  Just To Be Close To You—Commodores
  Sweet Love—Commodores
  Hot On The Tracks (LP)—Commodores
  Movin' On (LP)—Commodores
  House Party (LP)—Temptations

Joe Frank CAROLLO
  Everyday Without You—Hamilton, Joe
  Frank & Reynolds
  Winners And Losers—Hamilton, Joe
  Frank & Reynolds
  Fallin' In Love (LP)—Hamilton, Joe
  Frank & Reynolds

Richard CARPENTER
  Goofus—Carpenters
  I Need To Be In Love—Carpenters

There's A Kind Of Hush—Carpenters
A Kind Of Hush (LP)—Carpenters

Victor CARSTARPHEN
  Dance Your Troubles Away (LP)—
  Archie Bell & the Drells
  The Jacksons (LP)—Jacksons
  Summertime (LP)—MFSB
  Message In The Music (LP)—O'Jays

Lou CASABIANCA
  Automatic Man (LP)—Automatic Man

Jack CASADY
  (see HOT TUNA)

Harry Wayne CASEY (aka KC)
  Honey I—George McCrae
  I Like To Do It—KC & the Sunshine Band
  (Shake Shake Shake) Shake Your Booty
  —KC & the Sunshine Band
  That's The Way I Like It—KC & the
  Sunshine Band
  KC & The Sunshine Band (LP)—KC & the
  Sunshine Band
  Part 3 (LP)—KC & the Sunshine Band

Terry CASHMAN
  Baby, Baby I Love You—Terry Cashman
  Chain Gang Medley—Jim Croce
  Shannon—Henry Gross
  Someday—Henry Gross
  Springtime Mama—Henry Gross
  The Faces I've Been (LP)—Jim Croce
  Photographs & Memories: His Greatest
  Hits (LP)—Jim Croce
  Release (LP)—Henry Gross

Emilio CASTILLO
  You Ought To Be Havin' Fun—
  Tower Of Power
  Ain't Nothin' Stoppin' Us Now (LP)—
  Tower Of Power
  Live And In Living Color (LP)—
  Tower Of Power
  (see also TOWER OF POWER)

Leonard CASTON
  Happy—Eddie Kendricks

Jimmy CASTOR
  E-Man Groovin' (LP)—Jimmy Castor
  Bunch Featuring The Everything Man

Tom CATALANO
The Call—Anne Murray
Things—Anne Murray
And The Singer Sings His Song (LP)—
Neil Diamond
Keeping In Touch (LP)—Anne Murray
Together (LP)—Anne Murray
Helen Reddy's Greatest Hits (LP)—
Helen Reddy
Jonathan Livingston Seagull (LP)—
Soundtrack

Claude 'Coffee' CAVE
(see MANDRILL)

Morgan CAVETT
The Way I Want To Touch You—Captain
& Tennille
Love Will Keep Us Together (LP)—
Captain & Tennille

Malcolm CECIL
Beast From The East (LP)—Mandrill

Richy CECCOLINI
(see BLAZE)

David CHACKLER
**Did You Boogie With Your Baby (In The
Back Row Of The Movie Show)**—Flash
Cadillac & the Continental Kids

Roland CHAMBERS
Philadelphia Freedom (LP)—MFSB

Ron CHANCEY
Easy As Pie—Billy 'Crash' Craddock

Stephen CHAPIN
Greatest Stories Live (LP)—Harry Chapin
On The Road To Kingdom Come (LP)—
Harry Chapin

Blondie CHAPLIN
(see BEACH BOYS)

Michael/Mike CHAPMAN
Can The Can—Suzi Quatro
Living Next Door To Alice—Smokie
Action—Sweet
Fox On The Run—Sweet
Desolation Boulevard (LP)—Sweet

Craig CHAQUICO
(see JEFFERSON STARSHIP)

Manny CHARLTON
Love Hurts—Nazareth
Close Enough For Rock 'N' Roll (LP)—
Nazareth

Hair Of The Dog (LP)—Nazareth
Play 'N' The Game (LP)—Nazareth

Marshall CHESS
Fleetwood Mac In Chicago (LP)—
Fleetwood Mac

Nicky CHINN
Can The Can—Suzi Quatro
Living Next Door To Alice—Smokie
Action—Sweet
Fox On The Run—Sweet
Desolation Boulevard (LP)—Sweet

Hank CICALO
Uptown & Country—Tom Scott
New York Connection (LP)—Tom Scott

John CIPOLLINA
(see QUICKSILVER MESSENGER
SERVICE)

Mike CLARK
I Got To Know—Starbuck
Lucky Man—Starbuck
Moonlight Feels Right—Starbuck
Moonlight Feels Right (LP)—Starbuck

Stanley CLARKE
Journey To Love (LP)—Stanley Clarke
School Days (LP)—Stanely Clarke

Tony CLARKE
Blue Guitar—Justin Hayward &
John Lodge

Doug CLIFFORD
(see Don HARRISON BAND)

CLIMAX BLUES BAND
(Colin Cooper, Peter Haycock, Derek Holt,
Richard Jones & John Kuffley)
Gold Plated (LP)—Climax Blues Band

George CLINTON
**(Give Up The Funk) Tear The Roof Off
The Sucker**—Parliament
**Stretchin' Out In Bootsy's Rubber
Band (LP)**—William 'Bootsy' Collins
Hardcore Jollies (LP)—Funkadelic
Tales Of Kidd Funkadelic (LP)—
Funkadelic
The Clones Of Dr. Funkenstein (LP)—
Parliament
Mothership Connection (LP)—Parliament

Billy COBHAM
Life & Times (LP)—Billy Cobham
'Live' On Tour In Europe (LP)—Billy
Cobham/George Duke Band

Bud COCKRELL
(see PABLO CRUISE)

Dennis COFFEY
Daydreamer—C.C. & Company
Finger Lickin' Good (LP)—C.C. &
Company

Tommy COGBILL
And The Singer Sings His Song (LP)—
Neil Diamond

John COGHLAN
(see STATUS QUO)

Ray COLCORD
Get Your Wings (LP)—Aerosmith

Greg COLLIER
(see SILVER)

Phil/Philip COLLINS
(see BRAND X: GENESIS)

William/'Bootsy' COLLINS
Stretchin' Out In Bootsy's Rubber Band
(LP)—William 'Bootsy' Collins

COMMODORES
(William King, Ronald LaPraed,
Tom McClary, Walter Orange,
Lionel Richie & Milan Williams)
Just To Be Close To You—Commodores
Sweet Love—Commodores
Hot On The Tracks (LP)—Commodores
Movin' On (LP)—Commodores

Brian CONNOLLY
(see SWEET)

Norman CONNORS
Norman Connors Presents Aquarian
Dream (LP)—Norman Connors Presents
Aquarian Dream

Bruce CONTE
(see TOWER OF POWER)

Within THE CONTEMPO FAMILY
Armada Orchestra (LP)—Armada
Orchestra

Ry COODER
Chicken Skin Music (LP)—Ry Cooder

Stu COOK
(see Don HARRISON BAND)

Colin COOPER
(see CLIMAX BLUES BAND)

Denny CORDELL
Back To The Island—Leon Russell
Best Of Leon (LP)—Leon Russell
Will O' The Wisp (LP)—Leon Russell

Ritchie CORDELL
Let's Rock—Ellison Chase

Chick COREA
The Leprechaun (LP)—Chick Corea
Romantic Warrior (LP)—Return To
Forever

Don CORNELIUS
Soul Train '75'—Soul Train Gang

Richard CORNWELL
(see FATBACK BAND)

The CORPORATION
Anthology (LP)—Jackson 5ive

Don COSTA
The Osmonds Christmas Album (LP)—
Osmonds
Diana Ross (LP)—Diana Ross

Paul COTTON
(see POCO)

Tom/Tommy COUCH
Funny How Time Slips Away—
Dorothy Moore
Misty Blue—Dorothy Moore
Misty Blue (LP)—Dorothy Moore

Phil COULTER
Saturday Night—Bay City Rollers
Bay City Rollers (LP)—Bay City Rollers

David COURTNEY
David Courtney's First Day (LP)—
David Courtney

David COVERDALE
(see DEEP PURPLE)

Larry COX
Play On Love—Jefferson Starship
St. Charles—Jefferson Starship
With Your Love—Jefferson Starship
Dragon Fly (LP)—Jefferson Starship
Red Octopus (LP)—Jefferson Starship
Spitfire (LP)—Jefferson Starship

Dave/David CRAWFORD
  Bad Luck—Atlanta Disco Band
  Mighty High—Mighty Clouds Of Joy
  Young Hearts Run Free—Candi Staton
  Bad Luck (LP)—Atlanta Disco Band
  Kickin' (LP)—Mighty Clouds Of Joy
  Young Hearts Run Free (LP)—
  Candi Staton

Papa John CREACH
  (see JEFFERSON STARSHIP)

Lol CREME
  (see 10cc)

Jim CRETECOS
  Greetings From Asbury Park, N.J. (LP)—
  Bruce Springsteen
  The Wild, The Innocent & The E-Street
  Shuffle (LP)—Bruce Springsteen

Bob CREWE
  Sweet Talk—B.C. Generation
  Hollywood Hot—Eleventh Hour
  The Four Seasons Story (LP)—
  Four Seasons
  Gold (LP)—Frankie Valli

Peter CRISS
  (see KISS)

Steve CROPPER
  Can't Change My Heart—Cate Bros
  Union Man—Cate Bros
  Cate Bros (LP)—Cate Bros
  In One Eye And Out The Other (LP)—
  Cate Bros
  House Party (LP)—Temptations

David CROSBY
  Out Of The Darkness—David Crosby/
  Graham Nash
  Whistling Down The Wire (LP)—
  David Crosby/Graham Nash
  Wind On The Water (LP)—David Crosby/
  Graham Nash

CRUNCHY
  (see BLAZE)

Jerry CRUTCHFIELD
  Here's Some Love—Tanya Tucker

Bob CULLEN
  Anything You Want—John Valenti

Mike CURB
  Volare—Al Martino
  C'mon Marianne—Donny Osmond

  Ain't Nothing Like The Real Thing—
  Donny & Marie Osmond
  Deep Purple—Donny & Marie Osmond
  I Can't Live A Dream—Osmonds
  Disco Train (LP)—Donny Osmond
  Donny & Marie Featuring Songs From
  Their Television Show (LP)—Donny &
  Marie Osmond
  New Season (LP)—Donny & Marie
  Osmond
  Brainstorm (LP)—Osmonds

Bill CURTIS
  (see FATBACK BAND)

King CURTIS
  Confessin' The Blues (LP)—
  Esther Phillips

John CURULEWSKI
  (see STYX)

Tony D'AMATO
  Threads Of Glory—200 Years Of
  America In Words And Music (LP)—
  Various

John D'ANDREA
  Don't Fight The Hands (That Need You)—
  Hamilton, Joe Frank & Dennison
  Light Up The World With Sunshine—
  Hamilton, Joe Frank & Dennison
  Will You Love Me Tomorrow—
  Dana Valery

Jim DANDY
  (see BLACK OAK ARKANSAS)

Rick DANKO
  (see BAND)

Ron DANTE
  Street Singin'—Lady Flash
  I Write The Songs—Barry Manilow
  This One's For You—Barry Manilow
  Tryin' To Get The Feeling Again—
  Barry Manilow
  I (LP)—Barry Manilow
  II (LP)—Barry Manilow
  This One's For You (LP)—Barry Manilow
  Tryin' To Get The Feelin' (LP)—
  Barry Manilow

Russell DA SHIELL
  (see Don HARRISON BAND)

Pat DAUGHERTY
  (see BLACK OAK ARKANSAS)

Cliff DAVIES
Dog Eat Dog—Ted Nugent
Free For All (LP)—Ted Nugent

Raymond Douglas DAVIES
The Kinks' Greatest—Celluloid
Heroes (LP)—Kinks
The Kinks Present Schoolboys In
Disgrace (LP)—Kinks

Rhett DAVIES
Moon Madness (LP)—Camel

Richard DAVIES
(see SUPERTRAMP)

Carl DAVIS
Feelings—Walter Jackson
Feeling Good (LP)—Walter Jackson

Chip DAVIS
Convoy—C.W. McCall
There Won't Be No Country Music (There
Won't Be No Rock 'n' Roll)—C.W. McCall
Black Bear Road (LP)—C.W. McCall
Wilderness (LP)—C.W. McCall

Chuck DAVIS
Love Ballad—L.T.D.
Love To The World (LP)—L.T.D.

Clive DAVIS
Wham Bam (Shang-A-Lang)—Silver
Silver (LP)—Silver

Don DAVIS
One Piece At A Time—Johnny Cash & the
Tennessee Three
One Piece At A Time (LP)—Johnny Cash
& the Tennessee Three

Don DAVIS
I Hope We Get To Love In Time—
Marilyn McCoo & Billy Davis Jr.
You Don't Have To Be A Star (To Be In
My Show)—Marilyn McCoo &
Billy Davis Jr.
Disco Lady—Johnnie Taylor
Somebody's Gettin' It—Johnnie Taylor
We Can't Hide It Anymore—Larry Santos
Drama V (LP)—Ron Banks & the
Dramatics
Joy Ride (LP)—Dramatics
I Hope We Get To Love In Time (LP)—
Marilyn McCoo & Billy Davis Jr.
Eargasm (LP)—Johnnie Taylor

Hal DAVIS
Don't Leave Me This Way—
Thelma Houston
Love Hangover—Diana Ross
Any Way You Like It (LP)—
Thelma Houston
My Name Is Jermaine (LP)—
Jermaine Jackson
Anthology (LP)—Jackson 5ive
Diana Ross (LP)—Diana Ross
Diana Ross' Greatest Hits (LP)—
Diana Ross
I've Got A Feeling (LP)—Al Wilson

John DAVIS
When Love Is New—Arthur Prysock

John DAVIS
Whenever I'm Away From You—
John Travolta

Link DAVIS Jr.
(see ASLEEP AT THE WHEEL)

Martin DAVIS
Love, Life & Feelings (LP)—Shirley Bassey

Paul DAVIS
Superstar—Paul Davis
Thinking Of You—Paul Davis

Tim DAVIS
(see Steve MILLER BAND)

Roy DEA
9,999,999 Tears—Dickey Lee

John DEACON
(see QUEEN)

Bert DeCOTEAUX
Truckload Of Lovin' (LP)—Albert King
The Manhattans (LP)—Manhattans

DEEP PURPLE
(Tommy Bolin, David Coverdale,
Glenn Hughes, Jon Lord & Ian Paice)
Come Taste The Band (LP)—Deep Purple
(Ritchie Blackmore, David Coverdale,
Glenn Hughes, Jon Lord & Ian Paice)
Made In Europe (LP)—Deep Purple

Al DeLORY
The Best Of Glen Campbell (LP)—
Glen Campbell

Alan DENNISON
Everyday Without You—Hamilton, Joe
Frank & Reynolds
Winners And Losers—Hamilton, Joe
Frank & Reynolds
Fallin' In Love (LP)—Hamilton, Joe Frank
& Reynolds

Bill DENNY
Teddy Bear's Last Ride—Diana Williams

Eumir DEODATO
Peter Gunn—Deodato
Very Together (LP)—Deodato

Antonio Carlos DE OLIVEIRA
Morris Albert (LP)—Morris Albert

Rick DERRINGER
Let Me In—Derringer
Derringer (LP)—Derringer

Don DeVITO
Hurricane—Bob Dylan
Mozambique—Bob Dylan
Desire (LP)—Bob Dylan
Hard Rain (LP)—Bob Dylan

Barry DeVORZON
**Nadia's Theme (The Young & The
Restless)**—Barry DeVorzon &
Perry Botkin Jr.
Nadia's Theme (LP)—Barry DeVorzon
Nadia's Theme (LP)—Barry DeVorzon &
Perry Botkin Jr

Dennis DeYOUNG
(see STYX)

Jeff DEXTER
History—America's Greatest Hits (LP)—
America

Godfrey DIAMOND
Coney Island Baby (LP)—Lou Reed

Gregg DIAMOND
More, More, More—Andrea True
Connection
Party Line—Andrea True Connection
More, More, More (LP)—Andrea True
Connection

Joel DIAMOND
After The Lovin'—Engelbert Humperdinck
After The Lovin' (LP)—
Engelbert Humperdinck

Neil DIAMOND
And The Singer Sings His Song (LP)—
Neil Diamond

Denny DIANTE
Anytime (I'll Be There)—Paul Anka
Happier—Paul Anka
The Painter (LP)—Paul Anka
Times Of Your Life (LP)—Paul Anka

Jim DICKSON
Sleepless Nights (LP)—Gram Parsons/
Flying Burrito Brothers

Al DiMEOLA
Land Of The Midnight Sun (LP)—
Al DiMeola

Micky DOLENZ
(see MONKEES)

Floyd DOMINO
(see ASLEEP AT WHEEL)

Joel DORN
On The Track (LP)—Leon Redbone

Alan DOUGLAS
Midnight Lightning (LP)—Jimi Hendrix

Chip DOUGLAS (aka Douglas 'Farthing'
Hatelid)
The Monkees Greatest Hits (LP)—
Monkees

Jack DOUGLAS
Home Tonight—Aerosmith
Last Child—Aerosmith
Walk This Way—Aerosmith
(She's Just A) Fallen Angel—Starz
Get Your Wings (LP)—Aerosmith
Rocks (LP)—Aerosmith
Toys In The Attic (LP)—Aerosmith
Jump On It (LP)—Montrose
Radio Ethiopia (LP)—Patti Smith Group
Starz (LP)—Starz

Tom DOWD
Double Trouble—Lynyrd Skynyrd
Free Bird—Lynyrd Skynyrd
This Old Heart Of Mine—Rod Stewart
Tonight's The Night—Rod Stewart
The Road Goes On Forever (LP)—
Allman Brothers Band
Ten Years Of Gold (LP)—Aretha Franklin
Gimme Back My Bullets (LP)—
Lynyrd Skynyrd
One More From The Road (LP)—
Lynyrd Skynyrd
A Night On The Town (LP)—Rod Stewart
Atlantic Crossing (LP)—Rod Stewart
Live (LP)—Stephen Stills
Locked In (LP)—Wishbone Ash

Tyrone DOWNIE
(see Bob MARLEY & THE WAILERS)

Lamont DOZIER
Marvin Gaye's Greatest Hits (LP)—
Marvin Gaye

Daryl DRAGON
(see The CAPTAIN)

Pete DRAKE
Blast From Your Past (LP)—Ringo Starr

Skip DRINKWATER
Valentine Love—Norman Connors
You Are My Starship—Norman Connors
You Are My Starship (LP)—
Norman Connors

Gus DUDGEON
**Grow Some Funk Of Your Own/I Feel
Like A Bullet (In The Gun Of
Robert Ford)**—Elton John
Island Girl—Elton John
Sorry Seems To Be The Hardest Word—
Elton John
Don't Go Breaking My Heart—Elton John
& Kiki Dee
Changesonebowie (LP)—David Bowie
Blue Moves (LP)—Elton John
**Captain Fantastic & The Brown Dirt
Cowboy (LP)**—Elton John
Greatest Hits (LP)—Elton John
Here And There (LP)—Elton John
Rock Of The Westies (LP)—Elton John

George DUKE
I Heard The Blues She Heard My Cry (LP)
—George Duke
Liberated Fantasy (LP)—George Duke

'Live' On Tour (LP)—Billy Cobham/
George Duke Band

Aynsley DUNBAR
(see JOURNEY)

Gary DUNCAN
(see QUICKSILVER MESSENGER SERVICE)

Johnny DUNCAN
Dazz—Brick
Good High (LP)—Brick

Michael DUNFORD
(see RENAISSANCE)

Des DYER
Sky High (LP)—Jigsaw

Bob DYLAN
Hard Rain (LP)—Bob Dylan

Mallory EARL
Yellow Fever (LP)—Hot Tuna

Charles EARLAND
Odyssey (LP)—Charles Earland

EARTHBAND
(see Manfred MANN'S EARTHBAND)

EASY STREET
(Richard Brugess, Peter Marsh &
Ken Nicol)
I've Been Lovin' You—Easy Street

Dave EDMUNDS
Shake Some Action (LP)—
Flaming Groovies

Dennis EDWARDS
(see TEMPTATIONS)

Esmond EDWARDS
Hard Work—John Handy
Hard Work (LP)—John Handy
Mysteries (LP)—Keith Jarrett
Together Again...Live (LP)—Bobby Bland
& B.B. King

Manfred EICHER
Arbour Zena (LP)—Keith Jarrett
In The Light (LP)—Keith Jarrett

Bobby ELI
Laid Back Love—Major Harris
Happy Man—Impact
Mystic Dragons (LP)—Blue Magic
Jealousy (LP)—Major Harris
After The Lovin' (LP)—Engelbert
Humperdinck

Jay ELLIS
  Experience (LP)—Gloria Gaynor
  I've Got You (LP)—Gloria Gaynor

Terry ELLIS
  Locomotive Breath—Jethro Tull
  M.U. The Best Of Jethro Tull (LP)—
  Jethro Tull

Greg ELMORE
  (see QUICKSILVER MESSENGER SERVICE)

Geoff EMERICK
  Caledonia—Robin Trower
  Love Of My Life—Gino Vannelli
  Long Misty Days (LP)—Robin Trower
  The Gist Of Gemini (LP)—Gino Vannelli

Gregg ERRICO
  BLT—Lee Oskar
  Lee Oskar (LP)—Lee Oskar

Ahmet ERTEGUN
  Where Did Our Love Go—J. Geils Band
  Manhattan Transfer (LP)—Manhattan
  Transfer

Nesuhi ERTEGUN
  Confessin' The Blues (LP)—Esther Phillips

Richard EVANS
  Sophisticated Lady (She's A Different
  Lady)—Natalie Cole
  Natalie (LP)—Natalie Cole

Bob EZRIN
  I Never Cry—Alice Cooper
  Beth/Detroit Rock City—Kiss
  Flaming Youth—Kiss
  Shout It Out Loud—Kiss
  Alice Cooper Goes To Hell (LP)—
  Alice Cooper
  Destroyer (LP)—Kiss

Jack FAITH
  The Zip—MFSB
  Philadelphia Freedom (LP)—MFSB
  All Things In Time (LP)—Lou Rawls

John FARRAR
  Come On Over—Olivia Newton-John
  Don't Stop Believin'—
  Olivia Newton-John
  Every Face Tells A Story—
  Olivia Newton-John
  Let It Shine/He Ain't Heavy—He's My
  Brother—Olivia Newton-John
  Clearly Love (LP)—Olivia Newton-John
  Come On Over (LP)—Olivia Newton-John

Don't Stop Believin' (LP)—Olivia
Newton-John

Ricky FATAAR
  (see BEACH BOYS)

FATBACK BAND
  (Richard Cornwell, Bill Curtis,
  Johnny Flippin, Johnny King, Earl Shelton
  & George Williams)
  Night Fever (LP)—Fatback Band
  Raising Hell (LP)—Fatback Band

Victor FELDMAN
  (see L.A. EXPRESS)

Janna Merlyn FELICIANO
  Making Our Dreams Come True (Theme
  From 'Laverne & Shirley')—Cyndi Greco

Doug FERGUSON
  (see CAMEL)

Bryan FERRY
  Let's Stick Together (LP)—Bryan Ferry

Richard FINCH
  Honey I—George McCrae
  I Like To Do It—KC & the Sunshine Band
  Queen Of Clubs—KC & the Sunshine
  Band
  (Shake Shake Shake) Shake Your Booty
  —KC & the Sunshine Band
  That's The Way I Like It—KC & the
  Sunshine Band
  KC & The Sunshine Band (LP)—KC & the
  Sunshine Band
  Part 3 (LP)—KC & the Sunshine Band

Ben FINDON
  Love Really Hurts Without You—
  Billy Ocean

Andre FISCHER
  (see RUFUS FEATURING CHAKA KHAN)

Mick FLEETWOOD
  (see FLEETWOOD MAC)

FLEETWOOD MAC
  (Lindsey Buckingham, Mick Fleetwood,
  Christine McVie, John McVie &
  Stevie Nicks)
  Over My Head—Fleetwood Mac
  Rhiannon (Will You Ever Win)—
  Fleetwood Mac
  Say You Love Me—Fleetwood Mac
  Fleetwood Mac (LP)—Fleetwood Mac

Beau Ray FLEMING
Wanna Make Love (Come Flick My BIC)
—Sun

Dave FLETT
(see Manfred MANN'S EARTHBAND)

Mike FLICKER
Crazy On You—Heart
Dreamboat Annie—Heart
Magic Man—Heart
Dreamboat Annie (LP)—Heart

Johnny FLIPPIN
(see FATBACK BAND)

Dan FOGELBERG
Captured Angel (LP)—Dan Fogelberg

John C. FOGERTY
I Heard It Through The Grapevine—
Creedence Clearwater Revival
You Got The Magic—John Fogerty
Chronicle (LP)—Creedence Clearwater
Revival

Robben FORD
(see L.A. EXPRESS)

David FOSTER
Sherry—Keane Brothers
(see also ATTITUDES)

Kim FOWLEY
The Runaways (LP)—Runaways

Charles FOX
**Making Our Dreams Come True (Theme
from 'Laverne & Shirley')**—Cyndi Greco

Redd FOXX
You Gotta Wash Your Ass (LP)—
Redd Foxx

Rob FRABONI
Hello Old Friend—Eric Clapton
No Reason To Cry (LP)—Eric Clapton
Stingray (LP)—Joe Cocker

Peter FRAMPTON
Baby I Love Your Way—Peter Frampton
Do You Feel Like We Do—Peter Frampton
Show Me The Way—Peter Frampton
Frampton (LP)—Peter Frampton
Frampton Comes Alive! (LP)—
Peter Frampton

Ron FRANGIPANE
Our Pleasure To Serve You (LP)—
Stanky Brown Group

Aretha FRANKLIN
Ten Years Of Gold (LP)—Aretha Franklin
You (LP)—Aretha Franklin

Melvin FRANKLIN
(see TEMPTATIONS)

Colin FRECHTER
Rock And Roll Love Letter—Bay City
Rollers
Dedication (LP)—Bay City Rollers
Rock 'N' Roll Love Letter (LP)—
Bay City Rollers

Ed FREEMAN
The Best Of Tom Rush (LP)—Tom Rush

'Taff' FREEMAN
(see NEKTAR)

Ace FREHLEY
(see KISS)

David FREIBERG
(see JEFFERSON STARSHIP)

Glenn FREY
Rain, Oh Rain—Fools Gold
Fools Gold (LP)—Fools Gold

Jorgen FRITZ
Old Loves Die Hard (LP)—Triumvirat

Dominic FRONTIERE
**The Original Motion Picture Soundtrack
Performed By Gladys Knight & The Pips/
Gladys Knight in 'Pipe Dreams' (LP)**—
Gladys Knight & the Pips

Lew FUTTERMAN
Dog Eat Dog—Ted Nugent
Hey Baby—Ted Nugent
Free For All (LP)—Ted Nugent
Ted Nugent (LP)—Ted Nugent

Ethel GABRIEL
A Legendary Performer (LP)—Henry
Mancini

Andre GAGNON
Wow—Andre Gagnon

Rory GALLAGHER
Against The Grain (LP)—Rory Gallagher

Kenny GAMBLE
Enjoy Yourself—Jacksons
**Tell The World How I Feel About
'Cha Baby**—Harold Melvin & the
Blue Notes

Wake Up Everybody—Harold Melvin &
the Blue Notes
The Zip—MFSB
I Love Music—O'Jays
Livin' For The Weekend—O'Jays
Message In Our Music—O'Jays
Let's Make A Baby—Billy Paul
Nursery Rhymes—People's Choice
Groovy People—Lou Rawls
**You'll Never Find Another Love Like
Mine**—Lou Rawls
Dance Your Troubles Away (LP)—
Archie Bell & the Drells
The Jacksons (LP)—Jacksons
**All Their Greatest Hits! Collectors' Item
(LP)**—Harold Melvin & the Blue Notes
Wake Up Everybody (LP)—Harold Melvin
& the Blue Notes
Philadelphia Freedom (LP)—MFSB
Summertime (LP)—MFSB
Family Reunion (LP)—O'Jays
Message In The Music (LP)—O'Jays
When Love Is New (LP)—Billy Paul
We Got The Rhythm (LP)—People's
Choice
All Things In Time (LP)—Lou Rawls

Don GANT
  Havana Daydreamin' (LP)—Don Gant

Val GARAY
  Lifeline (LP)—Pablo Cruise

Jerry GARCIA
  (see GRATEFUL DEAD)

Stu GARDNER
  Yes, Yes, Yes—Bill Cosby
  **Bill Cosby Is Not Himself These Days
  Rat Own, Rat Own, Rat Own (LP)**—
  Bill Cosby

Art/Arthur GARFUNKEL
  My Little Town—Simon & Garfunkel
  Breakaway (LP)—Art Garfunkel
  Still Crazy After All These Years (LP)—
  Paul Simon
  Simon & Garfunkel's Greatest Hits (LP)—
  Simon & Garfunkel

David GARIBALDI
  (see TOWER OF POWER)

Tony GARNIER
  (see ASLEEP AT THE WHEEL)

David GATES
  Lost Without Your Love—Bread

Bob GAUDIO
  December, 1963 (Oh, What A Night)—
  Four Seasons
  Silver Star—Four Seasons
  Who Loves You—Four Seasons
  Fallen Angel—Frankie Valli
  We're All Alone—Frankie Valli
  Who Loves You (LP)—Four Seasons
  Our Day Will Come (LP)—Frankie Valli

Marvin GAYE
  Marvin Gaye's Greatest Hits (LP)—
  Marvin Gaye

Don GEHMAN
  Illegal Stills (LP)—Stephen Stills
  Live (LP)—Stephen Stills
  Long May You Run (LP)—Stills/Young
  Band

J. GEILS
  (see J. GEILS BAND)

J. GEILS BAND
  (Stephen Jo Bladd, J. Geils, Seth Justman,
  Danny Klein, Magic Dick & Peter Wolf)
  Live! Blow Your Face Out (LP)—
  J. Geils Band

GENESIS
  (Tony Banks, Phil Collins, Steve Hackett
  & Mike Rutherford)
  A Trick Of The Tail (LP)—Genesis
  (see also—Philip COLLINS: Steve
  HACKETT)

GENTLE GIANT
  (Gary Green, Kerry Minnear,
  Derek Shulman, Ray Shulman &
  John Weathers)
  Interview (LP)—Gentle Giant

Lowell GEORGE
  The Last Record Album (LP)—Little Feat

Phil GERNHARD
  Hell Cat—Bellamy Brothers
  Let Your Love Flow—Bellamy Brothers
  Satin Sheet—Bellamy Brothers
  Jasper—Jim Stafford
  **Bellamy Brothers Featuring 'Let Your
  Love Flow' (LP)**—Bellamy Brothers

Rinus GERRITSEN
  (see GOLDEN EARRING)

Barry GIBB
Maurice GIBB
Robin GIBB
(see BEE GEES)

Steve GIBSON
You've Got Me Runnin'—Gene Cotton

Mic GILLETTE
(see TOWER OF POWER)

Jack GILMER
Solitary Man—T.G. Sheppard

David GILMOUR
(see PINK FLOYD)

Larry GITTENS
(see KOOL & THE GANG)

Tompall GLASER
The Outlaws (LP)—Waylon Jennings,
Willie Nelson, Jessi Colter &
Tompall Glaser

Pat GLEESON
Coke (LP)—Coke Escovedo
Comin' At Ya' (LP)—Coke Escovedo

Gwen GLENN
My Name Is Jermaine (LP)—
Jermaine Jackson

The GLIMMER TWINS
(aka Mick Jagger/Keith Richard)
Fool To Cry—Rolling Stones
Hot Stuff—Rolling Stones
Black And Blue (LP)—Rolling Stones

Jeff GLIXMAN
Carry On Wayward Son—Kansas
Leftoverture (LP)—Kansas
Masque (LP)—Kansas

Roger GLOVER
Calling Card (LP)—Rory Gallagher
**The Butterfly Ball & The Grasshopper's
Feast (LP)**—Roger Glover & Guests

Graham GOBLE
It's A Long Way There—Little River Band
Little River Band (LP)—Little River Band

Donna GODCHAUX
Keith GODCHAUX
(see GRATEFUL DEAD)

Kevin GODLEY
(see 10cc)

Jack GOLD
Feelings (LP)—Johnny Mathis
I Only Have Eyes For You (LP)—
Johnny Mathis

Ken GOLD
You To Me Are Everything—Real Thing

GOLDEN EARRING
(Rinus Gerritsen, Barry Hay,
George Kooymans, Robert Jan Stips &
Cesar Zuiderwijk)
To The Hilt (LP)—Golden Earring

Stephan GOLDMAN
Barefoot Ballet (LP)—John Klemmer
Tough (LP)—John Klemmer

Jerry GOLDSTEIN
BLT—Lee Oskar
Summer—War
Lee Oskar (LP)—Lee Oskar
Greatest Hits (LP)—War
Why Can't We Be Friends? (LP)—War
Love Is All Around (LP)—War featuring
Eric Burdon

Cuba GOODING
Shame On The World (LP)—
Main Ingredient

Dickie GOODMAN
Mr. Jaws And Other Fables (LP)—
Dickie Goodman

Steve GOODMAN
Words We Can Dance To (LP)—
Steve Goodman

John GOODSALL
(see BRAND X)

Kelly GORDON
Ode To Billy Joe—Bobbie Gentry
The Best Of Glen Campbell (LP)—
Glen Campbell

Marc GORDON
Love Hangover—5th Dimension
**I've Got A Feeling (We'll Be Seeing
Each Other Again)**—Al Wilson
I've Got A Feeling (LP)—Al Wilson

Berry GORDY (Jr.)
Diana Ross (LP)—Diana Ross
Wings Of Love (LP)—Temptations

Graham GOULDMAN
(see 10cc)

Larry GRAHAM
The Jam—Graham Central Station
Ain't No 'Bout-A-Doubt It (LP)—
Graham Central Station
Mirror (LP)—Graham Central Station

Leo GRAHAM
Give It Up (Turn It Loose)—Tyrone Davis
Love And Touch (LP)—Tyrone Davis

George GRANTHAM
(see POCO)

Norman GRANZ
Porgy & Bess (LP)—Ray Charles &
Cleo Laine

GRATEFUL DEAD
(Jerry Garcia, Donna Godchaux,
Keith Godchaux, Mickey Hart,
Bill Kreutzmann, Phil Lesh & Bob Weir)
Steal Your Face (LP)—Grateful Dead

Dobie GRAY
If Love Must Go—Dobie Gray

Al GREEN
Full Of Fire—Al Green
Keep Me Cryin'—Al Green
Full Of Fire (LP)—Al Green
Al Green Is Love (LP)—Al Green
Have A Good Time (LP)—Al Green

Gary GREEN
(see GENTLE GIANT)

Roger GREENAWAY
Jeans On—David Dundas

Marlin GREENE
Boz Scaggs (LP)—Bob Scaggs

Dick GRIFFEY
Soul Train '75'—Soul Train Gang

Dave GRUSIN
Earl Klugh (LP)—Earl Klugh
Living Inside Your Love (LP)—Earl Klugh

James William GUERCIO
Another Rainy Day In New York City—
Chicago
If You Leave Me Now—Chicago
Chicago IX—Greatest Hits (LP)—Chicago
Chicago X (LP)—Chicago

Jeff GUERCIO
Flowing Free Forever (LP)—
Michael Murphey

John GUERIN
I'm Easy (LP)—Keith Carradine
(see also L.A. EXPRESS)

Steve HACKETT
Voyage Of The Acolyte (LP)—
Steve Hackett
(see also GENESIS)

Ron HAFFKINE
If Not You—Dr. Hook
A Little Bit More—Dr. Hook
Only Sixteen—Dr. Hook
(One More Year Of) Daddy's Little Girl—
Ray Sawyer
Bankrupt (LP)—Dr. Hook
A Little Bit More (LP)—Dr. Hook

Roy HALEE
To The Heart (LP)—Mark Almond
Simon & Garfunkel's Greatest Hits (LP)—
Simon & Garfunkel

Daryl HALL
Sara Smile—Daryl Hall & John Oates
Daryl Hall & John Oates (LP)—
Daryl Hall & John Oates

Rick HALL
Forever Lovers—Mac Davis
Tell It Like It Is—Andy Williams
Times Of Your Life (LP)—Paul Anka
Forever Lovers (LP)—Mac Davis

Bill HALVERSON
Michel Polnareff (LP)—Michel Polnareff
Live (LP)—Stephen Stills

Bill HAM
It's Only Love—Z Z Top
Point Blank (LP)—Point Blank
Fandango (LP)—Z Z Top

Dan HAMILTON
Everyday Without You—Hamilton, Joe
Frank & Reynolds
Winners And Losers—Hamilton, Joe
Frank & Reynolds
Fallin' In Love (LP)—Hamilton, Joe
Frank & Reynolds

Tom HAMILTON
(see AEROSMITH)

Barry HAMMOND
Breakfast Special (LP)—Pete Wingfield

Herbie HANCOCK
Man-Child (LP)—Herbie Hancock
Secrets (LP)—Herbie Hancock

Hagood HARDY
    The Homecoming (LP)—Hagood Hardy

Regi HARGIS
    (see BRICK)

Steve HARLEY
    Make Me Smile (Come Up And See Me)
    —Steve Harley & Cockney Rebel

Mark HARMAN
    Rose Of Cimarron—Poco
    Live (LP)—Poco
    Rose Of Cimarron (LP)—Poco

Major HARRIS
    Jealousy—Major Harris
    Jealousy (LP)—Major Harris

Norman HARRIS
    Ten Percent—Double Exposure
    He's A Friend—Eddie Kendricks
    Hold Back The Night—Trammps
    That's Where The Happy People Go—
    Trammps
    One For The Money—Whispers
    We're On The Right Track—South Shore
    Commission
    Ten Percent (LP)—Double Exposure
    Jealousy (LP)—Major Harris
    Goin' Up In Smoke (LP)—Eddie Kendricks
    He's A Friend (LP)—Eddie Kendricks
    Where The Happy People Go (LP)—
    Trammps
    One For The Money (LP)—Whispers

Don HARRISON
    (see Don HARRISON BAND)

Don HARRISON BAND
    (Doug Clifford, Stu Cook,
    Russell Da Shiell & Don Harrison)
    Sixteen Tons—Don Harrison Band
    The Don Harrison Band (LP)—
    Don Harrison Band

George HARRISON
    This Song—George Harrison
    The Best Of George Harrison (LP)—
    George Harrison
    Thirty Three & ⅓ (LP)—George Harrison
    Blast From Your Past (LP)—Ringo Starr

Bobby HART
    The Monkees Greatest Hits (LP)—
    Monkees

Bruce HART
    Free To Be...You And Me (LP)—
    Marlo Thomas

Carole HART
    Free To Be...You And Me (LP)—
    Marlo Thomas

Mickey HART
    (see GRATEFUL DEAD)

Rod HART
    C.B. Savage—Rod Hart

Don HARTMAN
    Drivin' Wheel—Foghat
    Night Shift (LP)—Foghat

Doni HARVEY
    (see AUTOMATIC MAN)

Jimmie HASKELL
    Sixteen Reasons—Laverne & Shirley

Annie HASLAM
    (see RENAISSANCE)

Douglas 'Farthing' HATELID
    (see Chip DOUGLAS)

Peter HAUKE
    Recycled (LP)—Nektar
    A Tab In The Ocean (LP)—Nektar

Tim HAUSER
    Manhattan Transfer (LP)—
    Manhattan Transfer

Bruce HAWES
    Ten Percent (LP)—Double Exposure

Barry HAY
    (see GOLDEN EARRING)

Peter HAYCOCK
    (see CLIMAX BLUES BAND)

Isaac HAYES
    Groove-A-Thon (LP)—Isaac Hayes
    Juicy Fruit (Disco Freak) (LP)—
    Isaac Hayes
    Disco Connection (LP)—Isaac Hayes
    Movement

Dan HEALY
    Kingfish (LP)—Kingfish

Jim HEALY
    Dazz—Brick
    Good High (LP)—Brick

John Anthony HELLIWELL
    (see SUPERTRAMP)

Levon HELM
(see BAND)

'Little' Jimmy HENDERSON
(see BLACK OAK ARKANSAS)

Michael HENDERSON
Drama V (LP)—Ron Banks & the
Dramatics
Joy Ride (LP)—Dramatics
Solid (LP)—Michael Henderson

Wayne HENDERSON
Fever (LP)—Ronnie Laws
Pressure Sensitive (LP)—Ronie Laws
Accept No Substitues (LP)—Pleasure

Scott HENNIGE
(see ASLEEP AT THE WHEEL)

Ken HENSLEY
(see URIAH HEEP)

David HENTSCHEL
A Trick Of The Tail (LP)—Genesis

Stan HERTZMAN
Silver Heels—Blaze

Tony HESTER
You're Fooling You—Dramatics
Drama V (LP)—Ron Banks & the
Dramatics
Joy Ride (LP)—Dramatics

Tommy HILL
Teddy Bear—Red Sovine
Teddy Bear (LP)—Red Sovine

Tony HILLER
Save Your Kisses For Me—Brotherhood
of Man

Roger HODGSON
(see SUPERTRAMP)

Brian HOLLAND
I' Gonna Let My Heart Do The
Walking—Supremes
Keep Holding On—Temptations
Marvin Gaye's Greatest Hits (LP)—
Marvin Gaye
Anthology (LP—Jackson 5ive
High Energy (LP)—Supremes
House Party (LP)—Temptations

Hans HOLLESTELLE
(see SPIN)

Jan HOLLESTELLE
(see SPIN)

Rupert HOLMES
Deep Cuts (LP)—Strawbs
Lazy Afternoon (LP)—Barbra Streisand

Derek HOLT
(see CLIMAX BLUES BAND)

Paul HORNSBY
Texas—Charlie Daniels Band
Fire On The Mountain—Marshall
Tucker Band
Everything That 'Cha Do (Will Come
Back To You)—Wet Willie
High Lonesome (LP)—Charlie Daniels
Band
Saddle Tramp (LP)—Charlie Daniels
Band
Long Hard Ride (LP)—Marshall Tucker
Band
Searchin' (LP)—Marshall Tucker Band
Volunteer Jam (LP)—Various
The Wetter The Better (LP)—Wet Willie

HOT TUNA
(Jack Casady, Jorma Kaukonen &
Bob Steeler)
Yellow Fever (LP)—Hot Tuna

Ron HOWDEN
(see NEKTAR)

Bones HOWE
Nighthawks At The Diner (LP)—
Tom Waits
Small Change (LP)—Tom Waits

Steve HOWE
Beginnings (LP)—Steve Howe

Garth HUDSON
(see BAND)

Leon HUFF
Enjoy Yourself—Jacksons
Tell The World How I Feel About 'Cha
Baby—Harold Melvin & the Blue Notes
Wake Up Everbody—Harold Melvin &
the Blue Notes
The Zip—MFSB
I Love Music—O'Jays
Livin' For The Weekend—O'Jays
Message In Our Music—O'Jays
Let's Make A Baby—Billy Paul
Nursery Rhymes—People's Choice
Groovy People—Lou Rawls
You'll Never Find Another Love Like
Mine—Lou Rawls

Dance Your Troubles Away (LP)—Archie Bell & the Drells
The Jacksons (LP)—Jacksons
All Their Greatest Hits! Collectors' Item (LP)—Harold Melvin & the Blue Notes
Wake Up Everybody (LP)—Harold Melvin & the Blue Notes
Philadelphia Freedom (LP)—MFSB
Summertime (LP)—MFSB
Family Reunion (LP)—O'Jays
Message In The Music (LP)—O'Jays
When Love Is New (LP)—Billy Paul
We Got The Rhythm (LP)—People's Choice
All Things In Time (LP)—Lou Rawls

Bob HUGHES
   Big Towne 2061 (LP)—Paris

Glenn HUGHES
   (see DEEP PURPLE)

HUGO (aka Hugo PERETTI)
   Funky Weekend—Stylistics
   You Are Beautiful—Stylistics
   Fabulous (LP)—Stylistics
   You Are Beautiful (LP)—Stylistics

Brian HUME
   (see PRELUDE)

Irene HUME
   (see PRELUDE)

Ian HUNTER
   All American Alien Boy (LP)—Ian Hunter

Willie HUTCH
   Concert In Blues (LP)—Willie Hutson

Leroy HUTSON
   Feel The Spirit (LP)—Leroy Hutson

Ralf HUTTER
   (see KRAFTWERK)

Jimmy IENNER
   I Only Want To Be With You—Bay City Rollers
   Yesterday's Hero—Bay City Rollers
   All By Myself—Eric Carmen
   Never Gonna Fall In Love Again—Eric Carmen
   Sunrise—Eric Carmen
   Sally—Grand Funk Railroad
   Take Me—Grand Funk Railroad
   Dedication (LP)—Bay City Rollers
   Eric Carmen (LP)—Eric Carmen
   Born To Die (LP)—Grand Funk Railroad

Grand Funk Hits (LP)—Grand Funk Railroad
Raspberries Best Featuring Eric Carmen (LP)—Raspberries

Suzee IKEDA
   The Temptations Do The Temptations (LP)—Temptations
   House Party (LP)—Temptations

Tommy IOMMI
   (see BLACK SABBATH)

Eddie IRONS
   (see BRICK)

Ernie ISLEY
Marvin ISLEY
O'Kelly ISLEY
Ronald ISLEY
Rudolph ISLEY
   (see ISLEY BROTHERS)

ISLEY BROTHERS
   (Ernie, Marvin, O'Kelly, Ronald & Rudolph Isley & Chris Jasper)
   For The Love Of You—Isley Brothers
   Harvest For The World—Isley Brothers
   Who Loves You Better—Isley Brothers
   Harvest For The World (LP)—Isley Brothers
   The Heat Is On Featuring Fight The Power (LP)—Isley Brothers

Clayton IVEY
   Any Way You Like It (LP)—Thelma Houston
   House Party (LP)—Temptations

Billy JACKSON
   It's Cool—Tymes

Brian JACKSON
   It's Your World (LP)—Gil Scott-Heron & Brian Jackson

Chuck JACKSON
   Inseparable—Natalie Cole
   Mr. Melody—Natalie Cole
   Sophisticated Lady (She's A Different Lady)—Natalie Cole
   The More You Do It (The More I Like It Done To Me)—Ronnie Dyson
   Inseparable (LP)—Natalie Cole
   Natalie (LP)—Natalie Cole
   Loving Power (LP)—Impressions

Jackie JACKSON
Marlon JACKSON
Michael JACKSON
Randy JACKSON
Tito JACKSON
(see JACKSONS)

Jermaine JACKSON
Mahogany (LP)—Soundtrack

JACKSONS
(Jackie, Marlon, Michael, Randy & Tito
Jackson)
The Jacksons (LP)—Jacksons

Erik JACOBSEN
The Best . . . Lovin' Spoonful (LP)—
Lovin' Spoonful

Mick JAGGER
(see GLIMMER TWINS)

JAIMOE
(see ALLMAN BROTHERS BAND)

Bob JAMES
More Than Ever (LP)—Blood, Sweat &
Tears
Primal Scream (LP)—Maynard Ferguson
Windjammer (LP)—Freddie Hubbard
Romeo And Juliet (LP)—Hubert Laws

Harvey JAMES
(see SHERBET)

Nick JAMESON
Fool For The City—Foghat
Slow Ride—Foghat
Fool For The City (LP)—Foghat
Rock And Roll Outlaws (LP)—Foghat

Hans JANSEN
(see SPIN)

Al JARDINE
(see BEACH BOYS)

Keith JARRETT
In The Light (LP)—Keith Jarrett

Felton JARVIS
Moody Blue/She Thinks I Still Care—
Elvis Presley
The Outlaws (LP)—Waylon Jennings,
Willie Nelson, Jessi Colter & Tompall
Glaser

Chris JASPER
(see ISLEY BROTHERS)

JCPI
Bigfoot—Bro Smith

JEFFERSON STARSHIP
(Marty Balin, John Barbata, Papa John
Creach, Craig Chaquico, Dave Freiberg,
Paul Kantner, Pete Sears & Grace Slick)
Play On Love—Jefferson Starship
St. Charles—Jefferson Starship (minus
Papa John Creach)
With Your Love—Jefferson Starship
(minus Papa John Creach)
Spitfire (LP)—Jefferson Starship (minus
Papa John Creach)
Dragon Fly (LP)—Jefferson Starship
Red Octopus (LP)—Jefferson Starship

David JENKINS
(see PABLO CRUISE)

Waylon JENNINGS
Can't You See—Waylon Jennings
Good Hearted Woman—Waylon & Willie
Diamond In The Rough (LP)—Jessi Colter
Jessi (LP)—Jessi Colter
A Little Bit More (LP)—Dr. Hook
Are You Ready For The Country (LP)—
Waylon Jennings
Waylon 'Live' (LP)—Waylon Jennings
The Outlaws (LP)—Waylon Jennings,
Willie, Nelson, Jessi Colter & Tompall
Glaser
Mackintosh & T.J. (LP)—Soundtrack

Billy JOEL
Turnstiles (LP)—Billy Joel

JOHNNYMELFI
Sun . . . Sun . . . Sun—Ja kki

Glyn JOHNS
Squeeze Box—Who
Joan Armatrading (LP)—Joan
Armatrading
Desperado (LP)—Eagles
On The Border (LP)—Eagles
Their Greatest Hits 1971-1975 (LP)—
Eagles
Fools Gold (LP)—Fools Gold
Anthology (LP)—Steve Miller Band
The Who By Numbers (LP)—Who

Harold JOHNSON
Any Way You Like It (LP)—Thelma
Houston

Bob JOHNSTON
Renegade—Michael Murphey
Flowing Free Forever (LP)—Michael Murphey
Swans Against The Sun (LP)—Michael Murphey
New Riders (LP)—New Riders Of The Purple Sage

Allen JONES
Shake Your Rump To The Funk—Bar-Kays
Too Hot To Stop (LP)—Bar-Kays

David JONES
(see MONKEES)

Marshall JONES
(see OHIO PLAYERS)

Percy JONES
(see BRAND X)

Quincy JONES
Get The Funk Out Ma Face—Brothers Johnson
I'll Be Good To You—Brothers Johnson
Look Out For # 1 (LP)—Brothers Johnson
Ten Years Of Gold (LP)—Aretha Franklin
I Heard That! (LP)—Quincy Jones
Mellow Madness (LP)—Quincy Jones

Richard JONES
(see CLIMAX BLUES BAND)

Danny JORDAN
All Roads (Lead Back To You)—Donny Most

David JORDAN
I Don't Want To Leave You—Debbie Taylor

JOURNEY
(Aynsley Dunbar, Gregg Rolie, Neal Schon & Ross Valory)
Look Into The Future (LP)—Journey

Seth JUSTMAN
(see J. GEILS BAND)

Paul KANTNER
(see JEFFERON STARSHIP)

Jeff KASENETZ
Let's Rock—Ellison Chase

Gary KATZ
The Fez—Steely Dan
Kid Charlemagne—Steely Dan
The Royal Scam (LP)—Steely Dan

Jerry KATZ
Let's Rock—Ellison Chase

Matthew King KAUFMAN
8.5 (LP)—Earth Quake

Jorma KAUKONEN
(see HOT TUNA)

Monte KAY
An Evening With Wally Londo Featuring Bill Slaszo (LP)—George Carlin

KAYAK
(Pim Koopman, Tom Scherpenzeel, Johan Slager, Bert Veldkamp & Max Werner)
Royal Bed Bouncer (LP)—Kayak

Kaplan KAYE
Listen To The Buddah—Ozo

Orrin KEEPNEWS
500 Miles High At Montreux (LP)—Flora Purim
Open Your Eyes You Can Fly (LP)—Flora Purim
Everybody Come On Out (LP)—Stanley Turrentine
Fly With The Wind (LP)—McCoy Tyner
Trident (LP)—McCoy Tyner

Jerry KELLER
The Monkees Greatest Hits (LP)—Monkees

Kenny KELLY
(see MANHATTANS)

Jim KELTNER
(see ATTITUDES)

Jerry KENNEDY
I'm So Lonesome I Could Cry—Terry Bradshaw
Kentucky Moonrunner—Cledus Maggard & the Citizen's Band
The White Knight—Cledus Maggard & the Citizen's Band
The White Knight (LP)—Cledus Maggard & the Citizen's Band

Kenny KERNER
Part Time Love—Gladys Knight & the Pips
The Best Of Gladys Knight & the Pips (LP)—Gladys Knight & the Pips
2nd Anniversary (LP)—Gladys Knight & the Pips
Kiss (LP)—Kiss
The Originals (LP)—Kiss

Ron KERSEY
  Jealousy—Major Harris
  Jealousy (LP)—Major Harris

David KERSHENBAUM
  Heart On My Sleeve—Gallagher & Lyle
  I Wanna Stay With You—Gallagher & Lyle
  Let's Live Together—Road Apples
  Fearless (LP)—Hoyt Axton
  Diamonds & Rust (LP)—Joan Baez
  From Every Stage (LP)—Joan Baez
  Gulf Winds (LP)—Joan Baez
  The End Of The Beginning (LP)—Richie Havens

Lee KERSLAKE
  (see URIAH HEEP)

Fred KEWLEY
  A Better Place To Be—Harry Chapin
  Greatest Stories Live (LP)—Harry Chapin

Chaka KHAN
  (see RUFUS FEATURING CHAKA KHAN)

Johnny KING
  (see FATBACK BAND)

William KING
  (see COMMODORES)

Barry KINGSTON
  Scotch On The Rocks—Band of the Black Watch
  Scotch On The Rocks (LP)—Band of the Black Watch

Donald KINSEY
  (see Bob MARLEY & THE WAILERS)

Charles KIPPS
  Melba (LP)—Melba Moore

Simon KIRKE
  (see BAD COMPANY)

William KIRKLAND
  Animal Notes (LP)—Crack the Sky
  Crack The Sky (LP)—Crack the sky

KISS
  (Peter Criss, Ace Frehley, Gene Simmons & Paul Stanley)
  Dressed To Kill (LP)—Kiss

Danny KLEIN
  (see J. GEILS BAND)

Gary KLEIN
  Prisoner (Captured By Your Eyes)—L.A. Jets

John KLEMMER
  Barefoot Ballet (LP)—John Klemmer
  Touch (LP)—John Klemmer

Moogy KLINGMAN
  Songs For The New Depression (LP)—Bette Midler

Bubba KNIGHT
  The Original Motion Picture Soundtrack Performed By Gladys Knight & The Pips/Gladys Knight In 'Pipe Dreams' (LP)—Gladys Knight & the Pips

Stanley KNIGHT
  (see BLACK OAK ARKANSAS)

Terry KNIGHT
  Grand Funk Hits (LP)—Grand Funk Railroad

Glen KOLOTKIN
  8.5 (LP)—Earth Quake

KOOL & THE GANG
  (Robert 'Kool' Bell, Ronald Bell, George M. Brown, Larry Gittens, Spike Mickens, Otha Nash, Claydes Smith, Dennis Thomas & Ricky West)
  Love And Understanding (Come Together)—Kool & the Gang
  Open Sesame—Kool & the Gang
  Love And Understanding (LP)—Kool & the Gang
  Open Sesame (LP)—Kool & the Gang

Al KOOPER
  Cry Tough (LP)—Nils Lofgren

Pim KOOPMAN
  (see KAYAK)

Danny KOOTCH
  (see ATTITUDES)

George KOOYMANS
  (see GOLDEN EARRING)

Paul KOSSOFF
  (see BACK STREET CRAWLER)

KOSTA
  (see BLAZE)

Eddie KRAMER
Hard Luck Woman—Kiss
Rock And Roll All Nite (Live Version)—
Kiss
Alive! (LP)—Kiss
Rock And Roll Over (LP)—Kiss
The Best Of Carly Simon (LP)—Carly
Simon

Joey KRAMER
(see AEROSMITH)

Cees KRANENBERG
(see SPIN)

Bill KREUTZMANN
(see GRATEFUL DEAD)

Roland KRUGER
Tonight's The Night—S.S.O.

Murray KRUGMAN
(Don't Fear) The Reaper—Blue Oyster
Cult
Agents Of Fortune (LP)—Blue Oyster Cult

John KUFFLEY
(see CLIMAX BLUES BAND)

Sid KULLER
America Is 200 Years Old . . . And There's
Still Hope! (LP)—Bob Hope

Michael KUNZE
Lady Bump—Penny McLean
Fly, Robin, Fly—Silver Convention
Get Up And Boogie—Silver Convention
No, No, Joe—Silver Convention
Madhouse (LP)—Silver Convention
Save Me (LP)—Silver Convention
Silver Convention (LP)—Silver
Convention

Steve KUPKA
(see TOWER OF POWER)

L.A. EXPRESS
(Max Bennett, Victor Feldman, Robben
Ford, John Guerin & David Luell)
L.A. Express (LP)—L.A. Express
(see also: John GUERIN)

David LaFLAMME
White Bird—David LaFlamme
White Bird (LP)—David LaFlamme

Ken LAGUNA
Johnny Cool—Steve Gibbons Band

Greg LAKE
I Believe In Father Christmas—Greg Lake

Dennis LAMBERT
Country Boy (You Got Your Feet In L.A.)
—Glen Campbell
Don't Pull Your Love/Then You Can
Tell Me Goodbye—Glen Campbell
Help Wanted—Hudson Brothers
The Princess And The Punk—Barry Mann
Free Ride—Tavares
Bloodline (LP)—Glen Campbell
The Best Of Glen Campbell (LP)—Glen
Campbell
Rhinestone Cowboy (LP)—Glen Campbell

Alan LANCASTER
(see STATUS QUO)

Jon LANDAU
Tenth Avenue Freeze-Out—Bruce
Springsteen
The Pretender (LP)—Jackson Browne
Born To Run (LP)—Bruce Springsteen

Jeff LANE
Ha Cha Cha (Funktion)—Brass
Construction
Movin'—Brass Construction
Can't Stop Groovin' Now, Wanna Do It
Some More—B.T. Express
Close To You—B.T. Express
Brass Construction (LP)—Brass
Construction
Brass Construction II (LP)—Brass
Construction
Energy To Burn (LP)—B.T. Express

Robert John LANGE
City Boy (LP)—City Boy

Ronald LaPRAED
(see COMMODORES)

Mel LARSON
Anthology (LP)—Jackson 5ive
Diana Ross' Greatest Hits (LP)—Diana
Ross

D.C. LaRUE
Ca-the-drals—D.C. LaRue
Ca-the-drals (LP)—D.C. LaRue

Andy LATIMER
(see CAMEL)

Derek LAWRENCE
Angel (LP)—Angel
Helluva Band (LP)—Angel

Stephen LAWRENCE
Free To Be . . . You And Me (LP)—Marlo
Thomas

Trevor LAWRENCE
That's The Way It Is (LP)—Nilsson

Tom LEADON
(see SILVER)

Mike LEANDER
Makes You Blind—Glitter Band

Chuck LEAVELL
(see ALLMAN BROTHERS BAND)

John LECKIE
Modern Music (LP)—Be Bop DeLuxe
Sunburst Finish (LP)—Be Bop DeLuxe

Dickey LEE
9,999,999 Tears—Dickey Lee

Geddy LEE
(see RUSH)

Robert E. LEE
Dazz—Brick
Good High (LP)—Brick

Gerrit Jan LEENDERS
Royal Bed Bouncer (LP)—Kayak

Kyle LEHNING
I'd Really Love To See You Tonight—
England Dan & John Ford Coley
Nights Are Forever—England Dan & John
Ford Coley
Nights Are Forever (LP)—England Dan &
John Ford Coley

Donovan LEITCH
Slow Down World (LP)—Donovan

John LENNON
Shaved Fish (LP)—John Lennon/Plastic
Ono Band

Craig LEON
The Ramones (LP)—Ramones
Escape From Babylon (LP)—Martha Velez

Glenn LEONARD
(see TEMPTATIONS)

Cory LERIOS
(see PABLO CRUISE)

Phil LESH
(see GRATEFUL DEAD)

Jeffrey LESSER
Deep Cuts (LP)—Strawbs
Lazy Afternoon (LP)—Barbra Streisand

Sylvester LEVAY
Madhouse (LP)—Silver Convention

Danny LEVIN
(see ASLEEP AT THE WHEEL)

Stewart LEVINE
Those Southern Knights (LP)—Crusaders
The Best Of The Crusaders (LP)—
Crusaders

Jack LEWIS
**An Evening With Wally Londo Featuring
Bill Slaszo (LP)**—George Carlin

Michael LEWIS
Let's Get It Together—El Coco

Nancy LEWIS
Monty Python Live At City Center (LP)—
Monty Python

Ramsey LEWIS
**What's The Name Of This Funk (Spider
Man)**—Ramsey Lewis

Henry LEWY
Save It For A Rainy Day—Stephen
Bishop

Marshall LIEB
Ode To Billy Joe—Bobbie Gentry

Goddard LIEBERSON
A Chorus Line (LP)—Original Cast

Alex LIFESON
(see RUSH)

Ronnie LIGHT
The Outlaws (LP)—Waylon Jennings,
Willie Nelson, Jessi Colter & Tompall
Glaser

Gordon LIGHTFOOT
The Wreck Of The Edmund Fitzgerald—
Gordon Lightfoot
Summertime Dream (LP)—Gordon
Lightfoot

Sandy LINZER
I'll Play The Fool—Dr. Buzzard's Original Savannah Band
Whispering/Cherchez La Femme/Se Si Bon—Dr. Buzzard's Original Savannah Band
Dr. Buzzard's Original Savannah Band (LP)—Dr. Buzzard's Original Savannah Band

Tommy LiPUMA
Breezin'—George Benson
This Masquerade—George Benson
Popsicle Toes—Michael Franks
Breezin' (LP)—George Benson
The Art Of Tea (LP)—Michael Franks
Glow (LP)—Al Jarreau
Stuff (LP)—Stuff

Michael LLOYD
Ain't Nothing Like The Real Thing—Donny & Marie Osmond
I Can't Live A Dream—Osmonds
Donny & Marie Featuring Songs From Their Television Show (LP)—Donny & Marie Osmond
New Season (LP)—Donny & Marie Osmond
Brainstorm (LP)—Osmonds

Andre LOCKE
(see MANDRILL)

Sam LOCRICCHIO
Eh! Cumpari—Gaylord & Holiday
Second Generation (LP)—Gaylord & Holiday

Mark LONDON
Too Young To Feel This Old (LP)—McKendree Spring

Jon LORD
(see DEEP PURPLE)

Jerry LOVE
Do It With Feeling—Michael Zager's Moon featuring Peabo Bryson

Mike LOVE
(see BEACH BOYS)

Herb LOVELLE
Stuff (LP)—Stuff

Wilfred LOVETT
(see MANHATTANS)

David LUCAS
(Don't Fear) The Reaper—Blue Oyster Cult
Agents Of Fortune (LP)—Blue Oyster Cult

David LUELL
(see L.A. EXPRESS)

LUIGI (aka Luigi CREATORE)
Funky Weekend—Stylistics
You Are Beautiful—Stylistics
Fabulous (LP)—Stylistics
You Are Beautiful (LP)—Stylistics

Robin LUMLEY
(see BRAND X)

Richard LUSH
Howzat—Sherbet

Warrick LYNN
Funky Kingston (LP)—Toots & the Maytals
Reggae Got Soul (LP)—Toots & the Maytals

Jeff LYNNE
Evil Woman—Electric Light Orchestra
Livin' Thing—Electric Light Orchestra
Showdown—Electric Light Orchestra
Strange Magic—Electric Light Orchestra
Face The Music (LP)—Electric Light Orchestra
A New World Record (LP)—Electric Light Orchestra
Ole Elo (LP)—Electric Light Orchestra

Leo LYONS
No Heavy Pettin' (LP)—UFO

Bill MABRY
(see ASLEEP AT THE WHEEL)

Tony MACAULAY
Falling Apart At The Seams—Marmalade

Dennis MACKAY/McKAY
Teaser (LP)—Tommy Bolin
Private Eyes (LP)—Tommy Bolin
Unorthodox Behaviour (LP)—Brand X
Spiders From Mars (LP)—Spiders from Mars
Go (LP)—Stomu Yamashta/Steve Winwood/Michael Shrieve

Tom MACKNO
(see BLAZE)

Teo MACERO
Agharta (LP)—Miles Davis

John MADARA
  The Hungry Years—Wayne Newton

MAGIC DICK
  (see J. GEILS BAND)

Tony MAIDEN
  (see RUFUS FEATURING CHAKA KHAN)

Eric MALAMUD
  You're My Everything—Lee Garrett

David MALLOY
  Rocky Mountain Music—Eddie Rabbitt

MANDRILL
  (Brian Allsop, Claude 'Coffee' Cave,
  Andre Locke, Tommy Trujillo, Carlos
  Wilson, Lou Wilson, Ric Wilson &
  Wilfredo 'Wolf' Wilson)
  Beast From The East (LP)—Mandrill

Chuck MANGIONE
  Bellavia (LP)—Chuck Mangione
  Encore—The Chuck Mangione Concerts
  —(LP)—Chuck Mangione
  Main Squeeze (LP)—Chuck Mangione
  The Need To Be (LP)—Esther Satterfield

MANHATTANS
  (Gerald Austin, Sonny Bivins, Kenny
  Kelly, Wilfred Lovett & Richard Taylor)
  I Kinda Miss You—Manhattans
  Kiss And Say Goodbye—Manhattans
  The Manhattans (LP)—Manhattans

Michael MANIERI
  Mary Hartman, Mary Hartman (Theme)—
  Deadly Nightshade

Barry MANILOW
  Street Singin'—Lady Flash
  I Write The Songs—Barry Manilow
  This One's For You—Barry Manilow
  Tryin' To Get The Feeling Again—Barry
  Manilow
  Weekend In New England—Barry
  Manilow
  I (LP)—Barry Manilow
  II (LP)—Barry Manilow
  This One's For You (LP)—Barry Manilow
  Tryin' To Get The Feelin' (LP)—Barry
  Manilow

Herbie MANN
  Surprises (LP)—Herbie Mann featuring
  Cissy Houston

Manfred MANN
  (see Manfred MANN's EARTHBAND)

Manfred MANN'S EARTHBAND)
  (Manfred Mann, Dave Flett, Colin
  Pattenden, Chris Slade & Chris Hamlet
  Thompson)
  Blinded By The Light—Manfred Mann's
  Earthband
  Spirit In The Night—Manfred Mann's
  Earthband
  The Roaring Silence (LP)—Manfred
  Mann's Earthband

Ken MANSFIELD
  Can't You See—Waylon Jennings
  Diamond In The Rough (LP)—Jessi
  Colter
  Jessi (LP)—Jessi Colter
  Are You Ready For The Country (LP)—
  Waylon Jennings

Bobby MANUEL
  Disco Duck—Rick Dees & His Cast Of
  Idiots

Richard MANUEL
  (see BAND)

Jerry MARCELLINO
  Anthology (LP)—Jackson 5ive
  Diana Ross' Greatest Hits (LP)—Diana
  Ross

Arif MARDIN
  Queen Of My Soul—Average White Band
  School Boy Crush—Average White Band
  Fanny (Be Tender With My Love)—Bee
  Gees
  Nights On Broadway—Bee Gees
  She's Gone—Daryl Hall & John Oates
  A Dose Of Rock And Roll—Ringo Starr
  Main Course (LP)—Bee Gees
  Bread And Roses (LP)—Judy Collins
  Ten Years Of Gold (LP)—Aretha Franklin
  Abandoned Luncheonette (LP)—Daryl
  Hall & John Oates
  A Street Called Straight (LP)—Roy
  Buchanan
  Soul Searching (LP)—Average White
  Band
  The Troublemaker (LP)—Willie Nelson
  Resolution (LP)—Andy Pratt
  Mackintosh & T.J. (LP)—Soundtrack
  Ringo's Rotogravure (LP)—Ringo Starr

Frank MARINO
  Mahogany Rush IV (LP)—Mahogany Rush

Bob MARLEY
  Escape From Babylon (LP)—Martha Velez
  (see also Bob MARLEY & THE WAILERS)

Bob MARLEY & THE WAILERS
  (Bob Marley, Aston 'Family Man' Barrett, Carlton Barrett, Tyrone Downie, Alvin 'Seeco' Patterson, Earl 'Chinna' Smith, Donald Kinsey & Al Anderson)
  Roots, Rock, Reggae—Bob Marley & the Wailers
  Rastaman Vibration (LP)—Bob Marley & the Wailers

Peter MARSH
  (see EASY STREET)

Bill MARTIN
  Saturday Night—Bay City Rollers
  Bay City Rollers (LP)—Bay City Rollers

Bobby MARTIN
  Touch & Go—Ecstasy Passion & Pain
  I Kinda Miss You—Manhattans
  Kiss And Say Goodbye—Manhattans
  The Manhattans (LP)—Manhattans
  Philadelphia Freedom (LP)—MFSB
  All Things In Time (LP)—Lou Rawls
  Live (LP)—Three Degrees

George MARTIN
  Amber Cascades—America
  Today's The Day—America
  Woman Tonight—America
  Let Me Down Easy—American Flyer
  Got To Get You Into My Life—Beatles
  Ob-La-Di, Ob-La-Da—Beatles
  Hearts (LP)—America
  Hideaway (LP)—America
  History—America's Greatest Hits (LP)—America
  American Flyer (LP)—American Flyer
  Abbey Road (LP)—Beatles
  The Beatles (White Album) (LP)—The Beatles
  The Beatles 1962-1966 (LP)—Beatles
  The Beatles 1967-1970 (LP)—Beatles
  Rock 'n' Roll Music (LP)—Beatles
  Sgt. Pepper's Lonely Hearts Club Band (LP)—Beatles
  Wired (LP)—Jeff Beck
  The Best Of George Harrison (LP)—George Harrison
  Born On A Friday (LP)—Cleo Laine

Henry Grumpo MARX
  Words (Are Impossible)—Donny Gerrard

Harry MASLIN
  Golden Years—David Bowie
  TVC 15—David Bowie
  Changesonebowie (LP)—David Bowie
  Station To Station (LP)—David Bowie
  Young Americans (LP)—David Bowie
  Hoppkorv (LP)—Hot Tuna

Dave/David MASON
  Certified Live (LP)—Dave Mason
  Split Coconut (LP)—Dave Mason

Jim MASON
  Livin' Ain't Livin'—Firefall
  You Are The Woman—Firefall
  Firefall (LP)—Firefall

Nick MASON
  (see PINK FLOYD)

Michael MASSER
  So Sad The Song—Gladys Knight & the Pips
  I Thought It Took A little Time (But Today I Fell In Love)—Diana Ross
  Theme From Mahogany 'Do You Know Where You're Going To'—Diana Ross
  The Original Motion Picture Soundtrack Performed By Gladys Knight & the Pips/ Gladys Knight In 'Pipe Dreams' (LP)—Gladys Knight & the Pips
  Diana Ross (LP)—Diana Ross
  Diana Ross' Greatest Hits (LP)—Diana Ross
  Mahogany (LP)—Soundtrack

Sherlie MATTHEWS
  Anthology (LP)—Jackson 5ive

Brian MAY
  (see QUEEN)

Curtis MAYFIELD
  Jump—Aretha Franklin
  Something He Can Feel—Aretha Franklin
  Let's Do It Again—Staple Singers
  New Orleans—Staple Singers
  Music From The Warner Bros. Motion Picture 'Sparkle' (LP)—Aretha Franklin
  Ten Years Of Gold (LP)—Aretha Franklin
  The Best Of Gladys Knight & The Pips (LP)—Gladys Knight & the Pips
  Give, Get, Take And Have (LP)—Curtis Mayfield
  Let's Do It Again (LP)—Staple Singers
  Pass It On (LP)—Staple Singers

Elliot F. MAZER
  Greatest Hits (LP)—Linda Ronstadt

Paul McCARTNEY
  Let 'Em In—Wings
  Silly Love Songs—Wings
  Band On The Run (LP)—Paul McCartney
  & Wings
  Venus And Mars (LP)—Wings
  Wings At The Speed Of Sound (LP)—
  Wings
  Wings Over America (LP)—Wings

Matthew McCAULEY
  Growin' Up—Dan Hill
  Dan Hill (LP)—Dan Hill

Tom McCLARY
  (see COMMODORES)

Van McCOY
  Night Walk—Van McCoy
  Party—Van McCoy
  This Is It—Melba Moore
  Everything's Coming Up Love—David
  Ruffin
  Heavy Love—David Ruffin
  Walk Away From Love—David Ruffin
  The Real McCoy (LP)—Van McCoy
  Melba (LP)—Melba Moore
  This Is It (LP)—Melba Moore
  Everything's Coming Up Love (LP)—
  David Ruffin
  Who I Am (LP)—David Ruffin

Eugene McDANIELS
  2nd Anniversary (LP)—Gladys Knight &
  the Pips
  This Mother's Daughter (LP)—Nancy
  Wilson

Pete McDONALD
  (see SPIDERS FROM MARS)

Ralph McDONALD
  Sound Of A Drum (LP)—Ralph McDonald

William E. McEUEN
  Dirt, Silver & Gold (LP)—Nitty Gritty
  Dirt Band

Gene McFADDEN
  Dance Your Troubles Away (LP)—
  Archie Bell & the Drells
  The Jacksons (LP)—Jacksons
  Summertime (LP)—MFSB
  Message In The Music (LP)—O'Jays

Edward McGEE
  (see TOWER OF POWER)

Dennis McKAY
  (see Dennis MACKAY)

John McLAUGHLIN
  Inner Worlds (LP)—Mahavishnu
  Orchestra/John McLaughlin
  Shakti with John McLaughlin (LP)—
  Shakti with John McLaughlin

Christine McVIE
  (see FLEETWOOD MAC: Christine
  McVIE)

John McVIE
  (see FLEETWOOD MAC)

Huey P. MEAUX
  Livin' It Down—Freddy Fender
  Vaya Con Dios—Freddy Fender
  You'll Lose A Good Thing—Freddy
  Fender
  Are You Ready For Freddy (LP)—Freddy
  Fender
  Before The Next Teardrop Falls (LP)—
  Freddy Fender
  If You're Ever In Texas (LP)—Freddy
  Fender
  Rock 'n' Country (LP)—Freddy Fender

Hank MEDRESS
  Cupid—Tony Orlando & Dawn
  Our Day Will Come—Frankie Valli
  Greatest Hits (LP)—Tony Orlando &
  Dawn
  To Be With You (LP)—Tony Orlando &
  Dawn
  Our Day Will Come (LP)—Frankie Valli

Patrick MEEHAN
  We Sold Our Soul For Rock 'n' Roll
  (LP)—Black Sabbath

Harold MELVIN
  All Their Greatest Hits! Collectors' Item
  (LP)—Harold Melvin & the Blue Notes

Bernard MENDELSON
  Disco Sax/For The Love Of You—
  Jimmy Person

Sergio MENDES
  Homecooking (LP)—Sergio Mendes &
  Brasil '77

Freddie MERCURY
  (see QUEEN)

Jim MESSINA
The Best Of Friends (LP)—Loggins &
Messina
Native Sons (LP)—Loggins & Messina

MIAMI STEVE VAN ZANDT
(see Miami Steve VAN ZANDT)

Spike MICKENS
(see KOOL & THE GANG)

Ralph MIDDLEBROOKS
(see OHIO PLAYERS)

Jimmy MILLER
That Was Only Yesterday (LP)—Gary
Wright: Spooky Tooth

Snuffy MILLER
The Blind Man In The Bleachers—
Kenny Starr

Steve MILLER
Fly Like An Eagle—Steve Miller Band
Rock 'n' Me—Steve Miller Band
Take The Money And Run—Steve Miller
Band
Fly Like An Eagle (LP)—Steve Miller Band

Steve MILLER BAND
(Tim Davis, Steve Miller, Jim Peterman,
Boz Scaggs & Bob Winkelman)
Anthology (LP)—Steve Miller Band
(see also: Boz SCAGGS)

Jackie MILLS
The Fonz Song—Heyettes

Bob MILLSAP
Hey Shirley (This Is Squirrely)—Shirley
& Squirely

Kerry MINNEAR
(see GENTLE GIANT)

Terence P. MINOGUE
Animal Notes (LP)—Crack The Sky
Crack The Sky (LP)—Crack The Sky

Tony MITCHELL
(see SHERBET)

Willie MITCHELL
Full Of Fire—Al Green
Keep Me Cryin'—Al Green
Full Of Fire (LP)—Al Green
Al Green Is Love (LP)—Al Green
Have A Good Time (LP)—Al Green

Fonce MIZELL
Love Ballad—L.T.D.
Donald Byrd's Best (LP)—Donald Byrd
Places And Spaces (LP)—David Byrd
Anthology (LP)—Jackson 5ive
Love To The World (LP)—L.T.D.

Larry MIZELL
Love Ballad—L.T.D.
Donald Byrd's Best (LP)—Donald Byrd
Places And Spaces (LP)—Donald Byrd
Love To The World (LP)—L.T.D.

Fred MOLLIN
Growin' Up—Dan Hill
Dan Hill (LP)—Dan Hill

Chips MOMAN
And The Singer Sings His Song (LP)—
Neil Diamond

Paddy MOLONEY
5 (LP)—Chieftains

Chips MOMAN
And The Singer Sings His Song (LP)—
Neil Diamond

Bob MONACO
Lydia Pense And Cold Blood (LP)—
Lydia Pense and Cold Blood
American Pastime (LP)—Three Dog
Night

Meco MONARDO
Experience (LP)—Gloria Gaynor
I've Got You (LP)—Gloria Gaynor

MONKEES
(Micky Dolenz, David Jones, Mike
Nesmith & Peter Tork)
The Monkees Greatest Hits (LP)—
Monkees

Vincent MONTANA Jr.
**The Game Is Over (What's The Matter
With You)**—Brown Sugar
Nice 'n' Naasty—Salsoul Orchestra
Tangerine—Salsoul Orchestra
You're Just The Right Size—Salsoul
Orchestra
Ten Percent (LP)—Double Exposure
Christmas Jollies (LP)—Salsoul Orchestra
Nice 'n' Naasty (LP)—Salsoul Orchestra
The Salsoul Orchestra (LP)—Salsoul
Orchestra

Mike MONTGOMERY
(see BACK STREET CRAWLER)

'Mo' MOORE
(see NEKTAR)

Warren 'Pete' MOORE
The Power Of Music (LP)—Miracles

Jacques MORALI
The Best Disco In Town—Ritchie Family
Arabian Nights (LP)—Ritchie Family

Patrick MORAZ
i (LP)—Patrick Moraz

Bob MORGAN
Moonlight Serenade—Bobby Vinton
Save Your Kisses For Me—Bobby Vinton
The Bobby Vinton Show (LP)—Bobby Vinton

Giorgio MORODER
Could It Be Magic—Donna Summer
Spring Affair—Donna Summer
Four Seasons Of Love (LP)—Donna Summer
A Love Trilogy (LP)—Donna Summer
Love To Love You Baby (LP)—Donna Summer

Johnny MORRIS
Lonely Teardrops—Narvel Felts

Ralph MOSS
The Best Of Gladys Knight & The Pips (LP)—Gladys Knight & the Pips

Mickie MOST
Don't Stop It Now—Hot Chocolate
You Sexy Thing—Hot Chocolate
Hot Chocolate (LP)—Hot Chocolate
Man To Man (LP)—Hot Chocolate

Thomas MOWERY
Scott Joplin's Treemonisha (LP)—Original Cast

Tim MULLIGAN
Zuma (LP)—Neil Young with Crazy Horse

Kevin MURPHY
(see RUFUS Featuring CHAKA KHAN)

Brent MYDLAND
(see SILVER)

Graham NASH
Out Of The Darkness—David Crosby/Graham Nash
Whistling Down The Wire (LP)—David Crosby/Graham Nash
Wind On The Water (LP)—David Crosby/Graham Nash

Larry NASH
Make Love To Your Mind—Bill Withers
Making Music (LP)—ill Withers

Otha NASH
(see KOOL & THE GANG)

Mike NATALE
This Old Man—Purple Reign

Randolph NAUERT
Junkfood Junkie—Larry Groce
Junkfood Junkie (LP)—Larry Groce

NEKTAR
(Roye Albrighton, Mick Brockett, 'Taff' Freeman, Ron Howden & 'Mo' Moore)
Recycled (LP)—Nektar
A Tab In The Ocean (LP)—Nektar

Bill NELSON
Modern Music (LP)—Be Bop DeLuxe
Sunburst Finish (LP)—Be Bop DeLuxe

Marty NELSON
Animal Notes (LP)—Crack The Sky
Crack The Sky (LP)—Crack The Sky

Willie NELSON
Remember Me—Willie Nelson
The Outlaws (LP)—Waylon Jennings, Willie Nelson, Jessi Colter & Tompall Glaser
Red Headed Stranger (LP)—Willie Nelson
The Sound In Your Mind (LP)—Willie Nelson

Freida NERANGIS
Every Beat Of My Heart—Crown Heights Affair
Foxy Lady—Crown Heights Affair
Dreaming A Dream (LP)—Crown Heights Affair

Mike/Michael NESMITH
(see MONKEES)

Don NEVINS
(see BRICK)

Stevie NICKS
(see FLEETWOOD MAC)

Ken NICOL
(see EASY STREET)

Harry NILSSON
Sandman (LP)—Nilsson

Jack NITZSCHE
**One Flew Over The Cuckoo's Nest
(LP)**—Soundtrack

Kenny NOLAN
Dancin' Kid—Disco Tex & the
Sex-o-lettes
I Like Dreamin'—Kenny Nolan

Laura NYRO
Smile (LP)—Laura Nyro

Berry OAKLEY
(see ALLMAN BROTHERS BAND)

John OATES
Sara Smile—Daryl Hall & John Oates
Daryl Hall & John Oates (LP)—Daryl
Hall & John Oates

Lucky OCEANS
(see ASLEEP AT THE WHEEL)

Chris O'CONNELL
(see ASLEEP AT THE WHEEL)

Michael O'DONOGHUE
NBC'S Saturday Night Live (LP)—
Original Cast

Eddie OFFORD
Beginnings (LP)—Steve Howe

Claus OGERMAN
Classical Barbra (LP)—Barbra Streisand

OHIO PLAYERS
(William Beck, Leroy Bonner, Marshall
Jones, Ralph Middlebrooks, Marvin
Pierce, Clarence Satchell & James
Williams)
Fopp—Ohio Players
Love Rollercoaster—Ohio Players
Rattlesnake—Ohio Players
Who'd She Coo—Ohio Players
Contradiction (LP)—Ohio Players
Gold (LP)—Ohio Players
Honey (LP)—Ohio Players

OISTER
Sincerely (LP)—Dwight Twilley Band

Milton OKUN
Baby, You Look Good To Me Tonight—
John Denver
Christmas For Cowboys—John Denver
Fly Away—John Denver
It Makes Me Giggle—John Denver
Like A Sad Song—John Denver
Looking For Space—John Denver
Afternoon Delight—Starland Vocal Band
California Day—Starland Vocal Band
Back Home Again (LP)—John Denver
Denver Gift Box (LP)—John Denver
An Evening With John Denver (LP)—
John Denver
Greatest Hits (LP)—John Denver
Rocky Mountain Christmas (LP)—
John Denver
Spirit (LP)—John Denver
Windsong (LP)—John Denver
Starland Vocal Band (LP)—Starland
Vocal Band

Mike OLDFIELD
Ommadawn (LP)—Mike Oldfield

Antonio Carlos DE OLIVEIRA
(see under D)

Ed O'LOUGHLIN
Midnight Love Affair (LP)—Carol
Douglas

Keith OLSEN
Over My Head—Fleetwood Mac
Rhiannon (Will You Ever Win)—
Fleetwood Mac
Say You Love Me—Fleetwood Mac
Hold On—Sons of Champlin
Fleetwood Mac (LP)—Fleetwood Mac
A Circle Filled With Love (LP)—Sons of
Champlin

Michael OMARTIAN
Devil With The Blue Dress—Pratt &
McClain with Brotherlove
Happy Days—Pratt & McClain with
Brotherlove
**Baretta's Theme (Keep Your Eye On The
Sparrow)**—Rhythm Heritage
Theme From S.W.A.T.—Rhythm Heritage
I've Got A Reason (LP)—Richie Furay
**Pratt & McClain Featuring 'Happy Days'
(LP)**—Pratt & McClain
Disco-Fied (LP)—Rhythm Heritage

Yoko ONO
Shaved Fish (LP)—John Lennon/
Plastic Ono Band

Walter ORANGE
(see COMMODORES)

Ozzy OSBOURNE
(see BLACK SABBATH)

US PRODUCER

Alan OSMOND
New Season (LP)—Donny & Marie Osmond
Disco Train (LP)—Donny Osmond
(see also OSMOND BROTHERS: OSMONDS)

Donny OSMOND
(see OSMOND BROTHERS: OSMONDS)

Jay OSMOND
(see OSMOND BROTHERS: OSMONDS)

Jimmy OSMOND
(see OSMONDS)

Marie OSMOND
(see OSMONDS)

Merrill OSMOND
Disco Train (LP)—Donny Osmond
(see also OSMOND BROTHERS: OSMONDS)

Wayne OSMOND
Disco Train (LP)—Donny Osmond
(see also OSMOND BROTHERS: OSMONDS)

OSMOND BROTHERS
(Alan, Donny, Jay, Merrill & Wayne Osmond)
Brainstorm (LP)—Osmonds
The Osmonds Christmas Album (LP)—Osmonds

OSMONDS
(Alan, Donny, Jay, Jimmy, Marie, Merrill & Wayne Osmond)
The Osmonds Around The World Live In Concert (LP)—Osmonds

PABLO CRUISE
(Bud Cockrell, David Jenkins, Cory Lerios & Stephen Price)
Lifeline (LP)—Pablo Cruise

Billy PAGE
Have You Ever Seen The Rain (LP)—Stanley Turretine

Gene PAGE
Have You Ever Seen The Rain (LP)—Stanley Turrentine

Jimmy PAGE
IV (LP)—Led Zeppelin
Presence (LP)—Led Zeppelin

Soundtrack From The Film 'The Song Remains The Same' (LP)—Led Zeppelin

Ian PAICE
(see DEEP PURPLE)

John PALLADINO
Solid Silver (LP)—Quicksilver Messenger Service
America Is 200 Years Old . . . And There's Still Hope! (LP)—Bob Hope

Chuck PANAZZO
(see STYX)

John PANOZZO
(see STYX)

Rick PARFITT
(see STATUS QUO)

Bobby PARIS
Ode To Billy Joe—Bobbie Gentry

Richard PARISSI
Play That Funky Music—Wild Cherry
Wild Cherry (LP)—Wild Cherry

Alan PARSONS
Make Me Smile (Come Up And See Me)—Steve Harley & Cockney Rebel
High Fly—John Miles
Music—John Miles
(The System Of) Doctor Tarr & Professor Fether—Alan Parsons Project
The Raven—Alan Parsons Project
January—Pilot
Year Of The Cat—Al Stewart
Somewhere I've Never Travelled (LP)—Ambrosia
Rebel (LP)—John Miles
Tales Of Mystery & Imagination: Edgar Allan Poe (LP)—Alan Parsons Project
Modern Times (LP)—Al Stewart
Year Of The Cat (LP)—Al Stewart

Gram PARSONS
Sleepless Night (LP)—Gram Parsons/Flying Burrito Brothers

Colin PATTENDEN
(see Manfred MANN'S EARTHBAND)

Alvin 'Seeco' PATTERSON
(see Bob MARLEY & THE WAILERS)

Billy PAUL
When Love Is New (LP)—Billy Paul

Lawrence PAYTON
   Catfish—Four Tops
   Catfish (LP)—Four Tops

Sandy PEARLMAN
   (Don't Fear) The Reaper—Blue Oyster Cult
   Agents Of Fortune (LP)—Blue Oyster Cult

Chas PEATE
   Brand New Love Affair—Jigsaw
   Love Fire—Jigsaw
   Sky High—Jigsaw
   Sky High (LP)—Jigsaw

Neil PEART
   (see RUSH)

Dan PEEK
   (see AMERICA)

Ray PENNINGTON
   Good Hearted Woman—Waylon & Willie
   Waylon 'Live' (LP)—Waylon Jennings
   The Outlaws (LP)—Waylon Jennings,
   Willie Nelson, Jessi Colter & Tompall
   Glaser

Christine PERFECT (aka Christine McVIE)
   The Legendary Christine Perfect Album
   (LP)—Christine McVie

Freddie PERREN
   Love Machine—Miracles
   Love Me—Yvonne Elliman
   You To Me Are Everything—Revelation
   Boogie Fever—Sylvers
   Cotton Candy—Sylvers
   Hot Line—Sylvers
   Don't Take Away The Music—Tavares
   Heaven Must Be Missing An Angel—
   Tavares
   Anthology (LP)—Jackson 5ive
   City Of Angels (LP)—Miracles
   Showcase (LP)—Sylvers
   Something Special! (LP)—Sylvers
   Sky High (LP)—Tavares

Joe PERRY
   (see AEROSMITH)

Lee PERRY
   Escape From Babylon (LP)—Martha Velez

Richard PERRY
   Stand Tall—Burton Cummings
   Breakaway—Art Garfunkel
   You Make Me Feel Like Dancing—Leo
   Sayer

Burton Cummings (LP)—Burton
   Cummings
   Breakaway (LP)—Art Garfunkel
   Coming Out (LP)—Manhattan Transfer
   Endless Flight (LP)—Leo Sayer
   The Best Of Carly Simon (LP)—Carly
   Simon
   Blast From Your Past (LP)—Ringo Starr

Houston PERSON
   Disco Sax/For The Love Of You—
   Houston Person

Jim PETERMAN
   (see Steve MILLER BAND)

J.C. PHILLIPS
   'Til It's Time To Say Goodbye—
   Jonathan Cain

Lenny PICKETT
   (see TOWER OF POWER)

Marvin PIERCE
   (see OHIO PLAYERS)

John PILLA
   Amigo (LP)—Arlo Guthrie

Michael PINDER
   The Promise (LP)—Michael Pinder

PINK FLOYD
   (David Gilmour, Nick Mason, Roger
   Waters & Richard Wright)
   The Dark Side Of The Moon (LP)—Pink
   Floyd
   Wish You Were Here (LP)—Pink Floyd

PLASMA MUSIC, INC.
   Firebird (LP)—Isao Tomita

Charles/Chuck PLOTKIN
   That's Why I Love You—Andrew Gold
   Still The One—Orleans
   Andrew Gold (LP)—Andrew Gold
   Waking And Dreaming (LP)—Orleans

Neely PLUMB
   The Sound Of Music (LP)—Soundtrack

POCO
   (Paul Cotton, George Grantham, Timothy
   B. Schmit & Rusty Young)
   Rose Of Cimarron—Poco
   Live (LP)—Poco
   Rose Of Cimarron (LP)—Poco

Richard PODOLOR
Strong Enough To Be Gentle—Black Oak Arkansas
X Rated (LP)—Black Oak Arkansas

Michel POLNAREFF
If You Only Believe (Jesus For Tonight)—Michel Polnareff
Lipstick—Michel Polnareff
Michel Polnareff (LP)—Michel Polnareff

Vini PONCIA
Better Days—Melissa Manchester
Just You And I—Melissa Manchester
Rescue Me—Melissa Manchester
Better Days & Happy Endings (LP)—Melissa Manchester
Help Is On The Way (LP)—Melissa Manchester

Jean-Luc PONTY
Aurora (LP)—Jean-Luc Ponty
Imaginary Voyage (LP)—Jean-Luc Ponty

Garth PORTER
(see SHERBET)

Joe PORTER
Any Way You Like It (LP)—Thelma Houston

Brian POTTER
Country Boy (You Got Your Feet In L.A.)—Glen Campbell
Don't Pull Your Love/Then You Can Tell Me Goodbye—Glen Campbell
Help Wanted—Hudson Brothers
The Princess And The Punk—Barry Mann
Free Ride—Tavares
Bloodline (LP)—Glen Campbell
The Best Of Glen Campbell (LP)—Glen Campbell
Rhinestone Cowboy (LP)—Glen Campbell

Joe POTTER
Any Way You Like It (LP)—Thelma Houston

Andrew POWELL
David Courtney's First Day (LP)—David Courtney

PRELUDE
(Brian Hume, Irene Hume & Ian Vardy)
For A Dancer—Prelude
Owl Creek Incident (LP)—Prelude

Elvis PRESLEY
Moody Blue/She Still Thinks I Care—Elvis Presley

Francis Rocco PRESTIA
(see TOWER OF POWER)

Leroy PRESTON
(see ASLEEP AT THE WHEEL)

Greg PRESTOPINO
Michel Polnareff (LP)—Michel Polnareff

Jim PRICE
KGB (LP)—KGB

Stephen PRICE
(see PABLO CRUISE)

Steve PRIEST
(see SWEET)

Spencer PROFFER
Times Of Your Life (LP)—Paul Anka

Johnnie PRUITT
E-Man Groovin' (LP)—Jimmy Castor Bunch featuring the Everything Man

QUEEN
(John Deacon, Brian May, Freddie Mercury & Roger Taylor)
Bohemian Rhapsody—Queen
Somebody To Love—Queen
You're My Best Friend—Queen
A Night At The Opera (LP)—Queen

QUICKSILVER MESSENGER SERVICE
(John Cipollina, Gary Duncan, Greg Elmore, David Freiberg & Dino Valenti)
Solid Silver (LP)—Quicksilver Messenger Service

Mick RALPHS
(see BAD COMPANY)

Bill RAMAL
Mr. Jaws & Other Fables (LP)—Dickie Goodman

Phil RAMONE
50 Ways To Leave Your Lover—Paul
Simon
Still Crazy After All These Years—Paul
Simon
My Little Town—Simon & Garfunkel
**Love Theme From 'A Star Is Born'
(Evergreen)**—Barbra Streisand
Breakaway (LP)—Art Garfunkel
Sanborn (LP)—David Sanborn
Still Crazy After All These Years (LP)—
Paul Simon
Second Childhood (LP)—Phoebe Snow
A Star Is Born (LP)—Soundtrack

Michael RANDALL
Diana Ross' Greatest Hits (LP)—Diana
Ross

Yvonne RANKIN
Inside (LP)—Kenny Rankin

Ray RANSOM
(see BRICK)

Paul RAYMOND
Wire Fire (LP)—Savoy Brown featuring
Kim Simmonds

Lou REED
Coney Island Baby (LP)—Lou Reed
Rock And Roll Heart (LP)—Lou Reed

Joe REISMAN
Symphonic Soul (LP)—Henry Mancini &
His Concert Orchestra

Lou REIZNER
All This And World War II (LP)—
Soundtrack
The Best Of Rod Stewart (LP)—Rod
Stewart

RENAISSANCE
(Jon Camp, Michael Dunford, Annie
Haslam, Terrence Sullivan & John Tout)
Live At Carnegie Hall (LP)—Renaissance

Lauren RENDER
Let's Get It Together—El Coco

Bob RENO
Let Her In—John Travolta
Whenever I'm Away From You—John
Travolta
John Travolta (LP)—John Travolta

Joe RENZETTI
**Did You Boogie With Your Baby (In The
Back Row Of The Movie Show)**—Flash
Cadillac & the Continental Kids

Gian Piero REVERBERI
Reverberi (LP)—Reverberi

Allen REYNOLDS
I'll Get Over You—Crystal Gayle

L.J. REYNOLDS
Drama V (LP)—Ron Banks & the
Dramatics
Joy Ride (LP)—Dramatics

Rickie Lee REYNOLDS
(see BLACK OAK ARKANSAS)

Keith RICHARD
(see GLIMMER TWINS)

Deke RICHARDS
Anthology (LP)—Jackson 5ive

Jack RICHARDSON
Night Moves (LP)—Bob Seger & the
Silver Bullet Band

Lionel RICHIE
(see COMMODORES)

Jimmy ROACH
Disco Sax/For The Love Of You—
Houston Person
Joy Ride (LP)—Dramatics

Robbie ROBERTSON
Don't Think . . . Feel—Neil Diamond
If You Know What I Mean—Neil Diamond
Beautiful Noise (LP)—Neil Diamond
(see also BAND)

Jimmy ROBINSON
Paris (LP)—Paris

William/'Smokey' ROBINSON
Open—Smokey Robinson
Quiet Storm—Smokey Robinson
A Quiet Storm (LP)—Smokey Robinson
Smokey's Family Robinson (LP)—
Smokey Robinson

Paul RODGERS
(see BAD COMPANY)

D.J. ROGERS
Say You Love Me—D.J. Rogers
On The Road Again (LP)—D.J. Rogers

Gregg ROLIE
(see JOURNEY)

Ritchie ROME
   The Best Disco In Town—Ritchie Family
   Arabian Nights (LP)—Ritchie Family

Larry ROSEN
   Earl Klugh (LP)—Earl Klugh
   Living Inside Your Love (LP)—Earl Klugh

Diana ROSS
   Diana Ross (LP)—Diana Ross
   Diana Ross' Greatest Hits (LP)—Diana
   Ross

T-Boy ROSS
   I Want You—Marvin Gaye
   Marvin Gaye's Greatest Hits (LP)—
   Marvin Gaye

Francis ROSSI
   (see STATUS QUO)

Paul A. ROTHCHILD
   Slow Dancing—Funky Kings
   Breaker-Breaker—Outlaws
   Lady In Waiting (LP)—Outlaws

Alan RUBENS
   Jealousy (LP)—Major Harris

David RUBINSON
   Going Down Slowly—Pointer Sisters
   Let It Shine—Santana
   Man-Child (LP)—Herbie Hancock
   Secrets (LP)—Herbie Hancock
   Chameleon (LP)—Labelle
   The Best Of The Pointer Sisters (LP)—
   Pointer Sisters
   Amigos (LP)—Santana
   It Looks Like Snow (LP)—Phoebe Snow
   Safety Zone (LP)—Bobby Womack

RUFUS featuring CHAKA KHAN
   (Andre Fischer, Chaka Khan, Tony
   Maiden, Kevin Murphy & Bobby Watson)
   Dance Wit Me—Rufus featuring Chaka
   Khan
   Sweet Thing—Rufus featuring Chaka
   Khan
   Rufus Featuring Chaka Khan (LP)—
   Rufus featuring Chaka Khan

Todd RUNDGREN
   Good Vibrations—Todd Rundgren
   Faithful (LP)—Todd Rundgren
   Another Live (LP)—Todd Rundgren's
   Utopia
   Grand Funk Hits (LP)—Grand Funk
   Railroad

RUSH
   (Geddy Lee, Alex Lifeson & Neil Peart)
   All The World's A Stage (LP)—Rush
   2112 (LP)—Rush

Tom RUSH
   The Best Of Tom Rush (LP)—Tom Rush

Leon RUSSELL
   Back To The Island—Leon Russell
   Rainbow In Your Eyes—Leon & Mary
   Russell
   Best Of Leon (LP)—Leon Russell
   Will O' The Wisp (LP)—Leon Russell
   Wedding Album (LP)—Leon Russell

Mary RUSSELL
   Rainbow In Your Eyes—Leon & Mary
   Russell
   Wedding Album (LP)—Leon & Mary
   Russell

Mike RUTHERFORD
   (see GENESIS)

William SALTER
   Sound Of A Drum (LP)—Ralph
   McDonald

Ian SAMWELL-SMITH
   History—America's Greatest Hits (LP)—
   America

Paul SAMWELL-SMITH
   The Best Of Carly Simon (LP)—Carly
   Simon
   Greatest Hits (LP)—Cat Stevens

Paul SANCHEZ
   (see BLAZE)

Johnny SANDLIN
   The Road Goes On Forever (LP)—
   Allman Brothers Band

Alan SANDOW
   (see SHERBET)

Clarence SATCHELL
   (see OHIO PLAYERS)

Boz SCAGGS
   Boz Scaggs (LP)—Boz Scaggs
   (see also Steve MILLER BAND)

Martin SCHAER
   Roxy Roller—Sweeney Todd
   Roxy Roller—Sweeney Todd featuring
   Brian Guy Adams

Bob SCHAPER
  Sincerely (LP)—Dwight Twilley Band

Warren SCHATZ
  Daylight—Vicki Sue Robinson
  Turn The Beat Around—Vicki Sue Robinson
  Never Gonna Let You Go (LP)—Vicki Sue Robinson
  Vicki Sue Robinson (LP)—Vicki Sue Robinson

Stephen Y. SCHEAFFER
  Baby Face—Wing & A Prayer Fife & Drum Corps
  Baby Face (LP)—Wing & A Prayer Fife & Drum Corps

Aram SCHEFRIN
  Ca-the-drals—D.C. LaRue
  Full Time Thing (Between Dusk & Dawn)—Whirlwind
  Ca-the-drals (LP)—D.C. LaRue

Tom SCHERPENZEEL
  (see KAYAK)

Timothy B. SCHMIT
  (see POCO)

Al SCHMITT
  Glow (LP)—Al Jarreau
  Farther Along (LP)—Spirit

Bill SCHNEE
  I've Got A Reason (LP)—Richie Furay
  Michel Polnareff (LP)—Michel Polnareff

Florian SCHNEIDER
  Radio-Activity (LP)—Kraftwerk

Jerry SCHOENBAUM
  You Are My Starship—Norman Connors
  You Are My Starship (LP)—Norman Connors

Tom SCHOLZ
  More Than A Feeling—Boston
  Boston (LP)—Boston

Neal SCHON
  (see JOURNEY)

Andy SCOTT
  (see SWEET)

Clive SCOTT
  Sky High (LP)—Jigsaw

Ken SCOTT
  Don't Touch Me There—Tubes
  Changesonebowie (LP)—David Bowie
  The Rise And Fall Of Ziggy Stardust (Spiders From Mars) (LP)—David Bowie
  Journey To Love (LP)—Stanley Clarke
  School Days (LP)—Stanley Clarke
  Crisis? What Crisis? (LP)—Supertramp
  Young And Rich (LP)—Tubes

Marty SCOTT
  Sequencer (LP)—Synergy

Tom SCOTT
  Uptown & Country—Tom Scott
  New York Connection (LP)—Tom Scott
  Tom Cat (LP)—Tom Scott & the L.A. Express

Gil SCOTT-HERON
  It's Your World (LP)—Gil Scott-Heron & Brian Jackson

Tony SCOTTI
  Hell Cat—Bellamy Brothers
  Let Your Love Flow—Bellamy Brothers
  Satin Sheets—Bellamy Brothers
  Bellamy Brothers Featuring 'Let Your Love Flow' (LP)—Bellamy Brothers

Troy SEALS
  If Love Must Go—Dobie Gray

Don SEARS
  Convoy—C.W. McCall
  There Won't Be No Country Music (There Won't Be No Rock 'n' Roll—C.W. McCall
  Black Bear Road (LP)—C.W. McCall
  Wilderness (LP)—C.W. McCall

Pete SEARS
  (see JEFFERSON STARSHIP)

John SEBASTIAN
  Hideaway—John Sebastian
  Welcome Back—John Sebastian
  Welcome Back (LP)—John Sebastian

Neil SEDAKA
  Breaking Up Is Hard To Do—Neil Sedaka
  Love In The Shadows—Neil Sedaka
  Steppin' Out—Neil Sedaka
  You Gotta Make Your Own Sunshine—Neil Sedaka
  The Hungry Years (LP)—Neil Sedaka
  Sedaka's Back (LP)—Neil Sedaka
  Solitaire (LP)—Neil Sedaka
  Steppin' Out (LP)—Neil Sedaka

Bob SEGER
Night Moves—Bob Seger & the Silver
Bullet Band
Nutbush City Limits—Bob Seger & the
Silver Bullet Band
Live Bullet (LP)—Bob Seger & the Silver
Bullet Band
Night Moves (LP)—Bob Seger & the
Silver Bullet Band

Tom SELLERS
You're My Everything—Lee Garrett
Wham Bam (Shang-A-Lang)—Silver
Silver (LP)—Silver

Jay SENTER
Helen Reddy's Greatest Hits (LP)—
Helen Reddy

Doc SEVERINSEN
Night Journey (LP)—Doc Severinsen

Bob SHAD
The Lonely One—Special Delivery
featuring Terry Huff

Brad SHAPIRO
Rise And Shine (LP)—Kokomo

Sidney SHARP
Sixteen Reasons—Laverne & Shirley

Mel SHAW
Hit The Road Jack—Stampeders

Tommy SHAW
(see STYX)

Earl SHELTON
(see FATBACK BAND)

Louie SHELTON
Baby, I'll Give It To You—Seals & Crofts
Get Closer—Seals & Crofts
Get Closer (LP)—Seals & Crofts
Seals & Crofts' Greatest Hits (LP)—
Seals & Crofts
Sudan Village (LP)—Seals & Crofts

SHERBET
(Daryl Braithwaite, Harvey James, Tony
Mitchell, Garth Porter & Alan Sandow)
Howzat—Sherbet

Billy SHERRILL
Since I Fell For You—Charlie Rich
'Til I Can Make It On My Own—Tammy
Wynette
Greatest Hits (LP)—Charlie Rich
Silver Linings (LP)—Charlie Rich

Sig SHORE
That's The Way Of The World (LP)—
Earth Wind & Fire

Glenn SHORROCK
It's A Long Way There—Little River
Band
Little River Band (LP)—Little River Band

Michael SHRIEVE
(see AUTOMATIC MAN)

Derek SHULMAN
(see GENTLE GIANT)

Ray SHULMAN
(see GENTLE GIANT)

Bunny SIGLER
Train Called Freedom—South Shore
Commission
Dance Your Troubles Away (LP)—Archie
Bell & the Drells
Message In The Music (LP)—O'Jays
All Things In Time (LP)—Lou Rawls

SILVER
(John Batdorf, Greg Collier, Tom
Leadon, Brent Mydland & Harry Stinson)
Silver (LP)—Silver

Shel SILVERSTEIN
The Outlaws (LP)—Waylon Jennings,
Willie Nelson, Jessi Colter & Tompall
Glaser

Tony SILVESTER
You To Me Are Everything—Broadway
Truckload Of Lovin' (LP)—Albert King

Kim SIMMONDS
Wire Fire (LP)—Savoy Brown featuring
Kim Simmonds

Gene SIMMONS
(see KISS)

Luther SIMMONS
Shame On The World (LP)—Main
Ingredient

Paul SIMON
  50 Ways To Leave Your Lover—Paul
  Simon
  Still Crazy After All These Years—
  Paul Simon
  My Little Town—Simon & Garfunkel
  Breakaway (LP)—Art Garfunkel
  Still Crazy After All These Years— (LP)
  —Paul Simon
  Simon & Garfunkel's Greatest Hits (LP)
  —Simon & Garfunkel

Valerie SIMPSON
  Come As You Are (LP)—Ashford &
  Simpson

Pete SINFIELD
  I Believe In Father Christmas—Greg
  Lake

Bob SKAFF
  Times Of Your Life—Paul Anka
  Times Of Your Life (LP)—Paul Anka

Chris SLADE
  (see Manfred MANN'S EARTHBAND)

Johan SLAGER
  (see KAYAK)

Grace SLICK
  (see JEFFERSON STARSHIP)

Dick SMEDLER
  All Roads (Lead Back To You)—Donny
  Most

Claydes SMITH
  Open Sesame (LP)—Kool & the Gang
  (see also KOOL & THE GANG)

Earl 'Chinna' SMITH
  (see Bob MARLEY & THE WAILERS)

Lonnie Liston SMITH
  Reflections Of A Golden Dream (LP)—
  Lonnie Liston Smith
  Renaissance (LP)—Lonnie Liston Smith
  Visions Of A New World (LP)—Lonnie
  Liston Smith

Mark K. SMITH
  Take A Hand—Rick Springfield

Michael L. SMITH
  Let's Be Young Tonight—Jermaine
  Jackson
  Any Way You Like It (LP)—Thelma
  Houston

My Name Is Jermaine (LP)—Jermaine
Jackson
The Temptations Do The Temptations
(LP)—Temptations

Norman SMITH
  Savage Eye (LP)—Pretty Things

Steve SMITH
  Man Smart, Woman Smarter—Robert
  Palmer
  Short Cut Draw Blood (LP)—Jim Capaldi
  Live (LP)—Bob Marley & the Wailers
  Pressure Drop (LP)—Robert Palmer
  Some People Can Do What They Like
  (LP)—Robert Palmer

John SNYDER
  1975: The Duets (LP)—Dave Brubeck &
  Paul Desmond

John SONNEVELD
  Grasshopper—Spin

John David SOUTHER
  Greatest Hits (LP)—Linda Ronstadt

Mark SPECTOR
  The Best Of Tom Rush (LP)—Tom Rush

Phil SPECTOR
  The Best Of George Harrison (LP)—
  George Harrison
  Shaved Fish (LP)—John Lennon/
  Plastic Ono Band

SPIDERS FROM MARS
  (Dave Black, Trevor Bolder, Pete
  McDonald & Woody Woodmansey)
  Spiders From Mars (LP)—Spiders From
  Mars

SPIN
  (Hans Hollestelle, Jan Hollestelle, Hans
  Jansen, Cees Kranenberg, Rein Van der
  Broek & Jan Vennik)
  Grasshopper—Spin

David SPINOZZA
  Mary Hartman, Mary Hartman (Theme)
  —Deadly Nightshade
  James Taylor's Greatest Hits (LP)—
  James Taylor

Glen SPREEN
  Rusty Weir (LP)—Rusty Weir

Bruce SPRINGSTEEN
  Tenth Avenue Freeze-Out—Bruce
  Springsteen
  Born To Run (LP)—Bruce Springsteen

Chris SQUIRE
   Fish Out Of Water (LP)—Chris Squire

Bill STAHL
   Little Drummer Boy—Moonlion

Chris STAINTON
   That Was Only Yesterday (LP)—Gary
   Wright: Spooky Tooth

Paul STALLWORTH
   (see ATTITUDES)

Paul STANLEY
   (see KISS)

Edwin STARR
   Abyssinia Jones—Edwin Starr

Ringo STARR
   Blast From Your Past (LP)—Ringo Starr

STATUS QUO
   (John Coghlan, Alan Lancaster, Rick
   Parfitt & Francis Rossi)
   Status Quo (LP)—Status Quo

Al STECKLER
   Our Pleasure To Serve You (LP)—Stanky
   Brown Group

Bob STEELER
   (see HOT TUNA)

Wolf STEPHENSON
   Funny How Time Slips Away—Dorothy
   Moore
   Misty Blue (LP)—Dorothy Moore

Charles STEPNEY
   Can't Hide Love—Earth Wind & Fire
   Getaway—Earth Wind & Fire
   Saturday Nite—Earth Wind & Fire
   Sing A Song—Earth Wind & Fire
   I Don't Wanna Lose Your Love—Emotions
   **What's The Name Of This Funk (Spider
   Man)**—Ramsey Lewis
   Free—Deneice Williams
   Spirit (LP)—Earth Wind & Fire
   Gratitude (LP)—Earth Wind & Fire
   Flowers (LP)—Emotions
   Don't It Feel Good (LP)—Ramsey Lewis
   Salongo (LP)—Ramsey Lewis
   This Is Niecy (LP)—Deniece Williams

Jim STERN
   Breakfast For Two—Country Joe
   McDonald
   Paradise With An Ocean View (LP)—
   Country Joe McDonald

Cat STEVENS
   Banapple Gas—Cat Stevens
   Greatest Hits (LP)—Cat Stevens
   Numbers (LP)—Cat Stevens

Ray STEVENS
   Young Love—Ray Stevens
   The Very Best Of Ray Stevens (LP)—
   Ray Stevens

Eric STEWART
   (see 10cc)

Michael STEWART
   Inside (LP)—Kenny Rankin

Rod STEWART
   The Best Of Rod Stewart (LP)—
   Rod Stewart

Robert STIGWOOD
   Gold Vol. 1 (LP)—Bee Gees

Stephen STILLS
   Illegal Stills (LP)—Stephen Stills
   Long May You Run (LP)—Stills-Young
   Band

Harry STINSON
   (see SILVER)

Robert Jan STIPS
   (see GOLDEN EARRING)

Richard STREET
   (see TEMPTATIONS)

Barbra STREISAND
   **Love Theme From 'A Star Is Born'
   (Evergreen)**—Barbra Streisand
   A Star Is Born (LP)—Soundtrack

John STRONACH
   Fools Gold (LP)—Fools Gold
   R.E.O. (LP)—R.E.O.

James STROUD
   Funny How Time Slips Away—Dorothy
   Moore
   Misty Blue—Dorothy Moore
   Misty Blue (LP)—Dorothy Moore

STYX
(Dennis DeYoung, Chuck Panozzo, John Panozzo, John Curulewski & James Young)
Lorelei—Styx
Equinox (LP)—Styx
(Dennis De Young, Chuck Panozzo, John Panozzo, Tommy Shaw & James Young)
Mademoiselle—Styx
Crystal Ball (LP)—Styx

Big Jim SULLIVAN
Angel (LP)—Angel
Helluva Band (LP)—Angel

Terrence SULLIVAN
(see RENAISSANCE)

SUPERTRAMP
(Bob C. Benberg, Richard Davies, John Anthony Helliwell, Roger Hodgson & Dougie Thomson)
Crisis? What Crisis? (LP)—Supertramp

Michael (B.) SUTTON
Down To Love Town—Originals
Any Way You Like It (LP)—Thelma Houston
My Name Is Jermaine (LP)—Jermaine Jackson

Micky SWEENEY
For A Dancer—Prelude
Owl Creek Incident (LP)—Prelude

SWEET
(Brian Connolly, Steve Priest, Andy Scott & Mike Tucker)
'Give Us A Wink!' (LP)—Sweet

Bill SZYMCZYK
Fooled Around And Fell In Love—Elvin Bishop
Struttin' My Stuff—Elvin Bishop
New Kid In Town—Eagles
Take It To The Limit—Eagles
Struttin' My Stuff (LP)—Elvin Bishop
Hotel California (LP)—Eagles
On The Border (LP)—Eagles
One Of These Nights (LP)—Eagles
Their Greatest Hits 1971-1975 (LP)—Eagles
Live! Blow Your Face Out (LP)—J. Geils Band

TALL 'T' PRODUCTIONS
The Temptations Do The Temptations (LP)—Temptations

Bernie TAUPIN
Ba-Fa (LP)—Hudson Brothers

Chip TAYLOR
And The Singer Sings His Song (LP)—Neil Diamond

Creed TAYLOR
Good King Bad (LP)—George Benson
The Other Side Of Abbey Road (LP)—George Benson
Benson & Farrell (LP)—George Benson & Joe Farrell
I Hear A Symphony (LP)—Hank Crawford
Three (LP)—Bob James
Feels So Good (LP)—Grover Washington Jr.

Richard TAYLOR
(see MANHATTANS)

Roger TAYLOR
(see QUEEN)

Ted TEMPLEMAN
I Cheat The Hangman—Doobie Brothers
It Keeps You Runnin'—Doobie Brothers
Takin' It To The Streets—Doobie Brothers
Wheels Of Fortune—Doobie Brothers
It Keeps You Runnin'—Carly Simon
The Best Of The Doobies (LP)—Doobie Brothers
Takin' It To The Streets (LP)—Doobie Brothers
Another Passenger (LP)—Carly Simon

TEMPTATIONS
(Dennis Edwards, Melvin Franklin, Glenn Leonard, Richard Street & Otis Williams)
House Party (LP)—Temptations

10cc
(Lol Creme, Kevin Godley, Graham Gouldman & Eric Stewart)
Art For Art's Sake—10cc
I'm Mandy Fly Me—10cc
Blue Guitar—Justin Hayward & John Lodge
How Dare You (LP)—10cc

Toni TENNILLE
Lonely Night (Angel Face)—Captain & Tennille
Muskrat Love—Captain & Tennille
Shop Around—Captain & Tennille
Song Of Joy (LP)—Captain & Tennille

Billy TERRELL
Venus—Frankie Avalon

Peter TESSIER
  Wow—Andre Gagnon

Mike THEODORE
  Daydreamer—C.C. & Company
  Finger Lickin' Good (LP)—C.C. &
  Company

Bob THIELE
  Reflections Of A Golden Dream (LP)—
  Lonnie Liston Smith
  Renaissance (LP)—Lonnie Liston Smith
  Visions Of A New World (LP)—Lonnie
  Liston Smith

Chris THOMAS
  Heart On My Sleeve—Bryan Ferry
  Love Is The Drug—Roxy Music
  Let's Stick Together (LP)—Bryan Ferry
  Siren (LP)—Roxy Music
  Viva! Roxy Music (LP)—Roxy Music

Dennis THOMAS
  (see KOOL & THE GANG)

Ray THOMAS
  Hopes Wishes & Dreams (LP)—Ray
  Thomas

Rocky THOMAS
  Born On A Friday (LP)—Cleo Laine

Chester THOMPSON
  (see TOWER OF POWER)

Chris Hamlet THOMPSON
  (see Manfred MANN'S EARTHBAND)

Dougie THOMSON
  (see SUPERTRAMP)

Pat THRALL
  (see AUTOMATIC MAN)

Russ TITELMAN
  Shower The People—James Taylor
  In The Pocket (LP)—James Taylor
  James Taylor's Greatest Hits (LP)—
  James Taylor

Peter TORK
  (see MONKEES)

Peter TOSH
  Legalize It (LP)—Peter Tosh

John TOUT
  (see RENAISSANCE)

TOWER OF POWER
  (Greg Adams, Ronnie Beck, Emilio
  Castillo, Bruce Conte, Mic Gillette, Steve
  Kupka, Edward McGee, Lenny Pickett,
  Francis Rocco Prestia & Chester
  Thompson)
  Ain't Nothin' Stoppin' Us Now (LP)—
  Tower of Power
  (Greg Adams, Emilio Castillo, Bruce
  Conte, David Garibaldi, Mic Gillette, Steve
  Kupka, Lenny Pickett, Francis Rocco
  Prestia, Chester Thompson & Hubert
  Tubbs)
  Live And In Living Color (LP)—Tower of
  Power

Ed TOWNSEND
  Marvin Gaye's Greatest Hits (LP)—
  Marvin Gaye
  Loving Power (LP)—Impressions

John TROPEA
  Tropea (LP)—Tropea

Robin TROWER
  Caledonia—Robin Trower
  Long Misty Days (LP)—Robin Trower

Butch TRUCKS
  (see ALLMAN BROTHERS BAND)

Tommy TRUJILLO
  (see MANDRILL)

Hubert TUBBS
  (see TOWER OF POWER)

Pierre TUBBS
  Gotta Be The One—Maxine Nightingale
  Right Back Where We Started From—
  Maxine Nightingale
  Right Back Where We Started From (LP)
  —Maxine Nightingale

Mike TUCKER
  (see SWEET)

Rich/Richard TUFO
  Loving Power (LP)—Impressions

Stanley TURRENTINE
  The Man With The Sad Face (LP)—
  Stanley Turrentine
  Everybody Come On Out (LP)—Stanley
  Turrentine
  Have You Ever Seen The Rain (LP)—
  Stanley Turrentine

Steven TYLER
  (see AEROSMITH)

Bjorn ULVAEUS
  Dancing Queen—Abba
  Fernando—Abba
  I Do, I Do, I Do, I Do, I Do—Abba
  Mamma Mia—Abba
  Greatest Hits (LP)—Abba

URIAH HEEP
  (Mick Box, David Byron, Ken Hensley,
  Lee Kerslake & John Wetton)
  High And Mighty (LP)—Uriah Heep

Dino VALENTI
  (see QUICKSILVER MESSENGER
  SERVICE)

Thomas J. VALENTINO
  A Fifth Of Beethoven—Walter Murphy
  & the Big Apple Band
  Flight '76—Walter Murphy Band
  A Fifth Of Beethoven (LP)—Walter
  Murphy Band

Ross VALORY
  (see JOURNEY)

Rein VAN DER BROEK
  (see SPIN)

Miami Steve VAN ZANDT
  I Don't Want To Go Home (LP)—
  Southside Johnny & the Asbury Jukes

Paul VANCE
  Without Your Love (Mr. Jordan)—
  Charlie Ross

Harry VANDA
  Yesterday's Hero—John Paul Young

Gino VANNELLI
  Love Of My Life—Gino Vannelli
  The Gist Of Gemini (LP)—Gino Vannelli

Joe VANNELLI
  Love Of My Life—Gino Vannelli
  The Gist Of Gemini (LP)—Gino Vannelli

Ian VARDY
  (see PRELUDE)

Derek VARNALS
  Hopes Wishes & Dreams (LP)—Ray
  Thomas

Bert VELDKAMP
  (see KAYAK)

Nikolas/Nik VENET
  Endless Summer (LP)—Beach Boys
  Spirit Of America (LP)—Beach Boys
  Greatest Hits (LP)—Linda Ronstadt

Jan VENNIK
  (see SPIN)

Mike VERNON
  Gold Plated (LP)—Climax Blues Band
  **The Legendary Christine Perfect Album
  (LP)**—Christine McVie
  Fleetwood Mac In Chicago (LP)—
  Fleetwood Mac

Tommy VICARI
  Starcastle (LP)—Starcastle

Tony VISCONTI
  Changesonebowie (LP)—David Bowie
  Young Americans (LP)—David Bowie
  Indiscreet (LP)—Sparks

WAILERS
  (see Bob MARLEY & THE WAILERS)

Phil WAINMAN
  Money Honey—Bay City Rollers
  Bay City Rollers (LP)—Bay City Rollers
  Dedication (LP)—Bay City Rollers
  Rock 'n' Roll Love Letter (LP)—Bay City
  Rollers

Loudon WAINWRIGHT III
  T-Shirt (LP)—Loudon Wainwright III

Rick WAKEMAN
  No Earthly Connection (LP)—Rick
  Wakeman

David T. WALKER
  On Love (LP)—David T. Walker

Joe WALSH
  Fools Gold (LP)—Fools Gold
  You Can't Argue With A Sick Mind (LP)
  —Joe Walsh

Dexter WANSEL
  The Jacksons (LP)—Jacksons
  Philadelphia Freedom (LP)—MFSB
  All Things In Time (LP)—Lou Rawls

Andy WARD
  (see CAMEL)

Bill WARD
  (see BLACK SABBATH)

Leon WARE
  After The Dance—Marvin Gaye
  I Want You—Marvin Gaye
  Marvin Gaye's Greatest Hits (LP)—
  Marvin Gaye
  I Want You (LP)—Marvin Gaye

Lenny WARONKER
The Wreck Of The Edmund Fitzgerald—Gordon Lightfoot
Shower The People—James Taylor
Gord's Gold (LP)—Gordon Lightfoot
Summertime Dream (LP)—Gordon Lightfoot
Sweet Harmony (LP)—Maria Muldaur
James Taylor's Greatest Hits (LP)—James Taylor
In The Pocket (LP)—James Taylor

Roger WATERS
(see PINK FLOYD)

Bobby WATSON
(see RUFUS Featuring CHAKA KHAN)

Johnny 'Guitar' WATSON
Ain't That A Bitch (LP)—Johnny 'Guitar' Watson

Stan WATSON
We're On The Right Track—South Shore Commission

John WEATHERS
(see GENTLE GIANT)

Dennis WEINREICH
I've Been Lovin' You—Easy Street

Bob WEIR
Kingfish (LP)—Kingfish
(see also GRATEFUL DEAD)

Tim WEISBERG
Live At Last (LP)—Tim Weisberg

Sam WEISS
When Love Is New—Arthur Prysock

Bruce WELCH
Devil Woman—Cliff Richard
I Can't Ask For Anymore Than You—Cliff Richard
I'm Nearly Famous (LP)—Cliff Richard

Jann WENNER
Boz Scaggs (LP)—Boz Scaggs

Tom WERMAN
Fire—Mother's Finest
Dog Eat Dog—Ted Nugent
Hey Baby—Ted Nugent
Mother's Finest (LP)—Mother's Finest
Free For All (LP)—Ted Nugent
Ted Nugent (LP)—Ted Nugent

Max WERNER
(see KAYAK)

Ricky WEST
(see KOOL & THE GANG)

Tommy WEST
Baby, Baby I Love You—Terry Cashman
Chain Gang Medley—Jim Croce
Shannon—Henry Gross
Someday—Henry Gross
Springtime Mama—Henry Gross
The Faces I've Been (LP)—Jim Croce
Photographs & Memories: His Greatest Hits (LP)—Jim Croce
Release (LP)—Henry Gross

John WETTON
(see URIAH HEEP)

Jerry WEXLER
Ten Years Of Gold (LP)—Aretha Franklin
You (LP)—Aretha Franklin
Phases And Stages (LP)—Willie Nelson
Mackintosh & T.J. (LP)—Soundtrack

Glenn WHEATLEY
It's A Long Way There—Little River Band
Little River Band (LP)—Little River Band

Harold WHEELER
Baby Face—Wing & A Prayer Fife & Drum Corps
Baby Face (LP)—Wing & A Prayer Fife & Drum Corps

Barry WHITE
My Sweet Summer Suite—Love Unlimited Orchestra
Baby, We Better Try And Get It Together—Barry White
Let The Music Play—Barry White
Music Maestro Please (LP)—Love Unlimited Orchestra
My Sweet Summer Suite (LP)—Love Unlimited Orchestra
Greatest Hits (LP)—Barry White
Is This Whatcha Wont? (LP)—Barry White
Let The Music Play (LP)—Barry White

Lenny WHITE
Venusian Summer (LP)—Lenny White

Maurice WHITE
Can't Hide Love—Earth Wind & Fire
Getaway—Earth Wind & Fire
Saturday Nite—Earth Wind & Fire
Sing A Song—Earth Wind & Fire
Flowers—Emotions
I Don't Wanna Lose Your Love—
Emotions
What's The Name Of This Funk (Spider
Man)—Ramsey Lewis
Free—Deniece Williams
Gratitude (LP)—Earth Wind & Fire
Spirit (LP)—Earth Wind & Fire
Flowers (LP)—Emotions
Don't It Feel Good (LP)—Ramsey Lewis
Salongo (LP)—Ramsey Lewis
This Is Niecy (LP)—Deniece Williams

John WHITEHEAD
Dance Your Troubles Away (LP)—
Archie Bell & the Drells
The Jacksons (LP)—Jacksons
Summertime (LP)—MFSB
Message In The Music (LP)—O'Jays

Norman WHITFIELD
It Should Have Been Me—Yvonne Fair
Car Wash—Rose Royce
Marvin Gaye's Greatest Hits (LP)—
Marvin Gaye
The Best Of The Pointer Sisters (LP)—
Pointer Sisters
Car Wash (LP)—Soundtrack

Brad WHITFORD
(see AEROSMITH)

Jack WIEDEMANN
I.O.U.—Jimmy Dean

George WILLIAMS
(see FATBACK BAND)

James WILLIAMS
(see OHIO PLAYERS)

Milan WILLIAMS
(see COMMODORES)

Otis WILLIAMS
(see TEMPTATIONS)

Paul WILLIAMS
Ordinary Fool (LP)—Paul Williams

Brian WILSON
It's O.K.—Beach Boys
Rock And Roll Music—Beach Boys
Endless Summer (LP)—Beach Boys

15 Big Ones (LP)—Beach Boys
Spirit Of America (LP)—Beach Boys
(see also BEACH BOYS)

Carl WILSON
(see BEACH BOYS)

Carlos WILSON
(see MANDRILL)

Dennis WILSON
(see BEACH BOYS)

Frank WILSON
Happy—Eddie Kendricks
Down To Love Town—Originals

Lou WILSON
(see MANDRILL)

Melvin WILSON
Love Potion (LP)—New Birth

Ric WILSON
(see MANDRILL)

Terry WILSON
(see BACK STREET CRAWLER)

Wilfredo 'Wolf' WILSON
(see MANDRILL)

Terry WILSON-SLESSER
(see BACK STREET CRAWLER)

Pete WINGFIELD
Breakfast Special (LP)—Pete Wingfield

Bob WINKELMAN
(see Steve MILLER BAND)

Edgar WINTER
Together (LP)—Johnny & Edgar Winter

Johnny WINTER
Captured Live (LP)—Johnny Winter
Together (LP)—Johnny & Edgar Winter

Richie WISE
Part Time Love—Gladys Knight & the
Pips
The Best Of Gladys Knight & The Pips
(LP)—Gladys Knight & the Pips
2nd Anniversary (LP)—Gladys Knight &
the Pips
Kiss (LP)—Kiss
The Originals (LP)—Kiss

Joe WISSERT
I Can't Hear You No More—Helen Reddy
Somewhere In The Night—Helen Reddy
It's Over—Boz Scaggs
Lowdown—Boz Scaggs
What Can I Say—Boz Scaggs
Gratitude (LP)—Earth Wind & Fire
Gord's Gold (LP)—Gordon Lightfoot
The Best . . . Lovin' Spoonful (LP)—
Lovin' Spoonful
Music, Music (LP)—Helen Reddy
Helen Reddy's Greatest Hits (LP)—
Helen Reddy
No Way To Treat A Lady (LP)—Helen
Reddy
Silk Degrees (LP)—Boz Scaggs

Bill WITHERS
Make Love To Your Mind—Bill Withers
Making Music (LP)—Bill Withers
Naked & Warm (LP)—Bill Withers

Bill WOLF
If I Only Could—Rowans

Peter WOLF
(see J. GEILS BAND)

Bobby WOMACK
Wedding Album—Leon & Mary Russell

Stevie WONDER
I Wish—Stevie Wonder
Fulfillingness' First Finale (LP)—Stevie
Wonder
Innervisions (LP)—Stevie Wonder
Songs In The Key Of Life (LP)—Stevie
Wonder

Ron WOOD
The Best Of Rod Stewart (LP)—Rod
Stewart

Terry WOODFORD
Any Way You Like It (LP)—Thelma
Houston
House Party (LP)—Temptations

Woody WOODMANSEY
(see SPIDERS FROM MARS)

Gary WRIGHT
Dream Weaver—Gary Wright
Love Is Alive—Gary Wright
Made To Love You—Gary Wright
The Dream Weaver (LP)—Gary Wright
That Was Only Yesterday (LP)—Gary
Wright: Spooky Tooth

Gregory WRIGHT
My Name Is Jermaine (LP)—Jermaine
Jackson

Richard WRIGHT
(see PINK FLOYD)

Sam WUHRER
(see BLAZE)

Bill WYMAN
Stone Alone (LP)—Bill Wyman

Stomu YAMASHTA
Go (LP)—Stomu Yamashta/Steve
Winwood/Michael Shrieve

Marvin YANCY
Inseparable—Natalie Cole
Mr. Melody—Natalie Cole
Sophisticated Lady (She's A Different
Lady)—Natalie Cole
The More You Do It (The More I Like
It Done To Me—Ronnie Dyson
Inseparable (LP)—Natalie Cole
Natalie (LP)—Natalie Cole
Loving Power (LP)—Impressions

Peter YARROW
Torn Between Two Lovers—Mary
MacGregor

Earl YOUNG
Ten Percent—Double Exposure
Hold Back The Night—Trammps
That's Where The Happy People Go—
Trammps
Ten Percent (LP)—Double Exposure
Where The Happy People Go (LP)—
Trammps

George YOUNG
Yesterday's Hero—John Paul Young

James YOUNG
(see STYX)

Jesse Colin YOUNG
On The Road (LP)—Jesse Colin Young

Neil YOUNG
Long May You Run (LP)—Stills-Young
Band
Zuma (LP)—Neil Young with Crazy Horse

Rusty YOUNG
(see POCO)

Micahel ZAGER
Do It With Feeling—Michael Zager's
Moon Band featuring Peabo Bryson

Frank ZAPPA
 Can You Do It—Grand Funk Railroad
 Good Singin' Good Playin' (LP)—Grand
 Funk Railroad
 Zoot Allures (LP)—Frank Zappa

Joe ZAWINUL
 Black Market (LP)—Weather Report

Cesar ZUIDERNIJK
 (see GOLDEN EARRING)

US PRODUCER

Miscellaneous Section

This section lists all the UK and US Number One singles and albums for 1976, the total weeks which each artist was at number one, the Top 50 Best Selling singles and albums in both the UK and the US, all the Gold and Platinum selling singles and albums in the UK and the US.

UK NO. 1 SINGLES OF 1976

January 3—January 24	Bohemian Rhapsody—Queen
January 31—February 7	Mamma Mia—Abba
February 14	Forever And Ever—Slik
February 21—February 28	December, 1963 (Oh, What A Night)—Four Seasons
March 6—March 20	I Love To Love (But My Baby Loves To Dance)—Tina Charles
March 27—May 1	Save Your Kisses For Me—Brotherhood of Man
May 8—May 29	Fernando—Abba
June 5	No Charge—J.J. Barrie
June 12—June 19	The Combine Harvester (Brand New Key)—Wurzels
June 26—July 10	You To Me Are Everything—Real Thing
July 17	The Roussos Phenomenon (EP)—Demis Roussos
July 24—August 28	Don't Go Breaking My Heart—Elton John & Kiki Dee
September 4—October 9	Dancing Queen—Abba
October 16—November 6	Mississippi—Pussycat
November 13—November 27	If You Leave Me Now—Chicago
December 4—December 18	Under The Moon Of Love—Showaddywaddy
December 25	When A Child Is Born (Soleado)—Johnny Mathis

Weeks at top of chart

ABBA (12)	TINA CHARLES (3)
ELTON JOHN &	CHICAGO (3)
KIKI DEE (6)	REAL THING (3)
BROTHERHOOD OF	SHOWADDYWADDY (3)
MAN (6)	FOUR SEASONS (2)
PUSSYCAT (4)	WURZELS (2)
QUEEN (4)	

J.J. BARRIE (1)
JOHNNY MATHIS (1)
DEMIS ROUSSOS (1)
SLIK (1)

UK NO. 1 ALBUMS OF 1976

January 3—January 10	**A Night At The Opera**—Queen
January 17	**The Best Of Roy Orbison**—Roy Orbison
January 24—February 28	**The Very Best Of Slim Whitman**—Slim Whitman
March 6—March 20	**Blue For You**—Status Quo
March 27—April 3	**Rock Follies**—Rock Follies
April 10	**Presence**—Led Zeppelin
April 17	**Rock Follies**—Rock Follies
April 24—June 19	**Greatest Hits**—Abba
June 26—July 3	**A Night On The Town**—Rod Stewart
July 10—September 10	**20 Golden Greats**—Beach Boys
September 17	**The Best Of The Stylistics, Vol. 2**—Stylistics
September 24	**Stupidity**—Dr. Feelgood
October 2—October 9	**Greatest Hits**—Abba
October 16—October 23	**Soul Motion**—Various
October 30	**The Soundtrack From The Film The Song Remains The Same**—Led Zeppelin
November 5	**Bert Weedon's 22 Golden Guitar Greats**—Bert Weedon
November 12—December 11	**20 Golden Greats**—Glen Campbell
December 18—December 25	**A Day At The Races**—Queen

Weeks at top of chart

ABBA (11)	ROCK FOLLIES (3)
BEACH BOYS (10)	STATUS QUO (3)
SLIM WHITMAN (6)	LED ZEPPELIN (2)
GLEN CAMPBELL (5)	ROD STEWART (2)
QUEEN (4)	VARIOUS (2)

DR. FEELGOOD (1)
ROY ORBISON (1)
STYLISTICS (1)
BERT WEEDON (1)

UK TOP 50 SINGLES OF 1976

1 Save Your Kisses For Me—Brotherhood of Man
2 Don't Go Breaking My Heart—Elton John & Kiki Dee
3 Mississippi—Pussycat
4 Dancing Queen—Abba
5 A Little Bit More—Dr. Hook
6 If You Leave Me Now—Chicago
7 Fernando—Abba
8 I Love To Love (But My Baby Loves To Dance)—Tina Charles
9 The Roussos Phenomenon (EP)—Demis Roussos
10 December, 1963 (Oh, What A Night)—Four Seasons
11 Under The Moon Of Love—Showaddywaddy
12 You To Me Are Everything—Real Thing
13 Forever And Ever—Slik
14 Sailing—Rod Stewart
15 Young Hearts Run Free—Candi Staton
16 The Combine Harvester (Brand New Key)—Wurzels
17 When Forever Has Gone—Demis Roussos
18 Jungle Rock—Hank Mizell
19 Can't Get By Without You—Real Thing
20 You Make Me Feel Like Dancing—Leo Sayer
21 Mamma Mia—Abba
22 Hurt—Manhattans
23 Silly Love Songs—Wings
24 Convoy—C.W. McCall
25 Kiss And Say Goodbye—Manhattans
26 You Just Might See Me Cry—Our Kid
27 Love Really Hurts Without You—Billy Ocean
28 You See The Trouble With Me—Barry White
29 Let 'Em In—Wings
30 No Charge—J.J. Barrie
31 Jeans On—David Dundas
32 Don't Take Away The Music—Tavares
33 Howzat—Sherbet
34 Rodrigo's Guitar Concerto De Aranjuez (Theme from 2nd Movement)—Manuel & the Music of the Mountains
35 Bohemian Rhapsody—Queen
36 Misty Blue—Dorothy Moore
37 Heaven Must Be Missing An Angel—Tavares
38 Dance Little Lady Dance—Tina Charles
39 I Am A Cider Drinker (Paloma Blanca)—Wurzels
40 Music—John Miles
41 Love Machine—Miracles
42 Aria—Acker Bilk, His Clarinet & Strings
43 Let's Stick Together—Bryan Ferry
44 In Zaire—Johnny Wakelin
45 The Killing Of Georgie—Rod Stewart
46 Girl Of My Best Friend—Elvis Presley
47 Play That Funky Music—Wild Cherry
48 You Don't Have To Go—Chi-Lites
49 I Only Wanna Be With You—Bay City Rollers
50 Arms Of Mary—Sutherland Brothers & Quiver

UK TOP 50 ALBUMS 1976

1   Greatest Hits—Abba
2   20 Golden Greats—Beach Boys
3   Forever And Ever—Demis Roussos
4   Wings At The Speed Of Sound—Wings
5   A Night On The Town—Rod Stewart
6   Live In London—John Denver
7   Laughter And Tears. The Best Of Neil Sedaka Today—Neil Sedaka
8   Their Greatest Hits 1971-1975—Eagles
9   20 Golden Greats—Glen Campbell
10 The Very Best Of Slim Whitman—Slim Whitman
11 The Best Of Roy Orbison—Roy Orbison
12 A Night At The Opera—Queen
13 Desire—Bob Dylan
14 Greatest Hits/2—Diana Ross
15 Instrumental Gold—Various
16 Frampton Comes Alive!—Peter Frampton
17 Changesonebowie—David Bowie
18 Rock Follies—Rock Follies
19 How Dare You—10cc
20 The Best Of Gladys Knight & The Pips—Gladys Knight & the Pips
21 Songs In The Key Of Life—Stevie Wonder
22 Atlantic Crossing—Rod Stewart
23 24 Original Hits—Drifters
24 A Little Bit More—Dr. Hook
25 Happy To Be—Demis Roussos
26 Bert Weedon's 22 Golden Guitar Greats—Bert Weedon
27 Tubular Bells—Mike Oldfield
28 Blue For You—Status Quo
29 Soul Motion—Various
30 The Best Of The Stylistics Vol. 2—Stylistics
31 Breakaway—Gallagher & Lyle
32 Trick Of The Tail—Genesis
33 Presence—Led Zeppelin
34 Passport—Nana Mouskouri
35 100 Golden Greats—Max Bygraves
36 Jailbreak—Thin Lizzy
37 The Dark Side Of The Moon—Pink Floyd
38 Diana Ross—Diana Ross
39 The Story Of The Who—Who
40 Simon & Garfunkel's Greatest Hits—Simon & Garfunkel
41 Arrival—Abba
42 Beautiful Noise—Neil Diamond
43 Carnival—Manuel & the Music of the Mountains
44 40 Greatest—Perry Como
45 The Best Of Helen Reddy—Helen Reddy
46 Motown Gold—Various
47 Wish You Were Here—Pink Floyd
48 Rolled Gold—Rolling Stones
49 Music Express—Various
50 The Best Of John Denver—John Denver

1976 UK PLATINUM & GOLD DISCS

The following are all certified by the B.P.I. (British Phonographic Industry). To qualify for a Platinum disc, a single must sell 1,000,000 copies and an album must register sales of £1,000,000. A Gold disc represents sales of 500,000 for a single, and sales worth £250,000 for an album.

PLATINUM SINGLES
Bohemian Rhapsody—Queen
Save Your Kisses For Me—Brotherhood of Man

PLATINUM ALBUMS
Once Upon A Star—Bay City Rollers
Venus And Mars—Wings
Rollin'—Bay City Rollers
40 Greatest—Jim Reeves
Greatest Hits—Abba
A Night On The Town—Rod Stewart
20 Golden Greats—Beach Boys
Arrival—Abba
Songs In The Key Of Life—Stevie Wonder
20 Golden Greats—Glen Campbell
The Greatest Hits Of Frankie Valli And The Four Seasons—Frankie Valli & the Four Seasons

GOLD SINGLES
Y Viva Espana—Sylvia
Fernando—Abba
Don't Go Breaking My Heart—Elton John & Kiki Dee
Dancing Queen—Abba
Mississippi—Pussycat
If You Leave Me Now—Chicago
Under The Moon Of Love—Showaddywaddy
When A Child Is Born (Soleado)—Johnny Mathis

GOLD ALBUMS
24 Original Hits—Drifters
The Cliff Richard Story—Cliff Richard
Shaved Fish—John Lennon/Plastic Ono Band
Blue Jays—Justin Hayward & John Lodge
This Is The Moody Blues—Moody Blues
Rolled Gold—Rolling Stones
All Around My Hat—Steeleye Span
Still Crazy After All These Years—Paul Simon
How Dare You—10cc
The Very Best Of Slim Whitman—Slim Whitman
The Best Of Roy Orbison—Roy Orbison
Very Best Of Bing—Bing Crosby
Desire—Bob Dylan
Wings At The Speed Of Sound—Wings
The Best Of Helen Reddy—Helen Reddy
Rock Follies—Soundtrack
Queen—Queen
Their Greatest Hits 1971-1975—Eagles
Presence—Led Zeppelin
Rock 'n' Roll—John Lennon

Black And Blue—Rolling Stones
Motown Gold—Various
A Trick Of The Tail—Genesis
Passport—Nana Mouskouri
Siren—Roxy Music
Santana's Greatest Hits—Santana
Welcome—Santana
A Kind Of Hush—Carpenters
Breakaway—Gallagher & Lyle
Rock 'n' Roll Music—Beatles
The Best Of Gladys Knight & The Pips—Gladys Knight & the Pips
Diana Ross—Diana Ross
The Best Years Of Our Lives—Steve Harley & Cockney Rebel
Laughter & Tears. The Best Of Neil Sedaka Today—Neil Sedaka
Happy To Be—Demis Roussos
My Only Fascination—Demis Roussos
The Best Of The Stylistics—Vol. 2—Stylistics
Frampton Comes Alive!—Peter Frampton
The Story Of The Who—Who
Beautiful Noise—Neil Diamond
Blood On The Tracks—Bob Dylan
20 Original Dean Martin Hits—Dean Martin
Soundtrack From The Film The Song Remains The Same—Led Zeppelin
His 20 Greatest—Gene Pitney
40 Greatest—Henry Mancini
Hotel California—Eagles
Diana Ross Greatest Hits/2—Diana Ross
Blue Moves—Elton John
Jailbreak—Thin Lizzy
A Little Bit More—Dr. Hook
I'm Nearly Famous—Cliff Richard
Serenade—Neil Diamond
Walk Right Back With The Everlys—Everly Brothers

US NO. 1 SINGLES IN 1976

January 3	**Saturday Night**—Bay City Rollers
January 10	**Convoy**—C.W. McCall
January 17	**I Write The Songs**—Barry Manilow
January 24	**Theme From Mahogany 'Do You Know Where You're Going To'**—Diana Ross
January 31	**Love Rollercoaster**—Ohio Players
February 7—February 21	**50 Ways To Leave Your Lover**—Paul Simon
February 28	**Theme from S.W.A.T.**—Rhythm Heritage
March 6	**Love Machine**—Miracles
March 13—March 27	**December, 1963 (Oh, What A Night)**—Four Seasons
April 3—April 24	**Disco Lady**—Johnnie Taylor
May 1	**Let Your Love Flow**—Bellamy Brothers
May 8	**Welcome Back**—John Sebastian
May 15	**Boogie Fever**—Sylvers
May 22	**Silly Love Songs**—Wings
May 29—June 5	**Love Hangover**—Diana Ross
June 12—July 3	**Silly Love Songs**—Wings
July 10—July 17	**Afternoon Delight**—Starland Vocal Band
July 24—July 31	**Kiss And Say Goodbye**—Manhattans
August 7—August 28	**Don't Go Breaking My Heart**—Elton John & Kiki Dee
September 4	**You Should Be Dancing**—Bee Gees
September 11	**(Shake Shake Shake) Shake Your Booty**—KC & the Sunshine Band
September 18—October 2	**Play That Funky Music**—Wild Cherry
October 9	**A Fifth Of Beethoven**—Walter Murphy & the Big Apple Band
October 16	**Disco Duck**—Rick Dees & His Cast of Idiots
October 23—October 30	**If You Leave Me Now**—Chicago
November 6	**Rock 'n' Me**—Steve Miller Band
November 13—December 25	**Tonight's The Night**—Rod Stewart

Weeks on top of chart

ROD STEWART (7)	BAY CITY ROLLERS (1)
	BEE GEES (1)
WINGS (5)	BELLAMY BROTHERS (1)
	RICK DEES & HIS CAST OF IDIOTS (1)
ELTON JOHN & KIKI DEE (4)	KC & THE SUNSHINE BAND (1)
JOHNNIE TAYLOR (4)	BARRY MANILOW (1)
	C.W. McCALL (1)
FOUR SEASONS (3)	STEVE MILLER BAND (1)
PAUL SIMON (3)	MIRACLES (1)
WILD CHERRY (3)	WALTER MURPHY & THE BIG APPLE BAND (1)
CHICAGO (2)	OHIO PLAYERS (1)
MANHATTANS (2)	RHYTHM HERITAGE (1)
DIANA ROSS (2)	JOHN SEBASTIAN (1)
STARLAND VOCAL BAND (2)	SYLVERS (1)

US NO. 1 ALBUMS IN 1976

January 3—January 10	Chicago IX—Chicago's Greatest Hits—Chicago
January 17—January 31	Gratitude—Earth Wind & Fire
February 7—March 6	Desire—Bob Dylan
March 13—April 3	Their Greatest Hits 1971-1975—Eagles
April 10	Frampton Comes Alive!—Peter Frampton
April 17	Their Greatest Hits 1971-1975—Eagles
April 24	Wings At The Speed Of Sound—Wings
May 1—May 8	Presence—Led Zeppelin
May 15—May 22	Black And Blue—Rolling Stones
May 29	Wings At The Speed Of Sound—Wings
June 5—June 12	Black And Blue—Rolling Stones
June 19—July 17	Wings At The Speed Of Sound—Wings
July 24	Frampton Comes Alive!—Peter Frampton
July 31—August 7	Breezin'—George Benson
August 14—August 28	Frampton Comes Alive!—Peter Frampton
September 4	Breezin'—George Benson
September 11—October 9	Frampton Comes Alive!—Peter Frampton
October 16—December 25	Songs In The Key Of Life—Stevie Wonder

Weeks at top of chart

STEVIE WONDER (11)	ROLLING STONES (4)
PETER FRAMPTON (10)	EARTH WIND & FIRE (3)
WINGS (7)	GEORGE BENSON (2)
	CHICAGO (2)
BOB DYLAN (5)	LED ZEPPELIN (2)
EAGLES (5)	
	FLEETWOOD MAC (1)

1 **Silly Love Songs**—Wings
2 **Don't Go Breaking My Heart**—Elton John & Kiki Dee
3 **Disco Lady**—Johnnie Taylor
4 **December, 1963 (Oh, What A Night)**—Four Seasons
5 **Play That Funky Music**—Wild Cherry
6 **Kiss And Say Goodbye**—Manhattans
7 **Love Machine**—Miracles
8 **50 Ways To Leave Your Lover**—Paul Simon
9 **Love Is Alive**—Gary Wright
10 **A Fifth Of Beethoven**—Walter Murphy & the Big Apple Band
11 **Sara Smile**—Daryl Hall & John Oates
12 **Afternoon Delight**—Starland Vocal Band
13 **I Write The Songs**—Barry Manilow
14 **Fly, Robin, Fly**—Silver Convention
15 **Love Hangover**—Diana Ross
16 **Get Closer**—Seals & Crofts
17 **More, More, More**—Andrea True Connection
18 **Bohemian Rhapsody**—Queen
19 **Misty Blue**—Dorothy Moore
20 **Boogie Fever**—Sylvers
21 **I'd Really Love To See You Tonight**—England Dan & John Ford Coley
22 **You Sexy Thing**—Hot Chocolate
23 **Love Hurts**—Nazareth
24 **Get Up And Boogie**—Silver Convention
25 **Take It To The Limit**—Eagles
26 **(Shake Shake Shake) Shake Your Booty**—KC & the Sunshine Band
27 **Sweet Love**—Commodores
28 **Right Back Where We Started From**—Maxine Nightingale
29 **Theme From S.W.A.T.**—Rhythm Heritage
30 **Love Rollercoaster**—Ohio Players
31 **You Should Be Dancing**—Bee Gees
32 **You'll Never Find Another Love Like Mine**—Lou Rawls
33 **Golden Years**—David Bowie
34 **Moonlight Feels Right**—Starbuck
35 **Only Sixteen**—Dr. Hook
36 **Let Your Love Flow**—Bellamy Brothers
37 **Dream Weaver**—Gary Wright
38 **Turn The Beat Around**—Vicki Sue Robinson
39 **Lonely Night (Angel Face)**—Captain & Tennille
40 **All By Myself**—Eric Carmen
41 **Love To Love You Baby**—Donna Summer
42 **Deep Purple**—Donny & Marie Osmond
43 **Theme From Mahogany 'Do You Know Where You're Going To'**—Diana Ross
44 **Sweet Thing**—Rufus featuring Chaka Khan
45 **That's The Way I Like It**—KC & the Sunshine Band
46 **A Little Bit More**—Dr. Hook
47 **Shannon**—Henry Gross
48 **If You Leave Me Now**—Chicago
49 **Lowdown**—Boz Scaggs
50 **Show Me The Way**—Peter Frampton

1   Frampton Comes Alive!—Peter Frampton
2   Fleetwood Mac—Fleetwood Mac
3   Wings At The Speed Of Sound—Wings
4   Their Greatest Hits 1971-1975—Eagles
5   Chicago IX—Chicago's Greatest Hits—Chicago
6   The Dream Weaver—Gary Wright
7   Desire—Bob Dylan
8   A Night At The Opera—Queen
9   History—America's Greatest Hits—America
10 Gratitude—Earth Wind & Fire
11 Face The Music—Electric Light Orchestra
12 Brass Construction—Brass Construction
13 Tryin' To Get The Feelin'—Barry Manilow
14 Still Crazy After All These Years—Paul Simon
15 Toys In The Attic—Aerosmith
16 Red Octopus—Jefferson Starship
17 Silk Degrees—Boz Scaggs
18 Fool For The City—Foghat
19 Breezin'—George Benson
20 Eric Carmen—Eric Carmen
21 Inseparable—Natalie Cole
22 Daryl Hall & John Oates—Daryl Hall & John Oates
23 Look Out For # 1—Brothers Johnson
24 Main Course—Bee Gees
25 Love Will Keep Us Together—Captain & Tennille
26 Windsong—John Denver
27 Helen Reddy's Greatest Hits—Helen Reddy
28 Ted Nugent—Ted Nugent
29 One Of These Nights—Eagles
30 Rufus Featuring Chaka Khan—Rufus featuring Chaka Khan
31 Alive!—Kiss
32 Mothership Connection—Parliament
33 Greatest Hits—John Denver
34 The Salsoul Orchestra—Salsoul Orchestra
35 Black And Blue—Rolling Stones
36 City Life—Blackbyrds
37 Rock Of The Westies—Elton John
38 Greatest Hits—Seals & Crofts
39 Takin' It To The Streets—Doobie Brothers
40 Song Of Joy—Captain & Tennille
41 Diana Ross—Diana Ross
42 Family Reunion—O'Jays
43 Movin' On—Commodores
44 Rocks—Aerosmith
45 Venus And Mars—Wings
46 Fly Like And Eagle—Steve Miller Band
47 Presence—Led Zeppelin
48 Aerosmith—Aerosmith
49 Dreamboat Annie—Heart
50 Breakaway—Art Garfunkel

1976 US PLATINUM & GOLD DISCS

The following are all certified by the R.I.A.A. (Recording Industry Association of America).
To qualify for a Platinum disc, a single must sell 2,000,000 copies and an album 1,000,000.
A Gold disc represents sales of 1,000,000 for a single, and 500,000 for an album.

PLATINUM SINGLES
Disco Lady—Johnnie Taylor
Kiss And Say Goodbye—Manhattans
Play That Funky Music—Wild Cherry
Disco Duck—Rick Dees & His Cast of Idiots

PLATINUM ALBUMS
Their Greatest Hits 1971-1975—Eagles
Desire—Bob Dylan
Frampton Comes Alive!—Peter Frampton
Presence—Led Zeppelin
Wings At The Speed Of Sound—Wings
Rock 'n' Roll Music—Beatles
Black And Blue—Rolling Stones
Rocks—Aerosmith
Breezin'—George Benson
Look Out For #1—Brothers Johnson
Chicago X—Chicago
Mothership Connection—Parliament
Beautiful Noise—Neil Diamond
Silk Degrees—Boz Scaggs
Song Of Joy—Captain & Tennille
Fly Like An Eagle—Steve Miller Band
Spitfire—Jefferson Starship
Spirit—John Denver
Spirit—Earth Wind & Fire
Hasten Down The Wind—Linda Ronstadt
Dreamboat Annie—Heart
Destroyer—Kiss
Soundtrack From The Film The Song Remains The Same—Led Zeppelin
Boston—Boston
A Night On The Town—Rod Stewart
The Outlaws—Waylon Jennings, Willie Nelson, Jessi Colter & Tompall Glaser
Run With The Pack—Bad Company
A New World Record—Electric Light Orchestra
Blue Moves—Elton John
Brass Construction—Brass Construction

GOLD SINGLES
Love Rollercoaster—Ohio Players
I Write The Songs—Barry Manilow
I Love Music—O'Jays
You Sexy Thing—Hot Chocolate
Proud Mary—Creedence Clearwater Revival
Theme From S.W.A.T.—Rhythm Heritage
Love To Love You Baby—Donna Summer
Fox On The Run—Sweet
Sing A Song—Earth Wind & Fire
Sweet Thing—Rufus featuring Chaka Khan

MISCELLANEOUS   389

50 Ways To Leave Your Lover—Paul Simon
December, 1963 (Oh, What A Night)—Four Seasons
Lonely Night (Angel Face)—Captain & Tennille
Love Hurts—Nazareth
Boogie Fever—Sylvers
Dream Weaver—Gary Wright
All By Myself—Eric Carmen
Right Back Where We Started From—Maxine Nightingale
Only Sixteen—Dr. Hook
Welcome Back—John Sebastian
I.O.U.—Jimmy Dean
Bohemian Rhapsody—Queen
Get Up And Boogie—Silver Convention
Silly Love Songs—Wings
Shannon—Henry Gross
Fooled Around And Fell In Love—Elvin Bishop
Sara Smile—Daryl Hall & John Oates
Afternoon Delight—Starland Vocal Band
Shop Around—Captain & Tennille
Don't Go Breaking My Heart—Elton John & Kiki Dee
You'll Never Find Another Love Like Mine—Lou Rawls
A Fifth Of Beethoven—Walter Murphy & the Big Apple Band
Summer—War
You Should Be Dancing—Bee Gees
Heaven Must Be Missing An Angel—Tavares
More, More, More—Andrea True Connection
Disco Duck—Rick Dees & His Cast of Idiots
I'd Really Love To See You Tonight—England Dan & John Ford Coley
(Give Up The Funk) Tear The Roof Off The Sucker—Parliament
Devil Woman—Cliff Richard
Let 'Em In—Wings
If You Leave Me Now—Chicago
Getaway—Earth Wind & Fire
Lowdown—Boz Scaggs
Teddy Bear—Red Sovine
You Don't Have To Be A Star (To Be In My Show)—Marilyn McCoo & Billy Davis Jr.
Tonight's The Night—Rod Stewart
Muskrat Love—Captain & Tennille
The Rubber Band Man—Spinners

GOLD ALBUMS
High On The Hog—Black Oak Arkansas
Wake Up Everybody—Harold Melvin & the Blue Notes
Rufus Featuring Chaka Khan—Rufus Featuring Chaka Khan
Numbers—Cat Stevens
Mona Bone Jakon—Cat Stevens
Love To Love You Baby—Donna Summer
No Way To Treat A Lady—Helen Reddy
A Christmas Album—Barbra Streisand
Face The Music—Electric Light Orchestra
Black Bear Road—C.W. McCall
Searchin' For A Rainbow—Marshall Tucker Band
Bare Trees—Fleetwood Mac
Inseparable—Natalie Cole

M.U. The Best Of Jethro Tull—Jethro Tull
Station To Station—David Bowie
The Dream Weaver—Gary Wright
Greatest Hits—Barry White
Will O' The Wisp—Leon Russell
A Night At The Opera—Queen
Red Headed Stranger—Willie Nelson
Fool For The City—Foghat
Bustin' Out—Pure Prairie League
Thoroughbred—Carole King
Brass Construction—Brass Construction
Eargasm—Johnnie Taylor
Apostrophe—Frank Zappa
Hair Of The Dog—Nazareth
City Life—Blackbyrds
2nd Anniversary—Gladys Knight & the Pips
Lazy Afternoon—Barbra Streisand
Come On Over—Olivia Newton-John
You've Never Been This Far Before—Conway Twitty
Here And There—Elton John
Takin' It To The Streets—Doobie Brothers
Bitches Brew—Miles Davis
Hideaway—America
Souvenirs—Dan Fogelberg
All The Love In The World—Mac Davis
Desolation Boulevard—Sweet
Harvest For The World—Isley Brothers
Contradiction—Ohio Players
Amigos—Santana
Twelve Dreams Of Dr. Sardonicus—Spirit
Ole ELO—Electric Light Orchestra
Love Trilogy—Donna Summer
Natalie—Natalie Cole
Music From The Warner Bros. Motion Picture 'Sparkle'—Aretha Franklin
Second Childhood—Phoebe Snow
All-Time Greatest Hits—Johnny Nash
A Kind Of Hush—Carpenters
Ted Nugent—Ted Nugent
Changesonebowie—David Bowie
Music, Music—Helen Reddy
Soul Searching—Average White Band
This One's For You—Barry Manilow
Native Sons—Loggins & Messina
All Things In Time—Lou Rawls
War's Greatest Hits—War
Get Closer—Seals & Crofts
15 Big Ones—Beach Boys
Wild Cherry—Wild Cherry
Frampton—Peter Frampton
Wired—Jeff Beck
The Royal Scam—Steely Dan
Children Of The World—Bee Gees
The Best Of B.T.O. (So Far)—Bachman-Turner Overdrive
Hard Rain—Bob Dylan

MISCELLANEOUS

Abandoned Luncheonette—Daryl Hall & John Oates
Dave Mason—Dave Mason
The Manhattans—Manhattans
Happiness Is Being With The Spinners—Spinners
Whistling Down The Wire—David Crosby/Graham Nash
The Clones Of Dr. Funkenstein—Parliament
In The Pocket—James Taylor
Message In The Music—O'Jays
I—Barry Manilow
A New World Record—Electric Light Orchestra
One More From The Road—Lynyrd Skynyrd
Agents Of Fortune—Blue Oyster Cult
A Fifth Of Beethoven—Walter Murphy Band
Summertime Dream—Gordon Lightfoot
Free To Be . . . You And Me—Marlo Thomas & Friends
Blue Moves—Elton John
For Earth Below—Robin Trower
Firefall—Firefall
Bigger Than Both Of Us—Daryl Hall & John Oates
Rock And Roll Outlaws—Foghat
Mystery To Me—Fleetwood Mac
Over-Nite Sensation—Mothers
Rock And Roll Over—Kiss
Four Seasons Of Love—Donna Summer
Free For All—Ted Nugent
Brass Construction II—Brass Construction
The Pretender—Jackson Browne
Jackson Browne—Jackson Browne
Ol' Blue Eyes Is Back—Frank Sinatra
Moondance—Van Morrison
The Best Of The Doobies—Doobie Brothers
Alice Cooper Goes To Hell—Alice Cooper
And I Love You So—Perry Como
Nights Are Forever—England Dan & John Ford Coley
Bicentennial Nigger—Richard Pryor
Don't Stop Believin'—Olivia Newton-John
Dr. Buzzard's Original Savannah Band—Dr. Buzzard's Original Savannah Band
Greatest Hits—Linda Ronstadt
That Christmas Feeling—Glen Campbell
The Best Of The Beach Boys, Vol. 2—Beach Boys
Daryl Hall & John Oates—Daryl Hall & John Oates
Hotel California—Eagles
Long Misty Days—Robin Trower
Wings Over America—Wings
Red Octopus—Jefferson Starship
Rocky Mountain Christmas—John Denver
Fleetwood Mac—Fleetwood Mac
Gord's Gold—Gordon Lightfoot

TRIVIA SECTION

This section is only for those who have nothing better to do than read this. Most of the following pieces of trivia will be of absolutely no interest or use to anybody!

DID YOU KNOW THAT?...

Hugo & Luigi and George David Weiss, who write all of the Stylistics hits, also wrote the Royal Guardsmen's 'Snoopy Vs. The Red Baron'.

Lou Adler, Herb Alpert and Sam Cooke originally wrote the song '(What A) Wonderful World' under the name of Barbara Campbell.

Status Quo's 'Wild Side of Life' was originally recorded by Hank Thompson in 1952, and was a UK hit for Josh MacRae in 1960.

Larry Russell Brown, who co-wrote Donny Osmond's 'C'mon Marianne', also co-wrote 'Tie A Yellow Ribbon Round The Old Oak Tree' and 'Knock Three Times' for Dawn.

'The Continental', a UK hit for Maureen McGovern in 1976, was the first song to be awarded an Oscar back in 1934.

Giorgio Moroder and Pete Bellotte, who write and produce all Donna Summer's hits, also wrote Chicory Tip's three big hits in 1972-3.

Georg Kajanus, lead singer and writer of Sailor, used to be in the group Eclection, but with the name George Hultgreen.

Larry Henley, who co-wrote Billie Jo Spears' 'Sing Me An Old Fashioned Song', was the lead vocalist on the Newbeats' 'Bread And Butter.'

'Baby Face' was a million seller for Art Mooney & his orchestra in 1948.

Steve Barri, who produced hits for Rhythm Heritage, John Sebastian and Pratt & McClain, was once in a duo called the Fantastic Baggys with P.F. Sloan.

Bones Howe, who produced Tom Waits' two US hit albums, wrote the Routers' hit 'Stingray' under the name of Gunther Heigal.

Tom Sellers who co-produced Lee Garrett's 'You're My Everything', was in a group called Gulliver, with Tim Moore—writer of the Bay City Rollers' 'Rock 'n' Roll Love Letter'—and Daryl Hall and John Oates.

Vini Poncia, who co-wrote Leo Sayer's 'You Make Me Feel Like Dancing', was a member of the Tradewinds, who had a US hit with

'New York's A Lonely Town (When You're The Only Surfer Boy Around)'.

Walter Becker and Donald Fagen, of Steely Dan, were once in Jay and the Americans' road band.

Showaddywaddy's 'Under The Moon Of Love' was originally a hit for its composer Curtis Lee back in 1961.

Mac Gayden, who wrote James and Bobby Purify's 'Morning Glory', wrote the Love Affair's 'Everlasting Love' with Buzz Cason.

The original version of 'He Ain't Heavy ... He's My Brother' was recorded by Kelly Gordon, who produced some of Glen Campbell's '20 Golden Greats'.

Peter Swettenham, co-producer of the Liverpool Express' hits, was a member of Grapefruit, who were the first rock group to be signed to the Beatles' Apple label.

Ron Dante, Barry Manilow's co-producer, was the lead vocalist on the Detergents' 'Leader Of The Laundromat'.

England Dan of England Dan & John Ford Coley is the brother of Jimmy Seals, of Seals & Crofts, who in turn were members of the Champs. Their big hit was 'Tequila', back in 1958.

Glen Campbell also spent some time with the Champs, before becoming one of Los Angeles' top session musicians. In fact the Beach Boys' 'Good Vibrations', which again was a hit in 1976, featured Campbell on lead guitar, Larry Knechtel, of Bread (and pianist on 'Bridge Over Troubled Water') on organ, Hal Blaine on drums—and it is believed Leon Russell was lurking around in the studio at the time as well.

The Atlanta Rhythm Section was formed out of the remnants of Classics IV, whose biggest US hit was 'Spooky'. Pablo Cruise was formed from Stoneground and It's A Beautiful Day, and Rufus from the American Breed.

The Doobie Brothers' producer, Ted Templeman, was a member of Harpers Bizarre.

Chip Taylor, who produced Neil Diamond's "And The Singer Sings His Song' LP, wrote the Troggs' 'Wild Thing'. He is also actor Jon Voight's brother.

Lenny Waronker, producer of James Taylor's 'Greatest Hits' and Gordon Lightfoot's 'The Wreck Of The Edmund Fitzgerald', is the son of Si Waronker, after whom one of the Chipmunks was named.

Kenny Young, of Fox, co-wrote 'Under The Boardwalk'.

Teddy Randazzo, who wrote and produced Little Anthony & the Imperials' minor UK hit, also wrote 'Yesterday Has Gone', which was Cupid's Inspiration's only hit.

Curtis Mayfield, who had many credits during 1976, wrote 'Um Um Um Um Um Um', which was a hit for both Major Lance and Wayne Fontana in 1964.

Moonlion's 'Little Drummer Boy' has been a hit three times before. First by the Harry Simeone Chorale in 1958, then by the Beverley Sisters the following year, and more recently by the Scots Dragoons Guards Band in 1972.

The Sandpipers' 'Hang On Sloopy' was originally a hit in the US by the Vibrations in 1964—and not by the McCoys. Their version was released the following year.

Carl Smith and Raynard Miner, writers of Melissa Manchester's 'Rescue Me', also wrote Jackie Wilson's 'Higher And Higher'.

Allen Toussaint, the top New Orleans writer and producer, wrote Lee Dorsey's two big hits—'Holy Cow' and 'Workin' In A Coalmine'.

Michael Stewart, who produced Kenny Rankin's 'Inside' LP, was a member of We Five, who had the original hit of 'You Were On My Mind'.

Mike Hawker, co-wrote the Bay City Rollers' 'I Only Want To Be With You', also co-wrote Helen Shapiro's 'Walkin' Back To Happiness'.

Albert Hammond, who co-wrote the Carpenters' 'I Need To Be In Love', was a member of Family Dogg, and also wrote Leapy Lee's 'Little Arrows'—which proves we can all have off-days.

... THERE'S NOT MANY PEOPLE THAT KNOW THAT!

*Not for sale in Canada.

0352   Star

396431	Frederick Anderson **ENGLAND BY BICYCLE**	95p
398914	J. Paul Getty **HOW TO BE RICH**	60p*
397829	**HOW TO BE A SUCCESSFUL EXECUTIVE**	60p*
397152	Nick Logan & Bob Woffinden **THE NME BOOK OF ROCK 2**	95p
398566	Harry Lorayne & Jerry Lucas **THE MEMORY BOOK**	60p*
39692X	Henry Miller **THE WORLD OF SEX**	60p
396407	Milligan & Hobbs **MILLIGAN'S BOOK OF RECORDS**	75p
396733	Sally O'Sullivan **THINGS MY MOTHER NEVER TOLD ME**	85p
397640	David Reuben **HOW TO GET MORE OUT OF SEX**	85p*
398779	Fiona Richmond **FIONA**	50p
300213	Ernest Tidyman **DUMMY**	45p*

0426   Tandem

191123	Eppstein (Editor) **THE BOOK OF THE WORLD**	£1.75*
08571X	Hyam Maccoby **REVOLUTION IN JUDAEA**	75p
163877	James Hewitt **ISOMETRICS AND YOU**	40p
168623	Xaviera Hollander **THE HAPPY HOOKER**	60p*
163443	**LETTERS TO THE HAPPY HOOKER**	60p*
168038	**XAVIERA GOES WILD**	75p*
166787	**XAVIERA, ON THE BEST PART OF A MAN**	60p*
17996X	Xaviera Hollander & Marilyn Chambers **XAVIERA MEETS MARILYN CHAMBERS**	60p*
124820	Charles Lindbergh **THE SPIRIT OF ST. LOUIS**	95p
124901	Fridtjof Nansen **FARTHEST NORTH**	£1.00
175158	Sakuzawa Nyoiti **MACROBIOTICS**	50p*
181204	L. Sprague De Camp **ANCIENT ENGINEERS (large format)**	£1.95*
134931	**THE WOMANLY ART OF BREAST FEEDING**	60p

*Not for sale in Canada.

0352 Star

396423	Mary Ann Ashe **RING OF ROSES**	60p
396938	Andre P. Brink **LOOKING ON DARKNESS**	95p
398663	Jackie Collins **THE WORLD IS FULL OF DIVORCED WOMEN**	50p
398752	**THE WORLD IS FULL OF MARRIED MEN**	50p
300671	Eric Corder **HELLBOTTOM**	75p*
300086	**THE LONG TATTOO**	40p*
398515	**RUNNING DOGS**	60p*
396857	Terry Fisher **IF YOU'VE GOT THE MONEY**	70p
39840X	Knight Isaacson **THE STORE**	60p
398981	Jeffrey Konvitz **THE SENTINEL**	70p*
396334	Gavin Lambert **THE SLIDE AREA**	75p
398299	Robin Maugham **THE SIGN**	55p*
397594	Clayton Moore **END OF RECKONING**	60p*
397608	**141 TERRACE DRIVE**	60p*
397543	**RIVER FALLS**	60p*
397667	**SECRET FIRE**	60p*
397659	**THE CORRUPTERS**	60p*
397551	**WESLEY SHERIDAN**	60p*
300809	Molly Parkin **LOVE ALL**	50p
397179	**UP TIGHT**	60p
396946	Judith Rossner **TO THE PRECIPICE**	85p*
397144	Alan Sillitoe **THE FLAME OF LIFE**	70p
398892	**THE GENERAL**	50p
300965	**THE LONELINESS OF THE LONG DISTANCE RUNNER**	50p
300949	**MEN, WOMEN AND CHILDREN**	50p
398809	**THE RAGMAN'S DAUGHTER**	50p
300981	**SATURDAY NIGHT AND SUNDAY MORNING**	50p
396415	Hubert Selby Jr. **THE ROOM**	75p
398884	Ernest Tidyman **STARSTRUCK**	60p*

*Not for sale in Canada.

0352	Star	

300698	Woody Allen **GETTING EVEN**	50p*
398973	Alida Baxter **FLAT ON MY BACK**	50p
397187	**OUT ON MY EAR**	60p
397101	**UP TO MY NECK**	50p
397632	Les Dawson **THE SPY WHO CAME**	50p
397020	Alex Duncan **VETS IN THE BELFRY**	50p
398612	**IT'S A VET'S LIFE**	60p
398795	**THE VET HAS NINE LIVES**	50p
396245	David Dawson **VET IN DOWNLAND**	60p
397535	Stephen John **WHAT A WAY TO GO!** (see also Tandem General Fiction)	50p
397314	King Kong **MY SIDE**	60p
397780	Spike Milligan **THE GREAT McGONAGALL SCRAPBOOK**	75p
397527	Jack Millmay **REVELATIONS FROM THE RAG TRADE** (See also Tandem General Fiction)	50p
396237	Stanley Morgan **INSIDE ALBERT SHIFTY**	70p
398965	**RUSS TOBIN'S BEDSIDE GUIDE TO SMOOTHER SEDUCTION**	60p
397454	**SKY-JACKED**	60p
396954	Harry Secombe **GOON FOR LUNCH**	60p
396148	Keith Waterhouse **MONDAYS, THURSDAYS (NF)**	60p

0426	Tandem	

158350	Tony Blackburn **A LAUGH IN EVERY POCKET**	40p
136616	**DARLING — YOU ARE A DEVIL!**	50p*
157710	Spike Milligan **THE BEDSIDE MILLIGAN**	35p
157982	**A BOOK OF BITS OR A BIT OF A BOOK**	35p
15827X	**A DUSTBIN OF MILLIGAN**	35p
158199	**THE LITTLE POT BOILER**	35p
158008	Spike Milligan & John Antrobus **THE BED-SITTING ROOM**	35p

*Not for sale in Canada.

Wyndham Books are obtainable from many booksellers and newsagents. If you have any difficulty please send purchase price plus postage on the scale below to:

Wyndham Cash Sales,
123 King Street,
London W6 9JG

OR

Star Book Service,
G.P.O. Box 29,
Douglas,
Isle of Man,
British Isles

While every effort is made to keep prices low, it is sometimes necessary to increase prices at short notice. Wyndham Books reserve the right to show new retail prices on covers which may differ from those advertised in the text or elsewhere.

Postage and Packing Rate
U.K. & Eire
One book 15p plus 7p per copy for each additional book ordered to a maximum charge of 57p.

These charges are subject to Post Office charge fluctuations.